TERM GRAPH REWRITING

Theory and Practice

TERM GRAPH REWRITING

Theory and Practice

Edited by

M. R. Sleep
University of East Anglia, UK

and

M. J. Plasmeijer and M. C. J. D. van Eekelen
University of Nijmegen, The Netherlands

JOHN WILEY & SONS
Chichester · New York · Brisbane · Toronto · Singapore

Other Wiley Editorial Offices

John Wiley & Sons, Inc., 605 Third Avenue,
New York, NY 10158-0012, USA

Jacaranda Wiley Ltd, G.P.O. Box 859, Brisbane,
Queensland 4001, Australia

John Wiley & Sons (Canada) Ltd, 22 Worcester Road,
Rexdale, Ontario M9W 1L1, Canada

John Wiley & Sons (SEA) Pte Ltd, 37 Jalan Pemimpin #05-04,
Block B, Union Industrial Building, Singapore 2057

British Library Cataloguing in Publication Data

A catalogue record for this book is available from the British Library

ISBN 0 471 93567 0

Produced from camera-ready copy supplied by the editors
Printed and bound in Great Britain by Bookcraft (Bath) Ltd

Contents

Preface

Term Graph Rewriting refers to techniques and theories for representing terms and term rewrite rules as graphs and graph rewrite rules. Many modern programming paradigms - most notably the functional and logic paradigms - have term rewriting at their heart, although the control regimes and semantics are very different. Practical implementations of these languages share subterms using pointers, and the machine code for such programs manipulates shared structures (called in this volume *term graphs*). The operational semantics of the resulting programs may be represented as a set of term graph rewriting rules. Reasoning about the correctness and efficiency of such representations relies on our ability to reason about term graph rewriting systems, and to relate them to other semantic models. Used in this way, term graph rewriting offers a model of computation which is closer to real implementations than pure term rewriting, but which avoids unnecessary machine detail.

Graph rewriting was the focus of a number of ESPRIT Basic Research Actions most notably SEMAGRAPH and COMPUGRAPH. These ESPRIT actions brought together and amplified European strengths in this area. Both projects led to exciting theoretical and practical advances for term graph rewriting reflecting the state of the art.

These advances were presented at the SemaGraph'91 symposium which took place at the University of Nijmegen during the period 10-12 December 1991. Other prominent workers in the field from the USA, Japan and elsewhere were invited to contribute to the symposium. The chapters in this book are based on selected contributions to the SemaGraph'91 symposium. Chapter 1 gives an introduction to term graph rewriting and an overview of the contents of the remaining chapters.

A number of individuals have contributed in a special way to the Symposium and the resulting book. Marielle van der Zandt and Yvonne Verhallen of Nijmegen University did much of the local organisation of the Symposium. Maureen Saward and Steve Rush of the University of East Anglia worked long hours to implement the changes required by copy editors and authors, and handled the mysteries of LaTeX for us. Paul Ling of East Anglia and Kristoffer Rose of DIKU provided additional advice on using LaTeX.

Last but not least we acknowledge the support of DGXIII of the CEC under the ESPRIT Basic Research Action programme via the following actions:

BRA3299 and *BRA7183* Computing by Graph Transformation (COMPUGRAPH).
BRA3074 and *BRA6345* The Semantics and Pragmatics of Extended Term Graph Rewriting (SEMAGRAPH).

Ronan Sleep, Rinus Plasmeijer and Marko van Eekelen (Editors)
UEA, Norwich, February 4th 1993

Contributors

P. Anderson : Grammatech Inc. One Hopkins Place, Ithaca, New York 14850, U.S.A.

Z.M. Ariola : Massachusetts Institute of Technology, 77 Massachusetts Avenue, Cambridge, Massachusetts 02139, U.S.A.

Arvind : Massachusetts Institute of Technology, 77 Massachusetts Avenue, Cambridge, Massachusetts 02139, U.S.A.

S. van Bakel : University of Nijmegen, Faculty of Mathematics and Informatics, Toernooiveld 1, 6525 ED Nijmegen, The Netherlands.

R. Banach : Manchester University, Dept. of Computer Science, Oxford Road, Manchester, M13 9PL, UK.

D. Bolton : City University, Computer Science Department, Northampton Square, London EC1V 0HB, UK.

S. Brock : University of East Anglia, School of Information Systems, Norwich NR4 7TJ, UK.

A. Corradini : Universita di Pisa, Dipartimento di Informatica, Corso Italia 40, 56125 Pisa, Italy.

W. Damm : Universität Oldenburg, FB10, Postfach 2503, W-2900 Oldenburg, Germany.

M. van Eekelen : University of Nijmegen, Faculty of Mathematics and Informatics, Toernooiveld 1, 6525 ED Nijmegen, The Netherlands.

J. Glauert : University of East Anglia, School of Information Systems, Norwich, NR4 7TJ, UK.

R. Goldsmith : University of East Anglia, School of Information Systems, Norwich NR4 7TJ, UK.

E. Goubault : Ecole Normale Superieure, 45 Rue d'Ulm, 75230 Paris, Cedex 05, France.

C. Hankin : Imperial College of Science, Department of Computing, 180 Queen's Gate, London, SW7 2BZ, UK.

T. Hardin : INRIA, Domaine de Voluceau Rocquencourt, P.O. Box 105, 78153 Le Chesnay, Cedex, France.

K. Hogsbro Rose : DIKU (TOPPS Group), University of Copenhagen, Universitetsparken 1, DK-2100 Copenhagen, Denmark.

P. Kelly : Imperial College of Science, Department of Computing, 180 Queen's Gate, London, SW7 2BZ, UK.

J.R. Kennaway : University of East Anglia, School of Information Systems, Norwich, NR4 7TJ, UK.

J.W. Klop : CWI, Kruislaan 413, 1098 SJ Amsterdam, The Netherlands.

P. Koopman : University of Leiden, Department of Computer Science, Leiden, The Netherlands.

M. Korff : Technical Universitat Berlin, Franklinstrasse 28/29, W-1000 Berlin 10, Germany.

H-J. Kreowski : Universität Bremen, Fachbereich Mathematik/Informatik, Postfach 33-04-40, D-2800 Bremen 33, Germany.

L. Leth : European Computer-Industry Research Centre, Arabellastrasse 17, D-8000 Munich 81, Germany.

M. Löwe : Technical Universitat Berlin, Franklinstrasse 28/29, W-1000 Berlin 10, Germany.

F. Lui : Universität Oldenburg, FB10, Postfach 2503, W-2900 Oldenburg, Germany.

P. McBrien : Imperial College, Department of Computer Science, 180 Queen's Gate, London, SW7 2BZ, UK.

D.L. McBurney : University of East Anglia, School of Information Systems, Norwich NR4 7TJ, UK.

E. Nöcker : University of Nijmegen, Faculty of Mathematics and Informatics, Toernooiveld 1, 6525 ED Nijmegen, The Netherlands.

T. Peikenkamp : Universität Oldenburg, FB10, Postfach 2503, W-2900 Oldenburg, Germany.

R. Plasmeijer : University of Nijmegen, Faculty of Mathematics and Informatics, Toernooiveld 1, 6525 ED Nijmegen, The Netherlands.

D. Plump : Universität Bremen, Fachbereich Mathematik/Informatik, Postfach 33 04 40, D-2800 Bremen 33, Germany.

J.C. Raoult : Université de Rennes, IRISA, Campus de Beaulieu, F-35042 Rennes-Cedex, France.

F. Rossi : Universita di Pisa, Dipartimento di Informatica, Corso Italia 40, 56125 Pisa, Italy.

M.R. Sleep : University of East Anglia, School of Information Systems, Norwich NR4 7TJ, UK.

S. Smetsers : University of Nijmegen, Faculty of Mathematics and Informatics, Toernooiveld 1, 6525 ED Nijmegen, The Netherlands.

B. Thomsen : European Computer-Industry Research Centre, Arabellastrasse 17, D-8000 Munich 81, Germany.

Y. Toyama : NTT Laboratories, Inunidani, Seika-cho, Soraku-gun, Kyoto 619-02, Japan.

F.J. de Vries : CWI, Kruislaan 413, 1098 SJ Amsterdam, The Netherlands.

A. Wagner : Technical Universität Berlin, Franklinstrasse 28/29, W-1000 Berlin 10, Germany.

H. Yamanaka : Institute for Advanced Study of Social Information Science, Fujitsu Laboratories Ltd, 1-17-25 Shin-Kamata, Ohta-Ku, Tokyo 144, Japan.

1

An Introduction to Term Graph Rewriting

J.R. Kennaway, J.W. Klop, M.R. Sleep and F.J. de Vries

1.1 INTRODUCTION AND HISTORICAL REMARKS

Rewriting is a method of computation. Let us give a very simple example from everyday arithmetic:

$$4 \times (2+5) - (2+5) \times 3 = 4 \times 7 - (2+5) \times 3 = 28 - (2+5) \times 3 = 28 - 7 \times 3 = 28 - 21 = 7.$$

In proceeding from the initial expression $4 \times (2 + 5) - (2 + 5) \times 3$ to the final result of 7, we at each stage select some subexpression for which we know how to perform a single computational step, replacing it by the result of that step. First $(2 + 5)$ is selected and replaced by 7, then the subexpression 4×7 is treated similarly, and so on until a final result is obtained which requires no further calculation. By introducing conditional rules, and rules for building and examining data structures, we obtain an expressive programming language.

There is a certain inefficiency in the above example computation. The subexpression $2 + 5$ appears twice, and is rewritten twice. A different representation of the whole expression might store $2 + 5$ just once, and make two references to it. When it is rewritten to 7, the effect is 'seen' by both references, and in a single computational step the expression becomes $4 \times 7 - 7 \times 3$. Thus, instead of representing the expression as a tree structure — a syntax tree — it may be represented as a graph instead, as in Figure 1.1. As a result, the amount of computation required to reach the normal form is in general reduced. This method of rewriting is called *term graph rewriting*, and is the subject of this book.

Term Graph Rewriting: Theory and Practice.
Eds. Ronan Sleep, Rinus Plasmeijer and Marko van Eekelen.

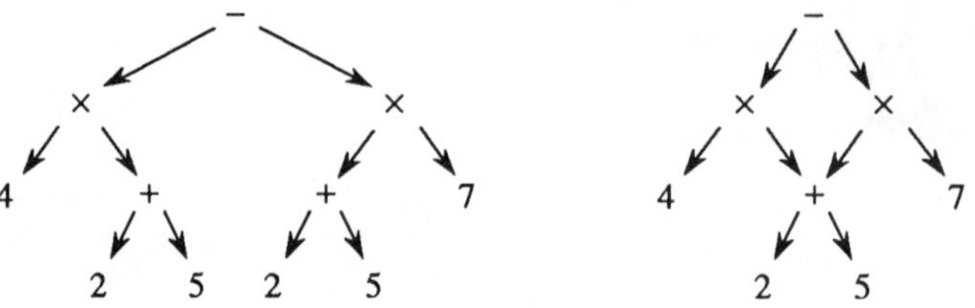

Figure 1.1 Tree and graph representations of $4 \times (2+5) - (2+5) \times 3$

1.1.1 History

Graph rewriting as a computational mechanism began with Wadsworth, who in his thesis [Wad71] proposed the idea of sharing in the setting of the lambda calculus. He used it to implement normal-order reduction for the lambda calculus, but showed that his implementation was not optimal. Lévy [Lév80] defined a notion of optimal reduction for lambda calculus, but did not give an implementation having this property. Such implementations were discovered independently by Lamping [Lam90] and Kathail [Kat90], and refined by Gonthier *et al.* [GAL92]. These works were all concerned with lambda calculus. Staples [Sta80] studied optimal evaluation for graph-like expressions and term rewriting. Barendregt *et al.* [BvEG+87] clarified the connection between graph based evaluation techniques (called *term graph rewriting*) and term rewriting, and established results about normalising strategies. All these treatments gave an operational description of rewrite steps.

A category-theoretic description of a rewrite step as a pushout in the category of term graphs (directed acyclic labelled graphs which represent terms) was first given by Raoult [Rao84], and refined by Kennaway in [Ken87]. Independently, Hoffmann and Plump [HP88] showed that Ehrig's double-pushout construction [Ehr79], in an equivalent ([CMR+91]) category of graphs called *jungles*, led to an equivalent form of term graph rewriting, called jungle rewriting. In the present volume, Corradini and Rossi use the same category to give a different translation of term rewrite rules to jungle rewrite rules, enabling them to treat both left-linear and non-left-linear rules in a uniform way. Kennaway [Ken91] and Löwe [Löw91] independently discovered that the double-pushout construction could be viewed as a single pushout in a category of term graphs and partial morphisms.

Sharing in term rewriting systems does not necessarily have to be expressed in the framework of graphs. Maranget [Mar92] has very recently considered so-called labelled term rewriting systems, T^lRSs. For orthogonal T^lRSs he can characterize the optimal derivations (i.e., informally, only contracting needed redexes, while avoiding duplication). He shows directly that for orthogonal T^lRSs there is an optimal reduction leading to normal form. For term graph rewriting this result has been obtained by Kennaway *et al.* [KKSdV90] via translations between term graph rewriting and infinitary term rewriting. As an application Maranget is able to show that lazy evaluation of the weak $\lambda\sigma$-calculus is optimal.

Currently much work on graph rewriting is centred around two European collaborations, both of which are supported by the ESPRIT Basic Research Programme. These are:

BRA 6345: Semantics and Pragmatics of Graph Rewriting (referred to below as *Semagraph*)
BRA 7183: Computing by Graph Transformation (referred to below as *Compugraph*)

Semagraph focuses primarily on term graph rewriting, while Compugraph has a wider scope. In the Semagraph project there is much more emphasis on the design of language systems based on term graph rewriting and efficient computer implementations. This has led to the development of two programming languages based on term graph rewriting, Dactl [GKS91] and Concurrent Clean [BEL+87, NSEP91]. Dactl, developed at the University of East Anglia, is a powerful low level language supporting fine grain control notions. Concurrent Clean, developed at the University of Nijmegen, is a high level lazy functional graph rewriting language with a very efficient implementation on both sequential as well as parallel hardware. The underlying graph rewriting semantics of Concurrent Clean made it possible to define a type system that indicates which parts of the graph can be overwritten without violating referential transparency on the language level. This has been used to incorporate unrestricted file-I/O, window based I/O and destructively updateable arrays [PAP93].

1.2 TERM GRAPH REWRITING

1.2.1 Operational descriptions

We begin by defining a category of *term graphs*. A term graph over a set of function symbols Σ consists of a set of nodes N, a tuple of members of N (the *roots* of the graph), a partial function *lab* from a subset of N to Σ, and a partial function *succ* from the same subset of N to N^*. Nodes outside the domain of *lab* and *succ* are called *variable* nodes. A homomorphism from a graph $G = (N_G, lab_G, succ_G)$ to a graph $H = (N_H, lab_H, succ_H)$ is a function f from N_G to N_H, such that for every non-variable node n of G, $lab_G(n) = lab_H(f(n))$ and $f(succ_G(n)) = succ_H(f(n))$ (where f is extended to tuples in the usual way). Note that f is not required to map variable nodes to variable nodes, nor root nodes to root nodes. These graphs and homomorphisms form the category of term graphs over Σ.

For any node n of a graph G, we write $G|n$ to denote the subgraph of G with n as its root, and containing that part of G accessible from n (i.e. closed under the *succ* function).

Single-rooted term graphs may be used to represent terms. A term may be read as a syntax tree, which is already a form of graph. However, instead of retaining the variable names which may occur in a term, we instead use variable nodes, in such a way that repeated occurrences of the same variable in a term are represented by multiple edges pointing to the same variable node of the graph. Figure 1.2 exhibits a simple example. Note that all three of the graphs in Figure 1.2 can be used to represent the given term. While multiple occurrences of a variable are always represented by a shared node, multiple occurrences of a non-variable subterm may be represented either as multiple subgraphs or as multiple references to a single subgraph. Thus in general a term can have several different graph representations. Among these are the representation which shares only repeated variables, never any larger repeated subterms, and the

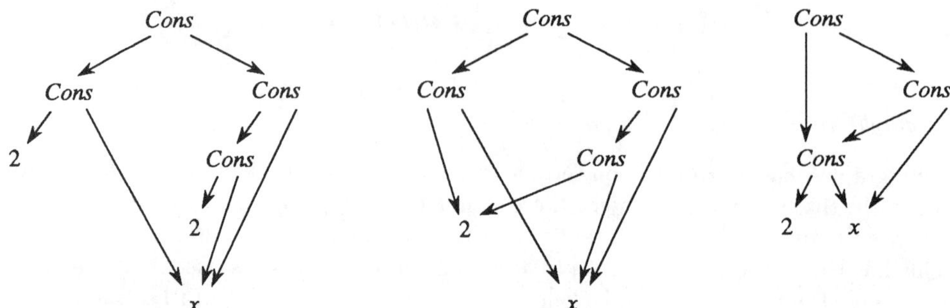

Figure 1.2 Three graph representations of $Cons(Cons(2, x), Cons(2, x), x)$

Figure 1.3 Two representations of $F(n) \rightarrow G(n-1) + H(n-1)$ as a graph rewrite rule

representation which shares as much as possible. All other representations lie between these (they form in fact a complete lattice with respect to a fairly obvious partial ordering by amount of sharing).

A *term graph rewrite rule* is a type of bi-rooted term graph. The two roots are called the *left root* and *right root*. The graph is subject to the following conditions. (i) The left root is not a variable node. (ii) Every variable node of the graph is accessible from the left root. (iii) The part of the graph which is accessible from the left root contains no sharing other than of variable nodes.

Term graph rewrite rules may be used to represent left-linear term rewrite rules. Given a term rewrite rule $L \rightarrow R$, we take graphs representing L and R, and merge them into a single graph by sharing nodes of L and R corresponding to the same variable. The roots of L and R become the left and right root of the graph. The graph representing L must be chosen to contain no sharing other than of variables, but the graph representing R need not be so limited. Repeated subterms of R may be represented by multiple edges pointing to the same subgraph in the graph rewrite rule. Figure 1.3 illustrates a term rewrite rule and two possible representations.

A term graph rewrite rule R is applied to a graph g by finding a homomorphism from $R \mid \mathit{left}(R)$ to g, adding to g a copy of every other node of R outside $R \mid \mathit{left}(R)$, deleting the node of g which $\mathit{left}(R)$ was mapped to, and replacing every edge pointing to that node by an edge pointing to the copy of $\mathit{right}(R)$. Figure 1.4 shows an example. Note that this representation of term rewrite rules does not handle non-left-linear rules. A repeated variable in the left hand side of a term rewrite rule implies a test for syntactic equality of the corresponding subterms of a redex of such a rule. The graph rewrite rule given by the above translation tests pointer equality, not syntactic equality.

With this restriction, this description was proved correct in [BvEG+87]. That is, in a left-linear system of rules, every reduction of a term to normal form by term

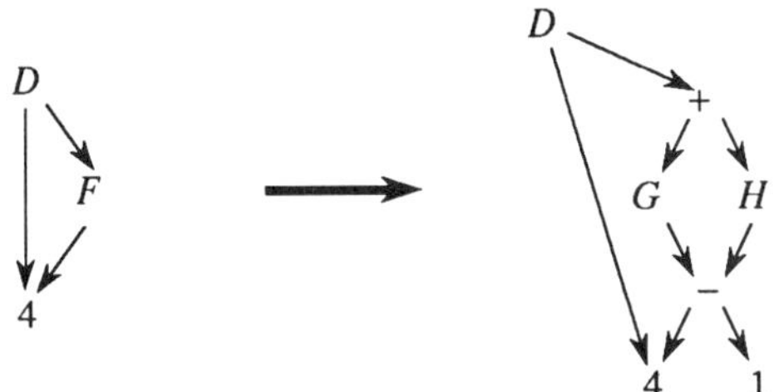

Figure 1.4 Applying the second rule of Figure 1.3 to the graph $D(n, F(n:4))$

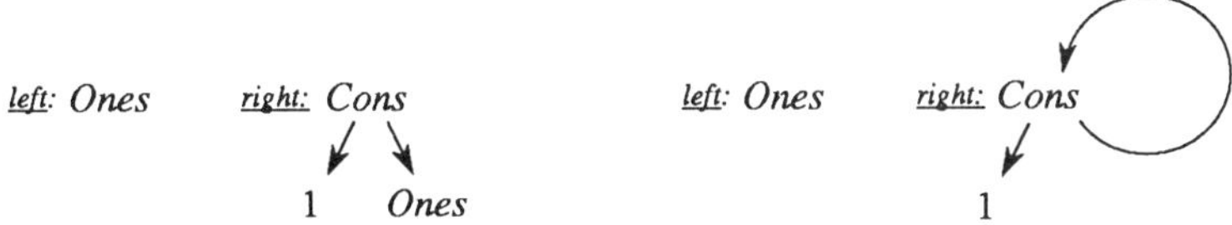

Figure 1.5 Acyclic and cyclic representations of $Ones \rightarrow Cons(1, Ones)$

rewriting is equivalent to interpreting the term as a graph, reducing the graph to normal form, and interpreting the resulting graph as a term.

The graph rewrite rules produced by the translation are always acyclic. An alternative translation may introduce cycles, if the right hand side of the rule contains a copy of the left hand side. Every reference to that subterm of the right hand side can be represented instead by an edge pointing to the right root of the graph. For example, the term rewrite rule $Ones \rightarrow Cons(1, Ones)$ can be represented by either of the two graph rewrite rules in Figure 1.5. The correspondence between this translation and term rewriting now requires consideration of infinite terms, since such terms arise when considering the unravelling of cyclic graphs. This is done in chapter 12 of this volume, entitled "The Adequacy of Term Graph Rewriting for Simulating Term Rewriting".

1.2.2 Category-theoretic descriptions

The 'Berlin school' has defined a notion of graph rewriting by means of category-theoretic constructions [ER80]. Given a category of graphs and graph morphisms such as that defined above, a rewrite rule is a pair of morphisms $L \leftarrow K \rightarrow R$. L is the *left hand side* of the rule, R is the *right hand side*, and K is the *interface graph*. An occurrence of this rule in a graph G is a morphism from L to G. Such an occurrence is rewritten by constructing the diagram of Figure 1.6, in which both squares are required to be pushouts. The graph H is the result of the rewrite. The effect is that

$$\begin{array}{ccccc} L & \leftarrow & K & \rightarrow & R \\ \downarrow & & \downarrow & & \downarrow \\ G & \leftarrow & D & \rightarrow & H \end{array}$$

Figure 1.6 Graph rewriting by a double pushout

$$\begin{array}{ccc} L & \Rightarrow & R \\ \Downarrow & & \Downarrow \\ G & \Rightarrow & H \end{array}$$

Figure 1.7 Graph rewriting by a single pushout

the part of L outside K is deleted from G, and is replaced by the part of R outside K.

An alternative description in terms of partial morphisms and a single pushout square has been given by Kennaway [Ken91] and independently by Löwe [Löw91]. In any category, a partial morphism from A to B is a morphism from a subobject of A to B: $A \hookleftarrow X \rightarrow B$. (To be precise, X is only determined up to isomorphism.) We write the partial morphism as $A \Rightarrow B$ when we do not wish to indicate X explicitly. The partial morphism is *total* if the subobject $X \hookrightarrow A$ is an isomorphism. A rewrite rule as used in the double-pushout construction can be seen as a partial morphism, provided $K \rightarrow L$ is one-to-one. An occurrence $L \rightarrow G$ is a total morphism. One may then consider the pushout of $L \hookleftarrow K \rightarrow R$ and $L \simeq L \rightarrow G$ in the category of graphs and partial morphisms, shown in Figure 1.7. This construction has been proved equivalent to the double-pushout construction, when the latter construction is defined [Ken91]. The conditions for existence of the single-pushout of partial morphisms are in fact less restrictive than for the double-pushout.

Term graph rewriting as defined in the previous section is then just the specialisation of the above constructions to the category of term graphs. A bi-rooted term graph G as in the previous section corresponds to a graph rewrite rule $L \leftarrow K \rightarrow R$ of the above sort, where $L = G \,|\, \mathit{left}(G)$, and K and R are the results of removing $\mathit{left}(G)$ from the domains of the labelling functions of L and G respectively. The morphisms from K to L and R are the obvious ones. Since $K \rightarrow L$ is an inclusion (i.e. it is 1–1 on nodes), $L \leftarrow K \rightarrow R$ is also a partial morphism $L \Rightarrow R$ in the same category. The occurrence $L \rightarrow G$ is also a partial morphism, whose domain is the whole of L, and the pushout of these two partial morphisms gives the same graph H, with the associated partial morphism from G to H being identical to $G \leftarrow D \rightarrow H$.

The above representation of term rewrite rules as graph rewrite rules only handles left-linear term rewrite rules. A somewhat different representation due to Corradini and Rossi is described in chapter 8 of this volume. This representation can describe non-left-linear rules. In the double-pushout formulation, L is taken to consist of a single labelled node, labelled with the principal function symbol of the left hand side of the term rewrite rule, and with an appropriate number of variable nodes as its successors. K consists of the same graph with empty label and successor functions, and R is as before. In this formulation, the 'occurrence' $L \rightarrow G$ exists whenever the principal function symbol of the rule occurs in G, even if the whole of the left hand side of the rule does not. The construction of H as the second pushout both performs the check that a redex is actually present, and makes the appropriate modification to the graph required by the rewrite. If a redex is not present, this pushout will not exist. In contrast, the second pushout of the previous construction always exists, the check for the existence of a redex being implied by the existence of the morphism $L \rightarrow G$.

It is worth noticing that these category-theoretic constructions cannot be performed for categories of terms or trees. Even when the graphs L and R of the double-pushout construction are trees, the interface graph K is not. In the single-pushout formulation, the relation between L and R would not be representable by any partial morphism from L to R in a category of trees. In addition, restricting R to be a tree would imply excluding non-right-linear term rewrite rules.

There are many different categories of graphs and graph morphisms besides the term graphs already described. An alternative formulation of essentially the same type of term graphs is as *hypergraphs.* A hypergraph is a graph whose 'edges' may have more than two ends, or just one end. For example an octopus can be represented by a single hyperedge with eight ends. Formally, a hypergraph consists of a set of nodes N, a set of hyperedges E, a connectivity function *vertexes*: $E \to N^+$, and a labelling function from E to a set Σ of labels. It may also have a distinguished tuple of members of N, its *roots.* It is a *term hypergraph* if it has one root, each node is accessible from the root, and each node is the first vertex of at most one hyperedge. Accessibility is defined in the obvious way: if a node n is the first vertex of a hyperedge e, the successors of n are defined to be all the other vertexes of e. The nodes accessible from n are the successors of n and the nodes accessible from them. It is clear that these hypergraphs are equivalent to the labelled ordered directed graphs we introduced previously.

Several other categories of graphs arise as categories of functors with codomain SET, the category of sets. For example, a node-labelled, edge-labelled graph can be described as a functor from the category $\bullet \leftarrow \bullet \underset{\rightarrow}{\overset{\rightarrow}{}} \bullet \rightarrow \bullet$ to SET. A graph morphism is then a natural transformation between such functors. The resulting category is in fact a topos, although this rich structure has currently not been made use of. Alternatively, a graph can be represented as a coalgebra of a functor T from SET to SET, that is, a morphism from a set A to the set TA. Morphisms of graphs are then certain commutative squares of morphisms in SET. If T is taken to be the functor mapping each set A to the set A^* of finite strings of members of A, then a coalgebra $f : A \to TA$ describes a directed graph in which each node $a \in A$ has as its successors the tuple $f(a)$. Other types of graph can be described by other functors on SET.

1.3 AN ANNOTATED DESCRIPTION OF THE REMAINING CHAPTERS

The chapters are divided into three classes. Several chapters on classical term rewriting address questions about term rewriting which have arisen in the course of the study of term graph rewriting. Chapters concerning the theory and semantics of graph rewriting itself form the second section, and language and implementation issues the third.

1.3.1 Chapters on classical term rewriting

Chapter 2. *Partial Type Assignment in Left Linear Applicative Term Rewriting Systems.*

A problem for type assignment for general term rewrite systems is that types may not be preserved by rewriting. This chapter presents a formal notion of type assignment for left linear applicative term rewriting systems. A necessary and sufficient condition is given to guarantee type preservation under rewriting. The rewrite rules used in typical functional programming languages satisfy this condition.

Chapter 3. *How to Get Confluence for Explicit Substitutions.*
When modelling implementations of functional languages, it is necessary to describe fully the substitution process needed to realise function application. This may be done by adding explicit conversion rules to the lambda calculus, and studying the properties of the resulting calculus. Careful design leads to a confluent calculus (the $\lambda\sigma\Uparrow\eta$ calculus) which adds explicit substitution rules to $\lambda\beta\eta$. Confluence is proved by the interpretation method.

Chapter 4. *An Infinitary Church-Rosser Property for Non-collapsing Orthogonal Term Rewriting Systems.*
The Church-Rosser property for orthogonal systems fails when infinite sequences of rewrites and terms of infinite size are allowed. A study of non-confluent examples suggests that this failure is caused by collapsing rules: that is, rules whose right hand sides consist of a variable. This chapter shows that confluence of transfinite orthogonal systems holds when collapsing rules are prohibited, or at most one collapsing rule is allowed, of the form $I(x) \rightarrow x$.

Chapter 5. *The Functional Strategy and Transitive Term Rewriting Systems.*
Most lazy functional languages use a reduction strategy derived from the textual presentation of a program. A left to right pattern-driven strategy — called here the *functional strategy* — is usually employed. Use of this strategy amounts to adopting the semantics associated with a priority rewrite system. It is shown that the strategy is normalising for the class of left-incompatible term rewrite systems. The notion of transitivity of indexes plays a key role.

1.3.2 Chapters on the theory and semantics of graph rewriting

Chapter 6. *Graph Rewriting Systems for Efficient Compilation.*
This chapter develops a practically motivated formal model of graph rewriting, and some basic results about partial correctness of important classes of optimisations used in real implementations. It illustrates the close relationship which has been established during recent years between theory and practice.

Chapter 7. *A Fibration Semantics for Extended Term Graph Rewriting.*
Dactl is a practical programming language which supports an extended term graph rewriting model of computation. Dactl extends the simpler term graph model of rewriting to include support for context-sensitive graph rewriting and explicit control over the rewriting strategy. This chapter investigates the relation between the operational semantics of Dactl and possible categorical descriptions.

Chapter 8. *A New Term Graph Rewriting Formalism: Hyperedge Replacement Jungle Rewriting.*
Most early approaches to modelling term rewriting with graphs used ordered, directed labelled graphs to represent terms. Associated with each node is a label and an ordered list of references to successor nodes. An alternative is to use hyperedges to represent the ordered list of successors. With this representation, the classical double pushout construction provides a sound and complete representation of term graph rewriting. In addition, it supports non-left linear term rewriting rules and unification.

Chapter 9. *Abstract Reduction: Towards a Theory via Abstract Interpretation.* Concurrent Clean is a term graph rewriting language with a very high performance implementation. Part of the reason for the high performance is the use of a powerful strictness analyser which uses abstract reduction. This chapter gives a preliminary theoretical account of the technique, starting from the lattice developed in Chapter 9. An preliminary comparison of abstract reduction and more conventional approaches to strictness analysis emerges.

Chapter 10. *A Lattice for the Abstract Interpretation of Term Graph Rewriting Systems.*
Abstract interpretation is an important technique for the static analysis of programs, but its application to analysing programs formulated as term graph rewriting systems requires new formal constructions. This chapter presents an abstract lattice of term graphs which can be used in the abstract interpretation of term graph rewriting systems. It considers a number of restrictions on abstract graphs which ensure completeness of the abstract lattice, and exhibits a Galois connection between the abstract lattice and the powerset of term graphs.

Chapter 11. *Event Structures and Orthogonal Term Graph Rewriting.*
For any normalisable graph in an orthogonal term graph rewrite system, the essentially different pieces of work which are required in its evaluation to normal form constitute an elementary event structure. The partial ordering of the event structure embodies the notion of the reduction of one redex contributing to the creation of another. Redexes can be reduced in any order compatible with this dependency relation. The associated state domain is the set of Levy-equivalence classes of needed reduction sequences starting from the given term graph. Its top element corresponds to reduction to normal form. The height of the partial ordering implies a lower bound on the time required to reach the normal form by parallel reduction, and the width implies an upper bound on the amount of parallelism that can be usefully employed.

Chapter 12. *The Adequacy of Term Graph Rewriting for Simulating Term Rewriting.*
A notion is defined, called 'adequacy', of what it means for one rewrite system to implement or simulate another. It is known that finitary rewriting of acyclic graphs is adequate, in this sense, for finitary orthogonal term rewriting. However, this is not true of transfinite rewriting, which necessarily arises when one considers cyclic graphs. The chapter shows that finitary cyclic graph rewriting is adequate for a restricted version of transfinite term rewriting, called rational term rewriting.

Chapter 13. *Translations into the Graph Grammar Machine.*
The notion of a graph grammar machine is introduced, and various translations of computational models into a particular graph grammar machine are constructed. Correctness is shown for the translations, leading to several undecidability results.

Chapter 14. *An Algebraic Framework for the Transformation of Attributed Graphs.*
The single pushout construction for graph transformation is extended to attributed graphs. This is done by decomposing an attributed graph into distinct structural and data type components, together with label operators which assign data type elements to structural items. Rules and transformations on these objects can be described by a careful combination of partial morphisms for the structure part and total morphisms on the data type component. The whole theory for the algebraic single pushout approach developed for non-attributed graphs carries over.

Chapter 15. *Hypergraph Rewriting: Critical Pairs and Undecidability of Confluence.*
The well-known critical pair lemma for term rewriting states that a term rewrite system is locally confluent if and only if every critical pair has a common reduct. This lemma provides a decision procedure for local confluence. In contrast, this chapter shows that the critical pair lemma does not hold for graph rewriting. A stronger sufficient condition is given for local confluence, but in general local confluence of graph rewrite systems is undecidable, even for terminating systems.

Chapter 16. *A Quick Look at Tree Transductions.*
Rewriting may be viewed as defining a relation on objects, and can be compared with other ways of defining relations. A rich source of approaches is found in the study of tree transductions. These include tree automata with output, tree grammars, and monadic second order formulae. These approaches are surveyed and compared.

1.3.3 Chapters on language and implementation issues

Chapter 17. *Paragon Specifications and Their Implementation.*
Paragon is a high level hardware architecture design language based on extended term graph rewriting. The extensions introduce process and object notions allowing complex concurrent interactions between objects representing different parts of the architecture to be described. A brief sketch of the syntax and semantics of Paragon is given, together with an implementation scheme for a subset of Paragon. The implementation scheme is illustrated with a small packet switch example.

Chapter 18. *MONSTR: Term Graph Rewriting for Parallel Machines.*
There are two fundamental reasons why graph rewriting is hard to map efficiently onto parallel machines: it requires shared memory, and each rewrite is notionally an atomic action. For certain classes of term graph rewrite system — most notably those associated with functional languages — it is possible to show that fine grain concurrent execution of graph rewriting does not violate the second requirement [Ken88]. However, more general forms of term graph rewriting expressible in languages such as LEAN or Dactl do not have this nice property, and an implementor needs to worry about the execution cost of preserving atomic semantics. The chapter closely examines the Dactl model of extended term graph rewriting, and defines a sublanguage which on the one hand is capable of efficiently simulating most of full Dactl, and on the other hand can be implemented efficiently on a distributed memory parallel machine.

Chapter 19. *A Graph Rewriting Model Enhanced with Sharing for OR-parallel Execution of Logic Programs.*
Most existing OR-parallel models of logic programming are based on extensions of the Warren Abstract Machine, mainly because these models make full use of the existing sequential Prolog implementation techniques. This chapter investigates a different approach using a graph rewriting model of OR-parallelism. The motivation is partly to explore new ways of sharing, and partly because graph rewriting provides a common framework for both logic and functional programming. Preliminary experiments suggest that performance can indeed be improved using the new sharing techniques introduced in this chapter, but that the overhead costs may be significant.

Chapter 20. *A New Process Model for Functions.*
Milner and others have developed concurrency models which support notions of 'mobile processes'. This makes it possible to translate lambda calculus expressions to process networks which realise fine grain distributed evaluation. Such networks can be described as concurrent graph rewriting systems, and this chapter demonstrates this by giving translations from lambda expressions to process networks and thence to the concurrent graph rewriting language Dactl. Experiments with this translation suggest that they are competitive, particularly so for eager computation.

Chapter 21. *Parallel Execution of Concurrent Clean on ZAPP.*
Techniques for implementing extended term graph rewriting systems on fast sequential machines have now reached the state where the Concurrent Clean system can be used to produce real application software with an excellent run time performance very rapidly. This chapter describes work to date on exploiting the explicit parallelism supported by the Concurrent Clean languages using a parallel distributed memory architecture. The result is a parallel compiler translating Concurrent Clean to transputer assembler code. Some of the key techniques are described, together with some early experimental results.

Chapter 22. *Graph-based Operational Semantics of a Lazy Functional Language.*
Plotkin-style Structured Operational Semantics is often used to formulate an operational semantics for a programming language. This chapter investigates an analogous approach called Graph-based Operational Semantics, and discusses its application to defining the operational semantics of a Lazy Functional Language.

Chapter 23. *Graph Rewriting Using the Annotated Functional Strategy.*
Practical evaluation strategies for functional languages are a compromise between theoretically elegant 'needed' strategies in which only necessary redexes are rewritten, and less elegant but much faster pattern-driven strategies controlled in part by textual ordering of definitions. Adding annotations to such a language makes it possible to explore the use of parallelism in a practical language. This chapter motivates and describes in some detail the operational semantics of the annotated graph rewriting language Clean. The practical effectiveness of the design decisions reported can be judged from the state of the art performance from Clean implementations.

Chapter 24. *Implementing Logical Variables and Disjunctions in Graph Rewrite Systems.*
Reasonably natural and efficient mappings of committed choice logic languages into graph rewrite systems have been demonstrated. However, the suitability of graph rewriting is not so clear when a Prolog-like model is used. The chapter presents a detailed discussion of the problems of implementing a backtracking logic language, and proposes and illustrates appropriate techniques.

Chapter 25. *Process Annotations and Process Types.*
Concurrent Clean is a language for parallel graph rewriting which uses explicit annotations to express control. With only two annotations, one for the creation of genuinely parallel processes and one for the creation of interleaved (pseudo-parallel) processes, complex concurrent programs can be concisely expressed. Both readability and writeability are enhanced by a specially designed type system. A number of programming examples are presented and the semantics discussed. Concurrent

Clean runs efficiently on a number of industry standard platforms, and has been used to rapidly produce efficient applications.

Chapter 26. *JALPA: A Functional Modular Programming Language Based on Extended Graphical Term Rewriting.*
JALPA is an experimental language based on a category of graphs and the notion of disjoint union. The category of graphs provides efficient mechanisms for global dynamic sharing of identical sub-expressions by pointers, and mathematically rigorous semantics. JALPA has two sorts of modularisation mechanisms: parameterised modules and hierarchically structured modules. The chapter reports preliminary results from an experimental interpreted implementation. The results suggest that JALPA can be implemented efficiently in the manner described.

REFERENCES

[BEL+87] T. Brus, M.C.J.D. van Eekelen, M. van Leer, M.J. Plasmeijer, and H.P. Barendregt. Clean - a language for functional graph rewriting. In *Proc. of Conference on Functional Programming Languages and Computer Architecture (FPCA '87)*, Springer-Verlag, Lecture Notes in Computer Science 274, pp. 364–384. Portland, Oregon, USA, 1987.

[BvEG+87] H. P. Barendregt, M. C. J. D. van Eekelen, J. R. W. Glauert, J. R. Kennaway, M. J. Plasmeijer, and M. R. Sleep. Term graph rewriting. In J. W. de Bakker, A. J. Nijman, and P. C. Treleaven (editors), *Proc. PARLE'87 Conference, vol.II*, Springer-Verlag, Lecture Notes in Computer Science 259, pp. 141–158, 1987.

[CMR+91] A. Corradini, U. Montanari, F. Rossi, H. Ehrig, and M. Löwe. Logic programming and graph grammars. In H. Ehrig, H.-J. Kreowski, and G. Rozenberg (editors), *Proc. 4th International Workshop on Graph Grammars and their Application to Computer Science*, Springer-Verlag, Lecture Notes in Computer Science 532, pp. 221–237, 1991.

[Ehr79] H. Ehrig. Introduction to the algebraic theory of graph grammars. In V. Claus, H. Ehrig, and G. Rozenberg (editors), *Proc. 1st International Workshop on Graph Grammars and their Application to Computer Science*, Springer-Verlag, Lecture Notes in Computer Science 73, pp. 1–69, 1979.

[ER80] H. Ehrig and B. Rosen. Parallelism and concurrency of graph manipulations. *Theoretical Computer Science*, **11**, pp. 247–275, 1980.

[GAL92] G. Gonthier, M. Abadi, and J.-J. Lévy. The geometry of optimal lambda reduction. In *19th Ann. ACM Symposium on Principles of Programming Languages*, 1992.

[GKS91] J.R.W. Glauert, J.R. Kennaway, and M.R. Sleep. Dactl: An experimental graph rewriting language. In H. Ehrig, H.-J. Kreowski, and G. Rozenberg (editors), *Proceedings, 4th International Workshop on Graph Grammars and their Application to Computer Science*, Springer-Verlag, Lecture Notes in Computer Science 532, 1991.

[HP88] B. Hoffmann and D. Plump. Jungle evaluation for efficient term rewriting. In J. Grabowski, P. Lescanne, and W. Weckler (editors), *Proc. Int. Workshop on Algebraic and Logic Programming*, vol. 49 of *Mathematical Research*, pp. 191–203. Akademie-Verlag, 1988.

[Kat90] V. Kathail. *Optimal Interpreters for Lambda-calculus Based Functional Languages.* PhD thesis, M.I.T., 1990.

[Ken87] J. R. Kennaway. On 'on graph rewritings'. *Theoretical Computer Science*, **52**, pp. 37–58, 1987.

[Ken88] J. R. Kennaway. The correctness of an implementation of functional dactl by parallel rewriting. In *UK IT 88 Conference Publication*, pp. 254–257. IEE/BCS for Information Engineering Directorate, Dept. Trade and Industry, London, 1988.

[Ken91] J. R. Kennaway. Graph rewriting in some categories of partial morphisms. In H. Ehrig, H.-J. Kreowski, and G. Rozenberg (editors), *Proc. 4th International Workshop on Graph Grammars and their Application to Computer Science*, Springer-Verlag, Lecture Notes in Computer Science 532, pp. 490–504, 1991.

[KKSdV90] J. R. Kennaway, J. W. Klop, M. R. Sleep, and F. J. de Vries. *Transfinite Reductions in Orthogonal Term Rewriting Systems.* Technical Report CS-R9041, Centre for Mathematics and Computer Science, Kruislaan 413, Amsterdam, 1990.

[Lam90] J. Lamping. An algorithm for optimal lambda calculus reduction. In *17th Ann. ACM Symposium on Principles of Programming Languages*, 1990.

[Lév80] J.-J. Lévy. Optimal reductions in the lambda-calculus. In J. P. Seldin and J. R. Hindley (editors), *To H.B. Curry: Essays in Combinatory Logic, Lambda Calculus and Formalism.* Academic Press, 1980.

[Löw91] M. Löwe. Algebraic approach to single pushout graph transformation. Technische Universität Berlin, 1991.

[Mar92] L. Maranget. *La Stratégie Paresseuse.* PhD thesis, University of Paris VII, 1992. D.Phil. thesis.

[NSEP91] E.G.J.M.H. Nöcker, J.E.W. Smetsers, M.C.J.D. van Eekelen, and M.J. Plasmeijer. Concurrent Clean. In *Proc. of Parallel Architectures and Languages Europe (PARLE'91)*, Springer-Verlag, Lecture Notes in Computer Science 505, pp. 202–219. Eindhoven, The Netherlands, 1991.

[PAP93] J.H.G. van Groningen P.M. Achten and M.J. Plasmeijer. High-level specification of i/o in functional languages. In *Proceedings, Glasgow 1992 International Workshop on Functional Languages*, Springer-Verlag, Lecture Notes in Computer Science, 1993.

[Rao84] J. C. Raoult. On graph rewritings. *Theoretical Computer Science*, **32**, pp. 1–24, 1984.

[Sta80] J. Staples. Computation on graph-like expressions. *Theoretical Computer Science*, **11**, pp. 171–185, 1980.

[Wad71] C. P. Wadsworth. *Semantics and Pragmatics of the Lambda-Calculus.* D.phil. thesis, University of Oxford, 1971.

2

Partial Type Assignment in Left Linear Applicative Term Rewriting Systems

S. van Bakel, S. Smetsers, and S. Brock

2.1 INTRODUCTION

In the recent years several paradigms have been investigated for the implementation of functional programming languages. Not only the Lambda Calculus [Bar84], but also Term Rewriting Systems [Klo90] and Graph Rewriting Systems [BvEG+87] are topics of research. Lambda Calculus (or rather combinator systems) forms the underlying model for the functional programming language Miranda[1] [Tur85], Term Rewriting Systems are used in the underlying model for the language OBJ [FGJM85], and Graph Rewriting Systems is the model for the language Clean [BvEvLP87, NSvEP91].

There exists a well understood and well-defined notion of type assignment on Lambda terms, known as the Curry type assignment system [CF58]. This type assignment system is the basis for many type checkers and inferers used in functional programming languages. For example the type assignment system for the language ML [Mil78], as defined by Milner forms in fact an extension of Curry's system. The type inference algorithm for the functional programming language Miranda works in roughly the same way as the one for ML. A real difference between these languages lies in the fact that Miranda also contains a type check algorithm, which is based on the type assignment system defined by Mycroft, an extension of Milner's type assignment system [Myc84, KTU88].

To provide a formal type system for all languages that use pattern matching this chapter presents a formal notion of type assignment on Left Linear Applicative Term

[1] Miranda is a trademark of Research Software Ltd.

Term Graph Rewriting: Theory and Practice.
Eds. Ronan Sleep, Rinus Plasmeijer and Marko van Eekelen.

Rewriting Systems. As shown in this chapter type assignment in Term Rewriting Systems in general does not satisfy the subject reduction property: i.e. types are not preserved under rewriting. The main result of this chapter, the formulation of a necessary and sufficient condition on rewrite rules to obtain subject reduction, could be used to prove that all rewrite rules that can be defined in a language like Miranda are safe in that respect. Also, if at first sight one could think that the generalization of type assignments from functional programming languages to Term Rewriting Systems would be straightforward, this is not true, as is shown from the conditions given to guarantee preservance of types under rewriting.

The type assignment system we present in this chapter is a partial system in the sense of [Pfe88], because we not only define how terms and rewrite rules can be typed, but also provide a type for each function symbol. There are several reasons to do so.

For symbols for which there is a rewrite rule (called defined symbols), and for symbols for which such a rule does not exist (called constants), there must be some way of determining what type can be used for an occurrence. Instead of for defined symbols investigating their rule every time the symbol is encountered, we can store the type of the symbol in a mapping from symbols to types, and use this mapping instead. Of course it makes no difference to assume the existence from the start of such a mapping from symbols to types, and to define type assignment using that mapping. This mapping is also convenient to make sure that types assigned to different occurrences of constants do not conflict.

In fact, the approach we take here is very much the same as the one taken by Hindley in [Hin69], where he defines the principal type scheme of an object in Combinatory Logic. Even his notion of type assignment could be regarded as a partial one. Moreover, since combinator systems can easily be translated into Left Linear Applicative Term Rewriting Systems, the results of this chapter, when restricting the allowed rewrite rules to those that correspond to combinators, are the same as in [Hin69].

We will define the Left Linear Applicative Term Rewriting Systems, as the subclass of Term Rewriting Systems that contain a predefined symbol *Ap*, and in which all rewrite rules are left linear. The definition of Applicative Term Rewriting Systems is not the one normally used, but more general: in the systems we consider, *Ap* is not the only function symbol.

The notion of type assignment on Left Linear Applicative Term Rewriting Systems is in fact defined on the tree representation of terms and rewrite rules, by assigning in a consistent way types to nodes and edges. The only constraints on this system are imposed by the relation between the type assigned to a node and those assigned to its incoming and outgoing edges. It is based on the Mycroft type assignment system as used in Miranda.

We will show that for every basis B, term M, type σ and substitution S: if $B \vdash M{:}\sigma$ (i.e. M is typeable by σ starting from the set B of typed term variables), then also $S(B) \vdash M{:}S(\sigma)$. We will also show that for every typeable term M, there is a principal pair $<P, \pi>$ for M, i.e. for every pair $<B, \sigma>$ such that $B \vdash M{:}\sigma$ there is a substitution S such that $S(<P, \pi>) = <B, \sigma>$.

Another result presented is that if $<B, \sigma>$ is the principal pair for M, and M' is obtained from M by replacing (in a consistent way) term variables by terms, and M'

is typeable by τ, then there is a substitution S such that: $S(\sigma) = \tau$, and for every $x{:}\rho$ occurring in B, the replacement of x is typeable by $S(\rho)$.

We will show that if type assignment is done in the most obvious, straightforward way, there are rewrite rules that are typeable, that match a term M typeable with σ, but for which the result of the application of the rewrite rule on M is not typeable with σ. We will formulate a condition that typeable rewrite rules should satisfy in order to guarantee preservance of types under rewriting. We will prove this condition to be necessary and sufficient.

The results discussed in this chapter were first presented in [vBSB92]. Readers interested in a more complete treatment are kindly referred to that paper.

2.2 LEFT LINEAR APPLICATIVE TERM REWRITING SYSTEMS

In this chapter we study Left Linear Applicative Term Rewriting Systems (LLATRS), which are a subclass of Term Rewriting Systems, as defined in [Klo90]. LLATRS are defined as the class of Term Rewriting Systems that (can) contain a special binary operator *Ap*, and in which all rewrite rules are left linear. To distinguish them from the Term Rewriting Systems that have *only* the function symbol *Ap*, we call the latter the *pure* Applicative Term Rewriting Systems.

The motivation for the use of Applicative Term Rewriting Systems instead of the general Term Rewriting Systems can be illustrated by the following example: If we would want to translate Combinatory Logic (CL)

$$\begin{array}{ll} S\ x\ y\ z & = x\ z\ (y\ z) \\ K\ x\ y & = x \\ I\ x & = x \end{array}$$

into a Term Rewriting System, then it could look like (making the implicit application explicit):

$$\begin{array}{lll} Ap\,(Ap\,(Ap\,(S,x),y),z) & \Rightarrow & Ap\,(Ap\,(x,z),Ap\,(y,z)) \\ Ap\,(Ap\,(K,x),y) & \Rightarrow & x \\ Ap\,(I,x) & \Rightarrow & x \end{array}$$

However, we prefer to see the symbols S, K and I as functions, with 3, 2 and 1 operands respectively. If we try to capture that view in our translation, we would need to define also the Curried versions of those symbols:

$$\begin{array}{lll} S\,(x,y,z) & \Rightarrow & Ap\,(Ap\,(x,z),Ap\,(y,z)) \\ Ap\,(S_2\,(x,y),z) & \Rightarrow & S\,(x,y,z) \\ Ap\,(S_1\,(x),y) & \Rightarrow & S_2\,(x,y) \\ Ap\,(S_0,x) & \Rightarrow & S_1\,(x) \\ K\,(x,y) & \Rightarrow & x \\ Ap\,(K_1\,(x),y) & \Rightarrow & K\,(x,y) \\ Ap\,(K_0,x) & \Rightarrow & K_1\,(x) \\ I\,(x) & \Rightarrow & x \\ Ap\,(I_0,x) & \Rightarrow & I\,(x) \end{array}$$

We consider the Applicative Rewriting Systems, because they are far more general than the subclass of systems in which there exists only the function symbol *Ap*. Since the Left Linear Applicative Term Rewriting Systems contain the subclass of the pure systems, all results obtained in this chapter are also valid for that subclass.

We take the view that in a rewrite rule a certain symbol is defined, and it is clear that the rules added to obtain the Curried versions of symbols in the translation of CL into a rewriting system are not intended as definitions for *Ap*, which is more or less a 'predefined function', but as definitions for the Curried versions.

However, in general Term Rewriting Systems are not sensitive for the names used for functions symbols. So the rewriting system given above is in fact the same as the one obtained by replacing all *Ap*s by F, and then all rewrite rules starting with F could be seen as rules that define F. In order to avoid this problem, we regard those rewriting systems that have a 'predefined' binary function, called *Ap*, which then cannot be renamed. The symbol *Ap* is neglected when we are looking for the symbol that is defined in a rewrite rule.

In the Lambda Calculus there is a clear difference between free and bound variables of a term. In Term Rewriting Systems a term variable x that occurs in the left-hand side of a rewrite rule can be seen as the binding occurrence of x, binding the occurrences of x in the right-hand side. However, in general x can occur more than once in the left-hand side, making the notion of *the* binding occurrence obscure. In this chapter we consider left linear rewriting systems, that contain only rewrite rules for which the left-hand side is linear (term variables occur only once), because for those rules the binding occurrence of a term variable is unique.

The following definitions are based on definitions given in [Klo90]. Definition 2.2.1 defines LLATRS, in the same way as the definition given by Klop for Term Rewriting Systems, extended with part a3 to express the existence of the predefined symbol *Ap*. Definition 2.2.2 defines a notion of rewriting on LLATRS, in the same way as the definition of rewriting given by Klop for Term Rewriting Systems, extended with part b(1)ii to express the left linearity of rewrite rules, part b(1)iv to express that the possible use of the symbol *Ap* in the left-hand side is restricted, and part c to define the notion of defined symbol of a rewrite rule. In fact, parts b(1)iv and c are related.

We introduce in some parts a different notation, because some of the symbols or definitions normally used are also used in papers on type assignment, but with a different meaning. For example, we use the word "replacement" for the operation that replaces term variables by terms, instead of the word "substitution", which will be used for operations that replace type variables by types.

Substitution and replacement are also operations defined in [CF58]. Both operations are there defined as operations on terms, where substitution is defined as the operation that replaces term variables by terms, and replacement is defined as the operation that replaces subterms by terms. Note that our definition therefore differs from the one given in [CF58].

To denote a replacement, we use capital characters like "R", instead of Greek symbols like "σ", which are used to denote types. We use the symbol "$\Rightarrow$" for the rewriting symbol, instead of "$\rightarrow$" which is used as a type constructor. We use the notion "constant symbol" for a symbol that cannot be rewritten, instead of for a function symbol with arity 0.

DEFINITION **2.2.1** *A* Left Linear Applicative Term Rewriting System *(LLATRS) is a pair* $(\Sigma, \mathbf{R})$ *of an* alphabet *or* signature Σ *and a set of* rewrite rules $\mathbf{R}$.

a. The alphabet Σ *consists of:*

(1) A countable infinite set of variables $x_1, x_2, x_3, \ldots$ *(or* $x, y, z, x', y', \ldots$*).*
(2) A non empty set Σ_0 *of* function symbols *or* operator symbols $F, G, \ldots,$ *each equipped with an "arity" (a natural number), i.e. the number of "arguments" it is supposed to have. We have 0-ary, unary, binary, ternary etc function symbols.*
(3) A special binary operator, called application *(Ap).*

b. The set of terms *(or* expressions*) "over"* Σ *is* Ter (Σ) *and is defined inductively:*

(1) $x, y, z, \ldots \in \text{Ter}(\Sigma)$.
(2) If $F \in \Sigma_0 \cup \{Ap\}$ *is an n-ary symbol, and* $T_1, \ldots, T_n \in \text{Ter}(\Sigma)$ $(n \geq 0)$*, then* $F(T_1, \ldots, T_n) \in \text{Ter}(\Sigma)$.

c. Terms in which no variable occurs twice or more, are called linear.

DEFINITION **2.2.2** *Let* $(\Sigma, \mathbf{R})$ *be a LLATRS.*

a. A replacement R *is a map from* Ter (Σ) *to* Ter (Σ) *satisfying*

$$R(F(T_1, \ldots, T_n))) = F(R(T_1), \ldots, R(T_n))$$

for every n-ary function symbol F (here $n \geq 0$*). So, R is determined by its restriction to the set of variables. We also write* T^R *instead of* $R(T)$.

b.(1) A rewrite rule $\in \mathbf{R}$ *is a pair (LHS, RHS) of terms* $\in \text{Ter}(\Sigma)$*. Often a rewrite rule will get a name, e.g.* $\mathbf{r}$*, and we write* $\mathbf{r} : LHS \Rightarrow RHS$*. Four conditions will be imposed:*

i. LHS is not a variable.

ii. LHS is linear.

iii. The variables occurring in RHS are contained in LHS.

iv. For every Ap in LHS, the left-hand argument is not a variable.

(2) A rewrite rule $\mathbf{r} : LHS \Rightarrow RHS$ *determines a set of* rewrites $LHS^R \Rightarrow RHS^R$ *for all replacements R. The left-hand side* LHS^R *is called a* redex*; it may be replaced by its "*contractum*"* RHS^R *inside a context* C[ ]*; this gives rise to* rewrite steps*:*

$$C[\, LHS^R \,] \Rightarrow_{\mathbf{r}} C[\, RHS^R \,].$$

(3) We call $\Rightarrow_{\mathbf{r}}$ *the* one-step rewrite relation *generated by* $\mathbf{r}$*. Concatenating rewrite steps we have (possibly infinite)* rewrite sequences $T_0 \Rightarrow T_1 \Rightarrow T_2 \Rightarrow \ldots$ *or* rewrites *for short. If* $T_0 \Rightarrow \ldots \Rightarrow T_n$ *we also write* $T_0 \Rrightarrow T_n$*, and* T_n *is a* rewrite *of* T_0.

c. *In a rewrite rule, the leftmost, outermost symbol in the left-hand side that is not an Ap, is called* the defined symbol *of that rule. If the symbol F is the defined symbol of* **r**, *then* **r** defines F. F *is* a defined symbol, *if there is a rewrite rule that defines* F. $A \in \Sigma_0$ *is called a* constant symbol *if A is not a defined symbol.*

Part b(1)iv of Definition 2.2.2 is added in order to avoid rewrite rules with left-hand sides like $Ap(x, y)$, because such a rule would not have a defined symbol.

PROPOSITION **2.2.3** *Let F be the defined symbol of the rewrite rule* $\mathbf{r}$: *LHS* $\Rightarrow$ *RHS. Then there are $n \geq j \geq 0$, and $T_1, \ldots, T_n$ such that:*

$$LHS = Ap(Ap(\ldots Ap(F(T_1, \ldots, T_j), T_{j+1}), \ldots), T_n).$$

and $T_1, \ldots, T_n$ are called the patterns *of* **r**.

We will consider rewriting systems that are *Curry-closed*, i.e. for every rewrite rule that defines the symbol F with arity $n \geq 0$, we will assume that there are n additional rewrite rules that define the function symbols F_0 upto F_{n-1} as follows:

$$\begin{array}{lll} Ap(F_{n-1}(x_1, \ldots, x_{n-1}), x_n) & \Rightarrow & F(x_1, \ldots, x_n) \\ Ap(F_{n-2}(x_1, \ldots, x_{n-2}), x_{n-1}) & \Rightarrow & F_{n-1}(x_1, \ldots, x_{n-1}) \\ \vdots & & \\ Ap(F_0, x_1) & \Rightarrow & F_1(x_1) \end{array}$$

The added rules with $F_{n-1}, \ldots, F_1, F_0$, etc. give in fact the "Curried"-versions of F.

We could have defined a closure operation on LLATRS, by adding rules and extending the alphabet Σ, but it is easier to assume that every LLATRS is Curry-closed. When presenting a rewrite system however, we will only show the rules that are essential: we do not show the rules that define the Curried-versions.

2.3 TREE REPRESENTATION OF TERMS AND REWRITE RULES

DEFINITION **2.3.1** *a. The tree representation of terms and rewrite rules is obtained in a straightforward way, by representing a term $F(T_1, \ldots, T_n)$ by:*

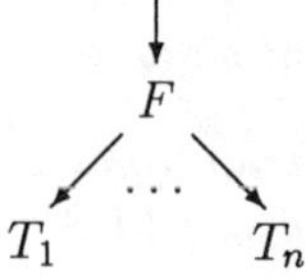

b. *The* spine *of a tree is defined as usual, i.e. the root node of the tree is on the spine, and if a node is on the spine, then its left most descendant is on the spine.*

c. *In the tree representation of a rewrite rule, the first node on the spine of the left-hand side, starting from the root node, that does not contain an Ap, is called the* defining node *of that rule. (Notice that if F is the defined symbol of a rewrite rule, then it occurs in the defining node of the tree representation of that rule.)*

We give some of the rewrite rules of CL in tree representation:

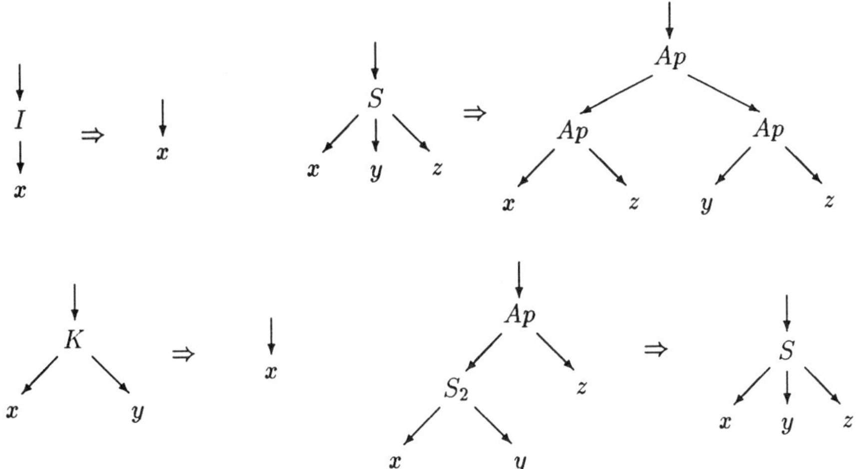

Rewrite rules can of course be more complicated than illustrated above by the rules for CL. In general, if the left-hand side of a rewrite rule is $F(T_1, \ldots, T_n)$, then the T_i need not be simple variables but can be terms as well, as for example in the rewrite rule $M(S_2(x, y)) \Rightarrow S_2(I_0, y)$. In tree representation, this rule looks like:

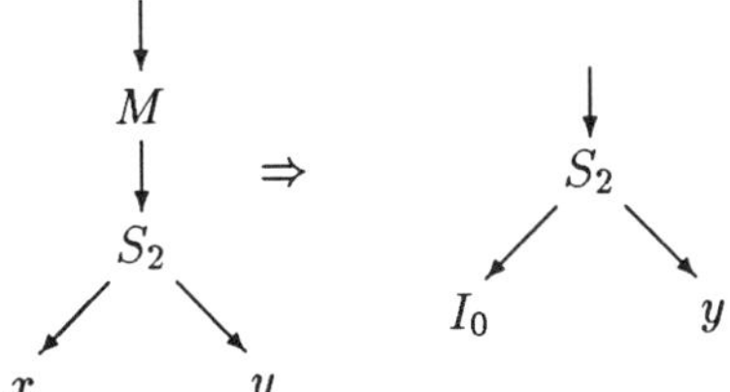

2.4 TYPE ASSIGNMENT IN LLATRS

In this section we present a notion of partial type assignment on LLATRS, based on the Mycroft type assignment system [Myc84, KTU88]. Assigning types to a LLATRS will consist of labeling the nodes and edges in the tree representation of terms and rewrite rules with type information. Types are assigned to nodes to capture the notion of "type of a function", "type of a constant" or "type of a variable", and are assigned to edges to capture the notion of "type of a subterm" (or tree). The edge pointing to the the root of a term is called the *root edge*.

The difference between Milner's and Mycroft's type assignment system lies in the way they handle recursion. Would we have used Milner's system, then we would have demanded that all occurrences of recursively defined objects are, within their definition, typed with the same type. Mycroft's approach is a more general one. Using his system the only requirement for recursive definitions would be to demand that the separate occurrences of the object within the definition are typed with types that are substitution instances of the type of the object.

There is one major difference between the notion of type assignment we introduce in this chapter and Curry's type assignment system. In that system a basis is usually defined as a mapping from term variables to types, or, equivalently, as a set of statements with distinct term variables as subjects. The bases allowed in the system we present, however, can contain several different statements for the same term variable. This in fact corresponds to the definition of ML-type assignment as given in [Dam85], and is used there for dealing with the let-construct. It could also be compared with using intersection types [BCD83] on free variables of terms. Unlike in Lambda Calculus, in Term Rewriting Systems this causes no difficulties, since there is no notion of "abstraction" in this world. Moreover, condition a2 of Definition 2.4.5 deals with this apparent anomaly. So in the system we present, it is possible to assign a type to the term $Ap(x, x)$.

2.4.1 Types

The type system we define in this subsection is based on the Curry type system, extended with type constants.

DEFINITION **2.4.1** *a.* *$\mathcal{T}_C$, the set of Curry types is inductively defined by:*

(1) All type variables $\varphi_0, \varphi_1, \ldots \in \mathcal{T}_C$.
(2) All type constants $c_0, c_1, \ldots \in \mathcal{T}_C$.
(3) If $\sigma, \tau \in \mathcal{T}_C$, then $\sigma \rightarrow \tau \in \mathcal{T}_C$.

b. A statement *is an expression of the form $M:\sigma$, where $M \in \text{Ter}(\Sigma)$ and $\sigma \in \mathcal{T}_C$. M is the* subject *and σ the* predicate *of $M:\sigma$.*

c. A basis *B is a set of statements with term variables, not necessarily distinct, as subjects. If a basis is denoted as $\{x_1:\rho_1, \ldots, x_n:\rho_n\}$, the x_i are distinct.*

In the notation of types, often outermost and rightmost brackets are omitted. We will use the symbol φ to denote a type variable and all other Greek characters to denote arbitrary types. Also, instead of φ indexed by a number, we will write the number.

DEFINITION **2.4.2** *a. A* substitution *$S : \mathcal{T}_C \rightarrow \mathcal{T}_C$ is as usual inductively defined by:*

(1) The substitution $(\varphi := \alpha)$, where φ is a type variable and $\rho \in \mathcal{T}_C$, is defined by:

i. $(\varphi := \alpha)(\varphi) = \rho$.

ii. $(\varphi := \alpha)(\varphi_0) = \varphi_0$, *if* $\varphi \neq \varphi_0$.

iii. $(\varphi := \alpha)(c_i) = c_i$.

iv. $(\varphi := \alpha)(\sigma \rightarrow \tau) = (\varphi := \alpha)(\sigma) \rightarrow (\varphi := \alpha)(\tau)$.

(2) If S_1 and S_2 are substitutions, then so is $S_1 \circ S_2$, where $S_1 \circ S_2(\sigma) = S_1(S_2(\sigma))$.

b. If for σ, τ there is a substitution S such that $S(\sigma) = \tau$, then τ is called a (substitution) instance *of σ.*

c. If σ is an instance of τ, and τ is an instance of σ, then σ is called a trivial variant *of τ. We identify types that are trivial variants of each other.*

d. $S(B) = \{x{:}S(\rho) \mid x{:}\rho \in B\}$.
e. $S(\langle B, \sigma\rangle) = \langle S(B), S(\sigma)\rangle$.

2.4.2 Type assignment

Type assignment on a LLATRS (Σ, R) is defined as the labeling of nodes and edges in the tree representation of terms and rewrite rules with types. If a node or edge is labeled with a type σ, we say that it is *typed* with σ, and σ is *assigned* to it.

In this labeling, we use that there is a mapping that provides a type in $\mathcal{T}_C$ for every $F \in \Sigma_0 \cup \{Ap\}$. Such a mapping is called an environment.

DEFINITION **2.4.3** *Let* (Σ, **R**) *be a LLATRS. A mapping* $\mathcal{E} : \Sigma_0 \cup \{Ap\} \rightarrow \mathcal{T}_C$ *is called an* environment *if* $\mathcal{E}(Ap) = (1\rightarrow 2)\rightarrow 1\rightarrow 2$, *and for every* $F \in \Sigma_0$ *with arity* n, $\mathcal{E}(F) = \mathcal{E}(F_{n-1}) = \ldots = \mathcal{E}(F_0)$.

DEFINITION **2.4.4** *Let* (Σ, **R**) *be a LLATRS.*

a. We say that $M \in \text{Ter}(\Sigma)$ is typeable by $\sigma \in \mathcal{T}_C$ with respect to $\mathcal{E}$, *if there exists an assignment of types to edges and nodes that satisfies the following constraints:*

(1) The root edge of M *is typed with* σ.
(2) If a node contains a symbol $F \in \Sigma_0 \cup \{Ap\}$ *that has arity* n $(n \geq 0)$, *then there are* $\sigma_1, \ldots, \sigma_n$ *and* σ, *such that this node is typed with* $\sigma_1\rightarrow\ldots\rightarrow\sigma_n\rightarrow\sigma$, *the* n *outgoing edges are from left to right typed with* σ_1 *up to* σ_n, *and the ingoing edge is typed with* σ.

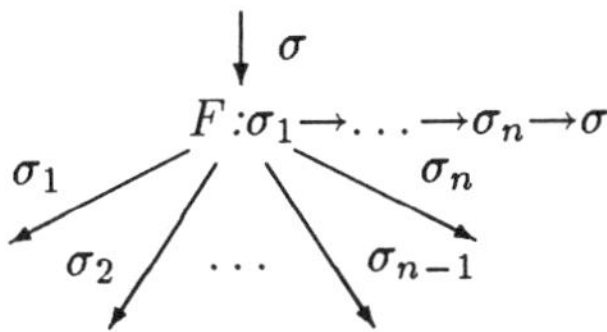

(3) If a node containing a symbol $F \in \Sigma_0 \cup \{Ap\}$ *is typed with* σ, *then there is a substitution* S, *such that* $S(\mathcal{E}(F)) = \sigma$.

b. Let $M \in \text{Ter}(\Sigma)$ *be typeable by* σ *with respect to* $\mathcal{E}$. *If* B *is a basis containing all statements with variables as subjects that appear in the typed tree for* $M{:}\sigma$, *we write* $B \vdash_{\mathcal{E}} M{:}\sigma$.

Notice that if $B \vdash_{\mathcal{E}} M{:}\sigma$, then B can contain more statements than needed to obtain $M{:}\sigma$.

DEFINITION **2.4.5** *Let* (Σ, **R**) *be a LLATRS.*

a. We say that **r**: $LHS \Rightarrow RHS \in \mathbf{R}$ *with defined symbol* F is naively typeable with respect to $\mathcal{E}$, *if the following constraints hold:*

(1) There are $\sigma \in \mathcal{T}_C$ *and basis* B *such that* $B \vdash_{\mathcal{E}} LHS{:}\sigma$ *and* $B \vdash_{\mathcal{E}} RHS{:}\sigma$.
(2) All nodes within **r** *containing the same term variable, are typed with the same type.*

(3) The defining node of **r***, containing* F*, is typed with* $\mathcal{E}(F)$*.*

b. We say that $(\Sigma, \mathbf{R})$ is naively typeable with respect to $\mathcal{E}$, *if for every* $\mathbf{r} \in \mathbf{R}$ *:* **r** *is naively typeable with respect to* $\mathcal{E}$*.*

Condition a3 is in fact added to make sure that the type provided by the environment for a function symbol F is not in conflict with the rewrite rules that define F. By restricting the type that can be assigned to the defining node to the type provided by the environment, we are sure that the rewrite rule is typed using that type, and not using a substitution instance.

It is easy to check that if F is a function symbol with artity n, and all rewrite rules that define F are typeable, then there are $\gamma_1, \ldots, \gamma_n, \gamma$ such that $\mathcal{E}(F) = \gamma_1 \rightarrow \ldots \rightarrow \gamma_n \rightarrow \gamma$.

In the rest of this chapter, we will assume the environment to be fixed, so we omit the subscript on $\vdash_{\mathcal{E}}$. Also, instead of saying "(naively) typeable with respect to $\mathcal{E}$", we just say "typeable". The use of an environment corresponds to the use of "axiom-schemes", and part a3 of Definition 2.4.4 to the use of "axioms" as in [Hin69].

A typical example for part a2 of Definition 2.4.4 is the function symbol Ap, which has the type $(1 \rightarrow 2) \rightarrow 1 \rightarrow 2$. So for every occurrence of Ap in a tree, there are σ and τ such that the following is part of the tree.

$$\begin{array}{ccc} & \downarrow \tau & \\ & Ap\colon (\sigma\rightarrow\tau)\rightarrow\sigma\rightarrow\tau & \\ \sigma\rightarrow\tau \swarrow & & \searrow \sigma \end{array}$$

2.4.3 The principal pair for a term

In this subsection we define the principal pair for a typeable term M with respect to $\mathcal{E}$, consisting of basis B and type σ, by defining the notion $pp(M)$ using Robinson's unification algorithm $unify_{\mathrm{R}}$ [Rob65]. (Notice that, from a formal point of view, we would have to define $pp_{\mathcal{E}}(M)$, but that again we are omitting the subscript $\mathcal{E}$.) In the following we show that for every typeable term, this is a legal pair and is indeed the most general one.

We recall the following well-known property of $unify_{\mathrm{R}}$.

PROPERTY **2.4.6** [Rob65] *If two types have an instance in common, they have a highest common instance which is returned by* $\mathrm{unify}_{\mathrm{R}}$*, so for all* σ, τ*: if* $S_1 = \mathrm{unify}_{\mathrm{R}}(\sigma, \tau)$ *and* S_2 *is a substitution such that* $S_2(\sigma) = S_2(\tau)$*, then there is a substitution* S_3 *such that* $S_2(\sigma) = S_3 \circ S_1(\sigma) = S_3 \circ S_1(\tau) = S_2(\tau)$*.*

DEFINITION **2.4.7** *We define, for every term* M *the notion* $pp(M) = \langle P, \pi \rangle$ *inductively by:*

a. For all x, φ*:* $pp(x) = \langle \{x{:}\varphi\}, \varphi \rangle$*.*

b. If for every $1 \leq i \leq n$*:* $pp(T_i) = \langle P_i, \pi_i \rangle$*,* $\mathcal{E}(F) = \sigma_1 \rightarrow \ldots \rightarrow \sigma_n \rightarrow \sigma$*, (we choose if necessary trivial variants such that the* $\langle P_i, \pi_i \rangle$ *are pairwise disjoint and these pairs share no type variables with* $\sigma_1 \rightarrow \ldots \rightarrow \sigma_n \rightarrow \sigma$*), and*

$$S = \mathrm{unify}_{\mathrm{R}}\,(\sigma_1 \rightarrow \ldots \rightarrow \sigma_n \rightarrow \sigma,\ \pi_1 \rightarrow \ldots \rightarrow \pi_n \rightarrow \varphi),$$

where φ *does not occur in any of the pairs* $<P_i,\ \pi_i>$, *nor in* $\sigma_1 \rightarrow \ldots \rightarrow \sigma_n \rightarrow \sigma$, *then:*

$$pp(F\,(T_1,\ \ldots,\ T_n)) = <S\,(P_1 \cup \ldots \cup P_n),\ S\,(\sigma)>.$$

For these notions the following properties hold:

THEOREM **2.4.8** (Soundness of substitution) *If* $B \vdash M{:}\sigma$, *then for every substitution* S: $S\,(B) \vdash M{:}S\,(\sigma)$.

We cannot show a soundness result for rewrite rules.
It is easy to verify that $pp(M) = <P,\ \pi>$ implies $P \vdash M{:}\pi$.

THEOREM **2.4.9** (Completeness of substitution) *If* $B \vdash M{:}\sigma$, *then there are* P, π, *and a substitution* S *such that:* $pp(M) = <P,\ \pi>$, *and* $S\,(P) \subseteq B$, $S\,(\pi) = \sigma$.

If F is the defined symbol of a rewrite rule, then the type $\mathcal{E}\,(F)$ dictates not only the type for the left and right-hand side of that rule, but also the principal type for the left-hand side, or, formally:

LEMMA **2.4.10** *If* F *is the defined symbol of the typeable rewrite rule* $\mathbf{r}$: $LHS \Rightarrow RHS$, *then there are* P, B, $\sigma_1,\ \ldots,\ \sigma_n$, *and* σ *such that*

$$\mathcal{E}(F) = \sigma_1 \rightarrow \ldots \rightarrow \sigma_n \rightarrow \sigma,\ pp(LHS) = <P,\ \sigma>,\ B \vdash LHS{:}\sigma \text{ and } B \vdash RHS{:}\sigma.$$

The following Lemma plays an important part in the proof that the condition, as defined in Definition 2.4.12, imposed on typeable rewrite rules is necessary and sufficient, as given in Theorem 2.4.13 and formulates the relation between replacements performed on a term and possible type assignments for that term.

LEMMA **2.4.11** *a. If* $pp(M) = <P,\ \pi>$, *and for the replacement* R *there are* B *and* σ *such that* $B \vdash M^{\mathrm{R}}{:}\sigma$, *then there is a substitution* S, *such that* $S\,(\pi) = \sigma$, *and for every statement* $x{:}\rho \in P$: $B \vdash x^{\mathrm{R}}{:}S\,(\rho)$.

b. If $B \vdash M{:}\sigma$, *and* R *is a replacement and* B' *a basis such that for every statement* $x{:}\rho \in B$: $B' \vdash x^{\mathrm{R}}{:}\rho$, *then* $B' \vdash M^{\mathrm{R}}{:}\sigma$.

2.4.4 Examples

Typed variants of some of the rewrite rules for CL. We have only inserted those types that are not immediately clear. Notice that we have assumed that

$\mathcal{E}\,(S) = (1 \rightarrow 2 \rightarrow 3) \rightarrow (1 \rightarrow 2) \rightarrow 1 \rightarrow 3$,
$\mathcal{E}\,(K) = 1 \rightarrow 2 \rightarrow 1$, and
$\mathcal{E}(I) = 1 \rightarrow 1$.

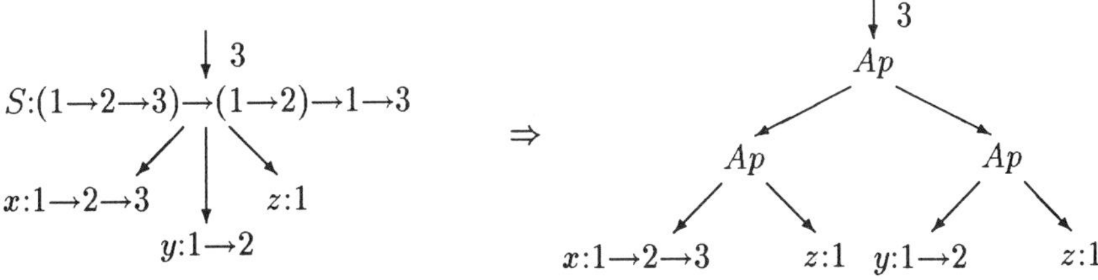

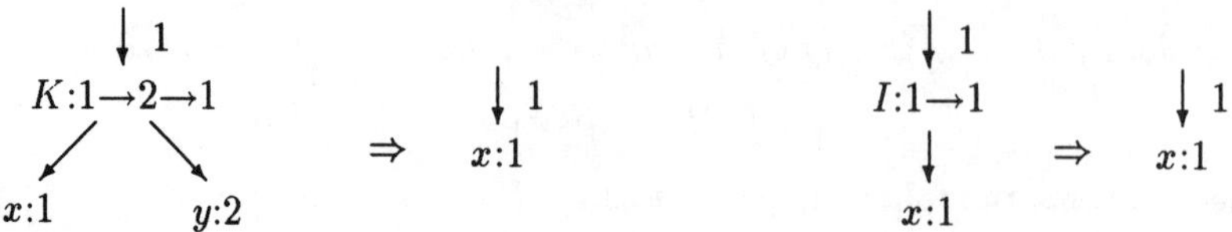

Using

$$
\begin{aligned}
\mathcal{E}(M) &= ((1\to 2)\to 3)\to(1\to 2)\to 2,\\
\mathcal{E}(S) &= (1\to 2\to 3)\to(1\to 2)\to 1\to 3, \text{ and}\\
\mathcal{E}(I) &= 1\to 1
\end{aligned}
$$

the rule for M can be typed as follows:

$\downarrow (1\to 2)\to 2$
$M{:}((1\to 2)\to 3)\to(1\to 2)\to 2$
$\downarrow$
$S_2{:}((1\to 2)\to 1\to 3)\to((1\to 2)\to 1)\to(1\to 2)\to 3$
$\swarrow \quad \searrow$
$x{:}(1\to 2)\to 1\to 3 \qquad y{:}(1\to 2)\to 1$

$\Rightarrow$

$\downarrow (1\to 2)\to 2$
$S_2{:}((1\to 2)\to 1\to 2)\to((1\to 2)\to 1)\to(1\to 2)\to 2$
$\swarrow \quad \searrow$
$I_0{:}(1\to 2)\to 1\to 2 \qquad y{:}(1\to 2)\to 1$

2.4.5 Patterns cause problems

Definitions 2.4.3, 2.4.4 and 2.4.5 define what a type assignment should be, just using the strategy as used in languages like for example Miranda. It is called *naive*, because it not sufficient to guarantee preservance of types under rewriting. (This is also called the "subject reduction property".) Not even typeability is kept under rewriting.

Take for example the definition of M, which can be typed as shown above. If we take the term $M(S_2(K_0, I_0))$ then it is easy to see that the rewrite is allowed, and that this term will be rewritten to: $S_2(I_0, I_0)$.

Although the first term is typeable in the following way:

$\downarrow (4\to 5)\to 5$
$M{:}((4\to 5)\to 4\to 5)\to(4\to 5)\to 5$
$\downarrow$
$S_2{:}((4\to 5)\to(4\to 5)\to 4\to 5)\to((4\to 5)\to 4\to 5)\to(4\to 5)\to 4\to 5$
$\swarrow \quad \searrow$
$K_0{:}(4\to 5)\to(4\to 5)\to 4\to 5 \qquad I_0{:}(4\to 5)\to 4\to 5$

the term $S_2(I_0, I_0)$ is not typeable with the type $(4\to 5)\to 5$. In fact, it is not typeable at all.

2.4.6 A necessary and sufficient condition for preservance of types under rewriting

By Definition 2.2.2, if a term M is rewritten to the term M' using the rewrite rule $LHS \Rightarrow RHS$, there is a subterm M_0 of M, and a replacement R, such that $LHS^{\mathrm{R}} = M_0$. M' is obtained by replacing M_0 by RHS^{R}. To guarantee the subject reduction property, we should accept only those rewrite rules $LHS \Rightarrow RHS$, that satisfy:

For all replacements R, bases B and types σ: if $B \vdash LHS^{\mathrm{R}}{:}\sigma$, then $B \vdash RHS^{\mathrm{R}}{:}\sigma$.

because then we are sure that all possible rewrites are safe.

In the notion of type assignment as presented in this chapter, it is easy to formulate a condition that rewrite rules should satisfy in order to be accepted.

DEFINITION **2.4.12** *a. We call a rewrite rule LHS* $\Rightarrow$ *RHS* safe *if:*

$$\text{If } pp(LHS) = <P, \pi>, \text{ then } P \vdash RHS{:}\pi.$$

b. The definition of a safe type assignment with respect to $\mathcal{E}$ *is the same as the one for a naive type assignment, by replacing in Definition 2.4.5 condition a1 and a2 by: If pp(LHS)* $= <P, \pi>$, *then* $P \vdash RHS{:}\pi$.

Notice that the notion $pp(M)$ is defined independently from the definition of typeable rewrite rules.

As an example of a rule that is not safe, take the definition of M. To obtain $pp(M\,(S_2\,(x,y)))$, we assign types to nodes in the tree in the following way:

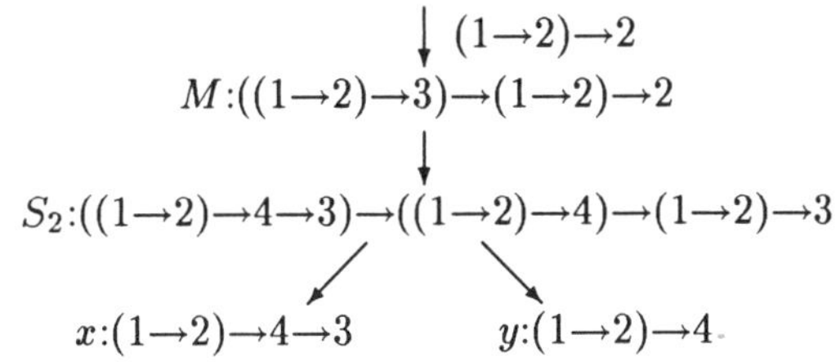

$$\downarrow (1\to2)\to2$$
$$M{:}((1\to2)\to3)\to(1\to2)\to2$$
$$\downarrow$$
$$S_2{:}((1\to2)\to4\to3)\to((1\to2)\to4)\to(1\to2)\to3$$
$$\swarrow \qquad\qquad \searrow$$
$$x{:}(1\to2)\to4\to3 \qquad\qquad y{:}(1\to2)\to4$$

If the right-hand side should be typed with $(1\to2)\to2$, the type needed for the node containing y is $(1\to2)\to1$.

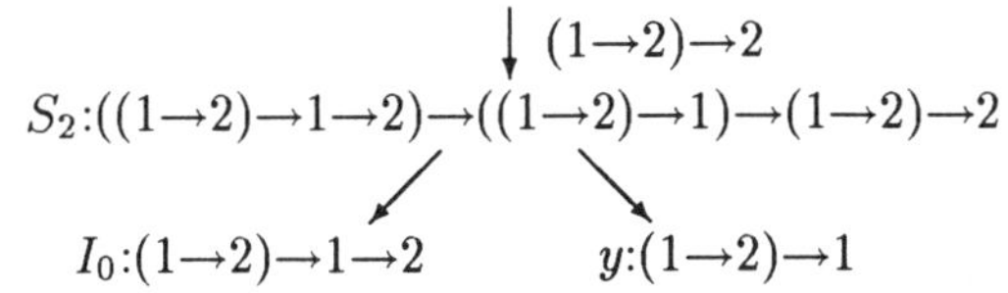

$$\downarrow (1\to2)\to2$$
$$S_2{:}((1\to2)\to1\to2)\to((1\to2)\to1)\to(1\to2)\to2$$
$$\swarrow \qquad\qquad \searrow$$
$$I_0{:}(1\to2)\to1\to2 \qquad\qquad y{:}(1\to2)\to1$$

In the type assignment of the rewrite rule the types assigned to the nodes containing x and y are therefore not the most general ones needed to find the type for the left-hand side of the rewrite rule. So this rule is not safe, and should therefore be rejected.

In the following Theorem, we prove that our solution is correct. The structure of the first proof depends greatly on the fact that for every type σ we can trivially find an $A \in \Sigma_0$, such that $\mathcal{E}\,(A) = \sigma$: we just pick a constant A, not already used. We do not require in the proof that for every symbol A there is a rewrite rule that defines A.

THEOREM **2.4.13** *a.* (The condition is necessary) *Let LHS, RHS* $\in$ Ter (Σ), *and* $\mathbf{r}$ *: LHS* $\Rightarrow$ *RHS be a typeable rewrite rule that is not safe. Then there there exists a replacement R, and a type* μ*, such that* $\vdash LHS^{R}{:}\mu$ *&* $\neg \vdash RHS^{R}{:}\mu$.

b. (The condition is sufficient) *Let LHS, RHS* $\in$ Ter (Σ), *and* $\mathbf{r}$ *: LHS* $\Rightarrow$ *RHS be a safe rewrite rule. Then for every replacement R, basis B and a type* μ*:*

$$B \vdash LHS^{R}{:}\mu \Rightarrow B \vdash RHS^{R}{:}\mu.$$

PROOF: *a.* Since $\mathbf{r}$ is typeable and left linear, we know that there are $\beta_1, \ldots, \beta_n$, τ, and distinct $x_1, \ldots, x_n$, such that: $\{x_1{:}\beta_1, \ldots, x_n{:}\beta_n\} \vdash LHS{:}\tau$ & $\{x_1{:}\beta_1, \ldots, x_n{:}\beta_n\} \vdash RHS{:}\tau$.

Then by Theorem 2.4.9, and Lemma 2.4.10 we know that there are bases P_l, P_r, types $\alpha_1, \ldots, \alpha_n$, δ and a substitution S_0, such that:

$$pp(LHS) = <P_l, \tau> \ \& \ pp(RHS) = <P_r, \delta> \ \& \ P_l = \{x_1{:}\rho_1, \ldots, x_n{:}\rho_n\} \ \&$$
$$S_0(\tau) = S_0(\delta) = \tau \ \& \ S_0(P_l) = S_0(P_r) = \{x_1{:}\beta_1, \ldots, x_n{:}\beta_n\}.$$

Let S_1 be the substitution such that for every i: $S_1(\varphi_i) = c_i$ (the ith type constant), μ be a type such that $S_1(\tau) = \mu$, $A_1, \ldots, A_n$ be constants such that for every $1 \leq i \leq n$, $\mathcal{E}(A_i) = S_1(\rho_i)$, and R be the replacement such that for every $1 \leq i \leq n$: $x_i^{R} = A_i$. Then by Lemma 2.4.11b: $\vdash LHS^{R}{:}\mu$. (Notice that LHS^{R} does not contain term variables.) Since $\mathbf{r}$ is not safe, we know that $\neg \{x_1{:}\rho_1, \ldots, x_n{:}\rho_n\} \vdash RHS{:}\tau$. Suppose towards a contradiction that $\vdash RHS^{R}{:}\mu$. Then by Lemma 2.4.11a there is a substitution S_2 such that $S_2(\delta) = \mu$ and for every $x{:}\gamma \in P_r$: $\vdash x^{R}{:}S_2(\gamma)$. By Definition 2.2.2b(1)iii for every $x{:}\gamma \in P_r$ there is a $1 \leq i \leq n$ such that $x = x_i$. Since S_1 replaces type variables by type constants, the type assigned to A_i can only be $S_1(\rho_i)$. This implies that for every $x{:}\gamma \in P_r$ there is a $1 \leq i \leq n$ such that $x = x_i$ and $S_2(\gamma) = S_1(\rho_i)$. It is straightforward to verify that, since S_1 replaces type variables by type constants, there is a substitution S_3 such that $S_2 = S_1 \circ S_3$. So for every $x{:}\gamma \in P_r$ there is a $1 \leq i \leq n$ such that: $x = x_i$ and $\rho_i = S_3(\gamma)$. But then by Lemma 2.4.8: $\{x_1{:}\rho_1, \ldots, x_n{:}\rho_n\} \vdash RHS{:}S_3(\delta)$. Moreover, $\mu = S_1(\tau) = S_2(\delta) = S_1 \circ S_3(\delta)$, so $\tau = S_3(\delta)$.

b. Since $\mathbf{r}$ is safe, there are P, π such that: if $pp(LHS) = <P, \pi>$, then $P \vdash RHS{:}\pi$ Suppose $pp(LHS) = <P, \pi>$, and R is a replacement such that there are basis B and type μ such that $B \vdash LHS^{R}{:}\mu$, then by Lemma 2.4.11a there is a substitution S such that $S(\pi) = \mu$ & $\forall\ x{:}\rho \in P$ [$B \vdash x^{R}{:}S(\rho)$]. But then by Lemma 2.4.8: $S(P) \vdash RHS{:}S(\pi)$ & $\forall\ x{:}\rho \in P$ [$B \vdash x^{R}{:}S(\rho)$]. So by Lemma 2.4.11b: $B \vdash RHS^{R}{:}\mu$. □

Notice that although the proof of part a uses explicitly the presence of type constants, the problem of loss of subject reduction also arises if type constants are not in the type system. However, we do not believe that it is possible to prove that the condition is also needed in that case.

REFERENCES

[Bar84] H. Barendregt. *The Lambda Calculus: its Syntax and Semantics.* North-Holland, Amsterdam, revised edition, 1984.

[BCD83] H. Barendregt, M. Coppo, and M. Dezani-Ciancaglini. A filter lambda model and the completeness of type assignment. *The Journal of Symbolic Logic*, **48**, 4, pp. 931–940, 1983.

[BvEG+87] H.P. Barendregt, M.C.J.D. van Eekelen, J.R.W. Glauert, J.R. Kennaway, M.J. Plasmeijer, and M.R. Sleep. Term graph rewriting. In *Proceedings of PARLE, Parallel Architectures and Languages Europe,* Eindhoven, The Netherlands, Springer-Verlag, Lecture Notes in Computer Science 259-II, pp. 141–158, 1987.

[BvEvLP87] T. Brus, M.C.J.D. van Eekelen, M.O. van Leer, and M.J. Plasmeijer. Clean - A Language for Functional Graph Rewriting. In *Proceedings of the Third International Conference on Functional Programming Languages and Computer Architecture,* Portland, Oregon, USA, Springer-Verlag, Lecture Notes in Computer Science 274, pp. 364–368, 1987.

[CF58] H.B. Curry and R. Feys. *Combinatory Logic*, vol. 1. North-Holland, Amsterdam, 1958.

[Dam85] L.M.M. Damas. *Type Assignment in Programming Languages.* PhD thesis, University of Edinburgh, Department of Computer Science, Edinburgh, 1985. Thesis CST-33-85.

[FGJM85] K. Futatsugi, J. Goguen, J.P. Jouannaud, and J. Meseguer. Principles of OBJ2. In *Proceedings 12th ACM Symposium on Principles of Programming Languages*, pp. 52–66, 1985.

[Hin69] J.R. Hindley. The principal type scheme of an object in combinatory logic. *Transactions of the American Mathematical Society,* **146**, pp. 29–60, 1969.

[Klo90] J.W. Klop. *Term Rewriting Systems.* Report CS-R9073, Centre for Mathematics and Computer Science, Amsterdam, 1990.

[KTU88] A.J. Kfoury, J. Tiuryn, and P. Urzyczyn. A proper extension of ML with an effective type-assignment. In *Proceedings of the Fifteenth Annual ACM SIGACT-SIGPLAN Symposium on Principles of Programming Languages*, pp. 58–69, San Diego, California, 1988.

[Mil78] R. Milner. A theory of type polymorphism in programming. *Journal of Computer and System Sciences*, **17**, pp. 348–375, 1978.

[Myc84] A. Mycroft. Polymorphic type schemes and recursive definitions. In *Proceedings of the International Symposium on Programming,* Toulouse, Springer-Verlag, Lecture Notes Computer Science 167, pp. 217–239, 1984.

[NSvEP91] E.G.J.M.H. Nöcker, J.E.W. Smetsers, M.C.J.D. van Eekelen, and M.J. Plasmeijer. Concurrent Clean. In *Proceedings of PARLE '91, Parallel Architectures and Languages Europe,* Eindhoven, The Netherlands, Springer-Verlag, Lecture Notes in Computer Science 506-II, pp. 202–219, 1991.

[Pfe88] F. Pfenning. Partial Polymorphic Type Inference and Higher-Order Unification. In *Proceedings of the 1988 conference on LISP and Functional Programming Languages*, Springer-Verlag, Lecture Notes in Computer Science 201, pp. 153–163, 1988.

[Rob65] J.A. Robinson. A machine-oriented logic based on the resolution principle. *Journal of the ACM*, **12**, 1, pp. 23–41, 1965.

[Tur85] D.A. Turner. Miranda: A non-strict functional language with polymorphic types. In *Proceedings of the Conference on Functional Programming Languages and Computer Architecture*, Springer-Verlag, Lecture Notes in Computer Science 201, pp. 1–16, 1985.

[vBSB92] S. van Bakel, S. Smetsers, and S. Brock. Partial Type Assignment in Left Linear Applicative Term Rewriting Systems. In J.-C. Raoult (editor), *Proceedings of CAAP '92. 17th Colloquim on Trees in Algebra and Programming,* Rennes, France, Springer-Verlag, Lecture Notes in Computer Science 581, pp. 300–321, 1992.

3

How to Get Confluence for Explicit Substitutions

T. Hardin

3.1 INTRODUCTION

It is well-known that λ-calculus is the theoretical base of functional programming languages since, in essence, a functional program consists of a set of applications of functions to arguments. The replacement of the formal parameters of functions by the actual ones is exactly a step of β-reduction and it is not so simple: clashes of names have to be avoided and we have to take care of the scopes of arguments of functions. These problems are hidden in λ-calculus because the substitution of variables by λ-terms is a built-in operation, defined at the level of the meta-language. For theoretical purposes, it suffices to consider β-conversions modulo renaming of bound variables (α-conversion). But this is not realistic in practise, where moreover, substitutions are delayed and recorded in environments. So, when modeling implementations of functional languages, it is necessary to fully describe the substitution process inside the language in order to be able to study their properties. Therefore the problem is twofold: design a language, extending λ-calculus, such that the substitution is a first-order citizen, and such that names' management is explicitely handled.

This problem is not new and several solutions have been proposed, since the early seventies. The important steps were the design of a name-free notation for λ-calculus by de Bruijn [Bru72], then the introduction of Categorical Combinatory Logic [Cur86] CCL by Curien and, during the last years, the definitions of $\lambda\sigma$-calculi [ACCL91, HL89]. We shall give a panorama of these different theories, from a rewriting point of view. The classical λ-calculus is a Combinatory Reduction System (see [Klo82]), that is, roughly, a Term Rewriting System with bound variables. CCL and the $\lambda\sigma$-calculi are very classical Term Rewriting Systems. The most important property that

Term Graph Rewriting: Theory and Practice.
Eds. Ronan Sleep, Rinus Plasmeijer and Marko van Eekelen.

an extension of λ-calculus has to verify is the Church-Rosser property. CCL is not weakly confluent but a restriction of the system, sufficient to compute β-reduction, is confluent on a subset of combinators containing λ-terms. The first version, called $\lambda\sigma$, of $\lambda\sigma$-calculus is not weakly confluent but is ground confluent. The second one, called $\lambda\sigma_{\Uparrow}$ (but also $\lambda\sigma$ when no confusion is possible), is fully confluent. We may untersdand the evolution from CCL to $\lambda\sigma_{\Uparrow}$ as a sequence of improvements to obtain Church-Rosser property and we shall present these theories following this guide-line and focusing on confluence. We restrict ourselves to the untyped versions of these three systems; typed versions of CCL are given in [Cur86] and [ACCL91] contains several type systems for $\lambda\sigma$. We shall not detail either weak $\lambda\sigma$-calculi, which are studied in [PLHL91]. In classical λ-calculus, the weak β-reduction is a restriction of β, which prevents reduction of β-redexes "under" the λs; it is the rule used to evaluate programs. This restriction is not sufficient to avoid captures ($(\lambda x.\lambda y.x)y$ reduces on $\lambda z.y$ and α-conversion $\lambda y.x =_\alpha \lambda z.x$ has to be performed before the reduction). Moreover, weak β-reduction is not confluent. In $\lambda\sigma$, this is possible, on one hand, to forbid substitutions under the λs (a simple way to avoid names'clashes), and on the other hand, to prevent applications of the rule (Beta) under the λs. The weak conditional $\lambda\sigma$-calculus autorizes no (Beta) step and no substitutions under the λs. The weak $\lambda\sigma$-calculus prevents only substitution under the λs and is given in two versions: the first one uses de Bruijn numbers, the second one keeps the variables'names. These weak calculi are confluent and compute weak head normal forms of λ-terms.

3.2 λ-CALCULI

3.2.1 The classical λ-calculus

DEFINITION **3.2.1** *The pure λ-calculus on a set V of variables, denoted by $\mathbf{\Lambda_V}$, is defined inductively as follows:*

$$a ::= x \mid \lambda x.a \mid aa$$

The β-rule is defined by:

$$(\lambda\, x.a)b \longrightarrow a\{\, x \leftarrow\, b\}$$

We suppose familiarity with this theory. For further details, see [Bar84, Klo82, Lév78]. We only give the complete definition of the substitution, in order to recall how intricate this definition is: all the following details are needed to avoid names'capture. Moreover, this definition belongs only to the meta-language of λ-calculus.

DEFINITION **3.2.2** *Let a and $b \in \mathbf{\Lambda_V}$. The set of free (resp. bound) variables of a is denoted by $FV(a)$ (resp. $BV(a)$). The substitution of b at all the free occurrences of x in a, denoted by $a\{x \leftarrow b\}$, is defined as follows:*

a. $x\{x \leftarrow b\} = b$ *and* $y\{x \leftarrow b\} = y$ *if* $y \not\equiv x$
b. $(a_1\, a_2)\{x \leftarrow b\} = (a_1\{x \leftarrow b\})\, (a_2\{x \leftarrow b\})$
c. $(\lambda\, x.a)\{x \leftarrow b\} = \lambda\, x.a$
d. $(\lambda\, y.a)\{x \leftarrow b\} = \lambda\, y.\, (a\, \{x \leftarrow b\})$ *if* $y \not\equiv x$ *and* $(\, y \notin FV(b)$ *or* $x \notin FV(a)\,)$

e. $(\lambda y.a)\{x \leftarrow b\} = \lambda z.(a\{y \leftarrow z\}\{x \leftarrow b\})$ *if* $y \not\equiv x$ *and* $(y \in FV(b)$ *and* $x \in FV(a))$; $z \notin V(ab)$.

The complicated points d. and e. are needed to prevent names'clashes: α-conversion has to be done before the substitution under a λ. If these substitutions are forbidden, they are no conflicts of names (see [PLHL91]).

The theoretical properties of $\mathbf{\Lambda_V}$ may be studied modulo α-conversion. This solution is unreasonable in implementations. But there is a simple way to avoid such names'conflicts, which was introduced by de Bruijn [Bru72, Bru78, Bal86, Ned92]: it is to suppress the names! To correctly perform β-reduction, it suffices to know what are the occurrences which have to be replaced. In $\mathbf{\Lambda_V}$, this is indicated by the identity between the name of the variable at a given occurrence and the name of the λs variable of the β-redex. It may also be indicated by the *binding height* of an occurrence, that is, by the number of λs one has to cross between this occurrence and its binder. If we decide to suppress also names of free variables $\{x_0, \ldots, x_n\}$ of a given term a, it suffices to consider a as a subterm of $\lambda.x_0 \ldots x_n.a$. We recall this notation below, because it is underlying all the theories which manage explicitly the substitution.

3.2.2 λ-calculus in de Bruijn notation

DEFINITION **3.2.3** *The set of λ-terms, $\mathbf{\Lambda}$, in de Bruijn's notation, is defined inductively as follows, where* $\mathtt{n}$ *is an integer greater or equal to 1*[1]*:*

$$a ::= \mathtt{n} \mid \lambda(a) \mid aa$$

The β-reduction is defined by:

$$\lambda(a)b \longrightarrow a\{1 \leftarrow b\}$$

In this formalism, names of variables have disappeared. A given occurrence u of a variable, say x, is replaced by the number n of symbols λ, whose occurences are "between" the binder of this x and u. For example, $\lambda x\ y.x(\lambda z.zx)y$ is written $\lambda(\lambda 2(\lambda 13)1$. Therefore explicit α-conversion is avoided but, as described below, numbers have to be adjusted when a substitution is performed. The *λ-height* of an occurrence u in a term a is the number of λs at prefix occurrences of u. It is denoted by $(|u|, a)$. A number p, at occurrence u, in a term a is bound iff $p \leq (|u|, a)$. So when reducing the redex $\lambda(a)b$, a number p at the occurrence u in a is affected by the substitution of b iff $p = (|u|, a) + 1$. Before replacing this p, the numbers of b have to be modified, to take care of the λ "above" u. This is done by the lift operation. Substitution, in de Bruijn's formalism, is defined as follows:

DEFINITION **3.2.4** *The substitution of b at the λ-height $(n-1)$ in a, denoted by $a\{\mathtt{n} \leftarrow b\}$, and the lift with n at the λ-height i, denoted by $t_i^n(a)$, are defined by induction as follows:*

[1] Some authors use 0 as the first de Bruijn number, see [Cur86] for example.

$$
\begin{array}{rcll}
(a_1a_2)\{\mathtt{n}\leftarrow b\} & = & a_1\{\mathtt{n}\leftarrow b\}\, a_2\{\mathtt{n}\leftarrow b\} & \\
\lambda a\{\mathtt{n}\leftarrow b\} & = & \lambda(a\{\mathtt{n+1}\leftarrow b\}) & \\
\mathtt{m}\{\mathtt{n}\leftarrow b\} & = & \mathtt{m}-\mathtt{1} \text{ if } \mathtt{m}>\mathtt{n} & (\mathtt{m}\in FV(a)) \\
 & & t_0^n(b) \text{ if } \mathtt{m}=\mathtt{n} & (\mathtt{m} \text{ bound by the } \lambda \text{ of the (Beta)-redex}) \\
 & & \mathtt{m} \text{ if } \mathtt{m}<\mathtt{n} & (\mathtt{m}\in BV(a))
\end{array}
$$

where:

$$
\begin{array}{l}
t_i^n(a_1a_2) = t_i^n(a)t_i^n(a_2) \\
t_i^n(\lambda a) = \lambda(t_{i+1}^n(a)) \\
t_i^n(\mathtt{m}) = \mathtt{m}+\mathtt{n}-\mathtt{1} \text{ if } \mathtt{m}\geq \mathtt{i}+\mathtt{1} \\
\qquad\qquad \mathtt{m} \text{ if } \mathtt{m}\leq \mathtt{i}
\end{array}
$$

Let us give an example: the term $\lambda x.((\lambda y.xy)x)$ is written $\lambda((\lambda(\mathtt{21}))\mathtt{1})$ in de Bruijn notation. It reduces to $\lambda x.xx$ or to $\lambda((21)\{\mathtt{1}\leftarrow\mathtt{1}\}) = \lambda(\mathtt{11})$ in de Bruijn notation.

Note that, in this de Bruijn setting, the substitution operation is still only defined in the meta-language. The only operation of this language remains the β-reduction. This is an important drawback when dealing with implementations. We need a more precise language accepting substitution as a first-class citizen for practical purposes.

3.2.3 λ-calculus with couples

As is well-known, couples and projections may be encoded by λ-terms, say C, *Fst* and *Snd*. The projection rules are then simply implemented by steps of β-reduction: $\mathit{Fst}\ (C\,a\,b) \xrightarrow{\beta^*} a$. But H. Barendregt [Bar74] has shown that it is impossible to prove the uniqueness of the construction inside the λ-calculus itself. So, if we want to ensure it, we are led to explicitly add three constants C, *Fst*, *Snd*, projection rules and a rule giving this uniqueness of the couple operation, which is called (SP): $C(\mathit{Fst}\ a)\,(\mathit{Snd}\ a) \longrightarrow a$. Remark that this rule is not linear, and such non-linear rules are known to create some difficulties in confluence problems. Indeed, in an untyped setting, this rule is very bad: as proved by J. W. Klop [Klo82](see also [Har89] and [PLHL91]), it destroys the confluence property. Note that this problem disappears when typing rules are added.

3.2.4 η-reduction

Classically, the λ-calculus is also endowed with another rewriting rule, the η-rule: $\lambda x.ax \ \rightarrow_\eta a$, if $x \notin FV(a)$. This rule η is an important tool, both from practical and theoretical points of view because it expresses extensionality: remark that $(\lambda x.a\,x)b \rightarrow_\beta a\,b$ so this abstraction of x in $a\,x$ is useless from a computational view point. To translate this rule in de Bruijn notation, we have to express the condition "$x \notin FV(a)$" and to do the update of numbers in the reduct a because the reduction removes the λ.

DEFINITION **3.2.5** *$a \in \Lambda$ verifies the* condition $C(\eta)$ *if and only if, for any occurrence u of a number p in a, $p \neq (|u|, a) + 1$.*

The decrementation *operation may be applied to any term a verifying $C(\eta)$. Its result is denoted by $a^{\downarrow}$. The term $a^{\downarrow}$ is obtained from a by replacing any number p at occurrence u in a by the number $(p-1)$ provided that p verifies $p > (|u|, M) + 1$.*

The η-reduction in Λ *is the rewriting relation defined by the rule:*

$$\lambda.(a\,1) \longrightarrow a^{\downarrow} \text{ if } a \text{ verifies } C(\eta)$$

DEFINITION **3.2.6** *The system $\beta\eta SP$ is the rewriting system defined on λ-calculus with couples by the rules β, η, (Fst), (Snd), and (SP).*

3.3 THE CATEGORICAL COMBINATORY LOGIC

The Categorical Combinatory Logic, CCL, was introduced by P.-L. Curien [Cur86] in 1983 as a syntactical model of Cartesian Closed Categories (CCC). It is well-known that these CCCs serve also as models of functional programming languages. CCL is a first-order theory, its operators come directly from categories: they are the composition "$\circ$", the identity id, the pairing $<\,,\,>$ and the projections Fst and Snd, the abstraction Λ and the applicator App. This algebra is endowed with a set of rules, called $CCL\beta\eta SP$, composed of four subsystems: a system containing only the rule (Beta) which starts the process of β-reduction, a system SL which serves to compute the substitution step by step, a system containing two rules (FSI) and (SP) ensuring uniqueness of pairing and a system containing the rules (AI) and (SΛ), which gives the uniqueness of the exponentiation and which is closed to the η-reduction rule of λ-calculus. The subsystem *Subst* is obtained by adding (FSI) and (SP) to SL, in order to obtain a weakly confluent system.

The system SL

(Ass)	$(x \circ y) \circ z$	$=$	$x \circ (y \circ z)$
(IdL)	$id \circ x$	$=$	x
(IdR)	$x \circ id$	$=$	x
(Fst)	$Fst \circ < x, y >$	$=$	x
(Snd)	$Snd \circ < x, y >$	$=$	y
(Dpair)	$< x, y > \circ z$	$=$	$< x \circ z, y \circ z >$
(DΛ)	$\Lambda(x) \circ y$	$=$	$\Lambda(x \circ < y \circ Fst, Snd >)$
(FSI)	$< Fst, Snd >$	$=$	id
(SP)	$< Fst \circ x, Snd \circ x >$	$=$	x
(Beta)	$App \circ < \Lambda(x), y >$	$=$	$x \circ < id, y >$
(AI)	$\Lambda(App)$	$=$	id
(SΛ)	$\Lambda(App \circ < x \circ Fst, Snd >)$	$=$	x

The λ-calculus with couples, endowed with $\beta\eta SP$ and CCL, endowed with $CCL\beta\eta SP$, are two equivalent equational theories (Curien [Cur86]). The translation of a λ-term, written in de Bruijn notation, into a CCL combinator is straightforward: $\mathtt{1} \Rightarrow Snd$, $\mathtt{n+1} \Rightarrow Snd \circ Fst^{n}$, $\lambda.a \Rightarrow \Lambda(a)$, $(a\,b) \Rightarrow App \circ < a, b >$ and pairing and projections are translated upon the corresponding operations. For example, the term

$\lambda y.(\lambda x.xy)y$, written in De Bruijn notation $\lambda((\lambda.\mathbf{1}\,\mathbf{2})\,\mathbf{1})$, is translated in the combinator $\Lambda(App \circ < \Lambda(App \circ < Snd, Snd \circ Fst >), Snd >)$. Therefore, the translation of a λ-term is a ground term of CCL, that is, a combinator.

An application of the rule (Beta) suppresses the redex, say $App \circ < \Lambda(a), b >$, build a new environment $< id, b >$ which retains the term b to be substituted (id plays the role of nil) and starts the substitution by composing a with this new environment. As environments are represented by pairs, λ-variables, translated in compositions of projections, may access in these environments. The rule (DΛ) pushes an environment y "under" a Λ: the λ-variables bound by this Λ are not concerned by the substitutions recorded in y (if $x = Snd$, then $x \circ < \_, Snd >$ rewrites on Snd), the numbers "inside" y are to be put under a new Λ so they have to be updated and this is done by the composition $y \circ Fst$.

Clearly, a β-step is computed in CCL by a (Beta)+SL derivation. But SL is not weakly confluent and we have to add (FSI) and (SP) to obtain weak confluence so we are led to consider (Beta)+*Subst*. Is this system confluent? The answer is no, due to the (SP) rule. However, it is possible to define a subsystem $\mathcal{E}$ of *Subst* and a subset, say $\mathcal{D}$, of CCL terms, closed under (Beta)+$\mathcal{E}$ derivations, such that this system remains confluent when restricted to $\mathcal{D}$. Moreover, translations of λ-terms belong to $\mathcal{D}$ and (Beta)+$\mathcal{E}$ is sufficient to compute substitutions. To obtain these results, a simple method was introduced by Hardin [Har89], it is called the *interpretation method*[2]. We recall it now.

3.3.1 The interpretation method

It is based upon the following simple lemma:

PROPOSITION **3.3.1** *Let R and $\mathcal{E}$ be reduction relations on a set X such that $\mathcal{E} \subseteq R^\star$ and $\mathcal{E}$ is canonical (confluent and terminating). Let $\mathcal{E}(M)$ denote the $\mathcal{E}$-normal form of M.*

If there exists a relation $\mathcal{E}(R)$ on the set of $\mathcal{E}$-normal forms, such that, if $M \longrightarrow_R N$, then $\mathcal{E}(M) \longrightarrow_{\mathcal{E}(R)} \mathcal{E}(N)$ and such that $\mathcal{E}(R) \subseteq R^\star$, then $\mathcal{E}(R)$ is confluent iff R is confluent.

The proof is as follows. Suppose that $M \longrightarrow_{R^\star} N$ and $M \longrightarrow_{R^\star} P$. We deduce by interpretation a $\mathcal{E}(R)$-derivation from $\mathcal{E}(M)$ to $\mathcal{E}(N)$ and another one from $\mathcal{E}(M)$ to $\mathcal{E}(P)$. Now, $\mathcal{E}(N)$ and $\mathcal{E}(P)$ have a common $\mathcal{E}(R)$-reduct. As $\mathcal{E} \subseteq R^\star$ and $\mathcal{E}(R) \subseteq R^\star$, these terms have a common $R^\star$-reduct. The other way is similarly obtained.

3.3.2 How to design $\mathcal{D}$

The subsystem *Subst* computes the substitution. It is weakly confluent and terminating. This last, difficult, result was first obtained by Hardin and Laville [HL86] and has been then reproved by different methods (see [CHR92] and [Zan92]). Now, CCL contains λ-calculus with couples and $CCL\beta\eta SP$ may simulate $\beta\eta SP$. So, in view of the non-confluence of $\beta\eta SP$, we may suppose that *Subst*+ (Beta) is not confluent. To obtain a positive confluence result, we have to remove the (SP) and (FSI) rules, which

[2] The method has been used independently elsewhere, e.g. in [BT88]

were added to SL to obtain weak confluence and to modify SL in such a way that substitutions remain completely computed by a canonical system. A careful examination of critical pairs of SL on one hand and of the substitution process on the other hand leads to remove (SP), (FSI) and (IdR), because this last rule has a critical pair with (DΛ) which needs (FSI) to be solved. To compute completely substitution, we have to add two instances of (IdR), the rules ($Fst \circ id \longrightarrow Fst$) and ($Snd \circ id \longrightarrow Snd$). Let $\mathcal{E}$ be the system obtained from *Subst* in this way: it is still canonical so we may define $\mathcal{E}$-interpretation. The next step is to add (Beta): bad step, $\mathcal{E}$+(Beta) is not even weakly confluent, due to a critical pair between (Ass) and (Beta), which would compel us to reintroduce (IdR). The solution is to restrict ourselves to a subset of ground terms such that this critical pair disappears when putting the terms in $\mathcal{E}$-normal form: this is the definition of $\mathcal{D}$. We omit the formal definition of this subset, which is quite technical, and refer to [Har89].

PROPOSITION **3.3.2** *Let $M \in \mathcal{D}$ be an (IdR)-redex and N its reduct. Then, $\mathcal{E}(M) \equiv \mathcal{E}(N)$.*

The proof may be found in [Har89]. Now, we build the interpretation of (Beta) on $\mathcal{D}$, it is called *simβ* and defined by: $M \longrightarrow_{sim\beta} N$ if $M \longrightarrow_{(Beta)} P$ and $\mathcal{E}(P) = N$.

PROPOSITION **3.3.3** *If $M \in \mathcal{D}$ and $M \longrightarrow_{(Beta)} N$, then $\mathcal{E}(M) \longrightarrow_{sim\beta^*} \mathcal{E}(N)$.*

It remains to prove the confluence of *simβ*: it is easy because this interpretation looks like the classical β and we can use Tait-Martin Löf method. From this result, we deduce the confluence of $\mathcal{E}$+ (Beta).

PROPOSITION **3.3.4** *a. $\mathcal{E}$+(Beta) is not weakly confluent.*

b. Restricted to the subset $\mathcal{D}$, $\mathcal{E}$+(Beta) is confluent.

c. Subst+ (Beta) is weakly confluent but not confluent.

d. Restricted to the subset of translations of λ-terms, Subst+(Beta) is confluent. Moreover, on translations of λ-terms, simβ coincides with β-reduction.

The proof is done by the interpretation method and may be found in [Har89].

3.4 THE $\lambda\sigma$-CALCULUS

CCL is the first known Term Rewriting System, which fully implements substitution but it is not completely satisfying: to study derivations of λ-terms, we have to work with the restriction to $\mathcal{D}$ and this is rather complicated. Moreover, functions and environments are both represented by combinators but their semantic is quite different. To respond to these problems, Curien designed first a calculus, called $\lambda\rho$ [Cur92], containing two sorts: `term` and `substitution` and then, extended it to obtain $\lambda\sigma$-calculus [ACCL91]. $\lambda\sigma$ is a Term Rewriting System with these two sorts, it is composed of a rule (Beta), which starts the substitution and of a subsystem, called σ, which performs the replacement. This system was introduced without references to CCL, but it turns out that, if we remove the sorts, this system is exactly $\mathcal{E}$+(Beta). So we explain now how this introduction of sorts leads to better confluence results.

DEFINITION **3.4.1** *The $\lambda\sigma$-terms are inductively defined by:*

$$\begin{array}{ll} \textit{terms} & a ::= \mathtt{X} \mid \mathtt{1} \mid ab \mid \lambda a \mid a[s] \\ \textit{substitutions} & s ::= \mathtt{x} \mid id \mid \uparrow \mid a \cdot s \mid s \circ t \end{array}$$

where `X` *et* `x` *are metavariables of sort* **term** *and* **substitution**.

A λ-term ab is translated onto the CCL combinator $App \circ < a, b >$. This combinator App is interesting from a categorical view point but it complicates the translation. If we accept to go away from the categorical world, then we may simply keep the application. Now, the CCL composition plays two roles: first, it serves to push the substitution (see rules (Beta),(DΛ)(Dpair), etc.), and so acts between a term and an environment, second, it serves to make computations between several substitutions (see the rule (Ass) for example). These uses are separated by the sorts: pushing an environment in a term is done by the operator [ ][3] while the composition of substitutions is still denoted by "$\circ$". Then the rule (Ass) is duplicated on the rules (Clos), which introduces the composition of substitutions, and (Ass).

$$\text{(Clos)} \quad a[s][t] \longrightarrow a[s \circ t] \qquad \text{(AssEnv)} \quad (s_1 \circ s_2) \circ s_3 \longrightarrow s_1 \circ (s_2 \circ s_3)$$

The pairing in CCL was used to code the λ-application and the environments. The rule (Beta) is now:

$$\text{(Beta)} \quad (\lambda a)\, b \longrightarrow a[b \cdot id]$$

The term a has to be evaluated in the environment defined by the substitution $b \cdot id$. Note that id is the right son of the binary operator $\cdot$ (called *cons*), it was the left son of the pairing in the CCL version: this explains some transpositions in the rules. It is just a matter of notational convention. Remark that the pairing of two terms is no longer a primitive operation: $\lambda\sigma$ does not contain λ-calculus with couples (but, as explained below, there is still a surjective pairing problem). Now, the access: `1` was coded by *Snd*, here we keep `1`; `n+1` became, in CCL, $Snd \circ Fst^n$ and is translated here on $\mathtt{1}[\uparrow^n]$. The role of $\uparrow$ is given by the following rule:

$$\text{(ShiftCons)} \quad \uparrow \circ (a \cdot s) \longrightarrow s$$

The rule (Dpair) is replaced by two rules:

$$\text{(App)} \quad (ab)[s] \longrightarrow (a[s]\; b[s]) \qquad \text{(MapEnv)} \quad (a \cdot s) \circ t \longrightarrow a[t] \cdot (s \circ t)$$

The two instances of (IdR) used in $\mathcal{E}$ become the following rules:

$$\text{(ShiftId)} \quad \uparrow \circ id \longrightarrow \uparrow \qquad \text{(VarId)} \quad \mathtt{1}[id] \longrightarrow \mathtt{1}$$

The rule (IdL) is now defined only for substitutions:

$$\text{(IdL)} \quad id \circ s \longrightarrow s$$

[3] One may read the term $a[s]$ as the term a in the environment defined by the substitution s.

The rule (DΛ) is called here (Abs):

$$\text{(Abs)} \quad (\lambda a)[s] \longrightarrow \lambda(a[1 \cdot (s \circ \uparrow)])$$

So, the $\lambda\sigma$-system is defined by:

(Beta)	$(\lambda a)\, b \longrightarrow a[b \cdot id]$
(App)	$(ab)[s] \longrightarrow (a[s]\, b[s])$
(VarId)	$1[id] \longrightarrow 1$
(VarCons)	$1[a \cdot s] \longrightarrow a$
(Clos)	$a[s][t] \longrightarrow a[s \circ t]$
(Abs)	$(\lambda a)[s] \longrightarrow \lambda(a[1 \cdot (s \circ \uparrow)])$
(IdL)	$id \circ s \longrightarrow s$
(ShiftId)	$\uparrow \circ\, id \longrightarrow \uparrow$
(ShiftCons)	$\uparrow \circ (a \cdot s) \longrightarrow s$
(AssEnv)	$(s_1 \circ s_2) \circ s_3 \longrightarrow s_1 \circ (s_2 \circ s_3)$
(MapEnv)	$(a \cdot s) \circ t \longrightarrow a[t] \cdot (s \circ t)$

The system $\lambda\sigma$ is ground confluent: the proof uses the interpretation method, see [ACCL91]. But, like $\mathcal{E}+$ (Beta), it is not weakly confluent, due to the lack of the rule (IdR).

Comparing $\lambda\sigma$ and CCL, the sorted version has two important avantages: first, it allows a clean semantic separation between terms and substitutions, second the $\lambda\sigma$-ground terms are exactly the λ-terms, and so the sorts avoid the restriction to $\mathcal{D}$. Moreover, the interpretation of $\lambda\sigma$ by σ is exactly the β-reduction.

To obtain weak confluence, we have to add the following rules, getting the system $\lambda\sigma_{SP}$:

(Id)	$a[id] \longrightarrow a$
(IdR)	$s \circ id \longrightarrow s$
(VarShift)	$1 \cdot \uparrow \longrightarrow id$
(SCons)	$1[s] \cdot (\uparrow \circ s) \longrightarrow s$

The rule (SCons) is a non-linear one and we encounter the same obstacle.

PROPOSITION **3.4.2** *a. $\lambda\sigma_{SP}$ is not confluent.*
b. When restricted to $\lambda\sigma$-terms containing no metavariables of sort `substitution`, *$\lambda\sigma_{SP}$ is confluent.*

The proof of the first point is given in [PLHL91], it is done with the interpretation method. Our term used for the counter-example in CCL (see [Har89]) was the translation of a term of λ-calculus with couples, it is no longer the case for the one we use here. However, this last term comes rather directly from a new counter-example in λ-calculus with couples (see [CH90]). The second point has been proved recently by Rios [Río92], also with the interpretation method.

3.5 THE $\lambda\sigma_{\Uparrow}$-CALCULUS

The next step is to define a Term Rewriting System, as good as $\lambda\sigma$ for λ-calculus, which is confluent. The rule (IdR) is needed to solve the critical pair between (Beta) and (AssEnv) (or (Ass)). The rule (SCons) (or (SP)), which destroys the confluence property, is needed to solve a critical pair induced by the one between (Abs) (or (DΛ)) and (IdR):

$$(\lambda(a)[id] \longrightarrow \lambda(a[\mathtt{1} \cdot (id \circ \uparrow)]) \longrightarrow \lambda(a[\mathtt{1} \cdot \uparrow])$$

We need the rule (Varshift) to solve this critical pair. But, (Varshift) has a critical pair with (MapEnv) which needs (SCons).

In fact, we get these troubles because the rule (Abs) introduces the binary operator *Cons*. This is to ensure correct computations of numbers: the first component is $\mathtt{1}$, ensuring that bound numbers in a will remain unchanged and the second component is $s \circ \uparrow$, preparing the update of numbers in s. There is no use to anticipate updates of numbers, when crossing a λ. Instead, we may only memorize the fact that a λ has just been crossed. This needs the introduction of a new unary operator $\Uparrow$, called *lift*.

Here is the syntax of the $\lambda\sigma_{\Uparrow}$-calculus, introduced in [HL89]. We use de Bruijn numbers instead of encoding them by $\mathtt{1}[\uparrow^n]$.

terms	$a ::= \mathtt{X} \mid \mathtt{n} \mid ab \mid \lambda a \mid a[s]$
substitutions	$s ::= \mathtt{x} \mid id \mid \uparrow \mid a \cdot s \mid s \circ t \mid \Uparrow(s)$

The constants $\mathtt{n}$ are integers greater than 1. The rule (Abs) is replaced by the following rule, called (Lambda):

$$\text{(Lambda)} \quad (\lambda a)[s] \longrightarrow \lambda(a[\Uparrow s])$$

We need rules to do updates of de Bruijn numbers when they are evaluated in an environment defined by a substitution $\Uparrow(s)$:

$$\text{(FVarLift1)} \quad \mathtt{1}[\Uparrow(s)] \longrightarrow \mathtt{1}$$

$$\text{(RVarLift1)} \quad \mathtt{n+1}[\Uparrow(s)] \longrightarrow \mathtt{n}[s \circ \uparrow]$$

and we rephrase the rules for *cons* with de Bruijn numbers:

$$\text{(FVarCons)} \quad \mathtt{1}[a \cdot s] \longrightarrow a$$

$$\text{(RVarCons)} \quad \mathtt{n+1}[a \cdot s] \longrightarrow \mathtt{n}[s]$$

A number is incremented with the following rule :

$$\text{(VarShift1)} \quad \mathtt{n}[\uparrow] \longrightarrow \mathtt{n+1}$$

The constant $\uparrow$ may suppress a $\Uparrow$ as follows:

$$\text{(ShiftLift1)} \quad \uparrow \circ \Uparrow(s) \longrightarrow s \circ \uparrow$$

Two substitutions having a $\Uparrow$ as top-symbol may be composed:

$$\text{(Lift1)} \quad \Uparrow(s) \circ \Uparrow(t) \longrightarrow \Uparrow(s \circ t)$$

Follows the complete system of rules of $\lambda\sigma_{\Uparrow}$. Remark that this system includes the rule (IdR) on substitutions and its version (Id) on the terms. If we keep the representation of de Bruijn numbers by $\mathtt{1}[\uparrow^n]$, then rules (VarShift) and (RVar) may be removed.

(Beta)	$(\lambda a)b$	$\longrightarrow$	$a[b \cdot id]$
(App)	$(ab)[s]$	$\longrightarrow$	$a[s]b[s]$
(Lambda)	$(\lambda a)[s]$	$\longrightarrow$	$\lambda(a[\Uparrow s])$
(Clos)	$(a[s])[t]$	$\longrightarrow$	$a[s \circ t]$
(VarShift1)	$\mathtt{n}[\uparrow]$	$\longrightarrow$	$\mathtt{n+1}$
(VarShift2)	$\mathtt{n}[\uparrow \circ s]$	$\longrightarrow$	$\mathtt{n+1}[s]$
(FVarCons)	$\mathtt{1}[a \cdot s]$	$\longrightarrow$	a
(FVarLift1)	$\mathtt{1}[\Uparrow(s)]$	$\longrightarrow$	$\mathtt{1}$
(FVarLift2)	$\mathtt{1}[\Uparrow(s) \circ t]$	$\longrightarrow$	$\mathtt{1}[t]$
(RVarCons)	$\mathtt{n+1}[a \cdot s]$	$\longrightarrow$	$\mathtt{n}[s]$
(RVarLift1)	$\mathtt{n+1}[\Uparrow(s)]$	$\longrightarrow$	$\mathtt{n}[s \circ \uparrow]$
(RVarLift2)	$\mathtt{n+1}[\Uparrow(s) \circ t]$	$\longrightarrow$	$\mathtt{n}[s \circ (\uparrow \circ t)]$
(AssEnv)	$(s \circ t) \circ u$	$\longrightarrow$	$s \circ (t \circ u)$
(MapEnv)	$(a \cdot s) \circ t$	$\longrightarrow$	$a[t] \cdot (s \circ t)$
(ShiftCons)	$\uparrow \circ (a \cdot s)$	$\longrightarrow$	s
(ShiftLift1)	$\uparrow \circ \Uparrow(s)$	$\longrightarrow$	$s \circ \uparrow$
(ShiftLift2)	$\uparrow \circ (\Uparrow(s) \circ t)$	$\longrightarrow$	$s \circ (\uparrow \circ t)$
(Lift1)	$\Uparrow(s) \circ \Uparrow(t)$	$\longrightarrow$	$\Uparrow(s \circ t)$
(Lift2)	$\Uparrow(s) \circ (\Uparrow(t) \circ u)$	$\longrightarrow$	$\Uparrow(s \circ t) \circ u$
(LiftEnv)	$\Uparrow(s) \circ (a \cdot t)$	$\longrightarrow$	$a \cdot (s \circ t)$
(IdL)	$id \circ s$	$\longrightarrow$	s
(IdR)	$s \circ id$	$\longrightarrow$	s
(LiftId)	$\Uparrow(id)$	$\longrightarrow$	id
(Id)	$a[id]$	$\longrightarrow$	a

The system $\sigma_{\Uparrow}$ is obtained by removing (Beta) from $\lambda\sigma_{\Uparrow}$ and is the system computing substitution. This system is canonical but the proof of its termination cannot be deduced from the one of *Subst*, which is, as we said previously, seriously difficult. Here, fortunately, the termination of $\sigma_{\Uparrow}$ can be etablished via a lexicographic ordering with two polynomial components (see [HL89] for details).

PROPOSITION **3.5.1** *a. The system $\lambda\sigma_{\Uparrow}$ is confluent.*

b. *The ground terms of sort* `term` *are exactly the* λ*-terms.*
c. *The interpretation of* $\lambda\sigma$ *by* $\sigma_{\Uparrow}$ *is* $sim\beta$*, which coincides on* λ*-terms with the classical* β*-reduction.*

The point a. was first obtained with the following lemma, coined in [Yok89] (see also [Oos92]):

LEMMA **3.5.2** *Let* R *and* S *be two relations defined on a same set* X*,* R *being canonical and* S *being strongly confluent. Suppose that if* $f \longrightarrow_S g$ *and* $\longrightarrow_R h$*, then* $g \longrightarrow_{R^*} k$ *and* $h \longrightarrow_{R^*SR^*}$*. Then, the relation* R^*SR^* *is confluent.*

We use this lemma with $S = \sigma_{\Uparrow}$ and a classical parallelization of (Beta) as R (see [HL89, PLHL91] for details). The proof of a. can also be done with the interpretation method (see [Har92]). This is more complicated but gives the point c. of this proposition.

The system $\lambda\sigma_{\Uparrow}$ may be extended with data constructors and the corresponding rules. For example, one may add two projections *Fst* and *Snd*, and a pairing operation $<,>$ together with the following rules. The termination and confluence properties remain valid.

(Fst)	$Fst(<a,b>)$	$\longrightarrow$	a
(Snd)	$Snd(<a,b>)$	$\longrightarrow$	b
(FstEnv)	$Fst(a)[s]$	$\longrightarrow$	$Fst(a[s])$
(SndEnv)	$Snd(a)[s]$	$\longrightarrow$	$Snd(a[s])$
(DPair)	$<a,b>[s]$	$\longrightarrow$	$<a[s],b[s]>$

3.6 η-REDUCTION IN $\lambda\sigma$-CALCULI

It is interesting to extend calculi of substitutions with a notion of η-reduction: this is useful for optimizations of code and also for computations of types in higher-order λ-calculi, for example. The theory $\beta\eta$ is confluent. So we expect to find a confluent extension. In CCC, the extensionality is expressed by the uniqueness of the exponentiation and is given, in CCL, by the rules (AI) and (SΛ). But $\mathcal{E}$+(Beta)+ (SΛ) +(AI) is not weakly confluent, even when restricted to $\mathcal{D}$. The subterm $M \circ Fst$ of the left member of (SΛ) makes critical pairs with several rules of *Subst* and an infinity of rules have to be added to ensure weak confluence. Instead, we may define the relation $c\eta$ by:

$$\Lambda(App \circ <M, Snd>) \longrightarrow_{c\eta} N \quad \text{if} \quad N \circ Fst =_{\mathcal{E}} M$$

Clearly, $c\eta$ contains the (SΛ) reduction. We may replace the reduction defined by (AI) and (SΛ) by the transitive closure of the relation (AI) $\cup\, c\eta$. We call it also $c\eta$.

PROPOSITION **3.6.1** $\mathcal{E} + (Beta) + c\eta$ *is confluent on* $\mathcal{D}$.

The proof is done by the interpretation method. The interpretation of $c\eta$ is a relation which coincides exactly with η-reduction on translations of λ-terms (see [Har87, Har89] for details).

The definition of $c\eta$ extends immediately to $\lambda\sigma$-calculi. Here, we have no longer to deal with rule (AI). The rule (SΛ) is translated onto $\lambda(a[\uparrow]1) \longrightarrow a$ and we encounter all the same difficulties, due to critical pairs. Therefore, the relation $c\eta$ is defined as follows:

$$\lambda(a1) \xrightarrow{c\eta} b \text{ if } a =_\sigma b[\uparrow]$$

PROPOSITION **3.6.2** *a.* $\lambda\sigma_{\Uparrow}+ c\eta$ *is confluent.*

b. $\lambda\sigma+ c\eta$ *is confluent.*

c. the interpretation of $c\eta$*, defined on* $\sigma_{\Uparrow}(\sigma)$*-normal forms by a step of* $c\eta$*-reduction followed by a derivation to* $\sigma_{\Uparrow}(\sigma)$*-normal forms, coincides on* λ*-terms with* η*-reduction.*

The proof is done by interpretation and needs the development of some technical lemmas like the following one, which ensures the correctness of the definition:

LEMMA **3.6.3** *Let* a *and* b *be two terms in* $\sigma_{\Uparrow}$*-n.f. Let* $p \geq 0$*. If* $a[\Uparrow^p(\uparrow)] =_{\sigma_{\Uparrow}} b[\Uparrow^p(\uparrow)]$ *then* $a \equiv b$*.*

Let s *and* t *be two substitutions in* $\sigma_{\Uparrow}$*-n.f. If* $s \circ \Uparrow^p(\uparrow) =_{\sigma_{\Uparrow}} t \circ \Uparrow^p(\uparrow)$*, then* $s \equiv t$*.*

A rather detailed proof is given in [Har92].

3.7 CONCLUSION

The $\lambda\sigma_{\Uparrow}\eta$-calculus is a first complete response to our request, which was to find a proper confluent extension of λ-calculus, computing explicitly substitutions and solving the names'problem. From a rewriting viewpoint, we have with the development leading from CCL to $\lambda\sigma_{\Uparrow}$ a real world example of how to improve confluence properties by modifications of the term rewriting system itself. Also, the interpretation method, which is a very simple trick, appears very powerful: it permits to reduce proofs on "complicated" terms to proofs on "regularized" terms.

From a λ-calculus viewpoint, the two systems are very interesting: they are used to describe and compare some abstract machines [ACCL91, Ler90], which are based on classical β-strategies. We have still to design new strategies, using their full power, that is, strategies which contain computations between substitutions. This is needed for optimizations (see [Bal86, Har87, Ned92]). These calculi are also a good framework to discuss optimality and sharing. We know that this is not possible to obtain Lévy's optimality with these systems [Fie90] because they are Term Rewriting Systems so subterms, which code function's bodies, have to be unshared before β-reduction. But, we may discuss a new kind of optimality, which refers to the number of elementary steps needed to compute the normal form of a given term, whenever it exists. We have also to fully unterstand what are the possible uses of the metavariables of $\lambda\sigma_{\Uparrow}$, which bring a really new capability of calculus: $\lambda\sigma_{\Uparrow}$ is a calculus of contexts. For example, if metavariables represent names of macros in a given text, then the pre-processing of a text is simply described by a first-order substitution applied to these metavariables.

Some open problems involve the rewriting and λ-calculus aspects: the most important one is to prove the termination of $\lambda\sigma$-calculi in a typed framework (see [ACCL91], which contains type systems for $\lambda\sigma$ and may be extended straigthforward to type $\lambda\sigma_{\Uparrow}$). This problem seems rather difficult: to prove the termination of typed λ-calculus is not so easy, this is the same for the termination of *Subst*, and these two points are subgoals of the desired proof.

REFERENCES

[ACCL91] M. Abadi, L. Cardelli, P-L. Curien, and J.-J. Lévy. Explicit substitutions. *Journal of Functional Programming*, **1**, pp. 4.375–416, 1991.

[Bal86] H. Balsters. *Lambda Calculus Extended with Segments.* PhD thesis, Eindhoven University, 1986.

[Bar74] H.P. Barendregt. Pairing without conventional restraints. *Zeitschr. J. Math And Logik und Grundlagen p Math*, **20**, pp. 289–306, 1974.

[Bar84] H. P. Barendregt. *The Lambda-Calculus*, vol. 103. Elsevier Science Publishing Company, 1984.

[Bru72] N.de Bruijn. Lambda-calculus notation with nameless dummies, a tool for automatic formula manipulation, with application to the church-rosser theorem. *Indag. Math.*, **34–5**, pp. 381–392, 1972.

[Bru78] N.de Bruijn. Lambda-calculus notation with namefree formulas involving symbols that represent reference transforming mappings. *Indag. Math.*, **40**, pp. 348–356, 1978.

[BT88] V. Breazu-Tannen. A combining algebra and higher-order types. In *Proc. LICS 88, Edinburgh*, 1988.

[CH90] P.-L. Curien and T. Hardin. *Yet another counterexample for λ-calculus with surjective pairing.* Technical report, forum Types, Communication, 1990.

[CHR92] P.-L. Curien, T. Hardin, and A. Rios. Strong normalisation of substitutions. In *MFCS92, Lecture Notes in Computer Science 629*, 1992.

[Cur86] P.-L. Curien. *Categorical Combinators, Sequential Algorithms and Functional Programming.* Research Notes in Theoretical Computer Science. Pitman, London, 1986.

[Cur92] P.-L. Curien. Environment machines. *Theoretical Computer Science*, **82**, 2, pp. 389–402, 1992.

[Fie90] J. Field. On laziness and optimality in lambda interpreters. In *ACM Conference on Principle of Programming Languages, San Francisco*, 1990.

[Har87] T. Hardin. *Résultats de Confluence pour les Règles fortes de la Logique Combinatoire Catégorique et Liens avec les Lambda-calculs.* PhD thesis, Université de Paris 7, 1987.

[Har89] T. Hardin. Confluence results for the pure strong categorical logic ccl. λ-calculi as subsystems of ccl. *Theoretical Computer Science*, **65**, pp. 291–342, 1989.

[Har92] T. Hardin. η-reduction for explicit substitutions. In *Algebraic and Logic Programming'92, Lecture Notes in Computer Science 632*, 1992.

[HL86] T. Hardin and A. Laville. Proof of termination of the rewriting system subst on c.c.l. *Theoretical Computer Science*, **46**, pp. 305–312, 1986.

[HL89] T. Hardin and J.J. Lévy. A confluent calculus of substitutions. In *France-Japan Artificial Intelligence and Computer Science Symposium, Izu (Japan)*, 1989.

[Klo82] J. W. Klop. *Combinatory Reduction Systems.* PhD thesis, Mathematisch Centrum Amsterdam, 1982.

[Ler90] X. Leroy. *The ZINC Experiment: an Economical Implementation of the ML Language.* Technical Report 117, INRIA, 78153, Le Chesnay Cedex, France, 1990.

[Lév78] J.-J. Lévy. *Réductions Correctes et Optimales dans le Lambda-Calcul.* PhD thesis, Université de Paris 7, 1978.

[Ned92] R.P. Nederpelt. *The Fine-Structure of Lambda Calculus.* Technical Report 92/07, Eindhoven University of Technology, Eindhoven, The Netherlands, 1992.

[Oos92] V. Van Oostrom. *Confluence by Decreasing Diagrams.* Technical report, Vrije Universiteit, de Boelelaan 1081a, 1081 HV Amsterdam, 1992.

[PLHL91] P.-L.Curien, T. Hardin, and J-J Lévy. *Confluence Properties of Weak and Strong Calculi of Explicit Substitutions.* Technical Report 1617, INRIA, 78153, Le Chesnay Cedex, France, 1991.

[Río92] A. Ríos. *Variations sur le Calcul Explicite de la Substitution.* PhD thesis, Université Paris 7, 1992.

[Yok89] H. Yokouchi. Relationship between λ-calculus and rewriting systems for categorical combinators. *Theoretical Computer Science*, **65**, 1989.

[Zan92] H. Zantema. *Termination of Term Rewriting by Interpretation.* Technical Report RUU-CS-92-14, Utrecht University, Utrecht, The Netherlands, 1992.

4

An Infinitary Church-Rosser Property for Non-collapsing Orthogonal Term Rewriting Systems

J.R. Kennaway, J.W. Klop, M.R. Sleep and F.J. de Vries

4.1 INTRODUCTION

There are at least two good reasons to study infinitary term rewriting. First, we believe that infinitary term rewriting is of interest for its own sake, as a natural extension of finitary term rewriting. Second, infinitary term rewriting provides a sound and thorough basis for term graph rewriting, a fruitful theoretical model for implementations of functional programming languages. Term graph rewriting has been defined by Barendregt and co-workers in [BvEG$^+$87] and has been adopted as the central model by the ESPRIT BRA project *SemaGraph*.

Term rewriting is a general model of computation. Computations can be finite and infinite. The usual focus is on successful finite computations: finite derivations ending in finite normal form. However, infinite computations computing a possible infinite answer are of interest as well: recursive procedures enumerating some infinite set: e.g. the natural numbers or the Fibonacci numbers. Until recently, infinite computations have hardly seriously been considered in the theory of term rewriting.

In functional programming languages like Miranda or ML it is possible to manipulate with lazy expressions representing infinite objects, like lists. Graph rewriting has been introduced as a theoretical framework to show the soundness of such computing.

Term Graph Rewriting: Theory and Practice.
Eds. Ronan Sleep, Rinus Plasmeijer and Marko van Eekelen.

Infinitary term rewriting is a foundation for graph rewriting (cf. [KKSdV93] for an elaboration of this point): some instances of graph rewriting on shared graphs actually represent infinite computations on infinite terms.

At present the theory of infinitary rewriting for orthogonal Term Rewriting Systems is rapidly emerging in a series of papers. Dershowitz, Kaplan and Plaisted have opened the series with [DK89, DKP89, DKP91]. They take a rather topological approach and study Cauchy converging reduction sequences. A number of their results (Compression Lemma, Infinitary Projection Lemma, Infinitary Church-Rosser property) depend on the rather strong notion of a top-terminating orthogonal Term Rewriting System. Dropping the condition of top-termination introduces problems. Farmer and Watro [FW91] observed the necessity of strong convergence for some instances of compressing and pointed out the link between infinitary term rewriting and graph rewriting.

In [KKSdV90b] we developed the theory of infinite term rewriting based on strongly converging reductions after presenting counter-examples to the desired general results for Cauchy converging sequences. For the theory involving strong convergence the Infinitary Projection Lemma, the Compressing Lemma and the Unique Normal Form Property are provable, whereas counter-examples exist for these results in case of Cauchy convergence. We also showed that despite the nice theory one can develop for strongly converging reductions the infinitary Church-Rosser property does not hold. The presented counter-example shows that also for Cauchy-converging reductions there is no infinitary Church-Rosser property for arbitrary orthogonal infinitary Term Rewriting Systems.

In this chapter we will prove the infinitary Church-Rosser property for strongly converging reductions for orthogonal infinitary Term Rewriting Systems of which all rules are non-collapsing, except for at most one rule of the form $I(x) \to x$. We think that our proof is instructive and conceptually clear.

The present account improves our treatment in the early version [KKSdV90a].

4.1.1 Overview of this chapter

In section 4.2 we briefly introduce infinitary Term Rewriting Systems (TRS). Then, in section 4.3, we define depth-preserving orthogonal Term Rewriting Systems and prove the infinitary Church-Rosser property for strongly converging sequences in such systems. Using Park's idea of hiaton we show in section 4.4 that any orthogonal TRS can be transformed into a depth-preserving orthogonal TRS, via the so called ϵ-completion. This enables us to prove the infinitary Church-Rosser property for orthogonal TRS consisting of non-collapsing rules with at most one unary collapsing rule. Finally, we discuss our results and relate them with those of Dershowitz, Kaplan and Plaisted.

4.2 INFINITARY ORTHOGONAL TERM REWRITING SYSTEMS

We briefly recall the definition of a finitary Term Rewriting System, before we define infinitary orthogonal Term Rewriting Systems involving both finite and infinite terms. For more details the reader is referred to [DJ90] and [Klo92].

4.2.1 Finitary Term Rewriting Systems

A *finitary Term Rewriting System* over a signature Σ is a pair $(Ter(\Sigma), R)$ consisting of the set $Ter(\Sigma)$ of finite terms over the signature Σ and a set of rewrite rules $R \subseteq Ter(\Sigma) \times Ter(\Sigma)$.

The *signature* Σ consists of a countably infinite set Var of variables $(x, y, z, \ldots)$ and a non-empty set of function symbols $(A, B, C, \ldots, F, G, \ldots)$ of various finite arities ≥ 0. Constants are function symbols with arity 0. The set $Ter(\Sigma)$ of *finite terms* $(t, s, \ldots)$ over Σ is the smallest set containing the variables and closed under function application.

The set $O(t)$ of *positions* of a term $t \in Ter(\Sigma)$ is defined by induction on the structure of t as follows: $O(t) = \{\lambda\}$, if t is a variable and $O(t) = \{\lambda\} \cup \{i \cdot u | 1 \leq i \leq n \text{ and } u \in O(t_i)\}$, if t is of the form $F(t_1, \ldots, t_n)$. If $u \in O(t)$ then the subterm t/u at position u is defined as follows: $t/\lambda = t$ and $F(t_1, \ldots, t_n)/i \cdot u = t_i/u$. The *depth* of a subterm of t at position u is the length of u.

Contexts are terms in $Ter(\Sigma \cup \{\Box\})$, in which the special constant $\Box$, denoting an empty place, occurs exactly once. Contexts are denoted by $C[\,]$ and the result of substituting a term t in place of $\Box$ is $C[t] \in Ter(\Sigma)$. A *proper* context is a context not equal to $\Box$.

Substitutions are maps $\sigma : Var \rightarrow Ter(\Sigma)$ satisfying the equation $\sigma(F(t_1, \ldots, t_n)) = F(\sigma(t_1), \ldots, \sigma(t_n))$.

The set R of *rewrite rules* contains pairs (l, r) of terms in $Ter(\Sigma)$, written as $l \rightarrow r$, such that the left-hand side l is not a variable and the variables of the right-hand side r are contained in l. The result l^σ of the application of the substitution σ to the term l is an *instance* of l. A *redex* (reducible expression) is an instance of a left-hand side of a rewrite rule. A reduction step $t \rightarrow s$ is a pair of terms of the form $C[l^\sigma] \rightarrow [r^\sigma]$, where $l \rightarrow r$ is a rewrite rule in R. Concatenating reduction steps we get a *finite reduction sequence* $t_0 \rightarrow t_1 \rightarrow \ldots \rightarrow t_n$ or an *infinite* reduction sequence $t_0 \rightarrow t_1 \rightarrow \ldots$.

4.2.2 Infinitary orthogonal Term Rewriting Systems

An *infinitary Term Rewriting System* (TRS, usually this abbreviation is reserved for the finitary Term Rewriting Systems only) over a signature Σ is a pair $(Ter^\infty(\Sigma), R)$ consisting of the set $Ter^\infty(\Sigma)$ of finite and infinite terms over the signature Σ and a set of rewrite rules $R \subseteq Ter(\Sigma) \times Ter(\Sigma)$. It takes some elaboration to define the set $Ter^\infty(\Sigma)$ of finite and infinite terms.

The set $Ter(\Sigma)$ of finite terms for a signature Σ can be provided with an metric $d : Ter(\Sigma) \times Ter(\Sigma) \rightarrow [0, 1]$. The *distance* $d(t, s)$ of two terms t and s is 0, if t and s are equal, and 2^{-k}, otherwise, where $k \in \omega$ is the largest natural number such that all nodes of s and t at depth less than or equal to k are equally labeled. The set of infinitary terms $Ter^\infty(\Sigma)$ is the metric completion of $Ter(\Sigma)$. (This is all well known, see for instance [AN80]). Substitutions, contexts and reduction steps generalize trivially to the set of infinitary terms $Ter^\infty(\Sigma)$.

To introduce the prefix ordering $\leq$ on terms we extend the signature Σ with a fresh symbol Ω. The prefix ordering $\leq$ on $Ter^\infty(\Sigma \cup \{\Omega\})$ is defined inductively: $x \leq x$ for any variable x, $\Omega \leq t$ for any term t and, if $t_1 \leq s_1, \ldots, t_n \leq s_n$, then $F(t_1, \ldots, t_n) \leq F(s_1, \ldots, s_n)$.

If all function symbols of Σ occur in R we will write just R for $(Ter^{\infty}(\Sigma), R)$. The usual properties for finitary Term Rewriting Systems extend verbatim to infinitary Term Rewriting Systems:

DEFINITION **4.2.1**

a. *A rewrite rule* $l \to r$ *is* left-linear *if no variable occurs more than once in the left-hand side* l.
b. R *is* non-overlapping *if for any two left-hand sides* s *and* t, *any position* u *in* t, *and any substitutions* σ *and* $\tau : Var \to Ter(\Sigma)$ *it holds that if* $(t/u)^{\sigma} = s^{\tau}$ *then either* t/u *is a variable or* t *and* s *are left-hand sides of the same rewrite rule and* $u = \lambda$ *(i.e. non-variable parts of different rewrite rules do not overlap and non-variable parts of the same rewrite rule overlap only entirely).*
c. *A (in)finitary Term Rewriting System* R *is* orthogonal *if its rules are left-linear and non-overlapping.*
d. *A rewrite rule* $l \to r$ *is* collapsing, *if* r *is a variable.*

It is well known (cf. [Ros73, Klo92]) that finitary orthogonal Term Rewriting Systems satisfy the *finitary Church-Rosser property*, i.e., ${}^*\!\!\leftarrow \circ \to^* \subseteq \to^* \circ {}^*\!\!\leftarrow$, where $\to^*$ is the transitive, reflexive closure of the relation $\to$. It is not difficult to see that infinitary orthogonal Term Rewriting Systems inherit this finitary Church-Rosser property. In this chapter we consider a generalization of the finite Church-Rosser property to infinite reductions. It is a rather subtle issue to decide on the appropriate class of infinite reductions. We will discuss this in the next section.

4.2.3 Projecting infinitary reductions

In a complete metric space like $Ter^{\infty}(\Sigma)$, Cauchy sequences of any ordinal length have a limit. (Such transfinite Cauchy sequences are an instance of Moore-Smith convergence over a net indexed by the ordinal length of the sequence, see e.g. the text book [Kel55].) It is a natural idea to introduce *(transfinite) converging* reductions, as Dershowitz, Kaplan and Plaisted have done in [DJ90]. These are transfinite reduction sequences whose elements form a Cauchy sequence.

DEFINITION **4.2.2** *A reduction of ordinal length* α *is a set* $(t_{\beta})_{\beta \leq \alpha}$ *of terms indexed by the ordinal* α *such that* $t_{\beta} \to t_{\beta+1}$ *for each* $\beta < \alpha$.

Note that when α is a limit ordinal, this definition does not stipulate any relationship between t_{α} and the earlier terms in the sequence. The obvious requirement to make is that the earlier terms should converge to t_{α}.

DEFINITION **4.2.3** *A reduction* $(t_{\beta})_{\beta \leq \alpha}$ *is* Cauchy converging, *written* $t_0 \to_{\alpha}^{c} t_{\alpha}$), *in the following cases.*

a. $t_0 \to_0^{c} t_0$,
b. $t_0 \to_{\beta+1}^{c} t_{\beta+1}$ *if* $t_0 \to_{\beta}^{c} t_{\beta}$,
c. $t_0 \to_{\lambda}^{c} t_{\lambda}$ *if* $t_0 \to_{\beta}^{c} t_{\beta}$ *for all* $\beta < \lambda$ *and* $\forall \epsilon < 0\, \exists \beta < \lambda\, \forall \gamma (\beta < \gamma < \lambda \to d(t_{\gamma}, t_{\lambda}) < \epsilon)$.

However, despite being apparently so natural, converging reductions are not well behaved even for orthogonal TRS.

- Converging reductions resist compression into converging reductions of length at most ω (cf. [FW91, KKSdV90b, DKP91]).
- Converging reductions do not project over finite reductions (cf. 4.2.4, [KKSdV90b, DKP91]).
- The infinitary Church-Rosser property does not hold (cf. 4.2.10, [KKSdV90b]).

The next example shows that the projection of a infinite converging reduction over a finite converging reduction need not be a converging reduction.

EXAMPLE **4.2.4** *[KKSdV90b, DKP91].*

$$\begin{array}{rl} \textit{Rules}: & A(x,y) \to A(y,x) \\ & C \to D \\ \textit{Sequences}: & A(C,C) \to A(C,C) \to A(C,C) \to A(C,C) \to \ldots \to_\omega A(C,C) \\ & A(C,D) \to A(D,C) \to A(C,D) \to A(D,C) \to \ldots \end{array}$$

Clearly $A(C,C) \to^c_\omega A(C,C)$. The second infinite reduction obtained by standard projection over the one step reduction $C \to D$ is not a converging reduction, and hence has no limit.

Strongly converging reductions, which generalize an idea in [FW91], have better properties. In [KKSdV90b] we have proved for orthogonal TRS that strongly converging reductions can be compressed and project over finite reductions. Informally, a strongly convergent reduction is such that for every depth d, there is some point in the reduction after which all contractions are performed at greater depth. By induction on α we define when a converging reduction $(t_\beta)_{\beta\leq\alpha}$ is strongly converging towards the limit t_α (notation $t_0 \to_\alpha t_\alpha$). By d_β we will denote the depth of the contracted redex in $t_\beta \to t_{\beta+1}$.

DEFINITION **4.2.5**

a. $t_0 \to_0 t_0$,
b. $t_0 \to_{\beta+1} t_{\beta+1}$ *if* $t_0 \to^c_{\beta+1} t_{\beta+1}$ *and* $t_0 \to_\beta t_\beta$,
c. $t_0 \to_\lambda t_\lambda$ *if* $t_0 \to^c_\lambda t_\lambda$ *and* $\forall\gamma < \lambda\ (t_0 \to_\gamma t_\gamma)$ *and* $\forall d > 0\, \exists\beta < \lambda\, \forall\gamma\ (\beta < \gamma < \lambda \to d_\gamma > d)$.

By $t \to_{\leq\alpha} s$ we denote the existence of a strongly converging reduction from t with limit s of length less than or equal to α.

We end this section with some positive facts about strongly converging reductions that we will need in the sequel of this chapter.

Farmer and Watro have provided a necessary and sufficient condition when an infinite sequence of strongly converging reductions of length $\omega + 1$ itself is strongly converging.

LEMMA **4.2.6** *[FW91]. Let $t_{n,0} \to_{\leq\omega} t_{n,\omega} = t_{n+1,0}$ be strongly converging for all $n \in \omega$. Let $d_{n,k}$ denote the depth of the contracted redex $R_{n,k}$ in $t_{n,k} \to t_{n,k+1}$. If for all n there is a d_n such that for all k it holds that $d_{n,k} > d_n$, and $\lim_{k\to\infty} d_k = \infty$, then there exists a term $t_{\omega,\omega}$ such that $t_{0,0} \to_{\leq\omega\times\omega} t_{\omega,\omega}$ via the strongly converging reduction $t_{0,0} \to_{\leq\omega} t_{0,\omega} = t_{1,0} \to_{\leq\omega} t_{1,\omega} = t_{2,0} \to_{\leq\omega} \cdots \to_{\leq\omega\times\omega} t_{\omega,\omega}$.* □

In order to state the Infinitary Projection Lemma for strongly convergent reductions we need the notion of descendant for transfinite reductions. We assume familiarity with the notion in finitary term rewriting of the descendants of of a position or set of positions by a finite reduction (cf. [HL91]). The existence of infinite terms does not complicate the notion, but for infinite sequences we must extend the definition to account for what happens at limit points.

DEFINITION **4.2.7** *Let R be a reduction sequence $t_0 \rightarrow_\alpha t_\alpha$ of length α. Denote the subsequence of R from t_{beta} to t_γ by $R_{\beta,\gamma}$ For a set of positions v of t_0 the set $v \setminus R$ of descendants of v by R in t_α is defined by induction on α. When α is finite, this is the standard notion. If α is a limit ordinal, then $v \setminus R$ is defined in terms of the sets $v \setminus R_{0,\beta}$ for all $\beta < \alpha$, as follows: $u \in v \setminus R$ if and only if $\exists \beta < \alpha\, \forall \gamma\, (\beta < \gamma < \alpha \rightarrow u \in v \setminus \gamma)$ If $\alpha = \lambda + n$ for a limit ordinal λ and a finite non-zero n, then $v \setminus R = v \setminus R_{0,\lambda} \setminus R_{\lambda,\lambda+n}$.*

When contemplating this definition, note that the strong convergence of $t_0 \rightarrow_\alpha t_\alpha$ implies that for any position $u \in O(t_\alpha)$, either u is in every $v \setminus \gamma$ for sufficiently large γ, or u is in none of them. This is not the case for merely converging reductions, as Example 4.2.4 illustrates.

LEMMA **4.2.8** *Infinitary Projection lemma [KKSdV90b]. Let $(t_n)_{n \in \omega}$ be a strongly converging reduction of t_0 with limit t_ω and let $t_0 \rightarrow s_0$ be a reduction of a redex R of t_0. Then there is a strongly converging reduction $(s_n)_{n \in A}$ with limit s_ω, where for all $n \leq \omega$, s_n is obtained by contraction of all descendants of R in t_n.* □

4.2.4 The infinitary Church-Rosser property

In the present infinitary context the natural generalization of the finite Church-Rosser property is to consider a peak of strongly converging reductions of arbitrary ordinal lengths.

DEFINITION **4.2.9** *An infinitary Term Rewriting System satisfies the infinitary Church-Rosser property for strongly converging reductions if for any peak $t \rightarrow_{\alpha_1} t_1$, $t \rightarrow_{\alpha_2} t_2$ there exists a joining valley $t_1 \rightarrow_{\beta_1} s$, $t_2 \rightarrow_{\beta_2} s$:*

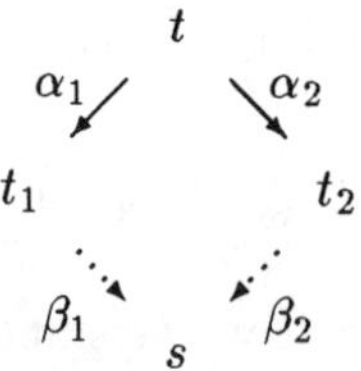

Since strongly converging reductions can be compressed into reductions of length at most ω the infinitary Church-Rosser property follows if we can show that peaks of length ω can be joined:

t

$\leq\omega$ ↙ ↘ $\leq\omega$

t_1 t_2

$\leq\omega$ ⋰ ⋱ $\leq\omega$

s

Despite the Infinitary Projection Lemma for strongly converging reductions, the infinitary Church-Rosser property does not hold for strongly converging reductions (nor for converging reductions) in orthogonal TRS. The following TRS are counter-examples to the infinitary Church-Rosser property for both convergence and strong convergence:

EXAMPLE **4.2.10** *[KKSdV90b]*

a. *Rules :*

$$A(x) \to x$$
$$B(x) \to x$$
$$C \to A(B(C))$$

Sequences :

$$C \to A(B(C)) \to A(C) \to_{\omega} A^{\omega}$$
$$C \to A(B(C)) \to B(C) \to_{\omega} B^{\omega}$$

b. *Rules :*

$$D(x,y) \to x$$
$$C \to D(A, D(B,C))$$

Sequences :

$$C \to D(A, D(B,C)) \to D(A,C) \to^{*} D(A, D(A,C)) \to^{*} \ldots$$
$$C \to D(A, D(B,C)) \to D(B,C) \to^{*} D(B, D(B,C)) \to^{*} \ldots$$

Note that in these examples the rules involving C are not strictly necessary: e.g. for the first example one may consider then the infinite term $(AB)^{\omega} = A(B(A(B(\ldots))))$ instead.

4.3 DEPTH-PRESERVING ORTHOGONAL TERM REWRITING SYSTEMS

In this section and the next we consider two natural classes of orthogonal TRS in which the infinitary Church-Rosser property holds for strongly converging sequences. The counter-examples suggest that collapsing rules are destroying the Church-Rosser properties. In the next section we will prove the Church-Rosser property for strongly converging reductions in orthogonal TRS without collapsing rules.

In this section however we will consider the more restricted but easier to deal with orthogonal TRS whose rules are depth-preserving.

DEFINITION **4.3.1** *A* depth-preserving *TRS is a left-linear TRS such that for all rules the depth of any variable in a right-hand side is greater than or equal to the depth of the same variable in the corresponding left-hand side.*

THEOREM **4.3.2** *Any depth-preserving orthogonal TRS has the infinitary Church-Rosser property for strongly converging sequences.*

PROOF. Let $t_{0,0} \to t_{0,1} \to \ldots \to_{\leq\omega} t_{0,\omega}$ and $t_{0,0} \to t_{1,0} \to \ldots \to_{\leq\omega} t_{\omega,0}$ be strongly convergent.

a. Using the Infinitary Projection Lemma for strongly convergent reductions we construct the horizontal strongly converging sequences $t_{n,0} \to^{*} t_{n,1} \to^{*} \ldots \to_{\leq\omega} t_{n,\omega}$ for $0 < n < \omega$, as depicted in figure 4.1. The vertical reductions are constructed similarly.

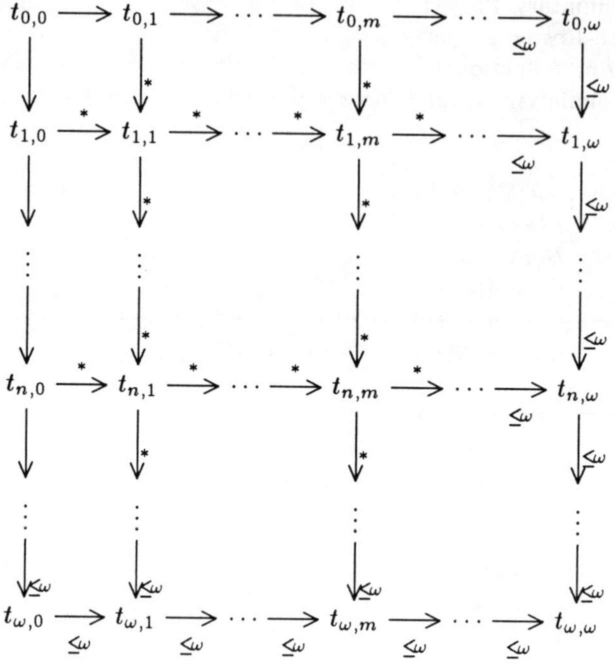

Figure 4.1

b. The construction of the Transfinite Projection Lemma also implies that the reduction $t_{n,\omega} \rightarrow_{\leq\omega} t_{n+1,\omega}$ is strongly converging.
By the depth-preserving property it holds for all $m, n \leq \omega$ that the depth of the reduced redexes in $t_{n,m} \rightarrow^* t_{n,m+1}$, which are all descendants of the redex $R_{0,m}$ in $t_{0,m} \rightarrow t_{0,m+1}$, is at least the depth of $R_{0,m}$ itself. Because $t_{0,0} \rightarrow t_{0,1} \rightarrow \ldots \rightarrow_{\leq\omega} t_{0,\omega}$ is strongly convergent we find by Lemma 4.2.6 that $t_{\omega,0} \rightarrow_{\leq\omega} t_{\omega,1} \rightarrow_{\leq\omega} t_{\omega,2} \ldots$ is strongly converging. Let us call its limit $t_{\omega,\omega}$.

c. In the same way the terms $t_{n,\omega}$ are part of a strongly converging sequence. The limit of this sequence is also equal to $t_{\omega,\omega}$, as can be seen with the following argument. Let $\epsilon > 0$. Because $(t_{\omega,n})_{n\leq\omega}$ is a Cauchy sequence, there is an N_1 such that for all $m \geq N_1$ we have $d(t_{\omega,m}, t_{\omega,\omega}) < \frac{1}{3}\epsilon$.
Because $t_{0,0} \rightarrow t_{1,0} \rightarrow \ldots \rightarrow_{\leq\omega} t_{\omega,0}$ is strongly converging, there is an N_2 such that for $n \geq N_2$ we have that $2^{-d_n} < \frac{1}{3}\epsilon$ where d_n is the depth of the redex R_n reduced at step $t_{n,0} \rightarrow t_{n+1,0}$. Since the descendants of this redex R_n occur at least at the same depth, and since the TRS R is depth-preserving, we get $d(t_{n,m}, t_{\omega,m}) < \frac{1}{3}\epsilon$ for all $m \leq \omega$ and all $n \geq N_2$.
For similar reasons there is an N_3 such that for all $n \leq \omega$ and all $m \geq N_3$ we have that $d(t_{n,\omega}, t_{n,m}) < \frac{1}{3}\epsilon$.
Concluding: Let N be the maximum of N_1, N_2 and N_3. Then for $n \geq N$ we find using the triangle inequality for metrics that

$$
\begin{aligned}
d(t_{n,\omega}, t_{\omega,\omega}) &\leq d(t_{n,\omega}, t_{n,n}) + d(t_{n,n}, t_{\omega,\omega}) \\
&\leq d(t_{n,\omega}, t_{n,n}) + d(t_{n,n}, t_{\omega,n}) + d(t_{\omega,n}, t_{\omega,\omega}) \\
&\leq \frac{1}{3}\epsilon + \frac{1}{3}\epsilon + \frac{1}{3}\epsilon \\
&\leq \epsilon.
\end{aligned}
$$

□

Observe that in this proof there are two places where it is essential that the reductions are strongly convergent. The first is the appeal to the Infinitary Projection Lemma. The second is in the argument that the sequences $(t_{\omega,n})_{n\in\omega}$ and $(t_{n,\omega})_{n\in\omega}$ have the same limit.

4.4 NON-COLLAPSING ORTHOGONAL TERM REWRITING SYSTEMS

DEFINITION **4.4.1** *A TRS R is non-collapsing if all its rewrite rules are non-collapsing, i.e. there is no rewrite rule in R whose right-hand side is a single variable.*

We will show that any non-collapsing orthogonal TRS satisfies the infinitary Church-Rosser property for strongly converging reductions. The proofs will use a variant of Park's notion of hiaton (cf. [Par83]). The idea is to replace a depth losing rule like $A(x, B(y)) \to B(y)$ by a depth-preserving variant $A(x, B(y)) \to B(\epsilon(y))$. In order to keep the rewrite rules applicable to terms involving hiatons, we also have to add more variants like $A(x, \epsilon^m(B(y))) \to B(\epsilon^{m+k+1}(y))$ for $k, m > 0$. By adding to a TRS all depth-preserving variants of its rewrite rules, we transform it into a depth-preserving TRS.

DEFINITION **4.4.2** *Let R be a TRS based on the alphabet Σ. Let Σ_ϵ be the extension of Σ with a fresh unary symbol ϵ.*

a. Let the ϵ-hiding function $\rho : Ter^\infty(\Sigma_\epsilon) \to Ter^\infty(\Sigma)$ be partially defined by induction as follows:

(1) $\rho(x) = x$,
(2) $\rho(f(t_1, \ldots, t_n)) = f(\rho(t_1), \ldots, \rho(t_n))$ for f in Σ and $t_i \in Ter^\infty(\Sigma_\epsilon)$ for $0 \leq i \leq n$,
(3) $\rho(\epsilon(t)) = \rho(t)$ for $t \in Ter^\infty(\Sigma_\epsilon)$.

Hence ρ is well-defined on terms in $Ter^\infty(\Sigma_\epsilon)$ containing no infinite string of ϵs.

b. A term $t \in Ter^\infty(\Sigma_\epsilon)$ is an ϵ-variant *of a term $s \in Ter^\infty(\Sigma)$ if $\rho(t) = s$, that is, if hiding the ϵs in t results in s.*

c. An ϵ-variant of a rule $l \to r$ is a pair of terms (l_ϵ, r_ϵ) such that

(1) $\rho(l_\epsilon) = l$.
(2) $\rho(r_\epsilon) = r$.
(3) the root symbol of l_ϵ is not ϵ.

(4) l_ϵ does not contain a subterm of the form $\epsilon(x)$ for any variable x.
(5) the root symbol of r_ϵ is not ϵ unless r is a variable,

d. *The ϵ-completion R^ϵ of R has alphabet Σ_ϵ. Its rules are the* depth-preserving *ϵ-variants of rules of R. We denote reduction in R^ϵ by $\rightarrow^\epsilon$.*

The proof of the following lemma is straightforward and omitted.

LEMMA **4.4.3** *The ϵ-completion of an orthogonal TRS is depth-preserving and orthogonal.* □

LEMMA **4.4.4** *Let R be a non-collapsing orthogonal TRS.*

a. *Let t_ϵ be an ϵ-variant of a term t of R. If t_ϵ strongly ϵ-converges in ω steps to some term s in R^ϵ, then s does not contain a branch ending in an infinite string of ϵs.*
b. *Let t_0 be the ϵ-variant of some term s_0. If $t_0 \rightarrow^\epsilon_\omega t_\omega$ is a strongly converging reduction in R^ϵ, then so is $s_0 \rightarrow_\omega s_\omega$ in R, where $s_i = \rho(t_i)$ for $0 \leq i \leq \omega$.*
c. *Let $t_0 \rightarrow_\omega t_\omega$ be a strongly converging reduction in R. Let s_0 be an ϵ-variant of t_0. Then there exists a strongly converging reduction $s_0 \rightarrow^\epsilon_\omega s_\omega$ in R^ϵ such that each s_i is an ϵ-variant of the corresponding t_i and similar for the reduction rules used.*

PROOF.

a. Since there are no collapsing rules, a string of ϵs can only be made longer by a reduction occurring at its top. Strong convergence implies that only finitely many such reductions can be made, and therefore that an infinite string of ϵs cannot be created.
b. Since t_0 is an ϵ-variant it does not contain an infinite string of ϵs. Neither does any of the t_i for $i \in \omega$, nor t_ω itself by the previous item 4.4.4(a). Hence, $\rho(t_n)$ is a well-defined term for all $0 \leq n \leq \omega$.
Because there are no infinite strings of ϵs in t_ω, every infinite path from the root of t_ω must contain infinitely many occurrences of members of Σ. Note also that t_ω is necessarily an infinite term.
Since by the previous item 4.4.4(a) t_ω contains no infinite string of ϵs, it must contain occurrences of members of Σ at arbitrarily great depth.
Given any finite number k, consider those occurrences v of t_ω, such that the path from the root to v contains at least k occurrences of symbols in Σ. By the preceding remarks, there must be at least one such occurrence. Let N_k be the minimum length of all such v. Because there are no infinite strings of ϵs, N_k must tend to infinity with k. Since $t_0 \rightarrow_\omega t_\omega$ is strongly converging there exists for any $k > 0$ an N such that for $n > N$, the depth of the redex reduced in $t_{n-1} \rightarrow t_n$ is at least N_k. This implies that the corresponding redex in $s_{n-1} \rightarrow s_n$ is at depth at least k, and hence $s_0 \rightarrow_\omega s_\omega$ is strongly convergent.
c. Trivial. The ϵ-variant s_0 of t_0 contains the corresponding ϵ-variant of the redex reduced in t_0. Apply an ϵ-variant of the corresponding rule. The resulting reduction satisfies the required properties. □

THEOREM **4.4.5** *Any non-collapsing orthogonal TRS satisfies the infinitary Church-Rosser property for strongly converging reductions.*

PROOF. Let R be an orthogonal TRS. Construct its ϵ-completion R^ϵ. By Theorem 4.3.2 the depth-preserving orthogonal TRS R^ϵ satisfies the infinitary Church-Rosser property. So if we start with two strongly converging reductions $t \twoheadrightarrow_{\leq\omega} s_1$ and $t \twoheadrightarrow_{\leq\omega} s_2$, then by Lemma 4.4.4(c) these reductions lift to two strongly converging reductions in R^ϵ, let us say $t \twoheadrightarrow^\epsilon_{\leq\omega} r_1$ and $t \twoheadrightarrow^\epsilon_{\leq\omega} r_2$. By Theorem 4.3.2 there exists a join u for the two lifted reductions such that $r_1 \twoheadrightarrow^\epsilon_{\leq\omega} u$ as well as $r_2 \twoheadrightarrow^\epsilon_{\leq\omega} u$. Erasing all ϵs using Lemma 4.4.4(b) we see that the term $\rho(u)$ is the join in R of $t \twoheadrightarrow_{\leq\omega} s_1$ and $t \twoheadrightarrow_{\leq\omega} s_2$. □

THEOREM **4.4.6** *An orthogonal TRS, each of whose rules is non-collapsing except for at most one rule of the form $I(x) \to x$, satisfies the infinitary Church-Rosser property for strongly converging reductions.*

PROOF. First, note that the proof of the previous theorem cannot be directly applied in the presence of the rule $I(x) \to x$. Consider the rules $A(x) \to I(x)$, $B(x) \to I(x)$, $I(x) \to x$. There are obvious reductions of the term $A(B(A(B(\cdots))))$ to both A^ω and B^ω. These lift to reductions ending with $A(\epsilon(A(\epsilon(\cdots))))$ and $\epsilon(B(\epsilon(B(\cdots))))$ respectively. If we now apply the Church-Rosser property of the depth-balanced system, we obtain reductions of these terms to $\epsilon(\epsilon(\epsilon(\epsilon(\cdots))))$, which cannot be lifted to strongly convergent reductions in the original system.

A simple modification of the previous proof establishes the present theorem. We modify the depth-preserving transformation by introducing two versions of ϵ: ϵ itself, and ϵ'. The rule $I(x) \to x$ is replaced by the depth-preserving version $I(x) \to \epsilon'(x)$. The other rules are transformed as before, except that wherever ϵ would appear on the left-hand side in the original transformation, either ϵ or ϵ' is used, in all possible combinations. On the right-hand sides, only ϵ is used. It is easy to see that the resulting system is depth-preserving and orthogonal, and hence that the infinite Church-Rosser property holds.

The distinction between ϵ and ϵ' can be thought of as labeling those occurrences of ϵ which arise from reductions of the I-rule.

Now consider two strongly converging reductions $t \twoheadrightarrow_{\leq\omega} s_1$ and $t \twoheadrightarrow_{\leq\omega} s_2$. As in the proof of the previous theorem, we obtain in R^ϵ a term u and two strongly converging reductions $r_1 \twoheadrightarrow^\epsilon_{\leq\omega} u$ and $r_2 \twoheadrightarrow^\epsilon_{\leq\omega} u$, where r_1 and r_2 are ϵ-variants of s_1 and s_2.

We cannot in general erase all the ϵs and ϵ's from these sequences to obtain a join for s_1 and s_2, since u may contain infinite branches of ϵs and ϵ's (which we shall call ϵ-branches for short). But we will show that we can transform these sequences in such a way as to eliminate such branches, after which the erasing process can be performed safely.

In every ϵ-branch in u, there must be infinitely many ϵ's. This follows for the same reason that in the non-collapsing case, no infinite branch of ϵs can arise.

Now consider an occurrence of ϵ' in an ϵ-branch of u. This must arise from a reduction by the rule $I(x) \to \epsilon'(x)$ at some point in each of the sequences $r_1 \twoheadrightarrow^\epsilon_{\leq\omega} u$ and $r_2 \twoheadrightarrow^\epsilon_{\leq\omega} u$. This reduction is performed on a subterm of the form $I(T)$, where T reduces to a ϵ-branch. By orthogonality, it is impossible for the reduction of the I-redex to be necessary for any later step of the sequence to be possible. If we omit it, the only effect is that certain occurrences of ϵ' later in the sequence are replaced by I.

We therefore omit from both $r_1 \to^{\epsilon}_{\leq\omega} u$ and $r_2 \to^{\epsilon}_{\leq\omega} u$ every I-reduction which gives rise to an occurrence of ϵ' in any ϵ-branch of u. This gives a term u' containing no such occurrences of ϵ', and reduction sequences $r_1 \to^{\epsilon}_{\leq\omega} u'$ and $r_2 \to^{\epsilon}_{\leq\omega} u'$. These sequences have the property that they contain no ϵ-branch anywhere. They may therefore be lifted to strongly convergent reductions in the original system, providing a strongly convergent joining of the original reduction sequences. □

4.5 CONCLUSION

The results of Dershowitz, Kaplan and Plaisted in [DKP91] imply that top-terminating orthogonal TRS satisfy the infinitary Church-Rosser property for Cauchy converging reductions which start from a finite term. (Cf. [DKP91]: combine their Theorem 3.3, Proposition 5.1, Theorem 6.4, and Theorem 6.3.) The property *top-termination*, that is, there are no derivations of infinite length starting from a finite term with infinitely many rewrites at topmost position, is rather strong and not very syntactic.

Our Theorems 4.4.5 and 4.4.6 show that for strongly converging reductions, orthogonal systems with no collapsing rules, other than possibly one of the form $I(x) \to x$, have the infinitary Church-Rosser property without conditions on the finiteness of the initial term. Theorem 4.4.6 is the best possible result for orthogonal TRS, since the counter-examples in 4.2.10 make it clear that no larger class of orthogonal TRS is Church-Rosser.

We do not know what the situation is for Cauchy converging reductions. For example, do non-collapsing orthogonal TRS have the infinitary Church-Rosser property for Cauchy converging reductions?

REFERENCES

[AGM92] S. Abramsky, D. Gabbay, and T. Maibaum (editors). *Handbook of Logic in Computer Science*, vol. II. Oxford University Press, 1992.

[AN80] A. Arnold and M. Nivat. The metric space of infinite trees: Algebraic and topological properties. *Fundamenta Informatica*, **4**, pp. 445–476, 1980.

[Boo91] R. V. Book (editor). *Proc. 4th Conference on Rewriting Techniques and Applications*, Springer-Verlag, Lecture Notes in Computer Science 488, Como, Italy, 1991.

[BvEG+87] H. P. Barendregt, M. C. J. D. van Eekelen, J. R. W. Glauert, J. R. Kennaway, M. J. Plasmeijer, and M. R. Sleep. Term graph rewriting. In J. W. de Bakker, A. J. Nijman, and P. C. Treleaven (editors), *Proc. PARLE'87 Conference, vol.II*, Springer-Verlag, Lecture Notes in Computer Science 259, pp. 141–158, Eindhoven, The Netherlands, 1987.

[DJ90] N. Dershowitz and J.-P. Jouannaud. Rewrite systems. In van Leeuwen [vL90], chapter 15.

[DK89] N. Dershowitz and S. Kaplan. Rewrite, rewrite, rewrite, rewrite, rewrite. In *Proc. ACM Conference on Principles of Programming Languages, Austin, Texas*, pp. 250–259, Austin, Texas, 1989.

[DKP89] N. Dershowitz, S. Kaplan, and D. A. Plaisted. Infinite normal forms (plus corrigendum). In G. Ausiello, M. Dezani-Ciancaglini, and S. Ronchi Della Rocca (editors), *Automata, Languages and Programming*, Springer-Verlag, Lecture Notes in Computer Science 372, pp. 249–262, Stresa, Italy, 1989.

[DKP91] N. Dershowitz, S. Kaplan, and D. A. Plaisted. Rewrite, rewrite, rewrite, rewrite, rewrite. *Theoretical Computer Science*, **83**, pp. 71–96, 1991. Extended version of [DKP89].

[FW91] W. M. Farmer and R. J. Watro. Redex capturing in term graph rewriting. In Book [Boo91], pp. 13–24.

[HL79] G. Huet and J.-J. Lévy. *Call-by-Need Computations in Non-ambiguous Linear Term Rewriting systems.* Technical report, INRIA, 1979.

[HL91] G. Huet and J.-J. Lévy. Computations in orthogonal rewrite systems I and II. In Lassez and Plotkin [LP91], pp. 394–443. (Originally appeared as [HL79].).

[Kel55] J. L. Kelley. *General Topology.* Van Nostrand, Princeton, 1955.

[KKSdV90a] J. R. Kennaway, J. W. Klop, M. R. Sleep, and F. J. de Vries. *An Infinitary Church-Rosser property for Non-collapsing Orthogonal Term Rewriting Systems.* Technical Report CS-9043, CWI, Amsterdam, 1990.

[KKSdV90b] J. R. Kennaway, J. W. Klop, M. R. Sleep, and F. J. de Vries. *Transfinite Reductions in Orthogonal Term Rewriting Systems.* Technical Report CS-R9041, CWI, Amsterdam, 1990.

[KKSdV93] J. R. Kennaway, J. W. Klop, M. R. Sleep, and F. J. de Vries. The adequacy of term graph rewriting for simulating term rewriting. In *this volume*, 1993.

[Klo92] J. W. Klop. Term rewriting systems. In Abramsky et al. [AGM92], pp. 1–116.

[LP91] J.-L. Lassez and G. D. Plotkin (editors). *Computational Logic: Essays in Honor of Alan Robinson.* MIT Press, 1991.

[Par83] D. Park. The "fairness problem" and nondeterministic computing networks. In J.W. de Bakker and J. van Leeuwen (editors), *Foundations of Computer Science IV, Part 2*, vol. 159 of *Mathematical Centre Tracts*, pp. 133–161. CWI, Amsterdam, 1983.

[Ros73] B. K. Rosen. Tree-manipulating systems and Church-Rosser systems. *Journal of the ACM*, **20**, pp. 160–187, 1973.

[vL90] J. van Leeuwen (editor). *Handbook of Theoretical Computer Science*, vol. B: Formal Models and Semantics. North-Holland, Amsterdam, 1990.

5

The Functional Strategy and Transitive Term Rewriting Systems

Yoshihito Toyama, Sjaak Smetsers, Marko van Eekelen and Rinus Plasmeijer

5.1 INTRODUCTION

An interesting common aspect of the functional languages Miranda [Tur85], Haskell [HWA+90], Lazy ML [Aug84] and Clean [BEL+87, NSEP91] is the similarity between their reduction strategies. The reduction order determined by these strategies can roughly be characterized as top-to-bottom left-to-right lazy pattern matching. This reduction order, in the following referred to as the *functional strategy*, is intuitively easy to understand and can efficiently be implemented. It is usually considered as an aspect of the language that is transformed during the compilation process to some standard reduction strategy (e.g. normal order reduction) in the underlying computational model (e.g. Lambda calculus). Several authors have pursued studies of this reduction order with different semantic transformations [Ken90, Lav87, PS90]. The language Clean is close to its underlying computational model (i.e. Term Graph Rewriting [BEG+87]). Therefore, it seems natural to define the functional strategy *directly* in the computational model rather than using a transformation to an equivalent system with a well-known strategy.

An important efficiency aspect of the functional strategy lies in the fact that evaluation of an actual argument is always forced (by applying the strategy recursively to that actual argument) when this argument is tried to match a non-variable in the corresponding formal pattern. A possible analysis of properties of the functional strategy may be performed using some kind of priority semantics as in [BBK87]. A

Term Graph Rewriting: Theory and Practice.
Eds. Ronan Sleep, Rinus Plasmeijer and Marko van Eekelen.

problem with these priority semantics is, however, the fact that important theoretical properties of standard term rewriting theory do not easily carry over to the priority world.

In this chapter the functional strategy is investigated within the standard framework of orthogonal Term Rewriting Systems. Thus we leave the overlapping situation between rules that usually appears in the functional strategy out of consideration. We believe that this approach is worthwhile as a first step since by this restriction we can rely upon the well-known concept of indexes when we try to explain why the functional strategy works well for a wide class of orthogonal Term Rewriting Systems. The concept of indexes was proposed by Huet and Lévy [HL79]. They introduced the subclass of strongly sequential orthogonal Term Rewriting Systems for which index reduction is normalizing. However, for reasons of efficiency their approach is not very feasible in a practical sense. An important problem they had to cope with is the fact that indexes in general, lack a certain transitivity property that seems to be essential for the efficiency of any reduction strategy.

This chapter studies transitivity properties of indexes by introducing so-called *transitive indexes*. The *transitive Term Rewriting Systems* are defined as a subclass of the strongly sequential Term Rewriting Systems for which each term not in strong head normal form has a transitive index. Furthermore, the notion *transitive direction* is introduced that is used in two different ways. First, it is shown that with the aid of these transitive directions a simple test on the left-hand sides of the rewrite rules can be expressed that is sufficient to characterize transitive Term Rewriting Systems. Second, transitive directions are the basis of a new strategy: the *transitive strategy*. This strategy is normalizing for transitive Term Rewriting Systems. Finally it is shown, using the introduced concepts, that the functional strategy is normalizing for a subclass of transitive Term Rewriting Systems: so-called *left-incompatible Term Rewriting Systems*.

5.2 TERM REWRITING SYSTEMS

In the following we will assume that the reader is familiar with the basic concepts concerning Term Rewriting Systems as introduced by [DJ90, Klo92, HL79]. The following definitions are based on definitions given in [Klo92]. In contrast with [Klo92] we use the notion "constant symbol" for a symbol that cannot be rewritten, instead of for a function symbol with arity 0.

DEFINITION **5.2.1** *A* Term Rewriting System *(TRS) is a pair* (Σ, R) *of an* alphabet *or* signature Σ *and a set of* rewrite rules R.

a. The alphabet Σ *consists of:*

(1) A countable infinite set of variables $x, y, z, \ldots$.

(2) A non empty set Σ_0 *of* function symbols *or* operator symbols $f, g, \ldots$, *each equipped with an "arity" (a natural number), i.e. the number of "arguments" it is supposed to have. We have 0-ary, unary, binary, ternary etc., function symbols.*

b. The set of terms *(or* expressions*) "over" Σ indicated by* $T(\Sigma)$ *or, if* Σ *is not relevant by* T*, is defined inductively:*

(1) $x, y, z, \ldots \in T(\Sigma)$.
(2) *If* $f \in \Sigma_0$ *is an n-ary symbol, and* $t_1, \ldots, t_n \in T(\Sigma)$ $(n \geq 0)$*, then* $f(t_1, \ldots, t_n) \in T(\Sigma)$.

c. Terms not containing a variable are called ground terms *(also:* closed terms*), and* $T_0(\Sigma)$ *is the set of ground terms. Terms in which no variable occurs twice or more, are called* linear.

d. A rewrite rule $\in R$ *is a pair* (l, r) *of terms* $\in T(\Sigma)$*. It will be written as* $l \to r$*. Often a rewrite rule will get a name, e.g.* $\mathbf{r}$*, and we write* $\mathbf{r} : l \to r$.

When the signature Σ is not relevant, a TRS (Σ, R) is indicated by the rewrite rules R only.

DEFINITION **5.2.2** *a. Consider an extra 0-ary constant* $\Box$ *called a* hole *and the set* $T(\Sigma \cup \{\Box\})$*. Then* $C \in T(\Sigma \cup \{\Box\})$ *is called a* context*. We use the notation* $C[\,, \ldots, \,]$ *for the context containing n holes* $(n \geq 1)$*, and if* $t_1, \ldots, t_n \in T(\Sigma)$*, then* $C[t_1, \ldots, t_n]$ *denotes the result of placing* $t_1, \ldots, t_n$ *in the holes of* $C[\,, \ldots, \,]$ *from left to right. In particular,* $C[\,]$ *denotes a context containing precisely one hole.*

b. $t \equiv s$ *indicates the identity of two terms t and s. s is called a* subterm *of t if* $t \equiv C[s]$*. We write* $s \subseteq t$*. s is a* proper subterm*, denoted by* $s \subset t$*, if* $s \subseteq t$ *and* $t \not\equiv s$

c. If a term t has an occurrence of some (function or variable) symbol e, we write $e \in t$*. The variable occurrence z in* $C[z]$ *is* fresh *if* $z \notin C[\,]$.

DEFINITION **5.2.3** *a. A* substitution σ *is a map from* $T(\Sigma)$ *to* $T(\Sigma)$ *satisfying* $\sigma(f(t_1, \ldots, t_n)) \equiv f(\sigma(t_1), \ldots, \sigma(t_n))$ *for every n-ary function symbol f. We also write* t^σ *instead of* $\sigma(t)$.

b. The set of rewrite rules R defines a reduction relation $\to$ *on T as follows:*

> $t \to s$ iff there exists a rule $\mathbf{r} : l \to r$, a context $C[\,]$ and a substitution σ such that $t \equiv C[l^\sigma]$ and $s \equiv C[r^\sigma]$.

The term l^σ *is called a* redex*, or more precisely an* $\mathbf{r}$*-redex. t itself* is *a redex if* $t \equiv l^\sigma$.

c. $\twoheadrightarrow$ *denotes the transitive reflexive closure of* $\to$.

d. Two terms t and $s \in T$ *are* overlapping *if there exist substitutions* σ_1 *and* σ_2 *such that* $t^{\sigma_1} \equiv s^{\sigma_2}$.

e. $t \in T$ *is a* normal form *(with respect to* $\to$*) if there exists no* $s \in T$ *such that* $t \to s$*. NF denotes the set of normal forms of T.*

f. A term t is in head-normal form *if there exists no redex* $s \in T$ *such that* $t \twoheadrightarrow s$.

DEFINITION **5.2.4** *A Term Rewriting System R is* orthogonal *if:*

a. For all rewrite rules $\mathbf{r} : l \to r \in R$*, l is linear*

b. For any two rewrite rules $\mathbf{r}_1 : l_1 \to r_1$ *and* $\mathbf{r}_2 : l_2 \to r_2 \in R$:

> $\mathbf{r}_1 \neq \mathbf{r}_2$ *then* l_1 *and* l_2 *are non-overlapping.*
> *For all* $s \subset l_2$ *such that s is not a single variable,* l_1 *and s are non-overlapping.*

Note. From here on we assume that every Term Rewriting System R is orthogonal.

5.3 STRONG SEQUENTIALITY

In [HL79] a class of orthogonal TRS is defined wherein needed redex are identified by looking at the left-hand sides only. These so-called *strongly sequential TRS* are based on the two notions *Ω-reduction* and *index* of which the definition is given in this section.

DEFINITION **5.3.1 (Ω-terms)** *a. Consider an extra constant* Ω*. The set* $T(\Sigma \cup \{\Omega\})$*, also denoted by* T_Ω*, is called the set of Ω-terms.* t_Ω *indicates the Ω-term obtained from a term* t *by replacing each variable in* t *with* Ω*.*

b. The pre-ordering $\succeq$ *on* T_Ω *is defined as follows:*

$$t \succeq \Omega \text{ for all } t \in T_\Omega,$$
$$f(t_1, \ldots, t_n) \succeq f(s_1, \ldots, s_n) \quad (n \geq 0) \quad \text{if } t_i \succeq s_i \text{ for } i = 1, \cdots, n.$$

We write $t \succ s$ *if* $t \succeq s$ *and* $t \not\equiv s$*.*

c. Two Ω-terms t *and* s *are* compatible, *denoted by* $t \uparrow s$*, if there exists some Ω-term* r *such that* $r \succeq t$ *and* $r \succeq s$*; otherwise,* t *and* s *are* incompatible, *which is indicated by* $t \# s$*.*

d. Let $S \subseteq T_\Omega$*. Then* $t \succeq S$ *(resp.* $t \uparrow S$*) if there exists some* $s \in S$ *such that* $t \succeq s$ *(resp.* $t \uparrow s$*); otherwise,* $t \not\succeq S$ *(resp.* $t \# S$*).*

DEFINITION **5.3.2 (Ω-systems)** *Let R be a Term Rewriting System.*

a. The set of redex schemata *of R is* $Red = \{ l_\Omega \mid l \to r \in R\}$*.*

b. Ω–reduction, *denoted by* $\to_\Omega$ *, is defined on* T_Ω *as* $C[s] \to_\Omega C[\Omega]$ *where* $s \uparrow Red$ *and* $s \not\equiv \Omega$*.*

c. The Ω-system R_Ω *(corresponding to R) is defined as a reduction system on* T_Ω *having* $\to_\Omega$ *as reduction relation.*

LEMMA **5.3.3** *For any R,* R_Ω *is* complete *(i.e.* confluent *and* terminating*)*

PROOF. Easy. See [Klo92]. □

DEFINITION **5.3.4 (Ω-normal form)** *a.* $\omega(t)$ *denotes the normal form of* t *with respect to* $\to_\Omega$ *. Note that due to Lemma 5.3.3* $\omega(t)$ *is well-defined.* NF_Ω *denotes the set of Ω-normal forms.*

b. $\bar{\omega}(f(t_1, \ldots, t_n)) \equiv f(\omega(t_1), \ldots, \omega(t_n))$*.*

The next technical lemma concerns Ω-reduction and the related definition of $\bar{\omega}$. It will be used in the proofs later on in this chapter.

LEMMA **5.3.5** *a. If* $t \succeq s$ *then* $\omega(t) \succeq \omega(s)$*.*

b. Let $C[\Omega] \in NF_\Omega$*. Then for all* $t \in NF_\Omega$*,* $C[t] \in NF_\Omega$

c. Let $\bar{\omega}(t) \equiv C[\Omega]$*, and* z *be a fresh variable. If* $C[z] \# Red$ *then* $C[z] \in NF_\Omega$*.*

PROOF.

a. By induction on the size of t.
b. Suppose $C[t] \notin NF_\Omega$. Then there exist a rule $r \in Red$ that is compatible with a subterm of $C[t]$. This subterm is a result of the combination of $C[\Omega]$ and t, i.e. $C[t] \equiv C'[C''[t]]$ such that $C''[t]$ is compatible with Red for some C' and C''. But, then $C''[\Omega]$ is also compatible with Red which is a contradiction to $C[\Omega] \in NF_\Omega$.
c. Trivial. □

The intuitive idea of $\rightarrow_\Omega$ is that it "approximates" ordinary reduction by considering left-hand sides only. All right-hand sides of rewrite rules in R_Ω are equal to Ω which represents any term. The "approximation" is expressed in the following lemma:

LEMMA **5.3.6** $t_1 \twoheadrightarrow t_2 \quad \Rightarrow \quad \omega(t_1) \preceq t_2$.

PROOF. By induction on the length of the reduction sequence from t_1 to t_2. □

The head-normal form property (Definition 5.2.3f) is in general undecidable. With the aid of Ω-reduction we can define a decidable variant of this property.

DEFINITION **5.3.7** *A term t is in* strong head-normal form *if $\omega(t) \not\equiv \Omega$.*

LEMMA **5.3.8** *If t is in strong head normal form then t is in head-normal form.*

PROOF. Let $t' \equiv \omega(t)$. Suppose t is not in head-normal form. Then there exists a term s such that $t \twoheadrightarrow s$ and $s \succeq Red$. Due to Lemma 5.3.6 $t' \preceq s$ so $t' \uparrow Red$. But also $t' \not\equiv \Omega$ and therefore $t' \rightarrow_\Omega \Omega$ which is a contradiction to $t' \in NF_\Omega$. □

DEFINITION **5.3.9 (Index)** *Let $C[\ ]$ be a context such that $z \in \omega(C[z])$ where z is a fresh variable. Then the displayed occurence of Ω in $C[\Omega]$ is called an* index *(notation $C[\Omega_I]$). Let $C[\Omega_I]$ and Δ be a redex occurrence in $C[\Delta]$. This redex occurrence is also called an index (notation $C[\Delta_I]$).*

DEFINITION **5.3.10 (Strong Sequentiality)** *A Term Rewriting System is* strongly sequential *if for each term $t \notin NF$, t has an index [HL79, Klo92].*

PROPOSITION **5.3.11** *Let R be strongly sequential. Then index reduction is normalizing.*

PROOF. See [HL79]. □

PROPOSITION **5.3.12** *For any strongly sequential TRS one has the following.*

a. $C_1[C_2[\Omega_I]] \Rightarrow C_1[\Omega_I]$ and $C_2[\Omega_I]$.
b. The reverse implication does not hold generally.

PROOF.

a. See [Klo92].
b. See example 5.3.13 □

In [HL79] an algorithm has been given that is capable of finding an index in a term t in $O(|t|)$ time. The main disadvantage of the algorithm is that after an index has been rewritten to a term t' the whole new term t' has to be considered again in order to determine the next index. So in general, the search cannot be started locally, i.e. at the position where the last index was found. This is in fact a consequence of Proposition 5.3.12b. This problem is illustrated by the next example:

EXAMPLE **5.3.13** Let $Red = \{f(1,1), g(f(\Omega,2)), h\}$. Now consider the term $g(h)$. Clearly, h is an index. Suppose h reduces to $f(\Delta_1, \Delta_2)$ where both Δ_1 and Δ_2 are redexes. Locally (i.e. when leaving the surrounding context out of consideration), both redexes are indexes. But for the whole term $g(f(\Delta_1, \Delta_2))$ only Δ_2 is an index.

LEMMA **5.3.14** *a. If* $C_1[\Omega_I]$ *and* $C_1[z] \preceq C_2[z]$ *(where z is fresh) then* $C_2[\Omega_I]$.
b. If $C_1[\Omega] \in NF_\Omega$ *and* $C_2[\Omega_I]$ *then* $C_1[C_2[\Omega_I]]$

PROOF.

a. By Lemma 5.3.5a, it follows that $\omega(C_1[z]) \leq \omega(C_2[z])$. Thus, we get $z \in \omega(C_2[z])$ as $z \in \omega(C_1[z])$
b. By Lemma 5.3.5b and $C_1[\Omega] \in NF_\Omega$, for any t, $\omega(C_1[t]) \equiv C_1[\omega(t)]$. Thus $\omega(C_1[C_2[z]]) \equiv C_1[\omega(C_2[z])]$. Since $z \in \omega(C_2[z])$ also $z \in C_1[\omega(C_2[z])]$. □

5.4 TRANSITIVITY

Example 5.3.13 indicates why indexes in strongly sequential system are not always transitive. A certain subterm t in a context $C[t]$ may reduce to a term t' without rewriting all indexes in t, but, resulting in a term $C[t']$ that is compatible with one of the elements of *Red*. In this section we formulate a restriction for TRS that avoids this problem. As will be shown, this criterion is sufficient for the transitivity property for indexes.

We first introduce a new concept of transitive indexes.

DEFINITION **5.4.1 (Transitive Index)** *The displayed index in* $C_1[\Omega_I]$ *is* transitive *if for any* Ω*-term* $C_2[\Omega_I]$, $C_2[C_1[\Omega_I]]$. *We indicate the transitive index with* $C_1[\Omega_{TI}]$. *We also call the redex occurrence* Δ *in* $C_1[\Delta]$ *a transitive index and indicate it with* $C_1[\Delta_{TI}]$.

Note that replacing $C_2[C_1[\Omega_I]]$ by $C_1[C_2[\Omega_I]]$ in Definition 5.4.1 would give a different notion. For example, let $Red = \{f(g(\Omega))\}$. Then $f(\Omega_{TI})$ by Definition 5.4.1 and the fact that $C_2[f(\Omega_I)]$ holds for any $C_2[\Omega_I]$. But, if we exchange C_1 and C_2 in this definition the displayed Ω in $f(\Omega)$ is not transitive anymore. Take, for example, the context $C_2[\Omega] \equiv g(\Omega)$. Clearly, $C_2[\Omega_I]$. However, in $f(g(\Omega))$, Ω is not an index.

Transitive indexes have the following transitivity property.

LEMMA **5.4.2** *If* $C_1[\Omega_{TI}]$ *and* $C_2[\Omega_{TI}]$ *then* $C_1[C_2[\Omega_{TI}]]$.

PROOF. Let $C_3[\Omega_I]$. From $C_2[\Omega_{TI}]$ it follows that $C_3[C_2[\Omega_I]]$. By the definition of transitivity and $C_1[\Omega_{TI}]$, $C_3[C_2[C_1[\Omega_I]]]$. □

As with indexes, transitivity of indexes remains valid for larger contexts.

Lemma **5.4.3** *If* $C_1[\Omega_{TI}]$ *and* $C_1[z] \preceq C_2[z]$ *(where z is fresh) then* $C_2[\Omega_{TI}]$.

Proof. This lemma follows immediately from the definition of transitive indexes and Lemma 5.3.14 a. □

The importance of transitivity is that it allows searching locally for indexes. Once an index has been found and rewritten, the search for the next index may continue at the same location where the last index has been found. As a consequence, rewriting can be performed in an efficient depth-first way. However, requiring that each term not in normal form should have a transitive index (analogous to the way strongly sequential systems are defined) appears to be too restrictive as can be seen in the next example:

Example **5.4.4** Let R be a TRS with $Red = \{f(g(\Omega))\}$. Consider the term $g(\Delta)$ where $\Delta \equiv f(g(1))$. In this term Δ is not a transitive index, since Δ is not an index in $f(g(\Delta))$.

Now the question is: "How to weaken the transitivity criterion for TRS?". The answer is given in the following reasoning. Suppose we have a TRS R and a strategy, for convenience called *hnf*, that delivers the redexes of a term t that should be reduced in order to obtain the head-normal form of t. Then it is easy to construct a normalizing strategy, say *nf*, for R: First, reduce a term t to head-normal form using *hnf* and then apply *nf* to all the arguments of the result.

The fact that the head-normal form property is undecidable makes it impossible for general TRS to give such a *hnf* strategy. The next definition of transitive TRS is based on the decidable strong head-normal form property.

Definition **5.4.5 (Transitive Term Rewriting Systems)** *A Term Rewriting System is* transitive *if each term t not in strong head-normal form has a transitive index.*

Proposition **5.4.6** *Let R be a TRS. If R is transitive then R is strongly sequential.*

Proof. We have to prove that every term t not in normal form contains an index. Therefore, we distinguish the following two cases:

$\omega(t) \equiv \Omega$: From the definition of transitivity of R it follows that t has a transitive index.

$\omega(t) \not\equiv \Omega$: . Since t is not a normal form there exists a context $C[,\cdots,]$ such that $t \equiv C[t_1,\cdots,t_n]$ and $\omega(t) \equiv C[\Omega,\cdots,\Omega]$ with every $t_i \succ \Omega$. Form the fact that R is transitive and $\omega(t_1) \equiv \Omega$, t_1 has an index. Applying Lemma 5.3.14 b , $C[t_1,\Omega,\cdots,\Omega]$ has an index and therefore (by Lemma 5.3.14 a) $C[t_1,\cdots,t_n]$ has also an index. □

The reverse of the previous proposition does not hold generally, i.e. not every strongly sequential system is also transitive.

Example **5.4.7** Let $Red = \{f(f(\Omega,0),1), f(2,f(3,\Omega))\}$. This TRS is strongly sequential. Now consider the term $f(\Delta_1,\Delta_2)$. Clearly, this term is not in strong head-normal form. But, Δ_1 is not a transitive index. Take, for instance, the context $f(\Omega_I,1)$. In $f(f(\Delta_1,\Delta_2),1)$ Δ_1 is not an index. For the same reason Δ_2 is not a transitive index.

The next problem is: "How can we localize transitive indexes?". The solution is given with the aid of the following definition of *transitive directions.*

DEFINITION **5.4.8 (Transitive direction)** *a. Let* $Q \subseteq T_\Omega$. *The displayed* Ω *in* $C[\Omega]$ *is a* direction *for* Q *if* $C[z] \# Q$. *We indicate a direction for* Q *with* $C[\Omega_Q]$.
b. Let $Red^* = \{p \mid \Omega \prec p \subseteq r$ *for some* $r \in Red\}$. *A* transitive direction *is defined as a direction for* Red^*. *We denote a transitive direction with* $C[\Omega_{TD}]$.

Transitive directions can be related to transitive indexes as follows.

LEMMA **5.4.9** *Let* $C[\Omega_{TD}]$ *and* $C[z] \in NF_\Omega$. *Then* $C[\Omega_{TI}]$.

PROOF. It is clear that $C[\Omega_I]$. We shall prove that the displayed index Ω is transitive, i.e. $C'[C[\Omega_I]]$ for any Ω-term $C'[\Omega_I]$. Let $\omega(C'[z]) \equiv C''[z]$. Note that $C''[z] \in NF_\Omega$ and that $\omega(C'[C[z]]) \equiv \omega(C''[C[z]])$. Now we show that $C''[C[z]] \in NF_\Omega$. Suppose $C''[C[z]] \notin NF_\Omega$. Then there exists some $r \in Red$ having a proper subterm r' not being Ω that is compatible with $C[z]$. However, this contradicts the assumption that $C[z] \# Red^*$. □

The next lemma explains how to use the previous one for finding an index.

LEMMA **5.4.10** *Let* $C[\Delta] \in T$. *If there exists some* $C'[z] \preceq C[z]$ *(where* z *is fresh) such that* $C'[z]$ *is divided into* $C'[z] \equiv C_1[C_2[\cdots C_n[z]\cdots]]$ $(n \geq 1)$ *where* $C_i[\Omega_{TD}]$ *for* $i = 2\cdots n$ *and* $C_i[z] \in NF_\Omega$ *for* $i = 1\cdots n$. *Then* $C[\Delta_I]$.

PROOF. By Lemma 5.4.9, $C_i[\Omega_{TI}]$ for $i = 2\cdots n$. Since $C_1[z] \in NF_\Omega$, we have $C_1[\Omega_I]$. By Definition 5.4.1 and Lemma 5.4.2, $C'[\Omega_I]$. From Lemma 5.3.14 a, it follows that $C[\Omega_I]$. □

It seems that the problem of finding transitive indexes has been postponed since we need transitive directions to determine transitive indexes. Lemma 5.4.11 in combination with Lemma 5.4.13 shows us where to look for transitive directions in a term that might be a candidate for being rewritten. Lemma 5.4.13 on its own, enables an efficient test for deciding whether or not a certain TRS is transitive.

LEMMA **5.4.11** *Let* $Red^{\prec} = \{p \mid \Omega \prec p \prec r$ *for some* $r \in Red\}$ *and let any* $t \in Red^{\prec}$ *have a transitive direction. Then for every* $s \in T_\Omega$ *such that* $s \uparrow Red \wedge s \not\succeq Red$, *s has a transitive direction.*

PROOF. Since $s \uparrow Red \wedge s \not\succeq Red$ there exists some $r \in Red$ such that $r \uparrow s \wedge s \not\succeq r$. Without loss of generality we may state that $r \equiv C[s_1,\cdots,s_m,\Omega,\cdots,\Omega]$ and $s \equiv C[\Omega,\cdots,\Omega,s_{m+1},\cdots,s_{m+n}]$ where $s_i \succ \Omega$ for $i = 1\cdots m+n, m > 0$ and $n \geq 0$. Since $C[\Omega,\cdots,\Omega,\Omega,\cdots,\Omega] \in Red^{\prec}$, $C[\Omega,\cdots,\Omega,\Omega,\cdots,\Omega]$ has a transitive direction. It is clear that this transitive direction must appear in the first m occurrences of Ω, say $C[\Omega_{TD},\cdots,\Omega,\Omega,\cdots,\Omega]$. $C[z,\Omega,\cdots,\Omega,\Omega,\cdots,\Omega] \preceq C[z,\Omega,\cdots,\Omega,s_{m+1},\cdots,s_{m+n}]$, hence $C[z,\Omega,\cdots,\Omega,s_{m+1},\cdots,s_{m+n}] \# Red^*$. □

LEMMA **5.4.12** *Let* $C[s] \in Red$, $s \succ \Omega$. *Then* $C[\Omega_I]$.

PROOF. From the non-overlapping property of R (Definition 5.2.4) it follows that $C[z] \in NF_\Omega$. □

Lemma 5.4.13 *Let R be a TRS. R is transitive iff every $t \in Red^{\prec}$ has a transitive direction.*

Proof.

$\Rightarrow$: Let $t \in Red^{\prec}$. Then $\omega(t) \equiv \Omega$. By assumption, t has a transitive index, say $t \equiv C[\Omega_{TI}]$. We will prove that $C[z] \# Red^*$. Assume that $C[z] \uparrow Red^*$. Then there exists an $s \in Red^*$ such that $C[z] \uparrow s$. This means that there exists a $r \in Red$ such that $r \equiv C'[s]$. Now consider the term $C'[C[z]]$. Since $C'[C[z]] \uparrow r$, $\omega(C'[C[z]]) \equiv \Omega$. From Lemma 5.4.12 it follows that $C'[\Omega_I]$. But then $\omega(C'[C[z]]) \equiv \Omega$ contradicts to $C[\Omega_{TI}]$. Hence it follows that $C[z] \# Red^*$.

$\Leftarrow$: By induction to the size of t we will prove that if $\omega(t) \equiv \Omega$ then t has a transitive index. The basis step is trivial. For the induction step we make a distinction between two cases:

$t \succeq Red$: We can take t itself as the transitive index.

$t \not\succeq Red$: Let $C[,\cdots,]$ be a context such that $t \equiv C[t_1, \cdots, t_n]$ with every $t_i \succ \Omega$ and $\bar{\omega}(t) \equiv C[\Omega, \cdots, \Omega]$ in which all Ω occurrences that correspond to subterms $s \succ \Omega$ of t are displayed. Since $C[\Omega, \cdots, \Omega] \not\succeq Red$ and $C[\Omega, \cdots, \Omega] \uparrow Red$, by Lemma 5.4.11, $C[\Omega, \cdots, \Omega]$ has a transitive direction. Applying Lemma 5.3.5 c and Lemma 5.4.9 it follows that this transitive direction is a transitive index. Again we distinguish two cases:

a. The transitive index Ω is displayed in $C[\Omega, \cdots, \Omega]$. Without any loss of generality we may assume that the first displayed Ω is the transitive index, i.e. $C[\Omega_{TI}, \cdots, \Omega]$. Since $\omega(t_1) \equiv \Omega$ we can apply the I.H.: t_1 has a transitive index. Thus, by Lemma 5.4.2, $C[t_1, \Omega, \cdots, \Omega]$ has a transitive index in t_1 and hence, by Lemma 5.4.3, $C[t_1, t_2, \cdots, t_n]$ has a transitive index in t_1.

b. The transitive index Ω is not displayed in $C[\Omega, \cdots, \Omega]$. This means that this transitive index corresponds to an Ω-occurrence in t. Now we can apply Lemma 5.4.3 immediately so, $C[t_1, \cdots, t_n]$ has a transitive index. □

Remark 5.4.14 • Strongly sequential orthogonal constructor systems [HL79, Klo92] are clearly transitive. We will prove later on that left-normal orthogonal systems [HL79, Klo92, O'D77] are transitive too.

• In [HL79] simple systems are defined as orthogonal Term Rewriting Systems satisfying $\forall t \in (Red^*)^{\prec} : \exists C[\,] : t \equiv C[\Omega_{TD}]$. Here $(Red^*)^{\prec} = \{p \mid \Omega \prec p \prec r \text{ for some } r \in Red^*\}$. It is clear that if R is simple then it is transitive, but the reverse direction is not the case from the following example. Let R have $Red = \{f(g(0, \Omega)), h(g(\Omega, 0))\}$. It is clear that R is transitive. However, $g(\Omega, \Omega) \in (Red^*)^{\prec}$ cannot make an incompatible term to Red^* by replacing an occurrence of Ω with z. Thus, R is not simple.

5.5 TRANSITIVE STRATEGY

This section presents a method for searching indexes of transitive systems. The key idea of our method is a marking of occurrences of subterms which are known to be in strong head-normal form. Of course, these marks are valid through reductions. Hence, we can repeatedly use the information indicated by marks for future searches of indexes.

DEFINITION **5.5.1** *Let (Σ, R)be a TRS.*

a. root *is a function from* T_Ω *to* Σ_0 *such that* root $(f(t_1, \cdots, t_n)) = f$

b. Let $D = \{root(l) \mid l \to r \in R\}$ *be the set of* defined function symbols. $D^* = \{f^* \mid f \in D\}$ *is the set of* marked function symbols *assumed that* $D^* \cap \Sigma = \emptyset$ *and* f^* *has the arity of* f. *It is clear that* $f^* \in D^*$ *is not a defined function symbol.* $T^* = T(\Sigma \cup D^*)$ *is the set of* marked terms.

c. Let t *be a marked term.* $e(t)$ *denotes the term obtained from* t *by erasing all marks.* $\delta(t)$ *denotes the* Ω*-term obtained from* t *by replacing all the maximal subterms having defined function symbols at the roots with* Ω. $\bar{\delta}(f(t_1, \ldots, t_n) \equiv f(\delta(t_1), \cdots, \delta(t_n))$ *for* $f \in \Sigma \cup D^*$.

DEFINITION **5.5.2** $t \in T^*$ *is* well-marked *if*

$$\forall s \subseteq t \; [root(s) \in D^* \Rightarrow e(\delta(s)) \in NF_\Omega].$$

LEMMA **5.5.3** *If* $t \in T^*$ *is well-marked then* $e(\delta(t)) \in NF_\Omega$.

PROOF. Trivial. □

LEMMA **5.5.4** *Let* $\forall s \subseteq t \; [root(s) \in D^* \Rightarrow e(\delta(s)) \# Red]$. *Then* t *is well-marked.*

PROOF. We will prove the Lemma by induction on the size of t. The basic step is trivial. Induction step: Let $t \equiv h(t_1, \cdots, t_n)$. From I.H., every t_i is well-marked. If $h \notin D$, t is well-marked. Assume that $h \in D^*$, say $h = f^*$. Then, $e(\delta(t)) \equiv f(e(\delta(t_1)), \cdots, e(\delta(t_n))) \# Red$. Since every $e(\delta(t_i)) \in NF_\Omega$, it follows that $e(\delta(t)) \in NF_\Omega$. □

LEMMA **5.5.5** *Let* t *be well-marked, and let* $e(\bar{\delta}(t)) = C[\Omega_{TD}]$. *Then* $C[z] \in NF_\Omega$.

PROOF. It follows directly from $C[z] \# Red$ and Lemma 5.5.3. □

DEFINITION **5.5.6** *Let* $t \equiv C[t_1, \cdots, t_p, \cdots, t_n] \in T^*$ *and* $t' \equiv e(C)[\Omega, \ldots, \Omega_{TD}, \ldots, \Omega]$. *Then we say that* t_p *is a* directed subterm of t with respect to t'.

DEFINITION **5.5.7 (Transitive reduction strategy)** *The* transitive strategy *has as input a term* $t \in T$. s *indicates a subterm occurrence of* t.

(1) *If* t *has no defined function symbol, terminate with "*$e(t)$ *is a normal form".*

(2) *Take the leftmost-outermost subterm of* t *having a defined function at the root as* s.

(3) *If* $e(\bar{\delta}(s)) \succeq Red$, *terminate with "*$e(s)$ *is an index of* $e(t)$*".*
(4) *If* $e(\bar{\delta}(s)) \uparrow Red$, *take a directed subterm of* s *with respect to* $e(\bar{\delta}(s))$ *as* s *and go to* (3).
(5) *Mark the root of* s *and go to* (1).

THEOREM **5.5.8** *Let* R *be transitive, and let* $t \in T$.

a. *The transitive strategy applied to* t *terminates with either "*t *is a normal form" (a) or with "*s *is an index of* t*" (b).*
b. *In case (a)* t *is a normal form. Otherwise (case (b)),* s *is an index of* t.

PROOF. A sketch of our proof is as follows. The loop consisting of (3)-(4) decreases the size of s. The loop consisting of (1)-(5) decreases the number of the defined function symbols in t. Thus, the transitive strategy eventually terminates at (1) or (3). If t is a normal form, the strategy cannot terminate at (3). Thus, it terminates at (1). Let t be not a normal form. Note that the root of a redex in t cannot be marked. Hence, the strategy eventually terminates at (3) with indicating "$e(t) \equiv e(C)[e(s)_I]$". From Lemma 5.5.4, t is well-marked. If at (4) $e(\bar{\delta}(s)) \uparrow Red$ and $e(\bar{\delta}(s)) \equiv C'[\Omega_{TD}]$, then, by Lemma 5.5.5 we obtain $C'[z] \in NF_\Omega$. If at (2) t has no defined function symbol at the root, then $e(\delta(t)) \in NF_\Omega$. Thus, by applying Lemma 5.4.10 it can be easily proven that $e(s)$ is an index of $e(t)$. □

5.6 FUNCTIONAL STRATEGY

The reduction order determined by the functional strategy is obtained via top-to-bottom, left-to-right pattern matching. In this section we will identify those TRS for which this way of pattern matching always delivers a transitive direction. Note that the fact that an Ω-occurrence in a term t is a transitive direction according to some rule R may not be affected by the rules "below" R. We will show that this requirement is met if each rule R' "below" R is *left-incompatible* with R.

DEFINITION **5.6.1 (Left-incompatibility)** *Let* $s, t \in T_\Omega$. *The* left-incompatibility *of* s *and* t, *indicated by* $t \#_< s$, *is defined as follows:*

- $t \not\equiv s$, $t \not\equiv \Omega$ $s \not\equiv \Omega$,
- $f = g \Rightarrow \exists i\, [\forall j < i\, [t_j \preceq s_j] \wedge t_i \#_< s_i]$
  where $t \equiv f(t_1, \cdots, t_n)$ *and* $s \equiv g(s_1, \cdots, s_m)$.

The above i *is called the* left-incompatible point.

EXAMPLE **5.6.2** Let $Red = \{f(\Omega, 1), f(1, 0)\}$. Then $f(\Omega, 1) \#_< f(1, 0)$, but not $f(1, 0) \#_< f(\Omega, 1)$. Furthermore, notice that in $f(\Delta_1, \Delta_2)$ only Δ_2 is an index. If the rule $f(\Omega, 1)$ is applied first then only Δ_2 is indicated as an index. This is not the case when $f(1, 0)$ is applied first; then both redexes are indicated.

LEMMA **5.6.3** *Let* $C[\Omega] \uparrow p$ *and let* $C[\Omega_{\{p\}}]$ *be the leftmost direction for* $\{p\}$. *Then*

$$p \#_< q \quad \Rightarrow \quad C[\Omega_{\{q\}}].$$

PROOF. By induction on the size of $C[\,]$. Basic step $C[\,] \equiv \Box$ is trivial. Induction step: Let $C[\Omega] \equiv f(t_1, \cdots, t_d, \cdots, t_n)$ where the indicated Ω occurs in t_d, say $t_d \equiv C_d[\Omega]$. Since $C[\Omega] \uparrow p$, $p \equiv f(p_1, \cdots, p_d, \cdots, p_n)$ and $p_i \uparrow t_i$ for $i = 1 \cdots n$. Since $p \#_< q$, we have the incompatible point k for p and q.

$d < k$: Then $p_d \preceq q_d$. Since $C_d[z] \# p_d$, we have $C[z] \# q_d$. Hence, $C[z] \# q$.
$d = k$: Since $C_d[\Omega_{\{p_d\}}]$ is the leftmost direction for $\{p_d\}$ and $p_d \#_< q_d$, we can apply I.H. to them. Thus, $C_d[\Omega_{\{q_d\}}]$ is obtained. Thus, $C[z] \# q$.
$d > k$: Since $C[\Omega_{\{p\}}]$ is the leftmost direction for $\{p\}$, we obtain $t_k \succeq p_k$. Since $p_k \#_< q_k$, we obtain that $t_k \# q_k$. Hence, $C[z] \# q$. □

DEFINITION **5.6.4** *An orthogonal TRS (Σ, R) is* left-incompatible *if it satisfies the following two conditions:*

- *Red can be expressed as a list $[p_1, \cdots, p_n]$ with $p_i \#_< p_j$ if $i < j$,*
- *$\forall p_i \in Red$, $q \in Red^+$ $[p_i \#_< q]$, where $Red^+ = Red^* - Red$.*

LEMMA **5.6.5** *Let R be a left-incompatible TRS with $Red = [p_1, \cdots, p_n]$. Let $C[\,]$ be a context such that $C[\Omega] \uparrow p_d$, $C[\Omega] \# p_i$ $(1 \le i < d)$ and let $C[\Omega_{\{p_d\}}]$ display the leftmost direction for $\{p_d\}$. Then $C[\Omega_{TD}]$.*

PROOF. Since $C[\Omega] \# p_i$ $(1 \le i < d)$, we have $C[\Omega_{\{p_i\}}]$ $(1 \le i < d)$. From the left-incompatibility, it follows that $p_d \#_< p_j$ $(d < j \le n)$ and $p_d \#_< q$ for $q \in Red^+$. Thus, by Lemma 5.6.3 we can show that $C[\Omega_{\{q\}}]$ for any $q \in Red^*$. □

COROLLARY **5.6.6** *Every left-incompatible system is transitive.*

PROOF. According to Lemma 5.4.13 it is sufficient to prove that each $t \in Red^{\prec}$ has a transitive direction. Let $t \in Red^{\prec}$. Then there exists some $p_d \in Red$ such that $t \# p_i$ $(i < d)$ and $t \uparrow p_d$. Since $t \not\succeq p_d$, t must have a direction for $\{p_d\}$. By Lemma 5.6.5, the leftmost direction of t for $\{p_d\}$ is a transitive direction. □

DEFINITION **5.6.7** *Let R be a left-incompatible TRS with $Red = [p_1, \cdots, p_n]$ and let $t \equiv C[t_1, \ldots, t_k, \ldots, t_n] \in T^*$ and $t' \equiv C[\Omega, \ldots, \Omega, \ldots, \Omega]$. Furthermore, let d be a number such that $e(C)[\Omega, \cdots, \Omega, \cdots, \Omega] \# p_i$ for $1 \le i < d$ and $e(C)[\Omega, \cdots, \Omega, \cdots, \Omega] \uparrow p_d$ (which means that p_d is the first compatible pattern in the list), and let $e(C)[\Omega, \cdots, \Omega_{\{p_d\}}, \cdots, \Omega]$ display the leftmost direction for $\{p_d\}$. Then we say that t_k is the* leftmost directed subterm of t with respect to t' and p_d.

DEFINITION **5.6.8 (Functional Reduction Strategy)** *The* functional strategy *has as input a term $t \in T$ and a TRS R which is left-incompatible with $Red = [p_1, \cdots, p_n]$. s indicates a subterm occurrence of t.*

(1) *If t has no defined function symbol, terminate with "e(t) is a normal form".*
(2) *Take the leftmost-outermost subterm of t having a defined function at the root as s.*
(3) *Find the first compatible pattern p_d to $e(\bar{\delta}(s))$ in the list Red if it exists; otherwise, mark the root of s and go to* **(1)**.

(4) *If* $e(\bar{\delta}(s)) \succeq p_d$, *terminate with "*$e(s)$ *is an index of* $e(t)$*".*
(5) *Take as* s *the leftmost directed subterm of* s *with respect to* $e(\bar{\delta}(s))$ *and* p_d, *and go to* (3).

THEOREM **5.6.9** *Let* R *be left-incompatible system and let* $t \in T$.

a. *The functional strategy applied to* t *terminates with either "*t *is a normal form" (a) or with "*s *is an index of* t*" (b).*
b. *In case (a)* t *is a normal form. Otherwise (case (b)),* s *is an index of* t.

PROOF. Note that if R is left-incompatible, then by Lemma 5.6.5 it is clear that the functional strategy is essentially same to the transitive strategy. Hence, the proof of this theorem is similar to the proof of Theorem 5.5.8. □

O'Donnell [O'D77] has proven that if an orthogonal Term Rewriting System R is left-normal then R is strongly sequential and leftmost-outermost reduction is normalizing. We now show that his result is a special case of the above theorem.

DEFINITION **5.6.10 (Left-normal TRS)** *a. The set* T_L *of the left-normal terms is inductively defined as follows:*

- $x \in T_L$ *if* x *is a variable,*
- $f(t_1, \cdots, t_{p-1}, t_p, t_{p+1} \cdots, t_n) \in T_L \quad (0 \leq p \leq n)$
  if $t_1, \cdots, t_{p-1} \in T_0$ *(i.e.* $t_1, \cdots, t_{p-1}$ *are groud terms),* $t_p \in T_L$, *and* $t_{p+1}, \cdots, t_n$ *are variables.*

b. *The set of the* left-normal schemata *is* $T_{L\Omega} = \{t_\Omega \mid t \in T_L\}$.
c. R *is* left-normal *(see also [O'D77, HL79, Klo92]) iff for any rule* $l \to r$ *in* R, l *is a left-normal term, i.e.* $Red \subseteq T_{L\Omega}$.

LEMMA **5.6.11** *Let* $p, q \in T_{L\Omega}$ *and* $p \# q$. *Then* $p \#_< q$.

PROOF. By induction on the size of q. Let $p \equiv f(p_1, \cdots, p_m, \Omega, \cdots \Omega)$ and $q \equiv f(q_1, \cdots, q_n, \Omega, \cdots \Omega)$ where p_i $(i < m)$ and q_j $(j < n)$ have no Ω occurrences. Since $p \# q$, there exists some k $(k \leq m, n)$ such that $p_i \equiv q_i$ $(i < k)$ and $p_k \# q_k$. Note that $p_k, q_k \in T_{L\Omega}$. Thus, from I.H., $p_k \#_< q_k$ follows. Therefore, $p \#_< q$. □

THEOREM **5.6.12** *Let* R *be a left-normal orthogonal Term Rewriting System. Then,* R *is a left-imcompatible system.*

PROOF. From $Red^* \subseteq T_{L\Omega}$, the orthogonality of R, and Lemma 5.6.11, we can easily show that R is left-incompatible. □

COROLLARY **5.6.13** *Let* R *be a left-normal orthogonal Term Rewriting System. Then the functional strategy applied to* $t \notin NF$ *indicates the leftmost-outermost redex of* t *as an index.*

PROOF. Follows directly from the definition of the functional strategy. □

EXAMPLE **5.6.14** The following R is left-incompatible but not left-normal. Hence, the functional strategy is normalizing for R. However, the leftmost-outermost reduction strategy is not.

$$R \begin{cases} f(c(x,0),c(0,x)) \rightarrow 1 \\ g \rightarrow 0 \\ \omega \rightarrow \omega \end{cases}$$

Now consider the term $f(c(\omega,g),c(g,\omega))$. It is clear that the functional strategy is normalizing and leftmost-outermost reduction not.

5.7 FUTURE WORK

With respect to the functional reduction strategy there exist two major problems that have to be solved. First, since the functional strategy is initially intended as a strategy for Priority Rewriting Systems, the adequacy of this strategy for Priority Term Rewriting Systems should be investigated. An additional problem comes from the fact that there does not always exist a well-defined semantics for a Priority Term Rewriting System. Second, implementations of (lazy) functional languages that are using this strategy appear to be efficient. It should be investigated whether this practical efficiency can be founded theoretically.

REFERENCES

[Aug84] L. Augustsson. A compiler for lazy ML. In *Proc. of ACM Symposium on LISP and Functional Programming*, pp. 218–227, 1984.

[BBK87] J.C.M. Baeten, J.A. Bergstra, and J.W. Klop. Term rewriting systems with priorities. In *Proc. of Conference on Rewriting Techniques and Applications*, Springer-Verlag, Lecture Notes in Computer Science 256, pp. 83–94. Bordeaux, 1987.

[BEG+87] H.P. Barendregt, M.C.J.D. van Eekelen, J.R.W. Glauert, J.R. Kennaway, M.J. Plasmeijer, and M.R. Sleep. Term graph reduction. In *Proc. of Parallel Architectures and Languages Europe (PARLE), vol.II*, Springer-Verlag, Lecture Notes in Computer Science 259, pp. 141–158. Eindhoven, The Netherlands, 1987.

[BEL+87] T. Brus, M.C.J.D. van Eekelen, M. van Leer, M.J. Plasmeijer, and H.P. Barendregt. Clean - a language for functional graph rewriting. In *Proc. of Conference on Functional Programming Languages and Computer Architecture (FPCA '87)*, Springer-Verlag, Lecture Notes in Computer Science 274, pp. 364–384. Portland, Oregon, USA, 1987.

[DJ90] N. Dershowitz and J.P. Jouannaud. Rewrite systems. In J. van Leeuwen (editor), *Handbook of Theoretical Computer Science*, vol. B, pp. 243–320. Elsevier, 1990.

[HL79] G. Huet and J.J. Lévy. *Call by Need Computations in Non-Ambiguous Linear Term Rewriting Systems.* Technical Report 359, INRIA, 1979.

[HWA+90] P. Hudak, P.L. Wadler, Arvind, B Boutel, J. Fairbairn, J. Fasel, K. Hammond, J. Hughes, T. Johnsson, R. Kieburtz, R.S. Nikhil, S.L. Peyton Jones, M. Reeve, D. Wise, and J. Young. *Report on the Functional Programming Language Haskell.* Technical report, Department of Computer Science, Glasgow University, 1990.

[Ken90] J.R. Kennaway. The specificity rule for lazy pattern-matching in ambiguous term rewriting systems. In *Proc. of 3rd European Symposium on Programming (ESOP)*, Springer-Verlag, Lecture Notes in Computer Science 432, 1990.

[Klo92] J.W. Klop. Term rewriting systems. In S. Abramsky, D. Gabbay, and T. Maibaum (editors), *Handbook of Logic in Computer Science*, vol. I. Oxford University Press, 1992.

[Lav87] A. Laville. Lazy pattern matching in the ML language. In *Proc. of 7th Conference on Software Technology and Theoretical Computer Science*, Springer-Verlag, Lecture Notes in Computer Science 287, pp. 400–419. Pune, India, 1987.

[NSEP91] E.G.J.M.H. Nöcker, J.E.W. Smetsers, M.C.J.D. van Eekelen, and M.J. Plasmeijer. Concurrent Clean. In *Proc. of Parallel Architectures and Languages Europe (PARLE'91)*, Springer-Verlag, Lecture Notes in Computer Science 505, pp. 202–219. Eindhoven, The Netherlands, 1991.

[O'D77] M.J. O'Donnell. *Computing in Systems Described by Equations.* Springer-Verlag, Lecture Notes in Computer Science 58. 1977.

[PS90] L. Puel and A. Suárez. Compiling pattern matching by term decomposition. In *Proc. of ACM conference on LISP and Functional Programming*, pp. 273–281, 1990.

[Tur85] D.A. Turner. Miranda: A non-strict functional language with polymorphic types. In *Proc. of Conference on Functional Programming Languages and Computer Architecture (FPCA '85)*, Springer-Verlag, Lecture Notes in Computer Science 201, pp. 1–16. Nancy, France, 1985.

6

Graph Rewriting Systems for Efficient Compilation

Z.M. Ariola and Arvind

6.1 INTRODUCTION

A modern trend in programming language theory has been to develop calculi to capture some specific aspects of functional language implementations. For example, several calculi for explicit substitution have recently been developed by Curien and Lévy [ACCL90, Cur86, Cur91, HL89, Hin77]. An attempt to formalize "weak reduction", i.e., the kind of reduction that is actually done by most functional language implementations, is described by Maranget [Mar91]. Barendregt *et al.*, have put forth a calculus to capture sharing in graph reduction implementation of Term Rewriting Systems (TRS) [BvEG+87a, BvEG+87b, Ken90, BvEvLP87]. In the same vein, we want to develop a calculus to capture the sharing of subexpressions in a more general class of languages.

Specification of sharing is desirable in the intermediate language used by a compiler for a purely functional language. Consider the function definition $\mathsf{F}\ x = x + x$ and the expression $\mathsf{F}(2{+}3)$. Any decent implementation, independent of the evaluation strategy (normal-order or applicative-order) it employs, will evaluate the subexpression $2+3$ only once. Dealing with sharing is important if the intermediate language is to be used to express and reason about optimizations. However, sharing becomes a necessity when a functional language is extended with side-effect operations, like I-structures [ANP89]. In general side-effects destroy "referential transparency" in the sense that the definition of an identifier cannot be substituted for each occurrence of the identifier in an unrestricted manner. Thus, the semantics of such a language requires a precise specification of sharing and substitution.

Term Graph Rewriting: Theory and Practice.
Eds. Ronan Sleep, Rinus Plasmeijer and Marko van Eekelen.

A way to capture sharing is to represent the expression as a graph instead of a linear text string or tree. This allows sharing of identical terms through pointers, and avoids repeated evaluation of identical terms as it is commonly done in normal-order reduction. Graph reduction for the λ-calculus was proposed by Wadsworth in order to bring together the advantages of both the applicative and the normal-order evaluation [Wad71]. Wadsworth also formally proved the correctness of his graph reduction technique. (As an aside, Wadsworth also showed that his graph reduction did not capture enough of sharing of expressions to lead to an optimal interpreter. More recently a new graph structure which allows sharing of "*contexts*", has been proposed by Kathail [Kat90]. This latter technique leads to provably optimal interpreters for the λ-calculus [Lév78]).

Much of the past work on graph rewriting has been to prove its correctness with respect to either the λ-calculus or Term Rewriting Systems (TRS). We see graph rewriting as a system in its own right, and want to explore its syntactic and semantic properties. We want to include graphs with cycles and rewriting rules that recognize or create cycles. This is not the case in either [Wad71] or [BvEG+87b] where only acyclic graphs are considered and thus, some important implementation ideas are ruled out.

In the following, we formally introduce Graph Rewriting Systems (GRS), and prove several syntactic properties of such systems. We also develop a term model for a restricted class of GRS along the lines of Lévy's term model for λ-calculus. The restricted GRS which we consider are adequate to describe sharing in combinatory systems but not the λ-calculus or the I-structures. In the last section we briefly discuss the applicability of our term model in showing the correctness of compiler optimizations.

This chapter is based on the PhD thesis of Zena M. Ariola [Ari92] where complete proofs and more examples with explanations may be found.

6.2 SYNTAX OF GRS

Our formalism for graph rewriting is based on the observation that a natural way to represent a graph textually is to associate an identifier to each node of the graph, and then write down all the interconnections as a *recursive let-block*. Equivalently we can say that we associate a name to each subexpression of a term. For example, the term $\mathsf{F}(+(2,2))$ will be expressed as:

$$\begin{aligned} \{\ & t_1 = +(2,2); \\ & t_2 = \mathsf{F}(t_1) \\ & \mathsf{In}\ t_2\} \end{aligned}$$

In applying the rule $\mathsf{F}(x) \longrightarrow \mathsf{G}(x,x)$, the name t_1, and not the expression $+(2,2)$, will be substituted for each occurrence of x, leading to the term:

$$\begin{aligned} \{\ & t_1 = +(2,2); \\ & t_2 = \mathsf{G}(t_1,t_1) \\ & \mathsf{In}\ t_2\} \end{aligned}$$

We will allow the substitution of $+(2,2)$ for each free occurrence of t_1 only when $+(2,2)$ becomes a *value*, i.e., 4. Thus, no duplication of work occurs during reduction. Therefore, we think that *an essential feature of a language for graph rewriting is the block construct with a suitable notion of substitutable values.*

SE	$\in$	Simple Expression
E	$\in$	Expression
F^k	$\in$	$\mathcal{F}^k$
Constant	$\in$	$\mathcal{F}^0$
SE	::=	*Variable* | *Constant*
E	::=	*SE*
	|	$\mathsf{F}^k\ (SE_1, \cdots, SE_k)$
	|	*Block*
Block	::=	$\{\ [Binding;]^*\ \mathsf{In}\ SE\}$
Binding	::=	$Variable = E$
Term	::=	*E*

Figure 6.1 Syntax of terms of a GRS with signature $\mathcal{F}$

The syntax of GRS terms is given in figure 6.1. Superscript on a function symbol indicates its "arity" i.e., the number of arguments it is supposed to have; constants are assumed to be function symbols of arity 0. The variable names on the left hand side of bindings in a block are required to be pairwise distinct. Furthermore the order of bindings in a block does not matter.

In the following $\mathtt{FV}(M)$ and $\mathtt{BV}(M)$ will denote the free and bound variables of term M, respectively. Moreover, if $M \equiv \{x_1 = e_1; \cdots x_n = e_n \ \mathsf{In}\ x\}$ and x is a variable, we will say that M is rooted at x. The root of a term plays a special role during its reduction. For example, consider the rule $\mathsf{F}(\mathsf{G}(x)) \longrightarrow \mathsf{0}$ and the term $\mathsf{F}(\mathsf{G}(1))$. During the reduction only the pointers to F (i.e., the root) are redirected to $\mathsf{0}$, and the subterm $\mathsf{G}(1)$ remains unaffected. We call the subterm $\mathsf{G}(x)$ the *precondition* of the above rule, which will be written in the GRS notation as follows:

$$\frac{x_2 = \mathsf{G}(x)}{x_1 = \mathsf{F}(x_2) \longrightarrow x_1 = \mathsf{0}}$$

DEFINITION **6.2.1 (GRS rule)** *A GRS rule τ is a set of preconditions, $x_1 = e_1, \cdots, x_n = e_n$, and a left-hand side, l, and a right-hand side, r, and is written as:*

$$\frac{x_1 = e_1 \mid \cdots \mid x_n = e_n}{x = l \quad \longrightarrow \quad x = r}$$

where

a. $e_i, 1 \leq i \leq n$, and l are terms of the form $\mathsf{F}^k(y_1, \cdots, y_k)$, where each y_i is either a variable or a constant and $k > 0$;

b. r is a term such that $\mathtt{FV}(r) \subseteq \mathtt{FV}(\{x_1 = e_1; \cdots x_n = e_n;\ x = l\ \mathsf{In}\ x\}) \cup \{x_1, \cdots, x_n, x\}$.

The term $\{x_1 = e_1; \cdots x_n = e_n;\ x = l \text{ In } x\}$ *is called the pattern of rule* τ, *and is denoted by* $\mathcal{P}(\tau)$.

The metavariables of a rule correspond to the free variables of its pattern. Notice that restriction (*a*) makes it impossible to give a GRS rule to rewrite a constant or a variable. However, we do not restrict the pattern of a rule to be a strongly connected rooted graph. Such a rule, referred to as a ***multi-rooted rule***, can be used to describe side-effect operations by keeping the state of the store directly in the term. For example, we can express the operation of reading location I of array X as follows:

$$\frac{x_1 = \mathsf{Store}(X, I, Z)}{x = \mathsf{Select}(X, I) \longrightarrow x = Z}$$

which can be assigned a natural interpretation that if there is a Store in the "context" of a Select then the Select can be rewritten to Z. It is for this reason that in our earlier work we had called our system a *Contextual Rewriting System* [AA89, AA91b, AA91a]. However, Jean-Jacques Lévy convinced us that our system basically described graph rewriting, so we renamed it simply a GRS.

DEFINITION **6.2.2 (GRS)** *A GRS is a structure* $(A(\mathcal{F}), R)$, *where* $A(\mathcal{F})$ *is the set of GRS terms defined over signature* $\mathcal{F}$, *and* R *is a set of GRS rules.*

6.3 BASIC RULES OF GRS

Analogous to the notion of α-equivalence in λ-calculus, we want to identify GRS terms whose differences may be regarded as merely syntactic noise. To that end we assume that all GRS come equipped with some basic set of "rules". These rules fall outside the syntax prescribed in Definition 6.2.1.

Substitution rules:

$$\frac{\mathsf{X} = \mathsf{V}}{\mathsf{X} \longrightarrow \mathsf{V}} \qquad \frac{\mathsf{X} = \mathsf{Y}}{\mathsf{X} \longrightarrow \mathsf{Y}} \quad \mathsf{X} \not\equiv \mathsf{Y}$$

where V is a constant. These rules formalize the notion of a substitutable expression and say that only constants and variables (provided X and Y are distinct variables) can be substituted freely. The corresponding binding can be deleted from the term when all such substitutions have been performed.

Degenerate cycle rule:

$$\mathsf{X} = \mathsf{X} \longrightarrow \mathsf{X} = \circ$$

This rule says that if we encounter a nonsensical binding like $x = x$ then we bind x to the special symbol $\circ$. The special symbol $\circ$ behaves just like a constant value and can be substituted freely.

Block Flattening rule:

$$\begin{array}{lcl} \{y\ =\ \{\ SS_1;\ SS_2;\ \cdots & & \{y\ =\ x' \\ \qquad\qquad\quad \text{In } x\} & \longrightarrow & SS_1'\ SS_2' \cdots \\ S_1;\ \cdots\ S_n & & S_1;\ \cdots\ S_n \\ \quad \text{In } z\} & & \quad \text{In } z\} \end{array}$$

where x' and SS_i' indicate renaming of all bound variables occurring in the internal block to avoid name clashes with the names in the surrounding scope.

Commutativity rule:

$$\{\cdots S_i;\ S_j \cdots \mathsf{In}\ x\} \longrightarrow \{\cdots S_j;\ S_i \cdots \mathsf{In}\ x\}$$

This rule says that the order of bindings in a block does not affect a term.

A term is said to be in *canonical form* if all the substitutions, the detection of degenerate cycles, and the flattening of blocks have been performed, and all bindings of the form $x = y$ and $x = v$ have been deleted. Consequently, two terms M and N are said to be *α-equivalent* if their canonical forms are the same up to renaming of bound variables and commutativity of bindings.

6.4 IDENTIFYING REDEXES AND REDUCTION

There are subtle issues involved in identifying redexes in a term. Consider the following two rules:

$$\tau_1 : \frac{x_1 = \mathsf{F}(0) \mid x_2 = \mathsf{F}(0)}{x = \mathsf{G}(x_1, x_2) \quad \longrightarrow \quad x = 0} \qquad \tau_2 : \frac{x_1 = \mathsf{F}(0)}{x = \mathsf{G}(x_1, x_1) \quad \longrightarrow \quad x = 0}$$

and the following two terms:

$$M \equiv \{\ t_1 = \mathsf{F}(0);\ t_2 = \mathsf{F}(0);\ t_3 = \mathsf{G}(t_1, t_2)\ \mathsf{In}\ t_3\} \qquad N \equiv \{\ t_1 = \mathsf{F}(0);\ t_2 = \mathsf{G}(t_1, t_1)\ \mathsf{In}\ t_2\}$$

Intuitively we can say that τ_1 matches M with the substitution "$x = t_3, x_1 = t_1, x_2 = t_2$", and τ_2 matches N with substitution "$x = t_2, x_1 = t_1$". Does rule τ_1 apply to N? Or does rule τ_2 apply to M? Rule τ_1 does indeed apply to the term N by matching both the preconditions by the same binding, that is, by considering the substitution "$x_1 = t_1, x_2 = t_1, x = t_2$". However, there will not be any variable substitution that makes τ_2 applicable to M. Thus, the preconditions of a rule can be satisfied by overlapping bindings. Moreover, the lhs of a rule can also overlap its precondition, as shown in the following example. Consider the term $M \equiv \{t = \mathsf{G}(t)\ \mathsf{In}\ t\}$ and the rule:

$$\frac{x_1 = \mathsf{G}(Y)}{x = \mathsf{G}\ (x_1) \quad \longrightarrow \quad x = 0}$$

The substitution "$x = t, x_1 = t, Y = t$" makes $\mathsf{G}(t)$ both a redex and its precondition!

We can capture the notion of a redex in terms of an ordering on terms. For this purpose we extend the syntax of GRS terms with a new "constant", called Ω, which matches any term and is less than or equal to any term in our ordering. The constant Ω, however, behaves differently than other constants because Ω *is not a substitutable value*. Thus, the term $\{t_1 = \Omega;\ t_2 = \Omega;\ t_3 = \mathsf{G}(t_1, t_2)\ \mathsf{In}\ t_3\}$ is not the same as $\{t_1 = \Omega;\ t_2 = \mathsf{G}(t_1, t_1)\ \mathsf{In}\ t_2\}$.

DEFINITION **6.4.1 (ω-ordering: $\leq_\omega$)** *Given GRS terms M and N in canonical form, rooted at z_1 and z_2, respectively, $M \leq_\omega N$ iff ∃ a function $\sigma : (\mathsf{BV}(M) \cup \mathsf{FV}(M) \cup \mathcal{F}^0) \rightarrow (\mathsf{BV}(N) \cup \mathsf{FV}(M) \cup \mathcal{F}^0)$ such that:*
a. $\forall c \in \mathcal{F}^0,\ \sigma(c) = c$;

b. $\forall x \in \mathtt{FV}(M)$, $\sigma(x) = x$;
c. $\forall x \in \mathtt{BV}(M)$, *if* x *is bound to* $\mathsf{F}^k(y_1, \cdots, y_k)$ *in* M *then* $\exists z, z = \sigma(x)$ *such that* z *is bound to* $\mathsf{F}^k(\sigma(y_1), \cdots, \sigma(y_k))$ *in* N;
d. $\sigma(z_1) = z_2$.

The function σ *is called the induced substitution.*

Notice that if a variable is bound to an Ω, condition (c) is automatically satisfied. Intuitively, $M \leq_\omega N$ if N can be obtained from M by replacing Ω with any other term or by increasing the sharing in M. Thus, $M \leq_\omega N$, where M and N are the terms in the example given at the beginning of this section.

We use ω-ordering as follows in defining a redex. We substitute Ω for all metavariables in the pattern of a rule. Such a term is called the *closure of a rule*. If term p is the closure of rule τ then a term M is said to be a τ-redex if $p \leq_\omega M$.

DEFINITION **6.4.2 (Closure of a rule)** *Given a GRS rule* τ, *the closure of* τ, *written as* $Cl(\tau)$, *is the term* $\{y_1 = \Omega; \cdots y_m = \Omega; t = \mathcal{P}(\tau) \text{ In } t\}$, *where* $\{y_1, \cdots, y_m\} = \mathtt{FV}(\mathcal{P}(\tau))$ *and* t *is a new variable.*

In the following, we will make use of the notation $M@x_i$, where $x_i \in \mathtt{BV}(M)$, which stands for the term M rooted at x_i, that is, the term $M@x_i$ is the same as M except that it is rooted at x_i. For example, if $M \equiv \{x_1 = e_1; \cdots x_n = e_n \text{ In } x\}$ then $M@x_i$ will be the term $\{x_1 = e_1; \cdots x_n = e_n \text{ In } x_i\}$.

DEFINITION **6.4.3 (Redex)** *A redex in a GRS term* M *is a triple* (τ, z, σ) *such that*
a. τ *is a GRS rule;*
b. $z \in \mathtt{BV}(M)$;
c. $Cl(\tau) \leq_\omega M@z$ *and* σ *is the induced substitution.*

DEFINITION **6.4.4 (Instance of a term)** *Given a GRS term* M *and a substitution* σ, *an instance of* M, *written as* M^σ, *is the term obtained by substituting* $\sigma(x)$ *for each free variable* x *of* M *and renaming each bound variable of* M.

Given a rule $\tau : \dfrac{x_1 = e_1 \mid \cdots \mid x_n = e_n}{x = l \rightarrow x = r}$, and redex (τ, z, σ) occurring in M, the reduction step consists of first allocating r^σ, that is, an instance of the rhs of rule τ using substitution σ. Subsequently, the term bound to the root of the redex is replaced by the newly instantiated term. The replacement operation is written as $M[z \leftarrow r^\sigma]$. The term so obtained is then *canonicalized*.

DEFINITION **6.4.5 (Reduction, $\longrightarrow$)** *Given a GRS term* M *in canonical form and rule* $\tau : \dfrac{x_1 = e_1 \mid \cdots \mid x_n = e_n}{x = l \rightarrow x = r}$, M *reduces to* N *by doing the* τ*-redex at* z *in* M *(written as* $M \longrightarrow N$*), iff* (τ, z, σ) *is a redex in* M *and* $N \equiv_\alpha M[z \leftarrow r^\sigma]$.

The instantiation of r in our system corresponds to the *build phase* of Barendregt system while our replacement operation corresponds to his *redirection phase*. However, there are subtle differences between the two systems. First of all, the *garbage collection phase* of Barendregt (that is, the deletion of nodes that are not reachable from the root), which in our system will correspond to the *dead code elimination*, is not performed in our GRS. The rationale being that we want to allow the so-called multi-rooted rules. The other difference arises in the presence of "projection" rules and cyclic graphs. For example, given the rule $x = \mathsf{I}(X) \longrightarrow x = X$, and the cyclic term $M \equiv \{t = \mathsf{I}(t) \text{ In } t\}$, following the Barendregt system, we will have, $M \longrightarrow M$. According to our system, $M \longrightarrow \{t = t \text{ In } t\}$, which, as explained before, will become $\circ$, a symbol to represent a "meaningless" term. This difference has a strong impact on the confluence of GRS, as we will see shortly.

6.5 CONFLUENT GRS

Not all GRS are confluent, however, we can show that for a restricted class, namely GRS without interfering rules, confluence is guaranteed. We introduce the notion of *compatible terms* which will be used, among other things, to define the notion of interference among rules. The idea is that terms which are not ordered, may still have a common upper bound. As we will see such terms can potentially interfere with each other.

DEFINITION **6.5.1 (Compatible terms, $\uparrow_\omega$)** *Given GRS terms M_1 and M_2 in canonical form, M_1 and M_2 are said to be ω-compatible, written as $M_1 \uparrow_\omega M_2$, if and only if $\exists M_3$ such that $M_1 \leq_\omega M_3$ and $M_2 \leq_\omega M_3$.*

For example, the term $\{t_1 = \Omega;\ t_2 = \Omega;\ t = \mathsf{G}(t_1, t_2) \text{ In } t\}$ is compatible with the term $\{t_1 = \mathsf{F}(0);\ t_2 = \mathsf{F}(0);\ t = \mathsf{G}(t_1, t_2) \text{ In } t\}$ but not with the term $\{t_1 = \mathsf{F}(0);\ t_2 = \mathsf{H}(0);\ t = \mathsf{G}(t_1, t_2) \text{ In } t\}$.

DEFINITION **6.5.2 (Interference)** *Given GRS rules τ_1 and τ_2, τ_1 is said to interfere with τ_2 iff $\exists x \in \mathsf{BV}(\mathcal{P}(\tau_1))$ such that*

a. if $\tau_1 \neq \tau_2$ then $Cl(\tau_1)@x \uparrow_\omega Cl(\tau_2)$;
b. if $\tau_1 = \tau_2$ and τ_1 is a single-rooted rule then $Cl(\tau_1)@x \uparrow_\omega Cl(\tau_2)$, where x is not the root of $\mathcal{P}(\tau_1)$.

For example, the rule $\tau\ :\ \dfrac{x_1 = \mathsf{L}(Y)}{x = \mathsf{L}(x_1) \longrightarrow x = 0}$ will interfere with itself because $Cl(\tau)@x_1 \uparrow_\omega Cl(\tau)$. Notice that the following two rules are non-interfering,

$$\frac{x_1 = \mathsf{G}(Y)}{x = \mathsf{F}(x_1) \longrightarrow x = 0} \qquad\qquad \frac{x_1 = \mathsf{G}(Y)}{x = \mathsf{D}(x_1) \longrightarrow x = 1}$$

It can be seen from this example that the preconditions of non-interfering rules are not affected by a reduction. We also note in passing that multi-rooted rules are always self-interfering, because they may cause an overlapping at the root.

In the following we will write a GRS with non-interfering rules as GRS_{NI}.

THEOREM **6.5.3** *Given a GRS_{NI} term M, if $M \longrightarrow M_1$ and $M \longrightarrow M_2$ then $\exists\ M_3$ such that $M_2 \longrightarrow M_3$ and $M_1 \longrightarrow M_3$.*

COROLLARY **6.5.4** *A GRS_{NI} is confluent up to α-equivalence.*

Consider the projection rules, $x = \mathsf{I}(X) \longrightarrow x = X$ and $x = \mathsf{J}(X) \longrightarrow x = X$ and the term $M \equiv \{x = \mathsf{I}(y);\ y = \mathsf{J}(x)\ \mathsf{In}\ x\}$, then $M \longrightarrow M_1 \equiv \{x = \mathsf{I}(x)\ \mathsf{In}\ x\}$ and $M \longrightarrow M_2 \equiv \{x = \mathsf{J}(x)\ \mathsf{In}\ x\}$. Notice that if both M_1 and M_2 are not reduced to $\circ$, the confluence property will be lost, as was observed in [KKSdV91]. Barendregt's graph reduction system is not confluent precisely because of the absence of such a reduction.

6.6 A GRAPH MODEL FOR GRS

We are interested in defining an equality on the set of terms such that the equality is useful in analyzing the correctness of compiler optimizations. Thus, we have to guarantee that if two terms M and N are equal, then the equality is preserved by putting them in the same context, i.e., $M = N \Longrightarrow \forall C[\Box], C[M] = C[N]$. This means that the equality has to be a *congruence* with respect to the formation rules of terms. Only then will equal terms be substitutable for each other, and, an optimization will be considered correct if it preserves equality.

An example of an equivalence relation on terms is *convertibility*. However, convertibility is too restrictive from a compiler's point of view, as shown by the following example:

$$M \equiv \{\ x = \mathsf{Cons}(y, z);\ y = \mathsf{F}(0);\ z = \mathsf{Cons}(y, \mathsf{Nil})\ \mathsf{In}\ x\}$$

$$N \equiv \{\ x = \mathsf{Cons}(y, z);\ y = \mathsf{F}(0);\ z = \mathsf{Cons}(w, \mathsf{Nil});\ w = \mathsf{F}(0)\ \mathsf{In}\ x\}$$

where M and N are in normal forms but not convertible to each other. However, if the internal representation of lists is ignored by an observer then both the terms represent the same *unfolded* list, $\mathsf{F}(0) : \mathsf{F}(0) : \mathsf{Nil}$. If the GRS containing these terms has a non left-linear rule, it may be possible to distinguish between such terms. Thus, such terms cannot be equated without disallowing non left-linear rules.

We should also notice that $N \leq_\omega M$, i.e., N has "less sharing" than M in the above example. Does it mean that N is "less defined" than M in the sense that one can *compute less* with N than with M? We would like to answer this question without delving into heavy duty model theory. We have carefully said "compute" to emphasize that we are interested in studying what a term represents from an operational point of view. In particular, we are interested in observing the gradual *syntactic building up of the final term.*

We introduce a function ω to compute the stable part of a term, that is, the part of the term that will not change as more reductions are performed on it. The ω function captures what Lévy has called the *direct approximation* of a λ-calculus term [Lév78], and Welch has called the *instantaneous semantics* of a term [Wel75]. Notice that as more reductions are performed the stable part should get larger, that is, if $M \longrightarrow M_1 \longrightarrow M_2 \cdots$ then $\omega(M) \leq_\omega \omega(M_1) \leq_\omega \omega(M_2) \cdots$. We remind the reader that $\leq_\omega$ is the syntactic ordering on terms that captures both the sharing, and the fact that Ω is less than any other term.

We collect all the stable or observable information gathered by reducing M in a set, called $W^*(M)$, and say that it represents the *information content* of M. We can now formulate our original question regarding the impact of sharing on a program's behavior as follows: *if N has less sharing than M then is $W^*(N)$ contained in $W^*(M)$?* As we shall see shortly, this is indeed the case in the absence of interfering rules.

It is also interesting to analyze if N is "less defined" than M implies that for all context $C[\square]$, $C[N]$ is "less defined" than $C[M]$. That is, is the equality induced by W^* a congruence? We will see that in the absence of interfering rules, the equality is also a congruence. Thus, we can conclude that the collection of stable information contained in GRS terms is indeed a model for GRS without interfering rules.

6.6.1 Instant semantics

The instant semantics of a GRS term M consists of computing its *stable part*, where stable part means the part of M which will not change by further reductions. The first intuitive solution that comes to mind is to replace all redexes in a term by Ω (since a redex subexpression can become any expression and Ω is less than all expressions). This solution has a problem as shown by the following example. Consider the rules:

$$\tau_1 : x = \mathsf{F}(Y, Y) \longrightarrow x = \gamma \qquad\qquad \tau_2 : x = \mathsf{I}(Y) \longrightarrow x = Y$$

and the following reduction:

$$\begin{array}{lll} M \equiv \{\ t = \mathsf{F}(t_1, t_2); & \longrightarrow & M_1 \equiv \{\ t = \mathsf{F}(t_1, t_1); \\ \quad\ \ t_1 = \mathsf{A}(0); & & \quad\quad\ t_1 = \mathsf{A}(0) \\ \quad\ \ t_2 = \mathsf{I}(t_1) & & \quad\quad\ \mathsf{In}\ t\} \\ \quad\ \ \mathsf{In}\ t\} & & \end{array}$$

The only redex in M is rooted at t_2. Suppose we replace it by Ω to obtain the stable term $M_2 \equiv \{\ t = \mathsf{F}(t_1, t_2);\ t_1 = \mathsf{A}(0);\ t_2 = \Omega\ \mathsf{In}\ t\}$. However, since the root of M_1 is a redex the stable information in M_1 is less than the stable information in M. This is contrary to our intuition that the information should increase with reduction. The problem is due to the presence of rule τ_2 which can introduce sharing. If we want to compute the instant semantics of a term without analyzing the RHS of rules then we have to assume that the Ω in M_2 can be replaced by the node with label A, and thus, can make the node with label F a τ_1-redex. Therefore we should not treat node F in M_2 as stable information. This example shows clearly that the first solution does not work. However, it does work for recursive program schema (RPS)!

The problem that the above example illustrates is that, even though M is not a redex it can become a redex when some redexes under it are performed. This phenomena is usually called *upward creation of redexes*. Reduction of a term in the λ-calculus or TRS can also result in the upward creation of redexes. However, upward creation of redexes is not possible in RPSs. To cope with this problem in the λ-calculus, Wadsworth [Wad71] and Lévy [Lév78] have introduced the notion of the ω-rule, which states:

$$\Omega\ M \longrightarrow \Omega$$

This simple ω-rule reduces any term that can become a redex (by upward creation) to Ω. However, the presence of non left-linear rules makes the generation of ω-rules for TRS and GRS difficult. Therefore, instead of introducing ω-rules, we introduce the notion of a *compatible redex* or an *ω-redex*. A compatible redex captures our intuition about why a term should be rewritten to Ω. It consists of analyzing a term to see if it can become a redex either by replacing Ω with some other term or by increasing the sharing in the term.

DEFINITION **6.6.1 (Compatible redex)** *A compatible redex in a GRS term M is a pair (τ, z) such that:*

a. τ is a rule;
b. $z \in \mathtt{BV}(M)$ and z is not bound to Ω;
c. $Cl(\tau) \uparrow_\omega M@z$ and $Cl(\tau) \not\leq_\omega M@z$.

z is called the root of the compatible redex.

Notice that because of condition (c), a compatible redex cannot be an ordinary redex. For the example given at the beginning of this section, we have that $Cl(\tau_1) \not\leq_\omega M_2$ and $Cl(\tau_1) \uparrow_\omega M_2$, thus, M_2 is a compatible redex and as such should be reduced to Ω.

DEFINITION **6.6.2 (ω-reduction, $\longrightarrow_\omega$)** *Given GRS terms M and N, M ω-reduces to N by doing the τ-compatible redex at z (written as $M \longrightarrow_\omega N$) iff (τ, z) is a compatible redex in M, and $N \equiv_\alpha M[z \leftarrow \Omega]$.*

A GRS term M is said to be in ω-normal form if it does not contain any compatible redexes.

PROPOSITION **6.6.3** *$\twoheadrightarrow_\omega$ is confluent and strongly normalizing.*

The stable part of a term M, i.e., $\omega(M)$, will then be computed by first replacing all distinct redexes occurring in M by Ω and then computing the ω-normal form of the term so obtained.

DEFINITION **6.6.4** *Given a GRS term M, M_Ω is the term $M[u_1 \leftarrow \Omega]\cdots[u_n \leftarrow \Omega]$ where $u_1 \cdots u_n$ are all the distinct redexes occurring in M.*

DEFINITION **6.6.5 (ω-function)** *Given a GRS term M, $\omega(M)$ is the ω-normal form of M_Ω.*

6.6.2 Meaning of a GRS term

We collect all observable information about GRS terms in a set called ω-graphs.

DEFINITION **6.6.6 (ω-graphs: Set of observations)** *Given a GRS, the set of all observations, called ω-graphs, is defined as:*

$$\omega\text{-}graphs = \bigcup\{\omega(M) \mid \forall \text{ GRS terms } M\}.$$

DEFINITION **6.6.7 (W^*: The information content of a GRS term)** *Given a GRS term M, $W^*(M) = \{a \mid a \in \omega\text{-}graphs, a \leq_\omega \omega(M'), M \twoheadrightarrow\}$.*

We have chosen to represent W^* by a set as opposed to the least upper bound of the set for technical reasons.

DEFINITION **6.6.8 ($\sqsubseteq_g$: Information ordering)** *Given GRS terms M and N, $M \sqsubseteq_g N$ iff $W^*(M) \subseteq W^*(N)$.*

If we want W^* to be our interpretation function W^* will have to satisfy some properties, that is, the meaning will have to be preserved by reduction, and it will have to be compositional. In other words:

$$\begin{array}{llll} \textbf{Soundness}: & M \twoheadrightarrow N & \Longrightarrow & M \equiv_g N \\ \textbf{Congruence}: & M \equiv_g N & \Longrightarrow & C[M] \equiv_g C[N] \end{array}$$

In order to show soundness we need to show some additional properties of the ω-function. In particular, we want to guarantee that the ω-function is monotonic with respect to $\leq_\omega$. From this it will follow that the ω-function is monotonic with respect to reduction.

THEOREM **6.6.9 (Soundness of $\equiv_g$)** *Given a confluent GRS and terms M and N, if $M \twoheadrightarrow N$ then $M \equiv_g N$.*

6.6.3 Impact of sharing on a program behavior

Before dealing with the question of congruence, let us digress and analyze the impact of sharing on a program behavior, that is, $M \leq_\omega N \Longrightarrow M \sqsubseteq_g N$? It turns out that in the presence of interfering rules the above will not hold. Consider the following GRS which has *confluent* but interfering rules:

$$\begin{array}{ll} \tau_1: & \dfrac{x_1 = \mathsf{B}(0) \mid x_2 = \mathsf{C}(0)}{x = \mathsf{A}(x_1, x_2) \longrightarrow x = 0} \\ \tau_2: & x = \mathsf{C}(0) \longrightarrow x = \mathsf{C}(0) \\ \tau_3: & x = \mathsf{B}(0) \longrightarrow x = \mathsf{C}(0) \end{array}$$

and the following terms:

$$M \equiv \{\ t_1 = \mathsf{A}(t_2, t_3);\ t_2 = \mathsf{B}(0);\ t_3 = \mathsf{B}(0)\ \mathsf{In}\ t_1\} \qquad N \equiv \{\ t_1 = \mathsf{A}(t_2, t_2);\ t_2 = \mathsf{B}(0)\ \mathsf{In}\ t_1\}$$

It is easy to see that $W^*(M) = \{\Omega, 0\}$, while $W^*(N) = \{\Omega, \{x_1 = \Omega;\ x_2 = \mathsf{A}(x_1, x_1)\ \mathsf{In}\ x_2\}\}$. Therefore, $M \leq_\omega N$ and $M \not\sqsubseteq_g N$.

THEOREM **6.6.10 (Monotonicity of $\sqsubseteq_g$ with respect to $\leq_\omega$)** *Given GRS_{NI} terms M and N, if $M \leq_\omega N$ then $M \sqsubseteq_g N$.*

6.6.4 Congruence

We want to show that $\equiv_g$ is a congruence, that is, if $M \equiv_g N$ then $\forall C[\Box], C[M] \equiv_g C[N]$. What can prevent $\equiv_g$ from being a congruence? In the definition of observable behavior we may have discarded something important, which may have an effect on the context enclosing the term. Suppose we have chosen to observe Booleans only, that is, we will distinguish between True and False, but not between 5 and 7. Thus, the two program $M \equiv 5$ and $N \equiv 7$ will trivially exhibit the same behavior. However, by putting them in the context $\{\ x = \Box;\ p =\leq (x, 5);\ y = \mathsf{Cond}(p, \mathsf{True}, \mathsf{False})\ \mathsf{In}\ y\}$ we will observe True when running $C[M]$ and False when running $C[N]$. It seems that we cannot discard any information that can be used to build terms.

A way of assuring that $\equiv_{\mathbf{g}}$ is a congruence is to show that for any context $C[\Box]$, the behavior of $C[M]$ can be inferred from the observations about M, that is,

$$\forall C[\Box], W^*(C[M]) = \bigcup\{W^*(C[P]) \mid P \in W^*(M)\}$$

In other words the context operation must be a continuous operation with respect to the observations. The proof that

$$\bigcup\{W^*(C[P]) \mid P \in W^*(M)\} \subseteq W^*(C[M])$$

follows automatically from the monotonicity of $\sqsubseteq_{\mathbf{g}}$ with respect to $\leq_\omega$. The other direction requires some more machinery.

We need to show that each observation of $C[M]$ can be obtained by plugging some observation of M, instead of M itself, in the context $C[\Box]$. There are two basic steps in the proof:

(i) Suppose $C[M] \twoheadrightarrow N$. Let $\mathcal{F}_1$ be the set of redexes in M that must be reduced to get to N, and let $\mathcal{F}_2$ be the set of all other redexes in M. The first step of the proof consists of showing that each reduction can be reordered such that we first reduce all the redexes in $\mathcal{F}_1$, that is, $\exists M'$, $C[M] \twoheadrightarrow C[M']$. Let $\mathcal{F}_3$ be the set of redexes in M' that are descendants of redexes in $\mathcal{F}_2$. We need to show that the rest of the reduction can be performed without reducing any redex in $\mathcal{F}_3$. Notationally we will say $C[M'] \overset{\not\twoheadrightarrow}{_{\mathcal{F}_3}} N$.

(ii) Next we need to show that the ω-function does not lose too much information. Let M_2 be the term obtained from M by setting all the redexes in $\mathcal{F}_2$ to Ω. We first prove that if $C[M] \overset{\not\twoheadrightarrow}{_{\mathcal{F}_2}} N$, then the same reduction can be carried out on $C[M_2]$. Since W* contains terms in ω-normal form, we also need to show that ω-reductions do not destroy the meaning of a term.

THEOREM 6.6.11 (Congruence of $\equiv_{\mathbf{g}}$) *Given GRS_{NI} terms M and N, if $M \equiv_{\mathbf{g}} N$ then $\forall C[\Box], C[M] \equiv_{\mathbf{g}} C[N]$.*

In the presence of interfering rules $\equiv_{\mathbf{g}}$ is not guaranteed to be a congruence. As an example, consider the following rules:

$$\begin{array}{ll} \tau_1: & x = \mathsf{B}(Y) \longrightarrow x = \mathsf{B}(Y) \\ \tau_2: & x = \mathsf{A}(Y) \longrightarrow x = \mathsf{A}(Y) \\ \tau_3: & \dfrac{x_1 = \mathsf{A}(Y)}{x = \mathsf{F}(x_1) \longrightarrow x = 1} \end{array}$$

then $\mathsf{A}(0) \equiv_{\mathbf{g}} \mathsf{B}(0)$, however, $\mathsf{F}(\mathsf{A}(0)) \not\equiv_{\mathbf{g}} \mathsf{F}(\mathsf{B}(0))$.

6.7 CONCLUSION

The motivation for this work came from a desire to formalize the compilation process of Id as a series of translations into simpler and simpler languages. To that end we have introduced the Kid (Kernel id) language [AA91b] and the P-TAC (Parallel Three Address Code) language [AA89]. We also provided the translation of Id into Kid and of Kid into P-TAC [AA91a]. P-TAC can be seen as an example of GRS, while Kid is more general due to the presence of λ-abstraction. This approach has lead to the formalization of compiler optimizations in terms of source-to-source transformations on these intermediate languages. Moreover, using the notion of information content of a term we have given a criteria for the (partial) correctness of these compiler optimizations [AA91b].

The results presented in this chapter (notably Theorems 2.6.10 and 2.6.11) can be applied in a straightforward manner to show the partial correctness of those optimizations that simply increase the sharing in a term. Examples of such optimizations include the common subexpression elimination, and the lifting of free expressions and loop invariants. We can also show the partial correctness of the cyclic Y-rule. In order to prove total correctness we need to discard sharing from our observations at the expenses of introducing more restrictions on the rules, as discussed in [Ari92].

We would like to extend GRS with λ-abstraction and to provide a term model that cover multi-rooted rules to express side-effect operations. This will provide a sound mathematical basis for the Id language. It will also be interesting to investigate the suitability of GRS as an intermediate language for other classes of languages, such as logic languages and imperative languages.

This work was done at the Laboratory for Computer Science at MIT, and at INRIA. Funding for this work has been provided in part by the Advanced Research Projects Agency of the U.S. Department of Defense under the Office of Naval Research contracts N00014-84-K-0099 (MIT) and N0039-88-C-0163 (Harvard), and in part by ESPRIT contract SEMAGRAPH/BRA 3074 (INRIA).

REFERENCES

[AA89] Z.M. Ariola and Arvind. P-tac: A parallel intermediate language. In *Proc. ACM Conference on Functional Programming Languages and Computer Architecture, London*, 1989.

[AA91a] Z.M. Ariola and Arvind. Compilation of id. In *Proc. of the Fourth Workshop on Languages and Compilers for Parallel Computing*, Springer-Verlag, Lecture Notes in Computer Science 589, Santa Clara, California, 1991.

[AA91b] Z.M. Ariola and Arvind. A syntactic approach to program transformations. In *Proc. ACM SIGPLAN Symposium on Partial Evaluation and Semantics Based Program Manipulation*, Yale University, New Haven, CT, 1991.

[ACCL90] M. Abadi, L. Cardelli, P.-L. Currien, and J.-J. Lévy. Explicit substitutions. In *Proc. ACM Conference on Principles of Programming Languages*, San Francisco, 1990.

[ANP89] Arvind, R.S. Nikhil, and K.K. Pingali. I-structures: Data structures for parallel computing. *ACM Transactions on Programming Languages and Systems*, **11**, 1989.

[Ari92] Z.M. Ariola. *An Algebraic Approach to the Compilation and Operational Semantics of Functional Languages with I-structures.* PhD thesis, Harvard University, 1992.

[BvEG+87a] H.P. Barendregt, M.C.J.D. van Eekelen, J.R.W. Glauert, J.R. Kennaway, M.J. Plasmeijer, and M.R. Sleep. Towards an intermediate language based on graph rewriting. In J. W. de Bakker, A. J. Nijman, and P. C. Treleaven (editors), *Proc. PARLE'87 Conference, vol.II*, Springer-Verlag, Lecture Notes in Computer Science 259, 1987.

[BvEG+87b] H.P. Barendregt, M.C.J.D. van Eekelen, J.R.W. Glauert, J.R. Kennaway, M.J. Plasmeijer, and M.R. Sleep. Term graph rewriting. In J. W. de Bakker, A. J. Nijman, and P. C. Treleaven (editors), *Proc. PARLE'87 Conference, vol.II*, Springer-Verlag, Lecture Notes in Computer Science 259, pp. 141–158, 1987.

[BvEvLP87] T. Brus, M.C.J.D van Eekelen, M.O. vam Leer, and M.J. Plasmeijer. Clean - a language for functional graph rewriting. In *Proc. ACM Conference on Functional Programming Languages and Computer Architecture*, Springer-Verlag, Lecture Notes in Computer Science 274, Portland, Oregon, 1987.

[Cur86] P.-L. Curien. Categorical combinators, sequential algorithms and functional programming. *Research Notes in Theoretical Computer Science*, 1986.

[Cur91] P.-L. Curien. An abstract framework for environment machines. *Theoretical Computer Science*, **82**, 1991.

[Hin77] R. Hindley. Combinator reductions and lambda reduction compared. *Zeitschr. f. math. Logik und Grundlagen d. Math. Bd*, **23**, pp. 169–180, 1977.

[HL89] T. Hardin and J.-J. Lévy. A confluent calculus of substitution. In *France-Japan Artificial Intelligence and Computer Science Symposium*, Izu, 1989.

[Kat90] V. Kathail. *Optimal Interpreters for Lambda-calculus Based Functional Languages.* PhD thesis, M.I.T., 1990.

[Ken90] J.R. Kennaway. Implementing term rewrite languages in Dactl. *Theoretical Computer Science*, 1990.

[KKSdV91] J.R Kennaway, J.W. Klop, M.R Sleep, and F.J. de Vries. Transfinite reductions in orthogonal term rewriting systems. In *Proc. RTA '91*, Springer-Verlag, Lecture Notes in Computer Science, 1991.

[Lév78] J.-J. Lévy. *Reductions Correctes et Optimales dans le Lambda-Calcul.* PhD thesis, Universite Paris VII, 1978.

[Mar91] L. Maranget. Optimal derivations in weak lambda-calculi and in orthogonal term rewriting systems. In *Proc. ACM Conference on Principles of Programming Languages*, Orlando, Florida, 1991.

[Wad71] C. Wadsworth. *Semantics And Pragmatics Of The Lambda-Calculus.* PhD thesis, University of Oxford, 1971.

[Wel75] P.H Welch. Continuous semantics and inside-out reductions. In *λ-Calculus and Computer Science Theory*, Springer-Verlag, Lecture Notes in Computer Science 37, Italy, 1975.

7

A Fibration Semantics for Extended Term Graph Rewriting

R. Banach

7.1 INTRODUCTION

In this chapter, we re-examine the problem of providing a categorical semantics for the core of the general term graph rewriting language DACTL. Partial success in this area has been obtained by describing graph rewrites as certain kinds of pushout. See [Ken87, HP88, HKP88, Ken91]. Nevertheless, none of these constructions successfully describe the whole of the operational models of [BvEG+87] where term graph rewriting was introduced, or of its generalization in the language DACTL itself [GKSS88, GHK+88, GKS91, Ken90]. The main stumbling blocks for all of these attempts have been examples such as the I combinator `root:I[a]` $\Rightarrow$ `a` when applied to a circular instance of itself `x:I[x]`. None of the hitherto proposed categorical formulations of TGR adequately capture the DACTL version of the rewrite (which is, reasonably enough, a null action), nor do they give a convincing story of their own (generally speaking the result of the rewrite is undefined). The aim of this chapter is to describe how these deficiencies may be overcome by using a different approach to the categorical semantics of rewriting. Instead of pushouts, we use a Grothendieck opfibration. Now Grothendieck opfibrations have strong universal properties, too strong to be applicable to all DACTL rewrites. Accordingly, a less universal construction describes the full operational core of DACTL rewriting. It turns out that the circular I example sits in between these two extremes.

In outline, the rest of the chapter is as follows. Section 7.2 describes the free rewriting core of the original DACTL model. Section 7.3 describes the categorical construction

Term Graph Rewriting: Theory and Practice.
Eds. Ronan Sleep, Rinus Plasmeijer and Marko van Eekelen.

and how it yields a Grothendieck opfibration. Surprisingly, it turns out that the garbage retention feature of DACTL is the key to the success of the construction. Section 7.4 reconsiders true DACTL rewriting and outlines the universal construction that describes it, including the circular I example. Section 7.5 concludes.

7.2 DACTL ABSTRACTED

In this section, we define the free rewriting core of DACTL rewriting, i.e. we ignore all issues pertaining both to markings, and (for simplicity) the pattern calculus. In addition, our terminology may appear a little unusual to those familiar with DACTL. Suppose an alphabet of node symbols $\mathbf{S} = \{S, T \ldots\}$ to be given.

DEFINITION **7.2.1** *A term graph (or just graph) G, is a triple (N, σ, α) where*

(1) *N is a set of nodes,*
(2) *σ is a map $N \rightarrow S$,*
(3) *α is a map $N \rightarrow N^*$,*

Thus $\sigma(x)$ maps a node to the node symbol that labels it, and $\alpha(x)$ maps each node to its sequence of successors. We write $A(x)$, the arity of a node, for the domain of $\alpha(x)$. Note that $A(x)$ is a set of consecutive natural members starting at 1, or empty. We allow ourselves to write $x \in G$ (instead of $x \in N(G)$) etc. Each successor node determines an arc of the graph, and we will refer to arcs using the notation (p_k, c), to indicate that the child c is the kth child of the parent p, i.e. that $c = \alpha(x)[k]$ for some $k \in A(p)$. When we speak of several graphs (or patterns, see below) simultaneously, as we will do in a moment, we will subscript N, $\sigma(x)$ and $\alpha(x)$ with the name of the graph in question in order to clarify which map we are refering to. Moreover, to be quite unambiguous when dealing with disjoint unions, the elements of such a union will always be tagged with either (1, -) or (2, -) to indicate their origin.

Let there be a symbol `Any`, not considered to be in **S**. We will assume the following invariant holds subsequently:

(ANY) $\sigma(x) = \texttt{Any} \Longrightarrow A(x) = \emptyset$.

A node labeled with `Any` is called implicit, a node labeled with a member of **S** is called explicit.

DEFINITION **7.2.2** *A pattern is a term graph containing zero or more implicit nodes.*

Thus every graph is a pattern (if we choose to regard it as such) but not vice versa.

DEFINITION **7.2.3** *A rule D is a triple (P, r, Red) where*

(1) *P is a pattern (called the full pattern of the rule).*
(2) *r is a node of P called the root. If $\sigma(r) = F$ then D is called a rule for F. The subpattern L of P, consisting of nodes and arcs accessible from (and including) r is called the left subpattern of (the full pattern P of) the rule D. All implicit nodes of P must be nodes of L.*

(3) *Red is a set of pairs, (called redirections) of nodes of P. These satisfy the invariants (RED-1), (RED-2) and (RED-3) below:*

(RED-1) *Red is the graph (in the set theoretic sense) of a partial function on P.*
(RED-2) $(l', r') \in Red \Longrightarrow l'$ *is an explicit node of L.*
(RED-3) *Let $(l_1, r_1), (l_2, r_2) \in Red$. If $l_1 \neq l_2$ and there is a homomorphism (see 2.4 below) $h : P \to Z$ such that $h(l_1) = h(l_2)$ then $r_1 = r_2$.*

The three invariants (RED-1) – (RED-3) assure the existence of rewrites as described below. To highlight the left subpattern of a rule, we will often write rules as $(incl : L \to P, root, Red)$.

To define the rewriting model, we must first define the notion of homomorphism of patterns and graphs. Note that 7.2.4 serves as well for graphs as it does for patterns.

DEFINITION **7.2.4** *Let P, Z be patterns. A map $h : P \to Z$ is a homomorphism if for all explicit $x \in P$*

$$\sigma(x) = \sigma(h(x)),\ A(x) = A(h(x)),\ \text{and for all } k \in A(x), h(\alpha(x)[k]) = \alpha(h(x))[k].$$

In brief, a rewrite of a graph G (G could just as easily be a pattern) according to a rule $D = (P, r, Red)$ proceeds through three stages. Firstly a homomorphism of the left subpattern L of P into G is located. This is the redex. Then copies of the other nodes and arcs of P are added to G in order to extend the homomorphism to one from the whole of P. Finally arcs whose destination is the image of the LHS of a redirection pair $(l, r) \in Red$, are swung over to arrive instead at the image of the corresponding RHS. More formally we have the definitions below.

DEFINITION **7.2.5** *Let $D = (P, r, Red)$ be a rule. Let G be a graph. Let L be the left subpattern of P. Let $m : L \to G$ be a homomorphism. Then $m(L)$ is a redex in G and $m(r)$ is the root of the redex. The homomorphism is called a matching of L to G.*

DEFINITION **7.2.6** *Assume the notation of 7.2.5. Let the graph G' be given by*

(1) $N_{G'} = (N_G \uplus N_P)/\approx$ *which is the disjoint union of N_G and N_P factored by the equivalence relation $\approx$, where $\approx$ is the smallest equivalence relation such that $(1, x) \approx (2, n)$ whenever $m(n) = x$.*

(2) $\sigma_{G'}(\{(1, x)\}) = \sigma_G(x)$,
$\sigma_{G'}(\{(2, n)\}) = \sigma_P(n)$,
$\sigma_{G'}(\{(1, x), (2, n_1) \ldots (2, n_q)\}) = \sigma_G(x)$.
Thus G' acquires symbols in such a way as to agree with both G and P; the representative in G' of an implicit node of P acquiring a symbol according to its image under m.

(3) $\alpha_{G'}(\{(1, x)\})[k] = \{(1, \alpha_G(x)[k]) \ldots\}$ *for* $k \in A(x)$,
$\alpha_{G'}(\{(2, n)\})[k] = \{(2, \alpha_P(n)[k]) \ldots\}$ *for* $k \in A(n)$,
$\alpha_{G'}(\{(1, x), (2, n_1) \ldots (2, n_q)\})[k] = \{(1, \alpha_G(x)[k]) \ldots\}$.
Thus G acquires arcs so as to agree with both G and P. The ... on the RHS of these cases indicate that the equivalence classes concerned need not be singletons.

LEMMA **7.2.7** *There is a homomorphism $m' : P \to G'$. Disregarding pedantry, m' extends $m : L \to G$. We call m' the extended matching.*

DEFINITION **7.2.8** *Assume the notation of 7.2.5 – 7.2.7. Let H be the graph given by*

(1) $N_H = N_{G'}$,

(2) $\sigma_H = \sigma_{G'}$,

(3)

$$\alpha_H(\{(1,x)\})[k] = \begin{cases} \{(2,y)\ldots\} & \textit{if } (u,y) \in Red \textit{ for some } y \in P \\ & \textit{and } u \in m'^{-1}(\alpha_{G'}(\{(1,x)\}[k]) \\ \alpha_{G'}(\{(1,x)\})[k] & \textit{otherwise} \end{cases}$$

$$\alpha_H(\{(2,n)\})[k] = \begin{cases} \{(2,y)\ldots\} & \textit{if } (u,y) \in Red \textit{ for some } y \in P \\ & \textit{and } u \in m'^{-1}(\alpha_{G'}(\{(2,n)\}[k]) \\ \alpha_{G'}(\{(2,n)\})[k] & \textit{otherwise} \end{cases}$$

$$\alpha_H(\{(1,x),(2,n_1)\ldots(2,n_q)\})[k] =$$

$$\begin{cases} \{(2,y)\ldots\} & \textit{if } (u,y) \in Red \textit{ for some } y \in P \\ & \textit{and } u \in m'^{-1}(\alpha_{G'}(\{(1,x)\ldots\}[k]) \\ \alpha_{G'}(\{(1,x),(2,n_1)\ldots(2,n_q)\})[k] & \textit{otherwise} \end{cases}$$

It is easy to show that this construction is consistent, by (RED-1) and (RED-3).

DEFINITION **7.2.9** *Let G be a graph, D be a rule, and m a matching of the left subpattern L of (the full pattern of) D to G. The graph H constructed via 7.2.5 – 7.2.8 is the result of the rewrite of G at the redex m(L) according to D.*

As an example of rewriting, we treat the circular I rewrite discussed already. In this rule the left subpattern $L =$ `root:I[a:Any]` is identical to the full pattern of the rule P, and the redirections are $Red = \{($`root`, `a`$)\}$. The graph $G =$ `x:I[x]` contains an instance of L. Since $L = P$, there are no nodes to be added at the contractum building stage so $G' = G$. To perform the redirections and complete the rewrite we look for the image of $\{($`root`, `a`$)\}$ in G'. This is $\{($`x`, `x`$)\}$. Therefore all nodes targeted at `x` must be redirected to `x`, a null action. So $H = G' = G$.

One feature of this model stands out, which is that no node is ever destroyed during rewriting. This means that copious quantities of garbage are generated. The attempts to describe graph rewriting using pushouts fail on the circular I example, precisely because they do some partial garbage collection in the arrows of the categories used. As the next section will show, the garbage retention feature of DACTL turns out to be an inspired design decision.

7.3 GRAPH REWRITING AS GROTHENDIECK OPFIBRATION

In this section we will recast some of the preceeding constructions into a categorical form using a Grothendieck opfibration.

Definition **7.3.1** *Let $\mathcal{P}$ be the category whose objects are (abstract) patterns and whose arrows are rules depicted by pairs of functions $(i, r) : L \to R$ satisfying the invariants (INJ), (RED), (HOM) below. L and R are called the left and right patterns of the rule (arrow) $(i, r) : L \to R$.*

(INJ) *$i : L \to R$ is a symbol/arity-preserving injection that is invertible on the implicit subpatterns of L and R, (i.e. "no new variables are introduced in the RHS of the rule").*

(RED) *$r : L \to R$ may only disagree with $i : L \to R$ on explicit nodes and satisfies*

$$\exists \text{ a homomorphism } h : L \to Z \text{ such that } h(x) = h(y) \iff [r(x) = r(y), \text{ or } r(x) = i(x) \text{ and } r(y) = i(y)].$$

(HOM) *(p_k, c) an arc of $L \iff (i(p)_k, r(c))$ an arc of R.*

Identities are just pairs of identities and composition is componentwise. It is trivial to check that $\mathcal{P}$ is a category.

We see that the arrows of $\mathcal{P}$ provide a component i that mimics the inclusion of the left subpattern into the full pattern of a DACTL rule of the previous section, and also a component r that mimics the redirection pairs of the previous treatment.

A subset of DACTL rules can be easily mapped to $\mathcal{P}$ arrows. This subset is characterized by the property (RED-P) below. We call this subset DACTL$^{\mathcal{P}}$.

(RED-P) x, y explicit and $\exists$ a homomorphism $h : L \to Z$ such that $h(x) = h(y) \implies [(x, t) \in Red \iff (y, t) \in Red]$.

There is an easy mapping from DACTL$^{\mathcal{P}}$ rules into arrows of $\mathcal{P}$. It is given by the next construction.

Construction **7.3.2** *Let $(incl : L \to P, root, Red)$ be a DACTL$^{\mathcal{P}}$ rule. Now DACTL rewriting semantics can just as easily be applied to instances of L in patterns as to instances in graphs. So let R be the pattern resulting from rewriting the identity instance of L in itself according to the rule. Then the arrow of $\mathcal{P}$ corresponding to the rule is (the abstract version of) $(i, r) : L \to R$ with (i, r) given by*

$$i(x) = \{(1, x), (2, x)\},$$
$$r(x) = \{(1, y), (2, y)\}, \text{ where } y = x \text{ unless } (x, y) \in Red.$$

Modulo the pedantry of disjoint unions, we have just applied the redirections *Red* to the pattern P.

We now give the $\mathcal{P}$ version of graph rewriting which we call the $\mathcal{P}$ rewriting construction, to distinguish it from the DACTL rewriting construction of the previous section.

Definition **7.3.3** *Let $\delta = (i, r) : L \to R$ be an arrow of $\mathcal{P}$, and let $g : L \to G$ be a rigid homomorphism of L into a graph G, by which we mean a homomorphism such that (RIG) below holds.*

(RIG) *x explicit, y implicit $\implies g(x) \neq g(y)$.*

Let the graph H be given by:

(1) *$N_H = (N_G \uplus N_R)/\approx$ where $\uplus$ is disjoint union and $\approx$ is the smallest equivalence relation such that $(1,x) \approx (2,n)$ whenever there is a $p \in L$ such that $x = g(p)$ and $n = i(p)$. Thus N_H is the pushout in $\mathcal{S}et$ of $R \xleftarrow{i} L \xrightarrow{g} G$.*
(2) $\sigma_H(\{(1,x)\}) = \sigma_G(x)$,
$\sigma_H(\{(2,n)\}) = \sigma_R(n)$,
$\sigma_H(\{(1,x),(2,n_1)\ldots(2,n_q)\}) = \sigma_G(x)$.

Before defining α_H, we pause to define $(j,s) : G \to H$ and $h : R \to H$

$$j(x) = \{(1,x)\ldots\},$$
$$s(x) = \begin{cases} \{(2,r(p))\ldots\} & \text{if } \exists p \in L \text{ such that } x = g(p) \text{ and } r(p) \neq i(p) \\ \{(1,x)\ldots\} & \text{otherwise} \end{cases}$$
$$h(n) = \{(2,n)\ldots\},$$

(3) $\alpha_H(\{(1,x)\})[k] = s(\alpha_G(x)[k])$,
$\alpha_H(\{(2,n)\})[k] = h(\alpha_R(n)[k])$,
$\alpha_H(\{(1,x),(2,n_1)\ldots(2,n_q)\})[k] = s(\alpha_G(x)[k])$.

LEMMA **7.3.4** *Definition 7.3.3 is consistent. Furthermore*

(a) *j is a symbol/arity-preserving injection,*
(b) *h is a rigid homomorphism,*
(c) *(j,s) is a redirection couple i.e. $[(x_k, y)$ an arc of G $\iff (j(x)_k, s(y))$ an arc of $H]$.*

LEMMA **7.3.5** *In the notation of 7.3.3, 7.3.4, $j \circ g = h \circ i$ and $s \circ g = h \circ r$.*

In general, the two rewriting models agree. We have the following result.

THEOREM **7.3.6** *Let $(incl : L \to P, root, Red)$ be a $DACTL^{\mathcal{P}}$ rule and let $(i,r) : L \to R$ be the corresponding $\mathcal{P}$ arrow. Let $g : L \to G$ be a rigid matching of L to a graph G. Then the abstract versions of the graphs H built by the two rewriting constructions are the same.*

We return to our primary objective of making a Grothendieck construction in the world of abstract patterns and graphs, via a universal property of $\mathcal{P}$ rewriting which makes it very reminiscent of a pushout.

THEOREM **7.3.7** *Using the notation of 7.3.3 – 7.3.5, let H' be a graph and suppose $(j', s') : G \to H'$ and $h' : R \to H'$ are such that*

(1) *j' is a symbol/arity-preserving injection,*
(2) *(j', s') is a redirection couple i.e. $[(x_k, y)$ an arc of G $\iff (j'(x)_k, s'(y))$ an arc of $H]$,*
(3) *h' is a homomorphism,*
(4) *$j' \circ g = h' \circ i$ and $s' \circ g = h' \circ r$,*
(5) *$i(a) = r(p)$ and $i(b) = r(q)$ and $g(a) = g(b) \Longrightarrow s'(g(p)) = s'(g(q))$,*

Then there is a unique pair of maps $(\theta, \rho) : H \to H'$ such that

(a) *θ is a symbol/arity-preserving node map,*

(b) *(θ, ρ) is a redirection couple i.e.* $[(p_l, c)$ *an arc of* H $\iff (\theta(p)_l, \rho(c))$ *an arc of* $H']$,

(c) *(θ, ρ) extend to a homomorphism on $h(R)$,*

(d) $j' = \theta \circ j$, $s' = \rho \circ s$, $h' = \theta \circ h = \rho \circ h$, *and* $\rho = \theta$ *on* $H - (s(G) \cup h(R))$.

Theorem 7.3.7 shows the pushout-like nature of the $\mathcal{P}$ rewriting construction. The graph H that it creates is universal up to isomorphism among ways of completing the squares referred to in Lemma 7.3.5 according to the conditions stated.

Now we are in a position to proceed with the Grothendieck construction.

DEFINITION **7.3.8** *For each object P of $\mathcal{P}$, we construct a category $\mathcal{G}^P$. The objects of $\mathcal{G}^P$ are pairs (G, g). Here G is an abstract graph and $g : P \rightarrow G$ is a rigid homomorphism. The arrows $\phi : (G, g) \rightarrow (G', g')$ of $\mathcal{G}^P$ are graph homomorphisms ϕ which preserve the redex, i.e. $g' = \phi \circ g$, and also are rigid i.e. $g(P) = \phi^{-1}(g'(P))$. The two notions of rigidity should cause no confusion.*

DEFINITION **7.3.9** *Consider an arrow $\delta = (i, r) : L \rightarrow R$ in $\mathcal{P}$, and (G, g) an object of $\mathcal{G}^L$. Let (H, h) be the object of $\mathcal{G}^R$ such that H is the unique abstract graph isomorphic to the result of rewriting the instance $g : L \rightarrow G$ according to rule δ using the $\mathcal{P}$ rewriting construction, and $h : R \rightarrow H$ is the obvious homomorphism. Let $Rew^\delta((G, g)) = (H, h)$.*

LEMMA **7.3.10** *$Rew^\delta : \mathcal{G}^L \rightarrow \mathcal{G}^R$ extends to a functor.*

THEOREM **7.3.11** *There is a functor $Rew : \mathcal{P} \rightarrow \mathcal{C}$ at such that*

$$Rew(P) = \mathcal{G}^P$$
$$Rew(\delta : L \rightarrow R) = Rew^\delta : \mathcal{G}^L \rightarrow \mathcal{G}^R$$

The existence of $Rew : \mathcal{P} \rightarrow \mathcal{C}at$ leads immediately to the construction of the Grothendieck category $\mathcal{G}(\mathcal{P}, Rew)$. The objects of $\mathcal{G}(\mathcal{P}, Rew)$ are pairs $((G, g), L)$ where L is an object of $\mathcal{P}$ and (G, g) is an object of $Rew(L)$. We can write such objects as $(g : L \rightarrow G)$. The arrows of $\mathcal{G}(\mathcal{P}, Rew)$ are pairs $(\phi, \delta) : (g : L \rightarrow G) \rightarrow (h : R \rightarrow H)$ where $\delta = (i, r) : L \rightarrow R$ is an arrow of $\mathcal{P}$, and $\phi : Rew^\delta(G) \rightarrow H$ is an arrow of $\mathcal{G}^R$. In slightly less combinatorial terms, an arrow (ϕ, δ) of $\mathcal{G}(\mathcal{P}, Rew)$ can be viewed as an abstract $\mathcal{P}$ rewrite of a redex $g : L \rightarrow G$ by a rule $\delta = (i, r) : L \rightarrow R$ giving $Rew^\delta((G, g))$, composed with a homomorphism ϕ. Thus it can be given by a pair $(j, s) : G \rightarrow H$ where $j = \phi \circ j^*$, $s = \phi \circ s^*$, and $(j^*, s^*) : G \rightarrow Rew^\delta(G)$ represents the effect of Rew^δ on G. Clearly $[(x_k, y)$ an arc of $G \iff (j(x)_k, s(y))$ an arc of $H]$. Such a pair (j, s) is strictly speaking a different thing from (ϕ, δ), but we will overlook this.

Composition of arrows $(\phi, \delta) : (g : L \rightarrow G) \rightarrow (h : M \rightarrow H)$ and $(\chi, \epsilon) : (h : M \rightarrow H) \rightarrow (k : N \rightarrow K)$ is defined by

$$(\chi, \epsilon) \circ (\phi, \delta) : (g : L \rightarrow G) \rightarrow (k : N \rightarrow K) = (\chi \circ Rew(\epsilon)(\phi), \epsilon \circ \delta)$$

Note that compared to our $\mathcal{P}$ rewriting construction, the arrows of $\mathcal{G}(\mathcal{P}, Rew)$ have an extra homomorphism "tacked onto the end". The fact that we can do this is purely a consequence of the fact that the individual Rew^δ functors mesh together to form the overall functor Rew. Readers unhappy about this can merely stick to the special case where all the $\mathcal{G}^P$ categories are discrete. The arrows of $\mathcal{G}(\mathcal{P}, Rew)$ will be called rewrites, or $\mathcal{G}$ rewrites if we wish particularly to distinguish them from $\mathcal{P}$ rewrites and DACTL rewrites. Of course from a categorical viewpoint, we might justifiably prefer them to be called corewrites or oprewrites.

Continuing the development, $\mathcal{G}(\mathcal{P}, Rew)$ is a fibered category. The fibers are the $\mathcal{G}^L$ categories and the projection $F : \mathcal{G}(\mathcal{P}, Rew) \to \mathcal{P}$ takes objects $(g : L \to G)$ to L, and arrows (ϕ, δ) to δ. This is an example of the canonical duality between split (op)fibrations and the Grothendieck categories built using the Grothendieck construction. Powerful universality properties that extend the universality properties that hold for pushouts pertain to this situation. For a little more discussion, of these issues, see the full version in [Ban93]. For a reasonably accessible description of the Grothendieck construction in its abstract form see [BW90].

7.4 TRUE DACTL REWRITING

In section 7.3 we developed a categorical formulation for a sublanguage of DACTL. Readers may legitimately wonder to what extent the full DACTL language shares the properties of DACTL$^{\mathcal{P}}$. The main problem encountered in applying the constructions of section 7.3 to the full language can be traced back to DACTL's capacity for ambiguous redirections. From the perspective of the Grothendieck construction, DACTL redirections can be ambiguous for two distinct reasons. The first concerns the priority mechanism that implicitly determines targets for redirection. Thus if $(x, t) \in Red$, and x and y both match the same graph node of the redex, but for no u do we have $(y, u) \in Red$, then the redirection in Red wins over the unstated identity redirection of y. A similar thing happens for implicit nodes of the pattern when they match the same graph node as some x such that $(x, t) \in Red$. Again the explicit redirection wins over the unstated identity redirection. Such phenomena prevent the commutativity needed for Lemma 7.3.5, and explain why the DACTL$^{\mathcal{P}}$ sublanguage contained specific conditions to prevent such behavior.

It might be imagined from this that the prospects for describing the whole language categorically were bleak. However this is not quite the case, and it is precisely the libertarian tendencies of implicit nodes that come to the rescue. Whenever a node of the left pattern has the capacity to be redirected in more than one way, we introduce a fresh implict node in the right pattern of the rule to act as its "mate". With a little care, we can exploit the capacity of implicit nodes to "match anything" in order to ensure that whatever actual redirection takes place, the mate node is able to accommodate it and to rescue the required commutativity. We thus make the syntactic form of rules reflect the actual ambiguity that comes from the semantics. We outline the construction informally below.

CONSTRUCTION **7.4.1** *Let $(incl : LP, root, Red)$ be a DACTL rule.*

[1] *Apply construction 7.3.2 and call the resulting pattern R2. Rename each node (which is an equivalence class built up out of a single node x say of P), as the corresponding x.*

[2] *For every implicit node x of R2, introduce a mate node. Redirect all images in R2 of arcs of L to x, to the mate. Call the resulting pattern R1.*

[3] *For every explicit node y of R1 such that y is not redirected in Red but y could match the same graph node as some x for which* $(x, t) \in$ *Red, introduce a mate node. Redirect all images in R1 of arcs of L to x, to the mate. Call the resulting pattern R.*

[4] *Let* $(i, r) : L \longrightarrow R$ *be the obvious maps.*

A rewriting construction (let us call it the D rewriting construction), similar to $\mathcal{P}$ rewriting can be designed that accurately reflects DACTL rewriting. We do not describe it in detail, but instead state the relevant universal property.

THEOREM **7.4.2** *In Theorem 7.3.7, let the rule under consideration be* $(i, r) : L \longrightarrow R$ *as manufactured in 7.4.1. Replace the (unstated) reference to* $\mathcal{P}$ *rewriting, by reference to D rewriting, remove the (unstated) reference to the rigidity of the matching of the redex* $g : L \longrightarrow G$*, and add an extra hypothesis*

(6) $i(a) = r(p)$ *and for all* $q \in g^{-1}(g(a)), r(q)$ *is a mate* $\Longrightarrow s'(g(p)) = s'(g(q))$ *for any such q.*

Then the theorem holds true in the modified form.

Theorem 7.4.2 describes a local form of universality that holds for D rewriting, but that does not extend to the global universality generated by a Grothendieck construction as discussed towards the end of section 7.3. The most important obstacle to the construction is the fact that there is an asymmetry between the patterns L and R of the rule constructed in 7.4.1. The pattern R contains mates while L does not. This blocks the translation of trivial DACTL rules (no contractum, empty redirections) to identity arrows in the base. Furthermore, even if $g : L \longrightarrow G$ is a rigid redex, there is no guarantee that the corresponding $h : R \longrightarrow H$ is rigid, again because of the mates. All things considered, it is remarkable that 7.4.2 holds at all.

One final enigma remains to be resolved before we close this discussion of rewriting, and that is the status of the circular instance of the I combinator. The most self evident feature of this example is that the matching $g : L \longrightarrow G$ which defines the rewrite is not rigid. It seems therefore, that we cannot but resort to the locally universal construction outlined above to describe it. While this is certainly possible, it is not the only thing that we can do. The circular I example actually occupies an intermediate position between the global universality of $\mathcal{P}$ rewriting, and the mates and local universality of D rewriting. The conditions that are imposed to make $\mathcal{P}$ rewriting globally universal are sufficient but not necessary to make it locally universal. The circular I example satisfies a set of weaker conditions, without having the rigidity property that gives global universality. These conditions can be summarized in the invariant (W-RIG) which stands for weak rigidity.

(W-RIG) p explicit, a implicit and $g(a) = g(p) \Longrightarrow r(p) = i(p)$ or $r(p) = i(a)$.

The circular I instance of the I combinator rule in $\mathcal{P}$ rewriting form clearly satisfies (W-RIG). It follows that the $\mathcal{P}$ rewriting construction is consistent for it, and describes the locally universal properties of this rewrite. Thus the $\mathcal{P}$ version of the rule is given by $(i, r) : L \longrightarrow R$ with L and R the same pattern described in the introduction; i being the identity, and r having $r(\texttt{root}) = r(\texttt{a}) = \texttt{a}$.

7.5 CONCLUSIONS

We have described how the essentials of the rather complex and perhaps unintuitive DACTL graph rewriting model may be recast as a universal solution to a particular categorical problem, and a familiar one for category theorists at that. This is particularly gratifying for the author whose previous experience with the DACTL model gave rise to the strong gut feeling that despite its somewhat convoluted operational description, a robust, elegant and convincing model lay behind the drudgery of contractum–build+redirect. Grothendieck (op)fibrations lie behind may constructions in mathematics, and are increasingly found in theoretical computer science these days. Their usefulness in separating "syntax" (contained in the base category) from "semantics" (in the Grothendieck category above) is perhaps their most appealing feature; we use both terms in quotes since we refer to situations more general than those just involving actual syntax and semantics of programming languages — any situation where we have a collection of "objects" and for each object we have to deal with a collection of its "instances" is a good candidate for a Grothendieck construction.

REFERENCES

[Ban93] R. Banach. Term graph rewriting and garbage collection using opfibrations. *To appear in: Theoretical Computer Science*, 1993.

[BvEG+87] H. P. Barendregt, M. C. J. D. van Eekelen, J. R. W. Glauert, J. R. Kennaway, M. J. Plasmeijer, and M. R. Sleep. Term graph rewriting. In *Proc. PARLE'87 Conference, vol.II*, pp. 141–158, 1987. Springer-Verlag, Lecture Notes in Computer Science 259.

[BW90] M. Barr and C. Wells. *Category Theory for Computing Science.* Prentice Hall, 1990.

[GHK+88] J.R.W. Glauert, K. Hammond, J.R. Kennaway, G.A. Papdopoulos, and M.R. Sleep. *DACTL: Some Introductory Papers.* Technical Report SYS-C88-08, School of Information Systems, UEA, Norwich, 1988.

[GKS91] J.R.W. Glauert, J.R. Kennaway, and M.R. Sleep. Dactl: An experimental graph rewriting language. In *Proc. 4th International Workshop on Graph Grammars and their Application to Computer Science*, Springer-Verlag, Lecture Notes in Computer Science 532, pp. 378–395, 1991.

[GKSS88] J.R.W. Glauert, J.R. Kennaway, M.R. Sleep, and G.W. Somner. *Final Specification of DACTL.* Technical Report SYS-C88-11, School of Information Systems, UEA, Norwich, 1988.

[HKP88] A. Habel, H-J. Kreowski, and D. Plump. Jungle evaluation. In *Fifth Workshop on Specification of Abstract Data Types*, Springer-Verlag, Lecture Notes in Computer Science 332, pp. 92–112, 1988.

[HP88] B. Hoffmann and D. Plump. Jungle evalulation for efficient term rewriting. In *Proc. International Workshop on Algebraic and Logic Programming*, vol. 49 of *Mathematical Research.* Akademie-Verlag, 1988.

[Ken87] J.R. Kennaway. On "on graph rewritings". *Theoretical Computer Science*, **52**, pp. 37–58, 1987.

[Ken90] J.R. Kennaway. Implementing term rewrite languages in Dactl. *Theoretical Computer Science*, **72**, pp. 225–250, 1990.

[Ken91] J.R. Kennaway. Graph rewriting in some categories of partial morphisms. In *Proc. 4th International Workshop on Graph Grammars and their Application to Computer Science*, Springer-Verlag, Lecture Notes in Computer Science 532, pp. 490–504, 1991.

8

A New Term Graph Rewriting Formalism: Hyperedge Replacement Jungle Rewriting

A. Corradini and F. Rossi

8.1 INTRODUCTION

We propose a new term graph rewriting formalism, called *hyperedge replacement jungle rewriting*, and we show that it allows to model Term Rewriting Systems (TRS) more faithfully than all the other term graph rewriting formalisms we are aware of.

Jungles are special acyclic directed hypergraphs (i.e., graphs where each arc can have any number of source and target nodes), and have been introduced in [Plu86, HKP88] to represent sets of terms with possibly shared subterms. In this sense they can be thought of as being the hypergraph correspondent of the well-known directed acyclic graphs (*dags*).

The *theory of graph rewriting* (or *graph grammars)* basically studies a variety of formalisms which extend the theory of formal languages in order to deal with structures more general than strings, like graphs and maps. A graph rewriting system is a collection of rules, each of which can be applied to a graph by replacing an occurrence of its left-hand side with its right-hand side. The form of graph rewrite rules and the mechanisms stating how a rewrite rule can be applied to a graph and what the resulting graph is, depend on the specific formalism. Among the various formulations of graph rewriting the so called "algebraic approach" [EPS73, Ehr87] is one of the most successful, mainly because of its flexibility. In fact, since the basic notions of

Term Graph Rewriting: Theory and Practice.
Eds. Ronan Sleep, Rinus Plasmeijer and Marko van Eekelen.

rule and rewriting step are defined in terms of diagrams and constructions in a category, they can be defined in a uniform way for a wide range of structures, simply by changing the underlying category. Moreover, many results can be proved once and for all using categorical techniques. *Jungle rewriting* is defined by applying the guidelines of the algebraic approach to graph rewriting to the category of jungles. The resulting formalism is only apparently similar to *jungle evaluation* as defined in [HKP88, HP91], which is actually the result of applying the algebraic approach to the category of hypergraphs, and then by restricting the attention to those hypergraphs which are jungles.

A *hyperedge replacement* jungle rewrite rule is a rule such that the left-hand side jungle consists of a single hyperedge. Graph rewriting formalisms satisfying the same restriction have been studied in [BC87, Hab89], but both consider arbitrary hypergraphs.

In summary, hyperedge replacement (HR-) jungle rewriting can be defined easily as a mixture of well-known notions. Despite that, its expressive power as a term graph rewriting formalism has not been explored before.

Term graph rewriting, i.e., the issue of representing TRS using graph rewriting, has been investigated by many papers in the literature. Some of them exploit the algebraic theory of graph grammars (like [PPEM87, HP91], which follow the so-called "double-pushout approach", and [Rao84, Ken87, Ken91], which use instead a single pushout construction); others employ a more operational presentation of graph rewriting e.g., [BvEG+87]. In general, term rewrite rules are translated into graph rewrite rules, while terms are represented either by dags or by jungles: usually the same term can be represented by many graphs which are not isomorphic. All the mentioned papers prove the soundness of their graph representation of rewrite rules, in the sense that if a graph rule which represents a term rule can be applied to a graph, then the corresponding term rule can be applied to the term represented by the graph. However, this translation is usually not complete with respect to applicability, i.e., it is possible that a graph cannot be rewritten with a graph rule, although the term it represents can be reduced by the corresponding term rewrite rule. Usually, this kind of completeness just holds for left-linear rules i.e., rules which do not have two occurrences of the same variable in the left-hand side. Some of those papers propose additional mechanisms which allow one to deal with non-left-linear rules, like *folding rules* as in [HKP88, HP91], or a generalization of the notion of *occurrence* as in [Ken87].

On the contrary, the jungle representation that we propose for TRS enjoys completeness with respect to applicability for non-left-linear rules as well, without resorting to additional mechanisms. As we will see, this is a consequence of the basic choice of performing the constructions which implement the rewriting (i.e., the pushout and the pushout complement, along the guidelines of the algebraic approach) directly in the category of jungles. In fact, the pushout in such a category corresponds to term unification, which is obviously powerful enough to model the pattern-matching mechanism needed to perform term rewriting. The possibility of modeling term unification in our framework suggests that Logic Programming as well may be represented by HR-jungle rewriting, but this topic goes beyond the scope of this chapter and is discussed in depth in [CR93].

The chapter is organized as follows. In section 8.2 we introduce the category of jungles, describe how jungles can be used to represent sets of terms, and analyse some relevant properties of the basic categorical constructions needed to apply the algebraic approach. Then section 8.3 presents the definition of hyperedge replacement jungle rewriting as the application of the algebraic approach to graph rewriting to the category of jungles, with the additional constraint of replacing exactly one edge at each rewriting step. Finally, section 8.4 presents our proposal for term graph rewriting together with the main results, showing that a Term Rewriting System can be represented by a hyperedge replacement jungle rewriting system in a sound way, which is complete with respect to applicability also for non-left-linear rules. For the sake of brevity, all the proofs are omitted: they can be found in the full paper [CR93].

8.2 THE CATEGORY OF JUNGLES AND ITS PROPERTIES

In this section we introduce the category of jungles, describe how one can use jungles to represent terms with possibly shared subterms, and explore some properties of the category (i.e., existence of pushouts and pushout complements) which are relevant for the definition of jungle rewriting along the guidelines of the algebraic approach to graph grammars. Most of the definitions and results of sections 8.2.1 and 8.2.2 are borrowed from the work by Hoffman and Plump ([HP91]) on *jungle evaluation*.

8.2.1 Categories of hypergraphs and jungles

A (directed) hypergraph straightforwardly generalizes a (directed) graph: it includes a set of nodes and a set of hyperarcs. Every hyperarc has a list of source nodes and a list of target nodes, instead of exactly one source and one target node. Nodes and hyperarcs are colored by elements of color sets. In this chapter we are interested just in hypergraphs whose nodes (resp. hyperarcs) are labeled by the sorts (resp. operators) of a many-sorted signature.

DEFINITION **8.2.1 (Many-sorted signatures)** *A* many-sorted signature $\underline{\Sigma}$ *is a pair* $\underline{\Sigma} = (S, \Sigma)$, *where* S *is a set of* sorts, *and* $\Sigma = \{\Sigma_{w,s}\}$ *is a family of sets of* operators *indexed by* $S^* \times S$. *If* $f \in \Sigma_{w,s}$ *then* s *is called the* type *of* f, w *is its* arity, *and* $|w|$ *(the length of* w*) is the* rank *of* f.

DEFINITION **8.2.2 (Hypergraphs)** *A* hypergraph G over $\underline{\Sigma}$ *is a tuple* $G = (V, E, s, t, m, l)$, *where* V *is a set of* nodes *(or* vertices*),* E *is a set of* hyperarcs *(or* hyperedges*),* s *and* $t : E \rightarrow V^*$ *are the* source *and* target *functions,* $l : V \rightarrow S$ *maps each node to a sort of* $\underline{\Sigma}$, *and* $m : E \rightarrow \Sigma$ *maps each arc to an operator of* $\underline{\Sigma}$. *A* path *in a hypergraph from node* v *to node* u *is a sequence of hyperarcs* $\langle e_1, \ldots, e_n \rangle$ *such that* $v \in s(e_1)$, $u \in t(e_n)$, *and for each* $1 < i \leq n$, $s(e_n) \in t(e_{n-1})$. *A hypergraph is* acyclic *if there are no non-empty paths from one node to itself. A hypergraph is* discrete *if it contains no edges. For a hypergraph* G, *indegree*$_G(v)$ *(resp. outdegree*$_G(v)$*) denotes the number of occurrences of a node* v *in the target strings (resp. source strings) of all edges of* G.

For the sake of simplicity, in this chapter we will often omit the prefix "hyper-", calling *hypergraphs* and *hyperarcs* simply *graphs* and *arcs*. A *jungle* is a hypergraph satisfying some additional conditions which makes it suitable to represent sets of (finite) terms with possibly shared subterms. The precise role played by these restrictions will be made clear in section 8.2.2.

DEFINITION **8.2.3 (Jungles)** *A* jungle over $\underline{\Sigma}$ *is a graph* $G = (V, E, s, t, m, l)$ *over* $\underline{\Sigma}$ *such that*

- *the labeling of the arcs is consistent with both the number and the labeling of the connected nodes, i.e.,* $\forall e \in E,\ m(e) \in \Sigma_{w,s} \Leftrightarrow l^*(s(e)) = s \wedge l^*(t(e)) = w$, *where* l^* *is the obvious extension of* l *to tuples;*
- *for each node* $v \in V$, $outdegree_G(v) \leq 1$;
- G *is acyclic.*

EXAMPLE **8.2.4 (Graphical representation of hypergraphs and jungles)** *Let* $\underline{\Sigma} = (S = \{list, nat\},\ \Sigma = \{\Sigma_{\epsilon,list} = \{EMPTY\},\ \Sigma_{\epsilon,nat} = \{0\},\ \Sigma_{nat \cdot list,list} = \{cons, rem\},\ \Sigma_{nat,nat} = \{succ\},\ \Sigma_{nat \cdot nat,nat} = \{+\},\ \Sigma_{list,nat} = \{car\}\})$ *(ϵ denotes the empty word of a free monoid). In figure 8.1 two hypergraphs over* $\underline{\Sigma}$ *are shown, which are called* G *and* H*, respectively.*

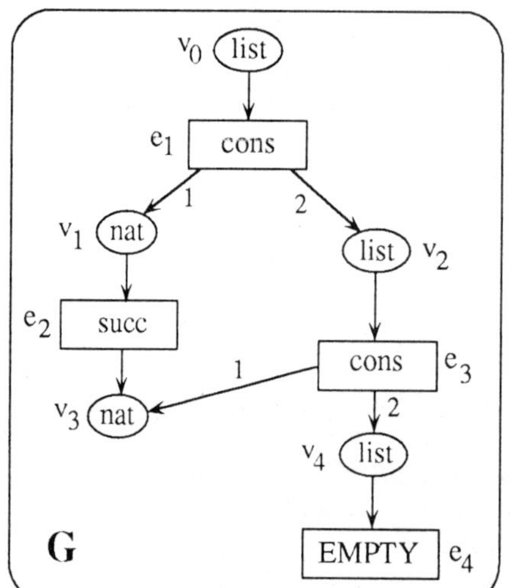

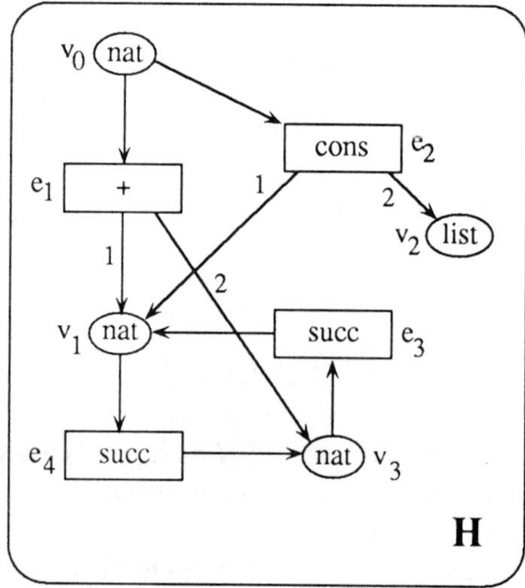

Figure 8.1 Examples of hypergraphs

In the graphical representation of hypergraphs we will use the following conventions. Arcs and nodes are represented by boxes and circles, respectively, with the colors written inside. The source (resp. target) nodes of an arc are connected to the arc itself by an arrow (sometimes called a *tentacle*) oriented towards the box (resp. towards the circle). When an arc has more than one source (resp. target), the incoming (resp. outgoing) tentacles are numbered. The graphical representation we use puts in evidence that hypergraphs can be regarded as directed bipartite graphs. It is easy to check that G above is also a jungle over $\underline{\Sigma}$, while H is not.

DEFINITION **8.2.5 (Hypergraph and jungle morphisms)** A morphism of hypergraphs (over $\underline{\Sigma}$) $f : G_1 \to G_2$ *consists of a pair of functions between arcs and nodes respectively, which are compatible with the source and target functions and which are color preserving. More precisely, if* $G_1 = (V_1, E_1, s_1, t_1, m_1, l_1)$ *and* $G_2 = (V_2, E_2, s_2, t_2, m_2, l_2)$ *are two graphs over* $\underline{\Sigma}$, *then* $f = (f_V : V_1 \to V_2, f_E : E_1 \to E_2)$ *is a morphism if* $s_2 \circ f_E = f_V^* \circ s_1$; $t_2 \circ f_E = f_V^* \circ t_1$; $m_2 \circ f_E = m_1$; *and* $l_2 \circ f_V = l_1$, *where* f_V^* *is the obvious extension of* f_V *to lists of nodes. A hypergraph morphism* $f = (f_V, f_E) : G_1 \to G_2$ *is* injective *(resp.* surjective*) iff both* f_V *and* f_E *are injective functions (resp. surjective). A morphism* f *is an* isomorphism *if it is both injective and surjective. Morphisms of jungles are defined exactly in the same way.*

DEFINITION **8.2.6 (Categories $\mathbf{HGraph}_{\underline{\Sigma}}$ and $\mathbf{Jungle}_{\underline{\Sigma}}$)** *The category whose objects are directed hypergraphs over* $\underline{\Sigma}$ *and whose arrows are hypergraph morphisms will be denoted by* $\mathbf{HGraph}_{\underline{\Sigma}}$. *The full subcategory of* $\mathbf{HGraph}_{\underline{\Sigma}}$ *including all jungles will be called* $\mathbf{Jungle}_{\underline{\Sigma}}$.

8.2.2 Representing terms by jungles

As it should be evident by the example in the previous section, there is a fairly obvious correspondence between the jungles over a signature $\underline{\Sigma}$ and the terms built over that signature. Although jungles have been used during the last years by people interested in graph term rewriting [Plu86, HKP88, HP91, Ken91] or in graph rewriting for logic programming [CMR+91, CRPP91], one cannot disregard the other main graphical representation of terms with shared subterms, namely *directed acyclic graphs* in the many variants, which have been used among others in [Rao84, PPEM87, Ken87, BC87]. The relationship between the two representations has been made precise in [CMR+91], where it has been shown that the category of jungles and that of dags over the same signature are equivalent. Thus, as far as one is concerned with results or constructions expressible in categorical terms, the use of jungles or dags is completely interchangeable. Our preference for jungles is therefore mainly a matter of taste. In the rest of this section we refer to a fixed many-sorted signature $\underline{\Sigma} = (S, \Sigma)$.

DEFINITION **8.2.7 (Terms, substitutions, unifiers)** *Let* $X = \{X_s\}_{s \in S}$ *be a family of pairwise disjoint sets of variables indexed by* S. *Then a* term of sort s *is an element of* $T_{\underline{\Sigma}_s}(X)$ *(the carrier of sort* s *of the free* $\underline{\Sigma}$*-algebra generated by* X*), that is a variable of* X_s, *or a constant in* $\Sigma_{\epsilon,s}$, *or* $f(t_1, \ldots, t_n)$, *if* $f \in \Sigma_{w,s}$, $w = s_1 \cdot \ldots \cdot s_n$, *and* t_i *is a term of sort* s_i *for each* $1 \leq i \leq n$. *The sort of a term* t *will be denoted by* $sort(t)$.

Given two families of S*-indexed sets of variables* $X = \{X_s\}$ *and* $Y = \{Y_s\}$, *a* substitution σ from X to Y *is a function* $\sigma : X \to T_{\underline{\Sigma}}(Y)$ *which is sort preserving. When* X *is finite,* σ *can be represented as* $\sigma = \{x_1/t_1, \ldots, x_n/t_n\}$, *where* $\sigma(x_i) = t_i$.

By the freeness property of $T_{\underline{\Sigma}}(X)$, *a substitution* $\sigma : X \to T_{\underline{\Sigma}}(Y)$ *can be extended in a unique way to a* $\underline{\Sigma}$*-homomorphism* $\sigma^{\#} : T_{\underline{\Sigma}}(X) \to T_{\underline{\Sigma}}(Y)$, *defined as* $\sigma^{\#}(x) = \sigma(x)$ *if* $x \in X$, *and* $\sigma^{\#}(f(t_1, \ldots, t_n)) = f(\sigma^{\#}(t_1), \ldots, \sigma^{\#}(t_n))$.

Given two substitutions σ *from* X *to* Y *and* τ *from* Y *to* Z, *their* composition *(denoted by* $\tau \circ \sigma$ *) is the substitution from* X *to* Z *defined as* $\tau \circ \sigma(x) = \tau^{\#}(\sigma(x))$. *In the rest of the chapter the extension of a substitution* σ *to terms will be denoted improperly by* σ *itself. A substitution* σ *from* X *to* Y *is a* variable renaming *if* $\sigma(x) \in Y$ *for each* $x \in X$ *and* σ *is a bijection. If* T *and* T' *are two sets of terms we will write*

$T \cong T'$ if they are identical up to a variable renaming. Given two substitutions σ and τ, σ is said to be more general *than τ if there exists a substitution ϕ such that $\phi \circ \sigma = \tau$. Two terms t and t'* unify *if there exists a substitution σ such that $\sigma(t) = \sigma(t')$. In this case σ is called a* unifier *of t and t'. The set of unifiers of any two terms is either empty, or it has a most general element (up to variable renaming) called the* most general unifier.

If G is a jungle, it should be quite obvious (look for example at the jungle G of figure 8.1) how to extract a term of sort s from each s-labeled node of G. Indeed, by Definition 8.2.3, each node has either exactly one outgoing tentacle or none. In the former case it is the root of a sub-jungle which represents a term, while in the latter case it represents a variable.

DEFINITION **8.2.8 (From nodes to terms)** *Let G be a jungle over $\underline{\Sigma}$. The* variables *of G are a family of S-indexed sets $Var(G) = \{Var_s(G)\}_{s \in S}$ defined as $Var_s(G) = \{v \in V_G \mid outdegree_G(v) = 0 \wedge l_G(v) = s\}$.*

The function $term_G$ associates with each node of G labeled by s a term in $T_{\underline{\Sigma}_s}(Var(G))$. It is defined inductively as follows:

- *$term_G(v) = v$, if $v \in Var_s(G)$,*
- *$term_G(v) = op(term_G(v_1), \ldots, term_G(v_n))$, if there exists $e \in E_G$ with $s_G(e) = v$, $t_G(e) = v_1 \cdot \ldots \cdot v_n$, and $m_G(e) = op \in \Sigma_{w,s}$.*

$TERM(G) = \cup_{s \in S} TERM_s(G)$ will denote the set of all terms associated with the nodes of jungle G, where $TERM_s(G) = \{term_G(v) | v \in V_G \text{ and } l_G(v) = s\}$. For each jungle G, the set $TERM(G)$ is closed under the subterm relation, i.e., if $t \in TERM(G)$ and t' is a subterm of t, then also $t' \in TERM(G)$. If G and G' are two isomorphic jungles, then we have $TERM(G) \cong TERM(G')$.

EXAMPLE **8.2.9 (Terms associated with a jungle)** *Consider the jungle G of figure 8.1. It contains just one variable v_3 of sort nat, thus $Var_{nat}(G) = \{v_3\}$ and $Var_{list}(G) = \emptyset$. The function $term_G$ is defined as $term_G(v_0) = cons(succ(v_3), cons(v_3, EMPTY))$; $term_G(v_1) = succ(v_3)$; $term_G(v_2) = cons(v_3, EMPTY)$; $term_G(v_4) = EMPTY$; and $term_G(v_3) = v_3$.*

While the collection of terms associated with a jungle is uniquely determined, each set of terms (closed under the subterm relation) may have many representations, since identical subterms can either be collapsed into a single subjungle or not (cf. [Rao84, PPEM87, HKP88]). Nevertheless, a minimal representation as jungle always exists, and it is characterized by the fact that function *term* is injective. The proof can be found in [HKP88], or in [CMR+91] for the equivalent case of dags.

DEFINITION **8.2.10 (Representing a set of terms by a jungle)** *Let T be a set of terms and let $\overline{T}$ be the closure of T under the subterm relation, i.e. $\overline{T} = \{t' \mid$ there is a term $t \in T$ such that t' is a subterm of $t\}$. Then a jungle G* represents *T iff $TERM(G) \cong \overline{T}$.*

PROPOSITION 8.2.11 (The fully collapsed jungle representing a set of terms) *Let T be a set of terms. Then the set of jungles representing T has a 'final element' $\mathcal{J}(T)$, the* fully collapsed jungle *of T. That is, for every jungle G which represents T there exists a unique jungle morphism $G \rightarrow \mathcal{J}(T)$. The jungle $\mathcal{J}(T)$ is uniquely determined up to isomorphisms, and is such that the function $term_{\mathcal{J}(T)} : V_{\mathcal{J}(T)} \rightarrow T_{\underline{\Sigma}}(Var(\mathcal{J}(T)))$ is injective.*

As jungles represent naturally collections of terms, jungle morphisms correspond to term substitutions.

DEFINITION 8.2.12 (The substitution induced by a morphism) *Let G and G' be jungles, and $h : G \rightarrow G'$ be a jungle morphism. Then the node component of h (i.e., $h_V : V_G \rightarrow V_{G'}$) induces a substitution $\sigma_h : Var(G) \rightarrow T_{\underline{\Sigma}}(Var(G'))$, defined as $\sigma_h(x) = term_{G'}(h_V(x))$. Moreover, the correspondence between jungle morphisms and term substitutions is preserved by composition, in the following sense: if $h : G \rightarrow G'$ and $k : G' \rightarrow G''$ are jungle morphisms then $\sigma_{k \circ h} = \sigma_k \circ \sigma_h : Var(G) \rightarrow T_{\underline{\Sigma}}(Var(G''))$.*

8.2.3 Categorical constructions in the category of jungles

In the theory of graph grammars a central role is played by two basic operations on graphs: the *gluing* of two graphs, which merges the graphs together identifying some selected arcs and nodes; and the *deletion* of a subgraph from a graph. These operations are cleanly formulated, in the algebraic approach to graph grammars, as simple categorical constructions, namely as *pushout* and as *pushout complement*, respectively.

In this section we summarize necessary and sufficient conditions for the existence of pushouts in the category of jungles, and we show that the pushout complement always exists under hypotheses which will be satisfied in the cases we are interested in. For the pushouts it is interesting to notice that although the category **HGraph**$_{\underline{\Sigma}}$ has all pushouts, they do not always exist in its full subcategory **Jungle**$_{\underline{\Sigma}}$; indeed, it is known in the "folklore" that the pushout in such categories (as for dags) corresponds to the existence of most general unifiers. We make this statement precise.

DEFINITION 8.2.13 (Pushout and pushout complement) *Given a category C and two arrows $b : K \rightarrow B$, $d : K \rightarrow D$ of C, a triple $\langle H, h : B \rightarrow H, c : D \rightarrow H\rangle$ as in figure 8.2 is called a* pushout *of $\langle b, d\rangle$ if:*

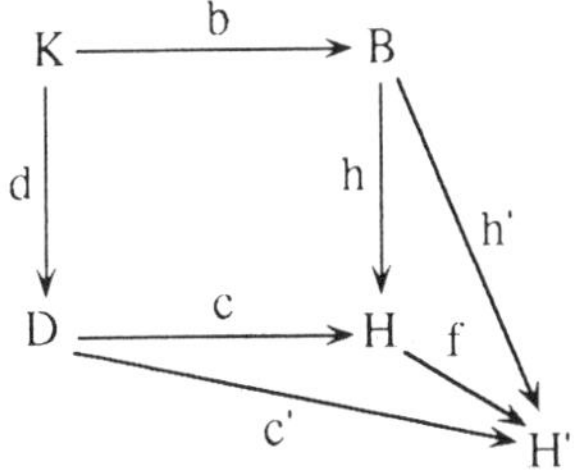

Figure 8.2 Pushout diagram

- *(commutativity property)* $h \circ b = c \circ d$;
- *(universal property) for all objects* H' *and arrows* $h' : B \to H'$ *and* $c' : D \to H'$, *with* $h' \circ b = c' \circ d$, *there exists a unique arrow* $f : H \to H'$ *such that* $f \circ h = h'$ *and* $f \circ c = c'$, *as in figure 8.2.*

In this situation, H *is called a* pushout object *of* $\langle b, d\rangle$. *Moreover, given arrows* $b : K \to B$ *and* $h : B \to H$, *a* pushout complement *of* $\langle b, h\rangle$ *is a triple* $\langle D, d : K \to D, c : D \to H\rangle$ *such that* $\langle H, h, c\rangle$ *is a pushout of* b *and* d. *In this case* D *is called a* pushout complement object *of* $\langle b, h\rangle$.

In any category, if the pushout object of two arrows exists then it is unique up to a unique isomorphism because of the universal property. On the contrary, since the pushout complement object is not characterized directly by a universal property, a pair of arrows can have many pushout complement objects which are not isomorphic, if any.

In the category of jungles, the pushout of two arrows exists iff the associated substitutions have a unifier. In this case, the pushout provides a most general unifier for those substitutions.

PROPOSITION **8.2.14 (Pushouts in $\mathbf{Jungle}_{\Sigma}$ as most general unifiers)**

a. *Let* $r : K \to R$ *and* $d : K \to D$ *be two jungle morphisms. Let* $\sigma_r : Var(K) \to T_{\Sigma}(Var(R))$ *and* $\sigma_d : Var(K) \to T_{\Sigma}(Var(D))$ *be the associated substitutions (see Definition 8.2.12). Then the pushout of* $\langle r, d\rangle$ *exists in* $\mathbf{Jungle}_{\Sigma}$ *if and only if there exist two substitutions* $\theta : Var(R) \to T_{\Sigma}(Y)$ *and* $\theta' : Var(D) \to T_{\Sigma}(Y)$ *which 'unify'* $\langle \sigma_r, \sigma_d\rangle$, *in the sense that* $\theta \circ \sigma_r = \theta' \circ \sigma_d$.
b. *If* $\langle g, f\rangle$ *is a pushout of* $\langle r, d\rangle$ *in* $\mathbf{Jungle}_{\Sigma}$ *then* $\langle \sigma_g, \sigma_f\rangle$ *is a most general unifier of* $\langle \sigma_r, \sigma_d\rangle$, *i.e., for each pair of substitutions* $\langle \theta, \theta'\rangle$ *such that* $\theta \circ \sigma_r = \theta' \circ \sigma_d$, *there exists a* σ *such that* $\sigma \circ \sigma_g = \theta$ *and* $\sigma \circ \sigma_f = \theta'$. *Moreover, jungle* H *is such that* $TERM(H) = \sigma_f(TERM(D)) \cup \sigma_g(TERM(R))$.

It is worth noting that the relationship between most general unifiers and universal constructions in a category has been stressed in many places (see for example [RB85] and [PPEM87]).

The characterization of sufficient conditions for the existence and uniqueness of the pushout complement of two arrows is a central topic in the theory of graph grammars, because it allows one to check the applicability of a rewrite rule to a graph. However, since in this chapter we are interested just in the application of the so called hyperedge replacement rewrite rules (as defined below in Definition 8.3.1), we consider just the pushout complements which arise from the application of a rewrite rule of that type. In this case a specific pushout complement can always be found (although in general it is not unique).

PROPOSITION **8.2.15 (Existence of certain PO-complements in $\mathbf{Jungle}_{\Sigma}$)** *Let* $l : K \to L$ *and* $g : L \to G$ *be two jungle morphisms such that*

- *jungle* L *consists of exactly one arc, say with label* f, *connected to* $n + 1$ *distinct nodes where* n *is the rank of* f;
- *jungle* K *is discrete and includes exactly* $n + 1$ *nodes; and*

- *the morphism $l : K \to L$ is a bijection on nodes.*

Then there exists a pushout complement of $\langle l, g\rangle$, say $\langle D, k : K \to D, d : D \to G\rangle$ which is obtained as follows. Jungle D is obtained from G by removing the arc which is the image of the unique arc of L via g; $d : D \to G$ is the obvious inclusion; and $k : K \to D$ is the unique morphism making the square commute.

8.3 HYPEREDGE REPLACEMENT JUNGLE REWRITING

In this section we introduce the basic concepts of the algebraic theory of graph rewriting [EPS73, Ehr87] for the specific case of the category of jungles. A jungle rewrite rule (analogously to term rewrite rules or string productions) describes how to replace the occurrence of a subjungle L in a jungle G with another jungle R. While in the case of terms or strings the embedding of R inside G is uniquely determined, this is not true in the more general case of graphical structures like jungles. Thus a third graph K is needed in order to give the connection points of R in G. In this chapter we will restrict our attention to hyperedge replacement rewrite rules, i.e., rules where the jungle in the left-hand side contains exactly one arc.

DEFINITION **8.3.1 (Hyperedge replacement jungle rewrite rules)**
A jungle (rewrite) rule $p = (L \stackrel{l}{\leftarrow} K \stackrel{r}{\rightarrow} R)$ *is a pair of jungle morphisms $l : K \to L$ and $r : K \to R$, where l is injective. The jungles L, K, and R are called the left-hand side (LHS), the interface, and the right-hand side (RHS) of p, respectively. A* hyperedge replacement (HR-) *jungle rewrite rule is such that L, K and l satisfy the hypotheses of Proposition 8.2.15, i.e., L has just one arc (say with label f) connected to $n+1$ distinct nodes where n is the rank of f, K is discrete and has $n+1$ nodes, and l is bijective on nodes. In a HR-jungle rule $p = (L \stackrel{l}{\leftarrow} K \stackrel{r}{\rightarrow} R)$ the jungles L, K and the morphism l are uniquely determined (up to isomorphisms) by the label of the unique arc of L. As a consequence, we will often represent p in a more compact way as*

$$p : f \rightsquigarrow (R, v_0, \ldots, v_n)$$

where f is the label of the arc of L, and $v_0, \ldots, v_n$ are distinguished nodes of R (possibly with $v_i = v_j$ for some $i \neq j$) which are the images through r of the $n+1$ nodes of K. We assume that nodes $v_0, \ldots, v_n$ correspond to the source and to the n target nodes of the unique edge of L, in this order.

Examples of HR-jungle rules will be given in section 8.4. The application of a rewrite rule p to a jungle G is modeled by a double pushout construction, following the classical algebraic approach to graph rewriting.

DEFINITION **8.3.2 (Direct rewriting)** *Given a jungle G, a jungle rewrite rule $p = (L \stackrel{l}{\leftarrow} K \stackrel{r}{\rightarrow} R)$, and an* occurrence *(i.e., a jungle morphism) $g : L \to G$, a* direct rewriting *from G to H based on g exists if and only if the diagram in figure 8.3 can be constructed, where both squares are required to be pushouts in* $\mathbf{Jungle}_{\underline{\Sigma}}$. *In this case, D is called the* context *jungle, and we write $G \Rightarrow_p H$.*

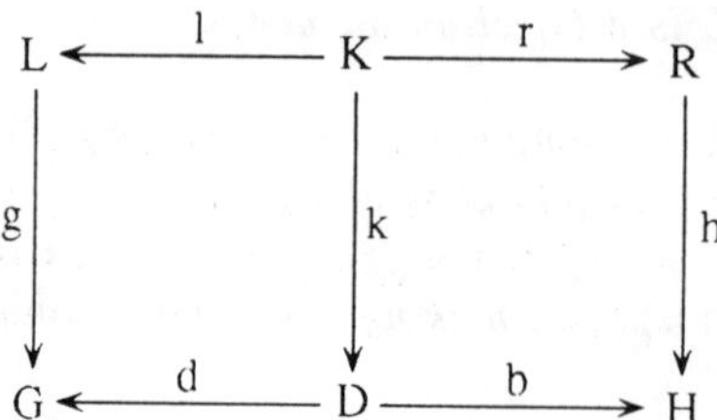

Figure 8.3 A double-pushout diagram

The double pushout construction can be interpreted as follows. In order to apply the rule p to G, we first need to find an occurrence of its LHS L in G, i.e., a jungle morphism $g : L \to G$. Next, to model the deletion of that occurrence from G, we construct the pushout complement of g and l, producing the context jungle D where the RHS R has to be embedded. This embedding is expressed by the second pushout.

It must be noticed that this construction can fail, since the required pushout and pushout complement do not always exist in the category of jungles. Nevertheless, in the case of a hyperedge replacement direct rewriting, since arrow $l : K \to L$ satisfies the hypotheses of Proposition 8.2.15 there always exists at least one pushout complement object. Therefore the application of a hyperedge replacement rewrite rule requires just the existence of the right-hand side pushout.

In the case of a hyperedge replacement direct rewriting $G \Rightarrow_p H$ there is a *track function* [HP91] from the nodes of G to the nodes of H.

DEFINITION **8.3.3 (Track function of a direct rewriting)** *Let p be a HR-jungle rule and $G \Rightarrow_p H$ be a direct rewriting. It is easy to check that morphism $d : D \to G$ (determined as in Proposition 8.2.15) is a bijection on nodes. Then the* track function *associated with $G \Rightarrow_p H$ is defined as $tr = b_V \circ d_V^{-1} : G_V \to H_V$.*

DEFINITION **8.3.4 (Jungle rewriting systems)** *A* jungle rewriting system *(over $\underline{\Sigma}$) is a finite set $\mathcal{R}$ of jungle rewrite rules in category* **Jungle**$_{\underline{\Sigma}}$. *A* hyperedge replacement *(shortly* HR-*) jungle rewriting system $\mathcal{R}$ is a jungle rewriting system where all the rewrite rules are hyperedge repacement rules.*

8.4 TERM GRAPH REWRITING VIA JUNGLE REWRITING

We present here our proposal for term graph rewriting, based on the graph rewriting formalism introduced in the last section. The main point is the translation of term rewrite rules into HR-jungle rules. Our representation substantially differs from all the others proposed in literature and, as we will show, it is more satisfactory in the sense that it allows one to manage non-left-linear rules uniformly, without resorting to additional mechanisms. After recalling the basic definitions about Term Rewriting Systems, we define the jungle representation $\mathcal{J}(t \to t')$ of a term rewrite rule $t \to t'$, and then we show that such representation is sound and complete with respect to applicability. The proofs of the statements in this section can be found in [CR93].

DEFINITION **8.4.1 (Term Rewriting Systems)** *A* (term) rewrite rule *(over a given signature $\underline{\Sigma} = (S, \Sigma)$) is a pair $t \to t'$ of terms such that $sort(t) = sort(t')$, t is not* *a variable, and all the variables in t' occur also in t. A rule $t \rightarrow t'$ is* left-linear *if all the variables occurring in t are distinct. A* (Term) Rewriting System *(TRS) is a finite set of rewrite rules $\mathcal{T} = \{t_i \rightarrow t'_i\}_{i \leq n}$. Given a rewriting system $\mathcal{T}$, a ground term s* rewrites *to a term s' (denoted by $s \rightarrow_{\mathcal{T}} s'$) iff there exists a rewrite rule $t \rightarrow t'$ in $\mathcal{T}$ and a substitution σ such that s has a subterm $s'' = \sigma(t)$, and s' is obtained from s by replacing s'' by $\sigma(t')$. Clearly, in this case s' is ground, too.*

For technical reasons we only consider the rewriting of *ground* terms, but this is not a real limitation. In fact, since the variables appearing in the term to be rewritten are never instantiated by the application of a rewrite rule, such variables can safely be considered as new constants.

Definition **8.4.2 (The HR-jungle rewriting system representing a TRS)** *Given a rewrite rule $f(t_1, \ldots, t_n) \rightarrow t'$, its* jungle representation *is the HR-jungle rewrite rule $\mathcal{J}(t \rightarrow t') = f \rightsquigarrow (R, v_0, \ldots, v_n)$, where*

- *$R = \mathcal{J}(\{t', t_1, \ldots, t_n\})$, i.e., R is the fully collapsed jungle representing the RHS and all the arguments of the LHS of the rule $t \rightarrow t'$.*
- *Nodes $v_0, \ldots, v_n$ are determined (see Proposition 8.2.11) by $term_R(v_0) = t'$ and $term_R(v_i) = t_i$ for $1 \leq i \leq n$.*

If $\mathcal{T} = \{t_i \rightarrow t'_i\}_{i \leq n}$ is a Term Rewriting System, its jungle representation *is the HR-jungle rewriting system $\mathcal{J}(\mathcal{T}) = \{\mathcal{J}(t_i \rightarrow t'_i)\}_{i \leq n}$.*

The jungle representation of a rewrite rule just defined may be understood more easily by resorting to a "normalized" presentation of the rule itself. If $f(t_1, \ldots, t_n) \rightarrow t'$ is a rule, its "normal" form is

$$f(x_1, \ldots, x_n) \rightarrow t' \text{ where } x_1 = t_1, \ldots, x_n = t_n,$$

with $x_1, \ldots, x_n$ fresh, distinct variables. The jungle representation $(L \xleftarrow{l} K \xrightarrow{r} R)$ of the rule can be considered as a direct translation of this normal form, since L represents exactly $f(x_1, \ldots, x_n)$, R represents the term t' and the arguments of the LHS $t_1, \ldots, t_n$, and morphism r forces the identifications $x_i = t_i$. Clearly, such a normalized presentation is equivalent to the original one (as proved below by the results of soundness and completeness), only thanks to the fact that the pushout in the category of jungles corresponds to term unification.

Example **8.4.3 (A jungle rewrite rule)** *Let Σ be the signature of lists of natural numbers introduced in Example 8.2.4. Then the term rewrite rule $car(cons(x, y)) \rightarrow x$ is represented by the jungle rewrite rule shown in figure 8.4, where we use the conventions of Definition 8.3.1. This representation should be compared with the normal form of such a rule, which is*

$$car(x_1) \rightarrow x \text{ where } x_1 = cons(x, y).$$

The next result states the soundness of our representation of term rewrite rules i.e., that every rewriting performed with the jungle representation of a term rule

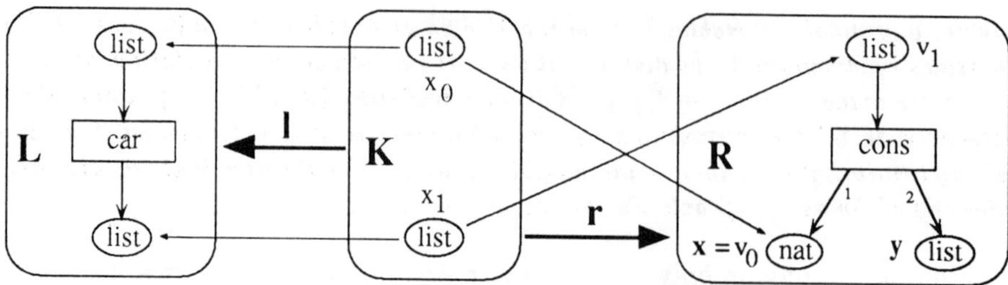

Figure 8.4 A sample jungle rule

corresponds to one or more applications of that rule. A similar result of soundness has been proved for many different term graph rewriting formalisms (see for example [BvEG+87, HP91].

THEOREM **8.4.4 (Soundness of jungle representation of rewrite rules)** *Let $p = L \xleftarrow{l} K \xrightarrow{r} R$ be the jungle representation of the term rewrite rule $t \rightarrow t'$ (i.e., $p = \mathcal{J}(t \rightarrow t')$), and let $G \Rightarrow_p H$ be a direct rewriting as in figure 8.3, with $Var(G) = \emptyset$. Then for each $v \in V_G$ we have that $term_G(v)$ rewrites to $term_H(tr(v))$ by n applications of the rule $t \rightarrow t'$, where n is the number of paths from v to the image through g of the (unique) root node of L.*

The next result states that whenever a term rewrite rule $t \rightarrow t'$ can be applied to a term s, then its jungle representation $\mathcal{J}(t \rightarrow t')$ can be applied to *any* jungle which represents s (possibly among other terms). This result does not hold (without additional conditions) for non-left-linear rules in all the related works on term graph rewriting we are aware of. The reason is that in all those proposals the LHS L of the graph rewrite rule representing a term rewrite rule $t \rightarrow t'$ (call it $\mathcal{G}(t \rightarrow t')$) is supposed to represent the whole term t. Now if $t = f(x,x)$, rule $t \rightarrow t'$ can be applied to the ground term $f(a,a)$ via the substitution $\sigma = \{x/a\}$. However, on the one hand L represents $f(x,x)$ as a jungle (or a dag) where the two occurrences of the variable x are shared, i.e., they are represented by the same node. On the other hand, there exists a jungle G such that $f(a,a) \in TERM(G)$, but there is no direct rewriting via $\mathcal{G}(t \rightarrow t')$. In fact, if G is the jungle representing $f(a,a)$ where the two occurrences of the constant a are represented by distinct edges, it is easy to check that there exists no graph morphism from L to G.

On the contrary, in our representation just the topmost operator of t is represented in L, with pairwise distinct variables as arguments. Practically, we use a left-linear representation of (possibly non-left-linear) rules: this is possible only thanks to the fundamental choice of performing all the constructions in the category of jungles.

PROPOSITION **8.4.5 (Completeness with respect to applicability)** *Let $\mathcal{J}(t \rightarrow t')$ be the jungle representation of a term rewrite rule $t \rightarrow t'$, G be a jungle (without variables) and $s \in TERM(G)$. If $t \rightarrow t'$ can be applied to term s, then there is a direct rewriting $G \Rightarrow_{\mathcal{J}(t \rightarrow t')} H$ for some jungle H.*

EXAMPLE **8.4.6 (Application of a non-left-linear rule)** *Consider the rule (over the signature of Example 8.2.4) $rem(x, cons(x,y)) \rightarrow rem(x,y)$, which is intended to model the deletion of the occurrences of a given number from a list. It is not left-linear.*

Clearly, the ground term $rem(0, cons(0, EMPTY))$ *rewrites to* $rem(0, EMPTY)$ *via that rule. The diagram in figure 8.5 shows that the jungle representation of the rule can be applied also to the jungle representing* $rem(0, cons(0, EMPTY))$ *where the two occurrences of '0' are represented by distinct edges. It should be noticed that as the result of the rewriting, the two distinct edges labeled by the constant '0' are merged together in the resulting jungle H.*

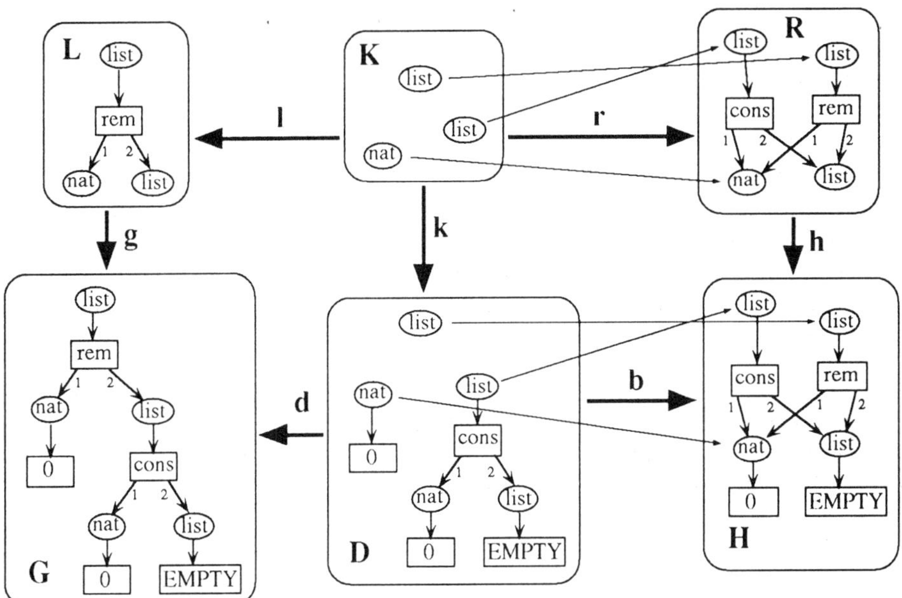

Figure 8.5 Successful application of a non-left-linear rule

The results of soundness of our jungle representation of TRS and of completeness with respect to applicability could allow us to restate in our framework most of the results about graph representation of Term Rewriting Systems, for example the completeness for confluent and terminating TRS [HP91]. However, this goes beyond the scope of this chapter.

8.5 CONCLUSIONS

In this chapter we introduced hyperedge replacement jungle rewriting, and investigated its expressive power as a term graph rewriting formalism, showing that it models Term Rewriting Systems in a faithful way. We proved the soundness of the jungle representation of Term Rewriting Systems, and also a result of completeness with respect to applicability which is stronger than similar results in the related literature, since it works also for non-left-linear rules.

Since term unification can be modeled by the pushout construction in the category of jungles, similar results of soundness and completeness also hold for the representation of Logic Programs through HR-jungle rewriting systems. These results are discussed in detail in [CR93]. The possibility of modeling in a uniform framework both Logic Programming and Term Rewriting Systems should allow representation of formalisms with both logical and functional aspects. Possible extensions in this direction include *conditional* term rewriting and the modeling of unification modulo an equational theory (*narrowing*). Another extension could consider *cyclic* jungles, suitable to model the rewriting of possibly infinite, rational terms.

REFERENCES

[BC87] M. Bauderon and B. Courcelle. Graph expressions and graph rewritings. *Mathematical System Theory*, **20**, pp. 83–127, 1987.

[BvEG+87] H. P. Barendregt, M. C. J. D. van Eekelen, J. R. W. Glauert, J. R. Kennaway, M. J. Plasmeijer, and M. R. Sleep. Term graph rewriting. In J. W. de Bakker, A. J. Nijman, and P. C. Treleaven (editors), *Proc. PARLE'87 Conference, vol.II*, Springer-Verlag, Lecture Notes in Computer Science 259, pp. 141–158, 1987.

[CMR+91] A. Corradini, U. Montanari, F. Rossi, H. Ehrig, and M. Löwe. Logic programming and graph grammars. In H. Ehrig, H.-J. Kreowski, and G. Rozenberg (editors), *Proc. 4th International Workshop on Graph Grammars and their Application to Computer Science*, Springer-Verlag, Lecture Notes in Computer Science 532, pp. 221–237, 1991.

[CR93] A. Corradini and F. Rossi. Hyperedge replacement jungle rewriting for term rewriting systems and logic programming. To appear in *Theoretical Computer Science*, 1993.

[CRPP91] A. Corradini, F. Rossi, and F. Parisi-Presicce. Logic programming as hypergraph rewriting. In S. Abramsky and T. S. E. Maibaum (editors), *Proc. TAPSOFT '91 (CAAP)*, Springer-Verlag, Lecture Notes in Computer Science 493, pp. 275–295, 1991.

[Ehr87] H. Ehrig. Tutorial introduction to the algebraic approach of graph-grammars. In H. Ehrig, M. Nagl, G. Rozenberg, and A. Rosenfeld (editors), *Proc. 3rd International Workshop on Graph Grammars and their Application to Computer Science*, Springer-Verlag, Lecture Notes in Computer Science 291, pp. 3–14, 1987.

[EPS73] H. Ehrig, M. Pfender, and H. J. Schneider. Graph-grammars: an algebraic approach. In *Proc. IEEE Conference on Automata and Switching Theory*, pp. 167–180, 1973.

[Hab89] A. Habel. *Hyperedge Replacement: Grammars and Languages.* Ph.d. thesis, University of Bremen, 1989.

[HKP88] A. Habel, H-J. Kreowski, and D. Plump. Jungle evaluation. In *Proc. 5th Workshop on Specification of Abstract Data Types*, Springer-Verlag, Lecture Notes in Computer Science 332, pp. 92–112, 1988.

[HP91] B. Hoffmann and D. Plump. Implementing term rewriting by jungle evaluation. *Informatique théorique et Applications / Theoretical Informatics and Applications*, **25**, pp. 445–472, 1991.

[Ken87] J. R. Kennaway. On 'on graph rewritings'. *Theoretical Computer Science*, **52**, pp. 37–58, 1987.

[Ken91] J. R. Kennaway. Graph rewriting in some categories of partial morphisms. In H. Ehrig, H.-J. Kreowski, and G. Rozenberg (editors), *Proc. 4th International Workshop on Graph Grammars and their Application to Computer Science*, Springer-Verlag, Lecture Notes in Computer Science 532, pp. 490–504, 1991.

[Plu86] D. Plump. *Im Dschungel: Ein neuer Graph-Grammatik-Ansatz zur effizienten Auswertung rekursiv definierter Funktionen.* Diplomarbeit, Fachbereich Mathematik-Informatik, Universität Bremen, 1986.

[PPEM87] F. Parisi-Presicce, H. Ehrig, and U. Montanari. Graph rewriting with unification and composition. In H. Ehrig, M. Nagl, G. Rozenberg, and A. Rosenfeld (editors), *Proc. 3rd International Workshop on Graph Grammars and their Application to Computer Science*, Springer-Verlag, Lecture Notes in Computer Science 291, pp. 496–514, 1987.

[Rao84] J. C. Raoult. On graph rewritings. *Theoretical Computer Science*, **32**, pp. 1–24, 1984.

[RB85] D. E. Rydeheard and R. M. Burstall. A categorical unification algorithm. In *Proc. of the Workshop on Category Theory and Computer Programming*, Springer-Verlag, Lecture Notes in Computer Science 240, 1985.

9

Abstract Reduction: Towards a Theory via Abstract Interpretation

Marko van Eekelen, Eric Goubault, Chris Hankin and Eric Nöcker

9.1 INTRODUCTION

In this chapter we present a framework for proving the correctness of the strictness analyser used in the Concurrent Clean system [NSvEP91]. Concurrent Clean is a lazy functional language based on term graph rewriting [BvEG+87]. Using the formal definitions of term graph rewriting several fundamental soundness and completeness results for using graph rewriting as an implementation optimization have been given. A very efficient implementation for Concurrent Clean has been developed, of which the strictness analyser is an important part. The strictness analyser for Concurrent Clean is based on graph rewriting using a technique called *abstract reduction* [Nöc90].

We use the same context-free grammar as [BvEG+87] (see Chapter 10) to denote term graphs.

In the following, we use the abstract lattice presented in Chapter 10. The lattice was called $A\text{-}G^d_M$ but we call it $A\text{-}G$ in the sequel. Recall that $A\text{-}G$ is related to $\wp(Graph)$ via a pair of adjoined functions, $(\alpha: \wp(Graph) \rightarrow A\text{-}G, \gamma: A\text{-}G \rightarrow \wp(Graph))$. Abstract graphs are built from:

$$Symbol^{\#} = \{F^{\#} \mid F \in Symbol, F \neq \Omega\} \cup \{Bot, Top, Union\}$$

(Bot and Top of arity 0, $Union$ of arity 2). We will make use of the shorthand notation for Unions and of the function $\#$, introduced in Chapter 10.

Term Graph Rewriting: Theory and Practice.
Eds. Ronan Sleep, Rinus Plasmeijer and Marko van Eekelen.

9.2 ABSTRACT REDUCTION AND THE FUNCTIONAL STRATEGY

Abstract reduction is defined in the context of functional Graph Rewriting Systems, of which Concurrent Clean is an example. The reader is referred to [NSvEP91] for an introduction to Clean.

In the following, let R be a set of rules:

$$R = R_1 \cup R_2 \cup \ldots \cup R_f$$

where each of the R_i defines some operator F_i, i.e. is a set of rules of the form:

$$R_i = \{r_{i,1}, \ldots, r_{i,j_i}\}$$

where $r_{i,k} = (g_{i,k}, n_{i,k}, n'_{i,k})$, $k = 1 \ldots j_i$, with $g_{i,k}|n_{i,k} = F_i(\ldots)$ [1]. In the following, we will drop the i index, when the context makes it clear which R_i we are considering.

Constructor symbols, in contrast to *operators*, are the symbols that do not label the root node of the left hand side of any rule of R (including the δ-rules). We consider any graph with an operator at its root as a *redex*, so we cannot deal directly with partial rewrite rules, in which such graphs can also be considered as normal forms. However, one can generally complete a partial rewrite system.

The functional strategy depends on the textual order of the rules; the matching algorithm selects the needed redexes "from top to bottom, and from left to right". If $g = F_i(\ldots)$ is the graph to be reduced, the strategy first tries to rewrite it by rule $r_{i,1}$, if not, by $r_{i,2}$, and so on. Then the arguments of $F_i(\ldots)$ are reduced from left to right, in order to match a rule $r_{i,k}$.

We will describe the behavior of the functional strategy with three operations:

$$\begin{array}{l} Match: Graph \times Graph \rightarrow \{tt, ff\} \\ Rewrite: Graph \times \wp(Rule) \rightarrow Graph \\ Reduce: Graph \times \wp(Rule) \rightarrow Graph \end{array}$$

The function *Reduce* reduces a graph to root normal form ("rnf"), *Rewrite* performs a rewrite step, and *Match* implements the matching algorithm. The functions are defined via the following equations (to be read top to bottom):

```
Reduce (g,r)          =  g                           if in_rnf (g)
                      =  Reduce (Rewrite (g,r),r)    otherwise

Match (g,p)           =  True                        if is_var(p)
                      =  Match(Reduce (g,R),p)       if ¬in_rnf(g)
                      =  False                       if root(g) ≠ root(p)
                      =  MatchArg(args(g),args(p))   otherwise

MatchArg ([ ],[ ])    =  True
MatchArg (g:gs,p:ps)  =  MatchArg(gs,ps)             if Match (g,p)
                      =  False                       otherwise
```

[1] Recall that the notation $g \mid n$ denotes the subgraph of g rooted at the node n.

```
Rewrite (g,r:rs)  =  Rewrite (g,rs)   if root(g) ≠ root(r)
                  =  Rewrite (g,rs)   if ¬MatchArgs(args(g),args(r))
                  =  tgr g r          otherwise
```

where *tgr* is the basic graph rewrite step [BvEG+87].

Now we describe the abstract reduction mechanism. Basically, it mimics the concrete one. An abstract graph may match several rules. Intuitively, an abstract reduction step should include (at least) all reduction steps that are possible for the concrete graphs represented by the abstract graph. That is, the following should hold:

$$t_1 \rightarrow^{\#} t_2 \Rightarrow \{g \mid h \rightarrow g, h \in \gamma(t_1)\} \subseteq \gamma(t_2)$$

This requirement is rather strong. The reduction mechanism we will define is not so precise. However, the important reductions are simulated. Sometimes, in a concrete graph more or less reductions can be done than in its corresponding abstract graph; this might be caused, for example, by a different form of sharing of subgraphs.

We will describe abstract reduction by defining abstract versions of the three functions defined above. That is, we will define:

$$\begin{aligned} &AMatch\colon A\text{-}G \times A\text{-}G \rightarrow Matching \\ &ARewrite\colon A\text{-}G \times \wp(ARule) \rightarrow A\text{-}G \\ &AReduce\colon A\text{-}G \times \wp(ARule) \rightarrow A\text{-}G \end{aligned}$$

9.2.1 Abstract rewriting

The function *AReduce* is easy to define. As in the concrete case it performs rewrite actions until the graph is in root normal form:

```
AReduce (g,r)  =  g                           if in_rnf (g)
               =  AReduce (ARewrite (g,r),r)  otherwise
```

An abstract graph is in root normal form if either:

- it is *Top* or *Bot*
- it is a *Union*, and all its arguments are in root normal form
- its root is a constructor symbol

Now we will define how an abstract rewrite step can be done. We will start our description by considering an abstract graph $g = F^{\#}v_1 \ldots v_n$, where F is a function symbol. This term represents a set of concrete graphs $\gamma(g)$, all starting with the same function symbol F. So, all concrete graphs will rewrite according to this function F. The abstract reduction step should simulate all those concrete rewrite steps. There are two problems:

- different expressions in $\gamma(g)$ can rewrite according to different rules of F
- for different expressions in $\gamma(g)$ the functional strategy can force the reduction of different subexpressions.

Suppose we have a function definition for a function F consisting of k alternatives:

$$\begin{array}{lllll} \text{F } p_{11} & \ldots & p_{1n} & \rightarrow & rhs_1 \\ & \ldots & & & \\ \text{F } p_{k1} & \ldots & p_{nn} & \rightarrow & rhs_k \end{array}$$

We define a corresponding abstract rewrite rule for $F^{\#}$ as follows:

$$\begin{array}{lllll} \#[\text{F } p_{11} & \ldots & p_{1n}] & \rightarrow & \#[rhs_1] \\ & \ldots & & & \\ \#[\text{F } p_{k1} & \ldots & p_{nn}] & \rightarrow & \#[rhs_k] \end{array}$$

That is, an abstract rewrite rule is derived from the concrete one by decorating the symbols. In the following we will omit the # suffix. Suppose the concrete graphs of g will rewrite according to the alternatives $i_1 \ldots i_m$ only. Then we can specify the abstract rewrite step *ARewrite* as follows:

$$\begin{array}{lll} \text{ARewrite (F } v_1 \ldots v_n) & = & \langle result_{i_1}, \ldots, result_{i_m} \rangle \\ \text{ARewrite } (\langle x_1 \ldots x_n \rangle) & = & \langle \text{ARewrite } (x_1) \ldots \text{ARewrite } (x_n) \rangle \end{array}$$

where $result_{i_j}$ is the result of an abstract rewrite step according to alternative i_j of the function F (using an abstracted version of *tgr*). Which alternatives are applicable, is determined by pattern matching using an auxiliary function *AMatchAlt*.

An abstract graph g matches a pattern p if all or some concrete graphs in $\gamma(g)$ match the pattern p. So, a match against a variable always succeeds. A matching algorithm for the abstract reduction should be safe, that is, if an abstract match yields false, then also all concrete matches should yield false. It is easy to define a simple abstract matching algorithm. A version that takes account of the functional strategy is more difficult. Consider, for example, the following function definition:

```
F Nil   →   Nil
F x     →   Cons x Nil
```

then the graph F Nil might rewrite as follows (since both alternatives match):

F Nil $\rightarrow^{\#}$ ⟨Nil, Cons Nil Nil⟩

and the graph F Bot might rewrite as follows (since the second alternative matches):

F Bot $\rightarrow^{\#}$ Cons Bot Nil

Both rewrites are, though safe, too pessimistic. In the first case in the concrete world the first alternative would have matched and the second alternative is therefore not tested. In the second example the pattern matching would not succeed because the argument has no root normal form (the result of F $\perp$ would be $\perp$). This behavior is the result of the functional strategy.

We will start by defining abstract matching in such a way that it returns enough information. Let g be an abstract graph, and p a pattern. We define, informally, the following four kinds of matches:

TotalMatch: all graphs in $\gamma(g)$ match p
NoMatch: no graph in $\gamma(g)$ matches p
BotMatch: the matching of all graphs in $\gamma(g)$ against p diverges
PartialMatch: some graphs in $\gamma(g)$ might match p

AMatch (g,p)	=	TotalMatch	if is_var (p)
AMatch (g,p)	=	AMatch(AReduce (g,R),p)	if $\neg$ in_rnf (g)
AMatch (Top,p)	=	PartialMatch	
AMatch (Bot,p)	=	BotMatch	
AMatch (g,p)	=	CombineUMatch(AMatch (g_i, p)) for all $1 \leq i \leq n$	if root(g) = Union
AMatch (g,p)	=	NoMatch	if root(g) $\neq$ root(p)
AMatch (g,p)	=	AMatchArgs(args(g),args(p))	otherwise

AMatchArgs ($g_1 \ldots g_n, p_1 \ldots p_n$) = CombineMatch (AMatch (g_i, p_i)) for $1 \leq i \leq n$

where:

CombineMatch($m_1 \ldots m_n$)	=	TotalMatch	if m_i = TotalMatch for all i
	=	NoMatch	if m_i = NoMatch for some i & m_j = TotalMatch for all j < i
	=	BotMatch	if m_i = BotMatch for some i & m_j = TotalMatch for all j < i
	=	PartialMatch	otherwise
CombineUMatch($m_1 \ldots m_n$)	=	TotalMatch	if m_i = TotalMatch for all i
	=	NoMatch	if m_i = NoMatch for all i
	=	BotMatch	if m_i = BotMatch for all i
	=	PartialMatch	otherwise

The functions *CombineMatch* and *CombineUMatch* combine matches of multiple patterns. Also in this case we can take into account that matching proceeds from left to right. For example, if a match results in a NoMatch then the result of the whole alternative will be NoMatch if all the previous matches resulted in a TotalMatch.

Now we can define when an alternative of a function can be chosen for the rewrite. We define the function *AMatchAlt*, that determines whether an alternative matches:

AMatchAlt (g,r)	=	AMatchArgs (args(g),args(p))	if root(g) = root(p)
		NoMatch	otherwise

Alternatives that are below an alternative that matches with a TotalMatch or a BotMatch can be ignored for the rewriting. That is, the $result_{i_j}$ in the definition of *ARewrite* are the results of the rewrites up to the first alternative that gives a NoMatch or TotalMatch. Because of the presence of unions it might be possible that an alternative can match in different ways. In practice, this means that the variables in the pattern must be bound in various ways.

We note that the new abstract matching algorithm is quite precise. However, it still can be made more accurate. The algorithm becomes much more complex in this case. An example of loss of information with the above definition is the following. Consider the function:

```
F Nil (Cons a b)  → ...
F x y             → ...
```

Then F Top Bot gives a PartialMatch on the first alternative. So, both alternatives are chosen. However, it is easy to see that in this case only the second one is needed: if this value would ever match the first argument pattern (Nil), then it would not terminate.

Now, we have a simple interpretation of NoMatch, BotMatch, PartialMatch and TotalMatch.

LEMMA **9.2.1** $\forall g, g' \in Graph$,

$$\begin{array}{lcll} AMatch(\#(g), \#(g')) & = & NoMatch & \Rightarrow \neg Match(g, g') \\ AMatch(\#(g), \#(g')) & = & BotMatch & \Rightarrow Match(g, g') \text{ diverges} \\ AMatch(\#(g), \#(g')) & = & TotalMatch & \Rightarrow Match(g, g') \\ AMatch(\#(g), \#(g')) & = & TotalMatch & \\ & & \vee PartialMatch & \Leftarrow Match(g, g') \end{array}$$

We have the following correctness result:

PROPOSITION **9.2.2** *AReduce is correct with respect to Reduce, i.e.*

$$\forall g \in Graph[\forall R \in Rule[Reduce(g, R) \in \gamma(AReduce(\#(g), R^{\#}))]]$$

9.3 LIMITS AND META-LIMITS

We can speak of the nth call to Rewrite. Then a *trace* beginning at the state $g \in Graph$, is

$$g = g_0 \rightarrow g_1 \rightarrow \ldots \rightarrow g_n \rightarrow \ldots$$

where g_n is the argument to the $n+1^{\text{th}}$ call to *Rewrite*. For finite traces, we will thus be able to do proofs by induction. Those among the g_is which are the result of the *Rewrite* called from *Reduce*(g, R) will be collected in a set of particular interest: $\{g_{u(i)} \mid i = 0\ldots\}$. From now on, we drop the subscript u in the traces, and will consider only these interesting parts of traces.

We can also define the notion of trace of an abstract computation beginning at state g (an abstract graph):

$$g = g_0 \rightarrow^{\#} g_1 \rightarrow^{\#} \ldots \rightarrow^{\#} g_n \rightarrow^{\#} \ldots$$

where g_n corresponds to the nth call to *ARewrite*.

In fact, we have much more than Proposition 9.2.2; we have a close relationship between the concrete traces and the abstract ones.

LEMMA **9.3.1** *Take $g \in Graph$, $g' \in A\text{-}G$, $g' = \#g$. Consider the concrete and abstract traces:*

$$\begin{array}{l} t : g = g_0 \rightarrow g_1 \rightarrow \ldots \rightarrow g_n \rightarrow \ldots \\ t' : g' = g'_0 \rightarrow^{\#} g'_1 \rightarrow^{\#} \ldots \rightarrow^{\#} g'_n \rightarrow^{\#} \ldots \end{array}$$

then "t is embedded in $\gamma(t')$", i.e.:

$$\forall i \geq 0[\exists j \geq i[g_i \in \gamma(g'_j)]]$$

The same conclusion holds with a much more general hypothesis. It is almost true for all g' such that $g \in \gamma(g')$, up to the restriction for g' having the same "sharing information" as g, defined as:

$$g' \text{ has the same sharing information as } g \Leftrightarrow U(g^a) \in \gamma(g'^a)$$

where the equality is defined up to permutation on the sharing annotation symbols [GH]. We can relax our definition of sharing, to consider the information important only in redexes: the representation of non-redex parts of a graph will obviously not have any influence on the trace of its reduction.

An implication of Lemma 9.3.1 is that we need to consider possibly infinite abstract traces, and infer the desired properties from abstract "limit" values. The implementation will obviously have to approximate such values.

Since we have a finite and deterministic way to construct traces and we always construct them from a regular set of states, we always get a kind of regularity in the trace.

DEFINITION **9.3.2** *Suppose we have an infinite abstract trace:*

$$t' : g'_0 \rightarrow^{\#} g'_1 \rightarrow^{\#} \ldots \rightarrow^{\#} g'_n \rightarrow^{\#} \ldots$$

and an abstract graph g', such that:

$$\forall g \in Graph[\forall j \geq 0[(g \in \gamma(g'_j)) \Rightarrow g \in \gamma(g')]]$$

then g' is called an upper limit *of t'. The least one is called the* limit.

Let $F(g) = g \sqcup g'$, where g' is such that $g \rightarrow^{\#} g' \rightarrow^{\#} \ldots$ is the abstract trace beginning at g. Then the limit of a trace beginning at g is just the least fixed point of F above g. (which can be computed using a widening operator [CC77]). Then we have:

LEMMA **9.3.3** *The limit of an abstract trace t' represents the finite concrete traces embedded in $\gamma(t')$, that is, if $g \in Graph$ such that it has a finite concrete trace:*

$$t : g = g_0 \rightarrow g_1 \rightarrow \ldots \rightarrow g_n,$$

$g' \in A\text{-}G$ such that $g \in \gamma(g')$ and g' has the same sharing information as g, l is the limit of the abstract trace beginning at g' then $g_n \in \gamma(l)$.

As Ω belongs to $\gamma(l)$, the limit represents also the infinite concrete traces embedded in $\gamma(t')$. Now, Proposition 9.2.2 can be restated for $AReduce^{\infty}(g, R^{\#})$, defined as an upper limit of the abstract trace beginning at state g, if it is infinite, or equal to $AReduce(g, R^{\#})$ if it is finite.

PROPOSITION **9.3.4** *$\forall g \in Graph.\forall g' \in A\text{-}G$ such that g' has the same sharing information as $g.\forall R \in Rule$.*

$$(g \in \gamma(g') \Rightarrow Reduce(g, R) \in \gamma(AReduce^{\infty}(g', R^{\#})))$$

For example, let List(A) be the graph:

```
x:⟨Nil, Cons A x⟩
```

whose concretization gives all monomorphic lists on base type A, and define the function Length by the rules:

Length Nil x → x
Length (Cons a b) x → Length b (Succ x)

where Cons, Succ and Nil are constructors. The abstract trace beginning at Length List(A) 0 is:

Length List(A) 0 $\rightarrow^{\#}$ ⟨0,Length List(A) (Succ 0)⟩
$\rightarrow^{\#}$ ⟨0,(Succ 0),Length List(A) (Succ (Succ 0)) ⟩
$\rightarrow^{\#}$ ...

then the limit is ⟨y:⟨0,Succ y⟩,Length List(A) x:⟨0,(Succ x)⟩⟩.

Thus we may be unable to detect some strictness information by just applying Proposition 9.3.4, because the abstract evaluation strategy is lazy, and thus a call to an operator may not be evaluated, if it is an argument of a constructor. We certainly can not compare the result of the abstract computation with anything, like *Bot*, to have the information we need in these cases. We have to continue the computation to normal form.

So we have to force evaluation of operators that may appear inside an expression. This will be done by the means of an evaluator E, defined as:

DEFINITION **9.3.5** *Let E be a function from Graph to Graph defined by:*

$$
\begin{array}{lll}
E(g) = g & \text{if } g \in Symbol \text{ and } g \text{ a constructor} \\
E(g) = E(Reduce(g,R)) & \text{if root of } g \text{ is an operator} \\
E(g) = C(E(g_1),\ldots,E(g_n)) & \text{if } g = C(g_1,\ldots,g_n) \text{ and } C \text{ is a constructor}
\end{array}
$$

E is called an unfolding evaluator.

But, because of sharing, E is not well defined: we must say in which order we compute $E(g_i')$. We want also to be able to compute such functions, or at least an approximation of them. Thus, we define formally a new notion of trace, called *meta-trace*, of an algorithm, which may not terminate, to compute it.

Let f be the function from *Graph* × *Graph* to *Graph* × *Graph** (finite sequence of graphs) defined by:

$$
\begin{array}{lll}
f(g,h) = & (g[h{:=}Reduce(h,R)];\ Reduce(h,R)) & \text{if } \neg\text{in\_rnf }(h) \\
 & (g;\ h_1\ldots h_n) & \text{if } h = C(h_1\ldots h_n) \\
 & (g;\ \emptyset) & \text{if h is a Symbol} \\
 & & \text{and a constructor}
\end{array}
$$

Now let F be the function from *Graph* × *Graph** to *Graph* × *Graph** defined by (let h be a subgraph of g):

$$F(g;h_1\ldots h_n) = (fst(x_n);\ x_1 = f(g,h_1), x_2 = f(fst(x_1),\ h_2)\ldots x_n = f(fst(x_{n-1}),h_n))$$
where $fst(g;h_1\ldots h_n) = g$

Now, a meta-trace beginning at state g is the sequence $(F^i(g;g))_{i\geq 0}$. A trace $(g_0;g_0) \longrightarrow \ldots \longrightarrow (g_n;h_1\ldots h_{m_n})$ is a partial meta-trace, unless we have $m_n = 0$ in which case it is a complete (and finite) one, and then we write $g_n = E(g_0)$. It is easy to see that a finite complete meta-trace is a maximal meta-trace (maximal in the sense, maximal number of arrows). Thus, we extend this definition in the case when there is no finite complete meta-trace beginning at (g_0, g_0). The union of all finite meta-traces is a meta-trace of length ω: it will be called an infinite complete meta-trace. We then extend the definition of E to this case: we will say that $E(g) = \Omega$. Finally, we simplify the notation. We write meta-traces as:

$$g = g_0 \longrightarrow g_1 \longrightarrow \ldots \longrightarrow g_n \longrightarrow \ldots$$

where the g_is are $fst(F^i(g;g))$. g_n corresponds intuitively to the state (in *Graph* or *A-G*) in which g is after the nth application of a rule that defines $E()$.

The definition of the meta-traces in the abstract case is similar. We can define an abstract unfolding evaluator, $E^{\#}$, acting on *A-G*, by the same equations, except that we use $AReduce^{\infty}$, instead of *Reduce*, in the second clause and add the following clause for Union:

$$\mathrm{E}^{\#}(\mathrm{g}') \quad = \quad \langle \mathrm{E}^{\#}(\mathrm{g}_1') \ldots \mathrm{E}^{\#}(\mathrm{g}_n') \rangle \quad \text{if } \mathrm{g}' = \langle \mathrm{g}_1' \ldots \mathrm{g}_n' \rangle$$

In the case of Length, the abstract meta-trace is:

```
Length List(A) 0
        ⟶# ⟨y:⟨0,Succ y⟩,Length List(A) x:⟨0,Succ x⟩⟩
        ⟶# ...
```

that is, constant after the second graph.

We define next what kind of infinite meta-traces we can deal with.

DEFINITION **9.3.6** *Let B be the function from Graph to Graph:*

$$\begin{array}{lcll} B(g) & = & \Omega & \textit{if } \neg in\_rnf\ g \\ B(g) & = & g & \textit{if } g \textit{ is a nullary constructor} \\ B(g) & = & C(B(g_1)\ldots B(g_n)) & \textit{if } g = C(g_1 \ldots g_n) \end{array}$$

Similarly, we have $B^{\#}$, from A-G to A-G, by just replacing Ω by Bot.
Then, l is an upper meta-limit *of $E^{\#}(g')$ (for g in A-G), if:*
$\exists T^{\#}$ *a meta-trace of $E^{\#}(g)$: $g' = g'_0 \longrightarrow^{\#} g'_1 \longrightarrow^{\#} \ldots \longrightarrow^{\#} g'_n \longrightarrow^{\#} \ldots$ such that:*
$\forall i[\gamma(B(g'_i)) \subseteq \gamma(l)]$.

We define the meta-limit of $E^{\#}(g')$, denoted by $E^{\#\infty}(g')$, as being the least upper meta-limit of $E^{\#}(g')$.

In the case of Length, $B^{\#}$ of the meta-trace beginning at Length List(A) 0 is Bot and then is constant equal to:

```
y:⟨0,Succ y⟩
```

Thus the meta-limit is y:⟨0,Succ y⟩.

The idea of the operator B is to do some kind of pending analysis [HY86]. But we know that for domains of height n, we have to consider up to n reductions, before deciding if a recursive call can be safely replaced by *Bot*. As we have a domain of infinite height, we collect the information of all "finite" pending analyses. This sequence is similar to the notion of Böhm tree found in the λ-calculus. Then we have:

LEMMA **9.3.7** $\forall g \in \gamma(g')$ *such that g' and g have the same sharing information*[2]*,*
$\forall T$ *meta-trace of $E(g)$:*
$g = g_0 \longrightarrow \ldots \longrightarrow g_n \longrightarrow \ldots$
we have $\forall i[B(g_i) \in \gamma(E^{\#\infty}(g'))]$. Moreover, the normal form (if it exists) of g belongs to $\gamma(E^{\#\infty}(g'))$.

[2] The sharing condition will in fact appear not to be necessary.

We now specialize our discussion to strictness analysis. We will consider two evaluators μ and ν on *Graph*, depending on a set of rules R, and compatible with the functional strategy; that is, evaluators that force evaluation inside some constructors, a bit like E defined above. More precisely:

DEFINITION **9.3.8** *Let C_0 be a subset of Symbol, composed uniquely of constructors. For c in C_0, let I_c be a finite sequence of distinct and non zero integers, bounded by the arity of c (denoted by $a(c)$), and whose length is less or equal than $a(c)$. Then C_0 and $(I_c)_{c\in C_0}$ define an evaluator μ on Graph, "compatible with the functional strategy", given by:*

$$\begin{array}{lll}
\mu(g) & = & \mu(\mathit{Reduce}(g,R)), \text{ if } \neg\text{in_rnf } g, \\
\mu(g) & = & g, \text{ if } g \text{ is a nullary constructor}, \\
\mu(g) & = & C(h_1 \ldots h_n), \\
 & & \text{if } g = C(g_1 \ldots g_n) \text{ where } C \in C_0 \\
 & & \text{and } h_i = \mu(g_i) \text{ if } i \in I_C,\ g_i \text{ otherwise}, \\
\mu(g) & = & g, \text{ otherwise}
\end{array}$$

Notice that the same remark applies to this definition as for Definition 9.3.5 and that E is an instance of the preceding scheme, with C_0 being the set of all constructors, and $I_c = (1, 2, \ldots, a(c))$ for all c in C_0. In a similar way, we can define the abstract version of the evaluator μ, $\#(\mu)$ or simply $\mu^{\#}$.

Such an evaluator corresponds to having constructors with strictness annotations on their arguments. We write $\mu[g] = \perp$ or Ω (*Bot* in the abstract case), if g is a graph with only constructors as nodes (or *Bot*) and if the strictness properties we have added to the constructors imply that g is actually *Bot*. We say also that g "is not preserved" by μ. The evaluator used in an implementation is actually $\mu[\mu(g)]$, written $\mu^*(g)$.

Now, the general notion in which we are interested in is, given two compatible evaluators μ and ν and a function call $F(g_1 \ldots g_i \ldots g_n)$, whether we can safely evaluate g_i by ν, before evaluating the function by μ, in order to compute $\mu(F(g_1 \ldots g_i \ldots g_n))$. Then we have:

PROPOSITION **9.3.9 (Strictness test)**

$$\begin{array}{l}
\mu[E^{\#\infty}(F^{\#}(\sqcup\{g' \mid \nu^{\#}[g'] = \mathit{Bot}\}))] = \mathit{Bot} \quad \Rightarrow \\
(\forall g \in \mathit{Graph}(\nu^*(g) = \perp \Rightarrow \mu^*(F(g)) = \perp))
\end{array}$$

that is,

$$\forall g \in \mathit{Graph}[\mu^*(F(g)) = \mu^*(F(\nu^*(g)))]$$

We will use in particular two instances of the latter proposition. First, let rnf be the evaluator to root normal form, (defined as the evaluator compatible with the functional strategy with C_0 equal to) then:

PROPOSITION **9.3.10 (First and higher order simple strictness test)**

$$E^{\#\infty}(F^{\#}(\mathit{Bot})) = \mathit{Bot} \Rightarrow \mathit{rnf}(F(\perp)) = \perp$$

so: $\mathit{rnf}(F(\mathit{rnf}(x))) = \mathit{rnf}(F(x))$

Second, following Geoffrey Burn [Bur87], we define four evaluators on lists: ξ_0, ξ_1, ξ_2, ξ_3. ξ_0 does no evaluation at all. ξ_1 evaluates to head-normal form. ξ_2 evaluates the spine of the list. ξ_3 evaluates the spine and every Cons cell to head-normal form. ξ_1, ξ_2, ξ_3 are evaluators compatible with the functional strategy and corresponding respectively to a fully lazy Cons, tail strict Cons, and head and tail strict Cons. Now, we have our test:

PROPOSITION **9.3.11 (List strictness test)**

$$\xi_i^*(F(\ldots l \ldots) = \xi_i^*(F(\ldots \xi_j^*(l) \ldots)) \Leftarrow E^{\#\infty}(F^{\#}(List(A) \ldots a(j) \ldots List(A))) \sqsubseteq a(i)$$

(where l, $\xi_j^*(l)$, $a(j)$ are k^{th} arguments of F or $F^{\#}$ and $\sqsubseteq$ is the ordering on A-G introduced in Chapter 10)

Now, we would like to use the information we have derived with these propositions in the computation of the strictness properties of other parts of the program. In order to do this, we put annotations on operators which we know the strictness properties of. We extend Definition 9.3.8, for C_0 containing also some operators $F \ldots$, and adding the rules:

$$\begin{array}{lcl} \mu(g) & = & Reduce(F(h_1 \ldots h_n), R), \\ & & \text{if } g = F(g_1 \ldots g_n) \\ & & \text{where } F \in C_0,\ F \text{ is an operator}, \\ & & \text{and } h_i = \mu(g_i) \neq Bot \text{ if } i \in I_F, g_i \text{ otherwise} \\ \mu(g) & = & Bot \text{ if } g = F(g_1 \ldots g_n) \\ & & \text{where } F \in C_0,\ F \text{ is an operator} \\ & & \text{and } \mu(g_i) = Bot \text{ for some } i \in I_F. \end{array}$$

Then Proposition 9.3.11 can be restated as:

PROPOSITION **9.3.12 (Modular strictness test)**

$$\mu[X^{\#\infty}(F^{\#}(\sqcup\{g' \mid \nu^{\#}[g'] = Bot\}))] = Bot \Rightarrow$$
$$(\forall g \in Graph[\nu^*(g) = \bot \Rightarrow \mu^*(F(g)) = \bot])$$

that is,

$$\forall g \in Graph[\mu^*(F(g)) = \mu^*(F(\nu^*(g)))]$$

where X is any evaluator, compatible with the functional strategy, defined by $C_0 = \{$all constructors $C \ldots$,some operators $F_i\}$, and $I_C = (1 \ldots a(C))$, I_{F_i} = any sequence of integers n_j such that F_i, as defined by the program R, is strict in its n_j^{th} argument.

9.4 PROPERTIES OF META-LIMITS

We now state the following useful properties of meta-limits:

9.4.1 Consistency of meta-limits

This first group of properties express the consistency of the notion of meta-limits with respect to reduction and the various relations between graphs introduced in Chapter

10. The first result means that sharing information is unnecessary. Let $g, g' \in A\text{-}G$. Then:

$$\begin{array}{lll} g \equiv g' & \Rightarrow & E^{\#\infty}(g) \equiv E^{\#\infty}(g') \\ g \sqsubseteq g' & \Rightarrow & E^{\#\infty}(g) \sqsubseteq E^{\#\infty}(g') \\ g \rightarrow g' & \Rightarrow & E^{\#\infty}(g) \sqsubseteq E^{\#\infty}(g') \\ limit(g) = g' & \Rightarrow & E^{\#\infty}(g) \sqsubseteq E^{\#\infty}(g') \end{array}$$

9.4.2 Substitution and meta-limits

Next, we show how meta-limits interact with substitution. We see that each of the above results is still applicable if we consider subgraphs (rather than the whole graph). The first result establishes that it is safe to replace any subgraph by Top. Let $g, g' \in A\text{-}G$, such that $g' = g|n$. Then:

$$E^{\#\infty}(g) \sqsubseteq E^{\#\infty}(g[n := Top])$$

$$\begin{array}{lll} g' \sqsubseteq h & \Rightarrow & E^{\#\infty}(g) \sqsubseteq E^{\#\infty}(g[n := h]) \\ g' \rightarrow h & \Rightarrow & E^{\#\infty}(g) \sqsubseteq E^{\#\infty}(g[n := h]) \\ limit(g') = h & \Rightarrow & E^{\#\infty}(g) \sqsubseteq E^{\#\infty}(g[n := h]) \\ E^{\#\infty}(g') = h & \Rightarrow & E^{\#\infty}(g) \sqsubseteq E^{\#\infty}(g[n := h]) \end{array}$$

9.4.3 Cycle/Bot introduction

Finally, we present two properties which are used extensively in the implementation to force termination of recursive programs. The first result allows the introduction of cycles into the meta-limit, the second is a result that supports the introduction of *Bot* (cf "pending analysis" [HY86]). Let $g, g', h \in A\text{-}G$, such that $g' = h|n$. Then:

$$\begin{array}{lll} g \rightarrow^k h, g' \sqsubseteq g & \Rightarrow & E^{\#\infty}(g) \sqsubseteq E^{\#\infty}(h[n := root(h)]) \\ g \rightarrow^k h, g' \sqsubseteq g, g' \text{ is needed in h} & \Rightarrow & E^{\#\infty}(g) \sqsubseteq Bot \end{array}$$

It is still a conjecture whether the last three properties are true for all functions we can define in Clean. For the moment, it seems that we can only prove them for certain classes of functions, like the class of mutually tail-recursive functions.

9.5 CONCLUSION

In general, it is rather difficult to estimate the practical power of a strictness analysis technique. In theory, often more information can be found than in practice:

- The computational complexity of the analysis can become so poor that only a limited amount of information can be found within the available time. This is a well-known problem in analyzers based upon abstract interpretation, where the domains can grow so big that the fixed point computations become intractable without some approximation techniques.
- Because of the above, implementations often compute an upper approximation of the theoretical ideal.

A good strictness analysis should give good results at least in the theoretical case (otherwise, they can certainly not be derived in practice). An implementation should be fast, and stay so if it is extended in some way. That is, changes should be easy to make, but in such a way that the good properties are not lost.

It is useful to consider the relative power of abstract reduction versus the more conventional approaches to strictness analysis. Consider the following example:

```
F x                →   Head (Cons x Nil)
Head (Cons x r)    →   x
```

By abstract reduction it is easily shown that F is strict in its argument. However, in abstract interpretation it is not usual to distinguish Nil from any other total list (for example see Wadler's 4-point domain [Bur87]); consequently, we lose the ability to detect such strictness. On the other hand, with the current use of abstract reduction, it is not possible to detect certain forms of context-sensitive [Bur87] strictness. This is critical when analysing higher-order functions and thus needs further investigation.

REFERENCES

[Bur87] G.L. Burn. *Abstract Interpretation and the Parallel Evaluation of Functional Languages*. PhD thesis, Imperial College, 1987.

[BvEG+87] H.P. Barendregt, M.C.J.D. van Eekelen, J.R.W. Glauert, J.R. Kennaway, M.J. Plasmeijer, and M.R. Sleep. Term graph rewriting. In *PARLE '87 (Volume II)*, Springer-Verlag, Lecture Notes in Computer Science 259, pp. 141–158, 1987.

[CC77] P. Cousot and R. Cousot. Abstract interpretation: A unified lattice model for static analysis of programs by construction of approximations of fixed points. In *4th POPL*, pp. 238–252, 1977.

[GH] E. Goubault and C. L. Hankin. A lattice for the abstract interpretation of term graph rewriting systems. In this volume.

[HY86] P. Hudak and J. Young. Finding fixpoints on function spaces. Manuscript, 1986.

[Nöc90] E.G.J.M.H. Nöcker. Strictness analysis based on abstract reduction. In *Proceedings of the Second International Workshop on Implementation of Functional Languages on Parallel Architectures*, pp. 297–321. University of Nijmegen Technical Report 90-16, 1990.

[NSvEP91] E.G.J.M.H. Nöcker, J.E.W. Smetsers, M.C.J.D. van Eekelen, and M.J. Plasmeijer. Concurrent Clean. In *PARLE '91 (Volume II)*, pp. 202–219. Springer-Verlag, Lecture Notes in Computer Science 506, 1991.

10

A Lattice for the Abstract Interpretation of Term Graph Rewriting Systems

E. Goubault and C. L. Hankin

10.1 INTRODUCTION

10.1.1 Abstract interpretation

Abstract interpretation is a semantics-based technique for static program analysis. By *static*, we mean that the analysis occurs at "compile-time". A program is interpreted using simple data which expose particular run-time properties. The results of the analysis might be used to:

- optimize the code produced from the program in some way
- verify that the program meets some "specification"
- verify that the program is free from certain kinds of bugs.

The importance of the *semantics-based* approach is that the results of the analysis can be proved to be an accurate reflection of the program's real behavior. We cannot expect to get precise information about the program behavior since almost any interesting question is reducible to known undecidable questions. Consequently the question of correctness of an abstract interpretation becomes an issue of *safety*: the abstract description of the program's behavior must include its true behavior.

The basic components of an abstract interpretation are:

A lattice of abstract values:
The program is executed using *abstract* data which enables us to capture the properties of interest. For technical reasons (see below), it is convenient if the abstract

Term Graph Rewriting: Theory and Practice.
Eds. Ronan Sleep, Rinus Plasmeijer and Marko van Eekelen.

values form a (complete) lattice. For example to detect strictness for first-order functions, two data values are all that is required ($\{0,1\}$, $0 \sqsubseteq 1$) [Myc81] - 0 to represent non-termination and 1 to represent possible termination.

Interpretations for operators:

Each of the operators in the program is interpreted using a non-standard interpretation. For example, in strictness analysis, + is given the interpretation $\wedge$ (meet) - this has the effect of propagating zeros, which accurately reflects that the result is undefined if either of the arguments is.

Correctness:

A variety of different approaches to showing correctness (safety) may be found in the literature. A standard approach [CC77] is to show that the abstract interpretation safely abstracts the *collecting* semantics. The collecting semantics may be seen as the most precise (but non-computable) abstract interpretation. While the standard semantics usually focuses on the input/output behavior of a program, the collecting semantics collects information about intensional behavior at certain selected *program points*. Typically, the program points may correspond to arcs in the flowchart representation of the program and the information collected at each point might be the set of states that exist when program execution reaches that point. Correctness is ensured by establishing a *Galois connection* (see later) between the collecting semantics domain and the abstract lattice and showing that the abstract operators are upper approximations of the operators induced by the Galois connection [CC77]. Completeness of the abstract lattice is important to ensure that least fixed points exist.

10.1.2 Term graphs

We will use the same context-free grammar as [BvEG+87] to denote term graphs:

```
graph  :=  node |
           node + graph
node   :=  A(node,...,node) |
           x |
           x: A(node,...node)
```

where A ranges over set of symbols, Symbol, and x ranges over a set of node identifiers, disjoint from Symbol. Any node identifier x which occurs in a graph must occur exactly once in the context:

x: A(node,...,node)

Node identifiers are represented by tokens beginning with a lower-case letter. We abbreviate A() to A.

A *Term Graph Program* is a sequence of left/right-oriented equations (rewrite rules) and an initial graph. See [BvEG+87] for details of the rewriting process; in that paper a graph rewrite is factored into four steps:

a. A redex is selected according to some *strategy*.
b. An instance of the right-hand side of the appropriate rule, with variables instantiated, is *built*.

c. Pointers to the root of the redex are *redirected* to the root of the instance.
d. Any nodes which are no longer accessible from the root of the graph are *garbage collected.*

In [Han91], we establish a general framework for the abstract interpretation of Term Graph Programs. In this setting, we identify rules with program points and collect information about the redexes which the rule has been used to reduce. An abstract interpretation requires the definition of a suitable lattice and the definition of safe interpretations for the four operators listed above. In [Han91], graphs were abstracted by sets of triples and the lattice structure was the usual powerset construction; for strictness analysis, we want to retain the graph structure of objects in the abstract lattice and our programme in this chapter is to establish an appropriate lattice.

10.1.3 Our approach

Thus our problem is to define a lattice of abstract graphs and to show how its elements can be related to sets of term graphs. There is a substantial literature, for example [Cou83], concerning orderings on trees. In the context of term graphs, the situation is complicated by the presence of sharing and cycles. Our approach, however is to try to use as much of the existing theory as possible.

[BvEG$^+$87] introduce an unravelling function, U, which maps any term graph into some, possibly infinite, regular tree. We will make extensive use of this function in the following.

Whenever we introduce a relation on graphs, we start by defining it for finite trees. This is then extended to infinite trees using standard techniques [Cou83], based on the observation that the infinite trees are generated from the left-closed sets of their finite approximants. Finally, we define the related term graph relation via the unravelling function (and its "inverse").

10.1.4 Summary

Our main motivation for this work was to provide a correctness proof for the strictness analyser proposed by Nöcker [Nöc90]. This chapter should be read in conjunction with Chapter 13 which contains a detailed consideration of the algorithm employed in [Nöc90].

In the next section we give a detailed account of our lattice construction. While the construction was inspired by [Nöc90], the techniques used are general and should be useful for a wide range of different static analyses of term graphs.

In section 3, we define a Galois connection between our abstract lattice and the powerset of term graphs. We conclude in section 4.

10.2 THE LATTICE OF ABSTRACT GRAPHS

We assume we have a special symbol Ω (used to represent non termination), of arity 0, in Symbol.

Tree (resp. F-Tree) is the set of (resp. finite) trees with nodes belonging to Symbol, and Graph, the set of finite graphs built on Symbol. The unravelling function U

[BvEG+87], maps Graph to a subset of Tree, consisting of "regular trees" in the sense of [Cou83].

Abstract graphs are built from:

$$\text{Symbol}^{\#} = \{\text{F}^{\#} \mid \text{F} \in \text{Symbol}, \text{F} \neq \Omega\} \cup \{\text{Bot, Top, Union}\}$$

(Bot and Top of arity 0, Union of arity 2); A-Tree (resp. FA-Tree), is the set of (resp. finite) trees with nodes belonging to Symbol$^{\#}$,"(resp. finite) abstract trees", and A-Graph, the set of finite graphs on Symbol$^{\#}$,"abstract graphs". As for concrete graphs, we have a map U$^{\#}$, between abstract graphs and regular abstract trees. Finally, we will make use of the function #, which is defined as:

$$\begin{array}{lcl} \#\text{: Symbol} \rightarrow \text{Symbol}^{\#} \\ \#\,\text{F} & = & \text{F}^{\#} \\ \#\,\Omega & = & \text{Bot} \end{array}$$

which is extended to Graph→A-Graph in an obvious way (node by node).

In the abstract interpretation framework, we need to define two complete lattices, an abstract and a concrete one, related by a Galois connection.

The concrete lattice will be $\wp$(Graph), ordered by set inclusion, $\subseteq$. It will represent sets of computations.

In the abstract lattice, whose carrier set is a subset of A-Graph, we want the Union node to represent a union of two graphs, Top to represent Graph, and Bot to represent $\{\Omega\}$, together with $\sqsubseteq$, being the counterpart of $\subseteq$. We could well define it as being an inverse image of some complete sublattice of $\wp$(Graph) but we would not be able to perform computations in such a lattice. Therefore, we describe this lattice in a purely syntactic way. Beginning by defining $\sqsubseteq$ on FA-Tree (on which we have structural induction) as $\sqsubseteq_t$, we will extend it to A-Tree, using the notion of admissible predicate [MNV72], and then transport the structure to A-Graph via the unravelling function.

Definition 10.2.1 *Let $\leq_t$ be the inductively defined, reflexive relation on FA-Tree×FA-Tree by :*
$\forall A[Bot \leq_t A \leq_t Top]$
$\forall A,B[A \leq_t Union(A,B)$ & $B \leq_t Union(A,B)]$
$\forall C[] [\forall A,B[A \leq_t B \Rightarrow C[A] \leq_t C[B]]]$
(where C[] is a context and the trees are written in the form of terms).

Then (FA-Tree,$\leq_t$) is a partially ordered set but is not a lattice in general. For example, if Symbol consists of two 0-ary functions A and B, then Union(A,B) and Union(B,A) are two incomparable minimal upper bounds of A and B. Our intuition is that they denote the same element and thus we are led to add several identities to our partially ordered set.

Definition 10.2.2 *Let $\equiv$ be the congruence defined on FA-Tree×FA-Tree by:*

a. *$\forall A,B,F[][Union(F[A],F[B]) \equiv F[Union(A,B)]]$*

b. Union is commutative:
$\forall A,B[Union(A,B) \equiv Union(B,A)]$

c. Union is associative:
$\forall A,B,C[Union(Union(A,B),C) \equiv Union(A,Union(B,C))]$
d. Union is idempotent
$\forall A[Union(A,A) \equiv A]$
e. Bot is the unit for Union
$\forall A[Union(A,Bot) \equiv A]$
f. Top is the zero for Union
$\forall A[Union(A,Top) \equiv Top]$

Let FA-T be the quotient of FA-Tree by $\equiv$. We write $\sqsubseteq_t$ for the relation induced by the one on FA-Tree, which is defined as:

$$x \sqsubseteq_t y \Leftrightarrow (\forall A\in x[\exists B\in y[A \leq_t B]] \ \&\ \forall B\in y[\exists A\in x[A \leq_t B]])$$

Now we have,

LEMMA **10.2.3** *$(FA\text{-}T,\sqsubseteq_t)$ is an upper semi-lattice with*
$[A]_\equiv \sqcup [B]_\equiv = [Union(A,B)]_\equiv$

We now extend these properties to A-Tree. First of all, we define what it means for a tree to be an approximation of an infinite tree.

DEFINITION **10.2.4** *Let ϵ be the reflexive relation defined on Tree$\times$Tree by:*
$\forall M[\Omega\ \epsilon\ M]$
$\forall C[][\forall M,N[M\ \epsilon\ N \Rightarrow C[M]\ \epsilon\ C[N]]]$
We define a similar reflexive relation, still called ϵ, on A-Tree$\times$A-Tree by:
$\forall M[Bot\ \epsilon\ M]$
$\forall C[][\forall M,N[M\ \epsilon\ N \Rightarrow C[M]\ \epsilon\ C[N]]]$

Thus, if M and N are in A-Tree and M ϵ N, then M is the same as N except that at some nodes where M has Bot, N has a non-Bot subtree. Then we have:

LEMMA **10.2.5** *ϵ is a partial order. Tree (resp. A-Tree) is isomorphic to the ϵ-ideal completion of F-Tree (resp. FA-Tree).*

It can be shown that every tree t is the ϵ-upper-bound of some chain of finite trees, called a *development* of t.

LEMMA **10.2.6** *Let P be a predicate, defined on finite trees, such that P is a homomorphism between the ordered structures (F-Tree,ϵ) and $\{tt,ff\}$ with the usual ordering. There is a unique extension of P to an admissible predicate P^*, defined on all trees, and having the same truth value as P on finite trees.*

Now, let A-T be A-Tree$/_\equiv$ and P(x,y) = 'x $\sqsubseteq_t$ y' defined on FA-Tree$\times$FA-Tree. Since:

$$x\ \epsilon\ y \Rightarrow P(x,y)$$

we can apply lemma 10.2.6 twice. We still write x $\sqsubseteq_t$ y for $P^*(x,y)$. It is not hard to see that $\sqsubseteq_t$ is a partial order on A-T.

We now define an order for abstract graphs.

Figure 10.1

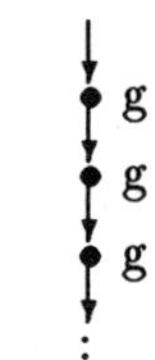

Figure 10.2

DEFINITION **10.2.7** *Let* $\sqsubseteq$ *be the relation defined on A-Graph×A-Graph by*
$\forall g, g' [g \sqsubseteq g' \Leftrightarrow [U^{\#}(g)]_{\equiv} \sqsubseteq_t [U^{\#}(g')]_{\equiv}]$

This is a pre-order; for example, consider the two graphs in Figure 10.1, both of which unravel to the same infinite tree shown in Figure 10.2, but they are clearly not identical. Let $\approx$ be the equivalence relation induced by $\sqsubseteq$, and (A-G,$\sqsubseteq$) be, by an abuse of notation, (A-Graph/$_\approx$,$\sqsubseteq$/$_\approx$). Then,

LEMMA **10.2.8** *(A-G,*$\sqsubseteq$*) is an upper semi-lattice with:*
$\perp = [Bot]_\approx$
$\top = [Top]_\approx$
$[g]_\approx \sqcup [g']_\approx = \{h \mid U^{\#}(h) \in [Union(U^{\#}(g), U^{\#}(g'))]_{\equiv}\}$

From now on, we will consider only regular trees, and abstract regular trees. Let us still call their collection Tree and A-Tree. U (resp. $U^{\#}$) is surjective now. Thus we have an inverse U^{-1}(resp. $U^{\#-1}$) from Trees (resp. A-Trees) to Graph (resp. A-Graph) modulo tree equivalency [BvEG+87]. Tree equivalency is obviously included in $\approx$. Therefore, lemma 10.2.8 says that the least upper bound in A-G is :
$[g]_\approx \sqcup [g']_\approx = [U^{\#-1}(\mathrm{Union}(U^{\#}(g), U^{\#}(g')))]_\approx$
However, we still do not have a complete lattice in general, even if, as we will do from now on, we suppose that Symbol$^{\#}$ is finite. Consider for example the following sequence of contexts:

$$\begin{array}{lcl} g_0[] & = & (a[]) \\ g_1[] & = & (a(a[])) \\ g_2[] & = & (a(a(b[]))) \\ & & \ldots \\ g_n[] & = & g_{n-1}[(b[])] \text{ if n is prime} \\ & & g_{n-1}[(a[])] \text{ otherwise.} \\ & & \ldots \end{array}$$

where a and b are symbols with arity one. Then u = $(g_n[Bot])_{n\geq 0}$ is an ascending sequence, and v = $(g_n[Top])_{n\geq 0}$ is a descending sequence, composed of upper bounds of the first one. One can prove, considering v, that the only possible candidate for the least upper bound (lub) of u is a graph whose unravelling is the infinite tree with bs at all prime depths, and a otherwise. The non-regularity of this tree makes it impossible to find a finite graph representing it. Thus we have a sequence which does not have any lub in our domain.

We could complete A-G but we will surely obtain an isomorphic copy of $\wp$(Graph): such a lattice is too big for practical use. Instead, we will extract from A-G a family of complete sublattices A-G^d_M, for M≥1, inspired by our last example. Notice that there are many other interesting complete subsets of A-G, which may not be sub-semi-upper-lattices of A-G[1]. In particular, any algorithm which uses abstract values lying in such a set could be proved correct by the same methods that we use in [vEGHN].

Definition **10.2.9** *Let s ∈ Symbol$^\#$ ∪ {Bot, Top}. We define depth(s,t), "the maximal depth of symbol s in term t", for t ∈ FA-Tree, by induction, as:*

$$\begin{array}{lcl} depth(s,t) & = & 1 \text{ if } t = s \\ depth(s,t) & = & 0 \text{ if } t \in Symbol^\# \cup \{Bot, Top\}, t \neq s \\ depth(s,F^\#(t_1,\ldots,t_n)) & = & 1 + max\{depth(s,t_i), i=1\ldots n\} \text{ if } s = F^\# \\ depth(s,F^\#(t_1,\ldots,t_n)) & = & 1 + max\{depth(s,t_i), i=1\ldots n\} \\ & & \quad \text{if } depth(s,t_i)>0 \text{ for some } i, \\ & & 0, \text{ otherwise} \\ depth(s, Union(t_1,t_2)) & = & max\{depth(s,t_1), depth(s,t_2)\} \end{array}$$

By extension on A-Tree, for s ≠ Bot:

$$depth(s,t) \quad = \quad max\{depth(s,t') \mid t' \in t\} \text{ (where the result may be infinite)}$$

We notice that for s = Top, t ≡ t′ ⇒ depth(Top,t) = depth(Top,t′), then we can now define $depth_{Top}$, "depth of Top", on A-G, by:

$depth_{Top}(g) = depth(Top, U^\#(g))$

and, finally, define A-G_M by:

A-G_M = {g | g ∈ A-G and $depth_{Top}(g) \leq M$}

The example we have given shows quite clearly, that not only Top, but also anything which can play the role of a local Top must have a similar restriction on its use. By local Top, we mean graphs such as:

x: Union((a x),(b x))

[1] We can take any structure which can be embedded, as an ordered set, in A-G.

whose concretization can contain a non-regular (infinite) tree; in this case, for instance, the tree in which b occurs at each prime depth. However, we cannot easily define the depth of such a compound expression. We choose simply not to allow such graphs:

x ∈ $A\text{-}G^d_M$ ⇔
x ∈ $A\text{-}G_M$ and for any Union node in x,
that is x = ...Union(x_1,x_2) ..., if from some subgraph of x_1,
there is a path to x_2 then there is no path from any subgraph
of x_2 to x_1 and vice versa.

We call the elements of $A\text{-}G^d_M$ deterministic (that is the reason for the superscript d), because in the terminology of regular expressions, we are forbidding objects containing $(f+g)^*$.

By these two restrictions, on the depth of Tops and determinism, we have ensured that there are no infinitely descending chains of the form used in the example. Now we have the result we want:

PROPOSITION **10.2.10** *($A\text{-}G^d_M$,⊑), $M \geq 1$, is a complete sublattice of (A-G,⊑)*

We conjecture that every complete sublattice of (A-G,⊑) is included in $A\text{-}G^d_M$, for some $M \geq 1$.

This domain gives a good account of the properties of the graphs used in [Nöc90]. We just list two of them, which can be inferred directly from the construction of our lattice (note that they hold already in A-G):

$<x_1,\ldots,x_n> \approx <\sigma(x_1,\ldots,x_n)>$[2]
where σ is any permutation on n elements

and

$x{:}<x,x_1,\ldots,x_n> \approx <x_1,\ldots,x_n>$

10.3 RELATING ABSTRACT GRAPHS TO THE REAL WORLD

We start by recalling the definition of a Galois connection:

DEFINITION **10.3.1 (Galois Connection)**
Let $(L, \sqsubseteq_L)$ and $(M, \sqsubseteq_M)$ be partially ordered sets. Then (α, γ) is a Galois connection *iff $\alpha \in L \rightarrow M$ and $\gamma \in M \rightarrow L$ are functions such that:*

$$\forall x \in L, y \in M[\alpha(x) \sqsubseteq_M y \Leftrightarrow x \sqsubseteq_L \gamma(y)]$$

In the setting of abstract interpretation, α is often called an abstraction *map and γ a* concretization *map.*

We define a Galois connection between A-G and ℘(Graph). We follow the same approach as in section 10.2; starting with finite trees, we extend the definition to trees and thence to graphs.

DEFINITION **10.3.2** *Let γ_{tree}: FA-Tree→ ℘(Tree) be inductively defined by:*

[2] We follow [Nöc90] by writing $<x_1,\ldots,x_n>$ for Union(x_1,Union(x_2,Union($\ldots$,Union(x_{n-1},x_n))))

$$
\begin{aligned}
\gamma_{tree}(Bot) &= \{\Omega\}\\
\gamma_{tree}(Top) &= Tree\\
\gamma_{tree}(F^{\#}(a_1,\ldots,a_n)) &= \{F(t_1,\ldots,t_n) \mid t_i \in \gamma_{tree}(a_i)\} \cup \{\Omega\}\\
\gamma_{tree}(Union(A,B)) &= \gamma_{tree}(A) \cup \gamma_{tree}(B)
\end{aligned}
$$

γ_{tree} is naturally extended to A-Tree:

$$\gamma_{tree}(x) = \bigcup_i \gamma_{tree}(x_i) \text{ where } (x_i)_i \text{ is the development of x}$$

which is valid because $x \epsilon y \Rightarrow \gamma_{tree}(x) \subseteq \gamma_{tree}(y)$.

Now, we notice that γ_{tree} is also well behaved with respect to $\equiv$:
$\forall A,B[A \equiv B \Rightarrow \gamma_{tree}(A) = \gamma_{tree}(B)]$
that is γ_{tree} naturally induces a map, also called γ_{tree}, from A-T to $\wp$(Tree).

DEFINITION **10.3.3** *Let* γ:*A-Graph*$\rightarrow \wp$*(Graph) be defined by:*
$\forall g[\gamma(g) = U^{-1}(\gamma_{tree}(U^{\#}(g)))]$

This definition can be extended to γ:A-G$\rightarrow \wp$(Graph) by

$$\gamma([g]_{\approx}) = U^{-1}(\gamma_{tree}(U^{\#}([g]_{\approx}))) = U^{-1}(\gamma_{tree}(U^{\#}(g)))$$

Define now α:$\wp$(Graph)$\rightarrow$A-G^d_M by

$$\forall S[\alpha(S) = \bigsqcup [U^{\#-1}(\#(U(S)))]_{\approx}$$

(where U and $U^{\#-1}$ are extended to powersets in the obvious way)

PROPOSITION **10.3.4** *(α,γ) is a Galois connection between $\wp$(Graph) and A-G^d_M, and* $\alpha \circ \gamma = id_{A-G^d_M}$[3].

10.4 CONCLUSION/DISCUSSION

Our construction makes heavy use of equivalences; in practice the abstract reduction mechanism uses particular representatives. Let $\cong$ denote tree-equivalency between elements of Graph, $\approx$ between elements of A-G^d_M. We can choose a particular representative, "canonical form", in the equivalence class of g (in Graph or in A-G^d_M) as follows:

a. if g $\in$ Graph, then

- $g \cong s \in$ Symbol
- $g \cong C(g_1,\ldots,g_n)$, C $\in$ Symbol, and the g_is can be chosen such that the shared nodes between them, are the same nodes shared in g.

b. if g $\in$ A-G^d_M, then

- $g \approx s \in$ Symbol$^{\#}$
- $g \approx C(g_1,\ldots,g_n)$, C $\in$ Symbol$^{\#}$ - {Union} and the g_is can be chosen such that the shared nodes between them, are the same nodes shared in g

[3] Mycroft uses the term *exactly adjoined pair* to refer to a Galois connection which satisfies this equality. Exact adjointness intuitively means that there are no redundant abstract values.

- $g \approx \text{Union}(g_1,g_2)$, where the roots of the canonical forms of g_1 and g_2 are not the same node.

We can also make apparent the sharing of symbols in our construction, even if at first glance, it seems that we have removed all this sharing information by unravelling graphs. The process is quite simple, it just consists in giving different names to the same labels that are on different nodes (we say that this name is not shared), by adding an annotations to labels. This amounts to adding some new symbols to Symbol; we denote the annotated version of a graph g by g^a.

A definition of a function, say f, like:

$$\begin{array}{lll} f(s) & = & \ldots\text{if s is a symbol} \\ f(C(g_1,\ldots,g_n)) & = & \ldots f(g_i)\ldots\text{if } C(g_1,\ldots,g_n) \text{ is a canonical form} \\ f(\text{Union}(g_1,g_2)) & = & \ldots f(g_1)\ldots f(g_2)\ldots\text{if Union}(g_1,g_2) \text{ is in canonical form} \end{array}$$

makes sense in the following way: it defines a function f on finite trees, by induction, in which the sharing information is artificially constructed (annotation on shared symbols, as above), then on infinite ones, by computing a limit, then on graphs. Thus if f is sensitive to the sharing information then we can still define it using the technical tools we have developed.

The constraints on elements of $A\text{-}G^d_M$ appear to be quite severe; the motivation is purely technical and it may appear that the constraints are unnecessary in practice. However, M can be seen as a parameter of the abstract interpretation which controls the accuracy of the analysis. Such parameterization is not uncommon in the abstract interpretation literature. For a certain class of properties, P, we could find an M that is big enough to ensure that the abstract computation to decide P(F), for some function F under analysis, would not lose any information in the abstract lattice.

REFERENCES

[BvEG+87] H.P. Barendregt, M.C.J.D. van Eekelen, J.R.W. Glauert, J.R. Kennaway, M.J. Plasmeijer, and M.R. Sleep. Term graph rewriting. In *PARLE '87 (Volume II)*, Springer-Verlag, Lecture Notes in Computer Science 259, pp. 141–158, 1987.

[CC77] P. Cousot and R. Cousot. Abstract interpretation: A unified lattice model for static analysis of programs by construction of approximations of fixed points. In *4th POPL*, pp. 238–252, 1977.

[Cou83] B. Courcelle. Fundamental properties of infinite trees. *Theoretical Computer Science*, **25**, pp. 95–169, 1983.

[Han91] C. Hankin. Static analysis of term graph rewriting systems. In *PARLE '91 (Volume II)*, Springer-Verlag, Lecture Notes in Computer Science 506, pp. 367–384, 1991.

[MNV72] Z. Manna, S. Ness, and J. Vuillemin. Inductive methods for proving properties of programs. In *Proceedings of the ACM Conference*, 1972.

[Myc81] A. Mycroft. *Abstract Interpretation and Optimising Transformations for Applicative Programs.* PhD thesis, University of Edinburgh, 1981.

[Nöc90] E.G.J.M.H. Nöcker. Strictness analysis based on abstract reduction. In *Proceedings of the Second International Workshop on Implementation of Functional Languages on Parallel Architectures*, pp. 297–321. University of Nijmegen Technical Report 90-16, 1990.

[vEGHN] M.C.J.D. van Eekelen, E. Goubault, C.L. Hankin, and E.G.J.M.H. Nöcker. Abstract reduction: Towards a theory via abstract interpretation. In this volume.

11

Event Structures and Orthogonal Term Graph Rewriting

J.R. Kennaway, J.W. Klop, M.R. Sleep and F.J. de Vries

11.1 INTRODUCTION

Several authors have hinted at a connection between transition systems such as are used to describe concurrency, and the reduction sequences that arise in term rewriting and Lambda calculus ([HL91, Sta89], and others). Here we make such a connection precise in the context of term graph rewriting. We construct for every normalizable term graph in an orthogonal term graph rewrite system, an elementary event structure. The events of this structure correspond to the different possible reduction steps that are required to reduce the term graph to normal form. The elements of the associated domain correspond to the possible needed reduction sequences which begin from the given term graph.

Similar connections have been remarked on for orthogonal term rewriting and Lambda calculus, but in those contexts, the possibility of one reduction duplicating another redex makes it more complicated to derive any sort of event structure, and the resulting events are less closely related to physical computations.

In proving the results of this chapter, we found the category-theoretic definition of graph rewriting which we introduced in [Ken91] very useful in avoiding irrelevant technicalities. In particular, it casts further light on the physical meaning of Lévy's equivalence relation on reduction sequences, which definitions in terms of tiling diagrams or permutation of reduction steps fail to do. Concrete definitions such as those of [Sta80, BvEG+87] would make these proofs much more complicated, and restrict

Term Graph Rewriting: Theory and Practice.
Eds. Ronan Sleep, Rinus Plasmeijer and Marko van Eekelen.

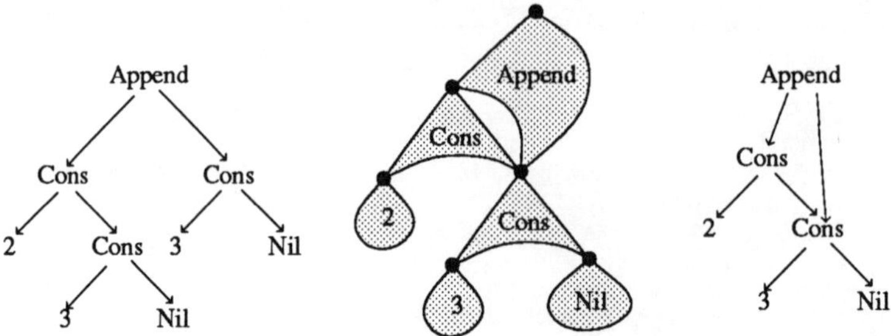

Figure 11.1 Terms and term graphs

them to one particular form of graph, while the more abstract definition may have application to other categories of graphs.

11.2 TERM GRAPH REWRITING

By term graph rewriting we mean, informally, one of the usual methods of implementing rewrite rules such as appear in functional languages such as ML or Miranda. The essential feature is that when a rewrite rule is applied whose right-hand side contains multiple occurrences of a free variable, the corresponding subterm of the expression being evaluated is not duplicated; instead multiple pointers are created to the original copy. The expression is therefore no longer a string or a tree, but a graph of a particular sort: a term graph. It is technically convenient to represent these as hypergraphs—that is, graphs in which each edge may have any positive number of vertexes.

DEFINITION **11.2.1** *Given a set Σ of function symbols, each having some arity (a non-negative integer), a* term graph *over Σ consists of a tuple (N, E, str), where N and E are sets, and str (structure) is a function from E to $\Sigma \times N \times N^*$. If $str(e) = (F, n, s)$, then the* vertexes *of e are n and the members of s. n is the* principal *vertex of e. (N, E, str) is subject to the following conditions:*

a. If $str(e) = (F, n, s)$ then the arity of F is the length of s.
b. Distinct hyperedges have distinct principal vertexes.

A node is empty *if it is not the principal vertex of some hyperedge. A graph is* closed *if it contains no empty nodes. We use empty nodes to represent free variables. While a separate alphabet of variable symbols is a convenient means of writing term graphs in textual form, it is only a notational device and not a part of the underlying model.*

A rooted *term graph is a graph together with one of its nodes. It is* garbage-free *if every node in the graph is accessible from the root. Accessibility is defined thus: n' is accessible from n if either $n = n'$, or $str(n) = (F, n'', s)$, and n' is accessible from n'' or from some member of s.*

Figure 11.1 illustrates a term represented as a term graph. On the left is the term shown as a tree. In the middle is a visual representation of the hypergraph, where each of the shaded ares is a hyperedge. On the right is an equivalent representation,

Term graph rewrite rule: $Append(Cons(x,y),z) \rightarrow Cons(x, Append(y,z))$

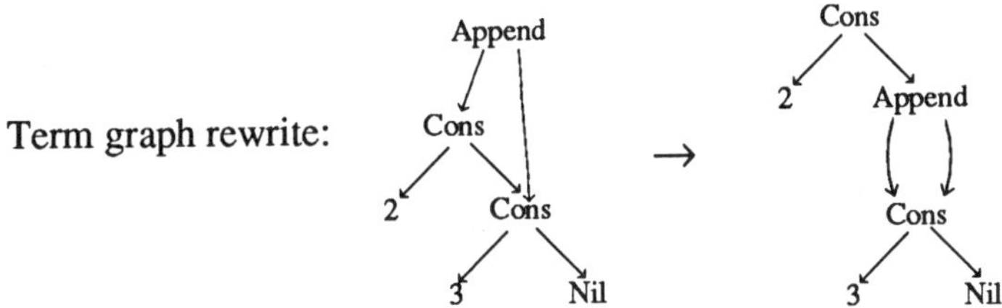

Figure 11.2 Term graph rewrite rule and rewrite

designed for its similarity to the tree picture. Instead of drawing the hyperedges explicitly, the function symbol of each hyperedge is attached to its principal vertex, from which arrows proceed to all the other vertexes of the hyperedge. In this example, the term graph has multiple references to the subgraph $Cons(3, Nil)$ where the term has multiple occurences of that subterm. However, a hypergraph is allowed to contain distinct isomorphic subgraphs—we do not require maximal sharing as is done e.g. in [HP88].

Formal definitions of term graph rewriting have appeared in [Sta80, BvEG$^+$87, Ken91]. We shall here take the notion to be sufficiently intuitive to require no further explanation beyond figures 11.1 and 11.2. However, the particular formalization which we gave in [Ken91] making use of category theory turns out to greatly simplify certain of the concepts and technical arguments which we shall later require, and we shall briefly describe this.

We do not require any advanced concepts of category theory, just the basic notions of category, functor, subobject, limit and colimit (the only limits and colimits we need are pullbacks and pushouts). The hypergraphs we have defined form a category when a notion of homomorphism is given. This notion is the obvious one: a mapping of the nodes and edges of one graph to another which preserves function symbols and connectivity. This category we call $\mathcal{J}$ (for *jungle*, a term coined in [HP88]).

Morphisms preserve structure, but rewrites are intended to change the structure of a graph. We therefore represent rewrite rules not as morphisms of $\mathcal{J}$, but as the morphisms of a derived category $\wp(\mathcal{J})$, the category of *partial morphisms* of $\mathcal{J}$.

DEFINITION **11.2.2** *In a category* **C**, *a* partial morphism *from A to B is a pair of morphisms $A \leftarrow X \rightarrow B$ where $X \rightarrow A$ is a monomorphism. (We may indicate monomorphisms by $\hookrightarrow$ or $\hookleftarrow$.) More precisely, it is an equivalence class of such pairs. $A \hookleftarrow X \rightarrow B$ and $A \hookleftarrow Y \rightarrow B$ are equivalent if there is an isomorphism $X \rightarrow Y$ such that $X \rightarrow Y \rightarrow B = X \rightarrow B$ and $X \rightarrow Y \hookrightarrow A = X \hookrightarrow A$.*

We write a partial morphism from A to B as $A \Rightarrow B$. We shall not always distinguish a partial morphism from a particular representative of the equivalence class.

The partial morphism $A \hookleftarrow X \rightarrow B$ is total *if $X \hookrightarrow A$ is an isomorphism. It is a* restriction *if $X \rightarrow B$ is an isomorphism.*

Assume that **C** *has the pullback of any pair of arrows of which one is a monomorphism. Then the composition of two partial morphisms $A \hookleftarrow X \rightarrow B$ and $B \hookleftarrow Y \rightarrow C$*

$$\begin{array}{ccccc} Z & \hookrightarrow & X & \hookrightarrow & A \\ \downarrow & & \downarrow & & \\ Y & \hookrightarrow & B & & \\ \downarrow & & & & \\ C & & & & \end{array}$$

Figure 11.3 Composition of partial morphisms

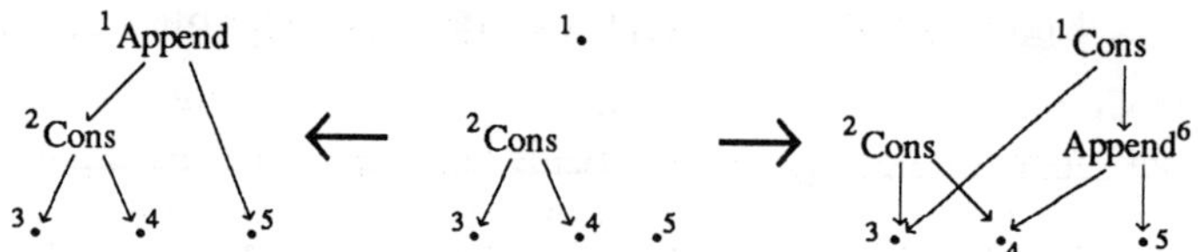

Figure 11.4 A term graph rewrite rule as a partial morphism

is the partial morphism $A \hookleftarrow X \hookleftarrow Z \to Y \to C$ *given by figure 11.3, in which the square* $ZXYB$ *is a pullback.*

Composition of partial morphisms is associative, and the partial morphisms $A \leftarrow_{id_A} A \to_{id_A} A$ *are identities for it. Thus the objects of* **C** *and partial morphisms form a category, which we denote by* $\wp(\mathbf{C})$.

DEFINITION **11.2.3** *A* term graph rewrite rule *is a partial morphism* $L \hookleftarrow X \to R$ *of* $\mathcal{J}$*, such that* X *is the subgraph of* L *obtained by omitting the root hyperedge (but retaining all the nodes), and such that every empty node of* R *is in the range of* $X \to R$. *A* redex *of this rule in a closed graph* G *is a total morphism from* L *to* G. *The hyperedges of* G *in the range of this morphism are* pattern-matched *by the redex. The* pre-reduct *of this redex is the graph* H *obtained as the pushout of* $L \Rightarrow R$ *and* $L \Rightarrow G$. *One may show that this graph always exists (although* $\wp(\mathcal{J})$ *does not have all pushouts).*

Figure 11.2 exhibited a term graph rewrite by the rule $Append(Cons(x, y), z) \to Cons(x, Append(y, z))$. Figure 11.4 displays the formulation of this rule as a partial morphism of $\mathcal{J}$. The attached numbers indicate the actions of the morphisms on nodes. Notice how empty nodes represent variables—we do not need a separate set of variable symbols.

Our definition of rewriting as a pushout of partial morphisms is not yet complete, hence the name pre-reduct. It omits the notion of garbage collection. To define this we must introduce the notion of a rooted graph.

DEFINITION **11.2.4** *A* rooted *graph is a (total) morphism* $\bullet \to G$*, where* $\bullet$ *is the graph with one node and no edges. It is* garbage-free *if every node of* G *is accessible from the node which is the image of the morphism* $\bullet \to G$. *The result of* garbage-collecting *this rooted graph,* $GC(\bullet \to G)$*, is a garbage-free rooted graph* $\bullet \to G'$ *such that there is a monomorphism* $G' \to G$ *such that* $\bullet \to G' \to G = \bullet \to G$*, and such that* G' *is the largest subgraph of* G *for which this is so. (Category theorists may note that this*

$$\begin{array}{ccccccc} & & L & \Rightarrow & R & & \\ & & \Downarrow & & \Downarrow & & \\ \bullet & \rightarrow & G & \Rightarrow & H & \Rightarrow & H' \end{array}$$

Figure 11.5 Reduction step

$$\begin{array}{ccccccccccccc} & & L_0 & \Rightarrow & R_0 & & L_1 & \Rightarrow & R_1 & & & & \\ & & \Downarrow & & \Downarrow & & \Downarrow & & \Downarrow & & & & \\ \bullet & \rightarrow & G_0 & \Rightarrow & G'_0 & \Rightarrow & G_1 & \Rightarrow & G'_1 & \Rightarrow & G_2 & \ldots \Rightarrow & G_n \end{array}$$

Figure 11.6 Reduction sequence

amounts to an adjoint to the inclusion of the category of garbage-free rooted graphs in the category of rooted graphs, the latter being the comma category $\bullet \downarrow \mathcal{J}$.)

Note that when G is closed, $GC(\bullet \rightarrow G) = \bullet \rightarrow G'$ where G' is the unique closed subgraph of G for which $\bullet \rightarrow G'$ is garbage-free.

In $\mathcal{J}$, $\bullet \rightarrow G$ factors through G'. In $\wp(\mathcal{J})$, we can also factor $\bullet \rightarrow G'$ through $\bullet \rightarrow G$ as $\bullet \rightarrow G \Rightarrow G'$, where $G \Rightarrow G'$ is the restriction morphism $G \hookleftarrow G' \cong G'$.

DEFINITION **11.2.5** *Given a rooted graph $\bullet \rightarrow G$, the result of reducing a redex $L \Rightarrow G$ of a rule $L \Rightarrow R$ is depicted in figure 11.5. The square $LRGH$ is a pushout, performing a pre-reduction as above. $\bullet \rightarrow G \Rightarrow H$ is in fact total, since the domain of $G \Rightarrow H$ includes all the nodes of G. We can therefore apply garbage-collection to it and obtain a rooted graph $\bullet \rightarrow H \Rightarrow H'$. This is the* reduct *of the redex.*

This defines a single reduction step. A reduction sequence can be constructed by stringing successive reductions together as in figure 11.6. One important feature of this definition of rewriting is that it gives additional information besides the final graph: it also gives a partial morphism from the initial graph to the final graph which has a concrete and intuitive meaning. Let the morphism be $G_0 \hookleftarrow X \rightarrow G_n$. Consider X as a subgraph of G_0. Then the nodes and hyperedges of G_0 outside X are those which the sequence erases. Hyperedges in X are preserved by the reduction. Nodes which are empty in X but nonempty in G are changed. Other nodes of X are preserved. The nodes and hyperedges of G_n outside the range of $X \rightarrow G_n$ are created by the reduction.

DEFINITION **11.2.6** *Let there be given two distinct redexes $L_1 \Rightarrow G$ and $L_2 \Rightarrow G$ of rules $L_1 \Rightarrow R_1$ and $L_2 \Rightarrow R_2$. They are* disjoint *if there is no hyperedge of G which is erased by reduction of one redex but pattern-matched by the other.*

A rule system is orthogonal *if no graph contains non-disjoint redexes.*

In the remainder of the chapter we restrict our attention to orthogonal systems.

11.3 REDUCTION GRAPHS

Besides the graphs with whose rewriting we are concerned, we deal with another sort of graph.

A *reduction graph* of a term graph t is a rooted directed graph labeled as follows. Each node is labeled with a term graph. For each arc, the term labeling its source is reducible in one step to the term labeling its target. The root of the graph is labeled with t, and all nodes are accessible from the root. It is possible for different nodes to be labeled with the same term.

We can consider several different reduction graphs of a term graph t. First, there is the *reduction tree* of t, denoted $RT(t)$. As its name implies, it is a tree. The out-arcs of each node are in $1-1$ correspondence with the set of all the redexes of the term graph labeling that node. These two properties uniquely identify $RT(t)$. Its nodes are in $1-1$ correspondence with the set of finite reduction sequences starting from t.

The *minimal reduction graph* of t, $MG(t)$, is obtained from $RT(t)$ by identifying together all nodes bearing the same label, and corresponding out-arcs of such nodes.

A third reduction graph concerns us here: the *Lévy graph* of t, or $LG(t)$. This stands midway between $RT(t)$ and $MG(t)$. Like $MG(t)$, it is obtained from $RT(t)$ via an equivalence relation on reduction sequences, but one finer than that associated with $MG(t)$: the relation of *Lévy-equivalence*. This is defined in the next section.

11.4 LÉVY-EQUIVALENCE

Consider the rewrite rule $A(B) \to C$ and the graph $D(A(x : B), A(x))$. The graph contains two redexes. There is an obvious sense in which we can reduce them both, in either order, and it is clear that the result is the same: $D(C, C)$. This notion is formalized as Lévy-equivalence. Lévy originally defined this for Lambda calculus [Lév78, Lév80], but it applies to orthogonal rewriting in general [HL91]. For term graph rewriting, it is rather simpler than for Lambda calculus or term rewriting, and our categorical formulation of rewriting makes it simple to define. The construction is performed by the following lemmas.

LEMMA **11.4.1** *In figure 11.7, let the squares $L_1R_1GG_1$ and $L_2R_2GG_2$ be pre-reductions of redexes $r_1 : L_1 \Rightarrow G$ and $r_2 : L_2 \Rightarrow G$. Then the pushout of $G \Rightarrow G_1$ and $G \Rightarrow G_2$ exists as the third square of that figure, and the rectangles $L_1R_1GG_2$ and $L_2R_2GG_1$ represent pre-rewrites of G_2 and G_1 respectively to G'.*

PROOF. By orthogonality, the node $r_1(root(L_1))$ of G cannot be the image by r_2 of any nonempty node of L_2. The domain of $G \Rightarrow G_1$ consists of every node of G except $r_1(root(L_1))$. Therefore $L_2 \Rightarrow G \Rightarrow G_1$ must be total. Its pushout with $L_2 \Rightarrow R_2$ therefore exists, and by standard facts about pushouts in general, it must be given by adjoining the pushout $L_2R_2GG_2$ with a pushout GG_1G_2G. Similarly, $L_1 \Rightarrow G \Rightarrow G_2$ is total, and the rectangle $L_1R_1G_2H$ must also be a pushout. □

LEMMA **11.4.2** *Let $\bullet \to G$ pre-reduce to $\bullet \to H$. Then $GC(\bullet \to G)$ reduces to $GC(\bullet \to H)$ by either a single step reduction or an empty reduction. ("Garbage collection commutes with reduction.")*

$$\begin{array}{ccccccc}
\bullet & & L_1 & \Rightarrow & R_1 & & \\
 & \searrow & \Downarrow & & \Downarrow & & \\
L_2 & \Rightarrow & G & \Rightarrow & G_1 & \Rightarrow & H_1 \\
\Downarrow & & \Downarrow & & \Downarrow & & \\
R_2 & \Rightarrow & G_2 & \Rightarrow & G' & & \\
 & & \Downarrow & & & \searrow\!\!\searrow & \\
 & & H_2 & & & & H
\end{array}$$

Figure 11.7

$$\begin{array}{cccccccc}
 & & L & \Rightarrow & R & & \\
 & & \Downarrow & & \Downarrow & & \\
\bullet & \rightarrow & G & \Rightarrow & H & \Rightarrow & H' \\
 & & \Downarrow & & \Downarrow & \nearrow\!\!\nearrow & \\
 & & G' & \Rightarrow & H'' & &
\end{array}$$

Figure 11.8

PROOF. It is enough to show this for a single step pre-reduction of $\bullet \rightarrow G$ to $\bullet \rightarrow H$. Let $GC(\bullet \rightarrow G) = \bullet \rightarrow G \Rightarrow G'$ and $GC(\bullet \rightarrow H) = \bullet \rightarrow G \Rightarrow H'$. If the root of L is not in the domain of $L \Rightarrow G \Rightarrow G'$, then the node changed by the reduction of $L \Rightarrow G$, and all nodes added by that reduction, are garbage in H. Thus $G' = H'$, and $GC(\bullet \rightarrow G')$ reduces to $GC(\bullet \rightarrow H')$ by the empty reduction.

Otherwise, take the pushout H'' of $G \Rightarrow H$ and $G \Rightarrow G'$ (see figure 11.8). H'' is also the pushout of $L \Rightarrow R$ and $L \Rightarrow G \Rightarrow G'$. Since $G \Rightarrow G'$ is a restriction morphism, so is $H \Rightarrow H''$. Therefore $H \Rightarrow H'$ factors through $H \Rightarrow H''$. Therefore $GC(\bullet \rightarrow G \Rightarrow G' \Rightarrow H'') = GC(\bullet \rightarrow G \Rightarrow H)$. □

LEMMA **11.4.3** *In figure 11.7, let G pre-reduce to G_1 and G_2, and reduce to H_1 and H_2, by reduction of the distinct redexes $r_1 : L_1 \Rightarrow G$ and $r_2 : L_2 \Rightarrow G$. Then H_1 and H_2 both reduce to the same graph H, which is obtained by garbage-collecting the pushout G' of $G \Rightarrow G_1$ and $G \Rightarrow G_2$.*

PROOF. From the preceding lemmas. □

The reductions of H_1 and H_2 to H constructed by this lemma are called the *projections* of r_2 over r_1 and of r_1 over r_2 respectively, denoted by r_2/r_1 and r_1/r_2. Projection of single reduction steps is extended to reduction sequences by the equations: $r/(r' \cdot s) = (r/r')/s$ and $(r \cdot s)/s' = (r/s') \cdot (s/(s'/r))$, where r and r' are single steps and s and s' are reduction sequences.

DEFINITION **11.4.4** *On finite reduction sequences,* Lévy equivalence *is the equivalence relation $\cong_L$ generated by the following axioms:*

a. $r \cdot (r'/r) \cong_L r' \cdot (r/r')$
b. $s \cong_L s' \Rightarrow s \cdot s'' \cong_L s' \cdot s'' \wedge s'' \cdot s \cong_L s'' \cdot s'$.

$$
LG(I(I(I(x)))) \qquad
\begin{array}{ccccccc}
 & \nearrow & I(I(x)) & \longrightarrow & I(x) & \searrow & \\
I(I(I(x))) & \longrightarrow & I(I(x)) & \times & I(x) & \longrightarrow & x \\
 & \searrow & I(I(x)) & \longrightarrow & I(x) & \nearrow &
\end{array}
$$

$$
MG(I(I(I(x)))) \qquad I(I(I(x))) \xrightarrow{3} I(I(x)) \xrightarrow{2} I(x) \xrightarrow{1} x
$$

Figure 11.9 Minimal and Lévy graphs of $I(I(I(x)))$

THEOREM **11.4.5** *[Lév78, Lév80] The above definition is equivalent to: $s \cong_L s'$ if and only if s/s' and s'/s are both the empty sequence.*

THEOREM **11.4.6** *Lévy-equivalent sequences determine the same partial morphism.*

PROOF. It is sufficient to verify this for the cases where the two sequences are related by one of the conditions of definition 11.4.4, which is immediate from the preceding lemmas. □

Note that the converse does not hold. By the above theorem, Lévy-equivalent sequences do the same thing to each node and hyperedge of their common initial graph, but in addition, they also do the same thing to each node or hyperedge they create. Sequences determining the same partial morphism need not do the latter.

Here is a simple example where the Lévy reduction graph of a term graph differs from its minimal reduction graph. Take the rule $I(x) \rightarrow x$ and the term $I(I(I(x)))$. The minimal and Lévy reduction graphs of this term are illustrated in figure 11.9. The numbers on the edges of the minimal graph indicate their multiplicity.

11.5 EVENT STRUCTURES

We now define event structures. These were invented by Winskel [NPW81, Win80] to give a semantics for Petri-nets.

There are several types of event structure. We will only require the simplest of them.

DEFINITION **11.5.1** *An* elementary event structure *is a finite or countable set E and a partial ordering $\leq$ of E. $\leq$ is called the* causality relation.

A left closed *subset of E is a subset X such that $e \leq e' \wedge e' \in X \Rightarrow e \in X$.*

$\mathcal{L}(E)$ denotes the set of left closed subsets of E, ordered by inclusion.

THEOREM **11.5.2** *[Win80] $\mathcal{L}(E)$ is a prime algebraic complete lattice.*

The intuition behind these definitions is that E is the set of events that can happen in the course of a computation. The partial ordering is a relation of dependency or causality: when $e < e'$, then e' cannot happen unless e has already happened. The members of $\mathcal{L}(E)$ thus represent possible computational states: a state is the set of events which have happened so far.

11.6 EVENT STRUCTURES FOR ORTHOGONAL TERM GRAPH REWRITING

11.6.1 Pre-events

The intuition underlying the following construction is that given a redex r of a graph G, and a reduction sequence $s : G \rightarrow G'$, if r/s is nonempty then it is in some sense the same piece of work as r, deferred to a later time.

DEFINITION **11.6.1** *A* pre-event *of a term graph G is a pair (s, r), where $s : G \rightarrow H$ is a reduction sequence and r is a redex of H. $Pre(G)$ is the set of all pre-events of G. For any reduction sequence s, the pre-events of s, denoted $Pre(s)$, are the events (s', r) such that $s' \cdot r$ is an initial segment of s.*

DEFINITION **11.6.2** *Two pre-events are equivalent if they can be proved so by the following axioms:*

a. $(s, r) \cong (s', r)$ *if* $s \cong_L s'$.
b. $(s, r) \cong (s \cdot s', r/s')$ *if* r/s' *exists.*

We now arrive at a theorem which is fundamental to the interpretation of term graphs as event structures. The rest of this section is devoted to its proof.

THEOREM **11.6.3** *No two distinct pre-events of a reduction sequence are equivalent.*

PROOF. We proceed by establishing properties of pre-events which are of minimal length in their equivalence class. Equivalent minimal pre-events are found to satisfy a much stronger equivalence relation. From this the theorem will follow.

DEFINITION **11.6.4** *A pre-event (s, r) is* minimal *if there is no $(s', r') \cong (s, r)$ with $|s'| < |s|$. A pre-event (s, r) is* irredundant *if every pre-event of s contributes to a later pre-event of $s \cdot r$. (Equivalently, if every pre-event of s is needed for the pre-event (s, r).)*

LEMMA **11.6.5** *Every minimal pre-event is irredundant.*

PROOF. Let (s, r) be a counterexample of minimal length. Let r_0 and r_1 be the first two steps of $s \cdot r$. By minimality of the counterexample, r_0 does not contribute to any later step. Therefore r_0 does not create r_1. Let $r_1 = r_2/r_0$. If $r_0 = s$ and $r_1 = r$, then $(\langle\rangle, r_2) \cong (r_0, r_1)$, contradicting minimality. Otherwise, $s = r_0 \cdot r_1 \cdot s' \cong_L r_2 \cdot (r_0/r_1) \cdot s'$. If r_0/r_1 is empty, then $(r_2 \cdot s', r) \cong (s, r)$ and $r_2 \cdot s'$ is shorter than s, contradicting minimality. Finally, if r_0/r_1 is nonempty, it does not contribute to any step of $s' \cdot r$, and so $((r_0/r_1) \cdot s', r)$ is a shorter counterexample. □

We can elaborate the above proof into an algorithm for transforming any pre-event (s, r) into an equivalent irredundant pre-event.

ALGORITHM **11.6.6** Firstly, note that if s is empty, (s, r) is irredundant.

For nonempty s, we will deal with each step of s, from the last backwards. At each stage, we will have transformed (s, r) into an equivalent pre-event $(s_0 \cdot r_0 \cdot s_1, r_1)$, where (s_1, r_1) is minimal. Initially, $s_0 \cdot r_0 = s$ and s_1 is empty (making (s_1, r_1) irredundant).

If $(\langle\rangle, r_0)$ contributes to some later step of $r_0 \cdot s_1 \cdot r_1$, then $(r_0 \cdot s_1, r_1)$ is irredundant. Otherwise, we need the following lemma, proved below.

LEMMA 11.6.7 *If $(\langle\rangle, r)$ does not contribute to any later pre-event of a sequence $r \cdot s$, then there is a sequence s' such that $s = s'/r$ and $|s| = |s'|$.*

Applying this lemma to the situation where $(\langle\rangle, r_0)$ does not contribute to any later step of $r_0 \cdot s_1 \cdot r_1$, we find that there is an $s_2 \cdot r_2$ such that $s_1 \cdot r_1 = (s_2 \cdot r_2)/r_0$ and $|s_2 \cdot r_2| = |s_1 \cdot r_1|$. This implies that projection over r_0 does not erase any step of $s_2 \cdot r_2$, and that in particular $r_1 = r_2/(r_0/s_2)$. Therefore $(r_0 \cdot s_1, r_1) \cong (s_2, r_2)$. Since (s_1, r_1) is irredundant, by Theorem 11.6.5 (s_2, r_2) is also. Furthermore $(s_0 \cdot r_0 \cdot s_1, r_1) \cong (s_0 \cdot s_2, r_2)$.

By continuing in this way, we process each member of s, obtaining in the end an equivalent irredundant pre-event (s', r').

PROOF OF LEMMA. If s is empty this is trivial. Otherwise $s = r' \cdot s'$, where r does not create r'. Then $r' = r''/r$ for some r'', and in the sequence $(r/r'') \cdot s'$, if r/r'' is nonempty, it does not contribute to any later pre-event of the sequence. s' is shorter than s, so by induction we may assume that there is an s'' such that $s' = s''/(r/r'')$ and $|s'| = |s''|$. Then $s = (r''/r) \cdot (s''/(r/r'')) = (r'' \cdot s'')/r$ and $|s| = |r'' \cdot s''|$ □

As a corollary, the above construction also provides us with a reduction sequence s'' such that $s' \cdot r' \cdot s''/s \cdot r$ is empty. s'' consists, roughly speaking, of the parts of s that were not needed for (s, r).

DEFINITION 11.6.8 *The number of steps of s which are needed for (s, r) is the* needed length *of (s, r).*

LEMMA 11.6.9 *If the minimization algorithm transforms (s, r) into (s', r'), then $|s'|$ is the needed length of (s, r).*

PROOF. Clear from the construction. □

DEFINITION 11.6.10 *Two pre-events (s, r) and (s', r') are* strongly equivalent *if $s \cong_L s'$ and $r = r'$.*

LEMMA 11.6.11 *If $(s, r) \cong (s', r')$ then the needed lengths of the two pre-events are equal. Furthermore, the respective results of applying the minimization algorithm to both are strongly equivalent.*

PROOF. It is sufficient to prove this when (s, r) and (s', r') are related by either of the axioms of Definition 11.4.4. Since the second part of the lemma implies the first, it is sufficient to prove only the second part.

For the second axiom, it is clear that the minimization algorithm will produce identical results given either (s, r) or $(s \cdot s', r/s')$.

For the first axiom, it is sufficient to take the case where $r = r'$ and $s = s_0 \cdot r_0 \cdot (r_1/r_0) \cdot s_1 \cong_L s_0 \cdot r_1 \cdot (r_0/r_1) \cdot s_1 = s'$. For s to be distinct from s', at least one of r_1/r_0 and r_0/r_1 must be nonempty. Assume r_1/r_0 is nonempty.

Applying the minimization algorithm, we may assume without loss of generality that (s_1, r) is minimal. We must show that the results of applying the algorithm on the one hand to r_1/r_0 and then r_0, and on the other hand to r_0/r_1 (if nonempty) and r_1, have the same length, and that this equality of length is preserved when we apply the algorithm to s_0. This may be shown by induction on $|s_1|$. When s_1 is nonempty, there

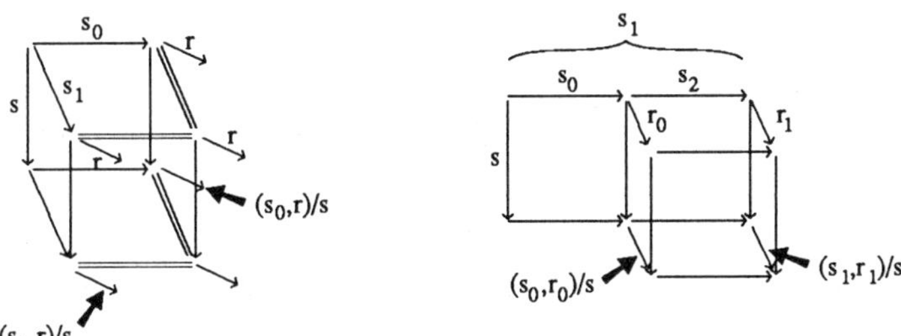

Figure 11.10

is a routine analysis of cases, according to which, if either, of r_0 and r_1/r_0 contributes to the first step of s_1. We omit the details. □

LEMMA **11.6.12** *a. An irredundant pre-event is minimal.*
b. Distinct redexes of the same term, considered as pre-events with empty history, are not equivalent.

PROOF. (i) If $(s,r) \cong (s',r')$ and (s,r) is irredundant, then from Lemmas 11.6.9 and 11.6.11, $|s \cdot r| \leq |s' \cdot r'|$, i.e. (s,r) is minimal.

(ii) Distinct redexes are minimal pre-events, yet not strongly equivalent. Hence (ii) follows from Lemma 11.6.11. □

LEMMA **11.6.13** *If* $(s_0, r_0) \cong (s_1, r_1)$ *and both* $(s_0, r_0)/s$ *and* $(s_1, r_1)/s$ *exist, then they are equivalent.*

PROOF. It is sufficient to show this for the two cases of the definition of equivalence of pre-events. Each of these in turn follows from the Cube Lemma; see figure 11.10. □

Finally, we complete the proof of Theorem 11.6.3.

$$\begin{aligned} (s_0, r_0) &\cong (s_0 \cdot r_0 \cdot s_1, r_1) \\ \Rightarrow (s_0, r_0)/s_0 &\cong (s_0 \cdot r_0 \cdot s_1, r_1)/s_0 \qquad \text{(Lemma 11.6.13)} \\ \Rightarrow (\langle\rangle, r_0) &\cong (r_0 \cdot s_1, r_1) \end{aligned}$$

Apply the minimization algorithm to $(r_0 \cdot s_1, r_1)$. This must yield a pre-event of the form $(\langle\rangle, r_2)$, such that $r_1 = r_2/(r_0 \cdot s_1)$. But $(\langle\rangle, r_0)$ and $(\langle\rangle, r_2)$ must be strongly equivalent, hence $r_0 = r_2$, and $r_2/(r_0 \cdot s_1)$ cannot exist. □

Informally, this theorem means that it is not possible for a reduction sequence to do the same piece of work twice. This theorem also shows the distinction between term graph rewriting and term rewriting. *Mutatis mutandis*, it is false for the latter, because of the possibility that reduction of one redex can make multiple copies of another, which may all be later reduced. By the definitions we have given, the reductions of each of these copies, considered as pre-events, would be equivalent. Reducing more than one of them would give a reduction sequence containing two or more equivalent pre-events, defeating the construction of an event structure, in which an event is something which can only happen once.

11.6.2 Events

DEFINITION **11.6.14** *An* event *of G is an equivalence class of pre-events of G. $Ev(G)$ is the set of events of G. $Ev(s)$ is the set of events which are represented by the members of $Pre(s)$.*

The pre-events of a graph have an immediate computational interpretation as the possible steps which may be executed by a reduction machine evaluating the graph. Theorem 11.6.3 implies that the more abstract events may be interpreted in the same way. Furthermore, if we consider a machine capable of executing distinct redexes concurrently, without necessarily any definite total ordering of its reductions beyond that implied by causality, then events precisely correspond to the steps which may be made by such a machine.

$Ev(s)$ does not quite describe the work done by s, since it is possible for some steps of s to erase parts of the graph in which some previous steps were performed, making those steps unnecessary.

DEFINITION **11.6.15** *An event e of a graph G is* needed *if $e \in Ev(s)$ for every reduction s of G to normal form. $Ev^0(G)$ is the set of needed events of G. A needed reduction sequence is one, all of whose events are needed. $LG^0(G)$ is the subgraph of $LG(G)$ obtained by restricting to needed reduction steps.*

$Ev^0(s)$ is the description we seek, as shown by the next theorem.

THEOREM **11.6.16** *$s \cong_L s'$ if and only if $Ev^0(s) = Ev^0(s')$.*

PROOF. The forwards implication is immediate from the definition of Ev^0.

For the converse, suppose $s_1 \not\cong s_2$. Choose sequences s_1 and s_2 Lévy-equivalent to s_1 and s_2 respectively and of minimal length. At least one of s_1/s_2 and s_2/s_1 must be nonempty. Supposing it is the first, consider the sequence $s_2 \cdot (s_1/s_2)$. By Theorem 11.6.3, no step in the second segment can be equivalent to any step of s_2. But every step of the second segment is equivalent to a step of s_1. Therefore $Ev(s_1') \neq Ev(s_2')$. But $Ev^0(s_1) = Ev^0(s_1) = Ev(s_1)$, and similarly for s_2, hence the theorem. □

11.6.3 The event structure of needed events

We now show that the notion of one redex creating another gives rise to a partial ordering of $Ev(t)$.

DEFINITION **11.6.17** *For e and e' in $Ev(G)$, define $e \leq e'$ if for every reduction sequence s starting from G, if $e' \in Ev(s)$ then $e \in Ev(s)$. (It is immediate that this is indeed a partial order.)*

The partial order has a concrete meaning.

DEFINITION **11.6.18** *In a sequence $s \cdot r \cdot s' \cdot r'$, the pre-event (s, r)* contributes to *the pre-event $(s \cdot r \cdot s', r')$ if there is a node n which is either the root of the contractum of r or is created by r, which is preserved by s', and such that n/s' is matched by r'.*

(s, r) is needed for *$(s \cdot r \cdot s', r')$ if it contributes to $(s \cdot r \cdot s', r')$ or if it contributes to a later step of $s \cdot r \cdot s'$ which is needed for $(s \cdot r \cdot s', r')$.*

THEOREM **11.6.19** *$e_0 < e_1$ if and only if there is a sequence of the form $s_0 \cdot r_0 \cdot s_1 \cdot r_1$ such that (s_0, r_0) is needed for $(s_0 \cdot r_0 \cdot s_1, r_1)$, and these two pre-events represent e_0 and e_1 respectively.*

PROOF. Let $e_0 < e_1$. By the definition of the ordering, there must be a sequence $s_0 \cdot r_0 \cdot s_1 \cdot r_1$ where (s_0, r_0) and $(s_0 \cdot r_0 \cdot s_1, r_1)$ represent e_0 and e_1 respectively. If (s_0, r_0) were not needed for $(s_0 \cdot r_0 \cdot s_1, r_1)$, then applying the minimization algorithm to $(s_0 \cdot r_0 \cdot s_1, r_1)$ would begin by transforming it to a form $(s_0 \cdot r_0 \cdot s_1, r_1)$ with (s_1, r_1) a minimal pre-event, and then eliminate r_0. The final result would be a pre-event (s_2, r_2) equivalent to $(s_0 \cdot r_0 \cdot s_1, r_1)$, and in which $Ev(s_2)$ is a subset of $Ev(s_0 \cdot r_0 \cdot s_1)$ not containing e_0 (since by Theorem 6.3, no other pre-event of $s_0 \cdot r_0 \cdot s_1$ can be equivalent to (s_0, r_0)). But this contradicts $e_0 < e_1$.

For the converse, suppose we have a sequence $s_0 \cdot r_0 \cdot s_1 \cdot r_1$ of the stated form. To establish the ordering of the events, we must show that for any pre-event (s_2, r_2) equivalent to $(s_0 \cdot r_0 \cdot s_1, r_1), s_2$ must contain a pre-event equivalent to (s_0, r_0). It is sufficient to do this for the cases where (s_2, r_2) is related to $(s_0 \cdot r_0 \cdot s_1, r_1)$ by one of the axioms for equivalence.

Axiom (i): $s_2 \cong_L s_0 \cdot r_0 \cdot s_1$. We may assume that s_2 and $s_0 \cdot r_0 \cdot s_1$ are related by an application of part (1) of Definition 2.2.1 to a part of $s_0 \cdot r_0 \cdot s_1$. If this part does not include r_0, then s_2 will have a pre-event $(s'_0, r_0$ equivalent to (s_0, r_0). Otherwise, there are two cases.

(a) There exist s_3 and $r_3 \neq r_0$ such that $s_2 = s_0 \cdot r_3 \cdot (r_0/r_3) \cdot s_3$, $s_1 = (r_0/r_3) \cdot s_3$, and $r_2 = r_1$. If r_0/r_3 is nonempty, then $(s_0 \cdot r_3, (r_0/r_3)) \cong (s_0, r_0)$. Otherwise, r_3 erases r_0. But this implies that r_3/r_0 erases every node which r_0 changes or creates. Therefore r_0 cannot contribute to any step of $s_1 \cdot r_1$ later than r_3/r_0. It cannot contribute to r_3/r_0 either, since this is a residual of a redex existing before r_0. This contradicts the hypothesis that (s_0, r_0) is needed for $(s_0 \cdot r_0 \cdot s_1, r_1)$.

(b) There exist s_3, r_3 and r_4 such that $s_0 = s_3 \cdot r_3, r_0 = r_4/r_3$, and $s_2 = s_3 \cdot r_4 \cdot (r_3/r_4) \cdot s_1$. Then $(s_3, r_4) \cong (s_0, r_0)$.

Axiom (ii): There are three subcases.

(a) There exists r_3 such that $s_2 = s_0 \cdot r_0 \cdot s_1 \cdot r_3$ and $r_2 = r_1/r_3$. Then s_2 contains the pre-event $(s_0, r_0$.

(b) There exist s_3 and r_3 such that $s_1 = s_3 \cdot r_3, r_1 = r_2/r_3$, and $s_2 = s_0 \cdot r_0 \cdot s_3$. Again, s_2 contains the pre-event (s_0, r_0).

(c) s_1 is empty, $s_2 = s_0$, and there exists r_2 such that $r_1 = r_2/r_0$. But this implies that $(s_0, r_0) \cong (s_0 \cdot r_0 \cdot s_1, r_1)$, contradicting Theorem 6.3. □

Finally, we have the required event structure and its associated configuration domain.

THEOREM **11.6.20** *$Ev^0(G)$ with the partial ordering inherited from $Ev(G)$ (of which it is a lower section) is an elementary event structure. Its associated domain of configurations is isomorphic to $LG^0(G)$. The resulting partial ordering of $LG^0(G)$ is identical to the ordering defined by Huet and Lévy [HL91]: $s \leq s'$ if and only if s/s' is empty.*

PROOF. It is immediate that $Ev^0(G)$ is a lower section of $Ev(G)$. Nodes of $LG^0(G)$ are in $1-1$ correspondence with Lévy-equivalence classes of needed reduction sequences, which by Theorem 6.6 are in $1-1$ correspondence with $Ev^0(G)$.

The configuration domain of $Ev^0(G)$ is the set of lower sections, ordered by the subset relation. Let s and s' be needed reduction sequences. If s/s' is empty, then $s' \cong_L s \cdot (s'/s)$, therefore $Ev^0(s) \subseteq Ev^0(s')$. Conversely, suppose $Ev^0(s) \subseteq Ev^0(s')$. In the sequence $s' \cdot (s/s')$, every step in the s/s' segment is equivalent to some step of s, hence by hypothesis to some step of s'. But by Theorem 6.3 there can be no such step. Therefore s/s' is empty, and $s \leq s'$. □

Thus a Lévy-equivalence class of needed reductions starting from G is equivalent to a lower section of the set of needed events of G.

11.7 RELATED WORK AND FURTHER DEVELOPMENTS

In [Sta89], Stark defines a notion of "concurrent transition system". This takes as basic a notion of an abstract residual operation on abstract transitions. However, his primary concern is the study of process networks. His paper only mentions in passing the possibility of constructing event structures from concurrent transition systems, and that orthogonal term rewriting and Lambda calculus reduction can give rise to examples of such structures. However, finding such structures in these contexts requires taking the basic transitions to be not ordinary reductions, but complete developments, which amounts to considering term graph reduction without the name. The construction—which is the purpose of this chapter—is still non-trivial.

We expect that the construction of event structures can also be applied in the presence of infinite graphs and transfinite rewriting, as set out in [KKSdV90]. The set $Ev^0(t)$ is generalized to the set of *Böhm-needed* redexes of t—those redexes which must be reduced in any reduction of t which obtains every part of its Böhm tree (a concept borrowed from Lambda calculus).

To extend this work to non-orthogonal systems, we would have to deal with the possibility of conflicts among events. While event structures with a notion of conflict are well known, all such structures in the literature depend on a conflict relation which is symmetric: if event e_1 conflicts with e_2, then e_2 conflicts with e_1. This is in general not the case for conflicts among redexes. Consider the rules $F(A) \rightarrow B$, $A \rightarrow C$. There is a conflict between these rules. The graph $F(A)$ may be reduced either to B or to $F(C)$. In this case, the conflict between the two redexes is symmetric. If one reduces either redex, the other no longer exists. However, consider the graph $D(x : F(y : A), y)$. This again contains two conflicting redexes. Reducing the redex at y breaks the redex at x. But reducing the redex at x gives the graph $D(x : B, y : A)$, in which the redex at y is still present. A type of event structure based on an asymmetric conflict relation is therefore required.

11.8 CONCLUSION

For any normalizable term graph t in an orthogonal term graph rewrite system, the essentially different pieces of work which are required in the evaluation of t to normal form form an elementary event structure. The partial ordering embodies the relation of one redex contributing to another. Redexes can be reduced in any order compatible with the dependency relation.

The associated state domain is the set of Lévy-equivalence classes of needed reduction sequences starting from t. The top element corresponds to the reduction of t to normal form. The height of the partial ordering of $Ev^0(t)$ implies a lower bound on the time required to reach the normal form by reduction, and the width implies an upper bound on the amount of useful parallelism that can be employed.

REFERENCES

[BvEG+87] H. P. Barendregt, M. C. J. D. van Eekelen, J. R. W. Glauert, J. R. Kennaway, M. J. Plasmeijer, and M. R. Sleep. Term graph rewriting. In J. W. de Bakker, A. J. Nijman, and P. C. Treleaven (editors), *Proc. PARLE'87 Conference, vol.II*, Springer-Verlag, Lecture Notes in Computer Science 259, pp. 141–158, Eindhoven, The Netherlands, 1987.

[HL79] G. Huet and J.-J. Lévy. *Call-by-Need Computations in Non-ambiguous Linear Term Rewriting systems.* Technical report, INRIA, 1979.

[HL91] G. Huet and J.-J. Lévy. Computations in orthogonal rewrite systems I and II. In Lassez and Plotkin [LP91], pp. 394–443. (Originally appeared as [HL79].).

[HP88] B. Hoffmann and D. Plump. Jungle evaluation for efficient term rewriting. In J. Grabowski, P. Lescanne, and W. Weckler (editors), *Proc. Int. Workshop on Algebraic and Logic Programming*, vol. 49 of *Mathematical Research*, pp. 191–203. Akademie-Verlag, 1988.

[Ken91] J. R. Kennaway. Graph rewriting in some categories of partial morphisms. In H. Ehrig, H.-J. Kreowski, and G. Rozenberg (editors), *Proc. 4th International Workshop on Graph Grammars and their Application to Computer Science*, Springer-Verlag, Lecture Notes in Computer Science 532, pp. 490–504, Bremen, Germany, 1991.

[KKSdV90] J. R. Kennaway, J. W. Klop, M. R. Sleep, and F. J. de Vries. *Transfinite Reductions in Orthogonal Term Rewriting Systems.* Technical Report CS-R9041, CWI, Amsterdam, 1990.

[Lév78] J.-J. Lévy. *Reductions Correctes et Optimales dans le Lambda-Calcul.* Thèse de doctorat d'état, Université Paris VII, 1978.

[Lév80] J.-J. Lévy. Optimal reductions in the lambda-calculus. In J. P. Seldin and J. R. Hindley (editors), *To H.B. Curry: Essays in Combinatory Logic, Lambda Calculus and Formalism.* Academic Press, 1980.

[LP91] J.-L. Lassez and G. D. Plotkin (editors). *Computational Logic: Essays in Honor of Alan Robinson.* MIT Press, 1991.

[NPW81] M. Nielsen, G. D. Plotkin, and G. Winskel. Petri nets, event structures, and domains, part 1. *Theoretical Computer Science*, **13**, 1981.

[Sta80] J. Staples. Computation on graph-like expressions. *Theoretical Computer Science*, **10**, pp. 171–185, 1980.

[Sta89] E. W. Stark. Concurrent transition systems. *Theoretical Computer Science*, **64**, pp. 221–270, 1989.

[Win80] G. Winskel. *Events in Computation.* PhD thesis, Dept. of Computer Science, University of Edinburgh, 1980.

12

The Adequacy of Term Graph Rewriting for Simulating Term Rewriting

J.R. Kennaway, J.W. Klop, M.R. Sleep and F.J. de Vries

12.1 INTRODUCTION

What does it mean to say that a Graph Rewrite System $(GRAPHS, \rightarrow_{graph})$ is an implementation of a Term Rewrite System $(TERMS, \rightarrow_{term})$? The intuitive answer is (cf. [vEB90]): everything which term rewriting can do can be performed by graph rewriting as well, modulo the unravelling of graphs to terms.

Unfortunately, if we insist on this notion, we soon discover that graph rewriting does *not* implement term rewriting. For example, consider rules such as $D(x) \rightarrow P(x,x), A \rightarrow B, P(A,B) \rightarrow C$. With term rewriting we get the sequence: $D(A) \rightarrow_{term} P(A,A) \rightarrow_{term} P(A,B) \rightarrow_{term} C$, so that $D(A) \rightarrow^* C$ using term rewriting. But with graph rewriting, the rule $D(x) \rightarrow_{graph} P(x,x)$ copies only a pointer to the subterm x, and the only possible graph rewriting of $D(A)$ is the sequence $D(A) \rightarrow_{graph} P(A,A) \rightarrow_{graph} P(B,B)$. So, unlike term rewriting, graph rewriting cannot rewrite $D(A)$ to C.

With term rewriting, two distinct copies of the argument x of the rule $D(x) \rightarrow P(x,x)$ are made, and can be treated differently in subsequent term rewriting.

With graph rewriting, such duplicating rules copy only pointers, and any subsequent rewrites of the subterm referenced by such a pointer is experienced by every term graph using that pointer. This is good for operational efficiency, but bad if we want to preserve term rewriting semantics. The main purpose of this chapter is to identify precisely a class of term rewriting systems whose semantics are preserved by graph rewriting implementations.

Term Graph Rewriting: Theory and Practice.
Eds. Ronan Sleep, Rinus Plasmeijer and Marko van Eekelen.

From the above examples, it is clear that term rewriting has more possibilities than graph rewriting. This suggests we treat graph rewriting as a constrained form of term rewriting in which certain term rewriting sequences are prohibited. *Rather than think of graph rewriting as implementing term rewriting, we should instead think of term rewriting implementing graph rewriting.* For certain classes of Term Rewriting System, the implementation works both ways, and there is a precise sense in which we can say that cyclic graph rewriting simulates term rewriting, and which works for a large class of Term Rewriting Systems called *rational orthogonal* systems.

12.1.1 Background

Several authors have written on the correctness of graph rewriting implementations of term rewriting [Sta80, BvEG+87, FW91]. Most restrict attention to acyclic graphs and orthogonal rule systems, although Farmer and Watro study the cyclic Y-combinator. In [BvEG+87] it is proved, for any orthogonal Term Rewrite System and its related Graph Rewrite System, that if an acyclic graph g unravels to a term t, then g has a normal form by acyclic graph rewriting if and only if t has a normal form by tree rewriting, and the normal form of g unravels to the normal form of t. There are a number of things one might want to improve in this result.

Simulate finite approximations to infinite reductions: the result only applies to terms which have a normal form, but this is in general undecidable. Lazy functional programming is based on finite approximations to infinite sequences, and our theory should deal with these.

Take advantage of cyclic graphs: most previous work is restricted to acyclic graph rewriting, but rewriting cyclic graphs has clear practical advantages, in some cases (e.g. for the Y combinator) reducing a transfinite number of rewrites to a finite number.

Cyclic graphs arise naturally as a result of certain optimizations in functional language implementation. Such graphs unravel to infinite terms, and their reduction sequences unravel to transfinite term reduction sequences. Infinitary term rewriting has recently received detailed attention [FW91, DK89, DKP89, DKP91, KKSdV91, KKSdV90a].

12.1.2 Overview

In this chapter we give a precise analysis of the relationship between cyclic term graph rewriting and infinitary term rewriting, for orthogonal rewrite systems. For non-orthogonal systems, graph rewriting and term rewriting differ significantly, although some of our results still hold.

Terms and computations of a finite acyclic Graph Rewriting System can be unravelled into terms and computations of a finitary Term Rewriting System. We will give an abstract definition of an adequate mapping between abstract reduction systems which captures the properties of the unravelling mapping. For example, *finite acyclic graph rewriting is adequate for finite term rewriting.*

The main result in [BvEG+87] is a corollary. To extend this to finitary cyclic graph rewriting, we have to consider *infinitary* term rewriting. Abstract reduction systems form a semantics only for finitary rewriting. By use of the weighted metric abstract reduction systems of [Ken92] as a semantics for infinitary rewriting we strengthen the adequacy concept so that it applies to finitary cyclic graph rewriting.

Our main result is that: *Finite graph rewriting is adequate for rational term rewriting.* In [KKSdV92] we show by means of an counter-example that: *Infinite graph rewriting is not adequate for infinite term rewriting.*

Our definition of an adequate mapping of one system to another adds to the abundance of concepts of simulation, in term rewriting (e.g. [BvEG+87, O'D85]), complexity theory (for an overview see [vEB90]) or programming languages [Mit91].

12.2 TERM REWRITING

In [KKSdV91] we develop a theory of infinitary orthogonal term rewriting. General introductions to term rewriting are [DJ90] and [Klo92]. Below we give only key definitions.

12.2.1 Infinitary Term Rewriting Systems

An *infinitary Term Rewriting System* over a signature Σ is a pair $(Ter^{\infty}(\Sigma), R)$ consisting of the set $Ter^{\infty}(\Sigma)$ of finite and infinite terms over Σ and a set of rewrite rules $R \subseteq Ter(\Sigma) \times Ter^{\infty}(\Sigma)$. Note that we require that the left-hand side of a rule is a finite term.

The definition of orthogonality for finitary Term Rewriting Systems extends verbatim to infinitary systems.

12.2.2 Strongly converging reductions

The set of terms over a signature can be made into a complete metric space (see for instance [AN80]). The metric (in fact, an ultrametric) is given by $d(t, s) = 0$ if t and s are equal, and is otherwise $1/2^k$, where k is the largest number such that the labels of all nodes of s and t at depth less than or equal to k are equally labeled. Now consider the following rule systems and reduction sequences.

a. $A \to B \to A \to B \to \ldots$, in a TRS with rules $A \to B$ and $B \to A$.
b. $D(E) \to D(S(E)) \to D(S(S(E))) \to \ldots$, in a TRS with rule $D(x) \to D(S(x))$.
c. $C \to S(C) \to S(S(C)) \to \ldots$, in a TRS with rule $C \to S(C)$.

The first example is a diverging reduction sequence. The second is a *weakly converging* reduction with limit $D(S^{\omega})$. The final example is *strongly converging* with limit S^{ω}. The distinction between the two types of convergence is that a weakly converging reduction need only converge in the topological sense, while a strongly converging reduction must satisfy the additional requirement that the depth of reduced redexes tends to infinity.

In [KKSdV91] we have shown that strongly converging transfinite reduction has a more well-behaved theory than weakly converging transfinite reduction. For this reason, we here consider only the former type of transfinite reduction. We write $t \to^{\omega} s$ (resp. $t \to^{\leq\omega} s$) to denote a strongly converging reduction of length ω (resp. at most

ω) from t to s. Concatenation of (a possibly infinite number of) reductions gives reductions of any ordinal length. For such a reduction of length α to be strongly converging we require that, considered as a mapping from $\alpha + 1$ to terms, it be continuous with respect to the usual topology on ordinals, that the depth of reduced redexes tends to infinity, and that every proper initial segment is also strongly converging. (The essential content of the last condition is that the depth of reduced redexes tends to infinity at every limit ordinal $\lambda \leq \alpha$.) We write $t \rightarrow^{\alpha} s$ for a strongly converging reduction of ordinal length α. While the notion of a reduction sequence longer than ω may seem devoid of computational content, the Compressing Lemma of [KKSdV91] shows that if t reduces to s by a strongly converging reduction of length greater than ω, it also reduces to s by a sequence of length at most ω. Finally, $t \rightarrow^{\infty} s$ denotes a strongly converging reduction of any finite or infinite length. Note that it is easily shown that the length is at most countable, and can be any countable ordinal.

12.3 GRAPH REWRITING

Graph rewriting is a common method of implementing term rewrite languages [Pey87]. It relies on the basic insight, that when a variable occurs many times on the right-hand side of a rule, one need only copy pointers to the corresponding parts of the term being evaluated, instead of making copies of the whole subterm. The reader familiar with graph rewriting may skip this section. Note however that we allow cyclic graphs; these correspond to certain infinite terms.

DEFINITION **12.3.1** *A term graph g over a signature $\Sigma = (F, V)$ is a quadruple $(nodes(g), lab(g), succ(g), roots(g))$, where $nodes(g)$ is a finite or infinite set of nodes, $lab(g)$ is a function from a subset of the nodes of g to F, $succ(g)$ is a function from the same subset to tuples of nodes of g, and $roots(g)$ is a tuple of (not necessarily distinct) nodes of g. Furthermore, every node of g must be accessible (defined below) from at least one root. Nodes of g outside the common domain of $lab(g)$ and $succ(g)$ are called empty.*

DEFINITION **12.3.2** *A path in a graph g is a finite or infinite sequence $a, i, b, j, \ldots$ of alternating nodes and integers, beginning and (if finite) ending with a node of g, such that for each m, i, n in the sequence, where m and n are nodes, n is the ith successor of m. The length of the path is the number of integers in it. If the path starts from a node m and ends at a node n, it is said to be a path from m to n. If there is a path from m to n, then n is said to be accessible from m. When this is so, the distance of n from m is the length of a shortest path from m to n.*

We may write $n : F(n_1, \ldots, n_k)$ to indicate that $lab(g)(n) = F$ and $succ(g)(n) = (n_1, \ldots, n_k)$. A finite graph may then be presented as a list of such *node definitions*.

For example, the list of node definitions $x : F(y, z), z : G(y, w, w), w : H(w)$ represents the graph shown in figure 12.1.

In such pictures, we may omit the names $x, y, z, \ldots$ as their only function in the textual representation is to identify the nodes. In particular, $x, y, z, \ldots$ do not represent variables: variables are represented by empty nodes. Different empty nodes need only be distinguished by the fact that they are different nodes; we do not

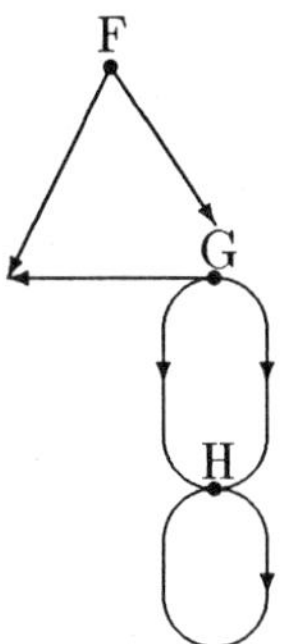

Figure 12.1 The graph $x : F(y, z), z : G(y, w, w), w : H(w)$

need any separate alphabet of variable names. Multiple references to the same variable in a term are represented in a graph by multiple references to the same empty node. The tabular description demonstrated above may conveniently be condensed, by nesting the definitions; for example, another way of writing the same graph is $F(y, z : G(y, w, w : H(w)))$. In general a graph may have more than one root. We will only use graphs with either one root (such graphs represent terms) and graphs with two roots (which represent term rewrite rules).

DEFINITION **12.3.3** *A graph homomorphism from a graph g to a graph g is a function f from the nodes of g to the nodes of g, such that for all nodes n in the domain of $lab(g)$, $lab(h)(f(n)) = lab(g)(n)$, and $succ(h)(f(n)) = succ(g)(n)$.*

Note that a graph homomorphism is not required to map the roots of its domain to the roots of its codomain. On graphs one can define many general graph rewrite mechanisms. We are concerned with one particular form: term graph rewriting.

DEFINITION **12.3.4** *A term graph is a graph with one root.*

A term graph rewrite rule is a graph with two, not necessarily distinct, roots (called the left and right roots), in which every empty node is accessible from the left root, and the subgraph containing those nodes accessible from the left root is a finite tree. The left- (resp. right-) hand side of a term graph rewrite rule r is the subgraph consisting of all nodes and edges accessible from the left (resp. right) root: notation $left(r)$ (resp. $right(r)$).

A redex of a term graph rewrite rule r in a graph g is a homomorphism from the left-hand side of r to g. The occurrence of the redex is the minimal occurrence of the node of g to which the left root is mapped. The depth of a redex is the length of the occurrence.

DEFINITION **12.3.5** *The result of reducing a redex of the rule r in a graph g at occurrence u is the graph obtained by the following construction.*

a. Construct a graph h by adding to g a copy of all nodes and edges of r not in $left(r)$. Where such an edge has one endpoint in $left(r)$, the copy of that edge in h is connected to the image of that endpoint by the homomorphism.
b. Let n_l be the node of h corresponding to the left root of r, and n_r the node corresponding to the right root of r. (These are not necessarily distinct.) In h, replace

every edge whose target is n_l by an edge with the same source and target n_r, obtaining a graph k. The root of k is the root of h, unless this is n_l, otherwise it is n_r.

c. *Remove all nodes which are not accessible from the root of k. The resulting graph is the result of the rewrite.*

We have now the ingredients to give the general definition of a Term Graph Rewrite System.

DEFINITION **12.3.6** *Let Σ be a signature. A Term Graph Rewrite System (GRS for short) is a pair $(G(\Sigma), R)$ where $G(\Sigma)$ is the set of graphs for the signature Σ, and R a set of term graph rewrite rules for the signature Σ.*

Having defined term graph rewriting and the notion of depth on term graphs, the concepts of normal form, infinitary rewriting, orthogonality, etc. carry over to term graphs.

As an example consider the rule $I(x) \rightarrow x$. and the graph $n : I(n)$ shown in figure 12.2.

Figure 12.2 The circular term graph $x : I(x)$

The graph $n : I(n)$ corresponds to the infinite term$I^\omega = I(I(I(\ldots)))$, and is a redex of the rule. This "circular I" graph reduces to itself according to Definition 12.3.5 above. Circular I is one instance of a class of redexes having the same behaviour, the *circular redexes.*

DEFINITION **12.3.7** a. *A redex of a rule r is circular if the roots of r are distinct and the homomorphism from $left(r)$ to g maps both roots of r to the same node. (This can only happen if the right root of r is accessible from the left root.)*

b. *A rule is a collapse rule if its right root is a variable.*

An example of a collapsing rule is $x : Head(Cons(y, z)) \rightarrow y$. An example of a non-collapsing rule which admits circular redexes is $x : F(y : F(z)) \rightarrow y$. Note that this rule conflicts with itself: it has two overlapping redexes in the graph F(F(F(G))). A circular redex of this rule is x:F(x).

PROPOSITION **12.3.8** *[KKSdV90a] In an orthogonal Term Graph Rewriting System, a rule has a circular redex if and only if it is a collapse rule.*

From now on we will consider term graphs and term graph rewriting only, and often we will simply call them graphs and graph rewriting.

12.3.1 Unravelling

Unravelling transforms (term) graphs to terms. Both graphs and computations can be unravelled. In [KKSdV92] we show that, for any Graph Rewrite System, if g reduces to g' by strongly convergent reduction, then $U(g)$ similarly reduces to $U(g')$ in the unravelled system. This is so even for non-orthogonal systems. Below we state key definitions and results.

DEFINITION **12.3.9** *The unravelling $U(g)$ of a graph g is the term representation of the following forest. The nodes of $U(g)$ are the paths of g which start from any of its roots. Given a node $a, i, b, j, \ldots, y$ of $U(g)$, if y is a nonempty node of g, then this node of $U(g)$ is labeled with the function symbol $lab(g)(y)$, and its successors are all paths of the form $a, i, b, j, \ldots, y, n, z$, where z is the nth successor of y in g. If y is empty, then it is labeled with a variable symbol, a different symbol being chosen for every empty node of g.*

Note that a cyclic graph will have an infinite unravelling. For example, the unravelling of the graph shown in the previous picture is the term $F(y, G(y, H^\omega, H^\omega))$.

It is easy to see that for a term graph g, $U(g)$ is a term, and for a graph rewrite rule r, $U(r)$ is a term rewrite rule. We can also apply the notion of unravelling to a whole rewrite system.

DEFINITION **12.3.10** *The unravelling of a Graph Rewriting System $(G(\Sigma), R))$ is the Term Rewriting System $(Ter^\infty(\Sigma)$,$U(R))$ whose rules $U(R)$ are the unravellings of the rules in R. This TRS is also denoted by $U(G(\Sigma), R)$; its set of terms is $U(G)$.*

So, given a signature Σ the operator U transforms GRSs over Σ into TRSs over Σ. Note that a GRS is orthogonal if and only if its unravelling is orthogonal.

PROPOSITION **12.3.11** *There is a homomorphism from $U(g)$ to g which takes the root of $U(g)$ to the root of g.*

The homomorphism is obtained by mapping each node of $U(g)$ (which is a finite path of g) to its final element. If g is acyclic, this is clearly the only homomorphism from $U(g)$ to g, but if g is cyclic there can be more than one: for example, if $g = x : A(A(x))$, there are two.

PROPOSITION **12.3.12** *A graph g in the GRS $(G(\Sigma), R)$ is a normal form if and only if its unravelling $U(g)$ is a normal form in $(Ter^\infty(\Sigma), U(R))$.*

THEOREM **12.3.13** *Let $g \to g'$ in a GRS. Then $U(g) \to_{\leq\omega} U(g')$ in the corresponding TRS. Moreover, the depth of every redex reduced in the term sequence is at least equal to the depth of the redex reduced in g.*

COROLLARY. Let $g \to_\alpha g'$ in a GRS for some infinite ordinal α Then $U(g) \to_{\leq\alpha} U(g')$ in the corresponding TRS.

12.3.2 Lifting.

Lifting transforms a Term Rewrite System into a Graph Rewrite System. We chose here a very simple lifting from the many GRS which unravel to the given TRS. We transform a term rule into a graph rewrite rule by sharing multiple occurrences of a variable in the right-hand side. This version is compatible with the one in [BvEG+87]. In contrast to unravelling, it does not have nice reduction preserving properties.

DEFINITION **12.3.14** *The lifting $L(Ter^{\omega}(\Sigma), R)$ of the TRS $L(Ter^{\omega}(\Sigma), R)$ is defined as the GRS $(G(\Sigma), R)$ where the elements of R are minimally shared, bi-rooted graphs, corresponding with the rules in R: reading the left- and right-hand sides of a term rule $T \to T'$ as trees, and then for each variable identifing all leaves of the two trees which bear that variable. The roots of the two trees become the roots of the graph.*

An example is provided by the following TRS:

$F(x) \to A(x, x)$
$A(D, D) \to B$
$C \to D$

The term $F(C)$ can reduce in the following way:

Term rewriting: $F(C) \to A(C, C) \to A(C, D) \to A(D, D) \to B$
Graph rewriting: $F(C) \to A(C, C) \to A(D, D) \to B$

Note that this example shows that there is not an exact counterpart of theorem 12.3.13 for lifting. Although $F(C)$ reduces to $A(C, D)$, the graph $F(C)$ in the lifted Term Rewrite System does not reduce to the graph $A(C, D)$, but reduces from $A(C, C)$ to $A(D, D)$ in a single step..

12.4 ADEQUACY: A PRECISE NOTION OF SIMULATION

Recall from the introductory remarks that graph rewriting may be viewed as a restricted form of term rewriting, and that while term rewriting can simulate graph rewriting, the reverse is not in general true. We want to develop some notion of simulation which captures some sense in which graph rewriting does simulate term rewriting.

Somewhat counter-intuitively, we start by writing down sensible conditions for a TRS to simulate a GRS. We will then strengthen these conditions to introduce some senses in which the GRS simulates a TRS.

If the Term Rewriting System is to simulate the Graph Rewriting System, the following requirements seems reasonable:

a. For every $g \in G$ there must be some term $U(g) \in T$.
b. If the graph $g \in G$ is a normal form, then the term $U(g)$ is also a normal form. Thus whenever the GRS reaches a dead end, so does the TRS.
c. Whenever $g \to_G g'$, then $U(g) \to^*{}_T U(g')$. That is, for every (single step) graph rewrite, there is a (perhaps multi-step) term rewriting sequence.

These three conditions allow a graph rewrite sequence to be simulated by a term rewriting sequence containing more steps, but this is in accord with the idea that the TRS is a "machine with finer grain instructions" than the GRS: that is, it can take the TRS several steps to simulate a single GRS step.

We now strengthen the three conditions so as to introduce some sort of notion of simulation of the TRS by the GRS:

a. For every $g \in G$ there must be some term $t \in T$. *Additionally require that* U *is surjective, so that there is some* $g \in G$ *for every* $t \in T$.
b. If the graph $g \in G$ is a normal form, then the term $U(g)$ is also a normal form. *Require the converse, as well, so that whenever* $U(g)$ *is a normal form, so is* g.
c. We have seen that because a TRS is finer grain than a corresponding GRS, there are some TRS sequences which have no corresponding GRS sequence. *However, we can often extend such TRS sequences, by further term rewriting, to a point where there is a corresponding graph sequence.* This suggests the following modified condition: *Whenever* $U(g) \rightarrow^*{}_{term} t'$*, then there exist* $t'' \in T$ *and* $g'' \in G$ *such that* $t' \rightarrow^*{}_{term} t''$ *and* $g \rightarrow^*{}_{graph} g''$.

The above discussion motivates the following definition of an adequate mapping:

DEFINITION **12.4.1** *A mapping* $U(G, \rightarrow) \rightarrow (T, \rightarrow)$ *is an adequate mapping if:*

a. U *is surjective.*
b. $g \in G$ *is a normal form if and only if* $U(g)$ *is a normal form.*
c. For $g \in G$*, if* $U(g) \rightarrow^*{}_{term} t'$ *then there is a* $g'' \in G$ *such that* $g \rightarrow^*{}_{graph} g''$ *and* $t' \rightarrow^*{}_{term} U(g'')$.

One test of the reasonableness of this definition is to check that term rewritings such as $t \rightarrow^*{}_{term} t_{nf}$ to normal form can be simulated by (adequate) graph rewriting:

a. find an element g of G such that $U(g) = t$. This is guaranteed by condition (a).
b. now term rewrite t to normal form t_{tnf}. By condition (c) there is a g'' such that g graph rewrites to g'' and t_{tnf} term rewrites to $U(g'')$. As t_{tnf} is a normal form, this means $t_{tnf} = U(g'')$, and by (b) g" is a normal form.

So, if there is a normalizing sequence for t by term rewriting, there is a corresponding normalizing sequence by graph rewriting. But the adequacy condition can do better than this. Let $t \rightarrow^* t'$ be a finite or infinite term rewriting sequence. Then, by condition (c), we can extend the term rewriting sequence to obtain $t \rightarrow^* t' \rightarrow^* t''$, such that there are g, g'' such that g graph rewrites to g'', and $t = U(g), t'' = U(g'')$. This means that not only can we simulate term rewritings to normal form, but also that we can simulate transfinite term rewriting sequences which develop increasing approximations to an infinite term. Such notions are common in lazy functional languages.

Our "adequacy" notion is one of many such notions of simulation, implementation etc., of one rewrite system in another, which we have encountered in the literature. The notions are compared in [KKSdV92].

12.5 ADEQUACY OF ACYCLIC GRAPH REWRITING FOR FINITE TERM REWRITING

We first state a result which is well known. Our proof is used as a basis for our more general result on cyclic graph rewriting and rational term rewriting. It depends on the notion of a complete development in an orthogonal rewriting system. Given a set of redexes of a term, a complete development of that set is a reduction sequence in which each step is the reduction of some residual of a member of the set, ending with a term containing no such residuals. A *Gross-Knuth* reduction of a term t is a complete development of all the redexes in t. We denote such a reduction sequence by $GKS(t)$ and its final term by $GK(t)$. Gross-Knuth reduction is similarly defined for graphs.

For finite terms and acyclic graphs, every set of redexes has a complete development. Note that while there may be many different orders in which the redexes may be reduced, the final result of a complete development of a given set of redexes is independent of the order. For infinite terms and cyclic graphs it is more complicated, as we shall see in the next section.

THEOREM **12.5.1** *Finite orthogonal acyclic graph rewriting is adequate for finite orthogonal term rewriting, via the unravelling mapping.*

PROOF. The first two adequacy conditions are trivially satisfied. For the cofinality condition, let there be given a reduction sequence $t_0 \to t_1 \to \ldots$, where $t_0 = U(g_0)$. For $i \geq 0$ let r_i be the one-step sequence from t_i to t_{i+1}. Construct a term reduction diagram and a graph reduction sequence inductively as follows.

$t''_0 = t_0$.
$T''_0 = r_0$.
$T''_i = r_i/(T_i \cdot T'_i) : t''_i \to^* t'_{i+1}$ (when $i \geq 1$).
$t'_1 = t_1$.
$T_1 = \langle\rangle : t_1 \to^* t'_1$.
$T_i = (T_{i-1} \cdot T'_{i-1})/r_{i-1} : t_i \to^* t'_i$ (when $i \geq 2$).
$T'_i = T''_{i-1}/(GKS(t''_{i-1})/T''_{i-1}) : t'_i \to^* t''_i$ (when $i \geq 1$).
$g_i = GK(g_{i-1})$ (when $i \geq 1$).

It is then easy to establish that $t''_i = U(g_i)$ for all $i \geq 1$, and hence that each t_i reduces to $U(g_i)$, by the sequence $T_i \cdot T'_i$. This proves cofinality. □

Here is an example of how the theorem fails for non-orthogonal rule systems.

Rules: $F(x) \to A(x,x), B \to C, B \to D$.

Term reduction sequence: $F(B) \to A(B,B) \to A(C,B) \to A(C,D)$.

By graph reduction, $F(B)$ can be reduced only to $A(x : B, x)$, $A(x : C, x)$, or $A(x : D, x)$. However, the term $A(C,D)$ cannot be reduced to the unravellings of any of these graphs.

Even for orthogonal systems, the adequacy relation fails for infinite terms and graphs. There exists a rewrite system containing an infinite graph g and an infinite reduction $U(g) \to^\infty t$, such that there is no graph g' for which $g \to^\infty g'$ and $t \to^\infty U(g')$. An example is given in [KKSdV92].

12.6 ADEQUACY OF FINITE GRAPH REWRITING FOR RATIONAL TERM REWRITING

Despite the failure of adequacy for infinite rewriting, we want to demonstrate the adequacy of cyclic graph rewriting for the transfinite term rewriting which cyclic graphs intuitively give rise to. We have mentioned that unrestricted transfinite rewriting does not allow such a result. Instead, we consider a restricted version of transfinite term rewriting which corresponds to finite cyclic graph rewriting: *rational* term rewriting.

DEFINITION **12.6.1** *A rational term is a term containing only finitely many non-isomorphic subterms. It can be shown (see [KKSdV92]) that a term is rational if and only if it is the unravelling of a finite graph. A rational set of nodes of a rational term is a set of nodes such that, if each of the nodes in the set is marked, the resulting term is still rational, taking the marks into account when testing isomorphism. A rational set of redexes of a rational term is a set of redexes whose roots are a rational set of nodes.*

THEOREM **12.6.2** *A set of nodes of a rational term t is rational if and only if there is a graph g unravelling to t, and a set of nodes of g which map by the unravelling to the given set of nodes of t.*

See [KKSdV92] for proof.

DEFINITION **12.6.3** *The rational term reduction sequences are defined by the following axioms:*

a. A strongly convergent complete development, of length at most ω, of a rational set of redexes, is rational.
b. A concatenation of finitely many rational reduction sequences is rational.
c. A subsequence of a rational reduction sequence is rational.
d. There are no other rational reduction sequences.

DEFINITION **12.6.4** *A* weakly collapsing *set of rewrite rules is a set which includes at most one rule whose right hand side is a variable, and such that that rule, if present, has the form $A(x) \to x$ for some function symbol A.*

THEOREM **12.6.5** *In weakly collapsing rewrite systems, finitary (cyclic) graph rewriting is adequate for rational infinitary term rewriting.*

We shall only give an idea of the proof here. It is easy to demonstrate that every rational reduction sequence is a finite concatenation of complete developments of rational sets of redexes. We imitate the proof of the adequacy theorem for acyclic graphs and finitary term rewriting, but in which each step $t_i \to t_{i+1}$ is a complete development of a rational set of redexes. The corresponding reduction from g_i to g_{i+1} is then the complete development of all redexes of g_i which are mapped by unravelling to the redexes reduced in t_i. The weakly collapsing condition on the system ensures that the result of such a complete development is independent of its order, as shown in [KKSdV92]. The necessity of this condition is illustrated by the following example.

Rules: $A(x) \to x$, $B(x) \to x$

Graph: $x : A(B(x))$

The Church-Rosser property fails here. The graph can reduce to either $x : A(x)$ or to $x : B(x)$, neither of which can reduce to anything but itself. Failure of the Church-Rosser property immediately leads to a failure of the adequacy property. Consider the graph $F(x, x), x : A(B(x))$. This reduces only to $F(x, x), x : A(x)$ or $F(x, x), x : B(x)$. Its unravelling is the infinite term $F(A(B(A(B(\ldots)))), A(B(A(B(\ldots)))))$. This can be reduced by a rational reduction sequence to $F(A(A(A(\ldots))), B(B(B(\ldots))))$. This term cannot be further reduced to the unravelling of either $F(x, x), x : A(x)$ or $F(x, x), x : B(x)$, contradicting the adequacy property.

The weakly collapsing condition is not as restrictive as it might at first appear. Every non-weakly collapsing system can be transformed into a weakly collapsing one by adding a new rule $I(x) \rightarrow x$, and replacing every right-hand side which is a variable x by $I(x)$. This transformation is closely similar to the way such rules are implemented in practice.

REFERENCES

[AGM92] S. Abramsky, D. Gabbay, and T. Maibaum (editors). *Handbook of Logic in Computer Science*, vol. II. Oxford University Press, 1992.

[AN80] A. Arnold and M. Nivat. The metric space of infinite trees: Algebraic and topological properties. *Fundamenta Informatica*, **4**, pp. 445–476, 1980.

[Boo91] R. V. Book (editor). *Proc. 4th Conference on Rewriting Techniques and Applications*, Springer Verlag, Lecture Notes in Computer Science 488, Como, Italy, 1991.

[BvEG+87] H. P. Barendregt, M. C. J. D. van Eekelen, J. R. W. Glauert, J. R. Kennaway, M. J. Plasmeijer, and M. R. Sleep. Term graph rewriting. In J. W. de Bakker, A. J. Nijman, and P. C. Treleaven (editors), *Proc. PARLE'87 Conference, vol.II*, Springer Verlag, Lecture Notes in Computer Science 259, pp. 141–158, Eindhoven, The Netherlands, 1987.

[DJ90] N. Dershowitz and J.-P. Jouannaud. Rewrite systems. In van Leeuwen [vL90a], chapter 15.

[DK89] N. Dershowitz and S. Kaplan. Rewrite, rewrite, rewrite, rewrite, rewrite. In *Proc. ACM Conference on Principles of Programming Languages, Austin, Texas*, pp. 250–259, Austin, Texas, 1989.

[DKP89] N. Dershowitz, S. Kaplan, and D. A. Plaisted. Infinite normal forms (plus corrigendum). In G. Ausiello, M. Dezani-Ciancaglini, and S. Ronchi Della Rocca (editors), *Automata, Languages and Programming*, Springer Verlag, Lecture Notes in Computer Science 372, pp. 249–262, Stresa, Italy, 1989.

[DKP91] N. Dershowitz, S. Kaplan, and D. A. Plaisted. Rewrite, rewrite, rewrite, rewrite, rewrite. *Theoretical Computer Science*, **83**, pp. 71–96, 1991. Extended version of [DKP89].

[FW91] W. M. Farmer and R. J. Watro. Redex capturing in term graph rewriting. In Book [Boo91], pp. 13–24.

[Ken92] J. R. Kennaway. *On transfinite abstract reduction systems.* Technical Report CS-R9205, Centre for Mathematics and Computer Science, Amsterdam, 1992.

[KKSdV90a] J. R. Kennaway, J. W. Klop, M. R. Sleep, and F. J. de Vries. *An Infinitary Church-Rosser property for Non-collapsing Orthogonal Term Rewriting Systems.* Technical Report CS-9043, CWI, Amsterdam, 1990.

[KKSdV90b] J. R. Kennaway, J. W. Klop, M. R. Sleep, and F. J. de Vries. *Transfinite Reductions in Orthogonal Term Rewriting Systems.* Technical Report CS-R9041, CWI, Amsterdam, 1990.

[KKSdV91] J. R. Kennaway, J. W. Klop, M. R. Sleep, and F. J. de Vries. Transfinite reductions in orthogonal term rewriting systems (extended abstract). In Book [Boo91], pp. 1–12. A longer version appears in [KKSdV90b].

[KKSdV92] J. R. Kennaway, J. W. Klop, M. R. Sleep, and F. J. de Vries. *On the adequacy of graph rewriting for simulating term rewriting.* Technical Report CS-R9204, Centre for Mathematics and Computer Science, Amsterdam, 1992.

[Klo92] J. W. Klop. Term rewriting systems. In Abramsky et al. [AGM92], pp. 1–116.

[Mit91] J. C. Mitchell. On abstraction and the expressive power of programming languages. In *Proc. Int. Conf. on Theoretical aspects of Computer Software*, Sendai, Japan, 1991.

[O'D85] M. J. O'Donnell. *Equational Logic as a Programming Language.* MIT Press, 1985.

[Pey87] S. L. Peyton Jones. *The implementation of functional programming languages.* Prentice-Hall, 1987.

[Sta80] J. Staples. Computation on graph-like expressions. *Theoretical Computer Science*, **10**, pp. 171–185, 1980.

[vEB90] P. van Emde Boas. Machine models and simulations. In van Leeuwen [vL90b], chapter 1.

[vL90a] J. van Leeuwen (editor). *Handbook of Theoretical Computer Science*, vol. B: Formal Models and Semantics. North-Holland, Amsterdam, 1990.

[vL90b] J. van Leeuwen (editor). *Handbook of Theoretical Computer Science*, vol. A: Algorithms and Complexity. North-Holland, Amsterdam, 1990.

13

Translations into the Graph Grammar Machine

H.-J. Kreowski

13.1 INTRODUCTION

In many areas of computer science, the relationships between languages or computational models play important roles. Quite often a relationship is established by translating the syntactic entities of one model into the syntactic entities of another model. Compilers are most famous instances of this kind. Another significant example is the notion of a reduction as used in complexity theory (see e.g. Mehlhorn [Meh84]). In the area of graph grammars, translations are frequently constructed to compare various computational models with graph grammars and various graph grammar models with each other. See e.g., Kreowski and Rozenberg [KR90], who expressed some graph grammar models in terms of structured graph grammars, Engelfriet and Rozenberg [ER90], who compared boundary NLC graph grammars with hyperedge replacement grammars, Kreowski and Reisig [Kre81, Rei81], who translated Petri-nets into graph grammars, Ehrig, Habel and Kreowski [EHK92], who modeled Chomsky grammars and semantic networks by graph grammars, and Janssens and Rozenberg [JR81], who reduced Post correspondence problems to node label controlled graph grammars etc.

In this chapter, a tentative approach is presented for a formal treatment of a translation into a graph grammar model. For this purpose, some basic features of graph grammar approaches and their derivation processes are put together into the notion of a graph grammar machine in section 13.2. In section 13.3, Chomsky grammars, Post correspondence problems and hyperedge-replacement grammars are translated into a particular graph grammar machine motivating the notion of correct translations as introduced in section 13.4. The idea of correctness is that the semantics of the syntactic

Term Graph Rewriting: Theory and Practice.
Eds. Ronan Sleep, Rinus Plasmeijer and Marko van Eekelen.

entities of the source model can be related in a nice way to the operational semantics of the graph grammars obtained by the translation. In section 13.5, some correctness results are applied to establish undecidability results for graph grammars. The results presented in this chapter have the character of "folklore". But to the knowledge of the author, most of them cannot be found in published literature. The hope is that the notions, constructions and observations in this chapter may serve as prototypes of similar considerations in the future.

13.2 THE GRAPH GRAMMAR MACHINE

In the literature, one encounters quite a lot of graph grammar and graph rewriting approaches that are different in motivation and technicalities (see e.g., the proceedings of the graph grammar workshops [CER79, ENR83, ENRR87, EKR91] for a survey). They nevertheless share some features that amount to the notion of a graph grammar machine in its elementary form:

a. A class $\mathcal{G}$ of graphs, hypergraphs or other graph-like structures containing all objects that may be processed eventually,
b. a decidable equivalence relation $\cong$ on $\mathcal{G}$ where related objects are called *isomorphic*,
c. a notion of a *rule* and its *application* establishing effectively, for any finite set P of rules, a binary relation $\underset{P}{\Longrightarrow}$ on $\mathcal{G}$, where $M \underset{P}{\Longrightarrow} N$ for $M, N \in \mathcal{G}$ is called a *direct derivation* from M to N,
d. for $n \geq 0$, the n-fold composition $\overset{n}{\underset{P}{\Longrightarrow}}$ of $\underset{P}{\Longrightarrow}$ with itself where $\overset{0}{\underset{P}{\Longrightarrow}}$ equals $\cong$, $\overset{1}{\underset{P}{\Longrightarrow}}$ equals $\underset{P}{\Longrightarrow}$ and $\overset{m+n}{\underset{P}{\Longrightarrow}}$ is the composition of $\overset{m}{\underset{P}{\Longrightarrow}}$ and $\overset{n}{\underset{P}{\Longrightarrow}}$, i.e. $A \overset{m+n}{\underset{P}{\Longrightarrow}} C$ if and only if there is some $B \in \mathcal{G}$ with $A \overset{m}{\Longrightarrow} B$ and $B \overset{n}{\Longrightarrow} C$,
e. the reflexive and transitive closure $\overset{*}{\underset{P}{\Longrightarrow}}$ of $\underset{P}{\Longrightarrow}$, i.e. the union of all $\overset{n}{\underset{P}{\Longrightarrow}}$, establishing a *derivation mechanism* on $\mathcal{G}$,
f. a set $\mathcal{T}$ of *output descriptions* such that each $T \in \mathcal{T}$ defines a decidable subset $\mathcal{O}_T \subseteq \mathcal{G}$ of output objects.

13.2.1 Graph grammar approach and graph grammar machine

a. A *graph grammar approach* is a system $\mathcal{A} = (\mathcal{G}, \cong, \mathcal{R}, \Longrightarrow, \mathcal{T}, \mathcal{O})$ where $\mathcal{G}$ is a class of graph-like objects, $\cong$ is a binary relation on $\mathcal{G}, \mathcal{R}$ is a class of rules, $\Longrightarrow$ is a mapping associating a binary relation $\underset{P}{\Longrightarrow}$ to each subset P of $\mathcal{R}, \mathcal{T}$ is a set of output descriptions and $\mathcal{O}$ is a mapping associating a subset $\mathcal{O}_T$ of $\mathcal{G}$ to each $T \in \mathcal{T}$ such that the conditions above are satisfied.
b. Each such graph grammar approach $\mathcal{A}$ defines a *graph grammar machine* $\mathcal{M}(\mathcal{A})$ that expects a finite set P of rules, a *start object* $Z \in \mathcal{G}$ and an output description T as inputs and yields a stream of output objects from the set

$$L(P, Z, T) = \{M \in \mathcal{O}_T | Z \overset{*}{\underset{P}{\Longrightarrow}} M\}$$

by enumerating $\overset{*}{\underset{P}{\Longrightarrow}}$ starting in Z and filtering the results through $\mathcal{O}_T$.

c. If $\mathcal{M}(\mathcal{A})$ gets additionally a natural number $k \in \mathbb{N}$ as input, the output can be restricted to the set $L(P, Z, T, k) = \{M \in \mathcal{O}_T \mid Z \overset{n}{\underset{P}{\Longrightarrow}} M \text{ for some } n \leq k\}$.

Remarks

a. The graph grammar machine may be illustrated by the following diagram.

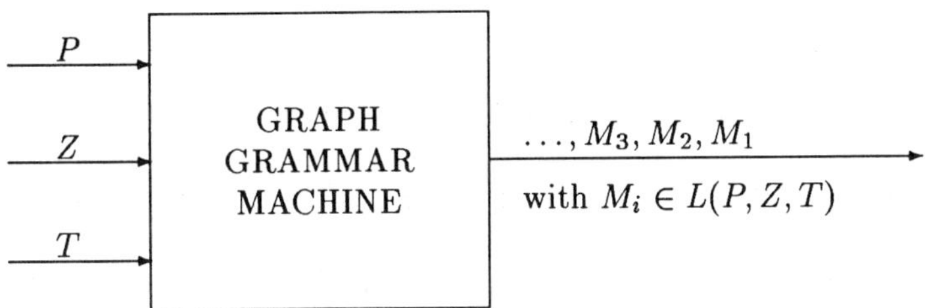

b. Most graph grammar approaches in the literature fit into the framework of the definition above although the kinds of graphs considered and the actual ways of rule-based rewriting may differ tremendously from case to case.
c. If labeled graphs are considered, the usual output description is a set T of terminal labels (a subset of all labels) specifying the set $\mathcal{O}_T$ of all graphs the nodes and edges of which are labeled in T only. But there are other possibilities like all irreducible graphs (to which no rule is applicable) or all graphs with certain properties like all planar graphs, all connected graphs, all k-colorable graphs, etc.
d. In a more sophisticated version of the graph grammar machine, one may assume that start objects belong to a subclass $\mathcal{I} \subseteq \mathcal{G}$, that the derivation process can be controlled in a suitable way to cut down its nondeterminism and that queries concerning quantitative and qualitative aspects of the expected outputs are possible.

13.2.2 Generated language and computed function

The idea of a graph grammar machine integrates the formal language and the computational point of view of rule-based systems.

Let $\mathcal{A} = (\mathcal{G}, \cong, \mathcal{R}, \Longrightarrow, \mathcal{T}, \mathcal{O})$ be a graph grammar approach.

a. If an input $G = (P, Z, T)$ of $\mathcal{M}(\mathcal{A})$ is considered as a *graph grammar*, $L(G) = L(P, Z, T)$ is the usual *generated language* of G.
b. Let $\mathcal{G}$ be equipped with a size function $size : \mathcal{G} \to \mathbb{N}$. Then a partial function $f : \mathcal{G} \to \mathcal{P}_{fin}(\mathcal{G})$, where $\mathcal{P}_{fin}(X)$ denotes the set of all finite subsets of a set X, is called $\mathcal{M}(\mathcal{A})$*-computed* with respect to P, T and a total computable function $b : \mathbb{N} \to \mathbb{N}$ if $f(Z) = L(P, Z, T, b(size(Z)))$ whenever $f(Z)$ is defined and $L(P, Z, T) = \emptyset$ otherwise.

13.2.3 Observation

The graph grammar machine provides an operational semantics for graph grammars and sets of rules together with output descriptions respectively. An obvious consequence of this situation is that each generated language is recursively enumerable and that each computed function is computable in the ordinary sense.

Let $\mathcal{A} = (\mathcal{G}, \cong, \mathcal{R}, \Longrightarrow, \mathcal{T}, \mathcal{O})$ be a graph grammar approach with a recursively enumerable class $\mathcal{G}$. Let G be a graph grammar and f be an $\mathcal{M}(\mathcal{A})$-computed function. Then the following hold.

a. $L(G)$ is recursively enumerable.
b. f is computable.

PROOF. The graphs isomorphic to Z can be enumerated by enumerating $\mathcal{G}$ and testing isomorphism. The relations $\underset{P}{\Longrightarrow}$ and hence $\overset{n}{\underset{P}{\Longrightarrow}}$ for all $n \geq 1$ can be constructed effectively by definition and construction. Altogether, all M with $Z \overset{*}{\underset{P}{\Longrightarrow}} M$ can be enumerated and tested for membership in $\mathcal{O}_T$. This proves the first statement. By assumption, there are P, T and $b : \mathbb{N} \to \mathbb{N}$ such that $f(Z) = L(P, Z, T, b(size(Z))$ if and only if $f(Z)$ is defined. By the same reasoning as above, $L(P, Z, T, b(size(Z))$ can be effectively constructed within a time bound depending on the size of Z only. □

13.2.4 Example machine

For the further considerations, the graph grammar machine is based on the so-called Berlin approach to graph rewriting (see e.g., Ehrig [Ehr79]). All specific results of this chapter are based on the graph grammar machine that is given by the following graph grammar approach.

a. Let $\mathcal{G}_C$ be the class of all *labeled directed graphs* (over C). Such a system M consists of a set V_M of *nodes*, a set E_M of *edges*, two functions $s_M, t_M : E_M \to V_M$ associating a *source* $s_M(e)$ and a *target* $t_M(e)$ to each $e \in E_M$, and two functions $l_M : V_M \to C$ and $m_M : E_M \to C$ *labeling* nodes and edges in some alphabet C. C is assumed to contain a default label that labels all nodes and edges if nothing else is fixed. In drawings of graphs, the default label is invisible.
b. For $M, N \in \mathcal{G}_C$, a *graph morphism* $f : M \to N$ consists of functions $f_V : V_M \to V_N$ and $f_E : E_M \to E_N$ such that $s_N(f_E(e)) = f_V(s_M(e))$, $t_N(f_E(e)) = f_V(t_M(e))$, $l_N(f_V(v)) = l_M(v)$, $m_N(f_E(e)) = m_M(e)$ for all $e \in E_M, v \in V_M$.

   If f_V and f_E are inclusions, M is a *subgraph* of N, denoted by $M \subseteq N$.

   If f_V and f_E are bijective, f is an *isomorphism*, and M and N are *isomorphic*, denoted by $M \cong N$.
c. A *rule* $r = (L, K, R, b)$ consists of three graphs $L, K, R \in \mathcal{G}_C$ with $K \subseteq L$ and a graph morphism $b : K \to R$.
d. Let P be a set of rules, $r = (L, K, R, b) \in P$, $M, N \in \mathcal{G}_C$ and $g : L \to M$ a graph morphism subject to the *gluing condition*

   (i) $a_M(e) \in g_V(V_L - V_K)$ for $e \in E_M$ and $a_M \in \{s_M, t_M\}$ implies $e \in g_E(E_L - E_K)$,
   (ii) $g_V(v) = g_V(v')$ for $v \neq v'$ implies $v, v' \in V_K$,
   (iii) $g_E(e) = g_E(e')$ for $e \neq e'$ implies $e, e' \in E_K$.

Then M *directly derives* N through r and g, denoted by $M \underset{P}{\Longrightarrow} N$ if N is isomorphic to the gluing of R and Z through b and d where Z is the subgraph of M with $V_Z = V_M - g_V(V_L - V_K)$ and $E_Z = E_M - g_E(E_L - E_K)$ and d is the restriction of g to the subgraphs K and Z.

The gluing is explicitly constructed by the disjoint union $R + Z$ of R and Z and by identifying the pairs of nodes $b_V(v), d_V(v)$ for $v \in V_K$ and the pairs of edges $b_E(e), d_E(e)$ for $e \in E_K$. The gluing condition makes sure that Z becomes a subgraph, that g can be restricted to K and Z and that M is isomorphic to the gluing of L and Z through the inclusion of K into L and d. By construction, one gets a graph morphism $h : R \to N$. In terms of category theory, the gluing construction is a pushout. If $M \in \mathcal{G}_C$ and l is a list of pairs of nodes and pairs of edges, then M/l denotes the graph obtained by identifying the items in the pairs.

e. Each $T \subseteq C$ serves as an output description by specifying as output objects all graphs labeled in T, i.e. $\mathcal{O}_T = \mathcal{G}_T$.

13.3 TRANSLATIONS

If each syntactic entity of some language or computational model can be translated into inputs of the graph grammar machine, the machine lends its operational semantics to the translated language. Clearly, this is meaningful in its own right only if the graph grammar machine is efficiently implemented or the translated language has not got any other formal semantics.

To demonstrate the principle, explicit translations of Chomsky grammars, Post correspondence problems and hyperedge replacement grammars are constructed. Clearly, the existence of such translations is not at all surprising because of the generality of the underlying graph grammar approach. Nevertheless, it may be of interest to see how it works.

13.3.1 Chomsky grammars

There is a simple way to consider a string w as a graph $w^\bullet$ that can be extented in such a way that string languages are mapped into graph languages and Chomsky grammars into graph grammars (cf. Ehrig, Habel, Kreowski [EHK92]). The translation given here is slightly more general because empty strings are included.

a. Given $w = x_1 \dots x_n \in C^*$ with $x_i \in C$ for $i = 1, \dots, n$ $(n \geq 0)$, the *string graph* $w^\bullet$ has the following form

$$\circ \overset{x_1}{\longrightarrow} \bullet \overset{x_2}{\longrightarrow} \bullet \dots \bullet \overset{x_n}{\longrightarrow} \diamond.$$

The node without incoming edges is denoted by $b(w^\bullet)$, the node without outgoing edges by $e(w^\bullet)$. In the case $n = 0$, w is the empty string λ, and $\lambda^\bullet$ has no edges, but one node $b(\lambda^\bullet) = e(\lambda^\bullet)$.

b. If $L \subseteq C^*$, $\{w^\bullet \mid w \in L\}$ is denoted by $L^\bullet$.

c. Let $p = (u, v)$ be a *production*, i.e. $u, v \in C^*$. Then p can be applied to $w \in C^*$ if $w = xuy$ for some $x, y \in C^*$ yielding $z = xvy$. Let P be a set of productions and $p \in P$. Then the application of p to w is denoted by $w \underset{P}{\longrightarrow} z$.

d. Let TWO be the totally disconnected graph with the two nodes b and e. Mapping b to $b(w^\bullet)$ and e to $e(w^\bullet)$ for $w \in C^*$ defines a graph morphism that will be denoted by $TWO \to w^\bullet$. It is an inclusion if and only if $w \neq \lambda$.

e. A *Chomsky grammar* $G = (N, T, P, S)$ consists of a set of *nonterminals* $N \subseteq C$, a set of *terminals* $T \subseteq C$, a set of productions P such that the left-hand side of each production contains at least a nonterminal, and $S \in N$.
$G = (N, T, P, S)$ generates the language $L(G) = \{w \in T^* \mid S \overset{*}{\underset{P}{\longrightarrow}} w\}$.

f. A Chomsky grammar can be translated into a graph grammar

$$G^\bullet = (P^\bullet = \{p^\bullet \mid p \in P\}, S^\bullet, T)$$

with $p^\bullet = (u^\bullet, TWO, v^\bullet, TWO \to v^\bullet)$ for $p = (u, v)$.

g. It is easy to see, that this translation has the following properties:

(i) $w \underset{P}{\longrightarrow} z$ through $(u, v) \in P$ if and only if $w^\bullet \underset{P^\bullet}{\Longrightarrow} z^\bullet$ through $(u, v)^\bullet$ and the inclusion of $u^\bullet$ into $w^\bullet$.

(ii) $S \overset{*}{\underset{P}{\longrightarrow}} w$ if and only if $S^\bullet \overset{*}{\underset{P^\bullet}{\Longrightarrow}} w^\bullet$.

(iii) $(L(G))^\bullet = L(G^\bullet)$.

Obviously, the statement (iii) follows from statement (ii) because $w \in T^*$ if and only if $w^\bullet \in \mathcal{G}_T$. And statement (ii) follows from statement (i). The latter holds because each graph morphism $g : u^\bullet \to w^\bullet$ is an inclusion and satisfies the gluing condition and $u^\bullet \subseteq w^\bullet$ if and only if there are $x, y \in C^*$ such that $w = xuy$ and

$$w^\bullet = (x^\bullet + u^\bullet + y^\bullet)/e(x^\bullet) = b(u^\bullet), e(u^\bullet) = b(y^\bullet).$$

13.3.2 Post correspondence problems

A *Post correspondence problem* $PCP = (U, V)$ is specified by two sequences $U = (u_1, \ldots, u_n)$ and $V = (v_1, \ldots, v_n)$ with $u_i, v_j \in A^*$ for $i, j = 1, \ldots, n$ and some alphabet A. A non-empty sequence $i_1, \ldots, i_k$ of indices is called a *solution* of PCP if $u_{i_1} \ldots u_{i_k} = v_{i_1} \ldots v_{i_k}$. It is well-known that the solvability of Post correspondence problems over alphabets with at least two elements is undecidable.

Choosing some output description T, a Post correspondence problem PCP can be translated into the graph grammar $trans(PCP)_T$ with the start graph $S^\bullet$ and the following rules:

$$\left.\begin{array}{l} r_i = (S^\bullet \supseteq TWO \subseteq (u_i S v_i^T)^\bullet) \\ \overline{r}_i = (S^\bullet \supseteq TWO \subseteq (u_i B v_i^T)^\bullet) \end{array}\right\} \text{for } i = 1, \ldots, n$$
$$\left.\begin{array}{l} r_x = ((xBx)^\bullet \supseteq TWO \subseteq B^\bullet) \\ \overline{r}_x = ((xBx)^\bullet \supseteq TWO \subseteq TWO) \end{array}\right\} \text{for } x \in A$$

where TWO and $TWO \subseteq w^\bullet$ are chosen as in subsection 13.3.1. S and B are two nonterminal symbols that do not belong to A. And w^T denotes the transposition of $w \in C^*$.

A rule of the first type of rules can be applied to the start graph: $S^\bullet \Longrightarrow (u_{i_1} S v_{i_1}{}^T)^\bullet$ for $1 \leq i_1 \leq n$. Because $S^\bullet$ is a subgraph of the result, one may repeat to apply rules of the first type:

$$S^\bullet \overset{k-1}{\Longrightarrow} (u_{i_1} \dots u_{i_{k-1}} S v_{i_{k-1}}{}^T \dots v_{i_1}{}^T)^\bullet \text{ for } 1 \leq i_j \leq n, j = 1, \dots, k-1.$$

with $v_{i_{k-1}}{}^T \dots v_{i_1}{}^T = (v_{i_1} \dots v_{i_{k-1}})^T$).
The only other applicable type of rules is $\overline{r}_i$ yielding

$$S^\bullet \overset{k}{\Longrightarrow} (uBv^T)^\bullet \text{ with } u = u_{i_1} \dots u_{i_k}, v = v_{i_1} \dots v_{i_k},\ u \neq \lambda \neq v,\ 1 \leq k.$$

Now, neither r_i nor $\overline{r}_i$ for any i is applicable, but r_x or $\overline{r}_x$ may be applicable for some $x \in A$. If $u = \overline{u}x_l \dots x_1$ and $v = \overline{v}x_l \dots x_1$ (i.e. $v^T = x_1 \dots x_l \overline{v}^T$), then one can apply $r_{x_1}, \dots, r_{x_{l-1}}$ in succession and $\overline{r}_{x_l}$ at the end:

$$(uBv^T)^\bullet \overset{l-1}{\Longrightarrow} (\overline{u}x_l B x_l \overline{v}^T)^\bullet \Longrightarrow \overline{u}^\bullet + (\overline{v}^T)^\bullet.$$

Here the derivation process gets stuck.

If $i_1, \dots, i_k$ is a solution of the given PCP, one has $u = v$ and can choose $\overline{u} = \lambda = \overline{v}$. Since $\lambda^\bullet$ is the totally disconnected graph with a single node, $\lambda^\bullet + \lambda^\bullet = TWO$ such that one gets a derivation

$$S^\bullet \overset{*}{\Longrightarrow} TWO.$$

If PCP has no solution, then any choice of the first k steps and of the decomposition of u and v ends with $\overline{u} \neq \lambda$ or $\overline{v} \neq \lambda$. In other words, each derivable graph contains edges. If the output condition T is chosen in such a way that $TWO \in \mathcal{O}_T$, the reasoning above shows the following statement.

(1) PCP is solvable if and only if $TWO \in L(trans(PCP)_T)$.

This statement can be rephrased if one takes into account that any derivable graph except TWO contains edges.

(2) PCP is solvable if and only if $L(trans(PCP)_T)$ contains a totally disconnected graph.

Again another formulation is obtained by employing a particular output condition. Let T_0 be the alphabet with the default label, then $\mathcal{O}_{T_0}$ contains all totally disconnected graphs and $L(trans(PCP)_{T_0}) = \{TWO\}$ or $L(trans(PCP)_{T_0}) = \emptyset$. This proves the following version of the statement.

(3) PCP is solvable if and only if $L(trans(PCP)_{T_0})$ is not empty.

Similar statements can be obtained by modifying the start graph and the rules. Choose, for example, the start graph $Z = (S\$)^\bullet / b((S\$)^\bullet) = e((S\$)^\bullet)$ where \$ is an extra symbol, i.e. Z is the cycle composed of the string graphs $S^\bullet$ and $\$^\bullet$. Replace, for each $x \in A$, the rule r_x by the rule

$$\hat{r}_x = ((xBx)^\bullet \supseteq TWO \xrightarrow{in} R_x = rev_B((xBx)^\bullet)$$

where $rev_c(M)$ is the graph obtained from M by reversing the direction of all c-labeled edges and in maps the node b to $s_{R_x}(e_B)$ and e to $t_{R_x}(e_B)$ for the edge e_B with $m_{R_x}(e_B) = B$. Finally, replace the rules $\overline{r}_x$ for $x \in A$ by the rule

$$\hat{r} = ((B\$)^\bullet \supseteq TWO \subseteq rev_{\pounds}(\pounds\$)^\bullet$$

where $\pounds$ is another special symbol.

Because $S^\bullet \subseteq Z$, the first k steps of a derivation can be done as above. The derived graph is a cycle composed of the string graphs $(uBv^T)^\bullet$ and $\$^\bullet$. If u and v can be decomposed as above, the rules $\hat{r}_{x_1}, \ldots, \hat{r}_{x_l}$ can be applied one after the other. The derived graph contains a cycle composed of the string graphs $(\overline{u}B\overline{v}^T)^\bullet$ and $\$^\bullet$. In addition, it consists of two copies of the string graph $(x_1 \ldots x_l)^\bullet$ where the first copy is attached to the source of the B-labeled edge of the cycle, and the second copy is attached to the target of this very edge. If PCP is not solvable, such graphs are the best one can get. If PCP is solvable, there are u and v with $u = v = x_1 \ldots x_l$, and the corresponding derived graph contains the only cycle $(B\$)^\bullet / b((B\$)^\bullet) = e((B\$)^\bullet)$ such that the rule $\hat{r}$ breaks the cycle if applied.

The reasoning above leads to further characterizations of the solvability of Post correspondence problems. Let $trans'(PCP)_T$ denote the graph grammar with output description T, start graph Z and the rules $r_i, \overline{r}_i, \hat{r}_x$ and $\hat{r}$. Let T_1 be the alphabet containing T_0, A and the special symbols \$ and $\pounds$, and let T_2 contain additionally B and S. Then $\mathcal{O}_{T_2}$ accepts all graphs derivable from Z while $\mathcal{O}_{T_1}$ does not accept graphs with edges labeled with B or S. If one takes into account that

(i) a Post correspondence problem has infinitely many solutions if it is solvable,
(ii) graphs derivable from Z contain cycles as long as they contain edges labeled with S or B, and
(iii) the labels S and B can disappear only if there are solutions,

then the following statements are shown.

(iv) PCP is solvable if and only if $L(trans'(PCP)_{T_1})$ is infinite.

(v) PCP is solvable if and only if $L(trans'(PCP)_{T_2})$ contains some cyclefree graphs.

Altogether, the examples may demonstrate sufficiently that the solvability of Post correspondence problems can be expressed by various graph-theoretic properties of the members of generated languages if one plays around a bit with the corresponding graph grammars.

13.3.3 Hyperedge replacement

Hyperedge replacement (see e.g., Habel [Hab89] or Drewes and Kreowski [DK91]) is one of the best studied graph grammar approaches with a context-free mode of rewriting. The basic idea is as follows: Choose a class of graphs of interest, for example, unlabeled undirected graphs. To be able to generate languages of such graphs they may be decorated by hyperedges in intermediate steps where the hyperedges are subject to eventual replacement by other decorated or undecorated graphs. A way to define hyperedge replacement is by translation into graph grammars.

a. An unlabeled undirected graph consists of a set V of nodes and a set E of edges each being a 2-element subset of V. A decorated graph H consists of an unlabeled undirected graph (V_H, E_H), a set Y_H of ***hyperedges***, a function $att_H : Y_H \to V_H^*$ ***attaching*** each hyperedge to a sequence of nodes, a ***labeling*** function $lab_H : Y_H \to C$, and a sequence $ext_H \in V_H^*$ of ***external nodes***. The class of all decorated graphs is denoted by $\mathcal{H}_C$.
b. A hyperedge replacement grammar $HRG = (N, P, Z)$ consists of a set of nonterminals $N \subseteq C$, a set P of rules and $Z \in \mathcal{H}_C$ as axiom. A rule $r = (A, R)$ is a pair with $A \in N$ and $R \in \mathcal{H}_C$.
c. A decorated graph H can be translated into a directed graph $D(H)$ by $V_{D(H)} = V_H + Y_H$, $E_{D(H)}$ consisting of two edges e^1 and e^2 for each $e = \{v, v'\} \in E_H$ with $s_{D(H)}(e^1) = t_{D(H)}(e^2) = v$ and $t_{D(H)}(e^1) = s_{D(H)}(e^2) = v'$, and n edges $y^1, \ldots, y^n$ for each $y \in Y_H$ with n being the length of $att_H(y) = v_1 \ldots v_n$ and $s_{D(H)}(y^i) = y$, $t_{D(H)}(y^i) = v_i$, $l_{D(H)}(y) = lab_H(y)$ for all $y \in Y_H, m_{D(H)}(y^i) = i$ for each $y \in Y_H$ and $i = 1, \ldots, n$, and all other edges carry the default label.
d. Let $n^\bullet$ for $n \in N$ denote the totally disconnected graph with the nodes $1, \ldots, n$, and $(A, n)^\bullet$ for $A \in N$ the graph with the $n+1$ nodes $0, \ldots, n$, the n edges $1, \ldots, n$ with 0 as source and i as target and label for each $i = 1, \ldots, n$. Moreover, 0 is labeled with A.
e. Now one can translate a hyperedge replacement grammar $HRG = (N, P, Z)$ into a graph grammar $D(HRG) = (D(P), D(Z), T)$ where T consists of the default label only and $D(P)$ contains the rule $D(r) = ((A, n)^\bullet, n^\bullet, D(R), b)$ for each $r = (A, R)$ with $ext_R = v_1 \ldots v_n$ and b mapping i to v_i for $i = 1, \ldots, n$.
f. $D(HRG)$ borrows its derivation process, given by the graph grammar machine, to HRG because the following holds:

   If $D(Z) \underset{D(P)}{\overset{*}{\Longrightarrow}} M$, then there is a unique $H \in \mathcal{H}_C$ with $D(H) = M^\circ$ where M° is M without loops.

13.4 CORRECT TRANSLATIONS

From the theoretical point of view, a translation is more interesting if the source language has some semantics of its own that can be compared with the outputs of the graph grammar machine. More precisely, the source language may have an operational semantics associating a value entity $V(X)$ (belonging to some value domain $\mathcal{V}$) to each syntactic input entity X while the translation transforms X into a graph grammar $T(X)$. Then the question is how $V(X)$ and $L(T(X))$ are related to each other.

13.4.1 The notion of correctness

Let T and V chosen as above. Let COMP be a set, called *comparison domain*, and R_1 and R_2 two functions, called *relators*, mapping value entities and graph languages respectively into COMP.

Then one may say that the translation T is *correct* with respect to V, R_1 and R_2 if $R_1(V(X)) = R_2(L(T(X)))$ for all input entities X of the source language.

In similar notions like simulation, implementation, reduction and compilation, the semantics of the source and the target are directly related to each other either by mapping source semantics to target semantics or the other way round. The correctness concept introduced above is a bit more flexible because the compatibility between source and target semantics may be expressed in a comparison domain which can coincide with the source domain or the target domain or may differ from both of them. Correctness seems to be closely related to the concept of adequacy as introduced by Kennaway, Klop, Sleep and de Vries [KKSdV] for graph rewriting. It may be worthwhile to look into technical details of this relationship.

The following examples may shed some light on the significance of the notion of correctness.

13.4.2 Chomsky grammars continued

Considering the translation of a Chomsky grammar G into the graph grammar $G^\bullet$ (given in 13.3.1), we have $(L(G))^\bullet = L(G^\bullet)$.

In other words, if the generated language is considered as the value of a Chomsky grammar, if all graph languages form the comparison domain, if the first relator transforms a string language L into its graph language version $L^\bullet$ and if the second relator is the identity on graph languages, the translation that transforms G into $G^\bullet$ is correct with respect to the generated string languages and the two relators.

13.4.3 Post correspondence problems continued

In 13.3.2, various translations of Post correspondence problems into graph grammars are given that differ slightly with respect to the chosen rules, output descriptions and start graphs. In each case, we have got a characterization of the solvability of Post correspondence problems that can be reformulated now in terms of correctness.

Consider the set of solutions $\Sigma(PCP)$ of a Post correspondence problem PCP as its value entity. Choose the Boolean values as comparison domain and the non-emptiness test NET as first relator. As second relator, we may consider one after the other one of the following predicates on graph languages L:

($PRED_1$) Is TWO in L?
($PRED_2$) Does L contain some totally disconnected graph?
($PRED_3$) Is L non-empty?
($PRED_4$) Is L infinite?
($PRED_5$) Does L contain some cyclefree graph?

Then the five characterizations of solvability of Post correspondence problems can be stated as correctness results.

(1) $trans(-)_T$ is correct w. r. t. Σ, NET and $PRED_1$.
(2) $trans(-)_T$ is correct w. r. t. Σ, NET and $PRED_2$.
(3) $trans(-)_{T_0}$ is correct w. r. t. Σ, NET and $PRED_3$.
(4) $trans'(-)_{T_1}$ is correct w. r. t. Σ, NET and $PRED_4$.
(5) $trans'(-)_{T_2}$ is correct w. r. t. Σ, NET and $PRED_5$.

13.5 USE OF TRANSLATIONS

A (correct) translation of some computational model into graph grammars provides two principal possibilities. First, all concepts and results for graph grammars can be carried over and reinterpreted for the source language. An example of this kind is the translation of hyperedge replacement grammars into graph grammars. It allows one to employ graph grammar concepts like parallel derivations, independence, canonical derivations and their properties for hyperedge replacement although the kind of graphs that are transformed are quite different. Another example of this kind concerns the translation of Petri-nets into graph grammars (cf. Kreowski [Kre81]). Details are omitted. They are beyond the scope of the chapter. Second, certain results for the translated model apply to graph grammars via the translation. In particular, undecidability results for the source language yield undecidability results for graph grammars. Based on the correctness results above, some examples are given in the next subsection.

13.5.1 Undecidability of emptiness, finiteness and membership

For Chomsky grammars the emptiness problem, the finiteness problem and the membership problem are undecidable (see e.g., Hopcroft and Ullman [HU79]). Using the translation of Chomsky grammars to graph grammars above and its correctness, the corresponding problems are undecidable for graph grammars, too.

a. It is undecidable whether or not, for an arbitrary graph grammar G, $L(G)$ is empty.
b. It is undecidable whether or not, for an arbitrary graph grammar G, $L(G)$ is finite.
c. It is undecidable whether or not, for an arbitrary graph grammar G and an arbitrary graph M, $M \in L(G)$.

PROOF. If CG is a Chomsky grammar, $L(CG)$ is empty (finite, contains $w \in T^*$) if and only if $L(CG^\bullet)$ is empty (finite, contains $w^\bullet$) due to the correctness result in 13.4.2. But the properties are undecidable for Chomsky grammars such that they cannot be decidable for graph grammars. □

Remark

Using the first, third and fourth correctness results in 13.4.3, one gets the same undecidability results by the reduction of the Post correspondence problems to graph grammars.

13.5.2 Undecidability of graph properties

Another example is the undecidability of the solvability of Post correspondence problems. Using the correctness results in 13.4.3, it turns out that it is undecidable for graph grammars whether the generated languages contain graphs with certain graph-theoretic properties.

a. It is undecidable whether or not, for an arbitrary graph grammar G, $L(G)$ contains totally disconnected graphs.
b. It is undecidable whether or not, for an arbitrary graph grammar G, $L(G)$ contains cycle-free graphs.

PROOF. Due to the correctness results (2) and (5) the decidability of totally disconnected graphs or cycle-free graphs would imply that solvability of Post corresponding problems is decidable. □

None of the undecidability results above is surprising. On the contrary, the point is the way of proving them. The proof technique will apply to many other, less obvious cases. For example, the translations $trans'(-)_{T_2}$ yields monotone graph grammars, i.e. the size of the left-hand side of each rule is never greater than the size of the right-hand side. This proves two further results where at least the second result is new and has not got the flavour of "folklore".

a. It is undecidable whether or not, for an arbitrary monotone graph grammar G, $L(G)$ is finite.
b. It is undecidable whether or not, for an arbitrary monotone graph grammar G, $L(G)$ contains cycle-free graphs.

REFERENCES

[CER79] Volker Claus, Hartmut Ehrig, and Gregorz Rozenberg (editors). *Graph-Grammars and Their Application to Computer Science and Biology.* Springer-Verlag, Lecture Notes in Computer Science 73, 1979.

[DK91] Frank Drewes and Hans-Jörg Kreowski. A note on hyperedge replacement. In *Proc. Graph Grammars and Their Application to Computer Science*, pp. 1–11. Springer-Verlag, Lecture Notes in Computer Science 532, 1991.

[EHK92] Hartmut Ehrig, Annegret Habel, and Hans-Jörg Kreowski. Introduction to graph grammars with applications to semantic networks. *Computers & Mathematics with Applications*, **23**, 6–9, pp. 557–572, 1992.

[Ehr79] Hartmut Ehrig. Introduction to the algebraic theory of graph grammars. In *Proc. Graph-Grammars and Their Application to Computer Science and Biology*, pp. 1–69. Springer-Verlag, Lecture Notes in Computer Science 73, 1979.

[EKR91] Hartmut Ehrig, Hans-Jörg Kreowski, and Gregorz Rozenberg (editors). *Graph Grammars and Their Application to Computer Science.* Springer-Verlag, Lecture Notes in Computer Science 532, 1991.

[ENR83] Hartmut Ehrig, Manfred Nagl, and Gregorz Rozenberg (editors). *Graph-Grammars and Their Application to Computer Science.* Springer-Verlag, Lecture Notes in Computer Science 153, 1983.

[ENRR87] Hartmut Ehrig, Manfred Nagl, Gregorz Rozenberg, and Azriel Rosenfeld (editors). *Graph-Grammars and Their Application to Computer Science.* Springer-Verlag, Lecture Notes in Computer Science 291, 1987.

[ER90] Joost Engelfriet and Gregorz Rozenberg. A comparison of boundary graph grammars and context-free hypergraph grammars. *Information and Computation*, **84**, pp. 163–206, 1990.

[Hab89] Annegret Habel. *Hyperedge Replacement: Grammars and Languages*. Dissertation, Universität Bremen, Fachbereich Mathematik und Informatik, 1989. Revised version as Springer-Verlag, Lecture Notes in Computer Science 643, 1992.

[HU79] John E. Hopcroft and Jeffrey D. Ullman. *Introduction to Automata Theory, Languages, and Computation*. Addison-Wesley, 1979.

[JR81] Dirk Janssens and Gregorz Rozenberg. Decision problems for node label controlled graph grammars. *Journal of Computer and System Sciences*, **22**, pp. 144–177, 1981.

[KKSdV] J. Richard Kennaway, Jan Willem Klop, M. Ronan Sleep, and Fer-Jan de Vries. The adequacy of term graph rewriting for simulating term rewriting. In this volume.

[KR90] Hans-Jörg Kreowski and Gregorz Rozenberg. On structured graph grammars I and II. *Information Sciences*, **52**, pp. 185–210 and 221–246, 1990.

[Kre81] Hans-Jörg Kreowski. A comparison between petri-nets and graph grammars. In *Lecture Notes in Computer Science 100*, pp. 306–317. Springer-Verlag, 1981.

[Meh84] Kurt Mehlhorn. *Data Structures and Algorithmus 2: Graph Algorithms and NP-Completeness*. Springer-Verlag, 1984.

[Rei81] Wolfgang Reisig. A graph grammar representation of nonsequential processes. In *Lecture Notes in Computer Science 100*, pp. 318–325. Springer-Verlag, 1981.

14

An Algebraic Framework for the Transformation of Attributed Graphs[1]

Michael Löwe, Martin Korff, and Annika Wagner

14.1 INTRODUCTION

In the last 20 years, graph grammars have been shown to be useful in practical software engineering and in theoretical research.

The impact of graph grammars on software specification is due to the fact that many aspects of complex software systems can be advantageously visualized and explained with graphical methods. Examples are control- and data-flow tables, graphical representations of the system architecture visualizing the inheritance hierarchy, the subsystem decomposition, and the usage relation, graphical pre- and postcondition specifications for operations on complex pointer structures, Petri-nets respectively high-level Petri-nets, actor systems, etc. Hence, we find a graphical component in almost every software development method.

Since graph grammars are able to describe the dynamic evolution of such graphical structures, they seem adequate as a comprehensive method for software specification. This has led to some proposals for graph-grammar-based software engineering, see among others [Nag87, ES85, Göt88, KLG91, Sch91]. "Graph-grammar-based" means here that the kernel of these methods is some notion of graph transformation which has, however, been extended by several non-graphical components in order to become suitable for the practical needs in "every-day" software engineering.

[1] This work has been partly supported by the ESPRIT Working Group No. 3299 "Computing by Graph Transformation (COMPUGRAPH)".

Term Graph Rewriting: Theory and Practice.
Eds. Ronan Sleep, Rinus Plasmeijer and Marko van Eekelen.

Theory-oriented research within the field of graph grammars has brought up results with respect to speed-up of graph algorithms [Hab89], extension of formal language theory to multidimensional structures (mainly done within the NLC-approach [Roz87]), logical specification of graph languages [Cou90a, Cou90b], efficient implementation of rewrite systems [HP88, Ken91], description and analysis of parallel and distributed systems (mainly done within the Algebraic Approach to graph transformation [Ehr79, Löw90]), etc. For a comprehensive description of these results and detailed reference lists compare [EL92a].

Unfortunately, the graph grammar approaches for practical applications are very different and more complex than the ones used for theoretical investigations. Thus, the main body of theoretical results is not immediately applicable to those application-oriented graph grammar specifications. This means that the well-known gap between practical requirements and theoretical results is reflected in the field of graph grammars itself.

In this chapter, we will try to close this gap. We propose an extension of the algebraic approach, which provides a rich theory for the analysis of sequential and parallel systems, by an attribute concept. Attributes are used in all graph grammar proposals for software engineering since they integrate structural (i.e. graphical) aspects of a system with data type aspects (i.e. calculation of values). This leads to compact descriptions in which e.g., well-known arithmetic operations need not artificially be coded into graphical structures. Similar concepts of combining structural and algebraic aspects can be found in the theory of attributed string grammars [Räi80] in algebraic high-level Petri-nets [DHP91, GJK90], which is a combination of Petri-nets and algebraic specifications, and in the specification language LOTOS [Lot89], which integrates CCS-like specifications for the structural part with algebraic specifications for the data type component. Our proposal for the integration of attributes into graph transformation preserves the fundamental derivation concept of the algebraic approach i.e., both the manipulation of the graphical structure and the calculation of the new attributes is going to be combined within a single pushout construction. By this careful combination, the results obtained in the Single-Pushout Approach [Löw90] are applicable also to attributed graphs.

The notion of single pushout graph transformation has originally been introduced by Raoult in 1984 [Rao84]. Currently, several variations of this approach are being developed in the UK [Ken87, GKS89, Ken91], in the Netherlands [Bro91], in Japan [MK91], and in Germany [Löw90, LE91, EL92b]. The algebraic approach to single pushout transformations [LE91] which will be used in this chapter generalizes the classical approach [Ehr79], since it admits transformations without gluing conditions. Moreover, it simplifies many proofs for important properties due to the very compact notion of direct derivation, which allows to abstract from intricate operational details.

The chapter is organized as follows: Section 14.2 discusses some examples which motivate the attribute concepts developed in this chapter. The notions from the universal theory of algebras necessary for the development of the theory are briefly reviewed in section 14.3. This section also contains basic notions of the algebraic approach to single pushout graph transformation. Attributed graphs and their transformation are introduced in section 14.4. We follow the framework that has been proposed for the double pushout approach in [Sch92]: An attributed graph is a pair consisting of a graph G and an algebra A together with some labeling operations which assign to graphical objects in G values taken from A. Morphisms between these objects are partial on the graph part and total on the algebraic component. They are required to be compatible with the labeling operators. It is shown that pushouts can always be constructed in the associated category and that suitable restrictions for the algebra component lead to "label-preserving" morphisms. Due to the same underlying construction for direct transformations, the theory developed for single pushout transformation carries over to attributed structures. Some conclusions of the presented approach to the transformation of attributed graphs are discussed in section 14.5. Especially we point out that a similar treatment on the basis of partial graphs and partial algebras could be promising in reducing the complexity of the applied constructions.

14.2 EXAMPLES FOR THE TRANSFORMATION OF ATTRIBUTED GRAPHS

This section sketches the concept of attribution (and its application in system specification) which is going to be introduced in the following paragraphs. The examples are meant to demonstrate the greater flexibility graph rewriting obtains if standard operations (for example, arithmetic operations on integer or real numbers) are directly applicable and need not to be coded on the graphical level. We already use the rule concept and layout which will be formally introduced in the sections 14.3 - 14.4 in order to provide a first glance at the intended graph grammar framework.

14.2.1 Switching in place/transition nets

A well-known device for the specification of parallel systems are Petri-nets [Rei85]. Their structure is normally given by graphical representations and their basic switching mechanisms can easily be modeled by the graph rewriting rule $S(n/m)$ in figure 14.1. The rule is actually a scheme, each n/m-instance of which describes the switching of a transition with n places as precondition and m places as postcondition. The model in figure 14.1 follows the design of [Kre81], which encodes the presence of a token on a place by an extra vertex. That the token is *on* a place, is represented by an edge connecting place and token. All vertices and edges for modelling places, transitions resp. the flow relation are preserved by the rule.

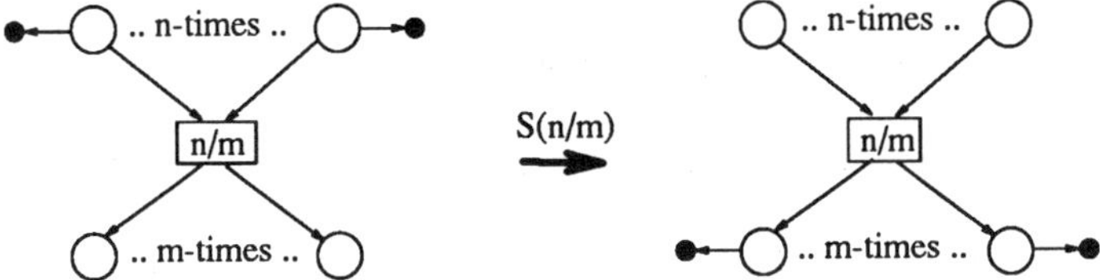

Figure 14.1 Basic switching mechanism

Although this model works well for this very simple type of a place/transition net, whose transitions consume and produce exactly one token at a time the graphical representation of the tokens seems not natural. The number of tokens on a place can better be seen as an attribute (of type "natural number") of the place. If we allow "weighted edges" as usual for place/transition nets, this leads to the rule S' in figure 14.2. It shows that the switching in a Petri-net does not change the structure of the net at all. It just manipulates the assignment of attribute values to the places.

The device for changing attributes is provided by an algebraic structure on the attribute values, in our example simply the plus operation on natural numbers. This algebraic structure gets more and more complex if we allow different types of tokens as in colored Petri-nets, or if we allow structured tokens as in high-level nets for example described in [DHP91][2]. The more complex the token structure, the less adequate a graphical encoding of the token structure. Even for the rule S', a purely graphical representation would not be easy to survey, respectively the complicated attribute representation would obscure the essential underlying structure of the net.

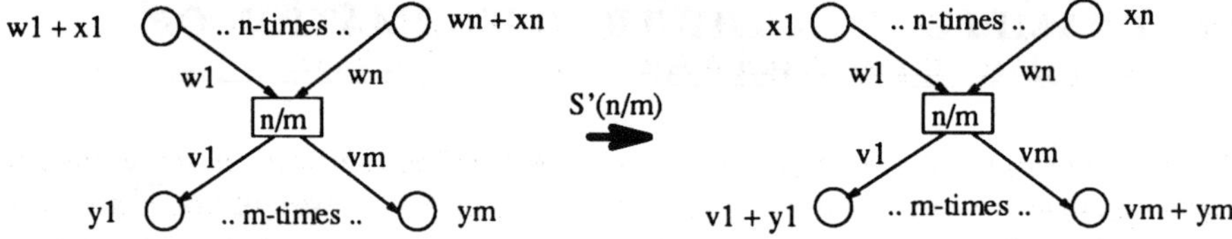

Figure 14.2 Weighted transition switching

14.2.2 Attributes for graphical layout

Another example in which attributes are helpful is the graphical layout of rule-generated graphs itself. As a simple example consider a set of graph rewriting rules which model the manipulation of the linked-list data type. If the change of the list-structure due to the application of rules shall be traced, we need a concrete and suggestive graphical representation of the list. The example in figure 14.3 uses a square to represent the list, black circles for listable items and white circles to symbolize the data stored in the listable items. The triangle represents the cursor.

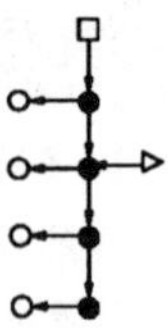

Figure 14.3 Graphical arrangement of a linked-list

With this conception, the list-manipulating rules must take care to preserve this general layout[3]. This can easily be modeled if two (real-valued) coordinates for each vertex are handled as attributes. We impose the following rules: black circles are drawn in a vertical lines i.e. their x-coordinate must be equal. A white circle has the same y value as the corresponding black one. A constant value c is assumed for their distance

[2] Almost all implementations of Petri-nets used these high-level concepts for tokens, compare for example [Itt87].

[3] It seems impossible to achieve that by some graphical coding.

on the x axis. The rule I for the insertion of new data into this type of attributed graphs is given in figure 14.4. The inserted black circle shall be placed right in the middle of its black neighbors. The example presupposes that all edges are drawn as straight lines[4]. The required algebraic structure for attributes in this field of application is real-valued arithmetic.

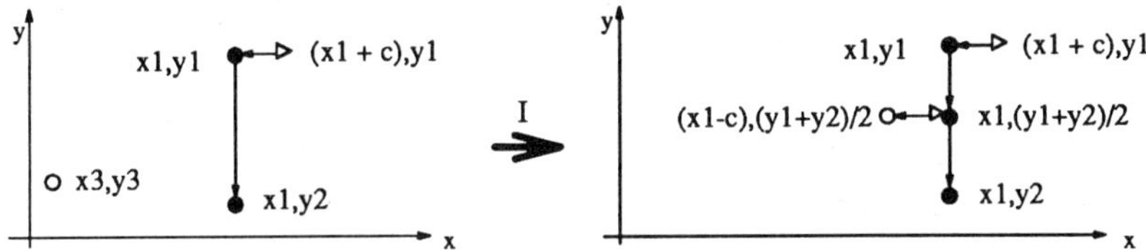

Figure 14.4 Attributes for graphical layout

The crucial point for this type of rules to work well is the pattern matching mechanism expressed e.g. by the term "$x1 + c$" in the rule's left-hand side which makes the rule applicable only if the actual attribute value for the cursor can be decomposed into a sum of $x1$ and c. The use of the same variable names in the rule's right-hand side indicates that the substitutions found for $x1, x3, y1, y2$, and $y3$ in the matching phase shall be used to construct the result of the direct derivation. How this mechanism can smoothly be integrated into the algebraic single-pushout approach to graph transformation [Löw90] is described in the following.

14.3 SHORT REVIEW OF BASIC NOTIONS AND RESULTS

The algebraic approach to graph transformation models graphs, hypergraphs and other graph-like structures as special types of algebras (see examples below). Rewrite rules and occurrences of rules are described by homomorphisms. The basic notions from universal algebra we need for this approach are the following.

A *signature* $SIG = (S, OP)$ consists of a set of sorts and a family of sets $OP = (OP_{w,s})_{w \in S^*, s \in S}$ of operation symbols.

For $op \in OP_{w,s}$, we also write $op : w \to s$. A *SIG-algebra* A is an S-indexed family $(A_s)_{s \in S}$ of carrier sets together with an OP-indexed family of mappings $(op^A)_{op \in OP}$ such that $op^A : A_{s_1} \times \ldots \times A_{s_n} \to A_s$ if $op \in OP_{s_1 \ldots s_n, s}$. If $w = s_1 \ldots s_n \in S^*$, we sometimes write A_w for $A_{s_1} \times \ldots \times A_{s_n}$.

A *homomorphism* $f : A \to B$ between two SIG-algebras A and B is a sort-indexed family of total mappings $f = (f_s : A_s \to B_s)_{s \in S}$ such that $op^B(f(x)) = f(op^A(x))$.

DEFINITION **14.3.1** *(Partial Homomorphism) A partial homomorphism $f : A \to B$ between SIG-algebras A and B is a homomorphism $f! : A(f) \to B$ from a subalgebra $A(f) \subseteq A$ to B.*

[4] We are currently doing first experiments at the Technical University of Berlin in this field of rule-controlled layout in graph rewriting. We use a prototype implementation of the single pushout approach as it is introduced here, which allows full graphical interaction in graph grammar editing and derivation [Bey91].

The category of all SIG-algebras and all partial homomorphisms between them is denoted by $\underline{SIG^P}$. $\underline{SIG}$ denotes the subcategory of $\underline{SIG^P}$ with the same class of objects and all total homomorphisms.

The single pushout approach to graph transformation as introduced in [LE91] is built up on these algebraic fundaments. Its central notion of ***graph structure signatures*** below is motivated by the following observations. *Directed graphs* can be seen as algebras with respect to the following signature:

GRAPH = **Sorts** V, E
Opns $s, t : E \rightarrow V$

This means that each graph G consists of a set of vertices G_V, a set of edges G_E, and two unary mappings $s^G, t^G : E_G \rightarrow V_G$ which provide source and target vertices for each edge.

Hypergraphs allow edges to be connected to a sequence $s_1 \ldots s_n$ of source vertices and a sequence $t_1 \ldots t_n$ of target vertices. Hence their edges form a family $E = (E_{n,m})_{n,m \in \mathbb{N}}$ sorted by the numbers n of source and m of target connections. This immediately leads to the signature for hypergraphs:

HYPERGRAPH = **Sorts** $V, (E_{n,m})_{n,m \rightarrow \mathbb{N}}$
Opns $(s_1, \ldots, s_n,\ t_1, \ldots, t_m : E_{n,m} \rightarrow V)_{n,m \in \mathbb{N}}$

It is easy to add vertex and edge labels in this algebraic framework which leads to slightly extended signatures LABELED GRAPH resp. LABELLED HYPERGRAPH. Homomorphisms between the corresponding algebras are meant to be identities on the label components. A remarkable property of all these signatures is that they contain *unary* operator symbols only.

DEFINITION **14.3.2** *(Graph Structure Signature) A* graph structure signature *GS is a signature which contains unary operator symbols only. All GS-algebras are called* graph structures.

The graph transformation approach of [Löw90, LE91], which uses partial morphisms in the sense of Definition 14.3.1 as rewriting rules, is applicable to all these graph-like structures[5]. The fundamental result for the single pushout approach to algebraic graph transformation which has been proven in [Löw90] which has been proven in [Löw90] is the following.

THEOREM **14.3.3** *(Co-completeness of $\underline{SIG^P}$) The category $\underline{SIG^P}$ of SIG-algebras and partial morphisms is finitely cocomplete if and only if SIG is a graph structure signature.*

The *initial object* in a category $\underline{SIG^P}$ of graph structures is the empty "graph" and pushouts can be built as described below.

PROPOSITION **14.3.4** *(Pushouts in Graph Structures) Let GS be a graph structure signature and $f : A \rightarrow B, g : A \rightarrow C \in \underline{GS^P}$. The pushout of f and g in $\underline{GS^P}$, i.e. $(D, f^* : C \rightarrow D, g^* : B \rightarrow D)$, can be constructed in four steps:*

[5] This is mainly due to the fact that the subalgebras of a given algebra A with respect to a graph structure signature are closed under union. Hence every family of subsets of the carriers of A contains a greatest subalgebra of A. This property is not guaranteed if constants or operators with more than one argument are involved.

a. *Construction of the* gluing object*: Let $\underline{A}$ be the greatest subalgebra of A satisfying (i) $\underline{A} \subseteq A(f) \cap A(g)$ and (ii) $x \in \underline{A}, y \in A$ with $f(x) = f(y)$ or $g(x) = g(y)$ implies $y \in \underline{A}$.*
b. *Construction of the* definedness area *of f^* and g^*: Let $B(g^*)$ be the greatest subalgebra of B whose carriers are contained in $B - f(A - \underline{A})$. Symmetrically, $C(f^*)$ is the greatest subalgebra in $C - g(A - \underline{A})$.*
c. Gluing*: Let $D = (B(g^*) \uplus C(f^*))_{/\equiv}$, where $\equiv$ is the least equivalence relation containing $\sim$, where $x \sim y$ if there is $z \in \underline{A}$ with $f(z) = x$ and $g(z) = y$.*
d. Pushout morphisms*: f^* is defined for all $x \in C(f^*)$ by $f^*(x) = [x]_\equiv$. The morphism g^* is defined symmetrically.*

If the definedness areas of partial homomorphisms are explicitly represented by inclusion morphisms, the whole situation in proposition 14.3.4 can be visualized in $\underline{GS}$ as it is done in figure 14.5. Note that the squares (1), (2), and (3) commute and (4) is a pushout in $\underline{GS}$ due to proposition 14.3.4 (c + d).

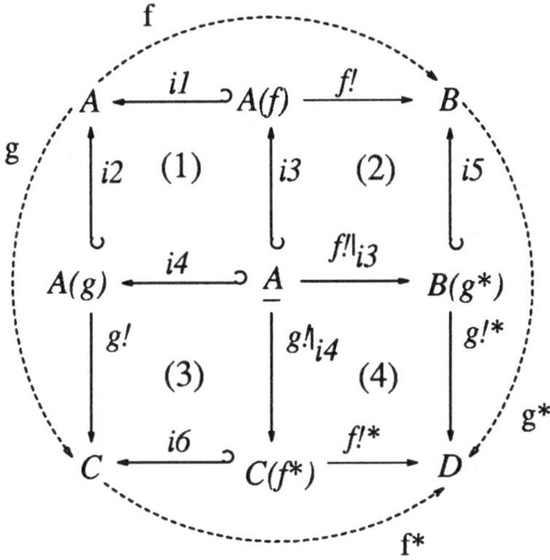

Figure 14.5 Pushout construction in $\underline{GS^P}$

These complex types of pushout constructions perform deletion, gluing, and addition of graphical elements within a single colimit construction. Hence they can be used to mathematically define the operational behavior of graph rewriting in a precise way:

DEFINITION **14.3.5** *(Rule, Occurrence, Derivation) Let GS be a graph structure signature. A rewriting* rule *$r : L \to R$ is a partial morphism in $\underline{GS^P}$. An* occurrence *for r in an object $G \in \underline{GS^P}$ is a total morphism $m : L \to G$. The* direct derivation *of G with the rule r at an occurrence m is the pushout of m and r in $\underline{GS^P}$. The corresponding pushout object is called* derived graph.

The intuition of a rule $r : L \to R$ is that all objects in $L - L(r)$ shall be deleted, all objects in $R - r(L)$ shall be added and $L(r)$ resp. $r(L)$ provides the gluing context. Note that the derivation with r deletes destructively due to proposition 14.3.4 (b), in the sense that all objects in G pointing (for example by source or target mappings) to deleted objects are deleted themselves; if two objects $x \in L - L(r)$ and $y \in L(r)$ in a rule's left hand side are identified by an occurrence, the effect of deletion is dominant.

14.4 TRANSFORMATION OF ATTRIBUTED GRAPHS

The mathematical model for the transformation of attributed graphs presented in this section directly follows from the intuition of attributed graphs given in section 14.2. Attributes are values taken from an attribute algebra, with which the graphical objects are labelled. Hence, the objects to be handled, i.e. the attributed graphs, are pairs of graphs and attribute algebras together with some labelling functions which connect the graphical and the algebraic structure. In order to keep the presentation simple we allow only one attribute for each graphical object.

Each graph is equipped with its own attribute algebra since the examples in section 14.2 show that different algebras are used on the level of rules and on the level of actual graphs. Consider for example figure 14.2. While the place-labels of place/transition nets are natural numbers, the labels used in the rule are terms over the signature of the natural numbers and a suitable set of variables. For example, the labels in rules are normally taken from "syntactical algebras", like term algebras or initial algebras in the considered class of attribute algebras, and the labels in the objects, which are going to be rewritten by the rules, are taken from some chosen fixed "semantical algebra".

The pattern matching mechanism i.e. the assignment of values to variables in the rules' left-hand sides, we have motivated in the example section, must be provided by the occurrences of the rule in an actual object. Since variable assignments, which are compatible with the term structure are special homomorphisms (from syntactical into semantical algebras), we design morphisms between attributed graphs as pairs consisting of a partial morphism for the graphical part and of a total homomorphism on the algebra component. The two components of a morphism are required to be compatible with the labeling functions.

The choice of total morphisms for the attribute component is due to Theorem 14.3.3 and the intention to describe rewriting of attributed graphs by pushout constructions on the extended morphism concept. These conceptional expositions are made precise in the following definitions.

14.4.1 Formal framework

DEFINITION **14.4.1 (Attribution)** *Let $GS = (S1, OP1)$ be a graph structure signature, let $S \subseteq S1$, and let $SIG = (S2, OP2)$ be an arbitrary signature. Then, a SIG-*attribution *of G is $ATTROP = (ATTROP_s : s \rightarrow s2_s)_{s \in S}$ where $s2_s \in S2$, i.e. an S-indexed family of operator symbols.*

DEFINITION **14.4.2 (Attributed graphs)** *If $ATTROP$ is a SIG-attribution of a graph structure signature GS, an attributed graph is a GS-graph with $ATTR$ibutes in SIG, i.e. an algebra with respect to the signature $ATTR = GS + SIG + ATTROP$. A* morphism *$f : A \rightarrow B$ between GS-graphs A and B having $ATTR$ibutes in SIG is* *a partial GS-morphism* $f1 : (A)_{GS} \to (B)_{GS}$[6] *together with a total SIG-morphism* $f2 : (A)_{SIG} \to (B)_{SIG}$ *satisfying for all operators* $(attr : s1 \to s2) \in ATTROP$ *and all* $x \in A(f1)_{s1} : f2(attr^A(x)) = attr^B(f1(x))$.

If we define composition of these morphisms by composition of the components and identities as pairs of component identities, the objects and morphisms with respect to Definition 14.4.2 form a category for each attribution $ATTROP$, denoted by $\underline{ATTR}$ in the following[7]. Note that the morphisms in $\underline{ATTR}$ are partial on the graph structure part only.

If the partial morphism $f1$ is represented by pairs of total morphisms as in figure 14.6 below, the required compatibility of the morphism components with the label operators can be represented by the commutativity of total morphisms in rectangle (1), i.e. $f2 \circ attr^A \circ i = attr^B \circ f1!$.

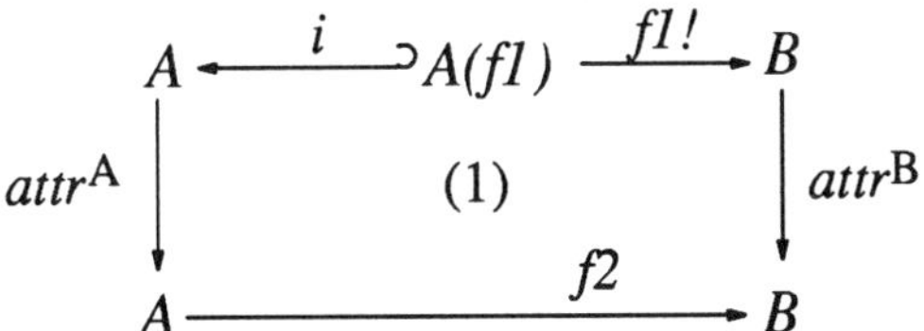

Figure 14.6 Compatibility requirement for $\underline{ATTR}$-morphisms

This idea is useful in the proof of the central theorem.

THEOREM **14.4.3 (Pushouts of attributed graphs)** *If $ATTROP$ is a SIG-attribution of GS, each pair $f : A \to B, g : A \to C$ of $\underline{ATTR}$-morpisms has a pushout $(D, f^* : C \to D, g^* : B \to D)$.*

PROOF. Construct the pushouts in $\underline{GS^P}$ of $(f)_{GS}$ and $(g)_{GS}$ and in $\underline{SIG}$ of $(f)_{SIG}$ and $(g)_{SIG}$ which provide $(D)_{GS}$ resp. $(D)_{SIG}$. (It is well-known that $\underline{SIG}$ has all colimits.) $\underline{GS^P}$is co-complete due to theorem 14.3.3. D can be enriched by attribute operators $attr^D : D_{s1} \to D_{s2}$ for each $(attr : s1 \to s2) \in ATTROP$ as it is indicated by figure 4.7 below. The foreground shows the $s1$-component of the $\underline{GS^P}$-pushout, the background the $s2$-component of the $\underline{SIG}$-pushout. Due to the chosen representation of partial morphisms by pairs of total mappings, as it has been introduced in section 3, figure 14.7 visualizes a situation in the category $\underline{SET}$ of sets and total mappings. By proposition 14.3.4 (c + d), D_{s1} is the pushout of x and y in $\underline{SET}$.

Since figure 14.7 commutes, $g2^*_{s2} \circ attr^B \circ i \circ x = f2^*_{s2} \circ attr^C \circ j \circ y$, which provides a unique mapping $attr^D : D_{s1} \to D_{s2}$ with $attr^D \circ g1!^*_{s1} = g2^*_{s2} \circ attr^B \circ i$ and $attr^D \circ f1!^*_{s1} = f2^*_{s2} \circ attr^C \circ j$. Hence, choosing the attribution of D as the family of

[6] $(A)_{GS}$ denotes the restriction of A to a subsignature i.e. $(.)_{GS}$ is the object part of the forgetful functor associated with the signature inclusion $GS \subseteq GS + SIG + ATTR$; for details compare [EM85].

[7] Note that $\underline{ATTR}$ cannot be defined as a comma category construction $(U \downarrow V)$ for suitable (forgetful) functors $U : \underline{GS^P} \to \underline{SET^P}$ and $V : \underline{SIG} \to \underline{SET^P}$. First the label operators are required to be total and second $f2 \circ lab^A = lab^B \circ f1$ is not required generally, but only on the area $f1$ is defined for. (For the notion of a comma category see [HS73]; $\underline{SET^P}$ denotes the category of sets and partial mappings.)

these unique completions for each single operator in ATTROP provides the required $\underline{ATTR}$-object D such that $g^* = ((g)^*_{GS}, (g)^*_{SIG})$ and $f^* = ((f)^*_{GS}, (f)^*_{SIG})$ become $\underline{ATTR}$-morphisms. Obviously $g^* \circ f = f^* \circ g$. Using the unique pushout morphisms on the $\underline{GS^P}$- and $\underline{SIG}$-component, it is easy to show that there is $u : D \rightarrow E$ with $u \circ g^* = g'$ and $u \circ f^* = f'$ for each triple $(E, g' : B \rightarrow E, f' : C \rightarrow E)$ such that $f' \circ g = g' \circ f$. Uniqueness follows from the uniqueness on each component. □

With this result, the single pushout approach to graph transformation given by Definition 14.3.5 can be extended to attributed graphs.

DEFINITION **14.4.4 (Single pushout transformation of attributed graphs)** *If ATTROP is a SIG-attribution of a graph structure signature GS, the single pushout approach to the transformation of attributed graphs can be formulated in the category $\underline{ATTR}$ as described above: A rewriting* rule $r : L \rightarrow R$ *is an $\underline{ATTR}$-morphism whose SIG-component is an isomorphism. An* occurrence $m : L \rightarrow G$ *of r in an attributed graph G is an $\underline{ATTR}$-morphism whose GS-component is total. The* direct derivation *of G with the rule r at an occurrence m is the pushout of r and m in $\underline{ATTR}$. The attributed graph H is called* directly derived graph *if H is the corresponding pushout object.*

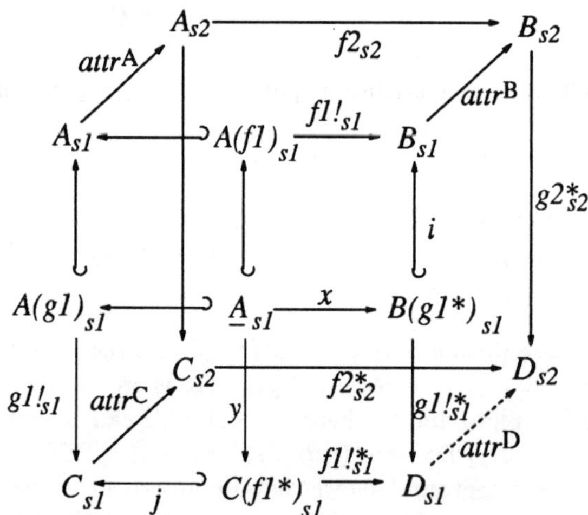

Figure 14.7 Construction of pushout attribution

It seems reasonable to allow only isomorphisms for the algebra part of rules r. This guarantees that the induced pushout morphism $r^* : G \rightarrow H$ between an object G and its direct derivation H is also isomorphic as far as the algebra of attributes is concerned (due to general results that pushouts extend isomorphisms to isomorphisms [HS73]). This reflects the idea that a direct derivation is intended to manipulate the graphical part of an object and the attributes of the graphical part but is not intended to change the algebra of actual attributes (compare examples of section 14.2).

Another approach would be to allow arbitrary rules, but as direct derivations only those pushouts which preserve (up to isomorphism) the algebra part of the derived object. This would provide a mechanism to formulate unification requirements as a precondition for rule application leading to a "logic programming style" for graph transformation on a very high level (compare also [CMR+91, CR991]).

We stick to the rule concept of Definition 14.4.4 since it allows rewriting at all occurrences without additional application conditions. All prerequirements for a rule to be applicable must therefore be formulated by appropriate patterns (graphical and algebraic) in the rules' left-hand sides. The advantages of *rewriting without gluing condition* are carefully elaborated in [Löw90] for the non-attributed case. The theory for sequential, parallel, and synchronized composition of rules becomes straightforward and less complex, notions and proofs become more compact and easy to survey. An enumeration of the results of [Löw90] carrying over to the attributed case is presented at the end of this section.

14.4.2 Formal review of the Petri-net example

With the notions accomplished now, we can provide a formal description of the Petri-net example in section 14.2.1 (figure 14.2). Attributes are taken from the algebra of natural numbers with the signature

$$\begin{array}{lll} \text{SIG} = & \texttt{Sorts} & nat \\ & \texttt{Opns} & 0, 1 :\rightarrow nat \\ & & + : nat, nat \rightarrow nat \end{array}$$

Graphical objects are places P and transitions T. Places are just vertices and transitions are hyperedges since they are connected to a sequence of places as preconditions and a sequence of places as postconditions. Hence $T = (T_{n,m})_{n,m \in \mathbb{N}}$ is sorted with respect to the number n of pre- and the number m of postconditions. Places and transitions constitute the static structure of a Petri-net which is not changed by the switching on the net. Therefore, we represent the assignment of the current number of tokens on a place to the place itself by an independent graphical object M which carries the attribute of a place. Summarizing, we obtain the following structure for the graphical part:

$$\begin{array}{lll} \text{GS} = & \texttt{Sorts} & P, (T_{n,m})_{n,m \in \mathbb{N}}, M \\ & \texttt{Opns} & (pre_1, \ldots, pre_n, post_1, \ldots, post_m : T_{n,m} \rightarrow P)_{n,m \in \mathbb{N}} \\ & & m : M \rightarrow P \end{array}$$

Only the carriers M for attributes get an attribution in $\underline{SIG}$:

$$\text{ATTR} = \text{GS} + \text{SIG} + \quad \texttt{Opns} \quad v : M \rightarrow nat$$

On the rule level, $T_{SIG}(X)$, i.e. the term algebra with respect to SIG over a family of large enough sets of variables X, is used to describe the switching mechanism. Actual Petri-nets are attributed with element from the SIG-algebra of the natural numbers.

Figure 14.2 can be interpreted as a visualization of a rule $r : L \rightarrow R$ in $\underline{ATTR}$ if we depict places in P by symbols o, transitions in T by □-symbols and their connections "pre" and "post" to places by directed edges. The attribute carriers are not explicitly represented. Instead each structure $\circ \overset{m}{\longleftarrow} \bullet \overset{v}{\longrightarrow} x$ is abbreviated by $\circ_x$. Hence the rule morphism r is the identity on all components of $\underline{ATTR}$ except M where it is empty, i.e. all attribute carriers of the left-hand side are deleted and the right-hand side adds *new* carriers for each place carrying the attribute which is the result of the switching.

Thus, the mechanism proposed by this example and the whole approach to attributed graph transformation follows the single assignment paradigm of [Ack79, MN84] for the update of attributes. Graphical elements cannot *change* their attributes. Instead each attribute update involves the *deletion* and *creation* of an object in the graph component.

14.4.3 Theoretical issues

But it is not just that this approach to the transformation of attributed graphs has been designed to meet the practical requirements. It has been carefully composed such that a single pushout construction serves as a model for direct derivations. Moreover by choosing rules to have isomorphisms on the algebra part, direct derivations have the shape of rules themselves since isomorphisms are preserved by pushouts. Finally all morphisms are total on the algebra component and therefore the property that pushouts preserve occurrences depends on the graph structure part only. Thus all results from single pushout graph rewriting [Löw90] which are essentially based on the properties mentioned above carry over to the attributed case. Among others there are:

a. Parallel independent transformations are locally confluent,
b. Transformation sequences with independent rules can be integrated into a single parallel step with parallel rules, which are just coproducts of rules,
c. Distinguished parallel steps can be sequentialized,
d. Transformation sequences can be substituted into bigger contexts,
e. Transformations with derived rules can be simulated by transformation sequences with the original rules,
f. Maximally parallelized transformation sequences are unique,
g. Confluence criteria for transformation systems can be based on critical pair confluence,
h. Subrule-structured transformations can be decomposed into subrule and remainder transformations,
i. Synchronized transformations can be decomposed into subrule and remainder steps,
j. Distributed derivations are equivalent with synchronized derivations of corresponding global states.

Thus, on one hand this extension of transformation to attributes actually extends the applicability of algebraic graph rewriting to a broader class of problems. On the other hand all well-known results and methods for the analysis of the chosen models in sequential, parallel and distributed environments are preserved.

14.5 CONCLUSIONS

In this chapter, the algebraic approach to graph transformation which is based on single pushout derivations has been extended to attributed graphs. Attributed graphs can be modeled in this framework by algebras consisting of two components. One part describes the structural aspects. The other one is dedicated to data type aspects. The connection between both components is established by "label operators" which assign data type elements to structural items, compare section 14.4. Rules and transformations on these objects can be described by a careful combination of partial morphisms for the structure part and total morphisms on the data type component.

As we have indicated in section 14.4, the whole theory for the algebraic single pushout approach developed for non-attributed graphs carries over to this generalized notion of graphs. The work presented in section 14.4 demonstrates that requirements coming from the field of graph grammar application in software engineering can smoothly be integrated into the pushout-based theory of graph grammars. We do not claim that all other concepts that have been designed in practice-oriented graph grammar approaches can adequately be modeled by pushout derivations. But it is an interesting question for future research how far the single pushout approach can serve as a unifying framework for different graph grammar models.

Research in this direction is very likely to stimulate the theory development itself. A major goal for a better integration of the graphical and the data type component in attributed graph transformation is to overcome the restrictions which are caused by the result of Theorem 14.3.3. A promising step in this direction is to pass over to partial graphs and partial algebras as it has been proposed in [LKW91]. In doing so, an explicit distinction between structural and data type aspects of the transformation becomes superfluous and the treatment becomes very straight forward as a transformation of partial algebras. In [LKW91] the existence of pushouts in the category of partial algebras and partial morphisms has been characterized. Since pushouts do not always exist, a detailed exposition of the theory for this approach can considerably be different from the results in [Löw90]. This has to be clarified by future research.

REFERENCES

[Ack79] W.B. Ackermann. Dataflow languages. In *AFIPS Confl. Proc. 48*. AFIPS Press, 1979.

[Bey91] M. Beyer. GAG: Ein graphischer Editor für algebraische Graphgrammatiksysteme. Diplomarbeit, Technical University of Berlin, Department of Computer Science, 1991.

[Bro91] P.M. van den Broek. Algebraic graph rewriting using a single pushout. In *Int. Joint Conf. on Theory and Practice of Software Development (TAPSOFT'91), Springer-Verlag, Lecture Notes in Computer Science 493*, pp. 90–102, 1991.

[CMR+91] A. Corradini, U. Montanari, F. Rossi, H. Ehrig, and M. Löwe. Graph grammars and logic programming. In Ehrig et al. [EKR91], pp. 221–237.

[Cou90a] B. Courcelle. Graph rewriting: An algebraic and logic approach. *Handbook of Theoretical Computer Science*, B:193–242, 1990.

[Cou90b] B. Courcelle. The monadic second-order logic of graphs I, recognizable sets of finite graphs. *Information and Computation*, 85:12–75, 1990.

[CR991] *On the Power of Contrext-Free Jungle Rewriting for Term Rewriting Systems and logic programming*, Proc. of the SEMAGRAPH Symposium 1991. Technical Report 91-25, University of Nijmegen, 1991.

[DHP91] C. Dimitrovici, U. Hummert, and L. Petrucci. Composition and net properties of algebraic high-level nets. In *Advances of Petri-Nets, Springer-Verlag, Lecture Notes in Computer Science 483*. 1991.

[Ehr79] H. Ehrig. Introduction to the algebraic theory of graph grammars. In *1st Graph Grammar Workshop, Springer-Verlag, Lecture Notes in Computer Science 73*, pp. 1–69, 1979.

[EKR91] H. Ehrig, H.-J. Kreowski, and G. Rozenberg, editors. *4th Int. Workshop on Graph Grammars and Their Application to Computer Science, Springer-Verlag, Lecture Notes in Computer Science 532.* 1991.

[EL92a] H. Ehrig and M. Löwe. Computing by graph transformation (compugraph): a survey. Technical Report 92/14, Technical University of Berlin, Department of Computer Science, 1992.

[EL92b] H. Ehrig and M. Löwe. Parallel and distributed derivations in the single-pushout approach. *Theoretical Computer Science*, 1992. accepted for publication.

[EM85] H. Ehrig and B. Mahr. *Fundamentals of algebraic specifications*, volume 1 of *Monographs in Computer Science*. Springer-Verlag, Berlin, 1985.

[ENRR87] H. Ehrig, M. Nagl, G. Rozenberg, and A. Rosenfeld, editors. *3rd Int. Workshop on Graph Grammars and Their Application to Computer Science, Springer-Verlag, Lecture Notes in Computer Science 291.* 1987.

[ES85] G. Engels and W. Schäfer. Graph grammar engineering: a method used for the development of integrated programming support tools. In *TAPSOFT'85, Springer-Verlag, Lecture Notes in Computer Science 186*, pp. 179–193, 1985.

[GJK90] D. Giesel, R. Jeschke, and J. Krüger. Entwurf und Implementierung eines Netzwerkzeugs zur Simulation algebraischer High-Level-Netze. Master's thesis, Technical University of Berlin, 1990.

[GKS89] J. Glauert, R. Kennaway, and R. Sleep. A Categorical Construction for Generalised Graph Rewriting. Technical report, School of Information Systems, University of East Anglia, Norwich NR4 7TJ, UK, 1989.

[Göt88] H. Göttler. *Graphgrammatiken in der Softwaretechnik*, volume 178 of *Informatik Fachberichte*. Springer-Verlag, 1988.

[Hab89] A. Habel. *Hyperedge replacement: Grammars and Languages.* PhD thesis, University of Bremen, 1989.

[HP88] B. Hoffmann and D. Plump. Jungle evaluation for efficient term rewriting. In J. Grabowski, P. Lescanne, and W. Wechler, editors, *1st International Workshop on Algebraic and Logic Programming*, pp. 191–203, Berlin, 1988. Akademie-Verlag.

[HS73] H. Herrlich and G. Strecker. *Category Theory.* Allyn and Bacon, Rockleigh, New Jersey, 1973.

[Itt87] G. Itter. Konzeption einer Fertigungsanlage mit Hilfe von Petri-Netzen. Technical report, TU-Berlin, IAI, FG Softwaretechnik, 1987.

[Ken87] R. Kennaway. On "On graph rewriting". *Theoretical Computer Science*, 52:37–58, 1987.

[Ken91] R. Kennaway. Graph rewriting in some categories of partial maps. In Ehrig et al. [EKR91], pp. 475–489.

[KLG91] S.M. Kaplan, J.P. Loyall, and S.K. Goering. Specifying concurrent languages and systems with Δ-grammars. In Ehrig et al. [EKR91], pp. 475–489.

[Kre81] H.-J. Kreowski. A comparison Between Petri-nets and Graph Grammars. In *Springer-Verlag, Lecture Notes in Computer Science 100*, pp. 1–, 1981.

[LE91] M. Löwe and H. Ehrig. Algebraic approach to graph transformation based on single pushout derivations. In *16th Int. Workshop on Graph Theoretic Concepts in Computer Science, Springer-Verlag, Lecture Notes in Computer Science 484*, pp. 338–353, 1991.

[LKW91] *Single-pushout transformation of attributed graphs: a link between graph grammars and abstract data types*, Proc. of the SEMAGRAPH Symposium 1991. Technical Report 91-25, University of Nijmegen, 1991.

[Lot89] ISO IS 8807: Information processing systems - Open Systems Interconnection - LOTOS - A formal description technique based on the temporal ordering of observational behaviour. *ISO*, 1989.

[Löw90] M. Löwe. *Extended Algebraic Graph Transformation.* PhD thesis, Technical University of Berlin, Department of Computer Science, 1990.

[MK91] Z. Mizoguchi and Y. Kawahara. Graph Rewritings without Gluing Conditions. Technical Report 33, Kyushu University, Fukuoka, Japan, 1991.

[MN84] B. Mahr and F. Nürnberg. DONALD - A Single Assignment Language For Non-Sequential algorithms. Technical Report 84/7, Technical University of Berlin, 1984.

[Nag87] M. Nagl. A software development environment based on graph technology. In Ehrig et al. [ENRR87], pp. 458–478.

[Räi80] K.-J. Räihä. Bibliography of attribute grammars. *SIGPLAN Notices*, 15(3):35–44, 1980.

[Rao84] J.-C. Raoult. On graph rewriting. *Theoretical Computer Science*, 32:1–24, 1984.

[Rei85] W. Reisig. *Petri nets*. Springer Verlag, 1985.

[Roz87] G. Rozenberg. An introduction to the NLC way of rewriting graphs. In *3rd Int. Workshop on Graph Grammars and Their Application to Computer Science, Springer-Verlag, Lecture Notes in Computer Science 291*, pp. 55–66, 1987.

[Sch91] A. Schürr. *Operationales Spezifizieren mit programmierten Graphersetzungssystemen.* Deutscher Universitätsverlag GmbH, Wiesbaden, 1991.

[Sch92] G. Schied. *Über Graphgrammatiken, eine Spezifikationsmethode für Programmiersprachen und verteilte Regelsysteme.* Arbeitsberichte des Institus für mathematische Maschinen und Datenverarbeitung (Informatik), University of Erlangen, 1992.

15

Hypergraph Rewriting: Critical Pairs and Undecidability of Confluence

Detlef Plump

15.1 INTRODUCTION

In their pioneering paper [KB70], Knuth and Bendix showed that confluence (or, equivalently, the Church-Rosser property) is decidable for terminating term rewriting systems. It suffices to compute all *critical pairs* $t \leftarrow s \rightarrow u$ of rewrite steps in which s is the superposition of the left-hand sides of two rules, and to check whether t and u reduce to a common term. This procedure is justified by the so-called critical pair lemma [Hue80] which states that a term rewriting system is locally confluent if and only if all critical pairs have a common reduct.

For (hyper)graph rewriting systems, however, no such simple characterization of local confluence is possible. The reason is that the embedding of derivations into "context" is more complicated than for tree rewriting. It is shown below that in the graph case, confluence of all critical pairs need not imply general local confluence. This phenomenon refutes a critical pair lemma published by Raoult [Rao84]. Okada and Hayashi [OH92] avoid the problem by giving a critical pair lemma under the strong restriction that distinct nodes in a graph must not have the same label.

In this chapter a critical pair lemma for general hypergraph rewriting is presented which provides a sufficient condition for local confluence. It requires that all critical pairs are confluent by derivations that satisfy certain conditions. The second part of this chapter reveals that a simple characterization of local confluence is indeed impossible: confluence is shown to be undecidable for terminating hypergraph rewriting systems.

Term Graph Rewriting: Theory and Practice.
Eds. Ronan Sleep, Rinus Plasmeijer and Marko van Eekelen.

15.2 HYPERGRAPH REWRITING

In this section the "Berlin approach" to graph rewriting is briefly reviewed (see [Ehr79] for a comprehensive survey), but all notions are lifted to the hypergraph case which is more flexible in applications. In particular, three theorems of the Berlin approach are recalled concerning the commutation, restriction, and extension of derivations. These results are essential tools in the proof of the critical pair lemma.

15.2.1 Hypergraphs and hypergraph morphisms

Let $\Sigma = \langle \Sigma_V, \Sigma_E \rangle$ be a *signature*, that is, Σ_V and Σ_E are sets (of node and edge labels), and each $\sigma \in \Sigma_E$ comes with a pair $type(\sigma) = \langle \alpha, \beta \rangle$ of strings $\alpha, \beta \in \Sigma_V^*$.

A *hypergraph* over Σ is a system $G = \langle V_G, E_G, l_G, m_G, s_G, t_G \rangle$, where V_G and E_G are finite sets of *nodes* and *hyperedges* (or *edges* for short), $l_G: V_G \to \Sigma_V$ and $m_G: E_G \to \Sigma_E$ are *labeling functions*, and $s_G, t_G: E_G \to V_G^*$ are functions that assign strings $s_G(e), t_G(e)$ of *source* and *target nodes* to each hyperedge e such that $type(m_G(e)) = \langle l_G^*(s_G(e)), l_G^*(t_G(e)) \rangle$. (The extension $f^*: A^* \to B^*$ of a function $f: A \to B$ maps the empty string to itself and $a_1 \dots a_n$ to $f(a_1) \dots f(a_n)$.)

G is said to be *discrete* if $E_G = \emptyset$.

In pictures of hypergraphs, nodes are drawn as circles and hyperedges as boxes, both with inscribed labels. Lines without arrowheads connect a hyperedge with its source nodes, while arrows point to the target nodes. For example, the graphical structure

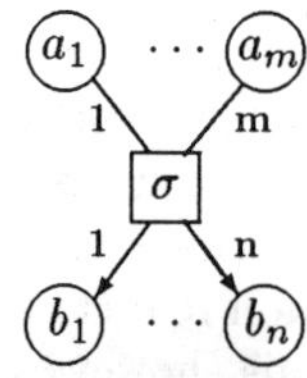

represents a hyperedge together with its source and target nodes, where $type(\sigma) = \langle a_1 \dots a_m, b_1 \dots b_n \rangle$. "Ordinary" edges with one source and one target node are frequently depicted as arrows, with labels written aside.

Let G,H be hypergraphs. Then G is a *subhypergraph* of H, denoted by $G \subseteq H$, if $V_G \subseteq V_H$, $E_G \subseteq E_H$, and l_G, m_G, s_G, t_G are restrictions of the corresponding functions of H.

A *hypergraph morphism* $f: G \to H$ consists of two functions $f_V: V_G \to V_H$ and $f_E: E_G \to E_H$ that preserve labels and assignments of source and target nodes, that is, $l_H \circ f_V = l_G$, $m_H \circ f_E = m_G$, $s_H \circ f_E = f_V^* \circ s_G$, and $t_H \circ f_E = f_V^* \circ t_G$. f is *injective* (*surjective*) if f_V and f_E are injective (surjective). f is an *isomorphism* if it is injective and surjective; in this case G and H are *isomorphic*, denoted by $G \cong H$. The subhypergraph of H with node set $f_V(V_G)$ and edge set $f_E(E_G)$ is denoted by fG. If $G \subseteq H$, then $G \hookrightarrow H$ denotes the inclusion morphism.

15.2.2 Rules and derivations

A *rule* $r = (L \supseteq K \to R)$ consists of three hypergraphs L,K,R and a morphism $K \to R$, where $K \subseteq L$.

A *hypergraph rewriting system* $\mathcal{G} = (\Sigma, \mathcal{R})$ consists of a signature Σ and a set $\mathcal{R}$ of rules with hypergraphs over Σ. For the rest of this section and the following section, $\mathcal{G}$ denotes an arbitrary hypergraph rewriting system.

Let G, H be hypergraphs. Given a rule $r = (L \supseteq K \to R)$ from $\mathcal{G}$ and a morphism $g: L \to G$, *G directly derives H through r and g*, denoted by $G \Rightarrow_{r,g} H$, if there are two hypergraph pushouts of the following form:

$$\begin{array}{ccccc} L & \hookleftarrow & K & \rightarrow & R \\ {\scriptstyle g}\downarrow & & \downarrow & & \downarrow \\ G & \hookleftarrow & D & \stackrel{c}{\rightarrow} & H \end{array}$$

(See [Ehr79] for the definition and construction of graph pushouts; the extension to hypergraphs is straightforward.) Intuitively, D is obtained from G by removing the nodes and edges in $gL - gK$, and H is constructed from D by identifying items in gK as specified by $K \to R$ and by adding the items in $R - K$.

The relations $\Rightarrow_r$ and $\Rightarrow$ are defined in the obvious way. $G \Rightarrow^\lambda H$ means $G \Rightarrow H$ or $G \cong H$. *G derives H*, denoted by $G \Rightarrow^* H$, if $G \cong H$ or there are hypergraphs $G_0,\ldots,G_n$ ($n \geq 1$) such that $G = G_0 \Rightarrow G_1 \Rightarrow \ldots \Rightarrow G_n = H$.

PROPOSITION **15.2.1** *Let G be a hypergraph, $r = (L \supseteq K \to R)$ be a rule, and $g: L \to G$ be a morphism. Then there exists a direct derivation $G \Rightarrow_{r,g} H$ if and only if the following two conditions are satisfied:*
Contact Condition. *No edge in $G - gL$ is incident to any node in $gL - gK$.*
Identification Condition. *For all items x, y in L, $g(x) = g(y)$ implies $x = y$ or $x, y \in K$.*

The following *track function* allows to "follow nodes through derivations". For a direct derivation $G \Rightarrow H$, $track_{G\Rightarrow H}: V_G \to V_H$ is the partial function defined by

$$track_{G\Rightarrow H}(v) = \begin{cases} c_V(v) & \text{if } v \in D, \\ \text{undefined} & \text{otherwise.} \end{cases}$$

For a derivation $G \Rightarrow^* H$, $track_{G\Rightarrow^* H} = i_V$ if $G \Rightarrow^* H$ by an isomorphism $i: G \to H$, and $track_{G\Rightarrow^* H} = track_{G_{n-1}\Rightarrow G_n} \circ \ldots \circ track_{G_0\Rightarrow G_1}$ if $G \Rightarrow^* H$ by a sequence $G = G_0 \Rightarrow G_1 \Rightarrow \ldots \Rightarrow G_n = H$.

$\mathcal{G}$ is *confluent* if for all hypergraphs G, H_1, H_2 with $H_1 \; {}^*\!\Leftarrow G \Rightarrow^* H_2$ there is a hypergraph M such that $H_1 \Rightarrow^* M \; {}^*\!\Leftarrow H_2$. $\mathcal{G}$ is *locally confluent* if for all direct derivations of the form $H_1 \Leftarrow G \Rightarrow H_2$ there is an M such that $H_1 \Rightarrow^* M \; {}^*\!\Leftarrow H_2$. Finally, $\mathcal{G}$ is *terminating* if it does not admit an infinite sequence $G_1 \Rightarrow G_2 \Rightarrow G_3 \Rightarrow \ldots$ of direct derivations.

15.2.3 Commutation, restriction, and extension of derivations

The following three theorems were originally formulated for graphs rather than for hypergraphs. But inspecting their proofs shows that they can be extended to the hypergraph case without further ado.

Theorem 15.2.2 (Commutation theorem [EK76]) *Let $H_1 \; {}_{r_1,g_1}\!\!\Leftarrow G \Rightarrow_{r_2,g_2} H_2$ be direct derivations through rules $r_i = (L_i \supseteq K_i \to R_i)$, for $i = 1,2$. If $g_1L_1 \cap g_2L_2 = g_1K_1 \cap g_2K_2$, then there is a hypergraph M such that $H_1 \Rightarrow_{r_2} M \; {}_{r_1}\!\!\Leftarrow H_2$.*

The following variant of the so-called Clip Theorem applies only to direct derivations, which suffices for the purposes of the present chapter.

Theorem 15.2.3 ([Kre77]) *Let $G \Rightarrow_{r,g} H$ be a direct derivation through a rule $r = (L \supseteq K \to R)$. If S is a subhypergraph of G such that $gL \subseteq S$, then $S \Rightarrow_{r,g'} U$ where g' is the restriction of g to S and $U \subseteq H$. Moreover, $track_{S\Rightarrow U}$ is the restriction of $track_{G\Rightarrow H}$.*

The next theorem allows a derivation to extend by arbitrary context, provided that context edges are not attached to nodes that are removed by the derivation. The present form of the theorem is tailored to the proof of the critical pair lemma.

Theorem 15.2.4 ([Ehr77, Kre77]) *Let $S \Rightarrow_{r,g} T \Rightarrow^* U$ be a derivation and G be a hypergraph with $S \subseteq G$. Let Boundary be the discrete subhypergraph of S that consists of all nodes that are touched by any edge in $G - S$. If $track_{S\Rightarrow T\Rightarrow^* U}$ is defined for all nodes in Boundary, then there is a derivation $G \Rightarrow_{r,\overline{g}} H \Rightarrow^* M$ such that $T \subseteq H$ and $\overline{g}$ is the extension of g to G. Moreover, M is defined by the pushout*

$$\begin{array}{ccc} \mathit{Boundary} & \xrightarrow{tr} & U \\ \downarrow & & \downarrow \\ \mathit{Context} & \rightarrow & M \end{array}$$

where $Context = (G - S) \cup Boundary$ is a subhypergraph of G, $Boundary \to Context$ is the inclusion of Boundary in Context, and tr is the restriction of $track_{S\Rightarrow T\Rightarrow^* U}$ to Boundary (considered as a morphism).

15.3 THE CRITICAL PAIR LEMMA

The quest for a critical pair lemma is motivated by the problem of testing hypergraph rewriting systems for (local) confluence. The idea is to infer the confluence of arbitrary divergent steps $H_1 \; {}_{r_1}\!\!\Leftarrow G \Rightarrow_{r_2} H_2$ from the confluence of those steps where G represents a "critical overlap" of the left-hand sides of r_1 and r_2. By the Commutation Theorem 15.2.2, such an overlap is critical only if it comprises nodes or edges that are removed by r_1 or r_2. This suggests the following definition of a critical pair.

Definition 15.3.1 (Critical pair) *Let $r_i = (L_i \supseteq K_i \to R_i)$ be rules, for $i = 1,2$. A pair of direct derivations of the form $T \; {}_{r_1,g_1}\!\!\Leftarrow S \Rightarrow_{r_2,g_2} U$ is a* critical pair *if $S = g_1L_1 \cup g_2L_2$ and $g_1L_1 \cap g_2L_2 \neq g_1K_1 \cap g_2K_2$. Moreover, $g_1 \neq g_2$ is required for the case $r_1 = r_2$.*

In the sequel, two critical pairs are not distinguished if they differ only by renaming of nodes and edges. The critical pairs arising from r_1 and r_2 can be computed by constructing all pairs of direct derivations $T \; {}_{r_1}\!\!\Leftarrow (L_1+L_2)_{/\approx} \Rightarrow_{r_2} U$ where $(L_1+L_2)_{/\approx}$

is a quotient of the disjoint union $L_1 + L_2$ that identifies at least one item in $L_1 - K_1$ (resp. $L_2 - K_2$) with some item in L_2 (L_1).

By the Commutation Theorem 15.2.2 a strong confluence property can be established for the case that $\mathcal{G}$ has no critical pairs at all. This is substantially different from term rewriting where only local confluence holds (see for example [Hue80]).

THEOREM **15.3.2** *Hypergraph rewriting systems without critical pairs are* strongly confluent, *that is, whenever* $H_1 \Leftarrow G \Rightarrow H_2$, *then there is a hypergraph* X *such that* $H_1 \Rightarrow^\lambda X \ {}^\lambda\!\Leftarrow H_2$.

PROOF. Let $H_1 \ {}_{r_1,g_1}\!\Leftarrow G \Rightarrow_{r_2,g_2} H_2$. If $g_1L_1 \cap g_2L_2 = g_1K_1 \cap g_2K_2$, then there are direct derivations $H_1 \Rightarrow_{r_2} M \ {}_{r_1}\!\Leftarrow H_2$ by Theorem 15.2.2. Assume therefore the contrary. The Clip Theorem 15.2.3 yields direct derivations $T \ {}_{r_1,g_1'}\!\Leftarrow (g_1L_1 \cup g_2L_2) \Rightarrow_{r_2,g_2'} U$ with $g_1'L_1 \cap g_2'L_2 \neq g_1'K_1 \cap g_2'K_2$. Because there are no critical pairs, $r_1 = r_2$ and $g_1 = g_2$ must hold. Then $H_1 \cong H_2$ since the result of a direct derivation is determined uniquely up to isomorphism. □

DEFINITION **15.3.3** *A critical pair* $T \Leftarrow S \Rightarrow U$ *is* joinable *if there is a hypergraph* X *such that* $T \Rightarrow^* X \ {}^*\!\Leftarrow U$.

It turns out that the joinability of all critical pairs of $\mathcal{G}$ does not guarantee local confluence. This problem may occur if $S \Rightarrow T \Rightarrow^* X$ and $S \Rightarrow U \Rightarrow^* X$ send some node in S to different nodes in X. As an example, let $\mathcal{G}$ contain the following two rules (the node indices 1,2 indicate the inclusion morphisms):

$r_1 =$

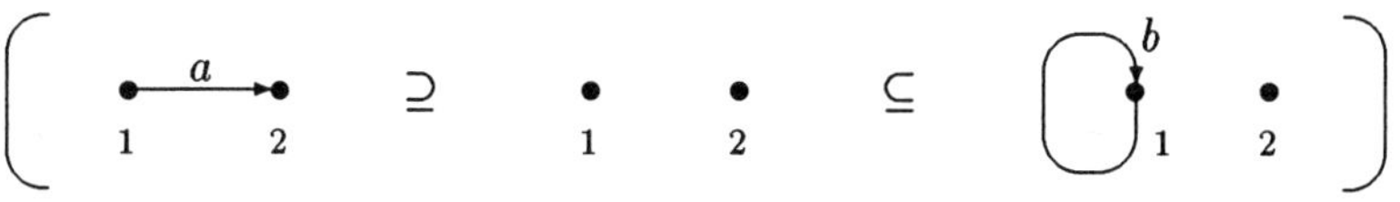

$r_2 =$

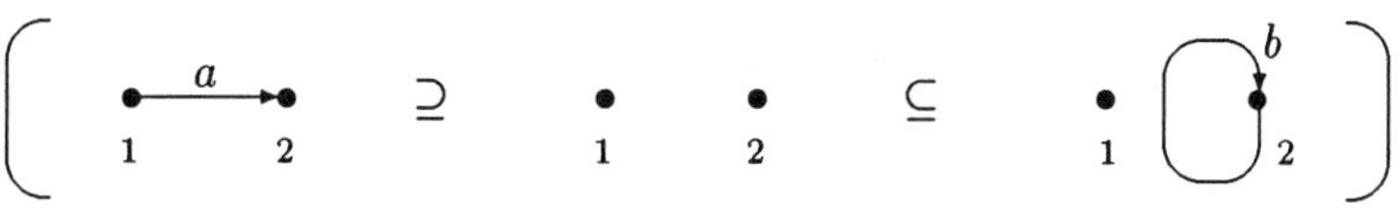

There are only two critical pairs, both being joinable:

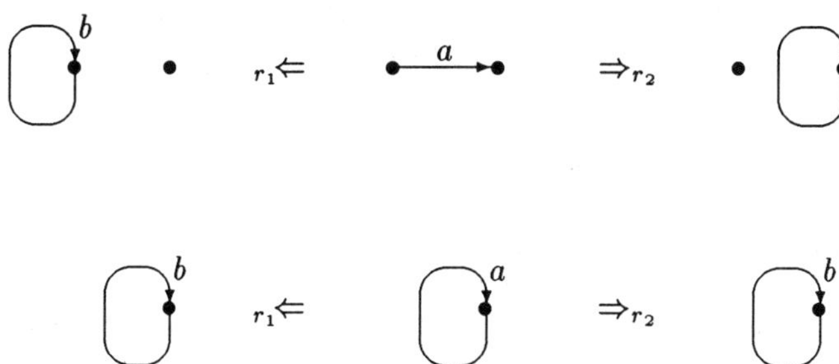

However, $\mathcal{G}$ is not locally confluent:

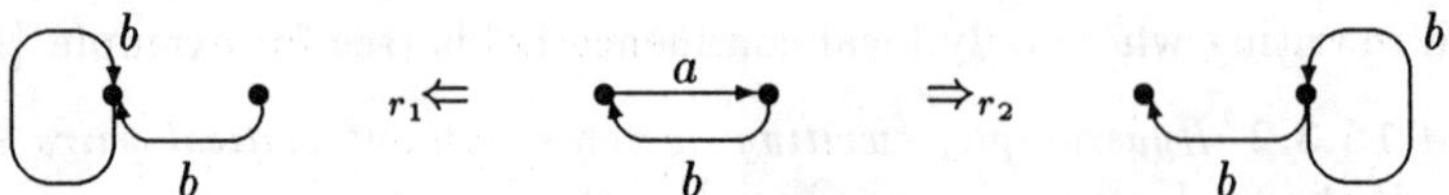

The outer hypergraphs are non-isomorphic and irreducible, hence they have no common reduct.

Here the embedding of the first critical pair into context destroys the isomorphism between the outer hypergraphs. This is possible because the two direct derivations of the critical pair—although resulting in the same hypergraph—have different track functions. In order to overcome this problem one can introduce the rules

$$r_3 = \left(\quad \supseteq \quad \emptyset \quad \subseteq \quad \emptyset \right)$$

$$r_4 = \left(\bullet \quad \supseteq \quad \emptyset \quad \subseteq \quad \emptyset \right)$$

which allow the outer hypergraphs of both critical pairs to the empty hypergraph to be reduced. r_3 and r_4 do not create new critical pairs, so all critical pairs have "confluent derivations with identical track functions". Still, this is not sufficient for local confluence: r_3 and r_4 cannot be applied to the outer hypergraphs of the last derivation pair because of the contact condition for direct derivations. In other words, the confluent derivations cannot be embedded into context since r_3 and r_4 remove nodes.

This example suggests that the confluent derivations of critical pairs should preserve certain nodes and send these to the same nodes in the common reduct.

DEFINITION **15.3.4** *Let $T \Leftarrow S \Rightarrow U$ be a critical pair, and let Protect(S) be the discrete subhypergraph of S that consists of all nodes v such that $track_{S\Rightarrow T}(v)$ and $track_{S\Rightarrow U}(v)$ are defined. Then $T \Leftarrow S \Rightarrow U$ is* strongly joinable *if there are derivations $T \Rightarrow^* X \;{}^*\!\!\Leftarrow U$ such that for all nodes v in Protect(S), $track_{S\Rightarrow T\Rightarrow^* X}(v)$ and $track_{S\Rightarrow U\Rightarrow^* X}(v)$ are defined and equal.*

LEMMA **15.3.5 (Critical Pair Lemma)** *A hypergraph rewriting system is locally confluent if all its critical pairs are strongly joinable.*

PROOF. Assume that all critical pairs of $\mathcal{G}$ are strongly joinable. Consider two direct derivations $H_1 \;{}_{r_1,g_1}\!\Leftarrow G \Rightarrow_{r_2,g_2} H_2$ through rules $r_i = (L_i \supseteq K_i \rightarrow R_i)$, $i = 1,2$. If $g_1L_1 \cap g_2L_2 = g_1K_1 \cap g_2K_2$, then there is a hypergraph M such that $H_1 \Rightarrow_{r_2} M \;{}_{r_1}\!\Leftarrow H_2$ by the Commutation Theorem 15.2.2 . Assume therefore $g_1L_1 \cap g_2L_2 \neq g_1K_1 \cap g_2K_2$. Assume further that $r_1 \neq r_2$ or $g_1 \neq g_2$, as otherwise $H_1 \cong H_2$. Let $S = g_1L_1 \cup g_2L_2$. By Theorem 15.2.3 there are restricted derivation steps $U_1 \;{}_{r_1,g'_1}\!\Leftarrow S \Rightarrow_{r_2,g'_2} U_2$ where g'_i is the restriction of g_i to S and $U_i \subseteq H_i$, for $i = 1,2$. Clearly these two steps constitute a critical pair. Hence, by assumption, there are derivations $U_1 \Rightarrow^* X \;{}^*\!\Leftarrow U_2$ such that $track_{S \Rightarrow U_1 \Rightarrow^* X}(v)$ and $track_{S \Rightarrow U_2 \Rightarrow^* X}(v)$ are defined and equal for each $v \in Protect(S)_V$.

Let *Boundary* be the discrete subhypergraph of S that consists of all nodes that are touched by any edge in $G - S$. Both $track_{G \Rightarrow H_1}$ and $track_{G \Rightarrow H_2}$ are defined for all nodes in *Boundary*, because $G \Rightarrow H_1$ and $G \Rightarrow H_2$ satisfy the contact condition. Then, in particular, $track_{S \Rightarrow U_1}$ and $track_{S \Rightarrow U_2}$ are defined on *Boundary*, that is, $Boundary \subseteq Protect(S)$. Hence, for $i = 1,2$, $track_{S \Rightarrow U_i \Rightarrow^* X}$ is defined on *Boundary*. Therefore, by Theorem 15.2.4, there are derivations $G \Rightarrow_{r_i,\overline{g_i}} \overline{H_i} \Rightarrow^* M_i$ with $U_i \subseteq \overline{H_i}$, for $i = 1,2$. $\overline{g_i}$ is the extension of g'_i to G, so $\overline{g_i} = g_i$ and consequently $\overline{H_i} \cong H_i$, for $i = 1,2$. Moreover, Theorem 15.2.4 states that, for $i = 1,2$, M_i is defined by the pushout

$$\begin{array}{ccc} Boundary & \xrightarrow{tr_i} & X \\ \downarrow & & \downarrow \\ Context & \longrightarrow & M_i \end{array}$$

where $Context = (G - S) \cup Boundary$, $Boundary \rightarrow Context$ is the inclusion of *Boundary* in *Context*, and tr_i is the restriction of $track_{S \Rightarrow U_i \Rightarrow^* X}$ to *Boundary* (considered as a morphism). Now $tr_1 = tr_2$ implies $M_1 \cong M_2$ since pushout objects are unique up to isomorphism. Thus $H_1 \Rightarrow^* M_1 \;{}^*\!\Leftarrow H_2$. □

In contrast to term and string rewriting, the critical pair lemma cannot provide a characterization of local confluence: the following example shows that even confluent and terminating systems may possess critical pairs that are not strongly joinable.

Let the label sets Σ_V and Σ_E be singletons, and let $\mathcal{G}$ contain only the following rule:

$r = (\quad \supseteq \quad \subseteq \quad)$

$\mathcal{G}$ is terminating because every rule application decreases the number of edges by one. To see that $\mathcal{G}$ is confluent, consider two derivations $H_1 \;{}^*\!\Leftarrow G \Rightarrow^* H_2$. Then either G contains no loop and $H_1 \cong G \cong H_2$, or G, H_1, H_2 contain at least one loop and have the same number of nodes. In the latter case holds $H_1 \Rightarrow^* M \;{}^*\!\Leftarrow H_2$ for the hypergraph M with $|V_G|$ nodes, one loop, and no other edges. So $\mathcal{G}$ is confluent. But the following critical pair is not strongly joinable (the nodes are numbered to indicate the track functions):

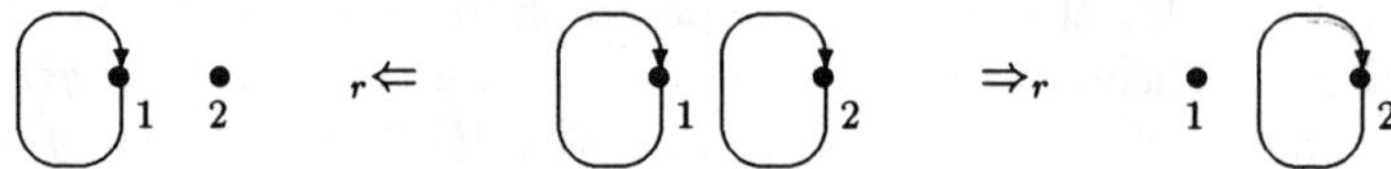

15.4 UNDECIDABILITY OF CONFLUENCE

The above example demonstrates that terminating and confluent hypergraph rewriting systems need not have strongly joinable critical pairs. So the well-known decision procedure for the confluence of terminating term rewriting systems—which reduces the terms of a critical pair to normal form and checks equality—cannot be adapted to the hypergraph case (by checking strong joinability of critical pairs). This leads to the question whether confluence is decidable at all for terminating systems. By the following result, the answer is negative.

THEOREM **15.4.1** *It is undecidable in general whether a finite, terminating hypergraph rewriting system is confluent.*

Here a hypergraph rewriting system $\mathcal{G} = \langle \Sigma, \mathcal{R} \rangle$ is said to be finite if Σ_V, Σ_E and $\mathcal{R}$ are finite sets.

The rest of this section is devoted to the proof of Theorem 15.4.1. The proof idea is inspired by the proof of Kapur, Narendran, and Otto [KNO90] that ground-confluence is undecidable for terminating term rewriting systems. In the following the Post Correspondence Problem (PCP) is reduced to the problem of deciding confluence for terminating hypergraph rewriting systems. Recall that the PCP is the following decision problem: Given two nonempty lists $A = \langle u_1, \ldots, u_n \rangle$ and $B = \langle v_1, \ldots, v_n \rangle$ of nonempty words over some alphabet Γ, decide whether there is a sequence $i_1, \ldots, i_k$ of indices such that $u_{i_1} \ldots u_{i_k} = v_{i_1} \ldots v_{i_k}$.

The pair $\langle A, B \rangle$ is called an *instance* of the PCP, and a sequence $i_1, \ldots, i_k$ as above is a *solution* of this instance. It is well-known that it is undecidable whether an arbitrary instance of the PCP has a solution (see for example [HU79]).

Let now $\langle A, B \rangle$ be an arbitrary instance of the PCP with $A = \langle u_1, \ldots, u_n \rangle$, $B = \langle v_1, \ldots, v_n \rangle$. The plan is to construct a finite, terminating hypergraph rewriting system $\mathcal{G}(A, B)$ that is confluent if and only if $\langle A, B \rangle$ has no solution.

Let $\Sigma_V = \{\bullet\}$ and $\Sigma_E = \Gamma \cup \{1, \ldots, n\} \cup \{\star, \bowtie, @, ?, \exists\}$; the types of the edge labels can be seen from the rules below. The rule set of $\mathcal{G}(A, B)$ is partitioned into subsets $\mathcal{R}_0, \mathcal{R}_1, \mathcal{R}_2$, and $\mathcal{R}_3$. $\mathcal{R}_0$ gives rise to a critical pair which stands for the choice to create an edge labeled by $\bowtie$ or to check a possible solution of $\langle A, B \rangle$. $\mathcal{R}_1$ tests whether a sequence of indices is a solution of $\langle A, B \rangle$, $\mathcal{R}_2$ detects ill-formed hypergraphs, and $\mathcal{R}_3$ performs "garbage collection".

$\mathcal{R}_0$ contains the following rules:

$\left(\boxed{\star} \to \bullet \quad \supseteq \quad \bullet \quad \subseteq \quad \boxed{\bowtie} \ \bullet \right)$

$\left(\boxed{\star} \to \bullet - \boxed{i} \to \bullet_{x} \quad \supseteq \quad \bullet_{x} \quad \subseteq \quad \boxed{@} \xrightarrow{3} \bullet - \boxed{i} \to \bullet_{x} \right)$ for $i = 1, \ldots, n$,

$\mathcal{R}_1$ contains the following rules:

$\left(\boxed{@} \xrightarrow{3} \bullet - \boxed{i} \to \bullet_{z} \quad \supseteq \quad x\bullet\ y\bullet\ \bullet_{z} \quad \subseteq \quad x\bullet \xrightarrow{u_i.1} \bullet \cdots \bullet \xrightarrow{u_i.p_i} \bullet,\ y\bullet \xrightarrow{v_i.1} \bullet \cdots \bullet \xrightarrow{v_i.q_i} \bullet,\ \boxed{@} \xrightarrow{3} \bullet_{z} \right)$

for $i = 1, \ldots, n$, where $u_i = u_i.1 \ldots u_i.p_i$ and $v_i = v_i.1 \ldots v_i.q_i$, with $u_i.j, v_i.j \in \Gamma$,

$\left(\boxed{@} \xrightarrow{3} \bullet \quad \supseteq \quad x\bullet\ y\bullet \quad \subseteq \quad \boxed{?} \right)$

$\left(x\bullet \xrightarrow{a} \bullet,\ y\bullet \xrightarrow{a} \bullet,\ \boxed{?} \quad \supseteq \quad x\bullet\ y\bullet \quad \subseteq \quad \boxed{?} \right)$ for all $a \in \Gamma$,

$\left(x\bullet \xrightarrow{a} \bullet,\ y\bullet \xrightarrow{b} \bullet,\ \boxed{?} \quad \supseteq \quad x\bullet\ y\bullet \quad \subseteq \quad x\bullet\ y\bullet\ \boxed{\bowtie} \right)$ for all $a, b \in \Gamma$ with $a \neq b$,

$\left(x\bullet \xrightarrow{a} \bullet \xrightarrow{m} \boxed{?} \quad \supseteq \quad x\bullet \quad \subseteq \quad x\bullet\ \boxed{\bowtie} \right)$ for $m = 1, 2$ and all $a \in \Gamma$,

$\left(\boxed{?} \quad \supseteq \quad \emptyset \quad \subseteq \quad \boxed{\exists} \right)$

$\mathcal{R}_2$ contains the following rules:

for $i = 1, \ldots, n$,

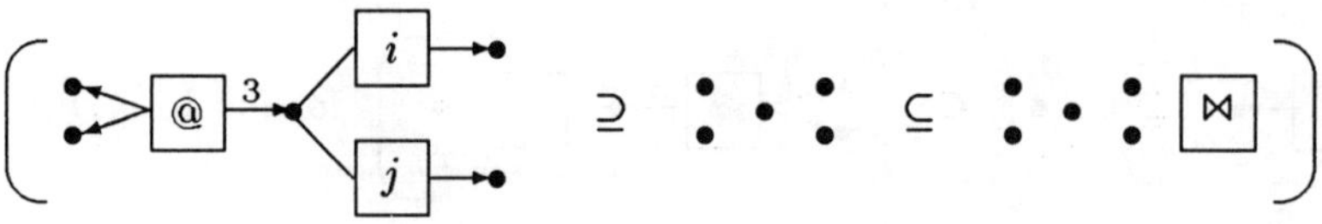

for all $i, j \in \{1, \ldots, n\}$,

for $m = 1, 2, 3$,

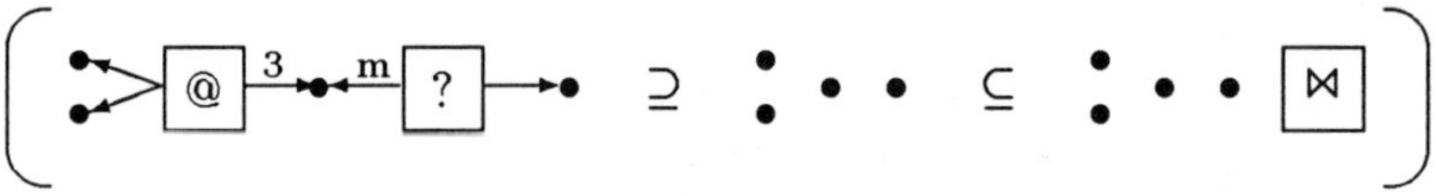

for $m = 1, 2$,

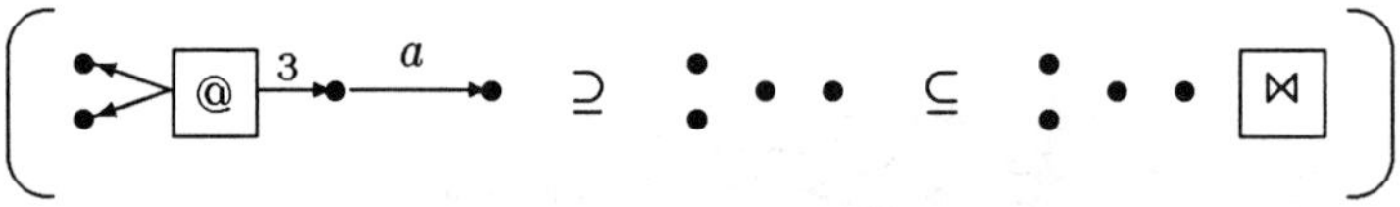

for all $a \in \Gamma$,

for all $a \in \Gamma$.

$\mathcal{R}_3$ contains the following "garbage collecting" rules:

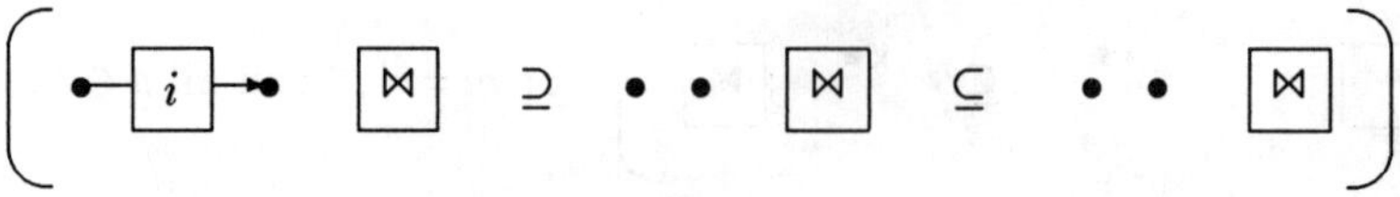

for $i = 1, \ldots, n$,

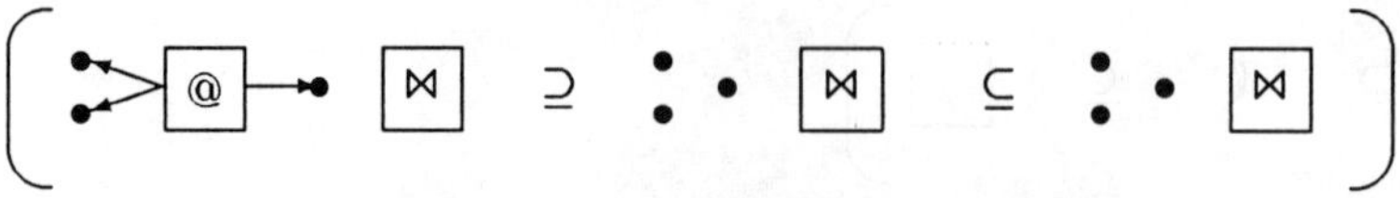

$$\left(\bullet\!\!\gtrless\!\boxed{?} \quad \boxed{\bowtie} \quad \supseteq \quad \begin{matrix}\bullet\\ \bullet\end{matrix} \quad \boxed{\bowtie} \quad \subseteq \quad \begin{matrix}\bullet\\ \bullet\end{matrix} \quad \boxed{\bowtie} \right)$$

$$\left(\bullet \xrightarrow{a} \bullet \quad \boxed{\bowtie} \quad \supseteq \quad \bullet\ \bullet \quad \boxed{\bowtie} \quad \subseteq \quad \bullet\ \bullet \quad \boxed{\bowtie} \right) \text{ for all } a \in \Gamma,$$

$$\left(\boxed{\exists} \quad \boxed{\bowtie} \quad \supseteq \quad \boxed{\bowtie} \quad \subseteq \quad \boxed{\bowtie} \right)$$

$$\left(\boxed{\bowtie} \quad \boxed{\bowtie} \quad \supseteq \quad \boxed{\bowtie} \quad \subseteq \quad \boxed{\bowtie} \right)$$

$$\left(\boxed{\bowtie} \quad \bullet \quad \supseteq \quad \boxed{\bowtie} \quad \subseteq \quad \boxed{\bowtie} \right)$$

In the following it is shown that $\mathcal{G}(A, B)$ is terminating (Lemma 15.4.2), and that $\mathcal{G}(A, B)$ is confluent if and only if $\langle A, B\rangle$ has no solution (Lemmas 15.4.4 and 15.4.6). This concludes the proof of Theorem 15.4.1 since $\mathcal{G}(A, B)$ is effectively constructible.

LEMMA **15.4.2** *$\mathcal{G}(A, B)$ is terminating.*

PROOF. Suppose that $\mathcal{G}(A, B)$ admits an infinite sequence $G_1 \Rightarrow G_2 \Rightarrow \ldots$ of direct derivations. No application of any rule in $\mathcal{G}(A, B)$ increases the number of edges with label in $\{\star\} \cup \{1, \ldots, n\}$, so there is some $l \geq 1$ such that the number of these edges is the same in all G_j with $j \geq l$. Consequently $G_l \Rightarrow G_{l+1} \Rightarrow \ldots$ contains no applications of the first three rule schemata. But all other rules in $\mathcal{G}(A, B)$ decrease the sum of the numbers of nodes and edges, and hence $G_l \Rightarrow G_{l+1} \Rightarrow \ldots$ cannot be infinite. □

LEMMA **15.4.3** *Every hypergraph containing an edge labeled by $\bowtie$ reduces to $\boxed{\bowtie}$.*

PROOF. Apply the rules in $\mathcal{R}_3$ and the first rule for $\mathcal{R}_0$ as long as possible. □

LEMMA **15.4.4** *If $\langle A, B\rangle$ has a solution, then $\mathcal{G}(A, B)$ is not confluent.*

PROOF. Let $i_1, \ldots, i_k$ be a solution of $\langle A, B\rangle$. Then

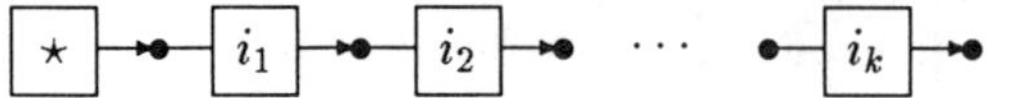

reduces to $\boxed{\bowtie}$ and $\boxed{\exists}$, both being irreducible. □

LEMMA **15.4.5** *If $\langle A, B\rangle$ has no solution and $G \Rightarrow H$ is a direct derivation through the second rule schema for $\mathcal{R}_0$, then $H \Rightarrow^* \boxed{\bowtie}$.*

PROOF. Call a sequence $e_1, \ldots, e_k$ of edges in H an *index chain* if (1) $m_H(e_j) \in \{1, \ldots, n\}$ for $j = 1, \ldots, k$, (2) $t_H(e_j) = s_H(e_{j+1})$ for $j = 1, \ldots, k-1$, and (3) $indegree(s_H(e_j)) = outdegree(s_H(e_j)) = 1$ for $j = 1, \ldots, k$. Let now $e_1, \ldots, e_k$ be the longest index chain in H such that e_1 is created by $G \Rightarrow H$. Then there is a derivation $H \Rightarrow^* H'$ through k successive applications of the first rule schema for $\mathcal{R}_1$, such that the jth step replaces e_j by two sequences of edges representing u_{i_j} and v_{i_j}, with $i_j = m_H(e_j)$. Let v be the third target node of the @-edge e created in the kth step. If v is a source or target node of any other edge, then $H' \Rightarrow H''$ through a rule in $\mathcal{R}_2$ and hence $H'' \Rightarrow^* \boxed{\bowtie}$ by Lemma 15.4.3. On the other hand, if e is the only edge incident to v, then e can be replaced by a ?-edge through the second $\mathcal{R}_1$-rule. The generated strings $u_{i_1} \ldots u_{i_k}$ and $v_{i_1} \ldots v_{i_k}$ cannot be equal as otherwise $i_1, \ldots, i_k$ were a solution of $\langle A, B\rangle$. Therefore an exhaustive application of the $\mathcal{R}_1$-rules for ?-edges results in a hypergraph containing a $\bowtie$-edge. Finally, this hypergraph reduces to $\boxed{\bowtie}$ by Lemma 15.4.3. □

LEMMA **15.4.6** *If $\langle A, B\rangle$ has no solution, then $\mathcal{G}(A, B)$ is confluent.*

PROOF. By Newman's Lemma (see e.g. [Hue80]) it suffices to show local confluence, since $\mathcal{G}(A, B)$ is terminating. Consider two direct derivations $H_1 \ {}_{r_1}\!\Leftarrow G \Rightarrow_{r_2} H_2$ through rules r_1,r_2 from $\mathcal{G}(A, B)$. Assume that the two steps are not independent in the sense of the Commutation Theorem 15.2.2 and that $H_1 \not\cong H_2$, as otherwise the existence of a common reduct is clear.

Case 1: $r_1, r_2 \in \mathcal{R}_2 \cup \mathcal{R}_3$. Then both H_1 and H_2 contain an edge labeled with $\bowtie$, hence they reduce to $\boxed{\bowtie}$ by Lemma 15.4.3.

Case 2: $r_1 \in \mathcal{R}_0 \cup \mathcal{R}_1$, $r_2 \in \mathcal{R}_2 \cup \mathcal{R}_3$. Then H_2 reduces to $\boxed{\bowtie}$. If H_1 contains a $\bowtie$-edge, then H_1 reduces also to $\boxed{\bowtie}$. Otherwise there is a direct derivation $H_1 \Rightarrow H_3$ through a rule in $\mathcal{R}_2$, so H_3 reduces to $\boxed{\bowtie}$.

Case 3: $r_1 \in \mathcal{R}_2 \cup \mathcal{R}_3$, $r_2 \in \mathcal{R}_0 \cup \mathcal{R}_1$. Analogously to case 2.

Case 4: $r_1, r_2 \in \mathcal{R}_0 \cup \mathcal{R}_1$. Then one of the rules, say r_1, is the first rule for $\mathcal{R}_0$ while r_2 is an instance of the second rule schema. By Lemmas 15.4.3 and 15.4.5, H_1 and H_2 reduce to $\boxed{\bowtie}$. □

15.5 CONCLUDING REMARKS

A task for further research is to find a sufficiently large subclass of terminating hypergraph rewriting systems for which confluence is equivalent to strong joinability of critical pairs. For the finite systems in such a class, confluence is decidable since strong joinability becomes decidable under termination.

A possible application of the critical pair lemma not considered in this chapter is the completion of non-confluent systems. One could set up a procedure which adds rules to a system until all critical pairs are strongly joinable, where the new rules should preserve the equivalence $\overset{*}{\Leftrightarrow}$ generated by $\Rightarrow$. The hypergraph rewriting systems submitted to such a procedure would have to be terminating, to ensure that strong joinability can be checked. This poses the question of how to test for termination of (hyper)graph rewriting systems, a topic to which apparently very little attention has been paid yet.

ACKNOWLEDGEMENT. I wish to thank Frank Drewes for pointing out an error in a previous version of the proof of Theorem 15.4.1.

REFERENCES

[Ehr77] Hartmut Ehrig. Embedding theorems in the algebraic theory of graph-grammars. In *Proc. Fundamentals of Computation Theory*, Springer-Verlag, Lecture Notes in Computer Science 56, pp. 245–255, 1977.

[Ehr79] Hartmut Ehrig. Introduction to the algebraic theory of graph grammars. In *Proc. Graph-Grammars and Their Application to Computer Science and Biology*, Springer-Verlag, Lecture Notes in Computer Science 73, pp. 1–69, 1979.

[EK76] Hartmut Ehrig and Hans-Jörg Kreowski. Parallelism of manipulations in multidimensional information structures. In *Proc. Mathematical Foundations of Computer Science*, Springer-Verlag, Lecture Notes in Computer Science 45, pp. 284–293, 1976.

[HU79] John E. Hopcroft and Jeffrey D. Ullman. *Introduction to Automata Theory, Languages, and Computation*. Addison-Wesley, 1979.

[Hue80] Gérard Huet. Confluent reductions: Abstract properties and applications to term rewriting systems. *Journal of the ACM*, **27**, 4, pp. 797–821, 1980.

[KB70] Donald E. Knuth and Peter B. Bendix. Simple word problems in universal algebras. In J. Leech (editor), *Computational Problems in Abstract Algebras*, pp. 263–297. Pergamon Press, 1970.

[KNO90] Deepak Kapur, Paliath Narendran, and Friedrich Otto. On ground-confluence of term rewriting systems. *Information and Computation*, **86**, pp. 14–31, 1990.

[Kre77] Hans-Jörg Kreowski. *Manipulationen von Graphmanipulationen*. Dissertation, Technische Universität Berlin, 1977.

[OH92] Yasuyoshi Okada and Masahiro Hayashi. Graph rewriting systems and their application to network reliability analysis. In *Proc. Graph-Theoretic Concepts in Computer Science*, Springer-Verlag, Lecture Notes in Computer Science 570, 1992.

[Rao84] Jean-Claude Raoult. On graph rewritings. *Theoretical Computer Science*, **32**, pp. 1–24, 1984.

16

A Quick Look at Tree Transductions

Jean-Claude Raoult

16.1 NOTATIONS

16.1.1 Trees

What is a tree? We guess that the reader is familiar with them although they are often mingled with terms. Terms are built over an alphabet F of *function symbols* graded by an *arity* function $\rho : F \to \mathbf{N}$ and a set X of *variables* the arity of which is assumed to be 0. The pair $\Sigma = (F, X)$ is called a *signature*. The set of terms over Σ is the smallest set satisfying

1) $X \subseteq T(F, X)$ and

2) $\rho(f) = n$ and $t_1, \ldots, t_n \in T(F, X)$ implies $f(t_1, \ldots, t_n) \in T(F, X)$

Condition 2 ensures that if $\rho(f) = 0$ then f is a term called a constant. The set of terms over Σ is denoted by $T(F, X)$, or simply T if no ambiguity results.

Trees are not terms. They are directed planar graphs, with vertices also called *nodes* and having a unique path from a root to each vertex, according to the following definitions.

DEFINITION **16.1.1** *An ordered graph is a set V of vertices together with a mapping $suc : V \to V^*$ assigning to a vertex a sequence of successors. If $suc(v) = v_1 \ldots v_n$, then v_i is the i-th successor of v and n is the out-degree of v.*

The graph is labeled *(or has coloured vertices) if there is a mapping $\kappa : V \to F \cup X$ such that the out-degree of a vertex is equal to the arity of its label.*

Term Graph Rewriting: Theory and Practice.
Eds. Ronan Sleep, Rinus Plasmeijer and Marko van Eekelen.

An arc is a triple (v, i, v') in which v' is the i-th successor of v. It is denoted by $v \xrightarrow{i} v'$ or simply $v \rightarrow v'$, loosing some information. Note that

1) there may not be two arcs $v \xrightarrow{i} v'$ and $v \xrightarrow{i} v''$, but

2) there may be two arcs $v \xrightarrow{i} v'$ and $v \xrightarrow{j} v'$.

A *path* of length n is a connected sequence of n arcs: $v_0 \xrightarrow{i_1} v_1 \xrightarrow{i_2} \ldots \xrightarrow{i_n} v_n$.

Definition **16.1.2** *A graph is a tree if*

1) there exists a root, from which there exists a path to any vertex, and

2) exactly one arc points to each vertex other than the root, and no arc points to the root.

There is a one-to-one correspondence between trees labeled by Σ and terms over Σ.

In the direction labeled tree $\mapsto$ term, it is called an *unravelling* of the tree and is defined by induction on the number of vertices: if the tree is reduced to its root, then its label c has arity 0 and $U(t) = c$. In general, the root has a label A of arity n and n successors $v_1, \ldots, v_n$; then $U(t) = A(U(t_1), \ldots, U(t_n))$ where t_i is the subtree of t having root v_i. This definition makes sense as soon as this recursion stops, i.e. for all acyclic graphs, in particular for trees.

In the direction term $\mapsto$ labeled tree, the set V is the set $D(t)$ of *occurrences* of the term t, which is a subset of $\mathbf{N}^*$ defined by induction on t. The labeling is also defined inductively. If the term is reduced to a variable x, then $D(x) = \{\varepsilon\}$ and has label x. In the general case, the term is $A(t_1, \ldots, t_n)$ and

$$D(t) = \{\varepsilon\} \cup \{1\}D(t_1) \cup \ldots \cup \{n\}D(t_n)$$

The root of the tree is ε and has label A.

It can be checked — and it has been checked several times (cf. for instance [Rao84]) — that these two correspondences are inverse mappings (up to a unique isomorphism), so that terms or trees are two different visions of the same thing. More interesting is the remark that the nodes of a tree correspond to places where values can be stored, e.g. addresses in the memory of a computer. See below the tree corresponding to $c(b(x, y), y, z)$.

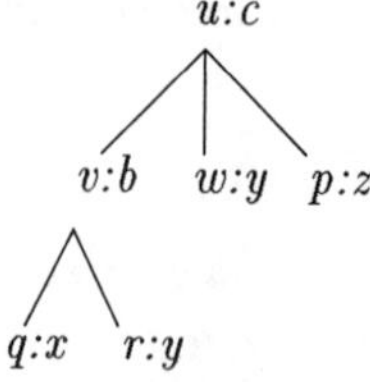

Figure 16.1 The tree corresponding to $c(b(x, y), y, z)$

There is an operation frequently used on trees (and terms) which we call *grafting*; it is a substitution with an implicit variable renaming.

DEFINITION **16.1.3** *Given a tree t, a variable x and a set L of trees, we denote by $t \cdot_x L$ the set of trees got by replacing in t the vertices having label x by trees in L, with the proviso that variables occurring in the trees of L have been renamed (for instance by indexing them by x) to avoid clashes with variables remaining in t. Or, inductively:*

$$x \cdot_x L = L$$
$$f(t_1, \ldots, t_n) \cdot_x L = \{f(t'_1, \ldots, t'_n);\ (\forall i)\ t'_i \in t_i \cdot_x L\}$$

Beware that different occurrences of x in t may be replaced by different trees in L. Of course, this warning does not apply to linear terms, in which variables occur at most once. Neither does it apply when L consists of a unique tree. This definition can be extended immediately to sequences $t_1 \ldots t_n$ of trees.

Example: $(f(x,z),z) \cdot_z f(x,y) = (f(x,z),z) \cdot_z f(u,v) = (f(x, f(u,v)), f(u,v))$

Instead of explicitly renaming the variables of s, we shall assume that the variables of t and s are different, unless otherwise stated, even if s is equal to t itself. As a result, if t and s are *linear*, i.e. if variables occur at most once in s, and at most once in t, then the grafting $t \cdot_x s$ is also linear.

A *tree morphism* in our setting is a mapping $T \to T$ compatible with the grafting:

DEFINITION **16.1.4** *A mapping $\mu : T \to T$ is a morphism if for all trees t and s, all variable x, it satisfies $\mu(t \cdot_x s) = \mu(t) \cdot_x \mu(s)$.*

16.1.2 Transductions

What is a tree transduction? It is a recursive relation $s \to t$ on trees: it should be decidable whether $s \to t$ or not. There is a trade-off between the properties that we expect from the transductions and their generality.

1) Do these transductions include the identity? This is a minimal requirement.
2) Are they preserved by composition? Can the succession of two transductions of some sort be realized by a single transduction of the same sort?
3) Can we undo the effect of a transduction with another transduction? Or (less stringent) is the inverse relation also a transduction?
4) Is the accessibility relation $s \to^* t$ recursive? Can one decide, given s and t, whether $s \to^* t$ or not?
5) Are they locally finite? Given any tree t, is there a finite number of trees t' corresponding to t under the transduction?

Even the simplest of transformations will not answer yes to all questions. For instance a vertex relabeling which is not one-to-one cannot be inverted.

Example: The relabeling $A \to A$, $B \to B$, $C \to B$ cannot be inverted: $A(B,B)$, $A(B,C)$, $A(C,B)$, and $A(C,C)$ all yield $A(B,B)$.

Tree homomorphisms, of which relabeling are special cases, will not be preserved by taking the inverse. But they contain the identity and are preserved by composition. Not only are homomorphisms locally finite, but each tree yields a unique image.

Another touchstone is the behavior of the transductions when their domain are restricted to filiform trees, in which each each node has exactly one successor, except the last one, which is labeled by a variable. These trees represent character strings, or words. Word transductions have been known for quite a time. For instance, the so-called *rational* transductions form an interesting subclass (see for instance [Ber79]). They satisfy all the above properties, except property 5; this is inevitable, if we want on one hand to associate a single tree to a whole family of trees, and on the other hand to keep preservation under the inverse.

Question 4 is very demanding. There is no general answer, but a partial one, at least in the case of character strings (we shall say "words"): the rational transductions because they show some regularity (see [Ber79]). Our goal is to extend this notion to trees, and eventually to graphs. In this respect, yet another question may be asked:

6) What are the images of regular, or rational, sets of trees (typical rational sets of trees are the parse trees of a given context-free language)? Are they rational again?

16.1.3 Tools

In the case of words, the oldest tool is probably the finite automaton with output, the "rational transducer". The relation $R = \{(a^p b^n, b^n a^q);\ n, p, q >= 0\}$ can be defined by the following automaton:

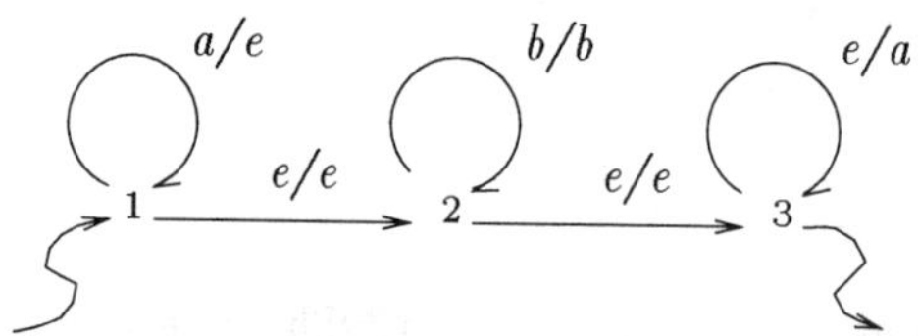

Figure 16.2 An automaton with output generating R

Or it can be generated by the following grammar:

$$\begin{array}{lll} A \to (a,\varepsilon)A & B \to (b,b)B & C \to (\varepsilon,a)C \\ A \to B & B \to C & C \to (\varepsilon,\varepsilon) \end{array}$$

Or it can be described by the following rational expression:

$$R = (a,\varepsilon)^*(b,b)^*(\varepsilon,a)^*$$

Or again, it can be represented by a pair of mappings (a "bimorphism") representing in some way the first and second projection of the relation, applied to a rational language representing the relation itself. In this case, set $K = x^*y^*z^*$ and

$$\begin{array}{ll} \phi(x) = a & \psi(x) = \varepsilon \\ \phi(y) = b & \psi(y) = b \\ \phi(z) = \varepsilon & \psi(z) = a. \end{array}$$

The equivalence between these four methods is fairly clear and has been proved long ago (see for instance [Ber79]). The relations thus defined satisfy questions 1, 2, 3 above.

In the case of trees, all these methods have been used with some success; but the results are much more complicated.

a. The simplest way of defining relations: tree rewritings, when suitably constrained, yield interesting families of transductions.
b. Finite automata with output have been studied mainly by [Eng75]. Unfortunately, root-to-leaf (left-to-right, or descending) and leaf-to-root (right-to-left or ascending) such automata are not equivalent in all cases. No obvious candidate wins the race.
c. Pairs of morphisms have been studied mainly by [AD82]. This is a rather abstract way of defining transductions, but Dauchet proves in his thesis that this method yields a good family of transformations. See [Rao92] for a survey of this method.
d. Grammars of relations, when suitably constrained, yield the most general family of transductions that may be called "rational". They are a more descriptive way of defining the same relations as [AD82].
e. Formulae describing the transformation are also good candidates, but here also, they have to be suitably constrained.

These methods will be developed in the next sections.

16.2 TRANSDUCTIONS USING TREE REWRITING

A tree rewriting is a relation over T which is compatible with the way trees are built. Whatever may be the definition of rewritings, the identity is a tree rewriting. Now whether rewritings are preserved by composition depends on which sort of rewriting is considered. All considered rewritings are finitely generated, by some *system*

$$\begin{cases} g_1 \to d_1 \\ \dots \\ g_n \to d_n \end{cases}$$

Frequently, the rewriting is limited to a single step, defined by: $c(s) \to c(t)$ if $s \to t$ and $c(x)$ is a term containing a unique occurrence of x. This is not preserved by composition: the succession of two single steps is obviously not a single step.

The rewriting may be a step of simultaneous parallel rewriting: here, the definitions concerning terms and trees do not correspond. Parallel rewriting of terms is defined by: $c(s_1, \dots, s_p) \to c(t_1, \dots, t_p)$ if $s_i \to t_i$ for $i = 1, \dots, p$ for any term c; or equivalently

$$\begin{aligned} s &= c(g_1\sigma_1, \dots, g_q\sigma_q) \\ t &= c(d_1\sigma_1, \dots, d_q\sigma_q) \end{aligned}$$

for some term $c(x_1, \dots, x_q)$ and substitutions $\sigma_1, \dots, \sigma_q$. No occurrence of a redex g_i is a prefix of another occurrence of a g_j. This sort of parallel rewriting is not preserved by composition.

Parallel rewriting for trees may be defined similarly: the redices are disjoint — but disjoint graphs. Their occurrences may be prefixes of one another, as long as no vertex is common to two redices. This notion may be expressed with graftings: $s \cdot_x s' \rightarrow t \cdot t'$ if $s \rightarrow t$ and $t \rightarrow t'$, or equivalently

$$s = s_1 \cdot_{x_1} g_1 \ldots s_q \cdot_{x_q} g_q \cdot_{x_{q+1}} s_{q+1}$$
$$t = s_1 \cdot_{x_1} d_1 \ldots s_q \cdot_{x_q} d_q \cdot_{x_{q+1}} s_{q+1}$$

Unfortunately, the situation is not better than for terms: parallel tree rewritings are not preserved by composition, as shown by the following example.

Example: Let $R = d(a(x)) \rightarrow b(a(x))$ and $S = a(b(x)) \rightarrow c(x)$. Then the following composition is not a tree rewriting, whether single of parallel:

$$a(d(a(\ldots(d(a(x))\ldots))) \rightarrow a(b(a(\ldots(b(a(x))\ldots))) \rightarrow c(\ldots(c(a(x)))\ldots)$$

The transitions of a Turing machine may be represented by the (term or tree) rewriting generated by finite system. And in the simulation, single step and parallel rewritings coincide. Therefore the accessibility relation is undecidable. For the same reason, none of them preserves the rationality of a set of trees. This sort of rewriting is too general.

Suffix rewritings for words ($u \rightarrow v \Rightarrow xu \rightarrow xv$) are rational transductions preserved by iteration, as proved by Caucal (cf. [Cau88]). On trees, Dauchet, Tison and others investigated suffix rewriting for trees: ground term rewriting (cf. [DTHL87] and [DT90] for two different methods). A *ground* term is a term which contains no variable: the generated rewriting operates on full subterms, without substitution. The resulting transductions have rational ranges and images, contain the identity and are preserved by composition and iteration. In [DT90], they show a strong result:

THEOREM **16.2.1** *Given a finite system of ground terms rewriting, any first order definable property over the relation* $s \rightarrow^* t$ *is decidable.*

The algorithm consists in associating a finite automaton (see the beginning of next section for a precise definition) with the formula, and running it on a superposition of the object and the image tree. Such a superposition is illustrated in the following figure.

Note that the transformation above is fairly simple: it is a "right rotation at the root", used in balanced trees. Nevertheless, the fact that the labels $0y$ and $y0$ do not belong to the same subtree of the superposition forbids any finite automaton to check the equality of two trees substituted for y. Therefore, this transformation cannot be implemented using their method.

16.3 TRANSDUCTIONS USING AUTOMATA WITH OUTPUT

Tree automata and tree languages are the topic of [GS84] to which we refer the reader for complements.

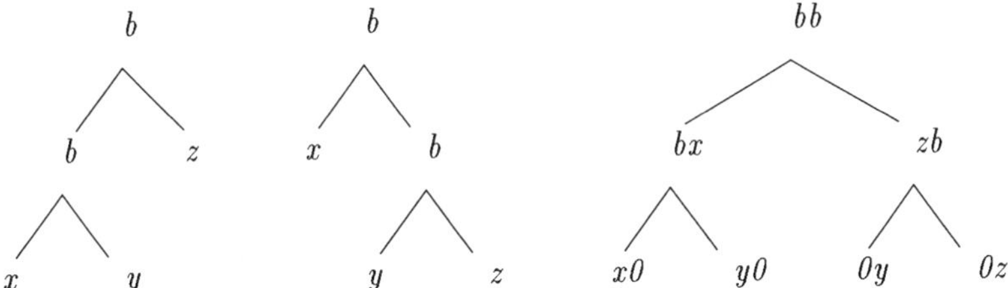

Figure 16.3 Two trees and their superposition

DEFINITION **16.3.1** *A tree automaton over F is a finite set Q of states together with a finite set Δ of* transitions *of the form $q_1 \dots q_n f q$ where $n = \rho(f)$.*

Given a tree t, a (successful) run of the automaton is a labeling $\chi : V \to Q$ of the vertices by the states compatible with the transitions: for all vertex v having label f and successors $v_1 \dots v_n$, the run χ must satisfy

$$\chi(v_1) \dots \chi(v_n) f \chi(v) \in \Delta$$

This representation suggests that the automaton is "ascending" from the leaves to the root. If instead the transitions have the form $q f q_1 \dots q_n$, the automaton is "descending" from the root to the leaves. Actually, the satisfiability condition for the runs is the same, so that there is no difference between the two approaches. The transitions look like pieces of a puzzle and the game may be played in any direction. The automaton accepts a tree if there is a run on the tree in which the root is labeled by given states (called initial if the automaton is "descending", called final if the automaton is "ascending"). A set of trees accepted by a finite automaton is called *rational* or sometimes *regular* or *recognizable*. For further results on tree automata, cf. [GS84].

For transducers, there is a difference between ascending and descending transducers. Ascending transducers look like tree automata with an output.

DEFINITION **16.3.2** *An ascending transducer is a finite set Q of states of arity one together with a finite set or transitions of the form*

$$f(q_1 x_1, \dots, q_n x_n) \to q t(x_{\sigma(1)}, \dots, x_{\sigma(p)})$$

where t contains no variable other than explicitly written and where σ is a mapping $[1, p] \to [1, n]$.

Descending tree transducers are defined symmetrically.

DEFINITION **16.3.3** *A (descending) transducer is a finite set Q of states of arity one together with a finite set of transitions of the form:*

$$q f(x_1, \dots, w_n) \to t(q_1 x_{\sigma(1)}, \dots, q_p x_{\sigma(p)})$$

where t contains no variable other than explicitly written and where σ is a mapping $[1, p] \to [1, n]$.

In both definitions, if σ is surjective, the transducer is *non-erasing*, otherwise it can delete an input tree (after processing it if it is ascending, before processing if it is descending). If σ is injective, the transducer is *linear*, otherwise it can duplicate an input tree (after processing it if it is ascending, before processing it if it is descending). For instance, a morphism μ has the format of a descending transducer with a single state and a single rule per function symbol (deterministic):

$$\mu f(x_1, \ldots, x_n)) = t(\mu x_1), \ldots, \mu x_n))$$

The main results concerning tree transducers are gathered in the following theorem in which A stands for ascending, D for descending, L for linear and N for non-erasing and H for homomorphic (a single state, deterministic); F^n stands for the n-fold composition of transducers of class F.

THEOREM **16.3.4** *The following arrows represent strict inclusions and only NLA, H and LA are closed under composition.*

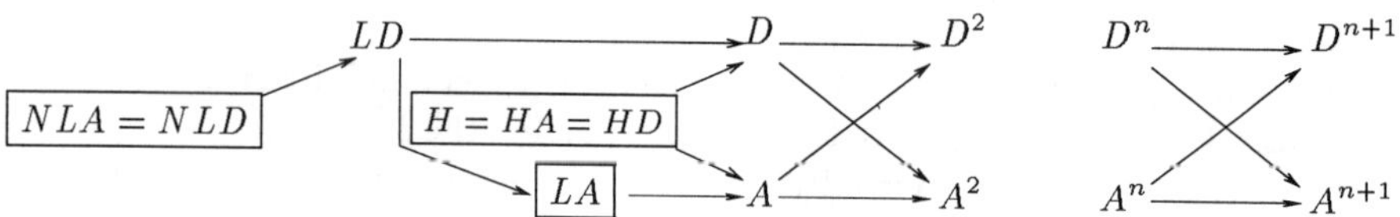

Figure 16.4 The hierarchy of transducers

Proofs in [Eng75]. An interesting family closed by composition is the class of linear ascending transducers.

For instance, consider the following ascending transducer with $Q = \{q\}$ over $F = \{b, a, c\}$ of respective arities 2,1,0:

$$\begin{aligned} b(qx, qy) &\rightarrow qa(x) \\ c &\rightarrow qc \end{aligned}$$

This transducer has a unique state, is ascending deterministic (at most one rule for each function symbol), linear but erasing and not total. It copies the left branch of a binary tree containing only bs and replaces all bs by as. This cannot be done by a descending transducer because deleting the right branch with a descending transducer allows the right subtree to be any tree — including trees containing as. This cannot be checked before processing. It is in LA but not in D.

All these transductions have a locally finite image. But if erasing is allowed, a given tree may be the image of an infinite number of trees. Therefore, it is not surprising that these classes are not preserved by taking the inverse. Restricted to words, all the above transductions yield rational transductions, but not all the rational word transductions. No class is preserved by iteration.

It can be checked easily (by suppressing the output) that the domain of all the above transducers is a rational set of trees; and for transducers in LA, the image of a rational set of trees is still rational.

16.4 TRANSDUCTIONS DEFINED BY GRAMMARS

A seemingly simple way of defining tree relations is by equations, or grammars. For instance, one can define three recursive relations B, C and I on terms by the following Prolog-like program

$$\begin{array}{rcl} B(x, b(u, v)) & \Leftarrow & C(x, u, v) \\ B(x, y) & \Leftarrow & I(x, y) \\ C(c(u, v, w), c(u', v', w'), z) & \Leftarrow & C(u, u', v'), I(v, w'), I(w, z) \\ C(b(x, y), u, v) & \Leftarrow & I(x, u), I(y, v) \end{array}$$

where I is the identity. Note that in this program, the right-hand sides of each clause contains only variables and no other variable than occurring on the left-hand side.

These relations are also solutions of equations, or generated by grammars, or again described by regular expressions. For instance, the definition in the example above can be rewritten as follows:

$$\begin{array}{rcl} B(x, y) & \Leftarrow & y = b(u, v), C(x, u, v) \\ & \vee & I(x, y) \\ C(x, y, z) & \Leftarrow & x = c(u, v, w), y = c(u', v', w'), C(u, u', v'), I(v, w'), I(w, z) \\ & \vee & x = b(u, v), I(u, y), I(v, z) \end{array}$$

or again by the following grammar:

$$\begin{array}{rl} B \rightarrow & (x, b(u, v)), Cxuv \\ | & (x, y), Ixy \\ C \rightarrow & (c(u, v, w), c(u', v', w'), z), Cuu'v', Ivw', Iwz \\ | & (b(u, v), y, z), Iuy, Ivz \end{array}$$

The definitions below describe this notation.

DEFINITION **16.4.1** *Given two graded sets F and R of function and relation symbols, a* parameterized relation *over F and R is a pair (v, S) where v is a linear tuple of trees in $T^*(F \cup X)$ and S, called the* synchronizing set, *is a set of formal relations of the form $Ax_1 \ldots x_n$ where $A \in R$ and $n = \rho(A)$ and all the arguments x_i are distinct and disjoint from the arguments of all other formal relations in S. Two parameterized relations differing only by the names of their variables will be considered equal.*

Parameterized relations over F and R can be denoted in different ways, for instance as above by a linear list of trees together with an indication of which variable belong to which relation symbol, like:

$$v(x_1, \ldots, x), Ax_1 \ldots x_n, By_1 \ldots x_p, Az_1 \ldots z_n$$

Parameterized relations can also be viewed as labeled (hyper)graphs, thanks to the following standard correspondence: associate a vertex with each subtree different from a variable. With every subtree $t = f(t_1, \ldots, t_n)$ associate a (hyper)arc of arity $n+1$ passing through the vertices associated with $t, t_1, \ldots, t_n$ in this order and labeled by f. Since variables occur at most once, they are identified with the vertices they label. Finally, all formal relations $Ax_1 \ldots x_n$ are identified with (hyper)arcs labeled by A and passing through $x_1, \ldots, x_n$ in this order. One may also add a source hyperarc passing through all vertices associated to the roots of the tuple. This correspondence is visualized in the figure below, where the graph is drawn and also written as a set of labeled hyperarcs. Notice that this last representation is close to a programme with unique assignment, in which the hyperarc $fxyz$ represents the statement $x := f(y, z)$.

$$w = (b(b(x,y)z), b(u, b(v, w))), Axu, Ayv, Azw, \qquad \text{or}$$
$$w = \{Rpr, bpqz, bqxy, brus, bsvw, Axu, Ayv, Azw\}$$

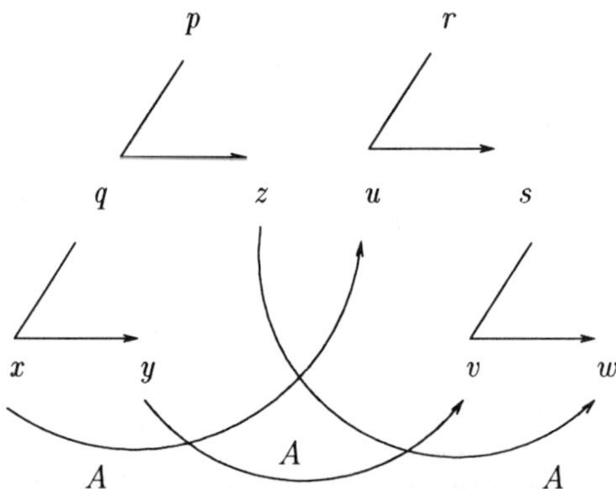

Figure 16.5 A drawing of the hypergraph w

To generate relations, we will replace a formal n-ary relation like Axy by a parameterized relation α.

DEFINITION **16.4.2** *A grammar of relations is a finite set of productions $A \to \alpha$ in which A is a predicate symbol, and α is a parameterized relation.*

As usual, the grammars generate a step of rewriting on parameterized relations $\beta \to \gamma$ in which one occurrence of a left-hand side of the grammar has been replaced by one of its right-hand sides. For instance, Axy is replaced by $\alpha = (gx, hyz), Bxyz$. In the notation of hypergraphs above, this is nothing other than hyperedge rewriting: $Auv \to \{gux, hvyz, Bxyz\}$.

Formally, rewriting a non-terminal into one of its right-hand sides will involve a grafting as defined in section 1: suppose $\beta = (w, S \cup \{Ax_1 \ldots x_n\}$ and $\alpha = (u, S')$ in which

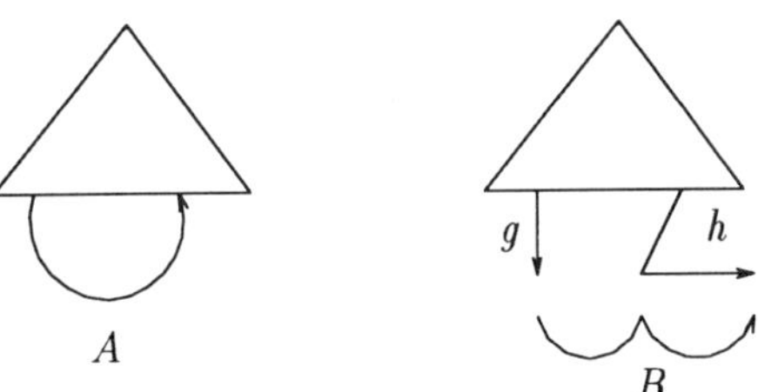

Figure 16.6 One step of derivation

u is a n-tuple of trees and the variables of α are disjoint from those of β; then

$$(w, S \cup \{Ax_1 \dots x_n\}) \to (w \cdot_{x_1 \dots x_n} u, S \cup S')$$

We shall use freely the terminology used in language theory, like non-terminal, language generated from an axiom, etc.

For instance, consider the following relation:

$$\begin{aligned} R \to \quad & (c(x,y,z), b(u,v)), Axyu, Izv \\ A \to \quad & (c(x,y,z), q, c(u,v,w)), Axyu, Izv, Iqw \\ \mid \quad & (b(x,y), z, c(u,v,w)), Ixu, Iyv, Izw \\ I \to \quad & (ax, ay), Ixy \mid (d,d) \end{aligned}$$

also depicted in the next figure.

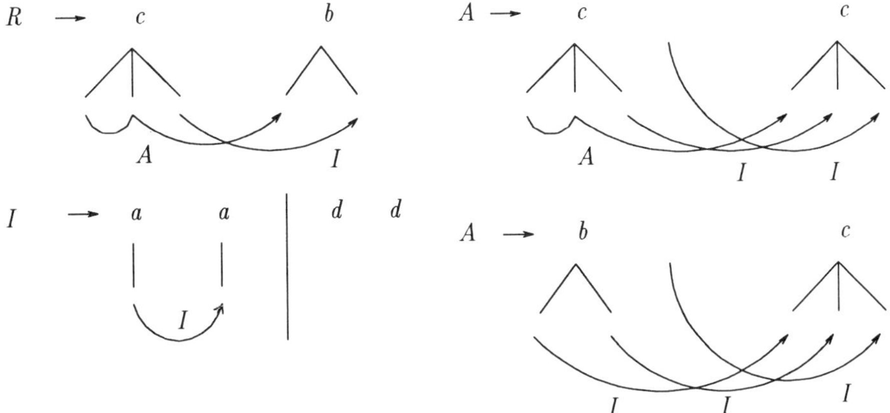

Figure 16.7 A grammar of relations; R and I are binary, A is ternary

Then a generated pair of trees is depicted below.

For all relations defined in this way, accessibility is decidable. But in general, the composition of two such relations need not be generated by a grammar. Introduce the following restriction.

DEFINITION **16.4.3** *A rational transduction is the relation generated by a grammar in which all non-terminals have all their arguments in two trees at most, one in each projection of the generated relation.*

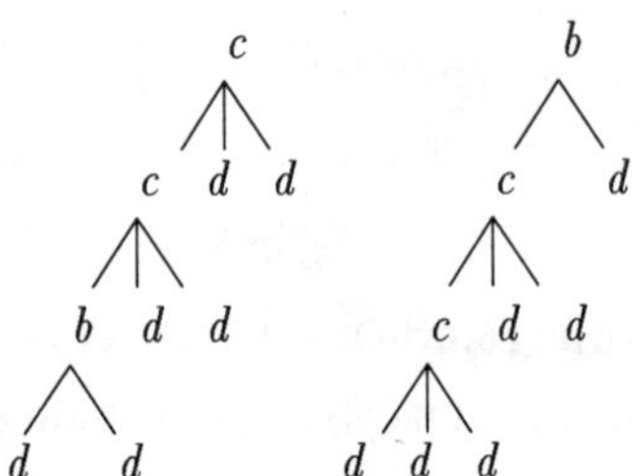

Figure 16.8 A pair of trees belonging to relation R

The above relations, for instance, are rational transductions. This definition is tuned to get the following result.

THEOREM **16.4.4** *Rational transductions contain the identity and are preserved by taking the inverse and the composition. Their ranges and images are rational sets of trees.*

For instance, the grammar above generates from R a rational transduction.

For an example of a grammar which does not generate a rational transduction, consider the following grammar:

$$\begin{array}{ll} R \rightarrow & (f(x), g(y, z)), Axyz \\ A \rightarrow & (a(x), a(y), a(z)), Axyz \mid (c, c, c) \end{array}$$

The second projection of the non-terminal A has two arguments in two different trees. For that matter, the generated relation is $\{(f(a^n(c), g(a^n(c), a^n(c)); n \geq 0\}$ and the second projection is not rational: no finite automaton can check that the two subtrees of the root g contain the same number of as.

16.5 TRANSDUCTIONS USING SECOND ORDER LOGIC

This method has been investigated mainly by Engelfriet in [Eng91], and by Courcelle (cf. [Cou91]), following the terminology of graphs — finite relational structures. Trees can be seen as (finite) models of a relational language defined as follows:

DEFINITION **16.5.1** *Given an alphabet F of function symbols we deduce an alphabet P of predicate symbols: for each $f \in F$, we define a unary symbol $c_f(x)$ and $\rho(f)$ binary symbols $s_i(x, y)$ for $(1 \leq i \leq \rho(f))$, with the intent that $c_f(x)$ holds if vertex x is labeled by f, and $s_i(x, y)$ holds if y is the ith successor of x.*

A first observation is that the domain of a finite automaton can be characterized by a sentence: a logical formula (see e.g. [Don70]).

THEOREM **16.5.2** *A set of trees is definable by a monadic second order formula over P if and only if this set is recognizable by a finite automaton.*

A tree transformation can also be specified by a tuple of monadic second order formulae over two alphabets P and P' of predicate symbols describing trees as defined above: $(\phi, \psi(x), (\theta_p(x_1, \ldots, x_n)_{p \in P'})$ where $n = \rho(p) = 1$ or 2. The image of a tree is described from the object, adding and deleting relations.

a. ϕ specifies the domain of the transduction: the object tree must satisfy ϕ: $t \models \phi$.
b. ψ specifies the vertex set of the image, as as subset of the vertex set of the object: $x \in t' \Leftrightarrow \psi(x)$.
c. θ_p specifies the set of vertices having label p if p is unary, the set of arcs labeled p if $p = s_i$ is binary.

Example: the right rotation at the root described in figure 16.3 can be defined logically as follows. We shall use two relations $r(x)$ asserting that x is a root and $p(x, y)$ asserting that y is a descendant of x (this last relation is second order)

$$\begin{aligned} r(x) = &\quad \neg\exists y(s_1(y,x) \vee s_2(y,x)) \\ p(x,y) = &\quad \forall X[\forall u \forall v((u \in X \wedge (s_1(u,v) \vee s_2(u,v)) \Rightarrow v \in X) \wedge x \in X \Rightarrow y \in X] \end{aligned}$$

Using r and p, we now define

$$\phi = \exists u[r(u) \wedge c_b(u) \wedge \exists z s_2(u,z) \wedge \exists v(s_1(u,v) \wedge c_b(v) \wedge \exists x s_1(v,x) \wedge \exists y s_2(v,y))]$$

This relation asserts that the object tree is a substitution of $b(b(x,y),z)$. We should also check that all vertices are labeled by b except the leaves, which are labeled by a (say).

$$\psi(x) = true$$

All vertices of t are used for t'.

$$\begin{aligned} \theta_{s_1}(x,y) = \quad & [r(x) \wedge \exists v(s_1(x,v) \wedge s_1(v,y))] \\ & \vee[\exists u(r(u) \wedge (s_1(u,x) \wedge s_2(x,y) \\ & \exists z(s_2(u,z) \wedge p(z,x) \wedge s_1(x,y) \\ & \vee \exists v(s_1(u,v) \wedge \exists z(s_1(v,z) \wedge p(z,x) \wedge s_1(x,y) \\ & \vee s_2(v,z) \wedge p(z,x) \wedge s_1(x,y)))] \end{aligned}$$

We let the reader define θ_{s_2}, in a way similar to θ_{s_1}. In the example above, (1) t' needs no other vertex than already present in t, and (2) the correspondence is functional: one t yields one t'. In the general case:

1) t' may be defined using k copies of t (k fixed for the transduction),
2) all the formulae may depend further on a finite set $\{X_1, \ldots, X_n\}$ of second order variables, to allow for several images for a single object t.

Note however that t is finite and that $X_1, \ldots, X_n$ have values in $\mathcal{P}(t)$, the power set of the set of nodes of t; therefore the number of associated t' will be finite also: these *definable* transductions are locally finite. Engelfriet in [Eng91] and Courcelle in [Cou91] prove the following result.

PROPOSITION **16.5.3** *The domain of a definable transduction is definable (recognizable). The composition of two definable transductions is a definable transduction.*

But the image of a definable transduction is in general not definable, and the inverse of a definable transduction is not necessarily definable either.

REFERENCES

[AD82] A. Arnold and M. Dauchet. Morphismes et bimorphismes d'arbres. *Theoretical Computer Science*, **20**, pp. 33–93, 1982.

[Ber79] J. Berstel. Transductions and context-free languages. In *Teubner Studienbücher*, Stuttgart, 1979.

[Cau88] D. Caucal. *Recritures suffixes de mots.* Technical Report 871, INRIA research report, 1988.

[Cou91] B. Courcelle. The monadic second order logic of graphs v: On closing the gap between definability and recognizability. *Theoretical Computer Science*, **80**, pp. 153–202, 1991.

[Don70] J. Doner. Tree acceptors and some of their applications. *Journal of Computer and System Sciences*, **4**, pp. 406–451, 1970.

[DT90] M. Dauchet and S. Tison. The theory of ground rewrite systems is decidable. In *Proc. of 5th IEEE symp. on LICS*, pp. 242–248, 1990.

[DTHL87] M. Dauchet, S. Tison, T. Heuillard, and P. Lescanne. *Decidability of the confluence of ground term rewriting systems.* Technical Report 675, INRIA research report, 1987.

[Eng75] J. Engelfriet. Bottom-up and top-down tree transformations — a comparison. *Mathematical Systems Theory*, **9**, 3, pp. 198–231, 1975.

[Eng91] J. Engelfriet. A characterization of context-free nce graph languages by monadic second order logic on trees. In H. Ehrig, H.-J. Kreowski, and G. Rozenberg (editors), *Proc. 4th International Workshop on Graph Grammars and their Application to Computer Science*, Springer-Verlag, Lecture Notes in Computer Science 532, pp. 311–327, 1991.

[GS84] F. Gecseg and M. Steinby. Tree automata. In *Akademiai Kiado, Budapest*, 1984.

[Rao84] J.-C. Raoult. On graph rewriting. *Theoretical Computer Science*, **32**, pp. 1–24, 1984.

[Rao92] J.-C. Raoult. A survey of tree transductions. In M. Nivat and A. Podelski (editors), *Tree automata and Languages*, pp. 311–326. Elsevier Science, 1992.

17

Paragon Specifications and Their Implementation

P. Anderson, D.J. Bolton and P.H.J. Kelly

17.1 INTRODUCTION

Current architecture description and verification methods primarily deal with static systems. Parallel systems need, however, to manage dynamic process creation, asynchronous message passing, and load balancing. Paragon provides a formalism with which to capture the architectural structure of a parallel application, and follow development of a parallel software and/or hardware implementation. A program is a set of class definitions each of which is defined by type information and a set of rewrite rules. Interaction between class instances is by means of synchronous and asynchronous message passing. Paragon is distinguished from other notations by its novel mixture of message passing and rewrite systems semantics.

This chapter introduces Paragon, and then addresses the bottom layers of refinement in specification of a concurrent or parallel hardware system: the design of static synchronous parallel processes to implement required behavior. We define a simple translation scheme for a defined subset of Paragon specifications which generates a program in a hardware description language.

The next section overviews the language through a discussion of applications, and a sketch of syntax and current operational semantics. A trivial routing switch example to be used throughout is also introduced. Section 17.3 outlines an implementation scheme for the simplest, static class of specifications. This includes a discussion of the restrictions required on specifications to allow definition of a translation to an Occam-based parallel system description language. Section 17.4 develops a simple strategy for buffering of asynchronous messages, leading into a translation for the switch example in

Term Graph Rewriting: Theory and Practice.
Eds. Ronan Sleep, Rinus Plasmeijer and Marko van Eekelen.

section 17.5. Section 17.6 concludes with further discussion of the restrictions required, which provide further insight into the nature of Paragon specifications.

17.2 OVERVIEW OF PARAGON

The development of Paragon arose from a need to understand the communications involved in parallel graph reduction architectures for functional programming language implementation. The objective was to design a parallel distributed memory abstract machine in which all remote memory access and communication is made explicit. Our starting point was initially a notation which incorporated pattern matching and rewriting of data structures, in the fashion of term rewriting. This notation has a natural interpretation as "term" graph rewriting, by interpreting copying in the right hand side of a rewrite rule as pointer, rather than structure, copying [BvEG+87a].

A graph rewrite system does not specify control flow clearly, although it does express potential behavior. For example, if we have the simple rewrite system:

S x y z → (x z) (y z)

we can augment this with control annotations in a DACTL-like manner [GKS87]:

S x y z → # !(x z) (y z)

where the # denotes suspension and ! denotes firing, or need. The Paragon rewrite rule which captures this behavior is:

⟨⟨S x y z⟩, ∅⟩ **given** need(client)
→ ⟨⟨left right⟩, {client}⟩
where left = **new**(⟨x z⟩), right = **new**(⟨y z⟩)
then left ! need (**self**)

Rules express a change of state, and here we use a pair to represent the current form of the object and the set of objects suspended pending this reduction (clearly several more rules are required to deal with an empty pending set, unwinding, and normal forms).

To control rewriting, and to introduce the concept of a process, rewrite rules may be guarded by message receipt carrying parameters (here the need message carries the needing client) and may be augmented by a set of messages to be sent should rewriting occur (here a need message to the fired object, carrying the current object **self** as the needing client). Thus rules may forward control to other rules. Objects may be dynamically generated with **new**, and incorporated into the new rewritten state as shown.

In a general graph-rewriting language, non-root overwriting can be used to model side-effects, as required for example to express resource management. In Paragon, message passing is used instead, thereby simplifying the semantics of rewriting. The resulting language differs from DACTL and Lean [BvEG+87b] in making side-effects explicit as message passing and differs from FP2 [SJ89] in allowing messages to be directed towards dynamically created objects.

The language has been applied to the problem of specifying parallel graph reduction architectures in several ways, and at several levels. It captures the route from a term rewrite system, annotated with control flow information, to a message-passing parallel implementation. This has been followed for a functional language implementation using a fixed combinator set machine [BHK89], and for a supercombinator reduction machine [BHK91]. A prototype for a parallel graph reduction architecture based on [BHK89] in the form of a simulator is described in [And91]. The specification of a functional language implementation using a fixed combinator set is used to derive a C implementation which simulates the execution of lazy functional programs taking full account of automatically generated strictness annotations. Below this level, simple refinements have been introduced to express the placement of logical processes on physical processing elements, together with a simple load balancing mechanism.

17.2.1 Class definitions and rules

A specification in Paragon consists of a set of class definitions, a set of associated data types, and a set of objects representing the initial state of the specified system. Data types are specified using a syntax borrowed from Miranda [Tur85], and define a free algebra with the named constructors. A class definition consists of the structure of the object defined as a data type and a set of rules which define the behavior of an object of that class when it receives a message. Classes and data types are written with constructors (possibly with arguments) or as tuples as follows:

data direction ::= North | East | South | West
class queue ::= EQ | PQ integer queue
class buffer ::= ⟨**vector** [North **upto** West] router,packet,direction⟩

The syntax of a Paragon rule is given in figure 17.1. A rule consists of a left-hand side and a right-hand side and has the following form:

$\mathcal{S}$ **given** m(x)
when $\mathcal{G}$
$\rightarrow$ $\mathcal{S}'$
then $\mathcal{C}$
where $\mathcal{B}$

This rule is applicable when an object of a particular class whose state matches the pattern $\mathcal{S}$ is passed a message m carrying arguments x. If the guard $\mathcal{G}$ evaluates to true, the rule fires, the object is transformed into $\mathcal{S}'$, and communications $\mathcal{C}$ are generated. Communications take the form obj ! message or obj !! message denoting synchronous and asynchronous message-passing respectively. $\mathcal{B}$ introduces some bindings of names used in $\mathcal{S}'$, $\mathcal{B}$ and $\mathcal{C}$. Expressions can contain references to **self** which refers to the object that is receiving the message, or to **nil** which refers to the null object. New instances of objects are created with the expression **new** (*class name,initial state*).

Rules can also be defined without a **given** clause, with the intention that the rule be applied "spontaneously" when the state matches $\mathcal{S}$ and the optional guard evaluates to true. An example of the use of such rules is given later.

```
⟨rule⟩      →  ⟨lhs⟩ ⇁ ⟨rhs⟩
⟨lhs⟩       →  ⟨state⟩ [ given ⟨message⟩ ] [ when ⟨guard⟩ ]
⟨message⟩   →  name [ ( ⟨state⟩ { , ⟨state⟩ } ) ]
⟨guard⟩     →  name = ⟨state⟩
            |  ⟨predicate⟩ | ⟨guard⟩∧⟨guard⟩ | ⟨guard⟩∨⟨guard⟩ | (⟨guard⟩)

⟨rhs⟩       →  ⟨state⟩ [ then ⟨tasks⟩ ] [ where ⟨bindings⟩ ]

⟨tasks⟩     →  name ! ⟨outgoing⟩                  synchronous
            |  name !! ⟨outgoing⟩                 asynchronous
            |  ⟨tasks⟩ || ⟨tasks⟩                 parallel composition
            |  ⟨tasks⟩ ; ⟨tasks⟩                  sequential composition
            |  ( ⟨tasks⟩ )

⟨outgoing⟩  →  name [ ( ⟨expr⟩ { , ⟨expr⟩ } ) ]
```

Figure 17.1 Paragon rules syntax

17.2.2 Example

As a trivial example we specify a simplified version of part of the interconnection network of a parallel graph reduction machine.

A packet traversing the network carries its contents and its destination address as a list of directions in which to go at each intervening switch. Each routing switch retains a vector representing the identities of neighbours in the network and a local destination representing the "client" processing element for the switch. The classes and data types required are as follows:

class switch ::= ⟨**vector** [1 **upto** 4] switch,pe⟩
data packet ::= ⟨[direction],contents⟩

A simple network can be constructed from an initial configuration as shown in figure 17.2, with connected processing elements omitted.

With the route message taking the incoming packet as an argument, the rules for the switch are specified as follows:

```
⟨nbours,client⟩   given route(⟨[ ],data⟩)              (Home)
→     self
                  then      client ! deliver (data)

⟨nbours,client⟩   given route(⟨d:dirs,data⟩)           (Forward)
→     self
                  then      nbours[d] !! route (⟨dirs,data⟩)
```

The first rule, labeled *(Home)*, is applicable when the list of directions is empty and hence the packet has reached its destination address. The second rule *(Forward)* matches when the list is non-empty and the first element from the path determines

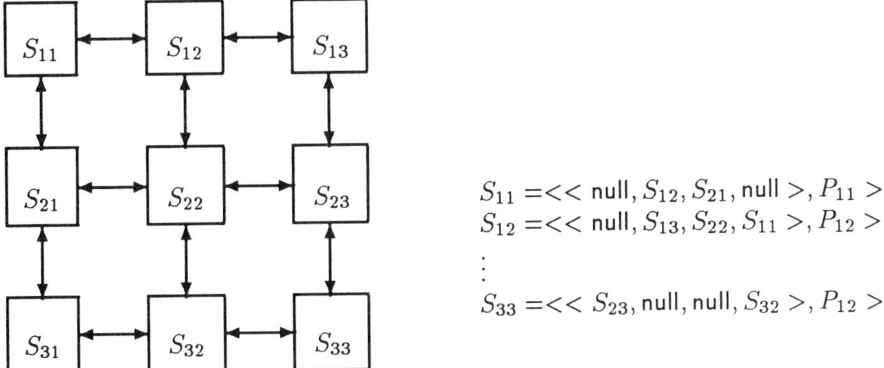

Figure 17.2 Simple network

the direction in which to forward the message by indexing the list. The message pass is asychronous to avoid deadlock.

17.2.3 Semantics sketch

A complete operational semantics based on those of POOL are presented in [BHK91]. Here we sketch the semantics to inform the implementation process described later.

The set of objects *Obj* includes standard objects and a set of programmer defined objects, *AObj*, to each of which is assigned a unique integer:

$$Obj = AObj \cup \mathcal{Z} \cup \{\mathbf{tt}, \mathbf{ff}\} \cup \mathbf{nil}$$

where $\mathcal{Z}$ is the set of integers, and **tt** and **ff** represent truth values.

The configurations used are elements of the form:

$$< X, \sigma, \tau, U > \in \mathcal{P}_{fin}(Activity) \times \Sigma \times Type \times Unit \cup err$$

where $\mathcal{P}_{fin}$ constructs the finite subsets of a given set.

Activity is a set of quadruples which records information about the current activity of each object. This takes one of two forms: $< Id, script, mess, env >$ or $< Id, result, mess, env >$, where *Id* is the identifier for the object, *script* is the script to be executed by the object, $result = Obj \cup Obj^*$ is a value produced by execution of a script (Obj^* is a tuple), *mess* contains the source of the message initiating activity, and $env = Id \rightarrow_{fin} result$ binds variables involved in pattern matching during rule selection. A *mess* has four forms: $< message, Id >$, where *Id* is the return address for a synchronous message; $< message, \mathbf{nil} >$, for asynchronous messages; **ok**, for acknowledgement of synchronous messages; and **nil**, indicating a dummy "message" to allow for spontaneous rewrites.

The state σ $(< \sigma_1, \sigma_2 >) \in \Sigma$ is represented by a pair of mappings:

$$(AObj \rightarrow_{fin} Obj^*) \times (AObj \rightarrow_{fin} (\mathcal{M}_{fin}(Messages)))$$

where σ_1 gives current bindings of variables for each object, and σ_2 gives the current message queue for each object represented as a finite multiset, with *Messages* of the same form as *mess*.

The function $Type = AObj \rightarrow_{fin} C_x$ gives the class name from which an object was generated, while *Unit* represents the class names $C_1, \ldots, C_n$ and the definitions $d_1, \ldots, d_n$ of their rules, so that the initial configuration of the system will be:

$$c_1 =< \emptyset, \sigma, \tau, U >$$

where

$$U =< C_1 : d_1;, \ldots, C_n : d_n > \quad \sigma_1(\mathbf{1}) = \{\mathbf{nil}, \ldots, \mathbf{nil}\}$$
$$\tau(\mathbf{1}) = C_n \quad \sigma_2(\mathbf{1}) = \emptyset$$

where the initial object with identifier **1** is an instance of the final class. There is a fairness assumption for rewriting, and terminal configurations are of the form:

$$c_{term} =< \emptyset, < \sigma_1, \lambda x.\emptyset >, \tau, U > \text{ s.t. } \neg\exists c \in Configurations.c_{term} \rightarrow c$$

so that there are no current activities, no messages waiting for processing, and no spontaneous rules applicable to any object.

The meaning of a specification is the set of all (finite and infinite) sequences of configurations $< c_1, c_2, \ldots, c_{term} >$ which satisfy the above constraints. In the semantics, the transition relation between configurations is defined by a series of axioms giving the meaning of basic components of the language and inference rules which allow the meaning of larger constructs to be be inferred by combining axioms. As an example we use the inference rule for adding new activities on message receipt.

The notation $X\backslash < \alpha, \_, \_, \rho >$ is used to represent a set X in which there are no activities associated with the object α. Inference rules are written with a main transition written below a horizontal bar, with transitions above the bar to be satified before the main transition.

$$\frac{\begin{array}{l} < X \cup \{< \alpha, o_1, \mu, \rho'' >\}, \sigma, \tau, U > \rightarrow < X \cup \{< \alpha, \underline{v_1}, \mu, \rho'' >\}, \sigma, \tau, U > \\ < X \cup \{< \alpha, o_2, \mu, \rho_1 >\}, \sigma, \tau, U > \rightarrow < X \cup \{< \alpha, \underline{v_2}, \mu, \rho_1 >\}, \sigma, \tau, U > \\ \vdots \\ < X \cup \{< \alpha, o_n, \mu, \rho_{n-1} >\}, \sigma, \tau, U > \rightarrow < X \cup \{< \alpha, \underline{v_n}, \mu, \rho_{n-1} >\}, \sigma, \tau, U > \\ < X \cup \{< \alpha, e, \mu, \rho_n >\}, \sigma, \tau, U > \rightarrow < X \cup \{< \alpha, \underline{\mathbf{tt}}, \mu, \rho_n >\}, \sigma, \tau, U > \\ < X \cup \{< \alpha, r, \mu, \rho_n >\}, \sigma, \tau, U > \rightarrow < X \cup \{< \alpha, \underline{t}, \mu, \rho_n >\}, \sigma, \tau, U > \\ match(l, \sigma_1(\alpha)) \wedge match(m', m) \wedge match(p_1, \sigma_1(\underline{v_1})) \wedge \ldots \wedge match(p_n, \sigma_1(\underline{v_n})) \end{array}}{\begin{array}{l} < X\backslash < \alpha, \_, \_, \rho >, < \sigma_1, \sigma_2[m \cup ms/\alpha] >, \tau, U > \rightarrow \\ \quad < X \cup \{< \alpha, s \ \mathbf{where} \ldots;, m, \rho_n >\}, < \sigma_1', \sigma_2[ms/\alpha] >, \tau, U > \end{array}}$$

This particular main transition will only apply if the left-hand side and message of a Paragon rule match the current state of α and the incoming message. The first group of transitions above the bar "evaluate" the objects $\underline{v_1}, \ldots, \underline{v_n}$ used in pattern matching (the underline indicates a value), then the guard (must be $\underline{\mathbf{tt}}$), and finally the tuple $\underline{t}$ corresponding to the new right hand side state r of α. The pattern matching predicate written immediately above the bar succeeds if an α rule left-hand side l matches the current state of α, if a rule message m' matches a waiting message m, and if rule patterns $p_1, \ldots, p_n$ match values $\underline{v_1}, \ldots, \underline{v_n}$ respectively.

Below the bar we see X updated with a tuple representing the script of communications s associated with the left-hand side of the matched rule, the accepted message m, and an environment ρ_n representing the accumulated substitutions to ρ, that is $\rho', \rho'', \rho_1, \ldots, \rho_n$, from matching (where ρ' is ρ with matching from $match(l, \sigma_1(\alpha))$ substituted). The state component σ_1' represents the updated bindings, and the accepted message m is withdrawn from σ_2.

Notice that this rule guarantees that objects respond to one message at a time and that the necessary pattern matching is an atomic action. This has implications for the implementation scheme to follow.

17.3 AN IMPLEMENTATION SCHEME

We are interested in constructing layered descriptions of parallel computer architectures. At the lowest layer we must therefore show that Paragon provides an unambiguous description of a possible hardware realisation. Initially, we confine our attention to Paragon systems which are both static (no objects created after configuration) and synchronous (all communications in rules are synchronous). Later, we will see that further restrictions on specifications are necessary to allow an efficient implementation, and we will also address the problem of implementing asynchronous message passing and dynamic object creation.

17.3.1 Implementing elements of Paragon descriptions

Each function specified in the Paragon system requires a feasible hardware implementation as follows:

Objects. For each object in the system we create an *object processor*, which manages the object's state (performs state rewrites, including spontaneous rewrites), handles all messages directed towards it, and and in consequence executes appropriate actions specified by the rules for the object.

A direct hardware implementation is possible when the specification is static so that the number and kind of object processors can be determined.

State. The state of each object is maintained in the corresponding object processor's local memory, represented in this scheme by a fixed-size variant record.

The need for a heap is avoided by restricting attention to non-recursive types, and the need for an object processor to refer to another's state is avoided by restricting pattern matching to the local object ("one-level" pattern matching) and the data structures it contains (which may not carry pointers).

Under these restrictions, data and objects can share the same representation: a tuple may be represented by a register containing a bitfield for each component.

Communication. We provide a physical channel for every potential communication between object processors.

The connections are unidirectional, with the receiving object processor acknowledging receipt when it has accepted the message and executed the associated rules.

Different messages received may be described by an appropriate block of logic implementing the alternative rules for each message sort.

Determining potential communication paths is troublesome in some cases, since Paragon allows the name of an object to be communicated in a message. The worst case would require a fully-connected network of channels, which is unacceptable: some kind of shared network would have to be introduced. Data-flow analysis can be used to determine which objects can communicate with one another to avoid this in most cases. Some special arrangement must be made to deal with parallel compositions of messages to the same destination.

Messages. Messages are represented in the same way as data, and are copied between object processors. Each communication channel is implemented using enough wires to accommodate the largest message which might be sent along it.

17.3.2 Summary of further restrictions

In addition to our requirement for specifications to be static and synchronous, the scheme presented requires further restrictions.

The left-hand side of a rule can refer to the names of other objects, but cannot demand pattern matching on their internal state. This avoids the need for the implicit critical region which would require locking during pattern matching to avoid inconsistent results, and to avoid non-local memory access.

It is awkward to handle messages which may be temporarily rejected by the target object, but accepted after some other message has been received (causing a change of state, for example). When pattern-matching and/or guard evaluation fails for all rules implemented by a message procedure the object processor must retain multiple messages (and message arguments) for each message sort received by the object, and then continually retry the message procedure. Each message must be assigned equal priority in attempted execution. We discount this possibility by restricting specifications to use only "total" (certain to be accepted) message passing.

Data structures can appear in an object's state, and in messages. In the hardware implementation a bit-vector representation is used, and structure copying results. This avoids inter-processor pointers, and garbage collection, but means recursive data types must be disallowed.

17.3.3 Translation scheme

The analysis presented leads us to a translation scheme from Paragon to a form of Occam [Inm88] suitable for compilation to a silicon layout [MK87]. The translations presented are intended to preserve the semantics described in [BHK91]. However, the restrictions discussed already define a particular treatment of the atomicity of pattern matching, and the schemes described in this section impose further decisions on, for example, the order of rule matching and the fair treatment of spontaneous rules.

To simplify description we augment Occam with enumerated and record types; these can be readily translated to true Occam BYTE or other types to express the representation of state as described above. The PAR construct will appear only at the outermost level, with the assumption that concurrent processes are implemented using one processing element for each process. For brevity, SEQs are omitted.

Object processors will be represented by Occam PROCs; we note [MK87] suggests that these can be implemented by body substitution or by conventional closed procedure calls of known fixed depth. Communication will be through variant protocol channels defined between object processors (one variant per message sort received). When the "name" of an object is communicated in messages or stored in an object state it is represented by the channel connected to its object processor. Each message sort received will also be represented as a PROC called by the object processor.

17.3.4 Object processors

A Paragon specification consists of classes whose behavior is described in terms of guarded message-receipt and "spontaneous" rules. We must translate each set of rules for a class into an appropriate set of object processors dealing with both message-receipt and spontaneous rules (spontaneous rules have no given clause, so should be applied whenever the object's state matches the left hand side).

The skeleton description for an object processor with both message-receipt and spontaneous rules is shown in figure 17.3. The processor is described in terms of an internal

```
PROC object-processor (CHAN OF Object-in in0,in1,...,inr,
                       CHAN OF BOOL sack0,sack1,...,sackr,
                       CHAN OF Object-out out0,out1,...,outs)
  Object-state state :
  Set up channels etc as appropriate
  WHILE TRUE
    ALT
      in0 ? message ; arguments
        Deal with spontaneous rule if necessary
        call procedure for message (pass state, and arguments)
        sack0 ! TRUE          Acknowledgement to sender
        .
        .
        .
      inr ? message ; arguments
        Similar to in0
      TRUE & SKIP
        Deal with spontaneous rule if necessary
:
```

Figure 17.3 Object processor description

record state and channel connections. Variant protocol channels $in_0,\ldots,in_r$ represent incoming messages (one variant per message sort received by the object), with successful message receipt and execution signalled to the sender via the $sack_0,\ldots,sack_r$ channels. Channels $out_0,\ldots,out_s$ represent objects to which messages are sent during execution of the message procedures, and will be assigned to appropriate internal object state components representing those objects.

Fair treatment of "spontaneous" rewrites is ensured through polling *both* when there is no message receipt ("TRUE & SKIP" in the Occam idiom) *and* immediately after each receipt.

17.3.5 Messages and associated rules

Consider the Paragon rule for a message m that communicates n arguments x. This is defined in Paragon by a set of k rules, each of the form $\mathcal{R}_j$, as follows:

$\mathcal{S}_j$ **given** m(x)
when $\mathcal{G}_j$
$\rightarrow$ $\mathcal{S}'_j$
then $\mathcal{C}_j$
where $\mathcal{B}_j$

We must translate alternative rules for a given message into a procedure in the target language as follows:

TM[$\mathcal{R}$] maps a set of Paragon rules for a given message onto a procedure.

TO[$\mathcal{S}$] maps an object on the left-hand side of a Paragon rule onto a set of statements that will both test if the current object matches and assign values to names in the pattern match (if necessary). If the match is successful, a flag success is set.

TB[$\mathcal{B}$] maps a set of Paragon **where** bindings onto a set of appropriate assignments.

TC[$\mathcal{C}$] will map the set of message passes onto appropriate set of communications via channels. We define a variant protocol channel which implements one variant per message defined for a class, carrying the message arguments in the rest of the protocol.

TG[$\mathcal{G}$] will map the set of Paragon guards onto a logical expression. These guards will operate not only on the variables bound by the message and on the state of the object, but also on the variables bound by the **TO** pattern-match and the required subset of those bound by the **TB where** bindings.

TS[$\mathcal{S}'$] will map an object onto statements in the target language which will rewrite the state so that it appropriately represents the structure of that object.

Figure 17.4 shows the result of **TM**[$\mathcal{R}$] for a message with k rules communicating n arguments x. The PROC has the same name as the message received and is defined in

```
PROC message-name (Object-state state, Typename x0,...,Typename xn-1)
  BOOL success :
  TO[S0]                        Pattern match
  IF
     success AND TG[G0]         Guards
        TB[B0]                  Bindings
        TS[S'0]                 Change state
        TC[C0]                  Communications
     TRUE
        TO[S1]
        IF
           success AND TG[G1]
              ...               And so on to translations for k-1
:
```

Figure 17.4 Result of translation function **TM**[$\mathcal{R}$] for k rules

terms of state, which represents the object receiving the message. Spontaneous rules have a similar translation to replace the phrase *Deal with spontaneous rule if necessary* in the object processor description (figure 17.3).

17.4 ASYNCHRONOUS MESSAGE PASSING

Paragon rules may specify asynchronous message transmission and dynamic creation of objects through **new**. Before we translate the simple example using the translation scheme developed above, we consider strategies for implementation of asynchronous systems; section 17.6 discusses dynamic systems.

Asynchronous message passing requires introduction of buffering to allow the sending object to proceed with further rewrites without waiting for the recipient to accept the message. In our scheme for buffering, one object manages a buffer represented by a queue of message/parameters pairs. Buffer objects receive add-message messages carrying such pairs from the sender, and need-message messages requesting them, from the receiver, respectively.

Such a buffer object buffer-d is introduced for all receivers d of asynchronous messages, and the sender's rules are modified so that the asynchronous communications d !! m(x) are replaced with buffer-d ! add-message(m,x). The state must be augmented with the name of its buffer process and a flag to manage buffer access. Also, rules for each receiver d must be modified by addition of a spontaneous rule and to accommodate the flag. The spontaneous rule applies when the object is ready to accept a message; it sends a need-message to which the buffer replies with the next message in its queue. The flag is required to prevent repeated firing of the spontaneous rule.

17.5 TRANSLATION OF SWITCH EXAMPLE

The example uses asynchronous message passing to avoid deadlock. We now transform the packet switch using the ideas developed in section 17.4 and then apply the implementation scheme from section 17.3 to produce an Occam description of the switch processor. First we modify the rules to introduce buffers for asynchronous messages:

⟨nbours-buffer,client,mybuffer,NOTSENT⟩ *Spontaneous*
→ ⟨nbours-buffer,client,mybuffer,NEEDSENT⟩
then mybuffer ! need-message

⟨nbours-buffer,client,mybuffer,NEEDSENT⟩ **given** route (⟨[ ],data⟩)
→ ⟨nbours-buffer,client,mybuffer,NOTSENT⟩
then client ! deliver(data) *At destination*

⟨nbours-buffer,client,mybuffer,NEEDSENT⟩ **given** route (⟨d:dirs,data⟩)
→ ⟨nbours-buffer,client,mybuffer,NOTSENT⟩
then nbours-buffer[d] ! add-message (route,dirs,data)

To translate these rules we introduce channel protocols and "records" as follows:

```
PROTOCOL Packet CASE route ; Directions ; Data :
PROTOCOL Switch
     CASE add-message ; Packet
     CASE need-message
     CASE deliver ; Data
:
RECORD Switch-state IS
     CHAN OF Switch nbours-buffer [1..4] ; CHAN OF Switch client ;
     CHAN OF Switch client ; Flag flag
:
```

In order to make asynchronous message buffering amenable to translation to Occam, the message buffers must be represented as an array managed as a circular buffer with a fixed length. If a fixed length buffer can be shown to be adequate, this scheme provides a reasonable hardware implementation. Figure 17.5 shows the translation of the rules using these definitions. Figure 17.6 shows the procedure for message route.

```
PROC switch-processor(CHAN OF Packet in [1..5], CHAN OF BOOL sack [1..5],
                              CHAN OF Switch out [1..6])
     Switch-state state :
     state.flag := NOTSENT
     state.nbours-buffer [1..4] := out [1..4]
     state.mybuffer := out [5]
     state.client := out [6]
     WHILE TRUE
          ALT
               in_i=1..5 ? route ; dirs ; data
                    IF
                         state.flag = NOTSENT
                              state.mybuffer ! need-message
                              state.flag := NEEDSENT
                    route (state, dirs, data)
                    sack[i] ! TRUE
               TRUE & SKIP
                    IF
                         state.flag = NOTSENT
                              state.mybuffer ! need-message
                              state.flag := NEEDSENT
:
```

Figure 17.5 Object processor for switch

17.6 CONCLUSIONS

The objective of developing the Paragon notation was to show how by a sequence of refinements, a parallel computer architecture could be derived from a specification of its primitive operations in terms of rewriting systems [BHK91]. Current work includes

```
PROC route (Switch-state state, Directions dirs, Data data)
    BOOL success := state.flag = NEEDSENT
    IF
        success
            state.flag := NOTSENT
            IF
                dirs = []
                    state.client ! deliver ; data
                dirs = (d:ds)
                    state.nbours-buffer[d] ! add-message ; route ; ds ; data
:
```

Figure 17.6 Translation of the route message

a translation of Paragon to Milner's π-calculus to provide an alternative semantics, and future work will include further implementation and case studies.

This chapter introduced Paragon and its semantics, and addressed the problem of bridging the final gap between a low-level Paragon description of an architecture, and the hardware itself. We have exhibited a fairly direct translation from specifications written in our high-level graph-rewriting notation into low-level parallel programs in which resource allocation is static, and computation and communication is made fully explicit. To emphasize the concreteness of this implementation, we have shown how a digital hardware system can be derived from the specification.

The restrictions on specifications to make them amenable to translation provide insight into the nature of Paragon, and we conclude by re-examining them.

Specifications were restricted to disallow dynamic object creation. A dynamic population of objects requires multiplexing of object processors and channels. Finding efficient allocation schemes raises significant design issues, including, for example, trade-offs between hardware cost and parallelism, and the general case requires garbage collection. We conclude that an automatic translation is not appropriate. Instead the specification must be refined to introduce explicit resource management; [Han89] shows an example using a distributed garbage collector.

For simplicity, we also disallowed all data structures which involve pointers. Pointer structures *within* an object processor's memory are not very troublesome, although in general garbage collection may be involved. Garbage collection may be avoided by copying entire data structures instead of copying pointers (intuitively this follows from the immutability of data structures; a more formal treatment could follow Barendregt et al. [BvEG+87a]). However, in general Paragon allows data structures to be passed in messages, and normally the intended meaning is that sharing of substructure occurs. Clearly, this raises many problems for a hardware realization.

Under the restriction to one-level pattern matching, a pattern in the LHS of a rule can refer to the name of another object pointed to from the state of the current object, but it cannot attempt to match against its state. This restriction removes awkward atomicity problems, but can be avoided at the expense of provision for an appropriate locking mechanism.

It also proves very difficult to handle messages which may temporarily be rejected by the target object. This can happen because the object's state does not match any rule which accepts the message, or because a guard fails. Our operational semantics defines sets of such outstanding messages with a (fair) polling mechanism. A hardware realization implementing such behavior seems unlikely to be efficient.

Finally, for a perfectly fair implementation, we require that exactly one rule be applicable given a particular set of incoming messages (including the empty set to include spontaneous rewrites). This is rather a strict constraint. Essentially it arises because each object processor has no internal parallelism, so can only test for the applicability of one rule at once, in a predetermined order. This is a generalization of the rewriting notion of sequentiality. As in functional programming, it very often turns out that a sequential order of testing is adequate for a particular application.

REFERENCES

[And91] Paul Anderson. *Computer Architecture for Wafer Scale Integration.* PhD thesis, Department of Computer Science, City University, London, 1991.

[BHK89] David Bolton, Chris Hankin, and Paul Kelly. Parallel Object-oriented Descriptions of Graph Reduction Machines (Extended Abstract). In E. Odijk, M. Rem, and J.-C. Syre (editors), *Proc. PARLE'89 Parallel Architectures and Languages Europe, vol. I*, Springer-Verlag, Lecture Notes in Computer Science 366, pp. 158–175, 1989.

[BHK91] D. Bolton, C.L. Hankin, and P.H.J. Kelly. An Operational Semantics for Paragon: A Design Notation for Parallel Architectures. *New Generation Computing*, **9**, pp. 171–197, July 1991.

[BvEG+87a] H.P. Barendregt, M.C.J.D. van Eekelen, J.R.W. Glauert, J.R. Kennaway, M.J. Plasmeijer, and M.R. Sleep. Term Graph Rewriting. In J. W. de Bakker, A. J. Nijman, and P. C. Treleaven (editors), *Proc. PARLE'87 Parallel Architectures and Languages Europe, vol. II*, Springer-Verlag, Lecture Notes in Computer Science 259, pp. 141–158, 1987.

[BvEG+87b] H.P. Barendregt, M.C.J.D. van Eekelen, J.R.W. Glauert, J.R. Kennaway, M.J. Plasmeijer, and M.R. Sleep. Towards an Intermediate Language for Graph Rewriting. In J. W. de Bakker, A. J. Nijman, and P. C. Treleaven (editors), *Proc. PARLE'87 Parallel Architectures and Languages Europe, vol. II*, Springer-Verlag, Lecture Notes in Computer Science 259, pp. 159–174, 1987.

[GKS87] J.R.W. Glauert, J.R. Kennaway, and M.R. Sleep. *DACTL: A Computational Model and Compiler Target Language based on Graph Reduction.* Report SYS-C87-03, School of Information Systems, University of East Anglia, 1987.

[Han89] Chris Hankin. *Specification of a Distributed Garbage Collection Algorithm.* ESPRIT Project 415 subproject B deliverable, document number 140, 1989.

[Inm88] Inmos Ltd. *Occam-2 Reference manual.* Prentice Hall International, 1988.

[MK87] David May and Catherine Keane. *Compiling Occam to Silicon.* Technical note 23, Inmos Ltd., 1000 Aztec West, Almondsbury, Bristol BS12 4SQ, UK., 1987.

[SJ89] Ph Schnoebelen and Ph Jorrand. Principles of FP2: Term Algebras for Specification of Parallel Machines. In J.W. de Bakker (editor), *Languages for Parallel Architectures*, pp. 223–273. Wiley, 1989.

[Tur85] D.A. Turner. Miranda: A non-strict functional language with polymorphic types. In *Proc. Int. Conf. on Functional Programming Languages and Computer Architecture*, Springer-Verlag, Lecture Notes in Computer Science 201, September 1985.

18

MONSTR: Term Graph Rewriting for Parallel Machines

R. Banach

18.1 INTRODUCTION

In this chapter, the primary issue addressed is the adoptability of generalized Term Graph Rewriting Systems (TGRS) as a fundamental computational model at the architectural level. This is a desirable thing to do since many currently fashionable programming styles (e.g. functional or logic) have easy translations into TGRS. Unfortunately, implementing the model on a parallel machine (an equally fashionable architectural style), is infeasable in its raw form. This is surprising because there are many implementations of fashionable programming styles on fashionable architectures that actually perform acceptably well. This indicates that perhaps the more troublesome features of the full TGR model are not really needed when one translates such languages into the TGR form. This hypothesis turns out to be correct, and gives rise to a program of work to indentify the little used, expensive aspects of general TGRS and to exclude them by carefully redefining TGR languages and/or their semantic models. Some aspects of this work are surveyed in this chapter.

The rest of the chapter is organized as follows. In section 18.2, we present an abstract version of a concrete TGR language, DACTL. In section 18.3 we present a sublanguage, MONSTR, and justify its selection on architectural grounds. In section 18.4, we discuss a number of semantic models for the MONSTR sublanguage, arguing that these more closely reflect the way a realistic parallel machine might execute MONSTR programs. We present the main soundness results that map computations according to these

Term Graph Rewriting: Theory and Practice.
Eds. Ronan Sleep, Rinus Plasmeijer and Marko van Eekelen.

more operational models, into computations according to the original semantics, thus giving a handle on correctness.

18.2 ABSTRACT DACTL

We present here a rather abstract and slightly simplified version of the language DACTL [GKSS88, GHK+88]. The abstraction takes us away from the tedium of concrete syntax and enables us to concentrate on the semantic issues. We assume we are given an alphabet $\mathbf{S} = \{S, T \ldots\}$ of node symbols. We write **SeqN** for the set of sets of naturals of the form $\{1 \ldots n\}$, where $\{1 \ldots 0\} = \emptyset$.

DEFINITION **18.2.1** *A(n abstract DACTL) term graph (or just graph) G, is a quintuple* $(N, \sigma, \alpha, \mu, \nu)$ *where*

(1) *N is a set of nodes,*
(2) *σ is a map $N \rightarrow S$,*
(3) *α is a map $N \rightarrow N^*$,*
(4) *μ is a map $N \rightarrow \{\varepsilon, *, \#, \#\#, \#\#\#, \ldots, \#^n \ (n \geq 1)\}$,*
(5) *ν is a map $N \rightarrow \{\varepsilon, \ \hat{}\ \}^*$,*

such that for all $x \in G$, $dom(\alpha(x)) = dom(\nu(x)) \in$ **SeqN**.

Informally, for each node we have its node symbol $\sigma(x)$ and its sequence of successors $\alpha(x)$. The node carries a node marking $\mu(x)$, and each arc to a successor (say the kth, $\alpha(x)[k]$) carries an arc marking, $\nu(x)[k]$. The maps μ, ν are referred to as the markings and are mainly concerned with encoding execution strategies, while N, σ, α are referred to as the graph structure and provide the main information content of the graph. For $x \in G$ (which we write in preference to $x \in N(G)$), the domain of $\alpha(x)$ or of $\nu(x)$ is called the arity of $x, A(x)$. We refer to an arc of the graph using the notation (p_k, c) to indicate that c is the kth child of p, i.e. that $c = \alpha(x)[k]$ and $k \in A(p)$.

For ease of use, the names are meant to be reasonably alliterative: σ for symbols, α for arcs, μ for markings, ν for notifications (see below).

We assume there is a special node symbol `Any`, not considered to be in **S**.

DEFINITION **18.2.2** *A rule R is a quadruple (G, r, Red, Act) where*

(1) *G is a graph, except that some nodes of G may be labeled with* `Any`, *and*

$$\sigma(n) = \texttt{Any} \Longrightarrow \alpha(n) = \varepsilon$$

(ε is the empty sequence, empty node marking, empty arc marking, according to context).

Nodes n with $\sigma(n) =$ `Any` *are called implicit whereas other nodes are explicit.*

(2) *r is a node of G called the root, and all implicit nodes are accessible from the root via a path of length at least one (so the root is explicit). If $\sigma(r) = S$, then R is a rule for S. For all nodes x accessible from (and including) r, $\mu(x) = \varepsilon$ and $\nu(x) = \varepsilon$ for all $k \in A(x)$.*

(3) *Red is a set of pairs, (called redirections) of nodes of G such that if $(x, y) \in Red$, then x is explicit and accessible from r. If $(x, y), (u, v) \in Red$ then $x = u \Longrightarrow y = v$*

and $x \neq u \Longrightarrow \sigma(y) \neq \sigma(v)$. *For* $(x, y) \in Red, x$ *is called the LHS and* y *the RHS of the redirection.*

(4) *Act is a set of nodes (called activations) of* G *such that for all* $x \in Act$, x *is accessible from the root* r.

The subgraph of G accessible from (and including) the root is called the pattern of the rule, and nodes of G not in the pattern are called contractum nodes. More generally a pattern is a rooted graph in which there may be some implicit nodes. By a graph we will normally mean an object without implicit nodes and not necessarily endowed with a root.

DEFINITION **18.2.3** *A matching of a pattern* P *with root* r *say, to a graph* G *at a node* $t \in G$, *is a map* $h : P \rightarrow G$ *such that*

(1) $h(r) = t$

(2) *If* $x \in P$ *is explicit then,* $\sigma(x) = \sigma(h(x)), A(x) = A(h(x))$, *and for all* $k \in A(x), h(\alpha(x)[k]) = \alpha(h(x))[k]$.

So a matching is a graph structure homomorphism in which **Any** nodes can match anything but explicit nodes must behave well. The same defintion will suffice for matching patterns to other patterns or, omitting mention of roots, for matching graphs to other graphs.

A system is just a set of rules. Rewriting proceeds via two stages, rule selection and rule execution.

DEFINITION **18.2.4** *Let* X *be a graph,* $t \in X$ *a node of* X *such that* $\mu(t) = *$, *and* $\mathbf{R}$ *a system. Let* $Sel = \{R \mid$ *there is an* $R \in \mathbf{R}$ *such that there is a matching* $h : P \rightarrow X$ *of the pattern* P *of the graph* G *of the rule* R *to* X *at* $t\}$. *Rule selection is some (otherwise unspecified) process for choosing a member of Sel assuming it is non-empty. It clearly only has force when there is more than one member of Sel. The chosen* R *makes* t *the root of the redex* $h(P)$ *and* R *the selected rule that governs the rewrite.*

Assuming we have a selected rule and redex, rule execution (or rewriting according to the rule governing the rewrite) proceeds in three phases: contractum building, redirection, and activation. Assume $X, t, R = (G, r, Red, Act)$ and h given as above.

DEFINITION **18.2.5** *Contractum building adds a copy of each contractum node of* G *to* X. *Node markings for such nodes are taken from* G. *Copies of arcs of* G *from contractum nodes to their successors are added in such a way that there is a graph structure homomorphism* h' *from the whole of* G *to the graph being created which agrees with* h *on* P. *Arc markings are again taken from* G. *Call the resulting graph* X' *and let* $i_{X,X'}$ *be the natural injection.*

DEFINITION **18.2.6** *Redirection takes each arc* (p_k, c) *such that* $c = h'(x)$ *for some* $(x, y) \in Red$ *and replaces it with* $(p_k, h'(y))$. *This can be done consistently since the LHSs of two distinct redirections cannot map to the same node of* X *since their node symbols are different by 18.2.2.(3). All such redirections are performed simultaneously. Let the resulting graph be called* X'' *and let* $i_{X',X''}$ *be the natural injection. Note that* $i_{X',X''}$ *is just an injective map on nodes rather than a graph structure homomorphism as for* $i_{X,X'}$. *We define the map* $r_{X',X''}$ *by* $r_{X',X''}(c) = i_{X',X''}(c)$ *unless* $c = h'(x)$ *for some* $(x, y) \in Red$, *in which case* $r_{X',X''}(c) = i_{X',X''}(h'(y))$.

DEFINITION **18.2.7** *Activation takes the nodes $y = i_{X',X''}(x)$ for $x = h'(u)$ with $u \in$ Act, and if $\mu(y) = \varepsilon$ then the node marking is changed to $*$. Unless $t'' = i_{X',X''}(h'(r))$ was one of these nodes, its marking is changed to ε. Call the resulting graph Y, and define $i_{X'',Y}$ as the natural injection.*

The result of the rewrite is the graph Y. For a more detailed exposition of contraction building and redirection, see [BvEG+87] 3.6 (i)-(ii), or [GKSS88] for a more detailed exposition of all the phases in a concrete syntax setting. Note that our notion of activation is a little different than that in [GKSS88], the pattern calculus (a feature of true DACTL we ignore), being at the heart of the matter. Also we have combined root quiescence and activation in our version of the activation phase, whereas root quiescence is done right at the beginning of the [GKSS88] definition. The reason for this is that it yields significant technical simplifications when graph markings are involved in inductive proofs of properties of executions (although the present chapter provides no evidence for this, due to its succinctness).

Suppose now that *Sel* is empty. Then instead of a rewrite, notification takes place.

DEFINITION **18.2.8** *Notification is the process whereby the node marking $\mu(t)$ is changed to ε, and for all arcs $(p_k, t) \in X$, if the arc marking $\nu(p)[k]$ is $\wedge$, then it is changed to ε, and if the node marking $\mu(p)$ is $\#^n$ (for $n \geq 1$) it is changed to $\#^{n-1}$, with $\#^0$ being understood as $*$. Call the resulting graph Y and let $i_{X,Y}$ be the natural injection.*

The result of the notification is the graph Y as before.

DEFINITION **18.2.9** *An initial graph is one which consists of an isolated node of empty arity, with the active ($*$) node marking, and labeled by the symbol* `Initial`.

DEFINITION **18.2.10** *An execution of a system* **R** *is a sequence of graphs $[G_0, G_1 \ldots]$ of maximum length such that G_0 is initial and for each $i \geq 0$ such that $i+1$ is an index of the sequence, G_{i+1} results from G_i by either rewriting or notification at some active node of G_i. Graphs occuring in executions are called execution graphs.*

By composing the various maps $i_{X,X'}$, $i_{X',X''}$ or $r_{X',X''}$, etc., we can track the history of a node through an execution of the system. Note that no node is ever destroyed.

So much for the definitions which give us the basic operational semantics of DACTL. The main problem with these semantics from a architectural point of view, is that an entire rewrite or entire notification must take place as a single atomic action. This places quite a burden on a parallel implementaion, when it has to cope with rewrites or notifications that might overlap with other rewrites or notifications. In particular, whatever an implementation does, it must in some acceptable way be equivalent to a serializable sequence of rewrites and notifications.

18.3 MONSTR

Now we present an abridged TGR language, MONSTR, first investigated in [BSW+88] and [BW89], which curtails some of the problems inherent in the DACTL definition. The definition is in terms of a list of restrictions on the general structure of DACTL.

First, we partition the symbol alphabet **S** into **F** ∪ **C** ∪ **V**, where **F** consists of functions which have rules but which cannot occur at subroot positions of patterns of rules; and **C** and **V**, consisting of constructors and variables (or stateholders), neither of which can occur at root positions of patterns of rules and therefore neither of which have rules; in addition constructors are not permitted to occur as the LHS of a redirection.

Next we insist that rules are of two kinds, normal rules and default rules. A default rule has a pattern which consists of an active function node and as many distinct implicit children as its arity dictates. Otherwise it is normal. Thus a default rule's pattern will always match at an active execution graph node labeled with the appropriate function symbol.

We insist that there is at least one default rule for every function symbol, and we allow a normal rule to be selected in preference to a default rule whenever either will match, but the latter aspect will be of no significance below.

DEFINITION **18.3.1** *MONSTR graphs, rules and systems must conform to the following list of restrictions.*

(1) *Symbols have fixed arities, i.e. the map* $x \rightarrow A(x)$ *factors through* $\sigma(x)$, *and thus* $A(x) = A(\sigma(x))$.
(2) *For each* $F \in \mathbf{F}$ *there is a subset* $M(F) \subseteq A(F)$ *such that* $k \in M(F)$ *iff for any normal rule for* F *with root* $r, \alpha(r)[k]$ *is explicit.*
(3) *For each* $F \in \mathbf{F}$ *there is a subset* $\Sigma(F) \subseteq A(F)$, *at most a singleton, such that if* $k \in \Sigma(F)$, *then for any normal rule for* F *with root* $r, \sigma(a(r)[k]) \in \mathbf{C} \cup \mathbf{V}$. *Otherwise, for explicit* $\alpha(r)[l], l \neq k, \sigma(a(r)[l]) \in \mathbf{C}$.
(4) *For each rule, any grandchild of the root is implicit.*
(5) *For every rule, no implicit node may have more than one parent in the pattern.*
(6) *Every node* x *in every rule is balanced, i.e.* $\mu(x) = \#^n$ *for some* $n \geq 1$ *iff* n *is the cardinality of* $\{k \in A(x) \mid \nu(x)[k] = \ \hat{}\ \}$.
(7) *Every arc* (p_k, c) *in every rule is state saturated, i.e. if* $\nu(p)[k] = \ \hat{}\ $, *then if* $\mu(c) = \varepsilon$ *then either* c *is explicit and* $\sigma(c) \in \mathbf{V}$, *or* $c \in Act$.
(8) *For every rule with root* $r, (r, t) \in Red$ *for some* t.
(9) *For every rule, if* $(x, y) \in Red$ *with* $\mu(y) = \varepsilon$ *and* $y \notin Act$ *then* y *is explicit and* $\sigma(y) \in \mathbf{V}$.
(10) *For every rule, if* $(y, z) \in Red$, *then* $y \notin Act$ *unless* $(x, y) \in Red$ *for some* x.

Despite the size of this collection of restrictions, a useful and expressive model of computation remains; in particular it is trivial to simulate a Turing Machine, giving us full computational power.

The restrictions on symbols and rules introduced in the preamble to 18.3.1 are there to impose some discipline on the generality of DACTL; designating symbols to be either functions, which perform rewrites but do nothing else; or constructors, which hold values but do nothing else (in particular they do not get redirected); or stateholders, which as their name implies, hold updatable values and can model standard notions of state.

Restrictions (1) – (5) are largely "geographical" in nature. They ease hardware construction, but also have an impact on problems arising from concurrent executions (see the discussion of the fine-grained MONSTR semantic model below). Restriction

(10) permits a smooth implementation of redirection by overwriting. Restrictions (6) – (9) have rather more immediate consequences; which also happen to aid overwriting.

THEOREM **18.3.2** *(Fundamental Properties) If a DACTL system obeys restrictions (6) – (9) of definition 18.3.1 then every execution graph is*

(1) *balanced,*
(2) *state saturated.*

18.4 ALTERNATIVE SEMANTIC MODELS

Having defined the MONSTR sublanguage of DACTL, we can now explore the consequences of executing MONSTR systems according to different operational semantics. The models we consider are the suspending MONSTR model, the fine-grained MONSTR model, fully coercing models, and serializable weak models.

18.4.1 The suspending MONSTR model

The suspending MONSTR model addresses one of the simpler problem areas of the DACTL semantic model, namely the fact that a rewrite can proceed independently of the markings of the subroot redex nodes. This is indeed problematic for implementations, because implementations that feature concurrent rewriting of distinct but perhaps overlapping redexes may well want to manipulate the graph in a more fine-grained way than the atomicity of the rewriting paradigm would allow, and this would tend to destroy serializability.

For $F \in \mathbf{F}$ we call $M(F)$ the map of F. Since all $M(F)$ arguments of F redexes are explicit, they must be examined during pattern matching. We insist that such arguments are idle i.e. have the ε node marking, before rewriting can occur. If this is not the case, then a suspension occurs.

DEFINITION **18.4.1** *Let $t \in X$ be an active function node and let $m > 0$ where m is the cardinality of $\{k \in M(\sigma(t)) \mid \mu(\alpha(t)[k]) \neq \varepsilon\}$. Then the suspension of t (on its non-idle map arguments) changes $\mu(t)$ to $\#^m$, and for each k such that $k \in M(\sigma(t))$ and $\mu(\alpha(t)[k]) \neq \varepsilon, \nu(t)[k]$ is changed to $\wedge$. Call the resulting graph Y and let the natural injection be $i_{X,Y}$ as before.*

Suspending MONSTR executions are thus sequences of graphs generated from an initial graph by rewrites, notifications and suspensions, and compared to DACTL executions, impose additional dependencies between rewrites. We note that since the root node of a suspension acquires as many # markings as it has out-arcs which acquire a ^ marking, balancedness is preserved and so suspending MONSTR executions enjoy the same fundamental properties as DACTL executions.

THEOREM **18.4.2** *Let G_i be a suspending MONSTR execution graph. Then there is a DACTL execution graph with graph structure isomorphic to that of G_i.*

THEOREM **18.4.3** *Suppose some suspending MONSTR execution terminates in a final graph where all the node and arc markings are ε. Then there is some DACTL execution that produces the same final graph.*

THEOREM **18.4.4** *Suppose for some suspending MONSTR execution, for each execution graph, the subgraph consisting of nodes and arcs having non-ε markings is acyclic. Then if the execution terminates, there is some DACTL execution that produces the same final graph.*

18.4.2 The fine-grained MONSTR model

Despite its suspension events, the suspending MONSTR model still insists that rewrites are done in a single atomic action, where they occur. The fine-grained MONSTR model breaks this atomicity of rewriting down into more primitive steps. On the whole, actions involving both of the pair of nodes at the two ends of an arc, are performed using message passing, and so correspond to more than one atomic action in the model. As the precise details are rather intricate we will content ourselves with a rather more informal presentation than hitherto.

We start with the notifications. In fine-grained MONSTR these are split into two sorts of action. Notification issuing, which quiesces the root and issues notification messages to the relevant parents; and notification events where such messages arrive and alter the node marking from $\#^n$ to $\#^{n-1}$ (or $*$). We have not said when the relevant arc marking gets altered. In reality it may be changed as part of either type of action, but doing so temporarily breaks one or other of the fundamental properties 18.3.2. This a technical nuisance, though not serious since parts of execution graphs where the invariant breaks down correspond $1-1$ with partially completed notifications (or other actions whose fine-grained versions also temporarily break the invariant).

Rewrites are broken up in a somewhat more complex manner. If the function labeling the root of the redex has no normal rules, then the rewrite moves immediately to the rewrite action below. Otherwise rewriting starts with read issuing, in which if t is the root of the redex and m is the cardinality of $C-args = M(\sigma(t)) - \Sigma(\sigma(t))$, then a read message is issued to each $C-args$ child of $t, \mu(t)$ is changed to $\#^m$, and for each $k \in C-args, \nu(t)[k]$ is changed to $\wedge$. This breaks fundamental property 18.3.2.(b). When such a message arrives at its destination, a read event takes place, in which if the argument is idle (say it is the kth), and a constructor, $\nu(t)[k]$ is changed to ε, and $\mu(t)$ changes from $\#^l$ to $\#^{l-1}$. If the argument is idle but not a constructor, the same thing happens but in addition a "FAIL" is recorded at the root of the redex. Here $\#^0$ is $*$ as before and if $\mu(t)$ indeed becomes $*$, then the rewrite is ready to perform the rewrite action below. If the argument is non-idle the read event is retried when the argument notifies. We see how fine-grained MONSTR suspensions are a more abstract model of these argument reading preliminaries, which are themselves a more abstract model of what happens at the machine level.

The rewrite action performs the heart of the rewrite and consists of three stages, all taking place within the confines of a single atomic action. First, if any FAILs have been recorded for the root of the redex, a default rule rather than the original normal rule is selected for matching and execution. This is because although the children at $C-args$ positions of the root might well have been redirected to constructor form by this time, the asynchronous nature of the argument reading process means that the rewriting mechanism cannot be aware of such a fact.

Second, assuming no FAILs, the pattern is matched including any stateholder argument $\alpha(t)[\Sigma(\sigma(t))]$. By hypothesis, enough arguments have been read to yield a verdict for any normal rule for $\sigma(t)$. All this proceeds unless the stateholder argument itself is non-idle in which case the rewrite suspends until notification by the stateholder argument.

Third, assuming no FAILs or suspension on the stateholder, a rule is selected in the usual way. The rule to be executed now having been fixed by one means or another, the contractum is built, the redirections are performed, and activation messages are issued to any nodes matched to pattern nodes in the activation set of the rule. Finally the root of the redex can be quiesced unless it turned out to be one of the nodes to be activated. This completes the description of rewrite actions.

The final type of action of interest is the activation event, in which an activation message arrives at its destination, and if the node marking of the destination is ε, changes it to $*$, activating the node.

Fine-grained MONSTR executions are thus generated by sequences of actions of the kind described above. With sufficient attention to detail the following results can be obtained.

DEFINITION **18.4.5** *Let R be a default rule with root r, and suppose the cardinality of $M(\sigma(r))$ is m. Suppose there is exactly one contractum node c, with $\sigma(c) = \sigma(r), \mu(c) = \#^m, \alpha(c)[k] = \alpha(r)[k]$ for $k \in A(r), \nu(c)[k] = \ ^\wedge$ for $k \in M(\sigma(r))$, and $\nu(c)[k] = \varepsilon$ for $k \in A(\sigma(r)) - M(\sigma(r))$. Suppose $Red = \{(r, c)\}$ and $Act = \{\alpha(r)[k] \mid k \in M(\sigma(r))\}$. Then R is a refiring rule.*

DEFINITION **18.4.6** *Let R be a normal rule with rule with root r and suppose $\sigma(\alpha(r)[k]) \in \mathbf{V}$ for $k \in \Sigma(\sigma(r))$, assumed non-empty. Suppose there is exactly one contractum node c, with $\sigma(c) = \sigma(r), \mu(c) = \#, \alpha(c)[k] = \alpha(r)[k]$ for $k \in A(r)$, and $\nu(c)[k] = \varepsilon$ for $k \in A(\sigma(r)) - \Sigma(\sigma(r))$ and $\nu(c)[k] = \ ^\wedge$ for $k \in \Sigma(\sigma(r))$. Suppose $Red = \{(r, c)\}$ and $Act = \emptyset$. Then R is a suspension rule.*

THEOREM **18.4.7** *Suppose for some system that*

(1) *every default rule for a symbol with non-empty arity is a refiring rule,*
(2) *every normal rule either,*

- **(a)** *does not match a stateholder (even if its $\Sigma(\sigma(root)) \neq \emptyset$), or*
- **(b)** *matches a stateholder (in its $\Sigma(\sigma(root))$ position) and redirects it to a non-idle node, or*
- **(c)** *is a suspension rule.*

Suppose also that

(ActF) *no activation message ever finds its destination to be an idle function node.*

Then if a fine-grained MONSTR execution terminates, there is a suspending MONSTR execution of the system that produces the same final graph, modulo garbage.

This is an opportune moment to briefly discuss garbage. Since nodes of the graph are never deleted during any execution step, copious quantities of garbage are generated. We define the live nodes of the graph to be base live nodes (which are active nodes, and constructors specifically designated as such), or nodes accessible from live nodes via ε-marked arcs, or nodes that can access live nodes via $^\wedge$-marked arcs. All others are garbage. This definition turns out to be sound.

18.4.3 Fully coercing models

Rewrites in the previous two models wait for active subcomputations to terminate (i.e. notify) before proceeding. This is the idea behind suspension. In this sense the two models are coercing in a rather weak sense. The fully coercing versions of the two models are coercing in a stronger sense, namely that they actively instigate subcomputations when they chance upon inactive subcomputations during pattern matching. Since constructors are regarded as ground objects, and stateholders are ground until some rewrite chooses to redirect them, the only nodes that denote the presence of inactive subcomputations are idle function nodes. Thus in the fully coercing version of suspending MONSTR, the root of a pattern match suspends not only on non-idle $M(\sigma(root))$ arguments, but also on those $M(\sigma(root))$ arguments which are idle functions; these are simultaneously made active. In the fully coercing version of fine-grained MONSTR, a similar thing happens when a read event encounters an idle function node. Instead of recording a FAILure, the event activates the function and completion of pattern matching is delayed until the child subcomputation notifies.

Of course, if no contractum node of any rule of a system is an idle function, then any semantic model that is at least as coercing as suspending MONSTR is fully coercing. The major point of significance concerning the fully coercing models follows.

THEOREM **18.4.8** *For fully coercing fine-grained MONSTR, Theorem 18.4.7 holds but without requiring the (run-time) condition (ActF).*

18.4.4 Serializable weak models

In all of the previous models, executions have been serial since the semantic models have been derived from the DACTL rewriting model, and rewriting models are conventionally sequential. On the other hand, the ultimate objective is to model the actions of an underlying parallel machine whose operation is in no way sequential. Sequentiallity thus plays two conflicting roles in our study of operational semantics. On the one hand, it is an objective, because we want to reduce the concurrent operation of the parallel machine to some serial rewriting sequence of the original DACTL semantic model if we can; on the other hand it is an obstacle, because for technical simplicity, we would like to work in the graph world as much as possible, but that world only offers us the sequential rewriting paradigm, which thus makes the modeling of concurrent behavior problematic.

To overcome the obstacle, we cannot avoid looking at the way a putative machine would represent and manipulate the graph. Such an examination would reveal the areas of conflict and hence of potential interference between different execution primitives. One could then lift the criteria necessary for non-interference to the graph world, and study them in the more convenient abstract setting.

For the particular architectural model we have in mind, the Flagship model [WW87, WWW+87, WSWW89], the problems boil down to the study of the interference of distinct redirections, given a minimal locking strategy for graph nodes. To see this, it is enough to review the definition of the redirection phase, which makes it plain that if the execution graph nodes matched to the LHS and RHS of a redirection are identical, then the redirection is a null action. To enforce this in a world of coded up graph representations with concurrently operating agents modifying the graph, requires both an identity test for node representations, and locking of appropriate parts of the coding to enable redirections to be performed atomically. Both of these are luxuries that an efficient implementation of the rewriting model would rather do without. The study of serializable weak models thus turns into the search for criteria that ensure that a system will execute safely in the absence of mechanisms in the semantic model to determine identity and enforce atomicity of redirection.

18.5 CONCLUSIONS

The reduction of the atomic semantics of the MONSTR subset of DACTL to semantics more in keeping with the behavior of a concrete architectural model such as the Flagship machine turns out to be a complex process. Most people who have attempted the reduction of abstract semantic models to more realistic ones would agree with this view. In fact it is not possible to do the reduction for the full MONSTR sublanguage as Theorem 18.4.8 might be taken to imply. It turns out that all points of difference between DACTL and machine semantics give rise to counter examples (usually quite easy to construct) that yield different results according to which semantic model is used. Nevertheless these counter examples are usually sufficiently pathological to inspire a search for criteria under which equivalence can be demonstrated, and to date, the search has been a fruitful one.

REFERENCES

[BSW+88] R. Banach, J. Sargeant, I. Watson, P. Watson, and V. Woods. The Flagship project. In *Proc. UK-IT-88 (Alvey Technical Conference) Information Engineering Directorate, IEE Publications*, pp. 242–245, 1988.

[BvEG+87] H. P. Barendregt, M. C. J. D. van Eekelen, J. R. W. Glauert, J. R. Kennaway, M. J. Plasmeijer, and M. R. Sleep. Term graph rewriting. In J. W. de Bakker, A. J. Nijman, and P. C. Treleaven (editors), *Proc. PARLE'87 Conference, vol.II*, Springer-Verlag, Lecture Notes in Computer Science 259, pp. 141–158, 1987.

[BW89] R. Banach and P. Watson. Dealing with state in Flagship: the MONSTR computational model. In C.R. Jesshope and D.K. Reinhartz (editors), *Proc. CONPAR-88, B.C.S. Workshop Series*, pp. 595–604. Cambridge University Press, 1989.

[GHK+88] J.R.W. Glauert, K. Hammond, J.R. Kennaway, G.A. Papdopoulos, and M.R. Sleep. *DACTL: Some Introductory Papers.* Technical report, School of Information Systems, University of East Anglia, Norwich, 1988.

[GKSS88] J.R.W. Glauert, J.R. Kennaway, M.R. Sleep, and G.W. Somner. *Final Specification of DACTL.* Technical Report SYS-C88-11, School of Information Systems, University of East Anglia, Norwich, 1988.

[WSWW89] I. Watson, J. Sargeant, P. Watson, and V. Woods. The Flagship parallel machine. In C.R. Jesshope and D.K. Reinhartz (editors), *Proc. CONPAR-88, B.C.S. Workshop Series*, pp. 125–133. Cambridge University Press, 1989.

[WW87] P. Watson and I. Watson. Evaluating functional programs on the Flagship machine. In *Proc. FLCA-87*, Springer-Verlag, Lecture Notes in Computer Science 274, pp. 80–97, 1987.

[WWW+87] I. Watson, V. Woods, P. Watson, R. Banach, M. Greenberg, and J. Sargeant. Flagship: A parallel architecture for declarative programming. In *Proc. 15th Annual International Symposium on Computer Architecture, Hawaii*, 1987.

19

A Graph Rewriting Model Enhanced with Sharing for OR-parallel Execution of Logic Programs

W. Damm, F. Liu and T. Peikenkamp

19.1 INTRODUCTION

OR-parallel execution of logic programs enables alternative solutions to a query to be found in parallel by allowing alternative clauses to be tried in parallel. As pointed out in [Con87], two major issues in the OR-parallel execution of logic programs are the combinatorial explosion in the number of processes and representation of multiple variable binding environments. Many different OR-parallel models [LBD+90] [Har90] [CWY91] have been proposed that aim to raise efficiency of OR-parallel execution by incorporating different strategies for the process control and environment management. Here it is not our intention to put forward some new schemes for process control and environment management. Instead, in orthogonal to the research efforts on these issues, we are seeking a further rise in efficiency of the OR-parallel execution from another dimension by exploiting sharing among different OR-processes. We will illustrate how this sharing can be significant in avoiding redundant computations of common computational paths among different OR-processes. Notably most existing OR-parallel models are based on the extension of the Warren Abstract Machine (WAM) as they all intend to make full use of the existing sequential Prolog implementation techniques. However, we adopt a rather different approach: a graph rewriting model for the OR-parallel execution of logic programs. Graph rewriting is a powerful computational model for

Term Graph Rewriting: Theory and Practice.
Eds. Ronan Sleep, Rinus Plasmeijer and Marko van Eekelen.

implementing declarative languages. In particular, it has almost become the standard model for supporting lazy functional languages. Graph rewriting has two distinct advantages: sharing can be easily represented by the shared graphs and parallelism is naturally exposed by the subgraphs. The main motivations for adopting a graph rewriting model instead of using an extension of the WAM for the OR-parallel execution of logic programs are twofold. First, the convenient way of representing shared computation of graph rewriting is of particular interest to us as we intend to exploit sharing among OR-parallel processes. Second, we intend to extend the model to support functional logic languages such as K-LEAF [BBG+87] and BABEL [MNRA89], and graph rewriting can provide a uniform model of computation for executing functions and logic predicates which are both allowed in a functional logic language. In fact, we are not the first to use graph rewriting to implement logic languages. There have been several interesting experiments reported in [Pap89] [GP88] [RCB87]. Moreover, there is an established framework DACTL [GKSS88] to deal with more general Term Graph Rewriting Systems in which both functional and logic programming can be supported. An interesting research being carried out is to represent our model by DACTL, but it is out of the scope of this chaper. The main issue discussed in this chapter is to enhance OR-parallel execution models with sharing.

19.2 INCORPORATING SHARING INTO THE OR-PARALLEL MODEL

19.2.1 What can be shared

In a graph rewriting model for functional languages, sharing is achieved by maintaining multiple references to a single shared subexpression graph. Once such a shared subgraph is evaluated and rewritten to its value by one of its demanders, the result of the evaluation can then be shared by all other demanders. The main issue of the actual implementation of sharing is to prevent the simultaneous re-evaluation of subgraphs. This has been discussed in detail in [Jon87] and [vEPS91]. However, sharing among OR-parallel processes which we are going to deal with is a bit more complicated and difficult than the sharing in a functional model.

In order to identify what can be shared, let us examine the OR-parallel execution[1] of a general goal statement which contains more than one subgoal:

:- ..., A, p(G_1,...,G_n),...

At some stage during the execution of the goal statement, many independent OR-processes $\pi_1, \ldots, \pi_k$, after having successfully solved the subgoal A, will then attempt to resolve the subgoal p(G_1,...,G_n) which is represented as a goal node in our graph rewriting model. Note G_1,...,G_n are also graph nodes representing the arguments of the goal. In most of the existing OR-parallel models, these independent OR-parallel processes $\pi_1, \ldots, \pi_k$ then proceed to resolve the subgoal p(G_1, ...,G_n) in their respective binding environments $\Phi_{\pi_1}, \ldots, \Phi_{\pi_k}$. Although there exist some computation paths common to all these OR-processes when resolving the goal p(G_1,...,G_n), different OR-processes will compute them independently, and thus some common

[1] We assume that the readers have some basic knowledge about OR-parallel execution of logic programs. A useful pointer to this is [War87].

computation might be performed over and over. For example, during the evaluation of the goal,

:- p(a),q(b)

if a number of m OR-parallel processes have successfully solved the goal p(a), then the goal q(b) will be computed m times. In order to avoid this redundant computation, a natural solution is to introduce sharing into the OR-parallel models, doing the common work for all OR-processes. We believe that this kind of sharing is non-trivial, and a significant amount of work can be saved if it is effectively implemented. This is based on the following observations:

a. The computation of $p(G_1, \ldots, G_n)$ sometimes may not need at all to access the environment in which it is evaluated. Thus, all the OR-processes $\pi_1, \ldots, \pi_k$ could repeat the same work even though they have completely different environments. For instance, the execution of the subgoal q(b) in the above example is fully independent of the environment in which it is evaluated.
b. If we take a close look at the environments of these independent OR-processes, we can find that they all consist of a common part Φ_c inherited from the head unification and a distinct part Φ'_i made by the respective process π_i during the resolution of the subgoal A. That is,

   $$\Phi_i = \Phi_c + \Phi'_i$$

   Obviously the inherited part Φ_c in the environments of different OR-processes can surely induce common computation paths in resolving the goal $p(G_1, \ldots, G_n)$.
c. Even if there would not be any common part in the environments, there would still exist some sharing in resolving the goal $p(G_1, \ldots, G_n)$. This is because the head unification between the goal $p(G_1, \ldots, G_n)$ and a clause is usually not "sensitive" to the actual values of the terms representing $G_1, \ldots, G_n$. This implies that the unification process is still common to all OR-processes even though they may have bound the goal arguments to completely different values. For instance, the arguments $G_1, \ldots, G_n$ may have been bound differently by different OR-parallel processes, the unification between the goal $p(G_1, \ldots, G_n)$ and a clause head $p(X_1, \ldots, X_n)$ is common to all the OR-parallel processes attempting the goal if $X_1, \ldots, X_n$ are distinct variables.
d. The OR-parallel execution of non-deterministic programs may have created a significantly large number of OR-processes when attempting the goal $p(G_1, \ldots, G_n)$. Thus even for a small amount of sharing, the effect of it can be "amplified" by the existence of a large number of OR-processes.
e. If the model is extended to support functional logic languages the effect of sharing will be even larger because the arguments of goals may contain function applications which may represent very large computations.

The sharing identified above can be exploited by the principle of graph rewriting. Figure 19.1 shows a subgoal P which is represented as a computational graph shared by two OR-parallel processes π_1, and π_2. The two processes may demand the evaluation of the subgoal P in their respective environment Φ_1 and Φ_2. Obviously, evaluating the subgoal P by rewriting the graph in any process environment may produce erroneous result for the other. As stated before, in OR-parallel models without this kind

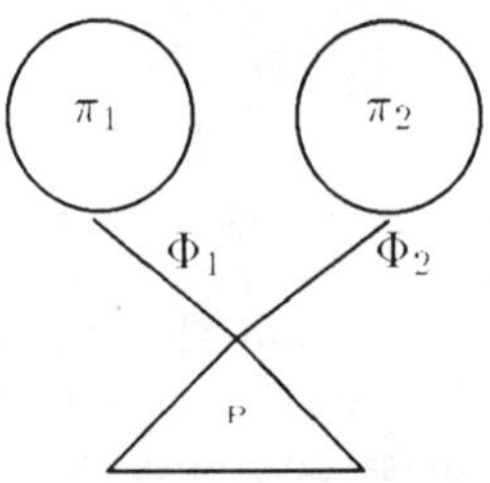

Figure 19.1 A computational graph shared by two OR-parallel processes

of sharing, each OR-parallel processes would simply copy the graph and evaluate it independently. However, as in a graph rewriting model for functional languages, copying an unevaluated shared subexpression is the potential cause for re-computation. In this context, if the rewrite of the graph is independent of the OR-parallel process environments or depends only on the commonly inherited part of them, then copying the graph and evaluating it for each process would introduce re-computation. In particular, it would cause extreme inefficiencies if the subgoal represents a large computation. Therefore the shared subgoal graph should, wherever possible, be rewritten independently of the OR-parallel process environments or in accordance with the commonly inherited part before any copying is attempted. Thus, on the one hand, the common computational path of different OR-parallel processes is computed once and shared by all, on the other hand, no erroneous rewriting is performed.

It can be seen that there are two fundamental differences between the shared computation in functional graph rewriting models and that in our model. First, sharing expressions do not carry any different environments into the shared subexpression, and thus the shared subexpression can be evaluated independently, and be rewritten by its value (normal form or weak head-normal form) in a functional model. While in our model, the evaluation of the shared subgoal graph may only be able to be rewritten partially as it may need to access the distinct parts of different process environments. In this case, the partially rewritten graph has to be copied and further rewritten in each process own environment in order to produce correct results. Second, in the functional model, the rewriting of a shared subexpression is deterministic, and it can be rewritten by its unique value, while in our model, the computation of subgoal may be non-deterministic as there may be more than one alternatives for the subgoal. However, their basic principles for handling sharing are the same: the common computational graphs are rewritten and evaluated only once. The above principle is illustrated in figure 19.2. The shared subgoal P is first rewritten to P' under the common environment Φ_c, and then the partially rewritten graph P' is copied by each demanding process and rewritten in its own environment $\Phi_c + \Phi_i' + \Phi_s$. Note that Φ_s is the resulting environment from rewriting P to P', and should be included to each process environment.

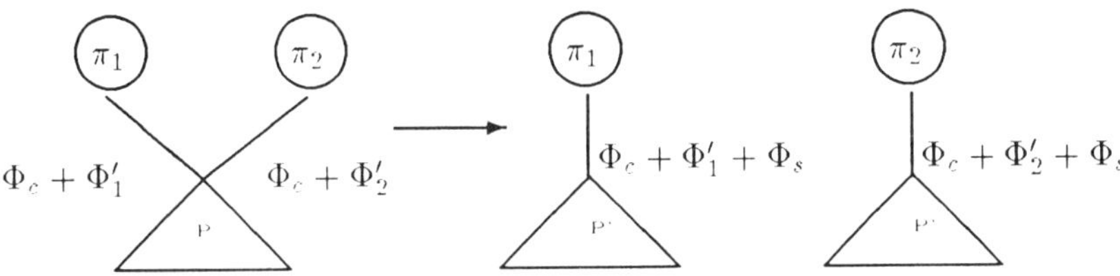

Figure 19.2 The principle of dealing with sharing

19.2.2 A strategy for sharing

A natural solution for implementing the above principle is to start a shared process to perform the common computation paths for all OR-processes using the common inherited environment. Upon its successful termination, each individual OR-process can combine with the shared process and proceed on its own. In order to design an effective strategy for sharing, we have set up the following three guidelines:

a. Achieve maximum degree of sharing;
b. Avoid any speculative work;
c. Minimize the effort for process combination.

The first guideline suggests that a shared process should do as much common work as possible. It should always perform rewriting wherever possible.

The second guideline implies that a shared process is started for resolving a goal only if at least one OR-process has successfully solved all the previous goals and arrived at this goal. This can make sure that the shared process is doing useful work because at least one OR-process needs the result. Moreover, a shared process should be suspended if it attempts to bind an unbound variable created before the shared process as it may have been bound (differently) by different OR-parallel processes. This is the fundamental difference between our model and an independent AND-parallel model in which AND-parallel processes perform computation independently and there is a significant synchronization problem when combining AND-processes.

The third guideline is, in fact, also guaranteed by what is needed to fulfill the second guideline: it will make sure that the shared processes may never produce bindings conflicting with those of the OR-processes to be combined with. Thus, to combine a shared process with a waiting process, we simply **concatenate** their binding environments.

In accordance with the above guidelines, our strategy is simple and straightforward: whenever a goal is attempted by one or more OR-processes, which have successfully solved the left siblings of the goal, a shared process is started to resolve the goal. The shared process may create its own child shared processes if there is more than one alternative, thus there may be many shared processes actually created. The other OR-processes must be blocked until the shared processes are suspended or have completed shared computations and arrived at the top-most query. In the case that a shared process is suspended, it must be combined with each OR-process blocked at its origin, and the combined process gets a copy of the suspended computation graph and evaluates it in its own environment. As stated before, a shared process is suspended when it intends to bind an unbound variable node created before its origin. If a shared process is completed, the solutions for the initial query can be collected from the environments created by the shared process and the waiting OR-processes at its origin.

19.3 THE EXECUTION MODEL WITH SHARING

19.3.1 The process-based execution

Processes traversing and rewriting the AND/OR tree are represented by process tokens, and transformation rules applied for a graph node will depend on the state of the processes. Here we assume that the model is implemented on an architecture with a global linear address space and a pool of processes which are executed by processors. There are two kinds of processes: non-shared and shared processes.

Each process token for a non-shared process contains three basic elements:

a. Process Label PL : number
b. Local Environment σ : var -> nodeID
c. Binding Array BA : nodeID -> nodeID

The process label PL is used to index variables in the clause. It is also used to mark the origin of a shared process in a shared process token. The value of PL is the depth of current position of the process token in the AND/OR tree. It is incremented when the process moves down across an OR-node and decremented when the process moves up across one.

The local environment σ stores local bindings from the head unification between a goal and a clause. It is used to initialize the subgoals in the clause body. The local environment represents mapping between variable names and locations (nodeIDs), and σ(x) returns the location of the root node of the heap term bound to x.

The binding array contains global bindings which will contribute to the composition of the final solution of the initial goal.

Besides the above three basic elements, a shared process token requires two extra elements: one is the process origin (PO), the other is the heap count (HC). The process origin PO is used to record where the shared process is started. It has the same value as the process label PL when the shared process is created. With this field, the shared process will be able to be correctly combined with the OR-processes waiting for it at its origin. The heap count HC contains the address of the first free memory cell in the heap when the shared process is created. With this field, the shared process will be able to identify whether an unbound variable node is created before or after the shared process is created by simply comparing the nodeID of the unbound variable node with the heap count HC.

The only operational difference between a non-shared process and a shared one lies in their different ways of performing rewriting a unification node when they intend to bind an unbound ancestor variable node. The former can make a local copy of the unbound variable node, bind it through the binding array, and rewrite the unification node to success. The latter has to be suspended, and the unification node is not allowed to be rewritten. Thus we can treat them uniformly by setting the heap count HC of a non-shared process to a number which will never cause the suspension of the non-shared process. In this way, we do not require an explicit distinction between a shared process and non-shared one, and thus every process (shared or non-shared) token contains five elements. Thus we need only a unique set of unification rules for both shared processes and non-shared processes. This is illustrated in the unification rules presented in the next section.

19.3.2 Graph rewriting rules

In our graph rewriting execution model, logic programs are viewed as sets of rewrite rules to be applied to an initial graph corresponding to a goal query. The state of the execution of a logic program is represented as an AND/OR computation tree[2], where processes dynamically traverse and rewrite the tree. The tree consists of a set of nodes. There are five basic types of nodes involving rewriting: goal nodes, unify nodes, OR nodes, AND nodes, and data nodes (terms). Accordingly we have defined a set of rewrite rules for transforming different graph nodes:

a. Rule for resolving a goal
b. Rule for OR-parallel execution
c. Rule for initializing a clause body
d. Rules for head unification

The rule for resolving a goal rewrites a goal node p(G_1,...,G_n) into an OR-node with different branches corresponding to different clauses whose main functor and arity match those of the goal. In figure 19.3, each alternative is a unify node, which

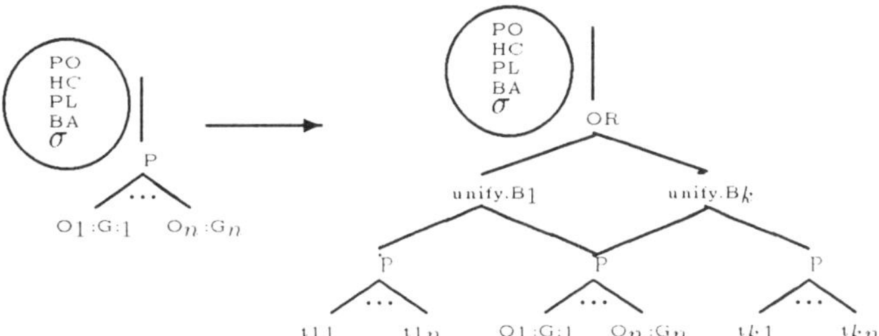

Figure 19.3 Rewrite rule for resolving a goal

represents the head unification between the goal and the head of a clause. If the head unification is successful, a graph for the corresponding clause body, B_j, is created for further execution. Otherwise, this alternative is simply discarded. Note that each unify node has a reference to the goal node p(G_1, ...,G_n). Thus the arguments of the goal are shared by all the alternatives. Although the effect of this kind of sharing is not so prominent in a pure logic programming framework, it could become significant in a functional logic framework, in which the arguments of a goal can contain complex function applications or large data structures. However this kind of sharing will not be thoroughly investigated until the model is extended to support functional logic languages.

[2] Due to the introduction of sharing, it is already a graph. But following the original terminology, here we still call it an AND/OR tree.

After a process has rewritten a goal node to an OR-node with k alternatives, the process (and the subsequent processes arriving at this OR-node) will split into k subprocesses to search all the alternatives in parallel for solutions. This situation is covered by the rule for OR-parallel execution in figure 19.4.

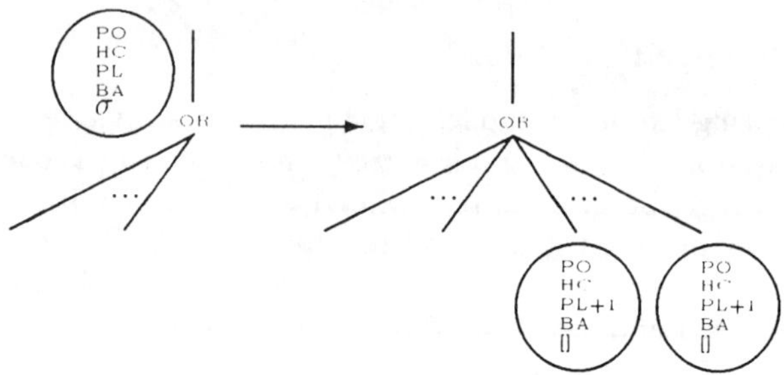

Figure 19.4 Rule for OR-parallel execution

As stated before, after a successful head unification, if the clause is a non-unit one, then the clause body must be initialized using the local environment generated during the head unification. In other words, a graph must be created for the clause body.

Assuming that the clause of the jth alternative has a clause body B_j which contains m conjunctive subgoals such as $Q_1, \ldots, Q_m$, we have a choice of creating the graph incrementally or completely. Here we choose to do it incrementally, i.e. a subgraph is created for a subgoal just before the subgoal is attempted for the first time in order to avoid allocating and reclaiming the storage for the graph created for the subgoals which may never be reached due to the failure of the subgoal being proved. The rule for initializing a clause body in figure 19.5 covers the above situation. It is worthwhile

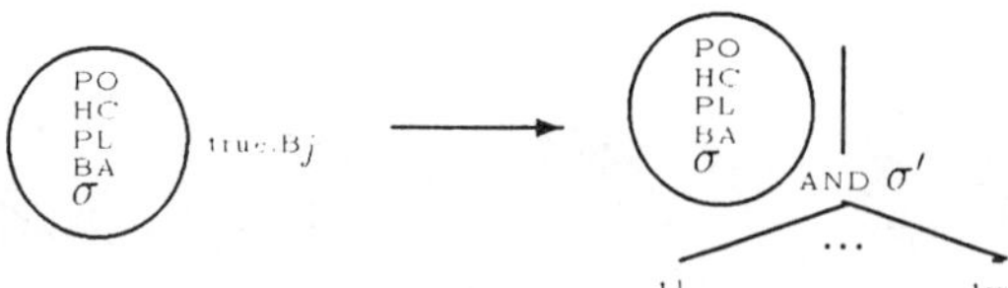

Figure 19.5 Rule for initializing a clause body

to point out that creating a graph for a clause body in our model is very similar to allocating heap cells in the standard WAM. The function Graph(t,σ) is used to create a graph for the clause body which is stored in the form of program "code". It takes a syntactic term t and a local environment σ as its arguments, and returns a root node identifier of the graph created for t and an updated local environment σ'. σ is the local environment from the head unification. During the creation of the graph for t, all the newly created unbound variable cells (nodes) for the variables which do not occur in the local environment σ must be recorded in the updated local environment σ'. It must be saved at the AND-node for the incremental graph creation of other conjunctive subgoals.

Rules for head unification specify how to rewrite a unify node according to the types of the terms to be unified. They also play an important role in the synchronization of shared processes. When a shared process intends to rewrite a unify node by binding an unbound ancestor node, it has to be suspended.

There are two groups of unification rules in the model: non-symmetric unification and symmetric unification. A non-symmetric unification is performed between a syntactic term from a clause head and a heap term (graph node) from the goal which is represented by a nodeID. The difference between a syntactic term and a heap term lies in that the former has not been allocated memory cell while the latter has been assigned a memory cell as a graph node. The symmetric unification performs unification between two heap terms, i.e. two nodeIDs. In fact, a symmetric unification node is transformed from a non-symmetric one in the case that a variable occurs more than once in the clause head.

The rules for a non-symmetric unification are shown in figure 19.6. They distinguish

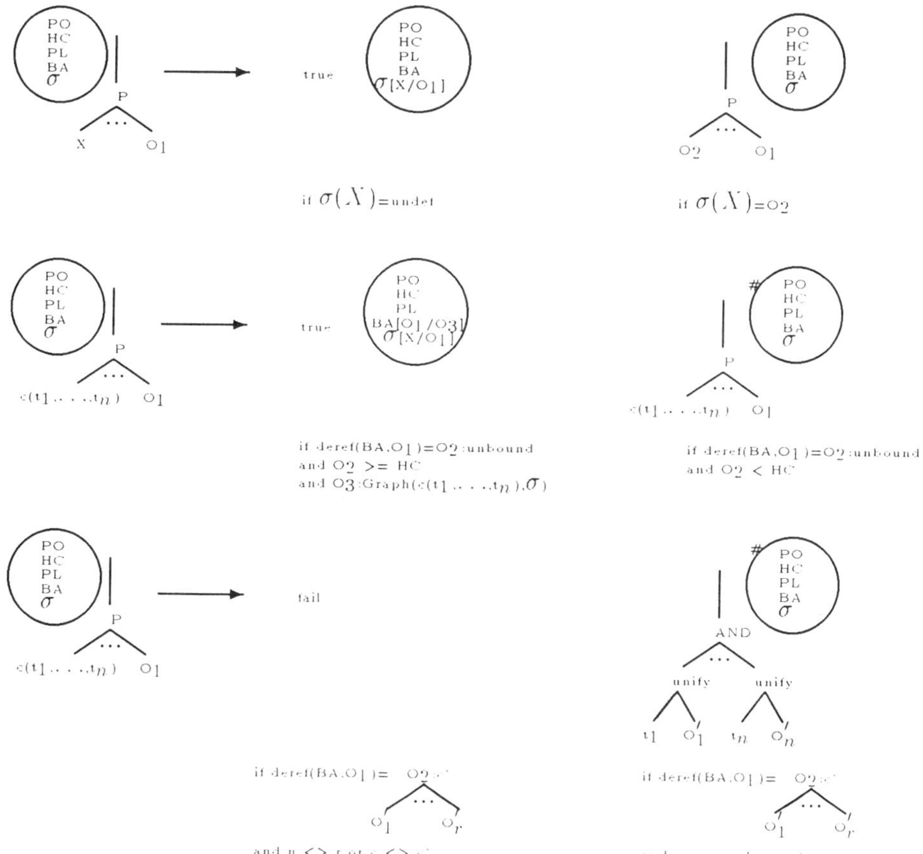

Figure 19.6 Rules for non-symmetric unification

two cases of syntactic terms to be unified: a variable represented by X or a constructor represented by c(t_1, ...,t_n). If it is variable and not bound yet (checked by looking up the local environment σ), which is indicated by σ=$\perp$, then the unify node is rewritten to a data node true, and the variable X is bound to the heap term and σ is updated accordingly. Otherwise the non-symmetric unification is transformed to a symmetric unification.

If the syntactic term is a constructor, a dereferencing operation must be performed on the nodeID of the heap term to decide its type. When it is also a constructor which has the same functor name and arity as these of the syntactic term, their corresponding arguments must be unified. However, if the heap term is an unbound variable, we have to check whether it is created before or after the origin of the process by comparing the heap count HC of the process and the nodeID O_2. If HC $\leq O_2$, which indicates variable is created after the orgin, then the process does not have to be suspended. It has the right to bind it through its own binding array. Otherwise ($O_2 \leq$ HC), the process must be suspended because O_2 may have been bound during visits of the left siblings of the current subgoal. As mentioned before, here we do not explicitly distinguish a shared process and a non-shared process. This is done by setting the heap count HC of a non-shared process to a number that never causes the suspension of the process.

The rules for a symmetric unification involve deferencing operations on one or both node IDs. If any of the two heap terms is an unbound variable node, we have to decide if the process should be suspended in the same way as described above. The other rules for symmetric unification in figure 19.7 are self-explanatory.

19.3.3 The management of shared processes

The mechanism for managing the creation, suspension, and combination of shared processes is realized by manipulating two queues associated with a goal node:

a. Waiting Process Queue (WPQ): it contains a list of waiting processes which have successfully solved all the left siblings of the goal and intended to resolve this goal.
b. Suspended Shared Process Queue (SSPQ) : it contains a list of suspended shared processes which have been started for solving the goal, and have been suspended after some computation.

When the first OR-process attempting a shared subgoal, it will find WPQ empty, which then triggers the creation of a shared process for the subgoal. The five elements of the process token for the shared process are initialized in the following way:

PO = d	where d is the current depth in the AND/OR tree
HC = addr	addr is the address of the first free memory cell in the heap
PL = d	where d is as above
σ = σ'	σ' is the updated local environment from the head unification and the initialization of the left siblings of the goal.
BA = ba	ba is the parent binding array

Any OR-process coming after will take the following actions

a. The process is put into the Waiting Process Queue.
b. The process is combined with each suspended shared process in the Suspended Shared Process Queue and resumes the computation from where the shared process was suspended.

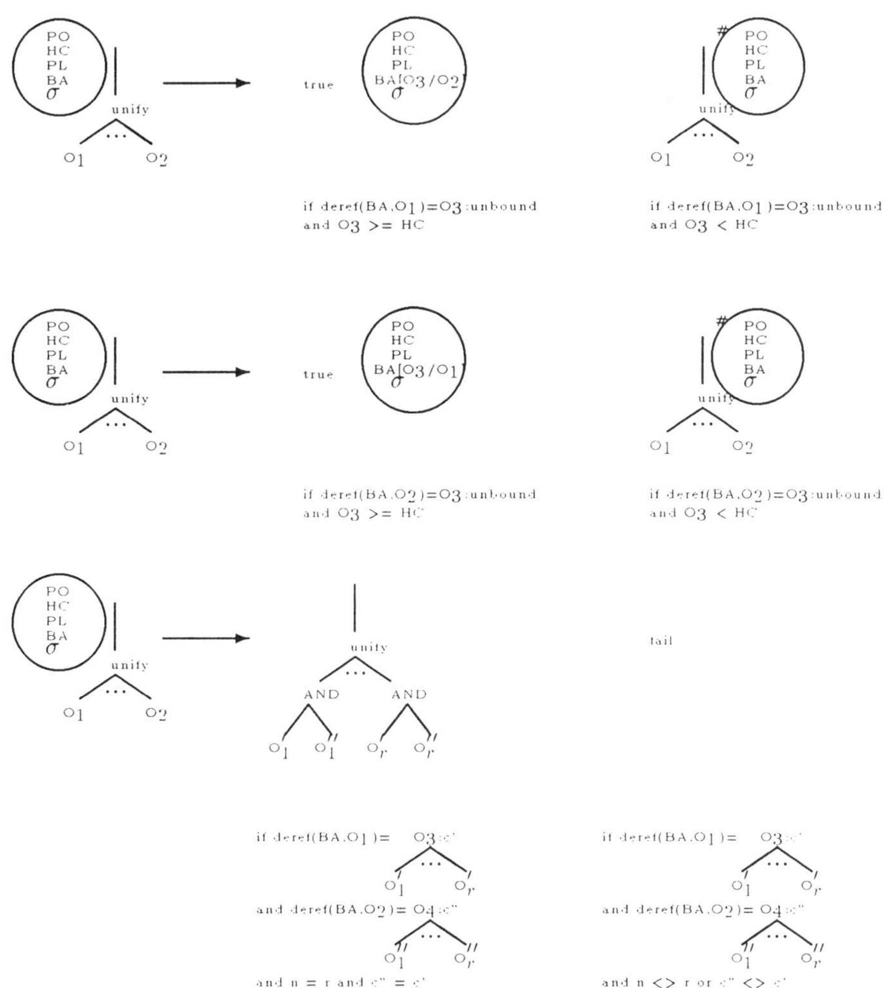

Figure 19.7 Rules for symmetric unification

Note that after the combination, all suspended shared processes should remain in the queue because other OR-processes which arrive later from the left sibling of the subgoal must be combined with them as well[3].

When a shared process is suspended, the following two actions are taken:

a. It is put into the Suspended Shared Process Queue at its origin
b. It is combined with each process waiting in the Waiting Process Queue at its origin, and the resulting combined processes resume the suspended computation.

---

[3] In an implementation a simple counting mechanism (recording the number of processes generated and not yet completed at a given OR-node) can be used to tell when this lists can be garbage-collected.

The combination of a suspended shared process P_s with a waiting process P_w at its origin forms a combined process P_{ws} to resume the suspended computation. Note that the shared process may have already reduced the subgraph significantly before becoming suspended. In order to allow other waiting processes at the same origin to be combined with the suspended shared process, both the suspended shared process and the remaining subgraph should be kept unchanged. Thus the combined process can resume the suspended computation by creating a new OR-branch copied from the suspended one. This is represented by the combination rule in figure 19.8. For clarity,

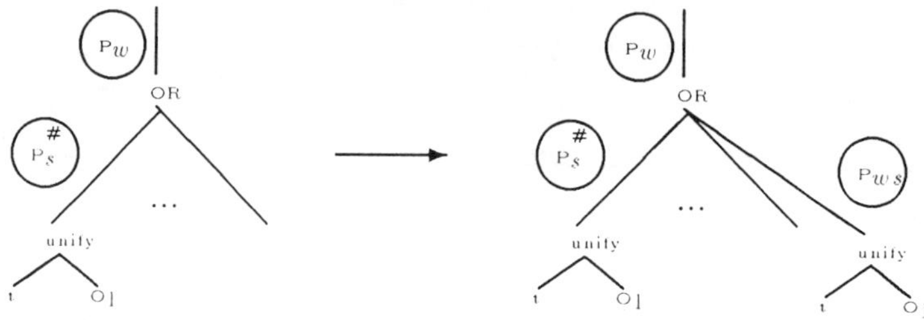

Figure 19.8 Rule for combining a suspended shared process and a waiting process

in figure 19.8, we do not explicitly represent WPQ and SSPQ in the combination rule. Instead, a suspended shared process P_s in a SSPQ is represented by keeping its process token marked by # where it was suspended, while a waiting process P_{w1} in WPQ is indicated by its process token at the origin of the shared process. Recall that both the suspended shared process and the waiting process must still be kept in their respective queues after the combination. This is represented in the figure by keeping the two process tokens at their previous positions.

The combined process from a waiting process and a suspended shared one is, in fact, a continuation of the waiting process. In other words, the combined process has the same process type as that of the waiting process. If the waiting process itself is a shared process, then the combined one is also a shared process which has the same process origin and heap count as those of the waiting shared process. Since the combined process will resume the suspended computation, it will inherit the process label and local environment of the suspended shared process. However, the global environment BA of the combined process must be derived by a composition of global environments of the waiting process and suspended shared process. Note that since the shared process can never produce conflicting bindings with the bindings in the binding arrays of the waiting processes, the entries in the binding array BA" are guaranteed to refer to the graph nodes which are not bound in BA'. Thus the binding arrays of waiting process and shared process can simply be concatenated.

19.4 PRELIMINARY SIMULATION RESULTS

In order to evaluate the model enhanced with sharing, we have designed two simulators: one for the pure OR-parallel model and one for the OR-parallel model enhanced with sharing. The simulators were written in the functional language ML. Although both simulators are very slow and still under optimization, they can provide us with some preliminary simulation results of a few simple programs. We have run three simple programs on both simulators. The first evaluates a query :- append(X,Y,[1,2,3,4]), the second evaluates a query :- main(X,Y,) where main is defined by the following program:

```
main(X,Y) :- p(X), q(Y), r(X,Y).
p(a). p(b). p(c).
q(a). q(b).
r(X,Y) :-s(X), s(Y).
s(a). s(b).
```

The third one is a 4-queen program. We have three group of data concerning with the execution time, the heap size used, and the unification operations during the execution of the above three programs. They are listed in table 1-3 in figure 19.9. During the

Table 1. Comparison of execution time (sec.)

Query	Pure OR-parallel Model	OR-parallel with sharing
append	0.54	0.55
main	0.56	0.43
queen4	67.26	55.89

Table 2. Comparison of number of heap cells

Query	Pure OR-parallel Model	OR-parallel with sharing
append	31	31
main	11	7
queen4	706	602

Table 3. Comparison of number of unification operations

Query	Pure OR-parallel Model	OR-parallel with sharing
append	37	37
main	35	15
queen4	4683	3887

Figure 19.9 Preliminary simulation results

evaluation of the query append, since there is only one subgoal in the clause body of append, there exists no sharing among OR-parallel processes, the number of unification operations and heap cells used are the same for both models. But the execution time for the pure model is shorter. This is due to the overhead on the management of shared processes. However the improvement made by the OR-parallel model with sharing over the pure OR-parallel model can be seen on the execution of the queries main and 4-queen. In the model enhanced with sharing, the unification operations performed for both queries are smaller due to the effect of sharing, the sizes of heap required are also smaller, and most importantly, the overall execution times are shorter.

19.5 CONCLUSION

Our OR-parallel execution model enhanced with sharing has two main characteristics: first, sharing is introduced without the need of introducing any complicated process synchronization mechanism, and second, sharing is achieved without inducing any speculative work. Although the model assumes a global address space, it can be implemented on a physically distributed architecture as long as a global virtual address space is provided. The extension of pure OR-parallel models with sharing is orthogonal to the major issues in pure OR-parallel models, and accordingly different strategies designed for controlling process granularity, ranging from controlling the number of parallel processes via the syntax of the program [CG86] to pruning unnecessary branches in the search tree [CH84], or task stealing can be incorporated into our model. We originally came to the concept of sharing in OR-parallel models when we were seeking an OR-parallel model for executing a class of functional logic languages exemplified by K - LEAF [BBG+87] in which the ability of sharing is considered to be even more vital.

So far, the preliminary simulation results have shown some promising aspects of the model enhanced with sharing. But they have also shown a sign of overhead for the management of shared processes. A more advanced evaluation on this overhead is particularly important in order to minimize the overhead if the sharing effect is not significant in a logic program.

REFERENCES

[BBG+87] M. Bellia, P.G. Bosco, E. Giovannetti, C. Moiso, and C. Palamidessi. A two level approach to logic plus functional programming integration. In *Proc. Conf. Parallel Architectures and Languages Europe*, Springer-Verlag, Lecture Notes in Computer Science 258, 1987.

[CG86] K.L. Clark and S. Gregory. PARLOG: Parallel programming in logic. *ACM Transactions on Programming Language Systems*, January 1986.

[CH84] A. Ciepielewski and S. Haridi. Control of activities in the or-parallel token machine. In *Proc. International Symposium on Logic Programming*, 1984.

[Con87] S. Conery. *Parallel Execution of Logic Programs.* Kluwer Academic Publishers, 1987.

[CWY91] V.S. Costa, D.H.D Warren, and R. Yang. *Andorra-I: A Parallel Prolog System that Transparently Exploits both And- and Or-parallelism.* Technical Report TR-91-03, University of Bristol, 1991.

[GKSS88] J.R.W. Glauert, J.R. Kennaway, M.R. Sleep, and G.W. Somner. *Final Specification of DACTL.* Technical Report SYS-C88-11, University of East Anglia, 1988.

[GP88] J.R.W. Glauert and G.A. Papadopoulos. A parallel implementation of GHC. In *Proc. Conf. Fifth Generation Computer Systems*, 1988.

[Har90] S. Haridi. A logic programming language based on the Andorra model. *New Generation Computing*, **7**, 2,3, 1990.

[Jon87] S.L. Peyton Jones. *The Implementation of Functional Languages.* Prentice-Hall, 1987.

[LBD+90] E. Lusk, R. Butter, T. Disz, R. Olson, R. Overbeek, and R. Stevens. The Aurora Or-parallel Prolog system. *New Generation Computing*, **7**, 2,3, 1990.

[MNRA89] J.J. Moreno-Navarro and M. Rodriguez-Artalejo. BABEL: A functional and logic programming language based on constructor discipline and narrowing. In *Proc.*

Conf. on Algebraic and Logic Programming, Springer-Verlag, Lecture Notes in Computer Science 343, 1989.

[Pap89] G.A. Papadopoulos. *Parallel Implementation of Concurrent Logic Languages Using Graph Rewriting Techniques.* PhD thesis, University of East Anglia, 1989.

[RCB87] T.J. Reynolds, A.S.K. Cheng, and A.J. Beaumont. BRAVE on GRIP. In *Proc. Workshop on Logic Programming and Reduction Workshop*, 1987.

[vEPS91] M.C.J.D. van Eekelen, M.J. Plasmeijer, and J.E.W. Smetsers. Parallel graph rewriting on loosely coupled machine architectures. In Kaplan and Okada (editors), *Proc. of Conditional and Typed Rewriting Systems (CTRS'90)*, pp. 354–369. Montreal, Canada, 1991.

[War87] D.H.D. Warren. Or-parallel models of prolog. In *Proc. International Joint Conference on Theory and Practice of Software Development*, Springer-Verlag, Lecture Notes in Computer Science 250, 1987.

20

A New Process Model for Functions

J.R.W. Glauert, L. Leth and B. Thomsen

20.1 INTRODUCTION

A number of studies have been made of the relationship between process notations and functional programming. Early work by Kennaway and Sleep used the LNET model [KS82], while Thomsen used higher-order processes [Tho89, Tho90]. Milner [Mil90], and Leth [Let91], show how an arbitrary λ–expression may be converted to a network of processes whose behaviour simulates reduction of the original λ–expression.

This work has been primarily motivated by a desire to explore the theoretical relationship between the formalisms, rather than to provide an efficient implementation of the λ-Calculus. Such work is of particular interest when considering implementation of a language such as Facile [GMP89] which aims to integrate functional and process styles. By encoding the functional components of a program as a network of processes, the complete language may be converted to processes for semantic purposes at least.

The studies based on extensions to CCS adopt a synchronous model of communication. Honda and Tokoro [HT91] show that asynchronous communication can be used to the same effect. The work presented here is able to take advantage of such asynchronous models.

This chapter describes a new translation of the λ-Calculus into a process notation, supporting a mixture of evaluation strategies using techniques similar to [Bur84]. Milner and Leth consider only the pure λ-Calculus while our new translation handles constant data values and their operations.

Programs in the process language may be translated very naturally into a generalized Graph Rewriting System (GRS). A translation to the practical GRS language Dactl is

Term Graph Rewriting: Theory and Practice.
Eds. Ronan Sleep, Rinus Plasmeijer and Marko van Eekelen.

presented. The style of execution of such a GRS is rather different from the traditional term-based translation of a functional language.

20.2 THE LAZY- AND EAGER- λ-Calculus

In this section we shall review some aspects of the Lazy-λ-Calculus [Abr88] and introduce the Eager-λ-Calculus. The syntax of both is slightly unconventional as we use an explicit left-associative operator, @, for application. The operator will be decorated to indicate which calculus is being considered.

$$e \ ::= \ x \mid \lambda x.\, e \mid e\,@\,e$$

where x is taken from a set of variable names.

20.2.1 The Lazy-λ-Calculus

Terms in the *Lazy-λ-Calculus* may be reduced according to the relation $\rightarrow_L$ defined as follows:

DEFINITION **20.2.1** *Let $\rightarrow_L$, lazy reduction, be the smallest relation satisfying:*

$$APPL: \ \frac{e \ \rightarrow_L \ e''}{c\,@\,c' \ \rightarrow_L \ e''\,@\,e'} \qquad\qquad BETA: \ (\lambda x.e)\,@\,e' \ \rightarrow_L \ e\,[e'/x]$$

The Lazy-λ-Calculus is inherently sequential. Reduction always occurs at the head of an application sequence, i.e. let $M \equiv M_0@M_1 \ldots\ M_n$ $(n > 0)$ where M_0 is not an application, then the only reduction possible is when $n \geq 1$ and $M_0 \equiv \lambda x.\, N$. In this case we have $M_0@M_1@M_2 \ldots\ M_n \rightarrow_L N\{M_1/x\}@M_2 \ldots M_n$ since we will generally consider that expressions to reduce are closed. There will always be a redex on the left spine unless the whole expression is an abstraction.

Note that the Lazy-λ-Calculus does not reduce the bodies of abstractions so it will only reduce expressions to weak head-normal form. This is not a problem when considering functional programming where functional normal forms are not usually of interest.

20.2.2 The Eager-λ-Calculus

Since we are interested in parallel evaluation of functional programs by translating them into a formalism for concurrent processes, we do not have great hopes if we solely base our work on the Lazy-λ-Calculus. A more eager evaluation strategy is obtained by adding an extra reduction rule $APPR$:

DEFINITION **20.2.2** *Let $\rightarrow_E$, eager reduction, be the smallest relation satisfying:*

$$APPL: \ \frac{e \ \rightarrow_E \ e''}{e\,@\,e' \ \rightarrow_E \ e''\,@\,e'} \qquad\qquad APPR: \ \frac{e' \ \rightarrow_E \ e''}{e\,@\,e' \ \rightarrow_E \ e\,@\,e''}$$

$$BETA: \ (\lambda x.e)\,@\,e' \ \rightarrow_E \ e\,[e'/x]$$

This allows reduction in both operator and operand in an application. We shall call this calculus the *Eager-λ-Calculus*. $\rightarrow_L$ is clearly contained in $\rightarrow_E$.

The Eager-λ-Calculus introduces some non-determinism to the reduction rules since for any application with redexes in the operand we may either reduce the operand or perform the reduction in $\rightarrow_L$. Since the Lazy-λ-Calculus is normalizing, the Eager-λ-Calculus may converge whenever the lazy calculus converges. However, if we continually choose redexes from $\rightarrow_E$ which are not needed, then a term with a weak head-normal form may not converge.

We should remark that the Eager-λ-Calculus is not the same as the *Call-by-Value-λ-Calculus*. Call-by-value reduction uses a restricted $BETA$ rule in which the operand must be a value, v, in the form $\lambda x.\, e$:

$$BETA: \ (\lambda x.e) @ v \rightarrow_V e[v/x]$$

This means that reduction of operator and operand may proceed non-deterministically, but reduction of a redex may only occur when both operator and operand have converged. Clearly there are terms for which the Call-by-Value-λ-Calculus diverges when the Lazy-λ-Calculus converges and the Eager-λ-Calculus may converge.

20.2.3 A mixed calculus

The translations presented in this chapter support a mixed language in which the Lazy-λ-Calculus and Eager-λ-Calculus live together in one calculus. In this case we annotate the application by $@_L$ or $@_E$ in $M@_LN$ or $M@_EN$ to indicate which evaluation strategy is to be used. The rules $APPL$ and $BETA$ apply to both forms of application while $APPR$ applies only to $@_E$. The effect is similar to [Bur84]. The intuition is that we may reduce any instance of the $BETA$ rule which can be reached by a path through the operator position of $@_L$ terms or either argument of $@_E$ terms.

Languages such a Concurrent Clean provide facilities which allow for limited eager evaluation and might well be given a semantics in the same way as the mixed calculus. Judicious use of the $@_E$ operator in positions where the operand is needed or strongly terminating will mean that the convergence properties of the program are the same as for the Lazy-λ-Calculus.

20.3 A PROCESS NOTATION

We present a process notation into which we will translate programs written in the mixed calculus described in the previous section. The notation has features corresponding to those of ECCS [EN84], the π-Calculus [MPW89] and LCCS [Let91]. All may be regarded as extensions to CCS allowing the communication of link names and hence allowing dynamic process networks to be generated.

The significant extension to these earlier notations is that we permit, as an atomic event, the communication of terms representing arbitrary tuples of values, although nothing more complicated than pairs is required for our translations below. This is very nearly equivalent to the Polyadic-π-Calculus [Mil91] although we would allow nested terms. We allow a received term to be matched to a pattern of names, or bound to a single name. Further work is required on a sort discipline for the calculus to ensure that names bound to structured values are never used as link names.

We are also very interested in the sub-calculus in which the process following an output action is always the inactive process. This is in essence the language of [HT91].

20.3.1 Syntax

The forms of agent, or process, allowed are a subset of those of LCCS with the addition of defined agents from the π-Calculus. In the syntax below, P and Q are agents, A an agent identifier, x a link, and y a value or link name:

Output $x!y.P$
Send value y on link x and continue with behaviour P.

Tupled Output $x!(q,r).P$
Send pair of values q and r on link x and continue with behaviour P.

Input $x?y.P$
Receive a value on link x and bind the value to y in subsequent behaviour P.

Tupled Input $x?(q,r).P$
Receive a pair of values on link x. Bind the first value to q and the second to r in subsequent behaviour P.

Restriction $P\backslash x$
x is the name of a link which may only be used within P. For many purposes this may be seen as the declaration of the link x.

Parallel Composition $(P|Q)$
P and Q continue concurrently and may interact via shared links. Binary composition is illustrated but an arbitrary number of agents may be composed including zero which gives inaction.

Agent Definition $P : A(x_1, \ldots, x_n) = Q$
A is an agent identifier of arity n which may be used in P. $x_1, \ldots, x_n$ may be free names in Q. Q may contain agent identifiers, including A, and free names from P.

Defined Agent $A(y_1, \ldots, y_n)$
A corresponding agent definition of the form $A(x_1, \ldots, x_n) = Q$ must be in scope. The defined agent behaves like $Q\{y_1/x_1, \ldots, y_n/x_n\}$.

Hence parallel composition and repetition are supported, but not summation (choice).

? and \ are name binding constructs yielding the obvious notion of free and bound names. We let $fn(P)$ denote the set of free names in P.

The form $\mathbf{rec}X.P$ is allowed as syntactic sugar for $X : X = P$.

20.3.2 Operational semantics

The operational semantics of the process notation is given in terms of a labelled transition system. There are four kinds of actions, ranged over by α: input actions $x?y$, output actions $x!z$, output of restricted name $x\backslash y$ and internal actions τ. We let $c(\alpha)$ denote the communication channel of an action, e.g. x above. ? and \ are name binders and $bn(\alpha)$ denotes the bound name of an action, e.g. y above.

The transition relation is defined as the smallest relation satisfying the axiom and rules in figure 20.1.

$$\text{Output} \quad x!y.P \xrightarrow{x!y} P$$

$$\text{Input} \quad x?y.P \xrightarrow{x?z} P\{z/y\}$$

$$\text{Res} \quad \frac{P \xrightarrow{\alpha} P'}{P\backslash x \xrightarrow{\alpha} P'\backslash x} \quad , x \neq c(\alpha)$$

$$\text{Open} \quad \frac{P \xrightarrow{y!x} P'}{P\backslash x \xrightarrow{y\backslash z} P'\{z/x\}} \quad , z \notin fn(P\backslash x)$$

$$\text{Par} \quad \frac{P \xrightarrow{\alpha} P'}{P \mid Q \xrightarrow{\alpha} P' \mid Q} \quad , bn(\alpha) \cup fn(Q) = \emptyset$$

$$\text{Com} \quad \frac{P \xrightarrow{x?y} P' \quad Q \xrightarrow{x!y} Q'}{P \mid Q \xrightarrow{\tau} P' \mid Q'}$$

$$\text{Close} \quad \frac{P \xrightarrow{x?y} P' \quad Q \xrightarrow{x\backslash y} Q'}{P \mid Q \xrightarrow{\tau} (P' \mid Q')\backslash y} \quad , y \notin fn(P)$$

$$\text{Agents} \quad \frac{P\{y_1/x_1, \ldots, y_n/x_n\} \xrightarrow{\alpha} P'}{A(y_1, \ldots, y_n) \xrightarrow{\alpha} P'} \quad , A(x_1, \ldots, x_n) = P$$

Figure 20.1 Operational semantics for process notation

20.4 TRANSLATION OF LAZY- AND EAGER-λ-CALCULUS

Milner [Mil90] provides encodings of the Lazy-λ-Calculus and the Call-by-Value-λ-Calculus in the π-Calculus. Only closed terms are considered. The encodings simulate particular reduction strategies.

We present a new scheme for translating λ–expressions to process networks. The language translated provides two forms of application operator and also supports constants denoted by k in the syntax. If all applications are $@_L$ then a lazy translation results, although it is not quite the same as that of Milner. The use of $@_E$ throughout yields a translation of the Eager-λ-Calculus.

20.4.1 The new translation scheme

$$
\begin{aligned}
[\![x]\!]_u &= \mathbf{rec}\,X.\,u?v\,.\,(\,x!v.()\,|\,X\,)\\
[\![k]\!]_u &= \mathbf{rec}\,X.\,u?v\,.\,(\,v!k.()\,|\,X\,)\\
[\![\lambda x.\,M]\!]_u &= \mathbf{rec}\,X.\,u?(x,q)\,.\,(\,[\![M]\!]_q\,|\,X\,)\\
[\![M\,@_L\,N]\!]_u &= (\,[\![M]\!]_f\,|\,f!(t,u).()\,|\,\mathbf{rec}\,X\,.\,t?v.(\,a!v.()\,|\,[\![N]\!]_a\,|\,X\,)\backslash a\,)\backslash f\backslash t\\
[\![M\,@_E\,N]\!]_u &= (\,[\![M]\!]_f\,|\,f!(a,u).()\,|\,[\![N]\!]_a\,)\backslash f\backslash a
\end{aligned}
$$

The pure λ-Calculus is not of great practical use. Constants, such as Boolean and integer data values, and operations on them must be added to make a practical functional language. Data values are represented by a set of names disjoint from those used for links. Functions such as the successor function will be represented by global names. A process network to implement these functions will exist in parallel with the program to be evaluated. The network for *succ* would be as follows:

$$\mathbf{rec}\,X.\,u?(x,q)\,.\,(\,X\,|\,(\,x!t.()\,|\,t?n\,.\,q?r\,.\,r!(n+1).()\,)\backslash t\,)$$

An occurrence of the name *succ* will be translated like a variable.

It is assumed that programs will reduce to data values. To retrieve the value from the translation of such a λ–expression it is necessary to send a channel to it and receive back the value on the channel. To extract the value from a program, P, we would produce a network of the form:

$$(\,[\![P]\!]_u\,|\,Read(\,u\,)\,)\backslash u\;:\;Read(\,w\,)\;=\;(\,w!c.()\,|\,c?v\,.\,Print(\,v\,)\,)\backslash c$$

and *Print* will display the final result.

20.4.2 Properties of the new scheme

The intuition behind the translation is that the translation of each syntactic construct is a process network with a special characteristic link, or ***handle***, through which the network will communicate. This link is denoted by u in the translations.

If the process represents a numeric constant, the value received on u will be a link on which the number is to be returned. If the process encodes an abstraction, u will be sent a pair of links. The first link of the pair is the handle on the argument, while the second link is to be the handle on the process which results when the argument is substituted in the body of the abstraction.

The encoding of an application links up an abstraction with an argument. Considering $@_E$ first, we see that neither the encoding of the operator nor operand are guarded. The process networks concerned will evolve independently. When the operator reaches weak head-normal form it will be waiting to receive input on its handle. The apply glue code in the translation sends the resulting abstraction a pair informing it of the operand and the channel which is to be the handle for the resulting network.

The encoding of $@_L$ guards the operand so that only when the operator actually requests the value of the operand will it be evaluated. The extra glue code acts as a buffer, passing on the request from the operator to the operand network.

A variable simply acts as a buffer, relaying information sent to it to the handle for the operand provided when the abstraction binding the variable was applied. The information sent will depend on the type of the result: if it is a constant then a single return link name will be sent; if it has a function type then a pair will be sent.

There are simplifications gained by communicating pairs of values. If only simple names may be communicated, extra temporary links are needed to prevent interleaving of messages from different agents able to the handle u, as in Milner's call-by-value scheme. The Polyadic-π-Calculus also overcomes these problems, though we must be aware that the sort of apparently similar links will depend on the type of the λ-expressions being translated.

All output actions in a translated network are followed by inaction. As a consequence no process is dependent on synchronized communication, and an asynchronous communication model would suffice. This can significantly reduce the complexity of a low-level implementation of such a process notation as will be shown later. [HT91] shows that sequentialization is possible using just asynchronous communication, though our use of tupled communication allows their scheme to be simplified.

20.4.3 Elimination of some recursion

It will be seen that a number of uses of the **rec** construct appear. These are needed to allow for multiple occurrences of the bound variable in the body of abstractions. When such abstractions are applied, the argument may be evaluated more than once with different arguments. These uses of **rec** are not always required. Indeed none would be required for the linear λ-Calculus.

To eliminate some of the superfluous recursion we may use a more sophisticated translation scheme based on the observation that terms in head position do not need recursion. In other words, when a variable or a λ-abstraction occurs as an operator in a λ-expression there is no need for multiple copies, whereas occurrence as an operand needs the possibility of producing various copies of the variable or the λ-abstraction.

The function application cannot be analyzed similarly, so recursion has to be provided in all cases. This gives us eight rules in the translation scheme; two for variables (without and with recursion), two for constants, two for λ-abstraction, and one for each of the applications. The translations involved with recursion are annotated with *:

$$
\begin{aligned}
[\![x]\!]_u &= u?v\,.\,x!v.() \\
[\![x]\!]_u^* &= \mathbf{rec}X.u?v.(x!v \mid X) \\
[\![k]\!]_u &= u?v\,.\,v!k.() \\
[\![k]\!]_u^* &= \mathbf{rec}\,X.\,u?v\,.\,(\,v!k.() \mid X\,) \\
[\![\lambda x.\,M]\!]_u &= u?(x,q)\,.\,[\![M]\!]_q \\
[\![\lambda x.\,M]\!]_u^* &= \mathbf{rec}\,X.\,u?(x,q)\,.\,(\,[\![M]\!]_q \mid X\,) \\
[\![M \mathbin{@_E} N]\!]_u &= [\![M \mathbin{@_E} N]\!]_u^* \\
&= (\,[\![M]\!]_f \mid f!(a,u).() \mid [\![N]\!]_a^*\,) \backslash f \backslash a \\
[\![M \mathbin{@_L} N]\!]_u &= [\![M \mathbin{@_L} N]\!]_u^*
\end{aligned}
$$

$$= \; ([\![M]\!]_f \,|\, f!(t,u).() \,|\, \mathbf{rec}\, X\,.\,t?v.(\,a!v.() \,|\, [\![N]\!]_a \,|\, X\,)\backslash a\,)\backslash f\backslash t$$

Note that the translation of $M \,@_L\, N$ only involves one level of recursion using **rec**. The recursion in $M \,@_E\, N$ comes indirectly through the use of $[\![N]\!]^*$.

20.5 PROCESS NOTATION AND GRAPH REWRITING

Process networks such as those described in this chapter may be easily translated into generalized Graph Rewriting Systems. The practical graph rewriting language Dactl [GKS91] is used as the target for our translation.

20.5.1 A standard form for process networks

In this section we define how to express a process network in a standard form which makes heavy use of defined agents. This form can then be implemented very easily as a GRS.

If A stands for an agent identifier then the forms we will allow are:

$$P ::= x!y.A \,\Big|\, x?y.A \,\Big|\, (A \,|\, \ldots \,|\, A) \,\Big|\, P\backslash x \,\Big|\, P : A = P$$

Also, we restrict agent definitions to the outermost level, so they may contain no free variables. It should be clear that any process expression can be converted to this form by inserting new agent identifiers and adding appropriate definitions. The transformation is in four stages. We will use forms of $\lambda x.x$ for illustration:

$$\mathbf{rec}\, X.\, u?(x,q)\,.\,(\,X \,|\, \mathbf{rec}\, Y.\, q?v\,.\,(\,Y \,|\, x!v.()\,)\,)$$

The first stage is to expand the syntactic sugar for **rec** which was defined such that $\mathbf{rec}X.P \equiv X : X = P$. This gives:

$$X : \quad X \;=\; u?(x,q)\,.\,(\,X \,|\, Y \,:\, Y \;=\; q?v\,.\,(\,Y \,|\, x!v.()\,)\,)$$

The second stage is to add extra agent definitions to satisfy the reduced syntax using the rule that $P \equiv A : A = P$ where A is a new agent identifier:

$$\begin{aligned} X : \quad & X \;=\; u?(x,q)\,.\,Z \,:\, Z \;=\; (\,X \,|\, Y \,:\, Y \;=\; q?v\,.\,W \,: \\ & W \;=\; (\,Y \,|\, Put \,:\, Put \;=\; x!v.\,Nil \,:\, Nil \;=\; ()\,)\,) \end{aligned}$$

The third stage is to add parameters to avoid free variables. This uses the rule that $X : X = P \equiv X(fn(P)) : X(fn(P)) = P\{(fn(P))/X\}$:

$$\begin{aligned} X(u) : \quad & X(u) = \; u?(x,q).\, Z(u,x,q) \,:\, Z(u,x,q) = \; (X(u) \,|\, Y(x,q) \,: \\ & Y(x,q) = \; q?v.\, W(x,q,v) \,:\, W(x,q,v) = \; (\,Y(x,q) \,|\, Put(x,v) \,: \\ & Put(x,v) = \; x!v.\, Nil \,:\, Nil \;=\; ()\,)\,) \end{aligned}$$

Finally, definitions can now be pulled to the top level:

$$
\begin{aligned}
X(u): \quad & X(u) = u?(x,q) \,.\, Z(u,x,q): \\
& Z(u,x,q) = (\,X(u) \,|\, Y(x,q)\,): \\
& Y(x,q) = q?v \,.\, W(x,q,v): \\
& W(x,q,v) = (\,Y(x,q) \,|\, Put(x,v)\,): \\
& Put(x,v) = x!v.\,Nil: \\
& Nil = ()
\end{aligned}
$$

All output operations are followed by a process denoting inaction. The *Put* action definition can be used for all output actions.

20.5.2 The graph rewriting language Dactl

Dactl provides a notation for describing computational objects as directed graphs, and for specifying computation in terms of pattern-directed rewritings of such graphs. It has been used in studies of the implementation of a range of language styles including functional programming, term rewriting languages [Ken90], and concurrent logic languages [GP88]. Graph rewriting also shows promise for supporting the integration of different programming styles; [GP91] reports early work on integration of functional and logic languages, while the work reported here arises from a collaborative study investigating integration of functional and process-based programming.

[GKS91] provides a thorough background to the Dactl language. Here we review the language features exploited in the translation of process networks to graph rewriting systems in this chapter. The nodes of a Dactl graph are labelled with a symbol which indicates that the node plays the role of an *operator* at the root of a rule application, a *data constructor*, or an *overwritable*. The role of operators and constructors will be familiar. The novel feature is the use of overwritable nodes which may be modified as a side-effect of rule application. This enables Dactl to express more computational models than the Term Graph rewriting which is discussed elsewhere in this book. Overwritables may model von Neumann storage cells, semaphores, and the logic variable. Overwritable nodes will be used in this chapter to model the contents of communication channels.

A Dactl graph may be represented by listing the definitions of the nodes giving their identifier, symbol, and a sequence of identifiers for the successor nodes. Repetition of identifiers is used to indicate sharing in a graph:

```
c: Chan[ n ],
n: Nil
```

Symbols are integers or identifiers starting in upper-case, while node identifiers start in lower-case. A node definition may replace one of the occurrences of the node identifier, and redundant identifiers may be removed allowing the equivalent shorthand form:

```
c: Chan[ Nil ]
```

Dactl rules contain a *pattern* to be matched and a body, or *contractum*, to replace the occurrence of the pattern in the graph, or *redex*. Patterns are Dactl graphs but may contain node identifiers lacking a definition which will match an arbitrary node.

The contractum of a rule contains new graph structure to be built, which may reference nodes matched by the pattern, and one or more *redirections*, which indicate that the source of the redirection should be overwritten by the target. In classic term rewriting rules there will always be a redirection overwriting the root of the redex with the root of the contractum. In such rules the pattern and contractum are separated by the symbol =>. This is shorthand for a form with an explicit overwrite using -> as separator.

To control the order of evaluation, attempts to match the rules against the graph only begin at *active* nodes, marked with a $*$ in the representation. If more than one rule matches, an arbitrary choice may be made about which rule to apply; fairness is not assumed. The contractum may use markings to nominate further nodes at which rewriting may take place. If multiple active nodes arise they may be considered in any order, or even in parallel if there is no conflict between possible rewritings.

A parallel composition of processes P and Q both using links x and y might be encoded by a graph:

```
*P[x y], *Q[x y]
```

Nodes may also be created *suspended*, indicated by one or more # markings, waiting for *notification* that a successor has been rewritten to a stable form. This enables a rule to create a data-flow graph in which certain nodes are active and will produce results which awaken parent nodes once all arguments are available. Each notification removes one suspension, the node becoming active when the last suspension is removed. Notification typically takes place when an active node has become a constructor or overwritable. Arcs which will form notification paths are marked with ^.

As a final illustration, we consider the modelling of links in our translation of the process notation. A channel will consist of an overwritable Chan whose argument is a list acting as a stack of available values. To output to the channel, a rule simply overwrites the channel to contain a list prefixed with the new value. To input from a channel, a rule must test for available input. If the channel contains the empty list, the operation is suspended until input is available. Otherwise the channel is rewritten containing the tail of the original list.

The rules for Put add a value at the head of the stack of values, while Get receives a value and then continues with process Use which may manipulate the value received:

```
RULE
      Put[c:Chan[v] d] -> c:= *Chan[Cons[d v]];
      Get[c:Chan[Cons[d v]]] -> *Use[d], c:= Chan[v];
      Get[c:Chan[Nil]] -> #Get[^c];
```

Below we illustrate the rules in action. The first attempt to read from the channel suspends on finding the empty channel Chan[Nil]. Note the final state with the channel empty again:

```
        *Get[c],  *Put[c 2],  c:Chan[n:Nil]
=>{3}  #Get[^c], *Put[c 2],  c:Chan[n:Nil]
```

```
=>{1}  #Get[^c],   c:*Chan[Cons[2 n:Nil]]
=>{-}  *Get[c],    c:Chan[Cons[2 n:Nil]]
=>{2}  *Use[2],    c:Chan[n:Nil]
=>...
```

The initial state of a link is **Chan[Nil]**, a channel with no messages available. Introduction of new channels is associated with restriction operators in process expressions.

The **Put** rule updates the channel **c** to contain the message referred to by **d** as the first message in its buffer. The effect of the active marker on the updated channel will be to unblock any process attempting to receive on this channel.

The two rules for **Get** describe the behaviour of a process guarded by an input action. The first rule corresponds to the case where there is input available. The value found in the channel is passed to the **Use** process which is made active. The channel is updated to reflect the fact that a message has been delivered. The final rule comes into play if the channel is empty. The **#** and **^** markings indicate that the **Get** process should be suspended until the channel **c** is updated by a **Put** process.

20.5.3 Translation of standard form networks to Dactl

The Dactl rules below illustrate the translation of the function $\lambda x.x$ applied to the constant value 3:

```
RULE
    INITIAL => *Read[z], *A[z], z:NewChan;
    A[z] -> *X[f], *Put[f Cons[a z]], *Const[a 3],
                f:NewChan, a:NewChan;
    X[u:Chan[Cons[Pair[x q] r]]] -> *Z[u x q], u:= Chan[r];
    X[u:Chan[Nil]] -> #X[^u];
    Z[u x q] -> *X[u], *Y[x q];
    Y[x q:Chan[Cons[v r]]] -> *W[x q v], q:= Chan[r];
    Y[x q:Chan[Nil]] -> #Y[x ^q];
    W[x q v] -> *Y[x q], *Put[x v];
    Const[u:Chan[Cons[v r]] k] -> *C[u k v], u:= Chan[r];
    Const[u:Chan[Nil] k] -> #Const[^u k];
    C[u k v] -> *Const[u k], *Put[v k];
    Read[z] => *Get[r], *Put[z r], r:NewChan;
```

All Dactl programs start with a graph containing a single active node with symbol **INITIAL**. This replaces process P above.

Processes generally correspond to GRS terms. The * marks an active process or rewritable term. Parallel composition, used by Z and W, is very straightforward. Restriction, used in A, corresponds to declaration of new links denoted by the term **NewChan**. The following pattern defines such new channels:

```
PATTERN
    NewChan = Chan[Nil];
```

All output actions involve the primitive **Put** described earlier. Processes guarded by an input action become two rules. The first extracts a value from a channel containing input, while the second applies when no input is available and blocks the process until an output action is performed on the channel.

To output a pair, the **Pair** constructor is used to build the pair, as in **A**. When a pair is input, (for example **x** and **q** in **X**), the pattern matches a pair of values for use in the body of the action (**Z** in this case).

The processes **Read** and **Put** are defined as follows:

```
RULE
    Put[c:Chan[v] d] -> c:= *Chan[Cons[d v]];
    Read[z] -> *Put[z r], *Print[r], r: NewChan;
    Print[x:Chan[Cons[v r]]] ->
        *PrintF["Result: %d" v], x:= Chan[r];
    Print[x:Chan[Nil]] -> #Print[^x];
```

The communication scheme is very simple because of the restricted use of the process model in the translation scheme: lack of a choice operator avoids the need to retract communication offers; ability to use asynchronous communication removes the need for synchronizing operations; and there is no need to maintain the order of available messages so a stack may be used.

The overall style of execution contrasts strongly with the more conventional Term Graph rewriting [BvEG+87] approach. Instead of representing an expression as a single rooted term, this style represents subexpressions as independent unrooted terms linked by shared references to nodes representing channels. In this way, execution corresponds more to the actions of the Chemical Abstract Machine [BB90] than a traditional graph reduction machine.

20.6 RESULTS

A translator has been developed which will convert "programs" in an extended λ-Calculus to the process notation. Several different translations from λ-Calculus to processes have been implemented. The process networks are converted to the sub-language which makes heavy use of agent definitions. This form is then converted to Dactl.

The mapping from process notation to Dactl does not handle non-trivial processes with output guards (only inaction may follow an output guard). This enables us to express the new translation directly, but the π-Calculus translations of Milner cannot be translated directly. A Form of the Lazy-λ-Calculus translation modified in a manner inspired by [HT91] has been produced. The translation is extended to handle constants. This has been called *PiLazy*:

$$\begin{aligned}
[\![x]\!]_u &= x!u.() \\
[\![k]\!]_u &= u?v\,.\,v!k.() \\
[\![\lambda x.M]\!]_u &= u?d.\,(\,d!a.() \mid a?x.\,u?v.\,[\![M]\!]_v\,)\backslash a \\
[\![M\,@_L\,N]\!]_u &= (\,[\![M]\!]_v \mid v!d.() \mid d?a.\,(a!t.() \mid v!u.() \mid \mathbf{rec}\,X\,.\,t?w.\,([\![N]\!]_w \mid X))\backslash t\,)\backslash d\backslash v
\end{aligned}$$

This translations were compared with *NewLazy* and *NewEager*. These correspond to the new translation converting all applications to lazy or eager form correspondingly.

In addition, the tupled communication of our notation was exploited to produce an improved version of *PiLazy*, called *ImpPiLazy*:

$$
\begin{aligned}
[\![x]\!]_u &= x!u.() \\
[\![k]\!]_u &= u?v\,.\,v!k.() \\
[\![\lambda x.M]\!]_u &= u?(x,v).\,[\![M]\!]_v \\
[\![M\,@_L\,N]\!]_u &= (\,[\![M]\!]_v \mid v!(t,u).() \mid \mathbf{rec}\,X\,.\,t?w.\,([\![N]\!]_w \mid X))\backslash t \backslash v
\end{aligned}
$$

The test programs used were:

IdTest : $(\lambda x.\,x)\,99$

Twice : $(\lambda twice.\lambda succ.\,twice\,twice\,succ\,0)\ (\lambda f.\lambda x.f\,(f\,x))\ (\lambda n.Succ(n))$

The efficiency measure used is the number of output actions made. In most cases, every output message is consumed.

Translation	*IdTest*	*Twice*
NewEager	4	49
NewLazy	5	80
PiLazy	7	94
ImpPiLazy	4	52

Note that the lazy translations allow no parallelism, so our main focus is on an eager translation, but with the aim of supporting laziness where it is required. Our translations are superior when function application is taking place, as in *Twice*. *PiLazy* does not perform well since we must avoid synchronous communication. However, the improved version *ImpPiLazy* is best for a purely lazy translation. We have not attempted to reduce recursion in the new translation.

20.7 CONCLUSIONS

A new scheme for translating λ-Calculus expressions to process networks has been presented. The new model allows mixing of lazy and call-by-value strategies. Simple data values and their operators may be incorporated in the translation.

Some early experimental results are presented based on a translation of process networks to Dactl. The results show that the new translation is superior for eager computation, and also performs well for lazy computation.

While implementation efficiency is not our primary concern, the final aim of this work is to investigate possible techniques for practical parallel implementation of languages integrating functional and process styles. The process notation we have developed may be related to graph rewriting opening the question of whether graph rewriting can form the basis for such practical implementations.

REFERENCES

[Abr88] S. Abramsky. The lazy lambda calculus. In D. Turner (editor), *Research Topics in Functional Programming*, pp. 65–116. Addison Wesley, 1988.

[BB90] G. Berry and G. Boudol. The chemical abstract machine. In *Proceedings, Principles of Programming Languages*, pp. 81–94, 1990.

[Bur84] F.W. Burton. Annotations to control parallelism and reduction order in the distributed evaluation of functional programs. *TOPLAS*, **6**, pp. 159–174, 1984.

[BvEG+87] H.P. Barendregt, M.C.J.D. van Eekelen, J.R.W. Glauert, J.R. Kennaway, M.J. Plasmeijer, and M.R. Sleep. Term graph rewriting. In J. W. de Bakker, A. J. Nijman, and P. C. Treleaven (editors), *Proceedings, PARLE'87 Conference*, Springer-Verlag, Lecture Notes in Computer Science 259, pp. 141–158, 1987.

[EN84] U. Engberg and M. Nielsen. *A Calculus of Communicating Systems with Label Passing.* Technical Report DAIMI PB-205, Computer Science Department, University of Aarhus, 1984.

[GKS91] J.R.W. Glauert, J.R. Kennaway, and M.R. Sleep. Dactl: An experimental graph rewriting language. In H. Ehrig, H.-J. Kreowski, and G. Rozenberg (editors), *Proceedings, 4th International Workshop on Graph Grammars and their Application to Computer Science*, Springer-Verlag, Lecture Notes in Computer Science 532, 1991.

[GMP89] A. Giacalone, P. Mishra, and S. Prasad. Facile: A symmetric integration of concurrent and functional programming. *IJPP*, **18**, 2, pp. 121–160, 1989.

[GP88] J.R.W. Glauert and G.A. Papadopoulos. A parallel implementation of GHC. In *Proceedings, International Conference on Fifth Generation Computer Systems, ICOT, Tokyo*, 1988.

[GP91] J.R.W. Glauert and G.A. Papadopoulos. Unifying concurrent logic and functional languages in a graph rewriting framework. In *Proceedings, 3rd Panhellenic Computer Science Conference. Athens*, 1991.

[HT91] K. Honda and M. Tokoro. An object calculus for asynchronous communication. In *Proceedings, ECOOP'91, Geneva*, 1991.

[Ken90] J.R. Kennaway. Implementing term rewrite languages in Dactl. *Theoretical Computer Science*, **72**, pp. 225–250, 1990.

[KS82] J.R. Kennaway and M.R. Sleep. Expressions as processes. In *Proceedings, Lisp and FP*, pp. 21–28, 1982.

[Let91] L. Leth. *Functional Programs as Reconfigurable Networks of Communicating Processes.* PhD thesis, Imperial College, London University, 1991.

[Mil90] R. Milner. Functions as processes. In *Automata, Languages, and Programming, Also Technical Report INRIA Sophia Antipolis, 1989*, Springer-Verlag, Lecture Notes in Computer Science 443, 1990.

[Mil91] R. Milner. *The Polyadic-π-Calculus: A Tutorial.* Technical Report TR ECS-LFCS-91-180, Edinburgh University, 1991.

[MPW89] R. Milner, J. Parrow, and D. Walker. *A Calculus of Mobile Processes, Parts I and II.* Technical Report TR ECS-LFCS-89-85, Edinburgh University, 1989.

[Tho89] B. Thomsen. A calculus of higher order communicating systems. In *Principles of Programming Languages*, pp. 143–154, 1989.

[Tho90] B. Thomsen. *Calculi for Higher Order Communicating Systems.* PhD thesis, Imperial College, London University, 1990.

21

Parallel Execution of Concurrent Clean on ZAPP

R.G. Goldsmith, D.L. McBurney and M.R. Sleep

21.1 INTRODUCTION

This chapter deals with the practical implementation of a programming system that exploits parallelism. The work so described draws together several fields of research, carried out at the University of East Anglia, UK and the University of Nijmegen, The Netherlands.

The Concurrent Clean on ZAPP system is designed to execute parallel programs on a distributed memory parallel processor. Two issues come to the fore in considering parallel programming systems. First, there must be a way to express an algorithm such that parallelism in the algorithm is described and second, there must be some way to distribute and manage the parallel tasks created by the program such that a reasonable gain is made.

Our work is based upon two schemes; the first, Concurrent Clean, is a functional programming language with annotations for specifying parallelism in programs. The second, called ZAPP, is a method for distributing work across a parallel machine. We use a generalized version of ZAPP to control how the parallel tasks specified in the Concurrent Clean program are executed on a distributed memory parallel architecture based on Transputers.

A distinctive feature of our implementation is the use of the Transputer process instructions to support concurrent graph rewriting directly. Selected nodes in the graph undergoing rewriting are represented by Transputer processes, and the Transputer's scheduling and communication mechanisms are used to synchronize reduction tasks.

Term Graph Rewriting: Theory and Practice.
Eds. Ronan Sleep, Rinus Plasmeijer and Marko van Eekelen.

21.1.1 Background

ZAPP [BS82] was originally proposed as a work distribution mechanism for exploiting divide and conquer parallelism on a distributed memory parallel architecture. In 1987, McBurney and Sleep [MS87] demonstrated the effectiveness of the ZAPP mechanism for a number of simple applications, using Transputer arrays.

This work demonstrated that very good performance could be obtained via ZAPP mechanisms. However, it did not do so in a truly programmable way because slight modifications to the basic "ZAPP kernel" were made for each new application.

To extend this work to a programmable form, collaboration began with the Dutch Parallel Reduction Machine project led by H.P.Barendregt and M.J.Plasmeijer. This project gave us the Modula2 source of a prototype compiler for a functional language (essentially Clean, where Clean is a predecessor to Concurrent Clean that has no facilities to express parallelism). In July 1989, we began developing the parallel compiler technology required to tie together the Dutch work on Clean and the British work on ZAPP. This collaborative work was supported by ESPRIT Basic Research Action 3074 (Semagraph).

21.2 THE ZERO ASSIGNMENT PARALLEL PROCESSOR (ZAPP) ARCHITECTURE

Our work attempts to combine an architectural mechanism (ZAPP) with an annotated graph rewriting language called Concurrent Clean. In this section and in section 21.3 we describe both of these components.

21.2.1 Overview of ZAPP

This section of the chapter introduces the essential features of ZAPP as originally proposed in [BS82] and modified in [MS87] and [MS89]. Later sections describe the modifications necessary to support distributed execution of annotated graph rewriting programs.

ZAPP is designed to distribute work efficiently to processing elements on a loosely coupled parallel processor. It was designed to support a *process tree* interpretation of the familiar *divide and conquer* paradigm.

ZAPP divides non-trivial tasks into smaller tasks which can be executed in parallel. It then waits for the results from the tasks it has spawned. When these results arrive, the current task will combine them and pass the result of the combining back to the task that created the current task. Thus, in divide and conquer on ZAPP, a tree of tasks is constructed, with trivial tasks as the leaves of the tree. The tree collapses as results are passed up the tree and the overall result is found at the root of the tree, by combining the results of the top-level child processes.

21.2.2 Parallel evaluation of functional languages

The referential transparency property of functional languages ensures that, for some expression in a functional program, subexpressions of the original expression can be evaluated in any order or even in parallel without affecting the overall result of the expression. To exploit this we treat the *evaluation* of a functional program as a task which may be split into other subtasks, that is, treat the evaluation of a functional program as a divide and conquer problem. For the task of evaluating an expression, each of those subexpressions to be evaluated in parallel will be a separate subtask. A (parent) process spawns a number of child processes, one for each subtask and waits until the results of the child processes are available. The parent process then combines the results from its children and forms the overall result which it passes back to its own parent.

Hence evaluating an expression in a functional language can be viewed as growing a tree of processes from the single process evaluating the initial complex problem. If we had an infinite tree of real processors, we could allocate one physical processor to each process arising from the divide and conquer process tree. Given only a finite number of processors, we need some scheme which can map a dynamically varying number of divide and conquer processes onto a fixed number of real processors. This is what ZAPP does. It is a *virtual tree architecture.*

When only a single processor is available, ZAPP must simulate all the logical processes in the divide and conquer process tree. When more processors are available, the logical processes can be distributed over a network to the individual processors and evaluated in parallel.

Communication in a divide and conquer process tree is only between parent and child. The child process is given data to work on when it is created. The child then works on the problem without further communication from the parent until the child has computed the result. The child notifies the parent that the result is available, and then dies. Throughout the lifetime of the child, its parent is suspended awaiting the results from all its children.

21.2.3 ZAPP architecture overview

A ZAPP machine consists of a number of connected processors (called ZAPP elements) each consisting of a von Neumann processor with its own private memory. In our case the von Neumann processor is a Transputer. There is no shared memory. The ZAPP elements communicate with one another by message passing.

Each ZAPP element executes a ZAPP kernel which supports a virtual tree of processes and implements process creation. ZAPP kernels balance the distribution of the process tree between themselves dynamically using local loading information.

The three steps in applying ZAPP to perform a calculation are:

Broadcast user program: Initialize ZAPP by broadcasting the user program to all processing elements. This includes code to divide problems into tasks and to combine results of tasks spawned.

Inject root problem: Inject the initial problem and data into a single ZAPP element. Call this the root element.

Extract result: Extract and report the final result from the root element.

21.2.4 Principles of ZAPP execution

Each ZAPP element evaluates the nodes of the process tree in a sequential depth first manner. Thus, with a single ZAPP element the nodes of the process tree are visited in the same order as a sequential recursive evaluation strategy.

Notice that breadth first expansion of the process tree would lead to memory requirements exponential in tree depth. The depth first strategy adopted by ZAPP avoids the space explosion problems of breadth first evaluation. The following remarks describe some of the features of the ZAPP system.

TASK POOLS

The processes of the process tree are held in one of three task pools called the Pending, Fixed and Blocked pools. Processes are placed in the Pending pool when they are spawned. Pending processes are processes which have not started executing; they can be executed on the same processor as they were created on or offloaded and executed on a different processor. Pending processes are the only processes which can be offloaded. The Fixed pool contains processes which have started executing together with those which have been offloaded (see below). Fixed processes cannot be offloaded. The Blocked pool contains processes which have been suspended while they wait for the results of their child processes. Processes start in the Pending pool, move to some Fixed pool, and (if they generate children) may visit the Blocked pool.

LOAD BALANCING

Load balancing is performed by all the ZAPP elements, each acting on local loading information. When a ZAPP element determines that it has too few active (Pending or Fixed) processes it requests tasks from its immediate neighbors. By immediate we mean processors directly connected by a physical link. A neighbor can choose to either respond by sending a task from its Pending pool or it can refuse the request. The neighbor does not pass such a request for more work to other ZAPP elements in the network. This restricts offloading to immediate neighbors, and is a key design decision in ZAPP. The benefit of this design decision is that at most one physical communication link is involved in offloading any ZAPP process. The drawback is that it restricts possible diffusion of work throughout the physical network. For suitable problems, the benefits outweigh the drawbacks.

OFFLOADING AND COPYING

Because ZAPP is a distributed memory architecture with no support for physically shared store, offloading a task actually means sending a complete descriptor of a task as a message from one processing element to another. In keeping with ZAPP's search for simplicity, only Pending tasks may be offloaded. By design, these tasks are always of the form *apply the divide and conquer function to the following data*, and consequently such tasks are defined by the data alone. Thus, a task's description is a copy of the task's data graph. In contrast a Fixed task, usually an executing process, would have some amount of state associated with it and would involve more work to offload. Returning a result to a parent on a different processor similarly requires a copy of the result being made and sent to the parent.

21.3 CONCURRENT CLEAN

The language Concurrent Clean is a functional term graph rewriting language which was developed at the University of Nijmegen. It is based on the earlier languages Clean and LEAN. Concurrent Clean is a language that programmers can use directly, but is aimed more at being an intermediate language, between languages with a richer syntax and various target machines, including the G-machine [Aug84], Nijmegen's PABC machine [NPS91] and our generalization of ZAPP. A Concurrent Clean program specifies rules by which transformations (rewrites) on the data graph representing the original problem are made. Evaluation of a program means making a sequence of rewrites on the data graph.

Concurrent Clean has a set of annotations which allow the programmer to express which expressions to evaluate in parallel. The semantics of Clean are extended to handle parallel rewriting. For a detailed description of Concurrent Clean the reader is referred to [NSvEP91].

21.3.1 Annotations for parallelism

At present, Concurrent Clean on ZAPP uses just two primitive task annotations which enable the programmer to mark subexpressions as *fixed* or *mobile* tasks. These tasks are evaluated in parallel with the current evaluation process. The execution model adopted by the architecture can choose to ignore such annotations if it sees fit, but must not add its own annotations to a program.

FIXED ANNOTATION

The FIXED or {F} annotation is used by the programmer to mark the root of a subgraph as a new fixed task which can only be evaluated on the same processor as it was created. The FIXED annotation indicates to the architecture:

a. that the execution of this task should be interleaved fairly with the execution of other tasks supported by the same processor,
b. that single processor, single memory execution is appropriate and that fast sequential coding may be beneficial.

MOBILE ANNOTATION

The MOBILE or {M} annotation is used to mark the root of a subgraph as a mobile task which is mobile in the sense that it can be evaluated on the same processor or on a different (remote) processor from the one it was generated on. The choice is left to the architecture. If a task is evaluated on a different processor from the one on which it was generated, the task is offloaded to its new home. Offloading in ZAPP is done by copying the subgraph rooted by the marked node to the new home of the task. The remote processor evaluates a copy of the subgraph rooted by the marked node.

In contrast, if the work is done on the same processor, no copy is made, and graph sharing via pointers to local memory occurs. This differs from the original Concurrent Clean operational semantics which insist on copying semantics even when no offload takes place. Our ZAPP implementation takes a similar approach to the passing back of results. Within a processor, this is done by pointer sharing whereas across inter-processor boundaries true copying takes place.

The central design decision taken by ZAPP as originally designed might be summarized as follows: use pointer sharing within a processor, but copy structures across processors.

The FIXED annotation should not be confused with the Fixed tasks of ZAPP. In Concurrent Clean, a FIXED annotation indicates that the task, when it is evaluated, can only be so on the processor that created the fixed task. In ZAPP, the Fixed tasks are merely those tasks that are being evaluated. Thus, tasks annotated as FIXED in a Concurrent Clean program will eventually be both Pending and Fixed tasks in the ZAPP system. The FIXED annotation indicates a fact about the task's future behavior, while being a ZAPP Fixed task indicates it current status.

WHY COPY?

Concurrent Clean adopts a graph rewriting model of computation in which a single global graph is modified by a series of sequential or parallel graph rewrites. Realistic physical implementations must simulate this global graph model using a network of physical processors each with some private local memory.

If there is just one physical processor with private memory, sharing of subgraphs between processes in the divide and conquer process tree can be achieved with great efficiency using sharing via pointers to memory locations. If there is more than one physical processor and memory, the issues become more complicated. At one extreme, the architecture might support virtual global memory which allows any processing element to access the local memory of all processing elements. At the other extreme lies the ZAPP architecture, which supports inter-processor communication only between processors which are connected by a direct physical link, and even then insists on offloading by copying.

The disadvantages of copying include:

Cost: the cost of copying is roughly proportional to the size of the structure. This might be very large.

Wastefulness: only a small proportion of the structure may be examined after copying. For example, copying the whole of the expression Head(verylonglist) would be very wasteful, as after copying just one list element would be used.

The advantages of copying are:

Bounded non-local cost: once a structure has been copied, it may be repeatedly accessed from local memory using fast sequential code.

Simplicity: administering inter-processor references efficiently and correctly is not easy. A copying scheme considerably simplifies the problem.

The main disadvantages of copying may be alleviated as follows:

Use copying carefully: provided there is lots of work to do on a copied structure, the copying cost can be a minor contribution to the total cost. Any operation such as matrix multiplication where the amount of work rises more than linearly in relation to structure size can be efficiently offloaded by copying.

Copy lazily: at the cost of complicating the housekeeping somewhat, we can copy structure elements only if they are actually needed.

21.4 IMPLEMENTING CONCURRENT CLEAN ON ZAPP (CCOZ)

Concurrent Clean On ZAPP (CCOZ) is an experimental implementation of Concurrent Clean on Transputers. The ZAPP and Concurrent Clean models differ in that ZAPP is only applicable to hierarchical process networks of the type generated by the divide and conquer function, whilst Concurrent Clean can create very general non-hierarchical process networks. However, the models are similar in that they take copies of subgraphs to be evaluated as offloaded tasks. The combined CCOZ model adds the expressive power of Concurrent Clean to the simple but effective dynamic scheduling of ZAPP.

21.4.1 Using ZAPP to execute concurrent Clean

CCOZ is implemented on a network of Transputers each of which executes a number of rewriting engines (called reducers) which rewrite subgraphs of the data graph (i.e. the tasks), using the rewrite rules of a program. The high-level management of these reducers (for example creation, communication and load balancing decisions) is performed by a CCOZ kernel. Each Transputer runs a single copy of the kernel. Low-level management of reducers (for example timeslicing and synchronization) is left to the Transputer itself, which directly supports such operations.

At the start of a computation, rewriting is initially performed by a single special reducer executing on a Transputer which has access to the outside world. This special reducer differs from other reducers in that it evaluates the initial data graph to normal form, printing out results as they are generated. Any reducers created during the execution of the program, other than the initial reducer, reduce their tasks to *root normal form* (RNF). Within a single reducer, rewriting is performed using fast sequential code on a single processor. If the program executed contains no task creation annotations then rewriting to normal form is performed entirely sequentially by this normalizing reducer.

Occasionally, as a result of reducing a redex with a rule containing process annotations, a reducer will spawn new tasks, specified as subgraphs to be evaluated to RNF. New reducers will be created to perform these tasks. Tasks are assigned to reducers (scheduled) for execution by the CCOZ kernel code which follows a depth first scheduling strategy (last in first out).

A FIXED annotation leads to a new reducer on the same processor which shares memory with the parent reducer. A MOBILE annotation may lead to a new reducer being established on a different processor, and (in the worst case) a copy of the relevant subgraph being taken.

Tasks marked as MOBILE can be transferred from one Transputer to another (ie. offloaded) by the CCOZ kernel to achieve load balancing. The load balancing mechanism employed is simple: CCOZ kernels request tasks from neighbors when they have too few according to a simple heuristic which, from previous experiments [MS87] appears to work well.

All communication between Transputers is by message passing and is performed through the CCOZ kernels. A subgraph (that is, the graph to be evaluated as a separate task) is copied from Transputer to Transputer in two phases. First, a local copy is taken which compacts the subgraph into contiguous memory locations and uses relative addresses. Next, the compacted copy is communicated to the recipient Transputer.

21.4.2 Representing reducers

The Transputer instruction set contains special provision for processes and process communication via synchronized point-to-point channels. For this series of experiments we decided to implement reducers as real Transputer processes, and to use the Transputer's scheduling and communication mechanisms to implement the synchronization of reducers.

This differs from the early ZAPP experiments, which used a single Transputer process to handle all the virtual subtrees running within a single Transputer.

Our choice was made mainly to explore the potential of the Transputer's support for processes rather than any definite quantitative argument.

21.4.3 Sequential rewriting code

The majority of code executed by a reducer is concerned with sequentially rewriting its task to RNF. The sequential rewriting code implements an abstract machine model similar to the G-machine [Aug84]. We assume the reader is familiar with this type of abstract machine, and also has some understanding of the architecture of the Transputer. The model uses a single stack and heap, as opposed to the three stacks and one heap of the G-machine and PABC machine. The heap is used to store a representation of the data graph. The stack holds return addresses and the arguments of rules (both pointers to heap nodes and basic unboxed values). The stack also performs an optimizing role by acting as a graph node cache for the heap.

The rewrite rules of the Concurrent Clean program are compiled into functions consisting of a matching section and a rewriting section. The matching part of a function tries to match parts of the data graph against the left hand side pattern of the related rewrite rule. On successful matching the rewriting code rewrites the matching piece of graph according to the right hand side pattern of the rule. The order in which matching and hence rewriting is performed, is determined by the reduction strategy which for Concurrent Clean is the pattern driven functional rewriting strategy of lazy functional languages.

An important objective of the compiler is to generate code which avoids constructing graphs in the heap whenever possible, using the stack instead. This optimization benefits greatly from using information on the strictness of rules ie. which arguments of a rule are always evaluated in evaluating the rule. All rules, whether user-defined or delta rules, which produce a result of basic type (integer, Boolean and so on) leave the unboxed result on top of the stack, instead of a pointer to the boxed result. Every rule with strict arguments which have a basic type expects to be invoked with the actual parameters, corresponding to those arguments, unboxed on the stack.

21.4.4 CCOZ element components

The major components of each CCOZ Processing Element implemented on a Transputer are a heap, rewriting and system code, reducers, task pools for pending, fixed and mobile tasks, a CCOZ kernel, and input and output processes. The heap is shared by all the reducers within an element and contains a representation of the data graph. All code is similarly shared. See figure 21.1. Note that the Transputers' scheduling lists corresponds to the ZAPP Fixed pool i.e. contains those tasks that are executing. Blocked tasks are attached to the program graph, at the root node of the graph of the task whose result they require. Note that there are two pools for pending tasks (one for pending tasks produced by the MOBILE annotation in the Concurrent Clean program and one for those tasks produced by the FIXED annotation), since only mobile pending tasks can be offloaded. Concurrent Clean only allows mobile tasks to be offloaded and the ZAPP mechanisms only offload those tasks that have not yet started executing.

Space prohibits detailed descriptions of the component processes in CCOZ. These may be found in [McB93]. The remarks below give some flavor of the mechanisms used.

REDUCER PROCESSES

Each reducer is implemented as a low priority process, with the reducer's stack implemented as the process's workspace. Memory is partitioned into two areas, one for the processes' workspace, and one for a shared heap. Garbage collection is done using a two space copying collector.

LOAD SHARING POLICY

Each kernel uses a very simple load sharing policy. When the number of tasks in its local task pools is below a threshold, and the number of reducers in its active set (the set of reducers which are ready to run but waiting their turn in the scheduling list of the Transputer) is also below threshold, it requests work from neighboring kernels. The neighbors can respond by offloading a task to the kernel's processor, or by refusing the request. An offloaded task is scheduled for evaluation immediately that it arrives at its destination. Once offloaded, a task can not be offloaded again. The heuristic used to decide whether to offload a task is simple; if the number of tasks in the pending mobile task pool is greater than a threshold, a task can be offloaded. Mobile tasks are selected for offloading according to a FIFO strategy. The threshold values used in each of the heuristics are small constants.

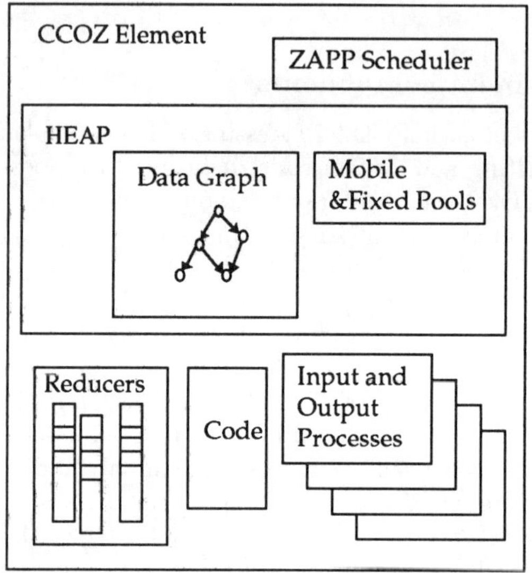

Figure 21.1 Schematic diagram of CCOZ kernel components

OFFLOADING AND INTER-PROCESSOR COPYING

The kernel code for offloading a mobile task makes appropriate housekeeping modifications to the graph, and initiates a copying process. This begins by making a local copy with relative, instead of absolute, addressing. An inter-processor transfer activity is then scheduled which results in some portion of the graph being established on the target processor. Depending on the task annotations inside the subgraph, this might be the whole subgraph, or at the other extreme, just the root node. The target processor then schedules a new reducer on the copied subgraph.

21.4.5 Creating tasks

New tasks are created by rewriting a redex with a rule containing task annotations. We will describe task creation using the full mechanism of CCOZ distributed graph reduction, although in practice heavy optimizations take place. An important optimization is that a reducer can pre-empt task creation. That is, if a graph is to be reduced as a separate task, and an already executing reducer demands the result of that task, if the task is not already scheduled for execution then the demanding reducer can go ahead with reducing the needed graph itself and the unexecuted task is removed from the pending pool. See [McB93] for further details. The full details of distributed graph reduction are complex, and we mention only some aspects below.

All reducers on a CCOZ element share the same heap and so can share parts of the data graph. Hence a subgraph annotated as a separate task may be available to several reducers. In order to prevent the duplication of work, when a subgraph is to be evaluated as a new task, special indirection nodes are inserted at the root of that subgraph. Reducers that need to use the annotated graph have to access the graph through the special indirection node and this allows us to implement synchronization for the reducers by associating particular actions with these special indirection nodes. Creating a task involves three operations:

a. construct the subgraph annotated as a task,
b. insert a special indirection node at the root of the subgraph,
c. add a task descriptor to the appropriate task pool.

The task descriptor refers to the root of the subgraph that is to be evaluated as a separate task. Thus, the reducer assigned to the task by the CCOZ kernel can get to the actual subgraph directly. Other reducers referencing the task annotated subgraph have to go through the special indirection node.

There are two types of special indirection node used as the root of tasks. The two types are called Defer (D_) and Defer_Copy (D_C). D_ nodes are used at the root of fixed tasks created by the FIXED annotation, whilst D_C nodes are used at the root of mobile tasks created by MOBILE annotation. Defer and Defer_Copy nodes contain Transputer channels, which are the method of synchronization and communication for the reducers.

The Defer and Defer_Copy nodes prevent the graph below the Defer or Defer_Copy node being shared or copied until that graph is in RNF (although there can be multiple references to the Defer or Defer_Copy node). Thus only the reducer directly assigned the task can reduce a graph rooted by a Defer or Defer_Copy node. The referential transparency of Concurrent Clean means that we only need to reduce a subgraph once, even if that subgraph is referenced several times. The Defer and Defer_Copy nodes enforce this. A reducer that tries to use a Defer or Defer_Copy node is demanding the reduced result of the graph rooted by the Defer or Defer_Copy node.

When a reducer comes across a Defer node, it suspends itself in a list on that node. When the reducer that is scheduled to reduce the subgraph below the Defer node finishes the reduction, the Defer node is converted into an (ordinary) indirection to the result graph and the reducers suspended on the Defer node are awoken. These are now free to access the result of the reduction. Hence, only one reducer will reduce the graph and other reducers simply use the result of the reduction.

Defer_Copy nodes act in a similar way, except that they are placed at the root of mobile tasks. Defer_Copy nodes indicate that the task is being evaluated on a remote processor and the result graph must be copied back from that processor. A reducer demanding the result of an offloaded mobile task is suspended in a list attached to the Defer_Copy node until the result graph is available in RNF. Once the result is available in RNF, it is copied back to the CCOZ element that offloaded the task. Deadlock is avoided since offloaded tasks are immediately scheduled for evaluation. Note that copying of the result is on demand, that is, the result of an offloaded task is only copied back to the offloading CCOZ element when the Defer_Copy node is accessed by a reducer. If the result were in RNF on a remote processor and yet not demanded, it would remain on the remote processor. If a mobile task is scheduled locally, the Defer_Copy node at the root of the task's graph is in effect converted to a Defer node when the task is scheduled.

For example, consider the following rewriting rules for computing the Nfib function:

```
Nfib(0) -> 1
Nfib(n) -> 1+Nfib(n-1)+Nfib(n-2)
```

Nfib is a modified version of the Fibonacci function: its value is the number of calls of Nfib required for evaluation in a naive implementation. This is true for 1, and inductively true for $n > 1$. If the time taken to evaluate **Nfib(n)** is t_n seconds, then the number of function calls per second (f.c.p.s.) is $Nfib(n)/t_n$.

The obvious way to exploit parallelism for Nfib is to evaluate the subexpression **Nfib(n-1)** in parallel with the subexpression **Nfib(n-2)**. This is expressed in the following Concurrent Clean version of the second of the rules above, in which the subexpression **Nfib(n-1)** is marked with a MOBILE annotation. Note that {M} is shorthand in Concurrent Clean for the MOBILE annotation and that {F} is shorthand for the FIXED annotation.

```
Nfib n -> ++I (+I (Nfib (-I n 2)) {M}(Nfib (-I n 1)))
```

The code for the RHS of the rule begins by creating a task for the subgraph **{M}(Nfib (-I n 1))**. First the subgraph **(Nfib (-I n 1))** is constructed, then a D_C node is inserted at the root of the constructed graph, and finally a new task descriptor record is added to the mobile task pool. When the housekeeping which will lead to parallel execution is complete, the code for the remainder of the rule is executed. This will lead to the evaluation of the other subexpression **(Nfib (-I n 2))** using a procedure call rather than process creation. Marking both subexpressions with {M} would lead to more parallel, but slower, code.

21.4.6 Copying tasks

When a rule containing task annotations is used to rewrite the graph, all the tasks specified in that rule are created at the same time. Thus a rule such as

```
J a b -> {M}G(a,{F}H(b))
```

will create two tasks (one mobile and one fixed) on the CCOZ element that used the rule. This task creation is performed before any reduction of the contractum graph is performed.

Previously, it was stated that offloading a task results in some portion of the subgraph representing that task being sent to another processor. We are now able to expand on this notion, using the above example. As can easily be seen, a complete copy of the graph rooted by the {M} annotation includes the subgraph rooted by the {F} annotation. Thus, a complete copy would duplicate the fixed task (since the offloading CCOZ element already has a task descriptor for the fixed task). When offloading the mobile task, we want to avoid implicitly copying the fixed task.

We therefore introduce some special procedure for copying Defer and Defer_Copy nodes, since these special indirections are at the roots of subgraphs to be reduced as separate tasks. When we have to offload a task, we do not want to copy any subgraphs of that task's graph that are rooted by Defer or Defer_Copy nodes i.e. that are tasks themselves. Instead, when making the local copy of a task's graph for offloading, if a Defer or Defer_Copy node is encountered, an new type of indirection to the original Defer (Defer_Copy) node is placed into the copy, indicating where on the offloading CCOZ element the Defer (Defer_Copy) node is. This new type of indirection is called a Defer_Force_Copy node. Copying does not progress below the Defer (Defer_Copy) node. Should a Defer_Force_Copy node be encountered in the original graph during the copying process, a new Defer_Force_Copy node referencing the Defer_Force_Copy in the original graph is placed in the copy. Copying does not progress below the original Defer_Force_Copy. Thus, chains of indirections can be built up, spanning several processors as work is diffused to other processors. This copy of the original graph, with its inter-processor references, is what is offloaded.

On the receiving CCOZ element, the offloaded task's graph is reduced as normal. However, when the reducer encounters one of the Defer_Force_Copy nodes, a message is sent to the CCOZ element that is referenced by the indirection, asking for a copy of the graph that it refers to. The reducer then suspends reduction until the graph is available. Depending on what the root node of the graph referenced by the inter-processor indirection is, a task is created to copy the graph back to the demanding processor. Defer (Defer_Copy) nodes on the offloading processor behave as normal and will allow a copy of the required graph to be taken only when it is in RNF (since we do not wish to duplicate tasks). However, if the subgraph requested through a inter-processor indirection is not yet scheduled for reduction, the processor that holds the requested graph is forced to schedule it there and then. Since the Defer (Defer_Copy) node on the offloading processor will correspond to a task annotation, the requested graph may have already been scheduled for reduction.

However, if an Defer_Force_Copy node refers to another Defer_Force_Copy node, then a task is created to get the graph referred to by the second Defer_Force_Copy node and then copy it back to the first demanding processor. The reason for the existence of chains of indirections is that work may diffuse over the whole machine, and yet CCOZ elements only communicate with their immediate neighbors. Thus, for a processor to use the result of a task executed on a processor not its neighbor requires a chain of indirections through adjacent processors, from the demanding processor to the processor that evaluated the task. Hence, demanding the result of an indirection always results in the creation of a task on the processor the indirection refers to, either to get the result of a task on that processor or to get that processor to copy a graph from another processor.

Thus for the example rule above, if both tasks were created on CCOZ element A, and the mobile task offloaded to CCOZ element B, the offloaded task references the data graph on CCOZ element A at the root of the fixed task.

The scheme detailed above for copying graphs for offloading also applies to the copying of result graphs (e.g. the situation when a reducer suspends on a Defer_Copy node). Thus, any subgraphs of a result graph rooted by Defer, Defer_Copy or inter-processor indirection nodes are not copied until they are in RNF and are demanded by another reducer. Again, the reason is to prevent duplication of work.

This means task annotations (specifically {F}) can be used to prevent the copying of redexes in result graphs and hence their duplication. A result graph can be copied as soon as it is in RNF and it has been demanded; yet there may be further redexes inside that graph. Thus, the result graph of a mobile task may bring unevaluated redexes back to its parent task. This copying of redexes can be unnecessary, since we could first evaluate the redexes and copy the results. Annotating such redexes as fixed tasks prevents useless copying, since the tasks cannot be copied as the {F} annotation inserts a Defer node. That is, if a offloaded task creates child fixed processes, these fixed processes remain on the CCOZ element that the parent task was offloaded to, until they are in RNF.

Full details of the copy scheme are described in [McB93].

21.4.7 Dynamic control of parallelism

Task creation is a relatively expensive operation, which we would like to avoid when there is little to be gained. When all processors are busy, and there is plenty of work in each task pool, there is little point in generating new tasks. Mechanisms which govern the exploitation of parallelism at run-time are sometimes called *throttling* mechanisms.

The elementary ZAPP architecture already contains some important throttling mechanisms. First, the depth first scheduling of tasks in the process tree restricts the number of tasks created at any given instant to a linear function of the tree depth. Second, ZAPP may decide to execute a task locally rather than offloading it to another processor. The first mechanism prevents an exponential growth with tree depth of the number of tasks in the pending pools. The second mechanism does not prevent task creation, but at least ensures that fast sequential execution using pointer sharing can be used instead of invoking offloading and graph copying mechanisms.

Throttling is not to be confused with eliminating tasks based on grain size. Grain size relates to the amount of work that can be done in a task, compared to the cost of creating that task. A task can pass the grain size test by having a large grain size and still fail the throttling test because all processing elements are busy and have adequate reserves of work in their task pools. Throttling requires information about loading which cannot easily be predicted at compile time, and so must be collected at run time.

CCOZ adds two new forms of throttling to those present in ZAPP. The idea is to generate two versions of code for each rule group which contains task annotations. The parallel version of the code will create tasks as indicated by the annotations in the rule group. The fast sequential version ignores the task annotations while compiling the code. At run-time the CCOZ kernel decides whether to use the parallel version or the sequential version.

This approach we have adopted for throttling means that all task annotations in a member of a rule group are either ignored or acted upon en masse. Annotations in the contractum of a rule member are not treated individually.

The heuristic function used in throttling is a simple threshold test. If the number of mobile tasks in the mobile list exceeds a small constant, the version of the code which does not spawn tasks is entered, otherwise the version which does spawn tasks is used. Throttling can be turned on or off as an option to the compiler.

The second throttling mechanism added by CCOZ is the task pre-emption scheme as mentioned in the section 21.4.5. Here although task creation is not avoided, the scheduling of a new task is avoided if the task to be performed by the new task can be safely done by an existing task. Thus we avoid interleaving tasks in some cases.

21.5 RESULTS

Below we present some of the results produced by a prototype of the CCOZ implementation. The results of experiments on a single Transputer running CCOZ are given first, followed by the results for multi-Transputer experiments.

21.5.1 Sequential results

Table 21.1 gives performance results of the prototype implementation with a single CCOZ kernel running on a single 20MHz T800 with 2MB of memory. Times are in seconds. The programs are all sequential versions.

Function	**Description**	**Result**
Nfib	$n = 30$	222165 f.c.s.
Naive Reverse	200 long list, 200 times	143 seconds
10 Queens		62.9 seconds
Quicksort	2000 elements	2.3 seconds

Table 21.1 Absolute performance of a CCOZ kernel on one Transputer

These figures give some indication of the absolute performance of a CCOZ kernel on a single Transputer. The raw function calls per second for NFib are impressive compared with earlier experiments using more direct methods.

21.5.2 Parallel results

The parallel programs bring into consideration the cost of creating and managing reducers and also the cost of copying graphs.

FUNCTION CALLS PER SECOND

This figure was measured using the following Concurrent Clean program for the Nfib function:

```
Start  -> Nfib 30;
Nfib 0 -> 1 |
Nfib 1 -> 1 |
Nfib n -> ++I (+I {M}(Nfib (--I n)) (Nfib (-I n 2)));
```

Runs took place using 1, 8 and 16 Transputers, with throttling turned on and turned off. The results are shown in table 21.2. The first column shows the number of CCOZ elements running in parallel. The second column shows whether or not throttling was used. The third column shows the runtime in seconds. The fourth column gives the observed performance as the number of function calls per second, and the final column shows the speedup.

Procs.	Thr.	t(secs)	f.c.p.s.	Speedup
1	off	29.79	90,370	1
1	on	13.06	206,036	1
8	off	3.89	692,582	7.66
8	on	1.81	1,490,818	7.24
16	off	2.01	1,340,563	14.83
16	on	1.04	2,601,465	12.63

Table 21.2 Function calls per second vs processors with and without throttling

PROGRAMMING CONTROL OVER GRAIN SIZE

The *granularity* of a task is important, especially in a system such has been described above. If a task takes longer to create or copy to another processor than it does to evaluate, then its granularity is small and it is a poor candidate for offloading.

Nfib is a good example of a problem with very fine grain size. However, we can write a version of Nfib which avoids creating small grains of work. This technique of programming out fine-grain tasks is illustrated by the following Concurrent Clean program:

```
TYPE
::T a ::= Constr a CHAR ;
GRS
Start -> Constr (Nfib 30) '\n';
Nfib 0 -> 1 |
Nfib 1 -> 1 |
Nfib n -> IF (<I n 15) (Snfib n) (Pnfib n) ;
Pnfib {!}n -> ++I (+I {M}(Nfib (--I n)) (Nfib (-I n 2))) ;
Snfib 0 -> 1 |
Snfib 1 -> 1 |
Snfib n -> ++I (+I (Snfib (--I n)) (Snfib (-I n 2))) ;
```

Table 21.3 summarizes the results of running this version of the Nfib program on 1, 8 and 16 Transputers with throttling turned on. Eliminating small grains from consideration as tasks improves the absolute performance of the program compared to the previous version, and for the 16 processor case the relative speedup is also improved.

Procs.	t(secs)	f.c.p.s.	Speedup
1	12.13	221,939	1
8	1.69	1,591,966	7.17
16	0.887	3,036,294	13.68

Table 21.3 Function calls vs processors with variable grain programming

QUEENS

The parallel Queens program in Appendix 1 was developed from a program described in [LV91]. The results of running this program are summarized in table 21.4. Note that throttling is turned off for these results. Grain-size control built into the program appears to eliminate the need for throttling for this program.

Procs.	t(secs)	Speedup
1	63.33	1
8	9.84	6.44
16	5.91	10.72

Table 21.4 Parallel queens performance

MATRIX MULTIPLICATION

Table 21.5 summarizes the results for a matrix multiplication program which forms the product of two 64x64 matrices. The times include the constant (unparallelizable) time taken to build the matrices initially.

Procs.	t(secs)	Speedup
1	5.79	1
8	1.67	3.41
16	1.5	3.87

Table 21.5 Matrix multiplication performance

21.6 CONCLUSIONS

A detailed scheme for programming and implementing parallel graph rewriting code has been briefly described, and some performance figures reported.

The raw function call rate for Nfib (about 221 939 fc/s per Transputer) and other simple functions is encouraging: even without the use of "grain control programming", the performance is already very much better than the figures for the original hand coded ZAPP experiments. Part of the improvement is due to significant advances in sequential compiler technology for graph rewriting. Some may be due to the direct use of process handling instructions in the Transputer.

For Nfib, good relative and absolute speedups were observed, and the use of programmable grain control provided a means of further improving performance.

For Queens and Matrix Multiply useful relative speedups were observed although there is clearly room for improvement. Both these applications involve data structure copying during offloading, and there is more work to do in this area.

It should be noted that the speedup factors for parallel results are affected by the use of the Transputer's fast on-chip memory. Parallel programs are forced to use external memory to hold many of the reducers' stacks and this slows the program down. However, if a parallel program is executed on *one* Transputer, the throttling mechanisms mean that it runs in an almost sequential fashion and thus most of its stack requirements can be allocated from the Transputer's on-chip memory. If the single Transputer parallel experiments are executed using external memory for the reducers stack, then there is a speedup factor of 13 for the 16 Transputer 10 Queens program and for Matrix Multiply on 8 and 16 Transputers, the speedup is 4.25 and 5.06 respectively.

Finally, our examples have illustrated the expressive power of the MOBILE and FIXED annotations ({M} and {F}). We also illustrated how the programmer could achieve considerable control of the grain size of offloaded work. This is particularly important for effective use of parallelism. While coarse-grain MIMD parallelism can make things go faster, very fine-grain parallelism can make things go much slower.

21.7 APPENDIX 1: PARALLEL QUEENS IN CONCURRENT CLEAN

```
TYPE
::Print a b ::= Constr a b;
GRS
Start -> Constr (Filtr (ParQueens 0 Nil)) '\n';
Filtr Nil -> 0 |
Filtr (Cons a b) -> Filtr b ;
Append Nil {!}x -> x |
Append (Cons x xs) ys -> Cons x (Append xs ys);
ParQueens 10 sub -> Cons sub Nil |
ParQueens 3 sub -> Loop 3 sub 1 |
ParQueens n sub -> Divide 10 1 10 n sub ;
Divide 0 {!}a {!}b n sub -> ParExtend n sub a |
Divide r a b n sub
-> Append {M}(Divide (-I a b1) a b1 n sub)
          {M}(Divide (-I a1 b) a1 b n sub) ,
          b1:/I (+I a b) 2, a1: ++I b1 ;
Queens 10 sub -> Cons sub Nil |
Queens n sub -> Loop n sub 1 ;
Loop n sub 11 -> Nil |
Loop n sub x -> Append (Extend n sub x) (Loop n sub (++I x)) ;
Extend n sub q -> IF (Safe 1 q sub)
  (Queens (++I n) (Cons q sub))
  Nil ;
ParExtend n sub q -> IF (Safe 1 q sub)
  (ParQueens (++I n) (Cons q sub))
  Nil ;
Safe {!}d q (Cons x xs) -> IF (AND  (<>I q x)
```

```
        (AND (<>I (Abs (-I q x)) d)
            (Safe (++I d) q xs)))
      TRUE
      FALSE |
Safe d q Nil -> TRUE ;
Abs {!}a -> IF (<I a 0) (*I -1 a) a;
```

REFERENCES

[Aug84] L. Augustsson. A compiler for Lazy ML. In *ACM Symposium on Lisp and Functional Programming*, 1984.

[BS82] F.W. Burton and M.R. Sleep. Executing functional programs on a virtual tree of processors. In *ACM Conference on Functional Programming Languages and Computer Architecture*, 1982.

[LV91] K.G. Langendoen and W.G. Vree. *Eight Queens Divided: an Experience in Parallel Functional Programming.* Technical Report TR CS-91-03, Dept. Computer Science, Univ. Amsterdam, 1991.

[McB93] D.L. McBurney. *Experiments with a Virtual Tree Architecture.* PhD thesis, UEA, School of Information Systems, Norwich, 1993.

[MS87] D.L. McBurney and M.R. Sleep. Transputer based experiments with the ZAPP architecture. In J.W.de Bakker, A.J. Nijman, and P.C. Treleaven (editors), *PARLE: Parallel Architectures and Languages Europe, vol I*, Springer-Verlag, Lecture Notes in Computer Science 259, pp. 242–256, 1987.

[MS89] D.L. McBurney and M.R. Sleep. Graph rewriting as a computational model. In A. Yonezawa and T. Ito (editors), *Concurrency: Theory, Language and Architecture*, Springer-Verlag, Lecture Notes in Computer Science 491, pp. 235–256, 1989.

[NPS91] E.G.J.M.H. Nöcker, M.J. Plasmeijer, and S. Smetsers. *The Parallel ABC Machine.* Technical Report Technical Report 91.07, Dept. Computing, Univ. of Southampton, 1991.

[NSvEP91] E.G.J.M.H. Nöcker, S. Smetsers, M.C. van Eekelen, and M.J. Plasmeijer. Concurrent Clean. In E.H.L. Aarts, J. van Leeuwen, and M. Rem (editors), *PARLE'91, Parallel Architectures and Languages Europe, vol I*, Springer-Verlag, Lecture Notes in Computer Science 506, 1991.

22

Graph-based Operational Semantics of a Lazy Functional Language

Kristoffer H. Rose

22.1 INTRODUCTION

This chapter proposes the use of term graph rewriting (TGR) as the basis for the specification formalism *graph operational semantics* (GOS) intended for lazy functional programming languages. We demonstrate how GOS is a compromise between theory and practice, i.e., formal solidity desirable in the design process, the detail required for implementation, and the compactness convenient for users, by using it to specify BAWL featuring the operational aspects of the language used in the standard text book *Introduction to Functional Programming* by Bird and Wadler [BW88].

But first we summarize BAWL and explain how it is susceptible to TGR; then we briefly sketch the background of this work before presenting an overview of the remainder of the chapter.

22.1.1 BAWL—a generic lazy functional programming language

Although it is not particularly large, *BAWL is not a toy language.* Consequently, we will not aim for a complete specification of all build-in operators, types, etc. of BAWL here, but just give an overview of the features particularly relevant to graph reduction.

Figure 22.1 shows a BAWL version of the "quicksort" algorithm as found in [BW88], and a list of integers to sort—thus evaluating the program should print the result list "$[1, 2, 3, 4, 5, 6, 7, 8]$". To be precise, the program defines and uses the function *sort* with a local definition of the infix list concatenation operator $+\!\!+$, assumes standard infix $<$

Term Graph Rewriting: Theory and Practice.
Eds. Ronan Sleep, Rinus Plasmeijer and Marko van Eekelen.

$$
\begin{array}{l}
sort\ [\,] \qquad\quad = [\,] \\
sort\ (x : xs) = sort\ [\,u \mid u \leftarrow xs; u < x\,] +\!\!+ [x] +\!\!+ sort\ [\,u \mid u \leftarrow xs; u \geq x\,] \\
\qquad\qquad\quad \textbf{where} \quad [\,] +\!\!+ ys \qquad\ = ys \\
\qquad\qquad\qquad\qquad\ (x : xs) +\!\!+ ys = x : (xs +\!\!+ ys) \\
?\ sort\ [2,4,6,8,7,5,3,1]
\end{array}
$$

Figure 22.1 Quicksort in BAWL

and $\geq$ relations over the standard mumeric type, constructors [] and infix : for lists of numbers, as well as standard list notation, notably "list comprehensions", i.e., the $[\,\_\mid\_\,]$ notation described in section 3.2 of [BW88] (originally called "ZF-expressions" in [Tur82]).

But we will not be concerned with such details here. Instead we will follow tradition and specify BAWL by giving a "Core BAWL" subset that is sufficiently powerful that all BAWL programs may be translated into it *linearly*, i.e., without duplication of code, and that has all the features that we wish to specify semantically. So Core BAWL is not a "low-level" language in the usual sense—in particular it includes full pattern matching. The only true simplification is that Core BAWL is *untyped* (to avoid the need for a static semantics): it just allows an unspecified set of constructors (each with a certain arity) and two special pattern forms for matching constructors. The first, $!x$, will only match arguments in head normal form (HNF), i.e., arguments where the root is on a form that is not evaluable (it may be a constructor or an application with insufficient arguments). This can be used to code the function *strict* of [BW88] as $strict\ f\ !x = f\ x$. The second, $(!!\ \_\ldots\_)$, will match any constructor value with components matching the individual $\_\ldots\_$ and can be used to code the *seq* function (using ; as a line delimiter): $seq\ (!!)\ x = x$; $seq\ (!!\ x_1)\ x = seq\ x_1\ x$; $seq\ (!!\ x_1\ x_2)\ x = seq\ x_1\ (seq\ x_2\ x)$, ... up to any finite constructor arity.

DEFINITION **22.1.1** *Let I range over the identifiers $\mathcal{I}$ and C over the constructors $\mathcal{C}$. The* Core BAWL programs *are defined inductively as follows ($X\ldots X$ means zero or more Xs):*

$$
\begin{array}{llcl}
\textit{Core BAWL program}: & B & ::= & \begin{array}{l} S \\ ?\ E \end{array} \\[1ex]
\textit{Script}: & S & ::= & \begin{array}{l} D \\ \vdots \\ D \end{array} \\[1ex]
\textit{Definition}: & D & ::= & \begin{array}{l} I\ P\ldots P\ =\ E\ \textbf{where}\ S \\ \vdots \\ I\ P\ldots P\ =\ E\ \textbf{where}\ S \end{array} \\[1ex]
\textit{Pattern}: & P & ::= & I \mid\ !I \mid (\,!!\ P\ldots P\,) \mid (\,C\ P\ldots P\,) \\
\textit{Expression}: & E & ::= & I \mid (\,C\ E\ldots E\,) \mid (\,E\ E\ldots E\,)
\end{array}
$$

where (1) the $I\ P\ldots P$ of each D should have the same I and number of Ps and (2) each C should be followed by the same number of Ps and Es everywhere.

In the rest of this chapter we will refer to this subset simply as BAWL; readers doubting that *sort* above can in fact be expressed in it may find the translation in figure 22.2 (a thorough explanation of the kind of translations we have used is given in chapter 3, 5, and 7 of Peyton Jones's book [PJ87]). The only variation is that we compile guards and tests into pattern matching rather than vice versa (the details may be found in [Ros92b, Ros91]).

$$
\begin{array}{l}
\mathit{sort}\ [\,] \quad = [\,] \ \ \textbf{where} \\
\mathit{sort}\ ((:)\ x\ xs) = ((+\!\!+)\ (\mathit{sort}\ (\mathit{cont}\ xs))\ ((+\!\!+)\ ((:)\ x\ [\,])\ (\mathit{sort}\ (\mathit{cont}'\ xs)))) \\
\quad \textbf{where}\ \ (+\!\!+)\ [\,]\ ys = ys \ \ \textbf{where} \\
\qquad\qquad (+\!\!+)\ ((:)\ x\ xs)\ ys = ((:)\ x\ ((+\!\!+)\ xs\ ys)) \ \ \textbf{where} \\
\qquad\qquad \mathit{cont}\ [\,] = [\,] \ \ \textbf{where} \\
\qquad\qquad \mathit{cont}\ ((:)\ u\ \mathit{rest}) = \mathit{res} \\
\qquad\qquad\quad \textbf{where}\ \ \mathit{res} = (\mathit{tmp}\ ((<)\ u\ x)) \\
\qquad\qquad\qquad\qquad \textbf{where}\ \ \mathit{tmp}\ \mathit{True} = ((:)\ u\ e') \ \ \textbf{where} \\
\qquad\qquad\qquad\qquad\qquad\quad \mathit{tmp}\ \mathit{False} = e' \ \ \textbf{where} \\
\qquad\qquad\qquad\quad e' = (\mathit{cont}\ \mathit{rest}) \ \ \textbf{where} \\
\qquad\qquad \mathit{cont}\ ((:)\ p\ \mathit{rest}) = (\mathit{cont}\ \mathit{rest}) \ \ \textbf{where} \\
\qquad\qquad \mathit{cont}'\ [\,] = [\,] \ \ \textbf{where} \\
\qquad\qquad \mathit{cont}'\ ((:)\ u\ \mathit{rest}) = \mathit{res} \\
\qquad\qquad\quad \textbf{where}\ \ \mathit{res} = (\mathit{tmp}\ ((\geq)\ u\ x)) \\
\qquad\qquad\qquad\qquad \textbf{where}\ \ \mathit{tmp}\ \mathit{True} = ((:)\ u\ e') \\
\qquad\qquad\qquad\qquad\qquad\quad \mathit{tmp}\ \mathit{False} = e' \\
\qquad\qquad\qquad\quad e' = (\mathit{cont}'\ \mathit{rest}) \ \ \textbf{where} \\
\qquad\qquad \mathit{cont}'\ ((:)\ p\ \mathit{rest}) = (\mathit{cont}'\ \mathit{rest}) \ \ \textbf{where} \\
?\ (\mathit{sort}\ ((:)\ 2\ ((:)\ 4\ ((:)\ 6\ ((:)\ 8\ ((:)\ 7\ ((:)\ 5\ ((:)\ 3\ ((:)\ 1\ [\,])))))))))
\end{array}
$$

Figure 22.2 Core BAWL version of *sort*

22.1.2 Evaluation of BAWL expressions by TGR

The top drawing of figure 22.3 depicts the term graph representation of the BAWL expression

$$
[1] +\!\!+ [2] \ \ \textbf{where} \ \ \begin{array}{lcl} [\,] +\!\!+ ys & = & ys \\ (x : xs) +\!\!+ ys & = & x : (xs +\!\!+ ys) \end{array}
$$

that we might need to evaluate during the execution of the *sort* program above (ignore the dotted lines for now). Each of the numbered nodes in the graph represents a subterm of the kind indicated by its label: The @-nodes denote application of a function to some arguments; Λ_2-nodes have the alternative (uniform) equations as subgraphs; and λ-nodes have the LHS and RHS (i.e., the left- and right-hand sides) of a single equation as left and right subgraphs[1] where ▪ denotes the position of the function itself.

The main difference between this representation and a traditional abstract syntax tree is that *variables are represented by pointers to their value*; in particular unbound variables are represented by pointers to the ?-node in the representation of the LHS where the variable is defined. For example, in the first equation the variable *ys* is represented by node *15*, in the second *x* is represented by node *20*, *xs* by *21*, and *ys* by *22*. This has the interesting property that *there is no distinction between binding and*

[1] The use of λ for this purpose is historical; = or even $\Rightarrow$ would be more appropriate for BAWL.

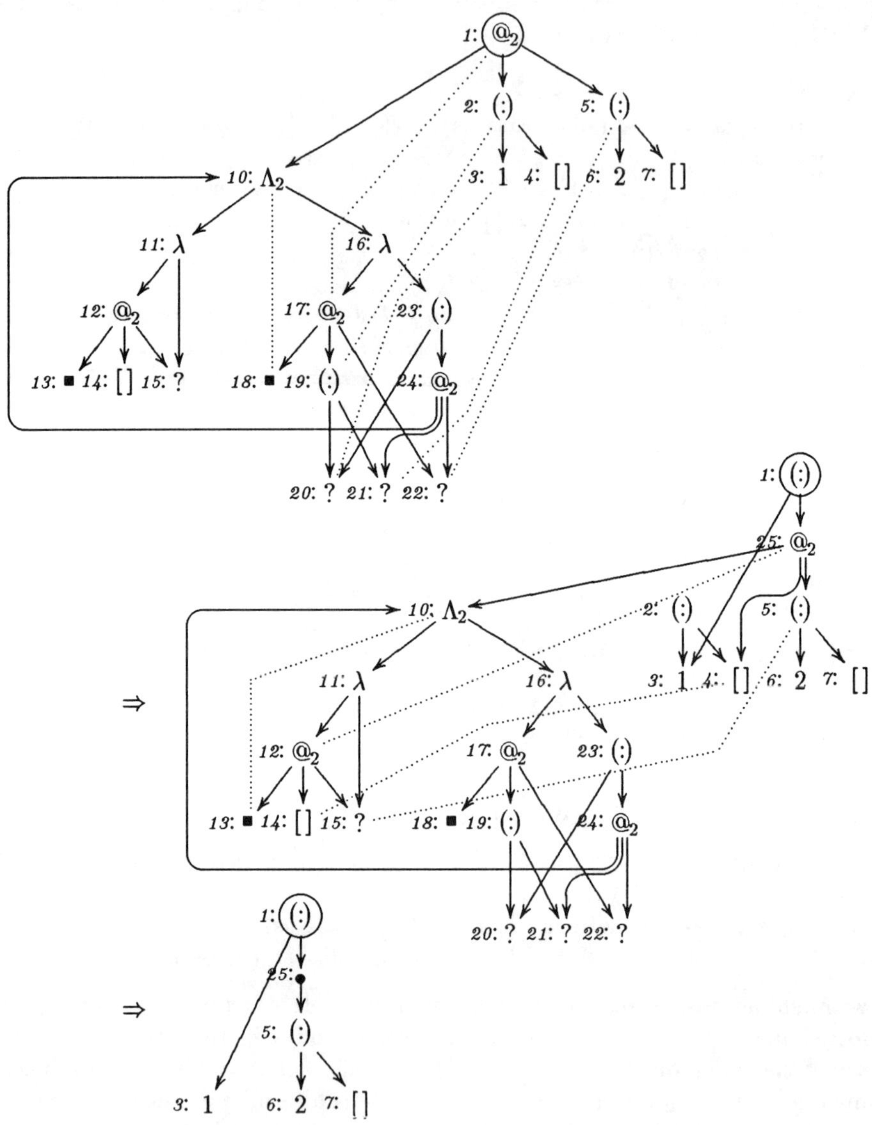

Figure 22.3 Term graph representation, matching, and reduction of BAWL expression

other forms of access to values. This is a crucial property that allows a much more uniform definition of suspensions, sharing, etc. as we shall see, by eliminating the need for auxiliary structure like environments and stores.

We want to reduce the application—so we compare the two LHS subgraphs (at *12* and *17*) with the application itself (at *1*). It is clear that (only) the LHS of the right equation fits: we match *17* to *1*, *18* to *10*, *19* to *2*, *20* to *3*, *21* to *4*, and *22* to *5* as shown by the dotted lines in the top graph; in the original program this corresponds to binding $x = 1$ (by mapping *20* to *3*), $xs = []$ (by mapping *21* to *4*), and $ys = [2]$ (by mapping *22* to *5*). The ▪ is convenient because it makes the comparison simpler.

Reducing an application is the same as replacing it with the body of the function (in this case the RHS at *23*) after substitution of the bound variables with whatever they were bound to. This is accomplished with the middle graph in figure 22.3 where we see how node *1* has been overwritten by a copy of node *23* that points to a fresh node *25*—we have *build new structure* on top of the arguments corresponding to the nodes unique to the RHS; the actual arguments remain shared. Notice how the (:)-node at *2* is no longer referenced by this expression—if it is not referenced from other parts of the graph then it has become garbage to be collected for reuse.

Anyway, there is now a new redex[2] in the graph as indicated by the dotted lines in the middle graph. There is one complication in this case, however: there are no unique nodes in the RHS and thus nothing to overwrite with! One way to solve this is by introducing *indirection nodes*, and this is what we have done in the reduced bottom graph of figure 22.3: node *25* has been overwritten by an indirection (the •) to the corresponding list argument (at *5*) that may thus remain shared. We have taken the liberty of removing the garbage (which includes the entire representation of the ++ function as well as node *2* and *4*) from this last graph.

It is clear that the above reduction captures many aspects of evaluation of lazy functional languages that are difficult to express in most other formalisms. This is the primary motivation for GOS and the subject of this chapter.

22.1.3 Background and related work

This chapter grew out of the desire in the author's thesis [Ros92b] to describe the semantics of graph reduction in lazy functional languages using graphs—even though this is an obvious idea most authors seem to prefer using stores, environment frames, substitutions, etc.

However, the idea has been around since [Wad71] who used it to implement the λ-calculus with acyclic sharing of common subterms. Modeling recursion by cyclic sharing was suggested for data by [Hoa75] and for functions by [Hug82]. This is also where the intuition of why graph reduction provides a useful model for lazy evaluation of functional languages is presented—"just keep all the subexpressions around, updating each to its proper value only as needed"—although it had to some extent been folklore since [McC60] and has been used extensively in implementations of functional languages. Examples are the Functional Abstract Machine [Car83], the G-machine [Joh84, BPJR88], Clean [BvEvLP87, KSvEP91], and DACTL [Ken88, GKS89]. All of these can be perceived as notations for algorithms that describe how graphs may be used to model the evaluation of the implemented language. Such notations have the advantage that they are directly executable. However, they are often not very readable since all the details of the implementation have to be present in the specification.

On the other hand, the idea has also been used in attempts to build models of functional languages and to prove properties of such models directly. Again starting from [Wad71] such attempts are naturally focused on models of the λ-calculus—a

[2] We will use the traditional word "redex" (reducible subexpression) rather than some abbreviation of "reducible sugraph" even though we will always refer to the latter.

rather large area of research, so we will just mention [Sta78] and [Lam90] as inspirational sources.

22.1.4 Overview

In section 22.2 we summarize the necessary TGR concepts in a notation convenient for our use, and we present the "minimal lazy rewrite" theorem that will prove useful later. We then specify the graph representation of BAWL programs in section 22.3 and present GOS by giving the dynamic semantics of BAWL in section 22.4—these two sections together outline a fully lazy operational semantics for BAWL. Finally we briefly discuss applications of GOS.

22.2 TERM GRAPH REWRITING

We briefly summarize term graphs and the notation of this chapter, impose a *match order* on them and define *rewriting* from this. The definitions in this chapter are based on those of [BvEG+87]; readers familiar with that paper (or other chapters in this book) will not find many surprises in this section except perhaps for the declarative definition of rewriting that is a compromise between the axiomatic one used by categorical treatments and the operational one used elsewhere.

We will make use of basic notation for sets, functions, relations, and orderings. In particular: Tuples satisfy $\langle x_1, \ldots, x_k\rangle.i = x_i$. A function $\phi: X \to Y$ has domain $\mathrm{Dm}(\phi)$ and range $\mathrm{Rg}(\phi)$; maps may be written $\{x \mapsto y, \ldots\}$ or even $\{\, x \mapsto y \mid p(x,y)\,\}$; restriction is written $\phi|_X$, and update $\phi[\psi]$ is ϕ updated with the mappings of ψ (so the mappings $\{\, x \mapsto \phi(x) \mid x \in \mathrm{Dm}(\phi) \cap \mathrm{Dm}(\psi)\}$ disappear). N is the set of natural numbers (including 0), and $\mathcal{I}$ is the set of identifiers.

DEFINITION **22.2.1** *Given a set of "labels" $\mathcal{L}$ with an associated "arity" function $\#: \mathcal{L} \to \mathsf{N}$ and a set of "nodeids" $\mathcal{N} = \{1, 2, \ldots\}$. A* term graph $\mathbf{g} \in \mathcal{G}_{\mathcal{L},\#}$ *is a "rooted labeled ordered directed graph", i.e., a structure ($N_\mathbf{g}$, $lab_\mathbf{g}$, $succ_\mathbf{g}$, $r_\mathbf{g}$) where*

$N_\mathbf{g}$	$\subset$	$\mathcal{N}$	the *nodeids*
$lab_\mathbf{g}$	:	$N_\mathbf{g} \to \mathcal{L}$	maps each node to its *label*
$succ_\mathbf{g}$	:	$N_\mathbf{g} \to N_\mathbf{g}^*$	maps each node to its *successor tuple*
$r_\mathbf{g}$	$\in$	$N_\mathbf{g}$	is the *root node*

that respects the label arities, i.e., $\forall n \in N_\mathbf{g} : succ_\mathbf{g} n = \langle n_1, \ldots, n_{\#(lab_\mathbf{g} n)}\rangle$. *We use the abbreviation* $\ell_\mathbf{g} = lab_\mathbf{g} r_\mathbf{g}$.

Note that (term) graphs are not required to be connected—we do not do implicit garbage collection as [BvEG+87] but as shown in that paper this is of no consequence. Graphs always have a connected part containing at least the root node, however: there is no "null graph". Also we only allow one root node in each graph; this can be circumvented by using a dummy root node where only its successors are of interest.

We manipulate (term) graphs using the following operations and concepts, although we will prefer to draw them.

DEFINITION **22.2.2** *a. The* ith successor graph *is* $\mathbf{g}.i = (N_\mathbf{g}, lab_\mathbf{g}, succ_\mathbf{g}, (succ_\mathbf{g} r_\mathbf{g}).i)$.

b. The reachable nodes *are defined by* $reach(\mathbf{g}) = reach'\langle \mathbf{g}, \emptyset \rangle$ *where*

$$\begin{aligned} reach'\langle \mathbf{g}, N\rangle &= \begin{cases} N & \text{if } r_{\mathbf{g}} \in N \\ N_1 \cup \cdots \cup N_k & \text{otherwise} \end{cases} \\ k &= \#\ell_{\mathbf{g}} \\ N_i &= reach'\langle \mathbf{g}.i, N \cup \{r_{\mathbf{g}}\}\rangle \quad \text{for } 1 \le i \le k \end{aligned}$$

c. The garbage collection *of a graph contains only the reachable nodes:* $gc(\mathbf{g}) = (N, lab_{\mathbf{g}}|_N, succ_{\mathbf{g}}|_N, r_{\mathbf{g}})$, *where* $N = reach(\mathbf{g})$. $\mathbf{g}$ *is* connected *iff* $\mathbf{g} = gc(\mathbf{g})$.

d. A (proper) subgraph $\mathbf{g}|n = gc(N, lab_{\mathbf{g}}, succ_{\mathbf{g}}, n)$ *for* $n \in reach(\mathbf{g})$.

e. Rerooting *a graph means "change the root nodeid to something else and 'redirect' all arrows from the old to the new root", defined by* $r{:}\,\mathbf{g} = (N, lab, succ, r)$ *where*

$$\begin{aligned} N &= \{r\} \cup (N_{\mathbf{g}} \setminus \{r_{\mathbf{g}}\}) \\ lab &= lab|_{N_{\mathbf{g}}\setminus\{r_{\mathbf{g}}\}}[r \mapsto \ell_{\mathbf{g}}] \\ (succ\, n).i &= \begin{cases} r & \text{if } n_i = r_{\mathbf{g}} \\ r_{\mathbf{g}.i} & \text{if } n_i \ne r_{\mathbf{g}} \wedge n = r \\ n_i & \text{if } n_i \ne r_{\mathbf{g}} \wedge n \ne r \end{cases} \\ & \quad \text{where } n_i = (succ_{\mathbf{g}} n).i \end{aligned}$$

f. An insertion $\mathbf{g}[\mathbf{x}] = \big(N_{\mathbf{g}} \cup N_{\mathbf{x}},\ lab_{\mathbf{g}}[lab_{\mathbf{x}}],\ succ_{\mathbf{g}}[succ_{\mathbf{x}}],\ r_{\mathbf{g}}\big)$ *is a way to replace parts of a graph* $\mathbf{g}$ *with the parts of* $\mathbf{x}$ *that have nodeids found in* $N_{\mathbf{g}}$.

g. A term graph set $\mathcal{G}_{\mathcal{L},\#}$ *is* arity monotonic *iff for all* $\ell, \ell' \in \mathcal{L}$ *we have that* $\ell \sqsubseteq \ell'$ *implies* $\#\ell \le \#\ell'$.

Choosing rerooting and insertion instead of the traditional "redirection" and "context" means that these operations are very close to operations available on graph reduction machines—and in fact the drawings we use can be represented as a string of insertions (constructing the "dominant graph") and rerootings (the "backpointers").

With this we are ready to define and use graph matching and rewriting.

DEFINITION **22.2.3** *Given* $\mathbf{p}, \mathbf{a} \in \mathcal{G}_{\mathcal{L},\#}$. $\sigma : N_{\mathbf{p}} \to N_{\mathbf{a}}$ *is a* rooted $\sqsubseteq$-match map from $\mathbf{p}$ to $\mathbf{a}$, *written* $\sigma \triangleright \mathbf{p} \xrightarrow{\sqsubseteq} \mathbf{a}$, *iff it satisfies* $\forall n \in reach(\mathbf{p})$:

$$lab_{\mathbf{p}}(n) \sqsubseteq lab_{\mathbf{a}}(\sigma(n)) \tag{22.1}$$

$$\sigma(succ_{\mathbf{p}}(n).i) = succ_{\mathbf{a}}(\sigma(n)).i \qquad \forall i \in \{1, \ldots, \#(lab_{\mathbf{p}}(n))\} \tag{22.2}$$

This is a generalization of the usual graph substitution concept in that it is parameterised over $\sqsubseteq$. In fact, matching with a *discrete* ordering corresponds to the "rooted homomorphism"—symbolically $\xrightarrow{=}$ is $\rightarrow$ of [BvEG+87]. Its symmetric closure is the "rooted isomorphism" ($\approx$) equivalence relation. Similarly, matching with a *flat* ordering (like $\xrightarrow{=_\perp}$) corresponds to the rooted homomorphism on "open graphs" of [BvEG+87] except that we include the "empty" $\perp$ nodes in the graph as actual nodes rather than leave them out. We discuss in [Hol90b] how our parametrization can be generalized to provide encoding of type systems.

It is easy to see that such a match is always unique (proof in [Ros92b]).

THEOREM **22.2.4** *Given* $\mathbf{p}, \mathbf{a} \in \mathcal{G}_{\mathcal{L},\#}$, $\mathcal{G}_{\mathcal{L},\#}$ *arity-monotonic. Then* $\sigma \triangleright \mathbf{p} \xrightarrow{\sqsubseteq} \mathbf{a}$ *iff*

$$\begin{array}{ll} \sigma(r_{\mathbf{p}}) = r_{\mathbf{a}} & \wedge\ \ \ell_{\mathbf{p}} \sqsubseteq \ell_{\mathbf{a}} \\ & \wedge\ \ \forall i \in \{1, \ldots, \#\ell_{\mathbf{p}}\} : \sigma' \triangleright \mathbf{p}'|r_{\mathbf{p}.i} \xrightarrow{\sqsubseteq} \mathbf{g}.i \\ & \qquad \text{where } \ \mathbf{p}' = \mathbf{p}[r_{\mathbf{p}} : \ell_{\mathbf{p}}\langle\rangle],\ \sigma' = \sigma[\mathbf{p}' \mapsto \mathbf{g}] \end{array}$$

This theorem is the key to rewriting by the "extending the match" idea used in the categorical models (probably described in other chapters of this book):

DEFINITION **22.2.5** *Given* $\mathbf{p}, \mathbf{a}, \mathbf{b} \in \mathcal{G}_{\mathcal{L},\#}$ *such that* $\sigma \triangleright \mathbf{p} \xrightarrow{\sqsubseteq} \mathbf{a}$. *Then* σ describes the term graph rewrite of $\mathbf{b}$ to $\mathbf{c}$, *written* $\sigma \triangleright \mathbf{p} \xrightarrow{\sqsubseteq} \mathbf{a} \triangleright \mathbf{b} \xrightarrow{\sqsubseteq} \mathbf{c}$, *iff*

$$\exists \sigma' : \sigma'|_{N_{\mathbf{p}}} = \sigma \quad \wedge \quad \sigma' \triangleright \mathbf{b} \xrightarrow{\sqsubseteq} \mathbf{c}$$

And in fact the constructive proof of Theorem 22.2.4 is an algorithm that produces the minimal contractum $\mathbf{c}$.

COROLLARY **22.2.6** *Given arity-monotonic* $\mathcal{G}_{\mathcal{L},\#}$ *with* $\sigma \triangleright \mathbf{p} \xrightarrow{\sqsubseteq} \mathbf{a}$. *Then* $\mathbf{c}_m$ *given by*

$$\begin{array}{l} \mathbf{c}_m = \sigma_m(gc(\mathbf{b})) \\ \sigma_m = rewrite\ \{\, n \mapsto n \mid n \in reach(\mathbf{b}) \setminus reach(\mathbf{p}) \,\}\ \mathbf{b} \\ \qquad \textbf{where} \quad rewrite\ \sigma\ \mathbf{b} = \sigma, \ \text{if } \mathbf{b} \in Dm(\sigma) \\ \qquad\qquad\qquad\qquad\qquad = \sigma_k, \ \text{if } \mathbf{b} \notin Dm(\sigma) \\ \qquad\qquad\qquad\qquad\qquad \textbf{where} \quad k\ = \#\ell_{\mathbf{b}} \\ \qquad\qquad\qquad\qquad\qquad\qquad\qquad c \ \text{ is a fresh nodeid} \\ \qquad\qquad\qquad\qquad\qquad\qquad\qquad \sigma_0 = \sigma[r_{\mathbf{b}} \mapsto c] \\ \qquad\qquad\qquad\qquad\qquad\qquad\qquad \sigma_i = rewrite\ \sigma_{i-1}\ \mathbf{b}.i \end{array}$$

satisfies $\forall \mathbf{c}, \mathbf{p} \xrightarrow{\sqsubseteq} \mathbf{a} \triangleright \mathbf{b} \xrightarrow{\sqsubseteq} \mathbf{c} : \mathbf{c}_m \xrightarrow{\sqsubseteq} \mathbf{c}$.

Essentially this is just the usual search for a "maximal glue component" but in the parameterized case; we will use this to specify fully lazy reduction later, but it may also be used for other things, e.g., when encoding a type system in $\sqsubseteq$ this can be used to find a most specific type.

The reader is invited to verify that $\{17 \mapsto 1,\ 18 \mapsto 10,\ 19 \mapsto 2,\ 20 \mapsto 3,\ 21 \mapsto 4,\ 22 \mapsto 5\} \triangleright \mathbf{g}|_{17} \xrightarrow{\sqsubseteq} \mathbf{g}|_{1}$ in the top graph of figure 22.3, provided the $\sqsubseteq$-ordering satisfies $\blacksquare \sqsubseteq \Lambda_2$, $? \sqsubseteq [\,]$, $? \sqsubseteq (:)$, $? \sqsubseteq 1$, and $? \sqsubseteq 2$.

22.3 GRAPH REPRESENTATION OF BAWL PROGRAMS

This section discusses and defines the term graph representation of BAWL programs. We first make a point of giving a perfectly naïve term graph representation and then we argue that the kind of matching and rewriting we wish to describe can be performed easily on this representation by imposing a suitable label ordering on it. Finally we comment on the how to interpret graph values as BAWL values.

We define the representation of (Core) BAWL programs as graphs in figure 22.4: the $\rho \vdash_X$ prefix should be read "the bindings $\{I \mapsto \mathbf{g}\}$ in ρ makes the following a well-formed X", where X is a syntactic BAWL component (of Definition 22.1.1) as shown. If

$$\frac{\rho[\rho'] \vdash_S S \qquad \rho[\rho'] \vdash_E E \rightsquigarrow \mathbf{e}}{\rho \vdash_B \begin{array}{c} S \\ ?\,E \end{array} \rightsquigarrow \mathbf{e}} \tag{22.1}$$

$$\frac{\rho \vdash_D D_1 \rightsquigarrow \mathbf{d}_1 \quad \cdots \quad \rho \vdash_D D_k \rightsquigarrow \mathbf{d}_k}{\rho \vdash_S \begin{array}{c} D_1 \\ \vdots \\ D_k \end{array}} \tag{22.2}$$

$$\frac{\rho_i \vdash_P P_{ij} \rightsquigarrow \mathbf{p}_{ij} \qquad \rho[\rho_i] \vdash_S S_i \qquad \rho[\rho_i] \vdash_E E_i \rightsquigarrow \mathbf{e}_i}{\rho \vdash_D \begin{array}{lcl} I\ P_{11} \ldots P_{1k} & = & E_1 \textbf{ where } S_1 \\ \vdots & & \\ I\ P_{n1} \ldots P_{nk} & = & E_n \textbf{ where } S_n \end{array} \rightsquigarrow \begin{array}{c} \Lambda_n \\ \swarrow \quad \cdots \quad \searrow \\ \lambda \qquad\qquad \lambda \\ @_k \quad \mathbf{e}_1 \qquad @_k \quad \mathbf{e}_n \\ \blacksquare\ \mathbf{p}_{11} \cdots \mathbf{p}_{1k} \quad \blacksquare\ \mathbf{p}_{n1} \cdots \mathbf{p}_{nk} \end{array}} \quad \forall ij \tag{22.3}$$

$$\frac{}{\rho \vdash_P I \rightsquigarrow r{:}\textcircled{?}}\ \rho(I) = r{:}\textcircled{?} \qquad \frac{}{\rho \vdash_P\ !I \rightsquigarrow r{:}\textcircled{!}}\ \rho(I) = r{:}\textcircled{!} \tag{22.4}$$

$$\frac{\rho \vdash_P P_i \rightsquigarrow \mathbf{p}_i}{\rho \vdash_P (X\ P_1 \ldots P_k) \rightsquigarrow \begin{array}{c} r{:}\textcircled{\ell} \\ \swarrow \quad \searrow \\ \mathbf{p}_1 \ \cdots\ \mathbf{p}_k \end{array}} \quad \forall i; \begin{cases} \ell = \,!!_k & \text{if } X = \,!! \\ \ell = C & \text{if } X = C \end{cases} \tag{22.5}$$

$$\frac{}{\rho \vdash_E I \rightsquigarrow \mathbf{e}}\ \rho(I) = \mathbf{e} \tag{22.6}$$

$$\frac{\rho \vdash_E E_i \rightsquigarrow \mathbf{e}_i}{\rho \vdash_E (\ C\ E_1 \ldots E_k\ ) \rightsquigarrow \begin{array}{c} r{:}\textcircled{C} \\ \swarrow \quad \searrow \\ \mathbf{e}_1 \ \cdots\ \mathbf{e}_k \end{array}} \quad \forall i \tag{22.7}$$

$$\frac{\rho \vdash_E E_i \rightsquigarrow \mathbf{e}_i}{\rho \vdash_E (\ E_0\ E_1 \ldots E_k\ ) \rightsquigarrow \begin{array}{c} r{:}\textcircled{@_k} \\ \swarrow \quad \searrow \\ \mathbf{e}_0 \ \cdots\ \mathbf{e}_k \end{array}} \quad \forall i \tag{22.8}$$

Figure 22.4 Graph representation of core BAWL

$\rightsquigarrow \mathbf{g}$ is specified then $\mathbf{g}$ is the corresponding graph representation. The representation is completely naïve, using a special label for each construction in Definition 22.1.1. The only trick used is the encoding of argument pattern abstractions using $@_i$ with a "dummy function plug" ▪, i.e., such that they look similar to the encoding of the applications they should match as mentioned in the introduction. It is not difficult to show that $\rho, \mathbf{e}$ can be found for any BAWL program B using (22.3) that invokes the other rules as appropriate.

Now we are just left with designing the label domain such that the graph representation gives us the matching and rewriting that we wish to use. The chosen ordering is shown in figure 22.5 as a Hasse diagram. The triangles between $!!_k$ and $\mathcal{C}_i$

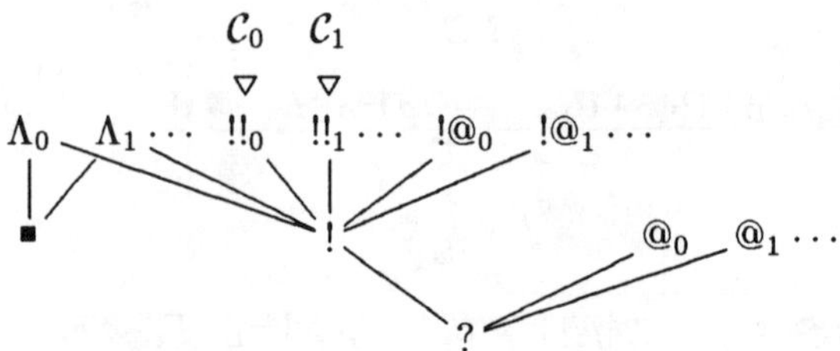

Figure 22.5 BAWL label ordering

just mean that $!!_k$ should be the only label lesser than the collection of constructors of arity k.

The only thing that is complicated in this is the recognition of partial applications since partial and complete applications are not distinguishable syntactically, and yet only partial ones are in HNF. As discussed in the following section we do it by dynamically "marking" them as different by updating @-nodes at the root of partial applications to !@-nodes that should be in HNF, i.e., match !-nodes. The added $!@_k$-nodes in the figure clearly satisfy this. Note that $!@_k$ do not represent anything according to the rules of figure 22.4 since the *syntax* does not distinguish between complete and incomplete applications.

The design means that we can make maximal use of graph rewriting in the following section, e.g., both matches indicated by dotted lines in figure 22.3 are handled by this.

We have not yet considered how to interpret a result graph as a BAWL value. But fortunately this is not complicated: the rules of figure 22.4 may be used "backwards" without any problems as long as we create variable names and change any !@-nodes into @-nodes as mentioned above. There is even a smallest BAWL program representing the value of any graph thanks to Corollary 22.2.6.

22.4 GOS—GRAPH OPERATIONAL SEMANTICS

This section gives the operational semantics of BAWL by specifying a reduction relation on the BAWL graph representation of the previous section. We have chosen to base GOS on "Structural Operational Semantics" style of [Plo81, Kah87], since the generality of relations make them well-suited for definitions over graphs.

We start by discussing the goal of the specification, in particular how it may be separated into a module specifying the evaluation strategy and a module specifying the evaluation step. The two main modules, pattern driven evaluation and the evaluation step, are then discussed separately. Finally, we discuss a technical point: indirections.

The purpose of this entire exercise is to achieve a semantic description of BAWL that captures and communicates those aspects of the language that we wish to emphasize on and experiment with. The following are the main features:

- *Lazy evaluation*: only structure that is needed by the user should be evaluated.

- *Pattern driven reduction strategy*: the pattern matching should be used to determine the evaluation order.
- *Fully lazy curried applications*: the individual evaluation "steps" are applications of curried functions to arguments with minimal duplication of data achieved by *destructive updating* whenever possible.

Fortunately the first point is a special case of the second provided the standard "driver function" *seq* (mentioned in the introduction) is available, so we will not discuss that any further. The other two will be described by the following relations:

- $\mathbf{p} : \mathbf{e} \Downarrow \mathbf{g}$: "The pattern graph **p** drives the converging of the expression graph **e** to the value graph **g**" (figure 22.6).
- $\mathbf{g} \Rightarrow \mathbf{g}'$: "The value graph **g** reduces in a single step to the value graph **g**′" (figure 22.7).

$$\boxed{\mathbf{p} : \mathbf{e} \Downarrow \mathbf{g}}$$

$$\frac{}{\mathbf{p} : \mathbf{g} \Downarrow \mathbf{g}} \qquad \mathbf{p} \xrightarrow{\sqsubseteq} \mathbf{g} \tag{22.9}$$

$$\frac{\mathbf{p}_1 : \mathbf{g}_1 \Downarrow \mathbf{g}_i' \quad \cdots \quad \mathbf{p}_k : \mathbf{g}_k \Downarrow \mathbf{g}_k'}{p\!:\!(\ell)\,[\mathbf{p}_1 \cdots \mathbf{p}_2] \;:\; g\!:\!(\ell)\,[\mathbf{g}_1 \cdots \mathbf{g}_2] \;\Downarrow\; g\!:\!(\ell)\,[\mathbf{g}_1' \cdots \mathbf{g}_2']} \qquad \ell \in \{@, !@\} \cup \mathcal{C} \tag{22.10}$$

$$\frac{\mathbf{g} \Rightarrow \mathbf{g}' \quad \mathbf{p} : \mathbf{g}' \Downarrow \mathbf{g}''}{\mathbf{p} : \mathbf{g} \Downarrow \mathbf{g}''} \tag{22.11}$$

Figure 22.6 The BAWL reduction strategy

Rule (22.11) is there to allow us to stop reduction when the pattern is "satisfied"—this requires a match and thus uses $\xrightarrow{\sqsubseteq}$ based on the label order from above. Rule (22.12) allows reduction of subgraphs driven by the corresponding subpatterns when the root labels are equal; the use of g on both sides of $\Downarrow$ ensures *destructive updating*, i.e., that all parts of the graph that refer to this constructed node will share the results of updating. Finally (22.13) is the rule for application and makes use of the "single step reduction" relation $\Rightarrow$ defined below. Notice that performing the reduction of an application does not depend on the pattern that drives the reduction. It is interesting to realize how simple it is to prove that this rule set uses destructive updating by induction over the possible proofs—the above three rules clearly satisfy this provided the $\mathbf{g} \Rightarrow \mathbf{g}'$ rules also do it!

Now for the evaluation step rules: (22.14) is the generic β-reduction rule where we reduce an application with at least the right number of arguments: First we let the pattern list (BAWL LHS) drive evaluation of the argument list until there is a match (the $\exists i$ is there to remind us that we have to search for the right i). Then we use the just established match to rewrite the corresponding body (BAWL RHS) to the contractum that should be the result of the entire operation! The rule as shown is not specified fully lazy—this is abstracted out—but it is easy to do this by explicitly inserting

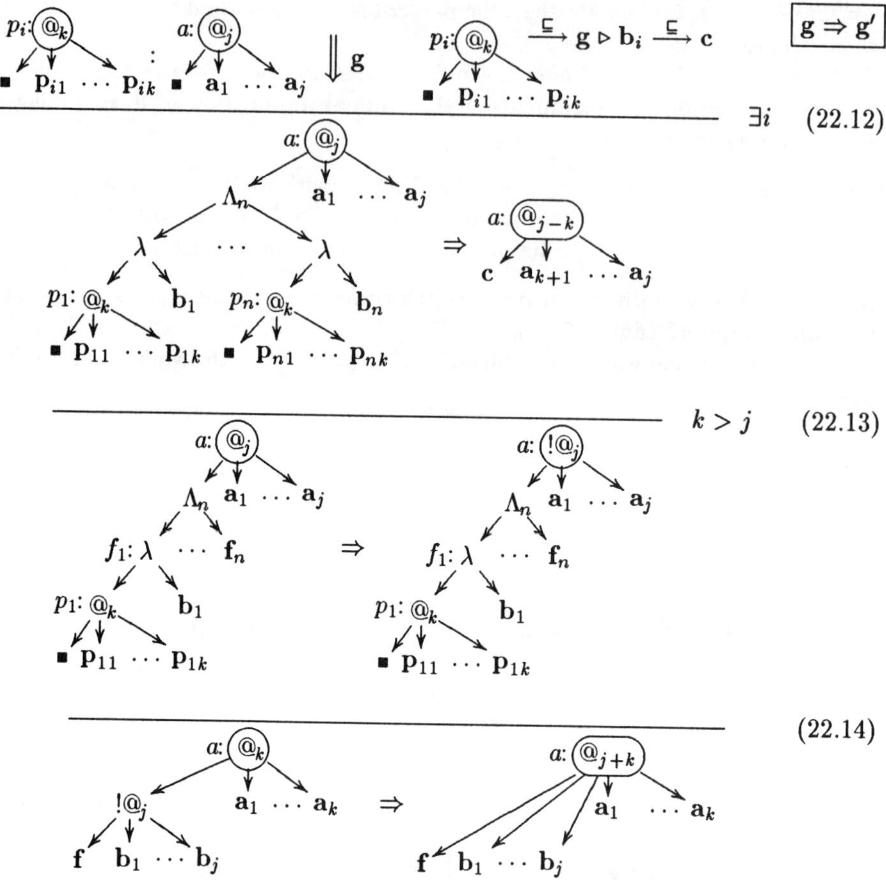

Figure 22.7 The BAWL evaluation step

the result of Corollary 22.2.6. (22.15) just updates an incomplete application when it is needed and (22.16) combines an incomplete application with the next outermost application; notice that this does not necessarily remove the partial application node itself.

Finally the promised discussion of *indirections*; fortunately this is easy. The thing to notice is that both (22.14) and (22.16) may succeed when $k = j$ in which case they leave a $@_0$-node as the root node. This node will either immediately merge with an underlying @-node by (22.16) or be updated to a $!@_0$-node by (22.15) that can only disappear in the same way. And a $!@_0$-node is indistinguishable from an indirection node; it even pattern matches as what it "points to"! The reader is invited to verify the example of figure 22.3 with the knowledge that $\bullet$ is in fact $@_0$ and $!@_0$.

There is only one situation where a $@_0$-node does not act as an indirection but instead as a ***suspension***, and that is when it points to a nullary function. Then the entire thing is a redex that can be reduced immediately by (22.14), thus a suspension. But it is important to realize that such a suspension will never be generated and then left alone by the evaluator since if it was generated then we still need to reduce it to get a match because it must come from another @-node that did not match!

However, there is a different, related issue: if the programmer specifies a BAWL *data definition* then this will be interpreted as a nullary function and consequently not be updated properly (instead each nullary "application" of the data will be updated). This is easily fixed, however, by adding a special case to the representation equations for data definitions such that the data is accessed directly (cf. [Ros92b, Ros91]).

22.5 DISCUSSION

We have sketched a specification of a definitely non-trivial lazy functional programming language, BAWL. The style of the presentation is of sufficient generality to express and manipulate the sharing properties of "real" programming languages in a direct way. We feel that this is a very promising direction that deserves further study, a study which we are currently undertaking.

Our approach as described here has been very "top-down": we started this by considering the needs of high-level lazy functional languages. Nevertheless, we have done some experiments with *implementation* of the presented ideas [Hol90a] in the form of a graph reduction machine called MATCHBOXES, and particularly coding the efficient match and rewrite algorithm as primitives in the machine seems to have some promise.

Finally, this author's attempt at a "theoretical bottom-up" approach starting from first principles [Ros92a] is still fairly fresh. Yet we hope that the two may meet.

REFERENCES

[BPJR88] G. L. Burn, S. L. Peyton Jones, and J. D. Robson. The spineless G-machine. In *1988 ACM Conference on LISP and Functional Programming*, pp. 244–258, Snowbird, Utah, July 1988, ACM.

[BvEG+87] H. P. Barendregt, M. C. J. D. van Eekelen, J. R. W. Glauert, J. R. Kennaway, M. J. Plasmeijer, and M. R. Sleep. Term graph rewriting. In J. W. de Bakker, A. J. Nijman, and P. C. Treleaven (editors), *PARLE '87—Parallel Architectures and Languages Europe vol. II*, vol. 256, pp. 141–158, Eindhoven, The Netherlands, June 1987, Springer-Verlag.

[BvEvLP87] T. Brus, M. C. J. D. van Eekelen, M. van Leer, and M. J. Plasmeijer. Clean—a language for functional graph rewriting. In G. Kahn (editor), *FPCA '87—Functional Programming Languages and Computer Architecture*, Springer-Verlag, Lecture Notes in Computer Science 274, pp. 364–387, Portland, Oregon, 1987.

[BW88] R. Bird and P. Wadler. *Introduction to Functional Programming*. Prentice-Hall, 1988.

[Car83] L. Cardelli. *The Functional Abstract Machine*. Technical Report TR-107, Bell Labs, 1983.

[GKS89] J. R. W. Glauert, J. R. Kennaway, and M. R. Sleep. *Final Specification of Dactl*. Report SYS-C88-11, University of East Anglia, Norwich, UK, 1989.

[Hoa75] C. A. R. Hoare. Recursive data structures. *Journal of Computer and Information Sciences*, **4**, pp. 105–132, 1975.

[Hol90a] K. H. Holm. *Graph Matching in Functional Language Specification and Implementation*. skriftlig rapport 90-1-3, DIKU, Universitetsparken 1, DK-2100 København Ø, Denmark, December 1990.

[Hol90b] K. H. Holm. Graph matching in operational semantics and typing. In A. Arnold (editor), *CAAP '90—15th Colloqvium on Trees and Algebra in Programming*,

Springer-Verlag, Lecture Notes in Computer Science 431, pp. 191–205, Copenhagen, Denmark, March 1990.

[Hug82] J. M. Hughes. Super-combinators. In *1982 ACM Symposium on LISP and Functional Programming*, pp. 1–10, Pittsburgh, Pennsylvania, August 1982, ACM.

[Joh84] T. Johnsson. Efficient compilation of lazy evaluation. *Sigplan Notices*, **19**, 6, pp. 58–69, June 1984.

[Kah87] G. Kahn. *Natural Semantics*. Rapport 601, INRIA, Sophia-Antipolis, France, February 1987.

[Ken88] J. R. Kennaway. Implementing term rewrite languages in Dactl. In M. Dauchet and M. Nivat (editors), *CAAP '88—13th Colloquium on Trees in Algebra and Programming*, Springer-Verlag, Lecture Notes in Computer Science 299, pp. 102–116, Nancy, France, March 1988.

[KSvEP91] P. W. M. Koopman, J. E. W. Smetsers, M. C. J. D. van Eekelen, and M. J. Plasmeijer. Efficient graph rewriting using the annotated functional strategy. In Plasmeijer and Sleep [PS91], pp. 225–250. (available as Nijmegen Tech. Report 91-25).

[Lam90] J. Lamping. An algorithm for optimal lambda calculus reduction. In *POPL '90—Seventeenth Annual ACM Symposium on Principles of Programming Languages*, pp. 16–30, San Francisco, California, January 1990, ACM.

[McC60] J. McCarthy. Recursive functions of symbolic expressions. *Communications of the ACM*, **3**, 4, pp. 184–195, April 1960.

[PJ87] S. L. Peyton Jones. *The Implementation of Functional Programming Languages*. Prentice-Hall, 1987.

[Plo81] G. D. Plotkin. *A Structural Approach to Operational Semantics*. Technical Report FN-19, DAIMI, Aarhus University, Aarhus, Denmark, 1981.

[PS91] M. J. Plasmeijer and M. R. Sleep (editors). *SemaGraph '91 Symposium on the Semantics and Pragmatics of Generalized Graph Rewriting*, Nijmegen, Holland, December 1991, Katholieke Universiteit Nijmegen. (available as Nijmegen Tech. Report 91-25).

[Ros91] K. H. Rose. Graph-based operational semantics for lazy functional languages. In Plasmeijer and Sleep [PS91], pp. 203–225. (available as Nijmegen Tech. Report 91-25).

[Ros92a] K. H. Rose. Explicit cyclic substitutions. In M. Rusinowitch and J.-L. Rémy (editors), *CTRS '92—3rd International Workshop on Conditional Term Rewriting Systems*, Springer-Verlag, Lecture Notes in Computer Science, Pont-a-Mousson, France, July 1992.

[Ros92b] K. H. Rose. *GOS—Graph Operational Semantics*. Speciale 92-1-9, DIKU, Universitetsparken 1, DK–2100 København Ø, Denmark, March 1992. (56pp).

[Sta78] J. Staples. A Graph-like Lambda Calculus for which Leftmost Outermost Reduction is Optimal. In V. Claus, H. Ehrig, and G. Rozenberg (editors), *1978 International Workshop in Graph Grammars and their Application to Computer Science and Biology*, Springer-Verlag, Lecture Notes in Computer Science 73, pp. 440–454, Bad Honnef, F. R. Germany, 1978.

[Tur82] D. A. Turner. Recursion Equations as a Programming Language. In J. Darlington, P. Henderson, and David A. Turner (editors), *Functional Programming and its Applications, an Advanced Course*, pp. 1–28. Cambridge University Press, 1982.

[Wad71] C. P. Wadsworth. *Semantics and Pragmatics of the Lambda Calculus*. PhD thesis, Programming Research Group, Oxford University, 1971.

23

Graph Rewriting Using the Annotated Functional Strategy

P.W.M. Koopman, J.E.W. Smetsers,
M.C.J.D. van Eekelen and M.J. Plasmeijer

23.1 INTRODUCTION

This chapter treats term graph rewriting using the annotated functional strategy. The functional is commonly used by *lazy* functional programming languages such as Miranda [Tur85] and Haskell [HJW+92]. Although this strategy is intuitively clear, no formal description of graph rewriting according to this strategy is available.

The functional strategy prescribes lazy evaluation, but forces the reduction of arguments before they are compared to the patterns in the rule alternatives. The priority of the rule alternatives is their textual order. The corresponding strategy for an equivalent lambda-term is left most. The translation of the rewrite system to lambda-calculus determines the priority of the rules and controls the pattern matching. For a graph rewrite system the description of this strategy is more complex since the expression to rewrite is graph instead of a tree and the rewrite rules are more complex than in lambda-calculus. In the graph rewrite systems considered here, the rule contains patterns and have a priority in order to avoid ambiguity. In lambda-calculus the only reduction rule is application.

Eager evaluation can be implemented much more efficiently than lazy evaluation. But it may lead to superfluous work and non-termination. Eager evaluation is safe for the arguments needed in every reduction of the function; the strict arguments. Rewrite rules can be annotated with strictness information. The annotated functional strategy

Term Graph Rewriting: Theory and Practice.
Eds. Ronan Sleep, Rinus Plasmeijer and Marko van Eekelen.

takes the annotations into account to deviate from the standard lazy evaluation and forces eager evaluation to strong root normal form.

This chapter gives operational semantics of reduction in a term graph rewrite system using the annotated functional strategy.

The functional language Miranda is used for the description of the functional strategy and the rewrite steps. This has as an advantage that the specifications can be partially checked for correctness by the Miranda compiler and can be executed to observe the dynamic behavior of the specified semantics.

The rewrite algorithm and the annotated functional strategy can be combined to yield a single efficient reduction algorithm. The elementary reduction step here is the reduction of a redex to root normal form. This algorithm is used in a very efficient implementation of lazy functional programming languages. Strictness annotations and type information are necessary to obtain this efficiency.

23.2 CLEAN

The graph rewrite language Clean, is the sequential subset of Concurrent Clean [BvEvL+87, vEP90, NSvEP91]. It is a lazy, modular, strongly typed, higher order functional programming language based on Term Graph Rewrite Systems [BvEG+87, BvEG+88, Klo92]. Clean is a functional programming language in its own right, but it is also used as an intermediate language in the compilation path from functional programming languages to concrete machines [KvEN+90, Koo90, PvE93].

A Clean program consists of a set of graph rewrite rules used to rewrite the initial graph. A graph consists of a set of nodes. Each node is labeled with an unique name; its **node-id**. Nodes consist of a constant, the **symbol**, and a (possibly empty) sequence of references to other nodes; the **arguments**. A rewrite rule states that an instance of the graph on the left-hand side (LHS), the redex **pattern**, can be transformed to the graph on the right-hand side (RHS); the **contractum**. The initial graph to be reduced by the Clean system is @0: Dataroot @1, @1: Start, this is usually abbrivated to Dataroot Start. The Dataroot is a *constructor*; there is no rewrite rule for this symbol. This implies that every useful Clean program contains a rule for the *function* Start. For convenience, objects of some basic types (Integers, Reals etc.) and rules manipulating these objects (addition etc.) are predefined. A predefined type and rewrite rule is (the sign == indicates that the rest of this line is a comment in Clean programs):

```
TYPE
:: BOOL → TRUE   ; == type definition for the Booleans
   BOOL → FALSE  ;
RULE
:: IF !BOOL x x → x ; == Type: a Boolean and 2 xes as argument; yields a x
   IF TRUE  t e → t ; == First alternative; if first argument is TRUE the result is t
   IF FALSE t e → e ; == Next alternative; if first argument is FALSE the result is e
```

The visible result of the reduction process consists of a printed *tree* representation of the graph in normal form. In order to shorten the descriptions some restrictions are made on the rewrite rules (generalization to full Clean is very simple):

- explicit node definitions at the textual outermost level are used for all shared nodes defined in a contractum pattern;
- the only predefined type considered here is BOOL for Boolean values;
- all rules are expected to be correctly typed according to the familiar polymorphic Milner-Mycroft type system [Mil78, Myc84];
- no partial functions are allowed in this subset and
- the guards introduced in version 0.8 of Clean are not yet incorporated in the description.

23.2.1 Example of a Clean program

A small self-contained example is shown to illustrate the kind of Clean programs possible. This example will be used as a running example in this chapter. A type representing Peano numbers and some functions using them are defined in Clean as:

```
TYPE
:: NUM             → ZERO              ; == a Peano number is either zero or,
   NUM             → S NUM             ; == the successor of a number
RULE
:: +P !NUM !NUM    → NUM               ; == addition; strict in its two arguments
   +P (S n) m      → S (+P n m)        ; == alternative 1; argument 1 must be S n
   +P zero m       → m                 ; == next alternative; no patterns
:: F !BOOL         → NUM               ; == F needs a strict BOOL; yields a NUM
   F c             → +P a b            , == the top of the RHS is an addition.
                     zero: ZERO        , == definitions of shared nodes used.
                     a: IF c b zero    , == note the cyclic dependencies
                     b: IF c (S zero) a ; == between a and b
:: Start           → NUM               ; == the start rule is the first rule executed.
   Start           → F FALSE           ; == Start can be rewritten to F FALSE.
```

23.2.2 The data structure used to represent the rewrite rules

For the formal description of the rewrite algorithm and the strategy in Miranda a data type to represent an *abstract syntax tree* (AST) of Clean is needed. This data structure is in close correspondence with the concrete syntax. The graph is represented by a sequence of trees.

```
clean        == [rewrite_rule]
rewrite_rule ::= TypedRule typerule rule | TypeRule typerule
typerule     == rule
rule         == [rulealt]
rulealt      ::= Rewrite graph_pat graph_pat
graph_pat    == [tree]
tree         ::= NODE annots node_id symbol fargs | NodeId annots node_id
annots       == [annot]
fargs        == [arg]
arg          == tree
annot        ::= Strict || The only annotation treated here.
```

```
symbol    ::= Function symbolid | Constructor symbolid | BOOLval bool
node_id   == [char] || An empty list denotes the absence of a node-id.
symbolid  == [char]
```

23.3 OPERATIONAL SEMANTICS OF A REWRITE STEP

Given a rule alternative, a graph and the root of the redex a rewrite can be performed. It is required that strict arguments (see below) are in (strong) *root normal form* (rnf) and the alternative is applicable; there is a *match* between the left-hand side (LHS) of the rule alternative and the actual graph.

A graph **matches** a rule alternative if it is an **instance** of the graph on the left-hand side; a mapping can be found between the pattern and the graph. A **mapping** is a function that associates node-ids in the graph to the node-id variables in the rewrite rule. This mapping preserves the node structure and constants in the pattern of the rule alternative must be equal to the corresponding symbols in the graph. Term graph rewriting means that the patterns of the rules are trees.

Node a is **reachable** from node b if either a is an argument of b or a is reachable from the arguments of b. A graph is **connected** if all nodes are reachable from the *root*. The graphs in the rewrite rules and the actual graph are always connected. By convention the first node in a list of definitions is the root.

A graph is in strong **root normal form** if the graph as a whole is not a redex nor can become a redex by reducing subgraphs. A graph in weak root normal form is not a redex, but can become a redex by reducing some of its arguments. A graph is in **normal form** if it does not contain any redex. The operational semantics of rewriting is defined by the following algorithm (see [BvEG+87]). **Rewrite Algorithm:**

1. Make a mapping from formal node-ids in the left-hand side of the rewrite rule to actual nodes in the graph.
2. Construct the graph corresponding to the right-hand side of the rule alternative (if present); the **contractum**. Formal node-ids are replaced by actual node-ids using the mapping from step 1.
3. All references to the root of the redex are **redirected** to the root of the contractum. If the root of the redex happens to be the root of the contractum the redex is **self-embedding**. Since such a self-embedding redex is a possible source of ambiguity [Ken91] its occurrence is regarded as an error.
4. Remove parts of the graph not reachable from the root. This removal of disconnected nodes is called **garbage collection**.

23.3.1 Examples of rewrite steps

Figure 23.1 shows two successive rewrite steps of the running example. Reduction of the initial graph according to the Start rule is shown in the upper part of figure 23.1. Rule F is applied to the graph obtained by the first reduction step. For each reduction step the initial graph, the graph with the contractum, the graph after redirection and the graph after garbage collection is shown.

The graph obtained after these two steps can be rewritten in various ways; the second alternative for the predefined condition can be applied to both nodes containing

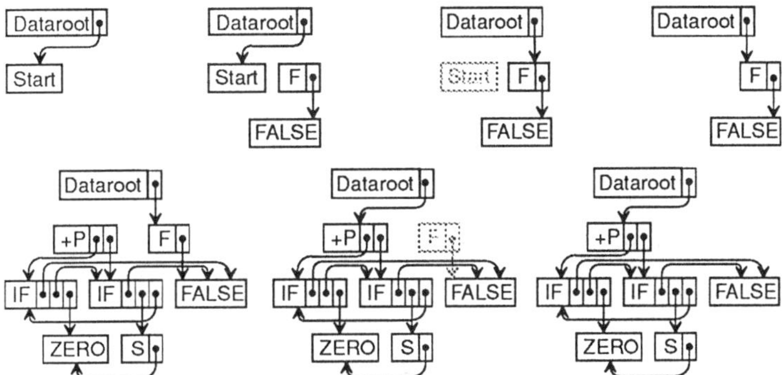

Figure 23.1 The first two rewrite steps of the running example

the symbol IF and the second alternative of +P can be applied. The reduction strategy discussed below determines which redex is chosen.

23.3.2 Data structure for the actual graph

A graph is represented by the abstract data type graph. This graph is a collection of named cells. Each cell is either empty or contains of a symbol and a list of actual node-ids: the arguments. Empty nodes are used during the construction of a graph. This abstract type is easier to handle during the rewrites than the graphs used in the rewrite rules. Moreover a clear distinction between the graphs in the rewrite rules and the actual graph is achieved by using separate data structures.

```
abstype graph, cell_id
 with   initial_graph   :: graph
        new_cell        :: graph → (cell_id, graph)
        store_cell      :: cell → graph → (cell_id, graph)
        update_cell     :: cell_id → cell → graph → graph
        get_cell        :: cell_id → graph → cell
        redirect        :: cell_id → cell_id → graph → graph
        collect_garbage :: graph → graph
        showgraph       :: graph → string
        showcell_id     :: cell_id → string
        root_id         :: cell_id
cell ::= Cell symbol [cell_id] | Empty_cell
```

23.3.3 Formal specification of the rewrite algorithm

A formal specification of one rewrite step is expressed in Miranda. The description becomes rather elaborated since rule alternatives are not simple compositions of elementary actions. The contractum is constructed node by node. The main function is called rewrite. The arguments of this function are the rule alternative to be applied, the root of the actual graph and the actual graph. The graph specified in the right-hand side is constructed and all references to the root are redirected to the root of the constructed graph. Finally, the garbage is removed. The result of the function rewrite is the updated graph.

```
rewrite :: rulealt → cell_id → graph → graph
rewrite (Rewrite lhs rhs) redex graph
 = collect_garbage (redirect redex reduct graph')
   where (reduct, graph') = construct_rhs rhs (mapping_lhs lhs redex graph) graph
```

The contractum specified in the right-hand side of a rule can be constructed in several ways. The algorithm shown here creates empty nodes for all shared nodes in the RHS and extends the mapping with these definitions. Then all formal node-ids have a mapping to actual addresses and the nodes can be filled. The result is a tuple containing a reference to the root and the new graph.

```
construct_rhs :: graph_pat → mapping → graph → (cell_id, graph)
construct_rhs [NodeId ann nid] mapping graph = (mapping nid, graph)
construct_rhs rhs mapping graph
 = (top, fill_cells rhs mapping' graph')
   where (top, mapping', graph') = create_cells rhs mapping graph

create_cells :: graph_pat → mapping → graph → (cell_id, mapping, graph)
create_cells (NODE ann nid sym args: nodes) mapping graph
 = (cid, record nid cid mapping', graph")
   where (cid, graph')                = new_cell graph
         (cid', mapping', graph") = create_cells nodes mapping graph'
create_cells [ ] mapping graph = (undef, mapping, graph)
```

A cell is filled by constructing its arguments and then updating it with the proper node. Arguments in the form of a node-id are constructed using the mapping. Arguments in the form of a node are constructed by constructing the node in the actual graph. These nodes cannot be shared since the only reference to them is at the point of definition. So, it is possible to construct a node with the proper contents immediately. The arguments are created from back to front (mainly for historical reasons).

```
fill_cells :: [tree] → mapping → graph → graph
fill_cells (NODE ann nid sym f_args: rest) mapping graph
 = fill_cells rest mapping (update_cell (mapping nid) (Cell sym a_args) graph')
   where (a_args, graph') = construct_args f_args mapping graph
fill_cells [ ] mapping graph = graph


construct_args :: fargs → mapping → graph → (cell_ids, graph)
construct_args (NodeId ann nid: f_args) mapping graph
 = (mapping nid: a_args, graph')
   where (a_args, graph') = construct_args f_args mapping graph
construct_args (NODE ann nid sym f_sub_args: f_args) mapping graph
 = (a_arg: a_args, graph''')
   where (a_args, graph')        = construct_args f_args mapping graph
         (a_arg, graph''')       = store_cell (Cell sym a_sub_args) graph"
         (a_sub_args, graph") = construct_args f_sub_args mapping graph'
construct_args [ ] mapping graph = ( [ ], graph)
```

To construct the mapping function the left-hand side graphof the rule and actual graph are scanned simultaneous to associate formal node-ids with actual addresses.

```
mapping == node_id → cell_id

mapping_lhs :: graph_pat → cell_id → graph → mapping
mapping_lhs [NODE ann nid f_sym f_args] top graph
 = map_args f_args a_args graph (record nid top new_mapping)
   where (Cell a_sym a_args) = get_cell top graph

map_args :: [arg] → [cell_id] → graph → mapping → mapping
map_args (NodeId ann f_id: f_args) (a_arg: a_args) graph mapping
 = map_args f_args a_args graph (record f_id a_arg mapping)
map_args (NODE ann id f_sym f_sargs: f_args) (a_arg: a_args) graph mapping
 = map_args f_args a_args graph mapping'
   where (Cell a_sym a_sargs) = get_cell a_arg graph
         mapping' = map_args f_sargs a_sargs graph (record id a_arg mapping)
map_args [ ] [ ] graph mapping = mapping

new_mapping :: mapping
new_mapping nid = error ("no mapping for: "++ nid)

record :: node_id → * → (node_id → *) → (node_id → *)
record "" cid mapping       = mapping || No node-id
record nid cid mapping name = cond (name=nid) cid (mapping name)
```

23.4 THE FUNCTIONAL STRATEGY

A reduction strategy is a function which takes a set of rewrite rules and the actual graph as arguments, and delivers the rule alternative and the place in the graph where it must be applied: the *redex*. The functional strategy tries to find a redex needed to reduce the graph to normal form. Reduction to normal form is achieved by depth first left to right application of reduction to root normal form. As stated before, a graph is in root normal form if the graph as a whole is not a redex nor can become a redex by reducing its subgraphs. The reduction to root normal form searches a rule corresponding to the symbol in the top node. When such a rule does not exist the graph is in root normal form. If a rule is found the alternatives are tried in textual order. Arguments are matched from left to right and an actual argument is reduced to root normal form before it is compared with a symbol in the LHS. In this way the functional strategy combines the discriminating position strategy [PvE93] with forcing evaluation to strong root normal form before matching in rewrite systems with priority rules [BBK87].

Consider the following example using the type NUM defined in section 23.2.1:

```
:: Start → Num                          ;
   Start → +P (+P (S zero) zero) zero ,
           zero: ZERO                   ;
```

This rule gets the intended semantics when the functional strategy is used. The argument +P (S zero) zero is reduced before it is matched to S n. The priority of

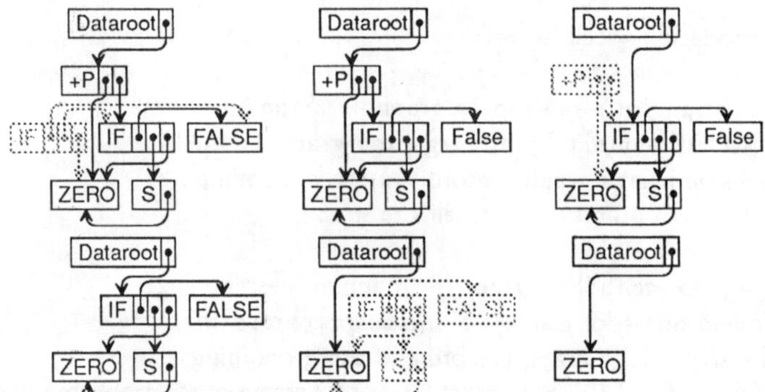

Figure 23.2 Reduction of the running example continued from figure 23.1

the rules guarantees that the first rule alternative of +P is applied, although both alternatives match the graph +P (S zero) zero.

The functional strategy is actually a practical compromise. The advantages are:

- it allows us to express computations in a user friendly manner: the priority of the rules makes rule alternatives similar to a control structure, and forcing evaluation before matching guarantees that the intended alternative is taken;
- it is relatively easy to explain and understand, a programmer will not often specify unintended infinite computations or a system where the wrong alternative is applied to an actual graph;
- as explained further on in this chapter and shown by state of the art compilers, it can be implemented very efficiently.

A disadvantage of this strategy is that the normal form is not always found. Sometimes it is possible to decide that an alternative is not applicable by
inspecting an argument further in the pattern while the functional strategy initiates an infitite reduction corresponding to the first pattern.

Using the functional strategy the reduction of the running example can be continued from figure 23.1. This strategy will indicate which rule alternative must be applied to what node.

23.4.1 Formal specification of the functional reduction strategy

The function functional_strat takes as arguments a set of rewrite rules (the Clean program), the actual graph and the cell_id of thetop of the redex.

```
functional_strat :: clean → graph → cell_id → redex
functional_strat clean graph top = nf_strat graph [top] [ ] clean
```

The type redex represents either a proper redex, the absence of a redex (the graph is in normal form), the impossibility to find a redex caused by a cyclic dependency or a dynamic type error.

```
redex ::= Redex rulealt cell_id | NoRedex cell_id | Cycle cell_id | TypeError cell_id
```

The type match represents the result of a match, it succeeds, fails, or cannot be determined because a subgraph needs to be reduced.

```
match ::= Match | NoMatch | Needs redex
```

The normal form strategy first performs a test to prevent cyclic applications. If the top has not been seen before, it must be brought in root normal form. If it is in root normal form the algorithm is applied depth first from left to right to the arguments. The function has two list of cell-ids as argument. The first list contains the nodes to inspect, the second list contains the inspected nodes.

```
nf_strat :: graph → [cell_id] → [cell_id] → clean → redex
nf_strat graph (top: rest) seen clean
 = nf_strat graph rest seen clean   , if member seen top
 = root_redex                       , if ~is_NoRedex root_redex
 = other_redex                      , if ~is_NoRedex other_redex
 = NoRedex top                      , otherwise
   where (Cell sym args) = get_cell top graph
         root_redex      = rnf_strat graph top [top] clean
         other_redex     = nf_strat graph (args ++ rest) (top: seen) clean
nf_strat graph [ ] seen clean = NoRedex undef
```

When the top node contains a function symbol, the root normal form strategy checks the rule corresponding to the symbol in the top. When the top node does not contain a function symbol, the symbol is a constructor and the graph is in rnf.

```
rnf_strat :: graph → cell_id → [cell_id] → clean → redex
rnf_strat graph top seen clean
 = check_rule (find_rule clean symbol) graph top seen clean , if is_function symbol
 = NoRedex top                                              , otherwise
   where symbol = cell_symbol (get_cell top graph)

find_rule :: [rewrite_rule] → symbol → rewrite_rule
find_rule (TypeRule rule: rules) symbol = find_rule rules symbol
find_rule (rule: rules) symbol = rule                     , if rule_symbol rule = symbol
                               = find_rule rules symbol , otherwise
find_rule [ ] symbol           = error ("No rule for " ++ show symbol)

check_rule :: rewrite_rule → graph → cell_id → [cell_id] → clean → redex
check_rule (TypedRule typerule alts) graph top seen clean
 = check_alts alts graph top seen clean

check_alts :: [rulealt] → graph → cell_id → [cell_id] → clean → redex
check_alts (alt: alts) graph top seen clean
 = Redex alt top                          , if match = Match
 = check_alts alts graph top seen clean , if match = NoMatch
 = redex                                  , otherwise
   where match                          = check_args f_args a_args graph seen clean
         (Needs redex)                  = match
         [NODE ann nid f_sym f_args]    = get_lhs alt
         (Cell a_sym a_args)            = get_cell top graph
check_alts [ ] graph top seen clean = TypeError top
```

Checking arguments is done from left to right. The type system guarantees that the arguments are present, therefore no test for the presence of an argument is needed. When the formal argument is a node-id it matches every actual graph. If the formal argument is a pattern (a node is specified) a test is performed to prevent cyclic searching for the current redex. Such a cycle is an error. If the actual argument is a redex it needs to be reduced now. When the actual and formal symbol are identical we proceed by checking the sub-arguments, otherwise the match fails.

```
check_args :: fargs → [cell_id] → graph → [cell_id] → clean → match
check_args (node: fargs) (aarg: aargs) graph seen clean
 = check_args fargs aargs graph seen clean, if match = Match
 = match                                   , otherwise
   where match = check_arg node aarg graph seen clean
check_args [ ] [ ] graph seen clean = Match

check_arg :: arg → cell_id → graph → [cell_id] → clean → match
check_arg (NodeId an nid) a_nid graph seen clean = Match
check_arg (NODE f_ann f_nid f_sym f_args) a_nid graph seen clean
 = Needs (Cycle a_nid)                      , if member seen a_nid & function || error
 = Needs (rnf_strat graph a_nid seen' clean) , if function
 = check_args f_args a_args graph seen' clean , if a_sym = f_sym
 = NoMatch                                   , otherwise
   where (Cell a_sym a_args) = get_cell a_nid graph
         seen'               = a_nid: seen
         function            = is_function a_sym
```

In the definitions above the following simple access functions are used:

```
is_strict :: arg → bool
is_strict (NodeId an id)    = member an Strict
is_strict (NODE an i s as) = member an Strict

cell_symbol :: cell → symbol
cell_symbol (Cell symbol args) = symbol

rule_symbol :: rewrite_rule → symbol
rule_symbol r = sym where (Rewrite [NODE an id sym args] rhs) = rule_alts r ! 0

rule_alts :: rewrite_rule → [rulealt]
rule_alts (TypedRule typerule rule) = rule

is_function :: symbol → bool
is_function (Function name) = True
is_function other_symbol    = False

is_NoRedex :: redex → bool
is_NoRedex (NoRedex id) = True
is_NoRedex other_redex  = False
```

```
cond c t e = t , if c
           = e , otherwise
```

This specification of the strategy is more complete than the description in words given above. For instance, here it is specified precisely how cycles are handled.

23.5 STRICTNESS ANNOTATIONS

A rewrite rule is said to be *strict* in some argument if the value of that argument is needed in every possible use of that rule. This knowledge can be used to reduce that argument to root normal form before the function is reduced. The eager reduction of a strict argument can be implemented more efficiently. Formally strictness is defined as follows:

DEFINITION **23.5.1** *A rewrite rule* F *of arity* n *is* **strict** *in its* i^{th} *argument if the (eager) evaluation of that argument does not change the termination behavior:*

$$\mathsf{F}\ a_1 \ldots a_{i-1} \bot a_{i+1} \ldots a_n = \bot$$

for all values of a_j $(j \neq i)$. *Bottom* ($\bot$) *denotes any expression without rnf.*

Strictness is in general undecidable. So, it is impossible to derive all strictness information, or to verify whether the strictness information provided is correct. In Clean there are two ways to add strictness information to a set of rewrite rules. *Global* strictness can be indicated by annotating the strict arguments in the type rule. All applications of that function are assumed to be strict in that argument. The second way to add strictness information is to place an annotation in the right-hand side of a rule. Such a *local* annotation indicates strictness for a specific function application. Using the *annotated* functional reduction strategy, strictness annotations force eager evaluation to root normal form of the corresponding graphs.

23.5.1 Strictness annotations in the type definition

A strictness annotation in a type definition forces the eager evaluation of the corresponding argument. The argument is reduced to root normal form before the rule alternatives are matched. The function check_rule in the formal specification above is replaced by:

```
check_rule :: rewrite_rule → graph → cell_id → [cell_id] → clean → redex
check_rule (TypedRule typerule alts) graph top seen clean
 = strict_redex                          , if ~is_NoRedex strict_redex
 = check_alts alts graph top seen clean  , otherwise
   where strict_redex = check_strict_args f_args a_args graph top seen clean
         [NODE ann nid f_sym f_args]  = lhs
         (Rewrite lhs rhs)            = typerule ! 0
         (Cell a_sym a_args)          = get_cell top graph
```

```
check_strict_args :: [arg] → [cell_id] → graph → cell_id → [cell_id] → clean → redex
check_strict_args (f_arg: f_args) (a_arg: a_args) graph top seen clean
 = Cycle a_arg                                        ,if strict & member seen a_arg
 = arg_redex                                          ,if strict & ~is_NoRedex arg_redex
 = check_strict_args f_args a_args graph top seen clean,otherwise
   where strict     = is_strict f_arg
         arg_redex = rnf_strat graph a_arg (a_arg: seen) clean
check_strict_args [ ] [ ] graph top seen clean = NoRedex top
```

Since reduction is defined as a sequence of individual rewrite steps no efficiency is gained by the strictness annotations in this algorithm. Only the order of these steps is influenced by this definition. The advantages in efficiency are clearly visible in the combined reduction algorithm discussed below.

The annotated functional strategy will interchange the last two reduction steps in our running example. The second argument of +P will be reduced before the redex rooted at +P since it is a global strict argument.

23.5.2 Strictness annotations in the right-hand side

The semantics of local strictness annotations in a rewrite rule is defined as:

DEFINITION **23.5.2** *A strictness annotation in a right-hand side prescribes the reduction to root normal form of the annotated subgraph before the root of that graph can be accessed*

Using the semantics of global strictness annotations in type definitions, this behavior can be achieved by the following program transformation:

Transformation

let G be a graph defining the RHS of a rewrite rule and n the node-id of a strict subgraph. The right-hand side is transformed to _Strict G' n, where G' is equal to G without the strictness annotation(s) on n. If a strict subgraph does not have a node-id a new node definition is constructed. The rewrite rule for _Strict is:

```
:: _Strict g !n → g ;
   _Strict g n  → g ;
```

In this way the semantics of local strictness annotations is expressed in the previously defined semantics of global strictness annotations. It is easy to show that the order of removing local strictness annotations is semantically irrelevant.

23.6 EXECUTION OF CLEAN PROGRAMS

Using the executable definitions of the strategy and a rewrite it is easy to construct an interpreter for Clean. This interpreter wil execute the single step semantics. The functional strategy is used to find a redex in the graph until no more redexes can be found. A rewrite step is performed for each redex indicated by the functional strategy.

```
reduce :: clean → graph → graph
reduce clean graph
 = step (functional_strat clean graph top)
   where
   (Cell graph [top])   = get_cell root_id graph
   step (Redex alt cid) = reduce clean (rewrite alt cid graph)
   step (NoRedex cid)   = graph || Normal form reached
   step (Cycle cid)     = error ("Cycle"++showcell_id cid++"in"++showgraph graph)
   step (TypeError cid)= error ("Error"++showcell_id cid++"in"++showgraph graph)
```

A trace of the reduction is obtained when the graph is shown after each reduction step. This is a very simple modification of the function step.

23.7 AN EFFICIENT REDUCTION ALGORITHM

The reduction algorithm given above reflects the semantics very clearly, but it can be optimized at many points. The general idea of these optimizations is to reduce the number of graph manipulations as much as possible. The most important optimizations are listed here.

As soon as the reduction of a node is initiated by the functional strategy its root normal form is needed. So, individual reduction steps can be combined to a reduction sequence to root normal form. In other words: the single step semantics is changed to a big step semantics where reduction to root normal form is the elementary action. Also the updates of the graph can be omitted until a root normal form is found. If the value of the root is needed in a rewrite step before it is in root normal form it is a cyclic computation and hence an error. Moreover, nodes need to be reduced to root normal form at most once. An attempt to reduce a node that is in root normal form can often be omitted when the status of nodes involved in a rewrite is recorded.

Redirection is semantically nice, but very inefficient. After every rewrite step the *whole* graph is updated by the function redirect. It is much more efficient to update the node containing the root of the redex with the root of the contractum.

Instead of a garbage collection after each rewrite step the garbage collection can be delayed until the normal form is reached or the graph space is exhausted. Since the functional strategy starts looking for a redex at the data root it is impossible to find a redex in the garbage. So, this garbage cannot even change the termination properties of the program. It is also known on theoretical grounds that it is safe to delay garbage collection [BvEG+87, Ken91].

Instead of matching a rule alternative and making a mapping if the match is found in two separate phases (the functions check_args and mapping_lhs), these actions can be combined in one pass.

It is not always necessary to create empty cells for all shared nodes before filling them as is done by create_cells. By building graphs from the leaves to the top, nodes can be stored in one action. Only for cycles an temporary empty node is needed.

For the combined reduction algorithm it is possible to gain efficiency for strict nodes. When all arguments are constructed it is possible, and more efficient, to reduce a strict subgraph at once, instead of first constructing its root and reducing it afterwards.

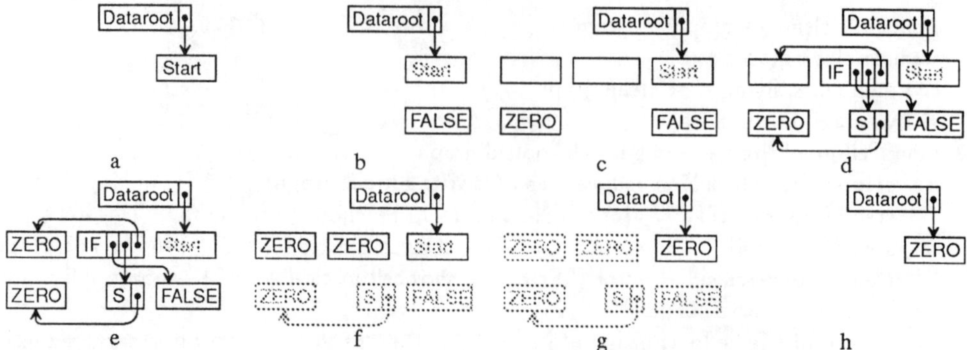

Figure 23.3 Reduction of the running example by the combined algorithm

a The initial graph. Identical to the initial graph in figure 23.1.
b The reduction of the node containing Start is initiated. The argument of F is constructed. If necessary it would have been reduced since it has a strictness annotation.
c The shared nodes in the contractum of F are created.
Node zero is filled first.
d Node b is filled, it cannot be reduced since it references the still empty node a.
e Node a is reduced and filled. The c is known to be in normal form (it is a strict argument of F). The algorithm for IF copies the contents of node zero since it is an redirection and both nodes might be shared.
f The function call _Strict ... b initiates reduction of b. Again a redirection; another copy of ZERO is made.
g Reduction according to +P, arguments are known to be in rnf. First alternative does not match. Redirection in next alternative is done by making a copy.
h The graph in normal form after garbage collection. Identical to the final graph in figure 23.2, as desired. Garbage collection is delayed until the normal form is reached.

It is possible to construct special cases in the algorithm for some frequently occurring predefined functions e.g., the predefined conditional IF and the rewrite rule for _Strict. The predefined rule for IF in a strict context will reduce its first argument, the condition, to root normal form. Depending on this value one of the other arguments will be reduced and the other one will be garbage. The optimized version reduces the condition before the other arguments are created. Reduction is continued with the needed branch and the other branch is never constructed. It is not necessary to build a node containing the symbol _Strict in a strict context. The effect of the rewrite rule is obtained by reducing the second argument before the first argument is treated. The very same node is used for _Strict and its first argument, this saves one redirection.

Due to space limitations it is not possible to give a detailed specification of the combined reduction algorithm. A description can be found in [KSEP91].

Reduction of the running example according to this algorithm is shown below. Compare this with the corresponding reduction shown in figures 23.1 and 23.2.

23.7.1 Compiling Clean

A compiler generates code to perform the graph manipulations which are descirbed above. A tailor-made abstract machine is defined as an intermediate level between the graph rewrite steps in Clean and concrete machine architectures. This stack-based abstract machine is called the ABC-machine [KvEN+90, Koo90, PvE93]. For a compiler, the gain from using the status information is even higher. Not only is the number of graph manipulations reduced, but this information is available at compile time. Compilers from Clean to code for the ABC-machine are described in [Koo90, Sme89, SNvGP91, PvE93]. Efficient compilers for ABC-code are available [vG90, SNvGP91].

23.8 DISCUSSION

This chapter gives a description of the operational semantics of a rewrite step and the annotated functional reduction strategy used in the graph rewrite language Clean. To our knowledge, this is the first formal description of the annotated functional reduction strategy for graph rewrite systems published. The formal specifications of these algorithms in Miranda are longer than informal descriptions. Apart from the well-defined semantics the formal specification in a functional programming language has two advantages. First, it is possible to check the partial correctness of the specification by an implementation of the description language. Second, the dynamic behavior of the specified algorithms can be observed.

The rewrite algorithm and the annotated functional reduction strategy can be combined into a single efficient reduction algorithm. Implementations of Clean based on this algorithm achieve state-of-the-art execution speed.

REFERENCES

[BBK87] J.C.M. Baeten, J.A. Bergstra, and J.W. Klop. Term rewriting systems with priorities. In *Proc. of Conference on Rewriting Techniques and Applications*, pp. 83–94. Bordeaux, 1987.

[BvEG+87] H.P. Barendregt, M.C.J.D. van Eekelen, J.R.W. Glauert, J.R. Kennaway, M.J. Plasmeijer, and M.R. Sleep. Term graph reduction. In *Proc. of Parallel Architectures and Languages Europe (PARLE)*, pp. 141–158. Eindhoven, The Netherlands, 1987.

[BvEG+88] H.P. Barendregt, M.C.J.D. van Eekelen, J.R.W. Glauert, J.R. Kennaway, M.J. Plasmeijer, and M.R. Sleep. Towards an intermediate language based on graph rewriting. *selected papers of the conference on Parallel Architectures and Languages Europe (PARLE)*, 1988.

[BvEvL+87] T. Brus, M.C.J.D. van Eekelen, M. van Leer, M.J. Plasmeijer, and H.P. Barendregt. Clean - a language for functional graph rewriting. In *Proc. of Conference on Functional Programming Languages and Computer Architecture (FPCA '87)*, pp. 364–384. Portland, Oregon, USA, 1987.

[HJW+92] P. Hudak, S.L. Peyton Jones, P.L. Wadler, B. Boutel, J. Fairbairn, J. Fasel, M.M. Guzman, K. Hammond, J. Hughes, T. Johnsson, R. Kieburtz, R.S. Nikhil, W. Partain, and J. Peterson. Report on the functional programming language haskell. *ACM SIGPLAN Notices*, **27**, 5, May 1992.

[Ken91] J.R. Kennaway. Graph rewriting in some categories of partial homomorphisms. In Kreowski Ehrig and Rozenberg (editors), *Proc. of 4th International Workshop on Graph-Grammars and Their Application to Computer Science*, pp. 490–504, 1991.

[Klo92] J.W. Klop. Term rewriting systems. In Abramsky, Gabbay, and Maibaum (editors), *Handbook of Logic in Computer Science*, vol. I. Oxford University Press, 1992.

[Koo90] P.W.M. Koopman. *Functional Programs as Executable Specifications.* PhD thesis, University of Nijmegen, 1990.

[KSEP91] P.W.M. Koopman, J.E.W. Smetsers, M.C.J.D. Eekelen, and M.J. Plasmeijer. Efficient graph rewriting using the annotated functional strategy. In *Proc. of Semagraph Symposium*, pp. 225–251. Nijmegen, The Netherlands, 1991.

[KvEN+90] P.W.M. Koopman, M.C.J.D. van Eekelen, E.G.J.M.H. Nöcker, Plasmeijer M.J., and Smetsers J.E.W. *The ABC-machine: A Sequential Stack-based Abstract Machine For Graph Rewriting.* Technical Report 90-22, University of Nijmegen, 1990.

[Mil78] R.A. Milner. Theory of type polymorphism in programming. *Journal of Computer and System Sciences*, **17**, 1978.

[Myc84] A. Mycroft. Polymorphic type schemes and recursive definitions. In *Proc. of 6th Int. Conf. on Programming*, pp. 217–239. Eindhoven, The Netherlands, 1984.

[NSvEP91] E.G.J.M.H. Nöcker, J.E.W. Smetsers, M.C.J.D. van Eekelen, and M.J. Plasmeijer. Concurrent Clean. In *Proc. of Parallel Architectures and Languages Europe (PARLE'91)*, pp. 202–219. Eindhoven, The Netherlands, 1991.

[PvE93] M.J. Plasmeijer and M.C.J.D. van Eekelen. *Functional Programming and Parallel Graph Rewriting.* International Computer Science Series. Addison Wesley, 1993.

[Sme89] J.E.W. Smetsers. *Compiling Clean to Abstract ABC-Machine Code.* Technical Report 89-20, University of Nijmegen, 1989.

[SNvGP91] J.E.W. Smetsers, E.G.J.M.H. Nöcker, J.H.G. van Groningen, and M.J. Plasmeijer. Generating efficient code for lazy functional languages. In *Proc. of Conference on Functional Programming Languages and Computer Architecture (FPCA '91)*, pp. 592–617. Cambridge, MA, USA, 1991.

[Tur85] D.A. Turner. Miranda: A non-strict functional language with polymorphic types. In *Proc. of Conference on Functional Programming Languages and Computer Architecture*, pp. 1–16. Portland, Oregon, USA, 1985.

[vEP90] M.C.J.D. van Eekelen and M.J. Plasmeijer. Concurrent functional programming. In *Proc. of Conference on Unix & Parallelism*, pp. 75–98., 1990.

[vG90] J.H.G. van Groningen. Implementing the abc-machine on m680x0 based architectures. Master's thesis, University of Nijmegen, 1990.

24

Implementing Logical Variables and Disjunctions in Graph Rewrite Systems

P.J.McBrien

24.1 INTRODUCTION

Graph Rewriting Systems (GRS) have been widely studied and used as the implementation vehicle for functional programming languages, some example implementations of GRS being DACTL [GKSS88] and the G-Machine [Joh84]. To date, the application of graph rewriting to the implementation of logic programming has met with somewhat less success, in part due to a concentration on the Prolog language which already has a successful implementation vehicle in the Warren Abstract Machine [War83] (usually referred to as the *WAM*). In this chapter the issues relating to the use of graph rewriting for implementing logic programming languages in the wider sense will be discussed.

The results presented in this chapter have been used as a basis for the definition and implementation of a graph rewriting language *TAM* [McB92] which supports directly the logical variable, operations to trail bindings of such variables (i.e. record for later reversal), and a special type of rewrite on graphs called *term rewriting on graphs* necessary to easily support logic languages. The implementation of the TAM is directed towards standard von Neumann architecture machines, and thus issues relating to the parallel evaluation of the graph rewriting will only be briefly dealt with.

We shall state informally what we mean by a logic programming language and its evaluation:

Term Graph Rewriting: Theory and Practice.
Eds. Ronan Sleep, Rinus Plasmeijer and Marko van Eekelen.

- a *logic programming language* P consists of a syntactic language L, and a set of directed equivalence rules R which express transformations or *reductions* which may be applied to terms of the language.
- the *evaluation* of P consists of taking some input term $i \in L$ with free variables v, applying the rules R in some specified manner to i until it is in some normal form, and then returning the normal form expression together with the bindings of v. If at any stage more than one rule may be applied, then the normal forms resulting from applying each of the rules should be found in turn.

The definition of a logic programming language is intentionally loose, and encompasses a much wider class of languages than those based on Horn-Clause logic, for which the title is usually reserved. Any computational logic which we may represent as term rewrite rules is acceptable.

In [BL86] a comparison between logic programming (restricted to the Horn-Clause subset) and functional languages was made, which revealed two fundamental differences between the approaches itemized below. Since the relationship between functional languages and GRS is both well established and close, these comments can be seen to be equally valid to the comparison of logic programming with GRS.

- **Determinism** logic programming uses a search-based computational model to achieve the effect of the non-deterministic evaluation of logical disjunctions, while functional languages have clear deterministic computational semantics.
- **Logical Variable** logic programs use unification (essentially bidirectional pattern matching), and allow variables to be treated like any other data, and thus be passed to and returned from functions. A corollary of this is that the local variables of a function may remain in existence outside the scope of the function.

A GRS is non-deterministic when no evaluation strategy is being used, but that is a "blind" non-determinism which will only follow "correct" reduction orders (i.e. ones not ending in failure) by chance. By contrast, the searching mechanism of logic programming means that the "correct" reduction order is always discovered (except for entering infinite loops or if "non-logical" features of the language are used).

The objective of [BL86] was to bring together logic programming and functional languages into a common formalism, and towards that aim it was suggested that functional languages be extended to include unification, and that logic programming be restricted in their use of both search-based computations and the logical variable. Many of the parallel logic programming languages [Sha87], such as GHC and Parlog may be regarded as meeting these criteria. They belong to a family of languages called *committed-choice* logic languages, which ease the problems associated with the parallel implementation of logic programming by making the rules of the program commit after the evaluation of some guard, and not be permitted to backtrack. Rules take the form:

$p(a_1, \ldots, a_n) \vdash guard_a | body_a.$

$p(a_1, \ldots, a_n) \vdash guard_b | body_b.$

All the rules for $p(a_1, \ldots, a_n)$ have their guards $guard_a, guard_b$ *etc,* evaluated in parallel, during which no variables from the program goal may be instantiated. The first guard to succeed causes the rule to commit, and the evaluation of all other guards to be stopped. Only then does evaluation of the rule body begin, which may instantiate variables from the goal. Thus we never need consider the backtracking of variable instantiations, since the only variables that are instantiated before a rule commits are those local to the rule, and thus can be ignored for the purposes of backtracking. After a rule commits there can be no backtracking on the choice made by the guard, hence the name "committed-choice".

Such languages readily lend themselves to implementation in GRS, and implementations of both GHC [GP88] and Parlog [Pap89] have been achieved in DACTL. These implementations provide for the logical variable and a unification algorithm, but due to the nature of the languages they implement, do not address the issues concerned with non-determinism (in the sense of always finding the "correct" clauses which lead to a solution). By contrast, the objective here is to implement all aspects of logic programming in GRS. While the inclusion of unification into GRS is a clear necessity which has already been achieved in several implementations, the provision of logical variables which work with some evaluation mechanism for disjunctions (search-based or otherwise) still needs to be investigated.

This chapter will develop a standard definition of GRS given in section 24.2, to allow for the implementation of all aspects of logic programming, including support for non-determinism. This will be conducted by firstly considering in section 24.3 how we may represent the logical variable in GRS, and then in section 24.4 discussing the issues relating to the evaluation of disjunctions.

24.2 GRAPH REWRITING

The GRS we shall be describing here are strictly speaking *labeled graphs* and *labeled term graphs*, but we shall refer to them simply as *graphs*. We shall also restrict ourselves to considering acyclic graphs, since the semantics of cyclic structures when considering logic programming languages, and in particular first order languages is not immediately apparent, and remains to be investigated.

The definitions a graph and graph rewriting are based on those in [BvEG+87], which should be consulted for examples and more precise definitions. A variation that is introduced here is that we class a certain number of zero arity functors as being constants — a distinction which becomes useful later. We also incorporate changes suggested in [Han91, McB92] which allows *selector functions* (such as $id(\mathbf{x}) \rightarrow \mathbf{x}$) to be dealt with correctly.

DEFINITION **24.2.1 (Labeled Graph)** *A rooted labeled graph G is defined as a tuple $(N, lab, succ, r)$ over an alphabet A, divided into functors F, variables V and constants C, where*

- *N is a finite set of nodes, where each $n \in N$ is identified by its* address *n.*
- *lab is the labeling a function $N \rightarrow A$, where we can speak of the member of A chosen as the* label *or* name *of the node. There must be at most one node n labeled by any variable $v \in V$.*
- *succ is the successor function $N \rightarrow N^*$, where the ordered set $\{n_1, \ldots, n_k\} \in N^*$ are the* successors *or* arguments *of the corresponding $n \in N$, and k is the* arity *of n. We may refer to a particular argument n_i by $succ(n)_i$, and refer to $succ(n)_i$ as being a* pointer *to n_i.*

- *$r \in N$ is nominated as the* root *node. We use $G|r$ as a shorthand for speaking of the subgraph rooted at r.*

Definition 24.2.2 presents our terminology for relating graphs with each other, and the way we can speak of graphs which differ only in the variables they contain as being in a sense equivalent.

DEFINITION **24.2.2 (Graph homomorphism, isomorphism and equivalence)** *A* homomorphism *is a mapping $h : N_1 \longrightarrow N_2$ between two graphs $g_1 = (N_1, lab_1, succ_1, r_1)$ and $g_2 = (N_2, lab_2, succ_2, r_2)$ which has the properties that for all nodes $n \in N_1$*

$lab_2(h(n)) = lab_1(n)$ *where* $lab_1(n) \notin V$

$succ_2(h(n)) = h(succ_1(n))$

We say that $h\{n_1, \ldots, n_k\} = \{h(n_1), \ldots, h(n_k)\}$, and by abuse of notation apply the homomorphism to graphs as a function i.e. $h(N, lab, succ, r)$ gives the graph g_2 formed by applying h to g_1.

An isomorphism *is any homomorphism h which has an inverse homomorphism h'' such that $g_2 = h(g_1)$ and $g_1 = h''(g_2)$. Thus we may say $h'' \circ h = h \circ h'' = id$, where id is the identity homomorphism for which $g = id(g)$ is obeyed for any g.*

A rooted homomorphism *is one which obeys $r_2 = h(r_1)$, and a* rooted isomorphism *is one where both the forward and inverse homomorphisms are rooted. Two graphs are* equivalent *if they have a rooted isomorphism, and we write $g_1 \simeq g_2$.*

The essence of a homomorphism is to make two graphs identical by replacing variables in one graph with any graph valid in the GRS. It can be seen that this is analogous to term substitution which serves to replace variables with any term of a TRS, so we may refer to a homomorphism as a *graph substitution*. Isomorphic graphs can differ only in the nodes labeled by members of V.

DEFINITION **24.2.3 (Graph rewriting)** *A graph rewrite rule is a triple (g_r, r_h, r_b) where g_r is an open labeled graph containing nodes r_h and r_b, which are the root nodes of the graphs* head *and* body. *Conventionally we write such a rule as* head $\longrightarrow$ body. *A variable may not be part of the* body *if it is not part of the* head.

The application of a graph rewrite rule to a graph g_0 has four steps:

a. matching *the rule against the graph g_0, which involves finding a node n and a homomorphism h such that $g_0|n = h(head)$ and $body - head = h(body - head)$ except for any instances of the* succ *function that point to elements of the* head. *We call $h(head)$ the* redex *and $h(body)$ the* contractum. *This homomorphism can be regarded as the "minimum" necessary, since it should leave the parts of the* body *not part of the* head *unchanged.*
b. *the* build phase, *where an isomorphic copy of $h(body - head)$ is made using the same homomorphism used to make* head *equal to the* redex *during matching. This copy is added to g_0 to give g_1.*
c. *the* redirection phase *updates the* succ *function and possibly the root of g_1 to give graph g_2 so that:*
   $\forall n, i.$ *if* $succ_1(n)_i = h(r_h)$ *then* $succ_2(n)_i = h(r_b)$ *else* $succ_2(n)_i = succ_1(n)_i$
   if $r_1 = h(r_h)$ *then* $r_2 = h(r_b)$ *else* $r_2 = r_1$

d. *the* garbage collection phase, *where any nodes* $n \in N_2$ *for which no path exists from* r_2 *to* n *are removed from* g_2 *to give* g_3.

24.3 THE LOGICAL VARIABLE

Of fundamental importance when implementing logic programming is the ability to handle the concept of a *logical variable*, which in the context of GRS we can define as follows:

DEFINITION **24.3.1 (Logical variable)** *A* logical variable *is a graph which we interpret as representing any unknown graph. The normal GRS restriction that no rewrite rule may contain a variable in the body which does not appear in the head is removed. Such* free variables *cause a new logical variable to be created in the graph as part of the normal contractum building phase.*

The graphical representation of formulae lends itself naturally to the representation of the logical variable, by simply allocating a special node label (here the name VAR is used) to represent a variable node, and then creating a node with that label for each variable. When the value of the variable is discovered during computation, then we substitute all occurrences of the variable with the value. This process of *variable instantiation* or *variable binding* could be easily achieved using the normal graph rewrite operation, where all pointers to the graph representing the variable are redirected to the value it is being bound to. This definition and use of the logical variable is similar to that found in DACTL implementations of logic programming [GP88, Pap89], where an *overwritable* symbol VAR is used for variables, and graph redirection used for variable instantiation. (An overwritable symbol is one which is not found as the root of any rewrite rule, but nevertheless may be changed by a redirection operation).

Since the definition of logic programming language requires that we are able to inspect the values taken by variables at the end of the computation, any "external" reference to a variable must also be updated by the redirection. Also the need to try several rules means that in some circumstances we need to be able to *backtrack* (i.e. reverse) the binding of variables during computation (as shall be seen in the section describing the evaluation of disjunctions), which requires that we must record all the nodes effected by redirection so that the action may be reversed.

At this point it may be thought that the graph rewrite operation is becoming a rather cumbersome procedure, but a well-known implementation procedure of *indirection functions* [PJ87] will be seen to overcome this problem, which will be called *identity functions* here to correspond with their intended semantics.

24.3.1 Identity Functions and Nodes

DEFINITION **24.3.2 (The identity functor and identity functions)** *Nominate a privileged functor* $\Im/1$ *as the* identity functor, *which for all graphs* t *of a GRS obeys the identity rule* $\Im(t) \simeq_{\Im} t$, *which says a node labeled with* $\Im/1$ *is regarded as being equivalent the node pointed to by its* $succ_1$ *entry. In particular, Definition 24.2.2 of homomorphism is changed to ignore nodes labeled with* $\Im/1$, *so that* $\forall n.(lab(n) = \Im) \rightarrow (h(n) = h(succ_1(n)))$

For pattern matching purposes, this has the consequence that if t is a potential redex then so is $\Im(t)$, and that during pattern matching phase of rewriting (q.v. Definition 24.2.3) we regard any node n with $lab(n) = \Im$ as being the node $succ_1(n)$. We may use the identity functions to produce a modified definition of graph rewriting in Definition 24.3.3 which uses the new functions to replace the redirection phase with an *indirection phase.* This definition also adjusts the garbage collection phase to take account of the fact that logical variables are referred to from outside the graph, and thus their instantiations must not be removed by garbage collection.

DEFINITION **24.3.3 (Graph rewriting using identity functions)** *The graph rewriting of Definition 24.2.3 is modified in steps (c) and (d) to be:*

c. *the* indirection phase *only updates the lab and succ function so that* $lab_2(h(r_h)) = \Im$ *and* $succ_2(h(r_h)) = h(r_b)$
d. *the* garbage collection phase, *which finds all nodes* $n \in N_2$ *for which no path exists from* r_2 *to* n, *and no path exists to* n *from any of the nodes representing the logical variables. Remove all such nodes from* g_2 *to give* g_3.

The effect of Definition 24.3.3 on the rewriting process for a rule $t \rightarrow s$ is that the root of the redex is *overwritten* with an indirection function $\Im$ pointing to s, whereas previously we would have redirected all pointers to the redex root to instead point at s. It is apparent that this gives a gain in efficiency since there is now no need to redirect any of the pointers to the redex, while the body s may have any address. Set against this, there will be an overhead of having to follow indirection nodes when accessing graphs. We will refer to the graph rewriting of Definition 24.2.3 as the *redirection method* and that of Definition 24.3.3 as the *indirection method.*

The two types of rewriting will produce identical results in all circumstances where the redex root would have been garbage collected in the redirection method, since it cannot then matter what the indirection method uses this node for. The redex root will be garbage collected unless it is also the contractum root, i.e. unless $h(r_h) = h(r_b)$.

This would be trivially true for rules where $r_h = r_b$, but otherwise will only occur when a selector function "removes" a path of length n from $h(r_h)$ to $h(r_b)$ from a cycle of length n, thus making $h(r_h) = h(r_b)$, e.g. we have a rule of the form $f(g(\mathbf{x})) \rightarrow \mathbf{x}$ and a cyclic graph $\mathbf{a} : f(g(\mathbf{a}))$. In this circumstance the indirection to the contractum root is incorrect, since rewriting using the redirection method should have left the redex root unchanged, but using the indirection method changes it to become $\Im(\Im(\Im(\Im(\ldots))))$.

The identity function $\Im$ is represented as a graph in exactly the same manner as any other function (here the name IEXP is used). When speaking of the graphical form of the identity function we can say that it represents an *indirection* to its argument. Any rewrite operation may use it to avoid the need for redirecting pointers, but when used for logical variables it has a useful side-effect. If we use indirection during rewriting, we instantiate a variable to value x by overwriting the variable node with $\Im(x)$. Inspecting the location of the variable at any later time during the computation will enable us to read the value $\Im(x)$ (which is equivalent to x), and if necessary change it. Example 24.3.4 illustrates the use of the indirection method during rewriting, and how the location of variables may always be read to find their current instantiation.

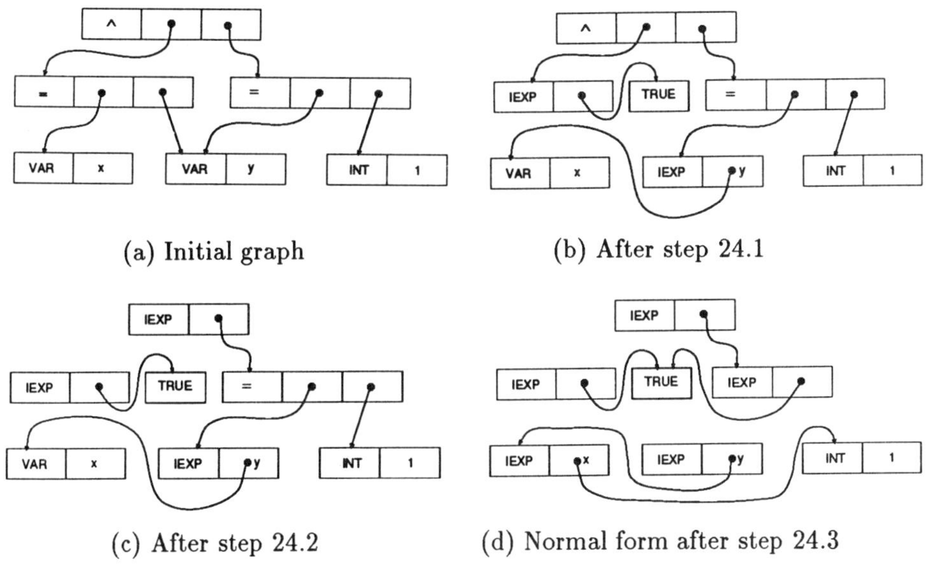

(a) Initial graph

(b) After step 24.1

(c) After step 24.2

(d) Normal form after step 24.3

Figure 24.1 Rewriting using indirection

EXAMPLE **24.3.4 (Rewriting using the indirection method)** *The graphs of following sequence of rewrites are illustrated in figure 24.1.*

$$\begin{aligned} \mathbf{x} = \mathbf{y} \wedge \mathbf{y} = 1 &\rightarrow \mathsf{TRUE} \wedge \mathbf{x} = 1 & (24.1)\\ &\rightarrow \mathbf{x} = 1 & (24.2)\\ &\rightarrow \mathsf{TRUE} & (24.3) \end{aligned}$$

a. The initial graph contains two VAR *nodes for the* **x** *and* **y** *variables.*

b. Equating **x** *and* **y** *requires two alterations to the graph. First, the node representing* **y** *is overwritten with an indirection to the node representing* **x** *(the opposite might equally have been done), and second the node representing an equality between the two variables is overwritten with an indirection to* TRUE.

c. The reduction of the conjunction makes the equality between **y** *and* 1 *the root of the graph via an identity function.*

d. The equality between a variable and a constant requires two actions. First, the variable is overwritten with an indirection to the node representing 1*, and second the equality node is replaced by an indirection to* TRUE *as the root of the graph.*

When reduction is complete we have TRUE *as the normal form, and inspecting the location of the variable* **x** *shows it instantiated with* $\Im(1)$, *and* **y** *with* $\Im(\Im(1))$, *both of which are equivalent (under* $\simeq_\Im$*) to* 1. *The answer can be read as* TRUE *with the substitutions* $1/\mathbf{x}$ *and* $1/\mathbf{y}$.

24.4 LOGICAL DISJUNCTIONS

A fundamental feature of logic programming languages is that we allow the variables of the computation to have a series of values associated with them corresponding to the value the variable takes in different disjuncts, and provide some method for that series of values to be presented to the user. This conflicts with the graphical representation of variables, which inherently represents a single value. Furthermore, the multiple values associated with variables may mean alternative rewrites apply to the same graph as the variable takes different values. In this section these problems are illustrated by presenting some examples, and then some general solutions are proposed.

24.4.1 Phantom Variable Bindings

If we naively apply graph rewriting to a disjunction which gives different values to the same variable, we find that the operation of binding a variable to a value in one disjunct will result in a *phantom variable binding*, where the same value is given to the variable in all other disjuncts.

EXAMPLE **24.4.1 (Phantom variable binding)** *We have the rewrite rule*

eq(x,g) :- var(x),ground(g),x:=g → TRUE

stating that where x *is a free variable and* **g** *is any ground term, then the* x *node may be overwritten with an indirection to the node representing the* **g**. *The following is then a "correct" result (in terms of the semantics of GRS) of applying our rule to a disjunction:*

or(eq(y,1),eq(y,2)) → or(TRUE,eq(1,2))

The binding of the variable y *in the* eq(y,1) *disjunct has also erroneously bound the* y *in the* eq(y,2) *disjunct.*

There are at least three possible solutions to this problem:

- **Backtracking** where the evaluation of different disjuncts is taken in turn, and a record is made on a *trail* of all variables bound during the evaluation of a particular disjunct. Thus when evaluation of it is complete, the variables may be returned to the state in which they were previously, before evaluation of the next disjunct begins. For this to work successfully, it is important that we use the indirection rewrite method, so that the location of a variable is always fixed, and thus references on the trail regarding the variable can be made to this fixed location.
- **Variable Substitution** where we use the equivalence that
$$\phi \vee \psi \equiv \phi \vee [n/n''][n''/n]\psi \text{ (where } n'' \notin \phi \vee \psi)$$
whenever variable n appears in both ϕ and ψ, so that there is no variable name clash between the two disjuncts. We may then apply rewrites to ϕ and $[n''/n]\psi$ without concern of phantom bindings occurring, and then use the outermost substitution to replace n'' with n in ψ.
- **Set Based Evaluation** where we store with each variable the set of values associated with it, and thus can represent the alternate values of various disjuncts directly.

24.4.2 Phantom Rewrites

The phantom variable effect discussed above is a manifestation of a more general problem concerned with sharing graphs between different disjuncts. Since each disjunct may have its own particular bindings for some variables, there is the possibility that different rewrite rules will apply to a certain redex in different disjuncts. The overwriting of the redex in one disjunct with the body of the rule may be incorrect for other disjuncts containing that redex, and result in *phantom rewrites* occurring.

EXAMPLE **24.4.2 (The phantom rewrite problem)**

$$(\mathbf{y}=1 \vee \mathbf{y}=2) \wedge \mathbf{x}=\mathbf{y} \rightarrow (\mathbf{y}=1 \wedge \mathbf{x}=\mathbf{y}) \vee (\mathbf{y}=2 \wedge \mathbf{x}=\mathbf{y}) \quad (24.4)$$
$$(\mathbf{y}=1 \wedge \mathbf{x}=\mathbf{y}) \quad (24.5)$$
$$\rightarrow (\mathsf{TRUE} \wedge \mathbf{x}=1) \quad (24.6)$$
$$\rightarrow \mathbf{x}=1 \quad (24.7)$$
$$\rightarrow \mathsf{TRUE} \quad (24.8)$$
$$\rightarrow (\mathbf{y}=1 \wedge \mathbf{x}=1) \vee (\mathbf{y}=2 \wedge \mathsf{TRUE}) \quad (24.9)$$
$$(\mathbf{y}=2 \wedge \mathsf{TRUE}) \quad (24.10)$$
$$\rightarrow \mathbf{y}=2 \quad (24.11)$$
$$\rightarrow \mathsf{TRUE} \quad (24.12)$$
$$\rightarrow (\mathbf{y}=1 \wedge \mathbf{x}=1) \vee (\mathbf{y}=2) \quad (24.13)$$

After step 24.4 backtracking is used to reduce the disjunction, beginning with the left-hand disjunct. In step 24.8 of the rewrite we redirect the **x** *variable to point at the number* 1, *and overwrite the equality with* TRUE. *However this will also change the same equality in the right-hand disjunct, so that when step 24.9 is reached, we see that the equality* **x=y** *present at step 24.4 has been erroneously changed to be* TRUE.

The example shows that a reduction applied to an expression shared between two disjuncts, which is valid in the context of the evaluation of one disjunct, may result in a semantically incorrect reduction in the other disjunct. Loosely speaking, we can state that no graph should be overwritten inside the scope of a disjunction, if the rewrite rule used depends on the instantiation of a variable made also inside the scope of the disjunction, unless enough information is recorded so that the rewrite may be fully reversed at some later stage.

In broad terms, there are three solutions to avoiding this problem:

- **Trailing Rewrite Operations** in the same way as Prolog trails the binding of logical variables, we could trail the graph nodes changed by a rewrite operation, and restore their previous values on backtracking. It is clear that such a trail would have a considerable implementation overhead since every rewrite operation would require at least one entry on the trail.
- **Graph Copying** where we do not permit expressions to be shared between disjuncts, and enforce a rule that when an expression x is "pushed" inside the scope of a disjunction by rewrite rules such as $x \wedge (y \vee z) \rightarrow (x \wedge y) \vee (x \wedge z)$, then at least one instance of x must be copied. The operation of such copying is obvious and intuitive for all types of graph node except the variable node. The variable node represents the concept of an unknown graph by its position in memory, and copying it would produce a new (i.e. different) variable. This is obviously related to how we handle variables, and we will return to this point later on.

- **Term Rewrites on Graphs** where the result of the rewrite does not overwrite the root of the redex, but instead is returned as a graph representing the reduced form of the redex. This is used only to update the pointer to the redex which was used during the original pattern matching of the rule against the redex. In the context of graph rewriting we may refer to such rules simply as term rewrites. The $\rightarrow$ (or for emphasis $\rightarrow_t$) operator will be used in the TAM-Rewrite language to indicate rules which work by term rewriting, and the $\rightarrow_g$ operator for rules which work by graph rewriting. Example 24.4.3 illustrates the difference in results produced by the two types of rewrite rules.
  The distinction between these two types of operation also appears in an early version of DACTL [GKS87], but at the time there seemed to be no clear semantics or practical use for providing distinct types of rewriting, and thus the distinction was dropped from the next version of DACTL [GKSS88].

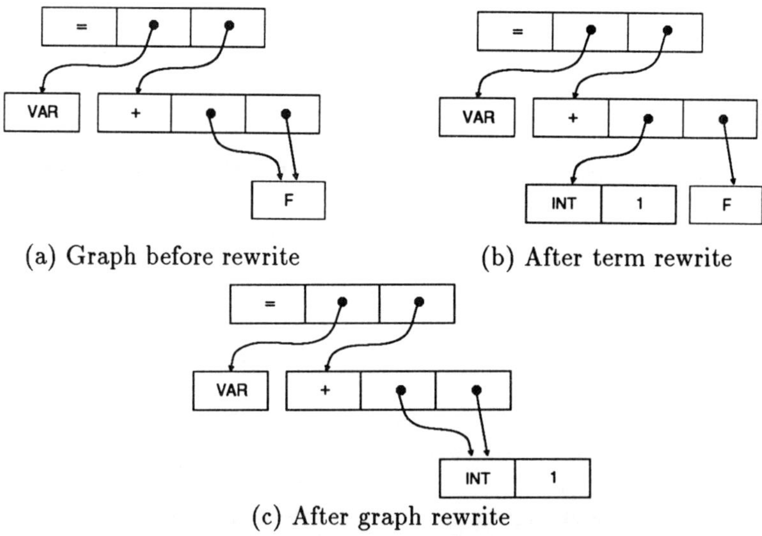

Figure 24.2 Using term and graph rewrites

EXAMPLE **24.4.3 (Term and graph rewriting** x=F()+F()) *Using the* term rewrite rule F() $\rightarrow_t$ 1 *we have the reduction* x=F()+F() $\rightarrow_t$ x=1+F(). *This is because the rewrite operation only redirects the pointer "involved" in the pattern matching to point to the contractum* 1, *leaving all other references to the redex* F() *unchanged in figure 24.2 (b).*

When using the graph rewrite rule F() $\rightarrow_g$ 1 *we get the reduction* x=F()+F() $\rightarrow_g$ x=1+1, *since the rewrite operation causes all pointers to the redex* F() *to be redirected to the contractum* 1 *in figure 24.2 (c).*

A comparison of *graph copying* and *term rewrites on graphs* as the solution to the phantom rewrite problem can be only subjective at this stage. It can be recognized that graph copying has a considerable overhead since it copies graphs which may never be overwritten, which is frequently the case in practice. For example, if we consider rules such as $\mathsf{FALSE} \wedge \mathbf{x} \rightarrow \mathsf{FALSE}$ and $\mathsf{TRUE} \vee \mathbf{x} \rightarrow \mathsf{TRUE}$, the graph matched by **x** could represent a large expression which is being "dropped", and thus if previously copied would have no pointers to it, and would be subject to garbage collection. In contrast, the term rewrite approach only "copies" (i.e. does not put an identity function in) the redex root node. Thus the worst case is that it "copies" a single node which is not shared.

24.4.3 Relating the Phantom Variable Binding and Phantom Rewrite Solutions

As stated before, the phantom rewrite effect is a more general instance of the phantom variable binding effect, and thus the choice between graph copying or term rewriting is related to the choice of solution for dealing with phantom variable bindings. This leads to there being two combined approaches to the execution of logic programming using graph rewriting, where either:

- *backtracking* should be used with *term rewrites*. During execution, we proceed by rewriting each disjunct in turn. Any redirections away from variable nodes made during the rewriting of one disjunct are always made using logical binds, i.e. backtrackable graph rewrites. Thus they may be reversed before proceeding with the rewriting of the next disjunct. Any other changes to part of the graph shared between disjuncts are made using term rewrites, thus preserving the structure of the graph in the context of the other disjuncts.
- *variable substitution* should be used with *graph copying*. In making a copy of the graph, any new variable formed would represent the substitution for the variable being "copied". Graph rewriting without any backtracking may then be used in a uniform manner for both variables and the general structure of the logical formula.

In making the choice of which overall method to use, we should also consider the computer architecture on which execution will take place. In broad terms, we may say that *sequential machines* will execute the term rewrite solution more efficiently than copying, due the latter tending to produce the wasted copies previously mentioned. By contrast *parallel machines* are in effect are continuously copying graphs in that they must pass graphs from one processor to another, and so might perform variable substitution without much overhead. For the purposes of this chapter we shall only investigate further term rewrites combined with the use of backtracking, since the aim of the work in [McB92] is an implementation on sequential machines.

24.4.4 Term Rewrites on Graphs

The previous subsection described the notion of a term rewrite on graphs in a practical context. In this subsection a more formal definition is given, by relating term rewrites to the definition of graph rewriting introduced by Definitions 24.2.3 and 24.3.3. Before this can be done, the concept of *context* in pattern matching must be defined.

DEFINITION **24.4.4 (Pattern matching contexts)** *The process of pattern matching a rule against a graph as described in Definition 24.2.3 involves searching the* *graph g for a subgraph $g_0|n$ matching the rule head. Unless n is the root, this process will arrive at the node n as $succ(n_c)_i$ of another node n_c. The* context *of the pattern matching may then be identified as the tuple $< n_c, i >$. If it is the root of the graph that matches the rule then the context is undefined.*

In Example 24.4.3 we see that the rewrite of F() has a context of the first successor of the + node, since that was the route used during pattern matching to find the redex. As presented so far, the choice of which F() we reach in pattern matching is arbitrary, but if we use DACTL-like control markings in the rewrite rules we may specify the route used to reach a node. In the example, writing x=(!F())+F() indicates the first *succ* of + is the context for any term rewrite on F(), while x=F()+(!F()) indicates the second *succ* is the context.

DEFINITION **24.4.5 (Term rewrites on graphs)** *A term rewrite on graphs behaves in exactly the same manner as a graph rewrite, except that the redirection phase (step (c) of Definition 24.2.3) will only change the instance of the* succ *function identified by the context $< n_c, i >$ of the rewrite, and does not change all instances of* succ *which point at the root of the redex.*

Note that to achieve the term rewrite on graphs we can not use the indirection technique of Definition 24.3.3, since that always has the effect of changing all the instances of the *succ* function which point at it. The behavior of a term rewrite on graphs is illustrated in Example 24.4.3.

24.4.5 Using Term and Graph Rewrites

From the preceding discussion it is apparent that the choice of using a term or graph rewrite rule for a particular reduction is critical to the correct implementation of a logic language. The purpose of this subsection is to describe guidelines for the choice of which type of rule to use in given situations. Before giving these guidelines, we need a definition of the elements of a logic programming language, which is given in Definition 24.4.6, and is based on that in [Hog91]. So as to avoid confusion with the terminology of term rewriting we shall refer to the "terms" of logic languages as *logical terms.*

DEFINITION **24.4.6 (Logical terms)** *The set of functors in Definition 24.2.1 are divided into* function *symbols S,* predicate *symbols P, and* connective *symbols C. For example, if $F = \{\mathsf{f}, \mathsf{g}, \mathsf{likes}, =, \mathsf{and}, \mathsf{or}, \mathsf{not}\}$ then we might have $S = \{\mathsf{f}, \mathsf{g}\}$, P={likes,=} and C={and,or,not}.*

A logical term *is a constant, variable or function made up using a function symbol and logical terms. e.g.* 1 mary john X f(1,f(mary))

An atomic formula *is a function made up of a predicate symbol and logical terms. e.g.* likes(john,mary) 1=2

A well-formed formula *(wff) is a function made up of a connective symbol and atomic formulae or wff. e.g.* and(likes(john,mary), likes(mary,john))

The discussion will be limited to consider only first-order languages, which have the restriction that a variable may only represent a logical term, and not any well-formed formulae of the language [Ric89]. The guidelines for performing rewrites on first-order languages are given in Theorem 24.4.7.

THEOREM **24.4.7 (Mixed use of term and graph rewrites)** *A graph rewrite rule may only be used in the evaluation of a first-order logic language when*

a. the variables in the head-pattern of the rule only match logical terms, and
b. the class of graph matched by the head-pattern can only be produced by graph rewriting operations.

The first clause of Theorem 24.4.7 dictates that we may use functors that are used to form a wff or predicates in a graph rewrite head pattern, but not the constants or any functors used to form terms. Thus only term rewrites may use constants in their head patterns, and if in the language being implemented we can assign the functor f/k to a variable, then f/k may not appear in a graph rewrite pattern. The second clause of Theorem 24.4.7 means that if a structure matched by a pattern can be formed by a term rewrite, then it is not safe to use a graph rewrite. The reason for this restriction is that a term rewrite could have been made to avoid breaking the theorem, and thus using the graph so produced to match against the pattern of a graph rewrite rule would indirectly break the theorem. An example will make this point clear. We have the rules:

$$\mathsf{not(not(x))} \quad \rightarrow_g \quad \mathsf{x} \tag{24.14}$$
$$\mathsf{g(1,x)} \quad \rightarrow_t \quad \mathsf{not(f(x))} \tag{24.15}$$

Starting with the graph not(g(1,x)) we may use rule 24.15 to reduce it to not(not(f(x))) and then rule 24.14 to reduce that to f(x). However, the second step uses a pattern structure that is produced using rule 24.14, which contains a term in its head pattern, and thus could vary according to the value taken by a variable. Rule 24.14 alone would not break the theorem, since the pattern not(x) could not be produced as the result of a term rewrite if no term rewrite has not/1 as the body root.

Note that a corollary of Theorem 24.4.7 is that any head pattern containing just variables as the pattern argument may be used in a graph rewrite rule. This intuitively corresponds to our understanding that a functor f/a is a unique entity, and that if we state an unqualified rule $f/a \rightarrow$ *body* about it then we can replace all instances of f/a with the *body*.

EXAMPLE **24.4.8 (The phantom rewrite problem solved)**

$$(\mathbf{y}=1 \vee \mathbf{y}=2) \wedge \mathbf{x}=\mathbf{y} \quad \rightarrow_g \quad (\mathbf{y}=1 \wedge \mathbf{x}=\mathbf{y}) \vee (\mathbf{y}=2 \wedge \mathbf{x}=\mathbf{y}) \tag{24.16}$$
$$(\mathbf{y}=1 \wedge \mathbf{x}=\mathbf{y}) \tag{24.17}$$
$$\rightarrow_t (\mathsf{TRUE} \wedge \mathbf{x}=1) \tag{24.18}$$
$$\rightarrow_t \mathbf{x}=1 \tag{24.19}$$
$$\rightarrow_t \mathsf{TRUE} \tag{24.20}$$
$$\rightarrow_t \quad (\mathbf{y}=1 \wedge \mathbf{x}=1) \vee (\mathbf{y}=2 \wedge \mathbf{x}=\mathbf{y}) \tag{24.21}$$
$$(\mathbf{y}=2 \wedge \mathbf{x}=\mathbf{y}) \tag{24.22}$$
$$\rightarrow_t (\mathsf{TRUE} \wedge \mathbf{x}=2) \tag{24.23}$$

$$\rightarrow_t \mathbf{x} = 2 \quad (24.24)$$

$$\rightarrow_t \mathsf{TRUE} \quad (24.25)$$

$$\rightarrow_t \quad (\mathbf{y} = 1 \wedge \mathbf{x} = 1) \vee (\mathbf{y} = 2 \wedge \mathbf{x} = 2) \quad (24.26)$$

The steps of Example 24.4.2 are repeated in Example 24.4.8, but using term or graph rewrites in accordance with Theorem 24.4.7, which dictates that only step 24.16 uses a graph rewrite. Notice that the use of a term rewrite in step 24.20 leads to the **x=y** *structure remaining in the second disjunct at step 24.21, and thus the correct reduction sequence is followed in steps 24.22 to 24.26.*

REFERENCES

[BL86] Marco Bellia and Giorgio Levi. The relation between logic and functional languages: A survey. *Journal of Logic Programming*, **3**, pp. 217–236, 1986.

[BvEG+87] H.P. Barendregt, M.C.J.D. van Eekelen, J.R.W. Glauert, J.R Kennaway, M.J. Plasmeijer, and M.R. Sleep. Term graph rewriting. In *Proc. PARLE'87 Conference II*, Springer-Verlag, Lecture Notes in Computer Science 259, pp. 141–158, 1987.

[GKS87] J.R.W. Glauert, J.R. Kennaway, and M.R. Sleep. DACTL: A computational model and compiler target language based on graph reduction. *ICL Technical Journal*, **5**, May 1987.

[GKSS88] J.R.W. Glauert, J.R. Kennaway, M.R. Sleep, and G.W. Somner. *Final Specification of DACTL.* Technical Report SYS-C88-11, Univ. of East Anglia, 1988.

[GP88] J.R.W. Glauert and G.A. Papadopoulos. A parallel implementation of GHC. In *Proceedings of the International Conference on Fifth Generation Computer Systems*, ICOT, Tokyo, 1988.

[Han91] Chris Hankin. Static analysis of term graph rewriting systems. In *PARLE '91 Conference Proceedings*, Springer-Verlag, Lecture Notes in Computer Science, 1991.

[Hog91] Christopher Hogger. *Essentials of Logic Programming*, vol. 1 of *Graduate Texts in Computer Science.* OUP, 1991.

[Joh84] T. Johnsson. Efficient compilation of lazy evaluation. In *Proceedings of the ACM Conference on Compiler Construction*, pp. 58–69, Montreal, June 1984.

[McB92] Peter McBrien. *Implementing Logic Languages by Graph Rewriting.* PhD thesis, Imperial College, 1992.

[Pap89] G.A. Papadopoulos. A fine-grain parallel implementation of PARLOG. In *TAPSOFT '89*, Springer-Verlag, Lecture Notes in Computer Science 352, pp. 313–327, Barcelona, Spain, 1989.

[PJ87] S.L. Peyton-Jones. *The implementation of functional programming languages.* Prentice-Hall, 1987.

[Ric89] Tom Richards. *Clausal Form Logic.* Addison Wesley, 1989.

[Sha87] Ehud Shapiro (editor). *Concurrent Prolog: Collected Papers.* MIT Press, 1987.

[War83] David H.D. Warren. *An Abstract Prolog Instruction Set.* Technical report, SRI, October 1983.

25

Process Annotations and Process Types

M.C.J.D. van Eekelen and M.J. Plasmeijer

25.1 INTRODUCTION

Functional languages have as advantage that, when a result is obtained, it will always be the *same* independent of the chosen order of reduction. This property makes functional languages well-suited for *interleaved* and *parallel* evaluation. For concurrent functional programming one certainly would like to have an analyzer that automatically marks expressions that can safely be executed in parallel. A strictness analyzer can be used for this purpose. But, other kinds of analyzers are needed to determine whether parallel evaluation of expressions is worthwhile. With the creation of a task a certain amount of overhead is involved depending on the number of processes created and the amount of communication that takes place between them. In order to gain efficiency tasks will have to represent a sufficiently large amount of work with limited inter-process communication. The amount of work performed by a task and the amount of communication between them is of course undecidable. The actual overhead also depends on the concrete machine architecture the program is running on. How to split up work efficiently is therefore very problem and machine dependent and often even difficult to solve for a human being.

So, we assume that the programmer *explicitly* has to define the concurrent behavior of the functional program, either in order to achieve a certain desired concurrent structure or to achieve a faster program. Furthermore, we assume that concurrent functional programs at least have to run conveniently on a widely available class of parallel machine architectures: multiple instruction-multiple data machines with a distributed memory architecture. Such a machine can consist of hundreds of processors (with local memory) connected via a communication network.

Term Graph Rewriting: Theory and Practice.
Eds. Ronan Sleep, Rinus Plasmeijer and Marko van Eekelen.

In spite of the conceptual possibilities, *concurrent functional programming* is still in its *infancy*. At the moment, none of the commercially available functional languages support concurrent programming. However, in several experimental languages concurrency primitives have been proposed in the form of annotations or special functions [Klu83, GKM86, HS86, Bur87, GKS87, VH88, DFH+91, NSvEP91]. With these primitives the default evaluation order of an ordinary functional program can be changed such that a concurrent functional program is obtained. There is not yet a common view on which kind of basic primitives are required for concurrent functional programming.

This chapter therefore does not reflect *the* way to achieve concurrency but it presents a promising method to define concurrency in an elegant way. The concurrent behavior of a program is defined by means of special high-level concurrency *annotations* with an associated *type system*. The annotations used in this chapter are derived from similar annotations that are based on the concept of *lazy copying* in *Term Graph Rewriting Systems* [vEPS91, BS92, PvE93]. Using the annotations together with the associated type system a very large class of process structures can be specified elegantly.

25.2 CONCURRENCY AND FUNCTIONAL PROGRAMMING

A concurrent program is a program in which parts of the program are running concurrently, i.e. *interleaved* or in *parallel* with each other. Such a part of the program is called a process. The algorithm that is executed by a program is called a task. With each task a certain amount of work is involved. In a concurrent program the task that has to be performed is split up in *subtasks* and each such a subtask is assigned to a concurrently executing process. Parallel processes are processes that perform their task at the *same* time. Interleaved processes perform their task *merged* in some unknown *sequential* order on a time-sharing basis.

Why concurrent functional programming?

Imperative programming languages have the disadvantage that one cannot always assign an *arbitrary* subtask in a program (such as a procedure call) to a process. A procedure call can have side-effects via access to global variables. Generally, unintended communication between processes may take place in this way such that the correctness of the program is no longer guaranteed.

The main disadvantage however, is that inter-process communication has to be defined *explicitly*. For distributed architectures message passing primitives have to be used (e.g. send and receive primitives or rendezvous calls). With these primitives all possible communication situations have to be handled. As a consequence, reasoning about such programs is often practically impossible.

Advantages of concurrent functional programming

In a functional language the evaluation of *any* expression (redex) can be assigned to a process. Since there are no side-effects, the outcome of the computation, the normal form, is independent of the chosen evaluation order. Interleaved as well as parallel evaluation of redexes is allowed albeit that some evaluation orders may influence the termination behavior of a program.

The fact that the evaluation order cannot influence the outcome of a computation gives additional flexibility and reliability for the evaluation of functional programs on parallel architectures. When a processor is defect or when it is overloaded with work it is always possible to change the order of evaluation and the number of tasks created in optimal response to the new actual situation that arises at run-time.

In a concurrent functional program a task assigned to a process consists of the evaluation of a function. Requiring no additional primitives, communication between processes takes place *implicitly* when one process needs a result calculated by another. This greatly facilitates reasoning about a concurrent program.

Besides the advantages mentioned above, a programmer of a concurrent functional program has the full power of a functional language at his disposal enabling him to write elegant and short programs.

Disadvantages of concurrent functional programming

In a concurrent functional programming language the programmer has to define how the concurrent evaluation of his program will take place. This means that a program in a functional language is no longer just an executable specification in which one does not have to worry about how expressions are being evaluated.

On the other hand, there are situations with respect to sequential functional programming in which a programmer cannot be totally unaware of the evaluation order of his program. For instance, patterns specified in a left-hand side of a function definition force evaluation. Whether or not a function can be called with an argument representing an infinite computation will depend on how the function is defined.

Most functional languages already have facilities to influence the default evaluation order (e.g. Miranda [Tur85], Haskell [HWA+90], Clean [BvEvL+87] and LML [Aug84]). In concurrent functional programming the programmer has to be even *more* aware of the evaluation order of a functional program. He should be able to control the reduction order in such a way that he can turn the program into the desired concurrent program. In the compilation process of functional languages so many transformations take place that for the average programmer it is very hard to predict in which order expressions are evaluated. For this reason for the control of the concurrent evaluation order the following approach is chosen:

Whenever a programmer decides to control the concurrent behavior of the program, he must explicitly specify which processes are to be created, what their task is, and how the original process should proceed. The programmer must have some understanding of the standard evaluation order, but he should not rely on knowledge of how the evaluation takes place in a particular implementation.

25.3 PROCESS ANNOTATIONS AND PROCESS TYPES

Suppose that one would like to increase the execution speed of the following function definition of the well-known fibonacci function by introducing parallelism in the computation. This definition will be used further *not* to achieve the most efficient parallel fib algorithm but to illustrate how various process structures can be specified.

```
fib:: num → num
fib 1 = 1
fib 2 = 1
fib n = fib (n - 1) + fib (n - 2),              if n > 2
```

Since both arguments of the addition have to be calculated before the addition can take place one could try to optimize the performance by calculating the two recursive calls of fib in parallel, each on a different processor. This is a typical example of **divide-and-conquer** parallelism.

To create a parallel process a function application is prefixed with a special annotation: {Par}. The precise semantics of this annotation is given in section 25.3.1. A process created with a {Par} will have as task the parallel evaluation of the annotated function to *normal form.*

With the {Par} annotation fib can be specified using divide-and-conquer parallelism

```
fib:: num → num
fib 1 = 1
fib 2 = 1
fib n = {Par} fib (n - 1) + {Par} fib (n - 2), if n > 2
```

The use of {Par} in such a recursive function definition creates a new process for each annotated function application in each call of the function. In this way a tree of processes is created. The bottom of the tree consists of processes that execute the non-recursive alternative of the function definition.

On many parallel architectures it will not be worthwhile to evaluate fib n in parallel in such a way. To turn the fine-grain parallelism into coarse-grain parallelism, in the example below a threshold is introduced that ensures that the processes at the bottom of the tree have some substantial amount of work to do.

Divide-and-conquer fibonacci with threshold:

```
fib:: num → num
fib 1 = 1
fib 2 = 1
fib n = {Par} fib (n - 1) + {Par} fib (n - 2), if n > threshold
      = fib (n - 1) + fib (n - 2),             if n > 2
        where threshold = 10
```

25.3.1 Creating parallel processes

The {Par}-annotation can be used in the body (the right-hand side) of any function definition to create a parallel process. When a function with a *{Par}-annotation* in its body is evaluated by a process (the father process) the steps described below are performed for each occurrence of {Par} in that body. After these steps have been performed the father process continues as usual with the regular evaluation of the function body. In order to simplify the semantic description {Par} is defined only for an argument that is a simple function application of the form: f a_1 a_2 ... a_n (so, {Par} is e.g. not defined on ZF-expressions). This is not a fundamental restriction.

A function application annotated with a {Par}-annotation is an example of an expression that is *known to be in Process Normal Form.* When an expression is in **Process Normal Form (PNF)** this means that, *when its evaluation is demanded,* it will either be in *normal* form or it will be reduced to *normal* form by one or more *processes.* Note that this deviates from the standard evaluation order in which only *head-normal form* reduction of subexpressions is demanded. In general, the PNF property is of course undecidable. However, it is possible to introduce a type system to achieve a decidable approximation of the PNF-property (*known to be* in PNF). Clearly, an expression annotated with a {Par}-annotation is known to be in PNF since a process will reduce it to normal form. There are more cases in which expressions are known to be in PNF. A complete survey of these cases is given in section 25.3.5. In the following we will use *in PNF* instead of *known to be in PNF* when there can be no confusion.

The following steps are performed when a {Par}-annotated function application {Par} f a_1 a_2 ... a_n is encountered in a function body during reduction:

a. First, the father process reduces each argument of f (from left to right) to *normal form* unless the argument is in PNF;
b. Then, a new process is created (the **child** process) that *preferably* runs in *parallel* on a *different* processor, evaluating f a_1 a_2 ... a_n to *normal form.*

When a process needs the information calculated by another process it has to *wait* until the result is available. As soon as part of the result has reached a normal form the information is passed to the demanding process (see also section 25.3.3).

Motivation for the chosen semantics

To reduce the complexity of the creation of the task and to reduce the overhead involved with inter-process communication, it is generally more efficient to evaluate the arguments of the function before the task is created. One has to keep in mind that a parallel task on a distributed memory architecture has to be copied to another processor. A small expression requires fewer communication than a large one. It is assumed that an expression in normal form often requires less space than the original redex (e.g., in the fib-example above fib 5 is a smaller expression than fib (6 - 1)).

When a task is created, all arguments of f are in PNF because they either have been reduced to normal form by the father process or they where already in PNF. When the father process is evaluating arguments there is a danger that the termination properties of the program are changed when they represent infinite calculations. This can be avoided by creating an additional process for the evaluation of such an argument. When an argument is in PNF the father process skips the evaluation of the argument since a process is taking care of it already or, upon demand, a process will take care of it in the future.

Usually, parallel processes are created to perform a substantial task. Therefore by default the task consists of the reduction of the indicated expression to normal form and not just to head-normal form.

25.3.2 Creating interleaved processes

Consider again the fib-example. In the presented solutions processes are not used in an optimal way. This is caused by the fact that the father process cannot do much useful work because it has to wait for the results of its child processes. A better solution would be to let the father process also reduce one of the two arguments.

The idea in the fib example below is that the first argument is reduced by the father process in parallel with the evaluation of the second argument.

```
fib:: num → num
fib 1 = 1
fib 2 = 1
fib n = fib (n - 1) + {Par} fib (n - 2),        if n > threshold
      = fib (n - 1) + fib (n - 2),              if n > 2
```

However, the solution assumes that the father process will continue with the evaluation of the first argument. In reality this may not be the case. As specified, the first argument will be calculated by the father process and the second one by another parallel process. But, if the father process happens to start with the calculation of the second argument, it will wait until the parallel child process has communicated the result. Hereafter the father can evaluate the first argument. So, although the specification is fulfilled, the desired parallel effect may not be obtained. The evaluation of the first argument is then not really performed *concurrently* with the evaluation of the second argument, but sequentially *after* the evaluation of the second argument has been completed by the parallel process.

The problem illustrated in the example arises because the programmer has made some (possibly wrong) assumptions on the precise evaluation order of the program. It is important not to make any assumptions like this. The problem can be solved by explicitly controlling the reduction order in such situations.

A new annotation is introduced that creates an *interleaved* executing child process on the same processor as the father process: the *{Self}-annotation.*

Divide-and-conquer fibonacci in which the father processor is forced to do some substantial work as well:

```
fib:: num → num
fib 1 = 1
fib 2 = 1
fib n = {Self} fib (n - 1) + {Par} fib (n - 2), if n > threshold
      = fib (n - 1) + fib (n - 2),               if n > 2
```

The {Self}-annotation can be used where a {Par} can be used: in the body (the right-hand side) of any function definition. When a function with some {Self}-annotations in its body is evaluated by the father process the appropriate step is performed for each occurrence of {Self} in that body.

When a {Self}-annotated function application {Self} f a_1 a_2 ... a_n is encountered in a function body during reduction, a **child** process is created as a subprocess that runs *interleaved* on the *same* processor as the father process with as task the evaluation of f a_1 a_2 ... a_n to *normal form*. Hence, a {Self}-annotated function application is in PNF.

Motivation for the chosen semantics

In many cases a better utilization of the machine capacity can be achieved when a subprocess is created on the same processor as the father process. The annotation is in particular handy to create **channel processes**. When several processes demand information from a particular process, it is useful to create a subprocess for each demanding process to serve the communication demand.

In contrast with the {Par}-annotation now the arguments a_1 a_2 ... a_n are not evaluated to normal form since no information has to be copied when the child process is created on the same processor.

The indicated expression f a_1 a_2 ... a_n is evaluated to normal form just as for processes created with the {Par}-annotation. This has the advantage that it makes communication transparent with respect to the kind of process that is communicating (created with {Self} or with {Par}).

25.3.3 Communication and lazy evaluation

A very important aspect of concurrent programming in functional languages is the property that communication is not defined explicitly but *implicitly* by making use of the lazy evaluation order: communication between processes takes place when one process needs a value that is being evaluated by another process.

In the sequential case when a value is needed, it is evaluated by the process itself. In the concurrent case when a value is needed that is being evaluated by another process, the demanding process has to *wait* until the value becomes available. Just as is the case when the result of an ordinary program is printed as soon as possible (communicated to an external device), communication between processes within a program can take place as soon as part of the result of a subtask is available: as soon as a head-normal form is reached. So, communication is lazy just as the evaluation is lazy. This property can be used to create information streams between processes.

A communication stream between processes. The definition of the function generator is assumed to be used also in several other examples in this chapter.

```
generator:: num → [num]
generator n = [n..100]

map (* 2) ({Par} generator 3)
```

When a father process needs a value of one of its child processes *and* the child process has produced a head-normal form, then the requested information is communicated to the father process (e.g. 3 :).

25.3.4 Expressive power of the process annotations

An advantage of functional languages is that it is relatively easy to define general tools for the creation of parallelism by using annotations like the {Par} in combination with the ordinary expressive power of higher order functions in these languages.

Divide-and-conquer parallelism can be expressed in a general way using higher order functions:

```
divconq:: (* → **) → * → (* → bool) → (** → ** → **) → (* → (*,*)) → **
divconq f arg threshold conquer divide
        = f arg,                                                    if threshold arg
        = conquer ({Self} divconq f left threshold conquer divide)
                  ({Par} divconq f right threshold conquer divide), otherwise
          where (left, right) = divide arg

pfib:: num → num
pfib n  = divconq fib n threshold (+) divide
          where threshold n = n ≤ 10
                divide n    = (n - 1, n - 2)
```

Function composition can be used to create pipelines of communicating processes.

Static pipeline of processes:

```
stat_pipe:: * → (* → **) → (** → ***) → (*** → ****) → ****
stat_pipe i f1 f2 f3 = f3 ({Par} f2 ({Par} f1 ({Par} i)))

stat_pipe (generator 3) (map fib) (map fac) (map (* 2))
```

With higher order functions general skeletons can be defined to create frequently occurring process structures (this is essentially different from the process skeletons in [DFH+91] which are inherently predefined). Often these are parallel variants of the basic building blocks used in sequential functional programming.

A general pipeline defined with the {Self}-annotation to force the construction of the pipeline:

```
parfoldr:: (* → ** → **) → ** → [*] → **
parfoldr f i [ ]     = i
parfoldr f i (x:xs)  = {Par} f x in where in = {Self} parfoldr f i xs

parfoldr map (generator 3) [(* 2), fac, fib]
```

The following parallel version of map implements vector-like processing since it creates a parallel process for each element in a given list.

```
parmap:: (* → **) → [*] → [**]
parmap f (x : xs)  = {Par} f x : {Self} parmap f xs
parmap f [ ]       = [ ]
```

then the expression parmap (twice fac) [0, 1, 2, 3] reduces to [1, 1, 2, 720].

A process can create one or more subprocesses with the {Self}-construct. These subprocesses (running interleaved on the same processor) can be used to serve communication channels with other processes. Each communication link of a process has to be served by a separate subprocess that reduces the demanded information to normal form. A process with its subprocesses in a functional language acts more or less like a process with its channels in a message passing language like CSP [Hoa78]. Serving subprocesses is like sending information over a channel to any process requesting that information.

Parallel quicksort. In this parallel version of the quicksort algorithm two child processes are created when the list to be sorted contains more than threshold elements (this is checked by the predicate too_few_elements that avoids walking down the complete list). Each child process sorts a sublist. The father process will supply the appropriate sublist to each of its child processes. The father process can perform both these tasks "simultaneously" with help of two subprocesses that run interleaved with each other.

```
sorter:: [num] → [num]
sorter list          = quick_sort list,     if too_few_elements list threshold
                     = par_quick_sort list, otherwise

threshold:: num
threshold            = 7

quick_sort:: [num] → [num]
quick_sort [ ]       = [ ]
quick_sort (x : xs)  = quick_sort [b | b ← xs ; b ≤ x]
                       ++ [x] ++ quick_sort [b | b ← xs ; b > x]

par_quick_sort:: [num] → [num]
par_quick_sort (x : xs = {Par} sorter ({Self} smalleq x xs)
                       ++ [x] ++ {Par} sorter ({Self} larger x xs)
                       where smalleq x xs = [b | b ← xs ; b ≤ x]
                             larger x xs  = [b | b ← xs ; b > x]

too_few_elements:: [num] → num → bool
too_few_elements [ ]      n = True
too_few_elements xs       0 = False
too_few_elements (x : xs) n = too_few_elements xs (n - 1)

sorter [6,3,1,4,2,7,3,12,5,1,4,97,3,2,17,6,93,114]
```

25.3.5 Specifying process types

The knowledge that an expression is in PNF is of importance when a new parallel process is created (see section 25.3.1). In the examples above, this knowledge was only *locally* used inside a function body. To make full use of the expressive power of functional languages it is necessary that the knowledge that an expression is in PNF can be expressed on a *global* level. For this purpose a special type attribute {proc} is introduced.

An expression has type {proc} T when it is of type T and furthermore *known* to be in PNF. This type can be used in the type definition of a function. An expression is said to have a process type when its type has the type attribute {proc}.

A tool to create a dynamic pipeline of processes of arbitrary length can be specified as follows making use of process attributes:

```
pipeline:: * → [* → *] → {proc} *
pipeline gen filters = npipe ({Par} gen) filters

npipe:: {proc} * → [* → *] → {proc} *
```

```
npipe in [ ]       = in
npipe in (x : xs)  = npipe ({Par} x in) xs

pipeline (generator 3) [map fib, map fac, map (* 2)]
```

In the function npipe, the father process knows that its first parameter is in PNF. So, when a new parallel process is created, evaluation to normal form of this parameter is not forced.

A type inferencer cannot derive that an argument of a function has a process type because it cannot be guaranteed that the function is always called with an actual argument in PNF. Therefore, process types have to be defined *explicitly* by the programmer. A type *checker* can then check the consistency of the type attributes and assign process types to subexpressions of function definitions accordingly. It is assumed that these actions are performed after the normal type inferencing/checking.

The following expressions **are known to be in PNF** and therefore a process type can be assigned to them:

- expressions of the form {Par} f $e_1 \ldots e_n$ or {Self} f $e_1 \ldots e_n$ for $n \geq 0$;
- an *argument of a function* if on the corresponding position in the type definition a process type is specified;
- a *result of a function* if on the corresponding position in the type definition a process type is specified;
- expressions of the form C a_1 a_2 $\ldots a_n$ where C is a constructor of which all the arguments a_i have a process type (**composition**);
- arguments a_i of an expression that has a process type and that is of the form C a_1 a_2 $\ldots a_n$ where C is a constructor (**decomposition**);
- expressions statically known to be in normal form, e.g. expressions not containing any function applications at all.

The decomposition case reflects the property that when a process is returning a complex value the information that a process is evaluating this value should not be lost when an object contained in this complex value is selected. This property is also referred to as the **decomposition property**. This decomposition property is often employed in more elaborate examples (see section 25.4).

Assume that g is of type [num], then using the decomposition property the expression x in

```
x where (x : xs) = {Par} g
```

is of type {proc} num.
With similar reasoning the following type specification is accepted:

```
phd:: {proc} [num] → {proc} num
phd (x : xs) = x
```

With the assigned process types the standard type substitutions and unifications are performed with the following two exceptions:

a. Where a process type is specified but a process type cannot be assigned, a process type error will occur.

This definition of pipeline will be rejected since in the right-hand side in the application of npipe for gen no process type is assigned while in the type definition of npipe a process type is specified:

```
pipeline:: * → [* → *] → {proc} *
pipeline gen filters = npipe gen filters

npipe::{proc} * → [* → *] → {proc} *
```

b. Where a non-process type is specified but a process type is assigned, no error will occur. In that case the specified type is used in substitutions and for unification (**deprocessing**). This deprocessing however, does not exclude the possibility that process types are substituted for type variables.

With the following definition:

```
f:: [num]→ num
f (x : xs) = x
```

the type of f ({Par} generator 3) is num due to deprocessing.
However, with the more general polymorphic definition:

```
f:: [*]→ *
f (x : xs) = x
```

the type of f ({Par} generator 3) is {proc} num due to decomposition and substitution.

The type system is such that in well-typed programs it is guaranteed that expressions that have a process type are in PNF.

25.4 CONCURRENT FUNCTIONAL PROGRAM EXAMPLES

In this section two more elaborate examples of concurrent functional programs are given. It is the purpose of the examples to show that more complex process topologies can also be expressed elegantly. It is not the intention to show how ultimate speed-ups can be achieved.

25.4.1 Sieve of Eratosthenes

The sieve of Eratosthenes is a classical example generating all prime numbers. In the parallel version a pipeline of processes is created. There is a process for each sieve. Those sieves hold the prime numbers in ascending order, one in each sieve. Each sieve accepts a stream of numbers as its input. Those numbers are not divisible by any of the foregoing primes in the pipeline. If an incoming number is not divisible by the local prime as well, it is sent to the next sieve in the pipeline. A newly created sieve process accepts the first incoming number as its own prime and returns this prime as result such that it can be printed. After that it starts sieving. A generator process is used to feed the first sieve in the pipeline with a stream (list) of increasing numbers greater than one.

In the programs below, two concurrent solutions for the sieve of Eratosthenes are given. In the first toy example only a fixed number (four) of sieve processes is created.

No more prime numbers can be found than the number of sieves created. So, only four prime numbers will be found. The program shows very clearly that each sieve process is returning two results in a tuple: the prime number and a stream of numbers that is communicated to the next sieving process.

Sieve of Eratosthenes with a fixed number of sieve processes in the pipeline.

```
static_sieving:: [{proc} num]
static_sieving          = [p1, p2, p3, p4]
                          where s0       = {Par} generator 2
                                (p1, s1) = {Par} sieve s0
                                (p2, s2) = {Par} sieve s1
                                (p3, s3) = {Par} sieve s2
                                (p4, s4) = {Par} sieve s3

sieve:: [num] → (num, [num])
sieve (prime : stream) = (prime, filter prime stream)

generator:: num → [num]
generator n             = [n..100]

filter:: num → [num] → [num]
filter n (x : xs)       = x : filter n xs, if x mod n ~= 0
                        = filter n xs,     otherwise
```

Notice that the local selector function (p_i, s_i) in static_sieving selects objects being evaluated by a (parallel) process. So, the argument $s_i$of a sieve is already under calculation by the previous sieving process. As explained in section 25.3.5 a process type can be assigned to the sieve arguments. In this way the wanted communication stream between the sieving processes is accomplished.

In the second more general solution as many sieves are created as necessary. Each time a new prime number is produced at the end of the pipeline a fresh sieve is created and the pipeline is extended. Each individual sieve works as described above.

Sieve of Eratosthenes with as many sieve processes as necessary in the pipeline.

```
dynamic_sieving:: [{proc} num]
dynamic_sieving         = npipe ({Par} generator 2)

npipe:: {proc} [num] → [{proc} num]
npipe [ ]               = [ ]
npipe in                = p : {Self} npipe s where (p, s) = {Par} sieve in
```

25.4.2 Warshall's algorithm

The parallel version of Warshall's solution for the *shortest path problem* is an interesting algorithm to test the expressiveness of parallel languages since it requires a special process structure containing a cycle [Aug85].

Given a graph G consisting of N nodes and directed edges with a distance associated with each edge. The graph can be represented by an $N \times N$ matrix in which the element at the ith row and in the jth column is equal to the distance from node i to node j. Warshall's shortest path algorithm is able to find the shortest path within this graph between any two nodes.

Warshall's shortest path algorithm:

A path from node j to node k is said to contain a node i if it can be split in two paths, one from node j to node i and one from node i to node k ($i \neq j$ & $i \neq k$). Let $SP(j,k,i)$ denote the length of the shortest path from node j to node k that contains only nodes less than or equal to i ($0 \leq i$ & $1 \leq j, k$ & $i,j,k \leq N$).
Then define:

$$
\begin{aligned}
SP\ (j,k,0) &= 0 \quad \textit{if } j = k \\
&= d \quad \textit{if there is an edge from } j \textit{ to } k \textit{ with distance } d \\
&= \infty \quad \textit{otherwise} \\
SP\ (j,k,i) &= \textit{minimum}\ (SP\ (j,k,i\text{-}1),\ SP\ (j,i,i\text{-}1) + SP\ (i,k,i\text{-}1))
\end{aligned}
$$

Define a matrix M as follows: $M[j,k] = SP\ (j,k,i)$ for some i. The final shortest path matrix can be computed iteratively by varying i from 0 to N using the equations described above. In the ith iteration for each pair of nodes it is exmined whether a shorter path exists via node i.

Observing the algorithm it can be concluded that during the ith iteration all updating can be performed in parallel. N parallel processes are created: one for each row updating its row during each iteration step. In the ith iteration all the parallel processes need to have access to row i as well as to their own row. This can be achieved by letting parallel process i distribute its own row as soon as the ith iteration starts. At the end of the distributed computation the rows of the solution are collected.

Initially, a parallel process rowproc$_i$ is created for each row of the matrix. Before rowproc$_i$ performs its ith iteration it distributes its own row to the other rowprocs. This is done in a cyclic pipeline, i.e. rowproc$_i$ sends its own row to rowproc$_j$ via rowproc$_{i+1}$, ..., rowproc$_{j-1}$ and rowproc$_j$ (counting modulo N from i to j).

This distributing, updating and iterating can be expressed in a parallel functional language by creating a cyclic process structure via a recursive local definition of a pair with as first element the final solution and as second element the output that will be produced by the Nth process after it is created.

```
matrix * == [ [*] ]

warshall:: matrix num → matrix num
warshall mat
  = shortest_paths
    where
    (shortest_paths, output_rowproc_N) = create_rowprocs #mat 1 mat output_rowproc_N

create_rowprocs::num→num→matrix num→{proc}[[num]]→([{proc}[num]],{proc}[[num]] )
create_rowprocs size k [row_N] input_left_rowproc
  = ([row_N_solution], output_rowproc_N)
    where (row_N_solution, output_rowproc_N)
              = {Self} iterate size k 1 row_N input_left_rowproc
create_rowprocs size k (row_k : restmat) input_left_rowproc
  = (row_k_solution : rest_solutions, output_rowproc_N)
    where
    (row_k_solution, output_rowproc_k) = {Self} iterate size k 1 row_k input_left_rowproc
    (rest_solutions, output_rowproc_N)
              = {Par} create_rowprocs size (k+1) restmat output_rowproc_k
```

```
iterate::num→num→num→[num]→[ [num]]→([num],[[num]])
iterate size k i row_k (row_i : xs)
  = (row_k, [ ]),                       if iterations_finished
  = (solution, row_k : rest_output), if start_sending_this_row
  = (solution, row_i : rest_output),  otherwise
    where iterations_finished       = i > size
          start_sending_this_row  = i = k
          (solution, rest_output) = iterate size k (i+1) next_row_k xs
          next_row_k               = row_k,                            if i = k
                                   = updaterow row_k row_i dist_k_i, otherwise
          dist_k_i                 = row_k!i

updaterow::[num] → [num] → num → [num]
updaterow [ ] rowi dist_j_i = [ ]
updaterow (dist_j_k : restrow_j) (dist_i_k : restrow_i) dist_j_i
  = minimum dist_j_k (dist_j_i + dist_i_k) : updaterow restrow_j restrow_i dist_j_i
    where minimum m n = m, if m < n
                      = n, otherwise

warshall  [ [    0,  100,  100,   13,  100 ] ,
            [  100,    0,  100,  100,    4 ] ,
            [   11,  100,    0,  100,  100 ] ,
            [  100,    3,  100,    0,  100 ] ,
            [   15,    5,  100,    1,    0 ] ]
```

25.5 DISCUSSION

With only *two* annotations, one for the creation of parallel processes and one for the creation of interleaved processes, due to the associated type system rather complicated concurrent programs can be specified in an elegant and readable way. Processes can be created dynamically. For the communication between processes no additional primitives are needed. Communication is demand driven: whenever a process needs information from another process the information is communicated as soon as it is available. Flexible and powerful tools for the construction of frequently occurring process topologies can be defined using the full expressive power of functional languages. Concurrent functional programs can be executed on any processor configuration, in parallel or just sequentially. In principle, the programmer can start with writing a sequential program. When this program is finished he can turn this program into a parallel version by creating processes for some of the function applications.

Of course, many problems remain that are connected with concurrent programming in general. Sometimes it is very difficult to tell for which function application it really is worthwhile to evaluate in parallel. In the worst case, the program has to be fully rewritten because the chosen algorithm was not suited for parallel evaluation at all.

Future research will concern the investigation of the practical usability and efficiency of the proposed language extensions in the context of the lazy functional graph rewriting language Concurrent Clean [NSvEP91]. The explicit use of sharing makes it possible to specify process topologies directly. Besides, for some applications one would like to have the possibility to create processes that reduce to head-normal form or to spine normal form instead of to normal form. Furthermore, it should be possible to assign a particular process to a specific concrete processor. With such a facility a concurrent program can be optimally tuned to the available parallel architecture. Certain applications require a better control on the kind of information (data or work in the form of redexes) that is passed from one process(or) to another. Finally, it can be important to have more control on the amount of communicated information as well as on the moment at which communication occurs.

REFERENCES

[Aug84] L. Augustsson. A compiler for lazy ML. In *Proc. of ACM Symposium on LISP and Functional Programming*, pp. 218–227, 1984.

[Aug85] L. Augusteijn. *The Warshall shortest path algorithm in POOL-T.* Technical Report Esprit project 415 A Doc. 0105, Philips Research Laboratories, Eindhoven, The Netherlands, 1985.

[BS92] Erik Barendsen and Sjaak Smetsers. *Graph Rewriting and Copying.* Technical Report 92-20, University of Nijmegen, 1992.

[Bur87] F.W. Burton. Functional programming for concurrent and distributed computing. *The Computer Journal*, **30-5**, 1987.

[BvEvL+87] T. Brus, M.C.J.D. van Eekelen, M. van Leer, M.J. Plasmeijer, and H.P. Barendregt. Clean - a language for functional graph rewriting. In *Proc. of Conference on Functional Programming Languages and Computer Architecture (FPCA '87)*, pp. 364–384. Portland, Oregon, USA, 1987.

[DFH+91] J. Darlington, A.J. Field, P.G. Harrison, D. Harpe, G.K. Jouret, P.L. Kelly, K.M. Sephton, and Sharp D.W. Structured parallel functional programming. In Glaser and Hartel (editors), *Proc. of Third International Workshop on the Implementation of Functional Programming Languages on Parallel Architectures*, pp. 31–51. Southampton, 1991.

[GKM86] J. Goguen, C. Kirchner, and J. Meseguer. Concurrent term rewriting as a model of computation. In *Proc. of Workshop on Graph Reduction*, pp. 53–94. Santa Fe, New Mexico, 1986.

[GKS87] J.R.W. Glauert, J.R. Kennaway, and M.R. Sleep. Dactl: A computational model and compiler target language based on graph reduction. *ICL Technical Journal*, **5**, 1987.

[Hoa78] C.A.R. Hoare. Communicating sequential processes. *Communications of the ACM*, **21**, 1978.

[HS86] P. Hudak and L. Smith. Para-functional programming: A paradigm for programming multiprocessor systems. In *Proc. of 12th ACM Symp. on Principles of Programming Languages*, pp. 243–254, 1986.

[HWA+90] P. Hudak, P.L. Wadler, Arvind, B. Boutel, J. Fairbairn, J. Fasel, K. Hammond, J. Hughes, T. Johnsson, R. Kieburtz, R.S. Nikhil, S.L. Peyton Jones, M. Reeve, D. Wise, and J. Young. *Report on the Functional Programming Language Haskell.* Technical report, Department of Computer Science, Glasgow University, 1990.

[Klu83] W.E. Kluge. Cooperating reduction machines. *IEEE Transactions on Computers*, **C-32/11**, 1983.

[NSvEP91] E.G.J.M.H. Nöcker, J.E.W. Smetsers, M.C.J.D. van Eekelen, and M.J. Plasmeijer. Concurrent Clean. In *Proc. of Parallel Architectures and Languages Europe (PARLE'91)*, pp. 202–219. Eindhoven, The Netherlands, 1991.

[PvE93] M.J. Plasmeijer and M.C.J.D. van Eekelen. *Functional Programming and Parallel Graph Rewriting.* International Computer Science Series. Addison Wesley, 1993.

[Tur85] D.A. Turner. Miranda: A non-strict functional language with polymorphic types. In *Proc. of Conference on Functional Programming Languages and Computer Architecture*, pp. 1–16. Portland, Oregon, USA, 1985.

[vEPS91] M.C.J.D. van Eekelen, M.J. Plasmeijer, and J.E.W. Smetsers. Parallel graph rewriting on loosely coupled machine architectures. In Kaplan and Okada (editors), *Proc. of Conditional and Typed Rewriting Systems (CTRS'90)*, pp. 354–369. Montreal, Canada, 1991.

[VH88] W.G. Vree and P.H. Hartel. *Parallel graph reduction for divide-and-conquer applications; Part I - programme transformations.* Internal Report D-15, University of Amsterdam, 1988.

26

JALPA: A Functional Modular Programming Language Based on Extended Graphical Term Rewriting

H. Yamanaka

26.1 INTRODUCTION

With the recent advances in the hardware technology, especially the VLSI technology, there has been growing interest in massively parallel machines. However, software for such machines has not become mature because of difficulties which arose from the sequential nature of imperative languages which are dominant in practical programming.

Functional languages are impartable for their comprehensibility and parallel nature, of which the essence is transparency, i.e. each program segment has a unique meaning independent of its occurrence in a program. So the programs can be very modular and enjoy parallel executions to save time. To be a bit optimistic, functional languages are one of the best choices for the future massively parallel programming in the large. And to fully exploit their parallelism, graph rewriting (or reduction) techniques have been developed and applied to implementing them [Pey87]. Graphical term rewriting is a mathematical framework for graph rewriting and gives mathematical descriptions to the implementation level concepts by employing those of category theory (or graph grammar) [Rao84, BvEG+87, Ken87, HP88].

However, there is a pessimistic aspect to the languages. The parallelism is too naive to help us to obtain the maximum efficiency on parallel machines. So some mechanisms or pragma have been required to implement such a language. In this chapter, we will

Term Graph Rewriting: Theory and Practice.
Eds. Ronan Sleep, Rinus Plasmeijer and Marko van Eekelen.

introduce a dynamic graph structure sharing mechanism, and claim that it can be an effective approach not only theoretically, but also practically.

So far, there have been functional languages based on TRS(Term Rewriting System) [Klo87], for example, ML [GMW79], HOPE [BMS80], Miranda [Tur85], OBJ2 [FGJM85], OBJ3 [GW88], etc., with little focus on GTRSs(Graphical Term Rewriting Systems). GTRS is a generalized computation model of TRS in a sense that TRS can manipulate only trees, whereas GTRS can manipulate graphs as well. GTRS is not only more general, but also a more abstract and efficient computation model than TRS. Moreover, it has the potential to make functional languages more natural and comprehensible while having implementation level semantics. However, it has received little attention for its potential. We have designed and implemented a new language based on GTRS.

GTRS could share identical subexpressions flexibly and efficiently, while they lack type checking and modularization mechanisms as a programming language. Type checking mechanisms can detect programming errors before execution, and modularization mechanisms are a must for programming in the large. In this respect, we have designed JALPA by introducing a many-sorted typing, parameterization of modules and an hierarchical module structure in GTRS preserving its natural clarity and transparency.

JALPA is basically a many sorted system. However, it has a mechanism for a polymorphic typing, i.e. type variables and the error sort included in every sort (excluding itself). This typing almost allows type checking at parse time. Parameterization of JALPA is very powerful. It allows us to pass functional arguments and module names as well as sorts. A significant feature of JALPA is an hierarchical module structure that each rewrite rule can have as a local module hierarchy (which can even include parameterized modules). Also, each parameterized module can have local module structures. Key concepts of programming in the large are modularity and encapsulation of data and operations. We believe the structure is powerful enough for large programming in practice.

In the following sections, we will first introduce definitions of GTRS, then the syntax of JALPA will be explained by examples of modularization. Its semantics will be introduced by mathematically rigorous descriptions. Lastly, implementation issues, especially, a global dynamic structure sharing method, will be presented.

26.1.1 Graphical term rewriting systems

A signature Σ is a pair $\langle S, F\rangle$, where S is a set of sorts or (types) and F is a set of function symbols. Each function symbol $f \in F$ is associated with a sort and an arity (rank) which are provided by following two functions, $sort: F \rightarrow S$ and $arity: F \rightarrow S^*$. Let X be a set of variable symbols, also each variable symbol is associated with a sort and arity ϵ.

A graph is a sextuple $G = \langle V, E, SE, TE, LV, LE\rangle$, where V is a set of nodes, E is a set of arcs, and $SE: E \rightarrow V$ and $TE: E \rightarrow V$ are source and target mappings respectively, $LV: V \rightarrow F \cup X$ is the mapping from nodes to their attached function or variable symbols and $LE: E \rightarrow N$ attaches the total order on arguments (there are no arcs labeled with an identical number whose source node is identical). G is called well-formed if $\forall e \in E$, $sort(LV(TE(e)))$ is equal to the $LE(e)$-th component of $arity(LV(SE(e)))$.

The (full) subgraph rooted by $v \in V$ is $G' = \langle V', E', SE|E', TE|E', LV|V', LE|E' \rangle$, where $V' = \{v' \in V | v'$ is reachable from v$\}$, $E' = E|V'$. (Note that $f|D$ is the function f of which domain is restricted to D.)

Let $G = \langle V_G, E_G, SE_G, TE_G, LV_G, LE_G \rangle$ and $H = \langle V_H, E_H, SE_H, TE_H, LV_H, LE_H \rangle$ be well-formed graphs. A homomorphism $f: G \to H$ is a pair of mappings $f = \langle f_V: V_G \to V_H, f_E: E_G \to E_H \rangle$ such that $f_V \circ SE_G = SE_H \circ f_E$, $f_V \circ TE_G = TE_H \circ f_E$, $LV_H \circ f_V = LV_G$, $LE_H \circ f_E = LE_G$. A homomorphism $f = \langle f_V, f_E \rangle$ is called injective (resp. surjective) if both f_V and f_E are injective (resp. surjective) mappings. If f is injective and surjective, f is called an isomorphism.

A mapping $f: G \to H$ is homomorphic at $s \in V_G$ if $LV_H(f_V(s)) = LV_G(s)$, and $\forall e \in E_G$ satisfying $SE_G(e) = s$, $LE_G(e) = LE_H(f_E(e))$. A graph morphism $(f, S): G \to H$ is a mapping $f: G \to H$ which is homomorphic at every node in S. The composition of two graph morphism $(f, S): G \to H$ and $(g, T): H \to J$ is $(g, T) \cdot (f, S) = (\langle g_V \cdot f_V, g_E \cdot f_E \rangle, S \cap f_V^{-1}(T))$. Note that if $S = V_G$, f is a homomorphism. $Graph(\Sigma \cup X)$ is the category whose objects and morphisms are graphs over $\Sigma \cup X$ and graph morphisms respectively.

A rewrite rule $f: L \to R$ is a graph morphism which is homomorphic at $S \subseteq L$ (a variable node in L must have a unique label). An occurrence $g: L \to G$ is a graph morphism which is homomorphic at all nodes of L except variable nodes. g is called applicable if for any variable node $v \in L_V$ of which label is !-prefixed, e.g. $!x$,$!y$, etc., the subgraph rooted by $g_V(v)$ is in normal form (which will be defined recursively later).

A redex is a pair $(f: L \to R, g: L \to G)$, where g is applicable, and the result of reducing this redex is the pushout of f and g if it exists. If there are no redexes in a graph, the graph is called in normal form, or a normal form.

If $Graph(\Sigma \cup X)$ is the category of all Dags (Directed Acyclic Graphs), the pushout always exists uniquely (up to isomorphism). Hereafter, we deal with only Dags by this reason.

Conveniently describing graphical terms (terms as graphs), we use the **where clause** to specify where to be shared. It is allowed to describe a graph rewrite rule as a pair of graphs with or without an **if clause**, which represents structure sharing between two terms in a rule.

Note that for GTRSs, we cannot deal with non-linear rules, variable nodes labeled with an identical symbol on each side are considered identical. This replaces syntactic comparison by pointer comparison. If we extended the reduction step to be preceded by an epimorphism (a surjective homomorphism), which collapses a graph to its smaller one before each reduction, the difference could be smaller. Whenever graphs are collapsed into the smallest, the comparisons are equivalent. In this implementation, we have adopted this extended reduction instead of the usual reduction in order to save time and space, and we think it is efficient enough by exploiting a structure hashing technique. We will describe the mechanism and performance issues in a later section.

26.2 SYNTAX OF JALPA

JALPA is designed so that programmers can program in both top-down and bottom-up styles. In top-down style programming, we can program downward from top level functions to the bottom functions. By the nature of graph reduction, even a piece of a program can be type-checked and evaluated any time. It strongly supports the stepwise refinement of partially developed modules. In the bottom-up approach, we can make up a program by concatenating many modules already developed, together with hierarchical name encapsulation and an import mechanism that instantiates parameterized modules. In short, a program in the large is yielded by gathering many small modules in this language. Despite the language modularity, the semantics are still purely functional and mathematical.

A program is a set of modules. A module is, roughly speaking, a pair consisting of a signature and a set of equations (representing graphical term rewrite rules). For example:

```
new nat;

  S: nat -> nat;
  0:     -> nat;
fib: nat -> nat;

init: fib($1);

fib(0)=0;
fib(S(x)) = {
  new pair;

  pair: nat,nat -> pair;
  head: pair -> nat;
  tail: pair -> nat;
     h: nat  -> pair;
     +: nat,nat -> nat;

  init: tail(h(x));

  h(u)     = pair(u,S(u)), if u=0; # h(0)=<fib(0),fib(1)>
  h(S(x)) = pair(z,+(y,z))
             where {
               y=head(u); # h(n+1)=<fib(n+1),fib(n+2)>
               z=tail(u); #  =<fib(n+1),fib(n)+fib(n+1)>
               u=h(x);    #  =<z,y+z> where <y,z>=h(n)
             }
  head(pair(x,y)) = x;
  tail(pair(x,y)) = y;
  +(x,y)  = {
    add: nat,nat -> nat;

    init: add(x,y);
```

```
    add(x,S(y)) = S(add(x,y));
    add(x,0)    = x;
  }
}
```

"`init: fib($1)`" is the starting point of computation of this program. Variables prefixed with "`$`" are input variables. "`new nat`" introduces a sort "`nat`" and can be referred to by other modules with a syntactic scope rule. "`S: nat -> nat`" is a declaration of a function "`S`" whose arity and sort are both "`nat`". "`where`" represents a graph structure sharing "`h(x)`". The module of "`fib(S(x))`" encapsulates auxiliary sort "`pair`" and functions "`h, pair, head, tail, +`".

JALPA strongly supports parameter passing of functions as well as sorts. Various data structures can be generated from a parameterized module. However, the main benefit is to support a kind of higher-order functions as follows:

```
pmod map[func:typeA->typeA,cell:typeA,typeB->typeC,bottom:->typeC] is {

    map: typeC->typeC;

    export map;

    map(cell(x,y))=cell(func(x),map(y));
    map(bottom())=bottom();
}
```

Module "`map`" will generate all functions that maps "`typeA`" elements by "`func`". For example, let "`double:nat->nat`" be a double function.

```
import double as map[double:nat->nat,cons:nat,list->list,nil:->list];
```

makes a function "`double.map`" that doubles each element of a list.

So far, we believe that parameterization as above is enough to support higher-order functions in practice. However, some people might say that they need to use "apply" as likely in LISP. We do not recommend using it, but JALPA has "apply" as a variadic polymorphic built-in function of which semantics are still first order. In short, we suppose "apply" to be defined as follows:

$$\{apply(''f'', x_1, x_2, \cdots, x_{n_f}) = f(x_1, x_2, \cdots, x_{n_f}) \mid f \in F\},$$

where $''f''$ is the string representation of a function f and f is also consistent with its arity.

Lastly, now JALPA has an environment which facilitates the handling of input and (ultimate) output variables, and practically we can use input variables in any program as global variables. If someone claims that functional variables must be used, we can say that they can be easily introduced in JALPA as environment variables. It is another way to parameterize programs without altering the semantic framework.

26.3 SEMANTICS OF JALPA

A JALPA program P has an initial graphical term $Init$, an entry of new sorts $Entry$, a set of import interface declarations $Import$ which instantiate parameterized modules by parameter passing, such that "*import x as pm*$[a1, a2, \cdots, an]$", a signature Σ, a set of rules R, (non-parameterized) modules $\{M_u | u \in O\}$, where $O \subseteq (N - \{0\})^+$, and parameterized modules $\{PM_u | u \in PO\}$, where $PO \subseteq (N - \{0\})^+$ and $O \cap PO = \emptyset$. Modules, parameterized or not, are connected hierarchically as a tree structure and each module can be identified by a tree address, i.e. $(N - \{0\})^+$. So a program is expressed by

$$P = \langle Init, Entry, Import, \Sigma, R, \langle M_u \rangle_{u \in O}, \langle PM_u \rangle_{u \in PO} \rangle$$

We introduce a partial order $\sqsubseteq$ on both modules by annotating $(N - \{0\})^*$ as follows:

a. The global module is M_ϵ (ϵ is the occurrence of length 0).
b. A module M occurred in M_u that is uniquely numbered as i is annotated as $M_{u \cdot i}$.

Each module M_u has a initial rule $init_u$, an entry of sorts $entry_u$, a signature Σ_u and a set of pure rules R_u, so $M_u = \langle init_u, entry_u, import_u, \Sigma_u, R_u \rangle$, where $init_u = \langle N_1, N_2 \rangle$. N_1 is the graphical term for entrance of this module and N_2 is the graphical term for the initial point of computation in it. Note that in M_ϵ we treat this as $init_\epsilon = \langle \phi, t \rangle$, where ϕ is a special constant that means the input port from external systems. $import_u$ is a set of import interfaces to instantiate a parameterized module. The import interface consists of a parameterized module name and its actual parameters. A parameterized module is

$$PM_u = \langle id_u, param_u, export_u, import_u, entry_u, \Sigma_u, R_u \rangle,$$

where id_u is a name and $param_u$ is a set of parameter which will be instantiated by parameter passing. Note that not only sorts but functions can be passed to the parameters. In JALPA, higher-order functions are not necessary because they can be obtained to instantiate a parameterized module by passing functions.

For convenience, we consider

$$P' = \langle Init, Entry, \emptyset, \Sigma', R', \langle M'_u \rangle_{u \in O'}, \emptyset \rangle,$$

where $O' \subseteq (N - \{0\})^*$. P' is obtained from instantiating parameterized modules by the import mechanism. The instantiation is the following:

a. A parameterized module and its descendant modules to be imported are copied preserving their hierarchical structure.
b. Sorts and functions in the structure are modified, such that exportable ones are prefixed with the importing name x, non-exportable ones introduced locally are prefixed with $\bar{x}$ ($\bar{x}$ prefixed ones cannot be referenced in the importing module), and non local ones are annotated by their introduced module address by α (defined later), e.g. $f \rightarrow x.f$, $s \rightarrow \bar{x}.s$, $g \rightarrow (g, 1.2.3)$, etc..
c. Parameters in the structure are replaced by actual parameters.
d. Contents of the root module are inserted into the importing one.

e. The copied descendant modules are linked to the importing one.

Now we start to define a target domain $\mathcal{D} = \langle INIT, \Sigma, X, R\rangle$, which is a set of flat GTRSs and a translation function $\mathcal{M}: P \to \mathcal{D}$. We define $\mathcal{M}$ as a quadruple $\langle \delta, \theta, \mathcal{V}, \alpha\rangle$. First, θ is a mapping that annotates each signature with its module occurrence. Let

$$\Sigma_u = \{f_k: s_{k1}, s_{k2}, \cdots, s_{kn_k} \to s_{kn_k+1}\}$$

then θ maps it to

$$\theta(\Sigma_u) = \{f_k^u: s_{k1}^{u1}, s_{k2}^{u2}, \cdots, s_{kn_k}^{un_k} \to s_{kn_k+1}^{un_k+1}\}$$

where $u_i = \delta(s_{ki}, u)$. And

$$\delta(s, u) = \sqcup\{v \in O' | v \sqsubseteq u,\ s \in Entry_v\},$$

where $\sqcup$ is the upper limit operator. (If Σ_u is not defined, let $\Sigma_u = \emptyset$.) Second, $\mathcal{V}$ is a mapping that collects variables in a graphical term. Its domain is extended to

$$\mathcal{V}(\langle N_1, N_2\rangle) = \mathcal{V}(N_1) \cup \mathcal{V}(N_2)$$

Lastly, α is a mapping that annotates an occurrence to each function symbol. Let $LV: V \to F \cup X$ be a labeling function of nodes and a graphical term g be $\langle V, E, SE, TE, LV, LE\rangle$.

$$\alpha(g, u \cdot i) = \langle V, E, SE, TE, LV', LE\rangle,$$

where $\forall v \in V$,

$$LV'(v, u \cdot i) = \begin{cases} (v, u \cdot i) & \text{if } v \text{ is defined in } M_{u \cdot i}; \\ v & \text{if } v = (f, w); \\ \alpha(v, u) & \text{otherwise.} \end{cases}$$

α is also extended as follows:

$$\alpha(\langle N_1, N_2\rangle, u \cdot i) = \{(\alpha(N_1, u), \alpha(N_2, u \cdot i))\}$$

Moreover, its domain is extended to modules

$$\alpha(M_u, u) = \alpha(init_u, u) \cup \alpha(R_u, u)$$

Note that we abbreviate the extension of α to sets of rules (it is straightforward).

Now we are ready to show the target domain. We introduce $\mathcal{I}$ that is a set of new input variables that are denumerable. In this system, $\mathcal{I}$ is treated as a set of new constants, which can be placed only in $\langle init_\epsilon\rangle$.

$$\Sigma = \bigcup_{u \in O'} \theta(\Sigma_u) \cup \mathcal{I},$$

where $O' = O \cup \{\epsilon\}$.
An initial graphical term, the starting point of computation, is

$$INIT = \alpha(Init_\epsilon)$$

A set of all variable symbols used in this system is

$$X = \bigcup_{u \in O'} (\mathcal{V}(init_u) \cup \mathcal{V}(R_u)),$$

where the domain of $\mathcal{V}$ is extended to rules and sets of rules. Finally we get a set of rules as follows:

$$R = \bigcup_{u \in O'} \alpha(M_u)$$

26.4 IMPLEMENTATION OF JALPA

We have a choice when we implement a GTRS. The choice is to implement it as an interpreter or a compiler. In general, the interpreter is flexible and convenient to be developed and improved, however, it is less efficient than the compiler. We believe that the best solution we may expect is to implement it as the interpreter and then to develop an efficient compiler in the sense of LISP. Moreover, it enables us to easily develop various strategy-based interpreters, e.g. Gross-Knuth (full development or simultaneous reduction of all redexes), call-by-name and call-by-value strategy-based ones. One may say that call-by-value strategy-based one is the fastest, however, in practice, it depends heavily on programs to be run and the implementation. Taking outermost strategies, we can use the stream-based programming to handle infinite data.

Recently, concurrent computation has become common among us with high performance computers. The JALPA interpreter is designed to be easily adaptable to such computation with a little modification extending the JALPA interpreter to be a multi-thread based one.

26.4.1 Cell and the graph representation

A cell is a unit of memory space to be allocated and has five elements. The first element is a reference count, the second element is a tag that represents many attributes, e.g. function symbol, variable symbol, basic type, constructor, normal form, etc., the next two elements are pointers to linked cells. Cells are connected by single direction links, but not bidirectional links. It means that an indirection node technique to replace multiply referred cells, while keeping its reference count, is adopted. The last element is a hash link pointer that enables one to easily maintain a linked list for hashing of graph structures when a graph is rewritten and then the linked list can be corrected immediately.

Reference count	Tag	Hash link pointer
Left pointer	Right pointer	———

Figure 26.1 Cell

In this implementation, a graphical term is represented as a cell holding the left pointer to a property list of a function and the right pointer to its argument list. The property list has at least its name, its sort and arity, associated graphical rules or executable segments and an associated hash table.

26.4.2 Garbage collection

The garbage collection has become common among high-level programming languages. In GTRS, we cannot help but take account of it. GTRS has an essential feature to scatter memory fragments and exhaust the memory space.

In the previous section, the decisive reason why we chose the cell structure is to efficiently collect garbage. In ordinary computation, reference counts of immediate cells are decremented if the cells keep their reference counts greater than 0. Otherwise, it is necessary to decrement those of all their descendants. For efficiency, since garbage collection cannot be avoided, we can postpone it by marking the immediate cells, so that it can be consistently decremented in the next garbage collection phase.

The first stage is to set all reference counts of unreferred cells to be 0 by dereferencing from the marked cells (explained above) and properly decrementing their reference counts.

The next stage is the reconstruction of the free cell list of all unreferred cells. The reconstruction is done by running and sweeping the linear memory space of the cell heap region as well as usual ones.

26.4.3 Graph matching

Graph matching could be an extension of tree matching. In case of tree matching, it is suffice to hold pairs of a variable and its corresponding node in the process. However, in case of graph matching, it is necessary to hold not only those pairs, but also some pairs of a non-variable node and its corresponding one because a graphical rule may map non-variable nodes homomorphically. Although this is not expensive because such nodes can be detected from rules in advance and considered as a kind of variable nodes or extended variable nodes. The significant difference is that in the matching of arcs, we should traverse some nodes of a rule more than once and for each traverse, we must check whether the nodes can be corresponded to the nodes as before or not (if they exist).

26.4.4 Structure sharing

Current implementation almost supports maximum structure sharing of identical subgraphs. It is based on a recursive hashing technique. Let g be a Dag, f be the label of the root node of g and $g_1, g_2, \cdots, g_n$ be proper child Dags of g. Then a hash function $hash: G \to N$ may be defined as follows:

$$hash(g) = \alpha(h(f), hash(g_1), hash(g_2), \cdots, hash(g_n)),$$

where $\alpha: N^+ \to N$ and $h: F \to N$.

However, essentially hash functions are arbitrary if they have space and time efficient algorithms and make few collisions. Usually all subgraphs have already been hashed and replaced by unique ones before each hashing, so the significant information is the addresses of their root cells because equality of any two subgraphs is almost identical to that of their root addresses.

$$hash(g) = \alpha(h(f), \#(g_1), \#(g_2), \cdots, \#(g_n)),$$

where $\#(g)$ is the address of the root cell of g.

a. The hash table is divided into pieces, so that each piece is assigned to a function symbol.
b. To evenly distribute graphs on the hash tables, we use two hash functions, and therefore 2-dimensional hash tables.

Built-in values are infinite, so we cannot deal with them as function symbols to be hashed. We use values instead of their addresses. it can be consistent if the matching algorithm is modified, so that if two subgraphs are built-in type values and their values are equal, then the matching algorithm treats them as if they are identical by pointer comparison.

Every new subgraph generated by a reduction is checked whether the identical subgraph occurs somewhere else or not. The hashing makes the check very efficient if no hash conflicts occur.

Hash tables are usually very sparse in practice, especially multidimensional ones. If we allocated an entire table at the beginning, it is very resource wasteful, because large memory space must be left unused. We use a sparse array treatment technique, that is, at the beginning we prepare only an array of pointers to 1-dimensional arrays which might be allocated later on demand. (If the arrays become garbage, they may be de-allocated at later garbage collections.)

26.4.5 Strategies

We have implemented four strategy-based interpreters, such that left-most innermost (call-by-value), left-most outermost (call-by-name), parallel outermost (simultaneous reduction of all outermost redexes) and Gross-Knuth (full development or simultaneous reduction of all redexes) strategy-based ones. For tree-reducible systems [BvEG+87], parallel-outer and Gross-Knuth strategies are both normalizing, moreover, the latter is optimal in reduction length. However, for some programs, left-most outermost and left-most innermost strategies are fast and efficient in practice, especially, the latter could be very fast.

26.4.6 Optimizations

We have few ways to improve efficiency of execution.

a. Each function symbol is linked to an association list whose first element is its print name and a list of rules whose left-most function symbols are identical to the symbol. The list is sorted by a total order that would make matchings efficient.

b. Each cell has a tag representing data types and information for efficient matching. The information is whether the cell is a constructor or not and whether the subterm rooted by the cell has been known as a normal form or not, and is updated dynamically by following rules:

Let $t = f(t_1, t_2, \cdots, t_n)$.

(1) If f is a constructor and its arguments are normal forms, variables or basic types, t is a normal form.
(2) If t is not a redex and its arguments are normal forms, t is a normal form.

c. It is often the case that inefficient rules are written for understandability. Even though in such a case, this optimization may get optimal efficiency. The method is to rewrite right-hand side terms of rules to their normal forms by applying all rules and replace right-hand side terms of the original rules to the terms obtained.

26.4.7 Evaluations

In this section, all data is measured on a Sun4/370 with 32MB main memory. The number of cells available is 400 000 and for each function, 256x64 buckets for 2-dimensional hashing can be allocated at maximum.

Strategy	Usual Reduction	Extended Reduction
Left-most innermost	2.80	5.28
Left-most outermost	2.30	3.35
Parallel outermost	2.14	3.75
Gross-Knuth	2.47	4.11

measurements in seconds
10 001 reductions
1025 buckets (total 6.25%) for hashing are used.
the length of the maximum linked list for hashing is 13.

Table 26.1 Append of 10 000 element lists

For the append program, it is no use to try to share identical subgraphs, and so table 26.1 is considered to show overhead of the structure sharing.

Strategy	Usual Reduction	Extended Reduction
Left-most innermost	2.56*[1]	0.78*[2]
Left-most outermost	41.1*[1]	7.91*[3]
Parallel outermost	20.4*[1]	10.35*[3]
Gross-Knuth	20.9*[1]	38.3*[3]

measurements in seconds
*[1] 15 624 reductions
*[2] 2615 reductions
*[3] 2628 reductions
roughly 1000 buckets (total about 6%) for hashing are used.
the length of the maximum linked list for hashing is 6.

Table 26.2 The 16th Fibonacci number

It is well-known that the Fibonacci program has exponential time complexity and can be transformed into a program of linear time complexity. It is a typical one suited for demonstrating structure sharing.

26.5 CONCLUSION

We have shown how to make a functional language based on graphical term rewriting modular for programming in the large, that is, how to translate parameterized and non-parameterized modules with an hierarchical structure into a flat GTRS.

Graphical rewriting allows us to evaluate a program in parallel and distributively while saving space and time by sharing common subexpressions. Moreover, in this implementation we have adopted an extended reduction which forces identical subexpressions globally and dynamically and showed that it is reasonable and tractable both theoretically and practically.

Parameterized modules facilitate the reuse of modules and higher-order programming easily. E.K.Blum, H.Ehrig *et al.* studied a theoretical framework of parameterized modules [BEPP87]. OBJ3 [GW88] strongly supports them. However, parameterized modules themselves do not have enough potential for programming in the large. In such cases, we must break down a program into many small modules. An hierarchical module structure is very helpful to reduce difficulties of treatment of such modules. We have designed JALPA so that lower-level modules implement higher-level modules with parameterized modules.

At present, an interpreter of JALPA is running on SunOS. Its compiler like the LISP type is under development. An implementation for concurrent execution of JALPA programs is planned.

REFERENCES

[BEPP87] E.K. Blum, H. Ehrig, and F. Parisi-Presicce. Algebraic specification of modules and their basic interconnections. *Journal of Computer and System Sciences*, **34**, pp. 293–339, 1987.

[BMS80] R.M. Burstall, D.B. MacQueen, and D.T. Sannella. HOPE: an experimental applicative languages. In *Proc. of 1st ACM Lisp Conference*, pp. 136–143, 1980.

[BvEG+87] H. P. Barendregt, M. C. J. D. van Eekelen, J. R. W. Glauert, J. R. Kennaway, M. J. Plasmeijer, and M. R. Sleep. Term graph rewriting. In *Proc. of PARLE'87*, Springer-Verlag, Lecture Notes in Computer Science 259, pp. 141–158, 1987.

[FGJM85] K. Futatsugi, J.A. Goguen, J. Jouannaud, and J. Messeguer. Principles of OBJ2. In *Proc. of 12th ACM POPL*, pp. 52–66, 1985.

[GMW79] M.J. Gordon, A.J. Milner, and C.P. Wadsworth. *Edinburgh LCF*. Springer-Verlag, Lecture Notes in Computer Science 78. 1979.

[GW88] J.A. Goguen and T. Winkler. *Introducing OBJ3*. Technical Report SRI-CSL-88-9, SRI International, 1988.

[HP88] B. Hoffmann and D. Plump. Jungle evaluation for efficient term rewriting. In *Proc. of Int. Workshop on Algebraic and Logic Programming*, Springer-Verlag, Lecture Notes in Computer Science 343, pp. 191–203, 1988.

[Ken87] J. R. Kennaway. On 'on graph rewritings'. *Theoretical Computer Science*, **52**, pp. 37–58, 1987.

[Klo87] J.W. Klop. *Term Rewriting Systems: a Tutorial*. Technical Report CS-N8701, Centre for Mathematics and Computer Science, Amsterdam, 1987.

[Pey87] S.L. Peyton Jones. *The Implementation of Functional Programming Languages*. Prentice-Hall, 1987.

[Rao84] J. C. Raoult. On graph rewritings. *Theoretical Computer Science*, **34**, pp. 1–24, 1984.

[Tur85] D. Turner. Miranda: a non-strict functional language with polymorphic types. In *Proc. of IFIP Int. Conference on Functional Programming Languages and Computer Architecture*, Springer-Verlag, Lecture Notes in Computer Science 201, pp. 1–16, 1985.

Index

Index compiled by Geoffrey C. Jones